To Keith, now and always
S. B.

To Tita, for her unconditional support
T. M. H.

Contents

Preface

This book has two intended audiences: students preparing for careers in computer science (and related fields) and students in other fields who want to learn about issues that arise from digital technology, the Internet, and other aspects of cyberspace. The book has no technical prerequisites. Instructors can use it at various levels, in both introductory and advanced courses about computing or technology.

Scope of This Book

Many universities offer courses with titles such as "Ethical Issues in Computing" or "Computers and Society." Some focus primarily on professional ethics for computer professionals. Others address a wide range of social issues. The bulky subtitle and the table of contents of this book indicate its scope. We also include historical background to put some of today's issues in context and perspective.

Students (in computer and information technology majors and in other majors) will face a wide variety of issues in this book as members of a complex technological society, in both their professional and personal lives. We believe it is important for students to see and understand the implications and impacts of the technology.

The last chapter focuses on ethical issues for computer professionals. The basic ethical principles are not different from ethical principles in other professions or other aspects of life: honesty, responsibility, and fairness. However, within any one profession, special kinds of problems arise. Thus, we discuss professional ethical guidelines and case scenarios specific to computing professions and we include two of the main codes of ethics and professional practices for computer professionals in an Appendix. We placed the professional ethics chapter last because we believe students will find it more interesting and useful after they have as background the incidents, issues, and controversies in the earlier chapters.

Each of the chapters in this book could easily be expanded to a whole book. We had to leave out many interesting topics and examples, so we placed some of these topics in exercises and hope these will spark further reading and debate.

Changes for the Fifth Edition

For this fifth edition, we updated the whole book, removed outdated material, added many new topics and examples, and reorganized several topics. New material appears throughout. We mention here some major changes, completely new sections and topics, and some that we extensively revised.

- This edition has more than 75 new exercises.

- Chapter 1 has a new section on self-driving cars (a topic that appears again in later chapters). In this chapter, we introduce the Internet of Things, another topic that reappears in later chapters.

- New, expanded, or extensively revised topics in Chapter 2 include implanting tracking chips in people, national ID systems, extensive government surveillance programs made public by leaked NSA documents, new surveillance technologies, blocking online ads and ethical controversies about doing so, and the European Union's "right to be forgotten." We reorganized Section 2.3 and added more Fourth Amendment issues and significant court decisions about searching cellphones and tracking people by tracking their phones.

- In Chapter 3, we expanded the section on how companies handle objectionable content, added recent controversial examples of leaks of sensitive material, and expanded the discussion of net neutrality.

- In Chapter 4, we expanded discussion of exemptions to the DMCA, added copyright cases in several countries related to news excerpts, added the court decision and arguments in the lawsuit against Google for copying millions of books, and updated and added several patent cases.

- We extensively reorganized and updated Chapter 5. We added a case study (the Target breach). Other new sections cover hacking methods and why the digital world, including the Internet of Things, is so vulnerable. The new section on security includes, among other topics, what cybersecurity professionals do, responsible disclosure of vulnerabilities, the role of users in security, and the controversies over impenetrable encryption and backdoors for law enforcement. The chapter has many new examples throughout.

- Chapter 6 has a large new section on the sharing economy and gig work.

- Chapter 7 has new sections on hurdles to expanding Internet access in poor and developing countries and on various issues about control of our devices and data. We added new examples and more discussion of biased and distorted information in cyberspace.

- In Chapter 8, we updated the section on voting systems, added a section with a new case study (the HealthCare.gov website), added issues about software controls in cars, and added a discussion of the accidental bombing of a Doctors Without Borders hospital.

- In Chapter 9, we added a discussion of the Volkswagen "defeat device" scandal and updated the scenarios.

This is an extremely fast-changing field. Clearly, some issues and examples in this book are so current that details will change before or soon after publication. We do not consider this to be a serious problem as specific examples illustrate the underlying issues and arguments. We encourage students to bring in current news reports about relevant issues to discuss in class. Finding so many ties between the course and current events adds to their interest in the class.

Controversies

This book presents controversies and alternative points of view: privacy vs. access to information, privacy vs. law enforcement, freedom of speech vs. control of content on the Net, pros and cons of offshoring jobs, market-based vs. regulatory solutions, and so on. Often the discussion in the book necessarily includes political, economic, social, and philosophical issues. We encourage students to explore the arguments on all sides and to be able to explain why they reject the ones they reject before they take a position. We believe this approach prepares them to tackle new controversies. They can figure out the consequences of various proposals, generate arguments for each side, and evaluate them. We encourage students to think in principles, rather than case by case, or at least to recognize similar principles in different cases, even if they choose to take different positions on them.

Our Points of View

Any writer on subjects such as those in this book has some personal opinions, positions, or biases. We believe strongly in the principles in the Bill of Rights. We also have a generally positive view of technology. Don Norman, a psychologist and technology enthusiast who writes on humanizing technology, observed that most people who have written books about technology "are opposed to it and write about how horrible it is."[*] We are not among those people. We think that

---

[*]Quoted in Jeannette DeWyze, "When You Don't Know How to Turn on Your Radio, Don Norman Is On Your Side," *The San Diego Reader*, Dec. 1, 1994, p. 1.

technology, in general, has been a major factor in bringing physical well-being, liberty, and opportunity to billions of people. That does not mean technology is without problems. Most of this book focuses on problems. We must recognize and study them so that we can reduce the negative effects and increase the positive ones.

For many topics, this book takes a problem-solving approach. We usually begin with a description of what is happening in a particular area, often including a little history. Next comes a discussion of why there are concerns and what the new problems are. Finally, we give some commentary or perspective and some current and potential solutions to the problems. Some people view problems and negative side effects of new technologies as indications of inherent badness in the technology. We see them as part of a natural process of change and development. You will see many examples of human ingenuity, some that create problems and some that solve them. Often solutions come from improved or new applications of technology.

At a workshop on Ethical and Professional Issues in Computing sponsored by the National Science Foundation, Keith Miller, one of the speakers, gave the following outline for discussing ethical issues (which he credited to a nun who had been one of his teachers, years ago): "What? So what? Now what?" That describes the organization of many sections of this book.

An early reviewer of this book objected to one of the quotations at the beginning of a section. He thought it was untrue. So, perhaps we should make it clear that we agree with many of the quotations—but not with all of them. We chose some to be provocative and to remind students of the variety of opinions on some of the issues.

We are computer scientists, not attorneys. We summarize the main points of many laws and legal cases and discuss arguments about them, but we do not give a comprehensive legal analysis. Many ordinary terms have specific meanings in laws, and often a difference of one word can change the impact of a provision of a law or of a court decision. Laws have exceptions and special cases. Any reader who needs precise information about how a law applies in a particular case should consult an attorney or read the full text of laws, court decisions, and legal analysis.

Class Activities

The course I (SB) designed in the Computer Science Department at San Diego State University requires a book report, a term paper, and an oral presentation by each student. Students do several presentations, debates, and mock trials in class. The students are very enthusiastic about these activities. Many of the Class Discussion Exercises at the ends of the chapters are good for these purposes. Many others in the General Exercises sections are also good for lively class discussions.

We both consider it an extraordinary pleasure to teach this course. At the beginning of each semester, some students expect boredom or sermons. By the end, most say they have found it eye-opening and important. They have seen and appreciated new arguments, and they understand more about the risks of computer technology and their own responsibilities. Many students send us news reports about issues in the course long after the semester is over, sometimes after they have graduated and are working in the field.

Additional Sources

The notes at the ends of the chapters include sources for specific information in the text and, occasionally, additional information and comment. We sometimes put one endnote at or near the end of a paragraph with sources for the whole paragraph. In a few places, the endnote for a section is on the section heading. We have checked all the Web addresses, but files move, and inevitably some will not work. Usually, a search on the author and a phrase from the title of a document will locate it. Also, we found that a search on the title of an article will often lead to a free version in cases where the URL brings up a page requiring a subscription.

Pearson Education maintains a website (www.pearsonhighered.com/baase) with supplements for instructors, including PowerPoint slides and a test bank. For access to instructor material, please contact your Pearson Education sales representative or visit the site, where you will find instructions.

Feedback

This book contains a large amount of information on a large variety of subjects. We have tried to be as accurate as possible, but, inevitably, there will be errors. We appreciate corrections. Please send them to timhenry@acm.org or GiftOfFire@sdsu.edu.

Acknowledgments

I am grateful to many people who provided assistance for this edition. I thank Charles Christopher, for a steady stream of excellent articles on legal issues; Ricardo Bilton of Digiday.com and Jessica Toonkel of Thomson Reuters, for asking me about the ethics of blocking online ads and thus bringing the topic to my attention; Jean Martinez-Nelson, for conversations on a variety of topics in the book and for encouragement; Julian Morris, for reading a section; Jack Revelle, for bringing topics and examples to my attention; Diane Rider, for the idea for Figure 1.2; Carol Sanders, for her unexpected and challenging perspectives, for telling me about articles relevant to the book, for reading a chapter, and for her encouragement; Jack Sanders, for reading a chapter and for his analytical insights and thoughts on various topics; Vernor Vinge, for valuable discussions and for sending relevant articles; and various friends and neighbors who listened to me talk about self-driving cars, virtual pornography, and smartphone patents when they were expecting casual conversation over a shared meal.

This edition includes material from earlier editions, and I remain grateful to all who helped with those. I thank Michael Schneider and Judy Gersting for asking me to write a chapter in this area when the field was new and Jerry Westby for encouraging me to expand it to a book.

I thank the team at Pearson who worked on this book: Tracy Johnson for overseeing the project and for finding Tim Henry to work with me on this edition, Erin Ault for her excellent job managing the production process, Marta Samsel for finding photos and creating Figure 1.2, Kristy Alaura, and the others behind the scenes who handled the many tasks that must be done to produce a book.

Above all, I thank Keith Mayers for helping with research, reading chapters, being patient, running errands, finding things to do while I worked (building furniture this time), and still and always being my sweetheart.

S. B.

In addition to the many people Sara thanks above, I am very grateful to my wife, Tita Mejia, for her tremendous patience and support as I attempted to balance family and writing and for allowing me to take on this project with so many topics that are near and dear. Also, Frank Carrano for starting me on this path and to Sara for her mentoring, ideas, high standards, and patience.

T. M. H.

Unwrapping the Gift

Prologue

Prometheus, according to Greek myth, brought us the gift of fire. It is an awesome gift. It gives us the power to heat our homes, cook our food, and run the machines that make our lives more comfortable, healthy, and enjoyable. It is also awesomely destructive, both by accident and by arson. The Chicago fire in 1871 left 100,000 people homeless. In 1990, the oil fields of Kuwait were intentionally set ablaze. Since the beginning of the 21st century, wildfires in the United States have destroyed millions of acres and thousands of homes. In spite of the risks, in spite of these disasters, few of us would choose to return the gift of fire and live without it. We have learned, gradually, how to use it productively, how to use it safely, and how to respond more effectively to disasters, be they natural, accidental, or intentional.

Computer technology is the most significant new technology since the beginning of the Industrial Revolution. It is awesome technology, with the power to save lives, to make us healthier, and to create large amounts of new wealth. It helps us explore space, communicate easily and cheaply, find information, create entertainment, and do thousands of other tasks. As with fire, this power creates powerful problems: potential loss of privacy, multimillion-dollar thefts, and breakdowns of large, complex systems (such as air traffic control, communications networks, and banking systems) on which we have come to depend. In this book, we describe some of the remarkable benefits of computer and communication technologies, the ways they change our lives, the problems associated with them, and the means for reducing the problems and coping with their effects.

1.1 The Pace of Change

> *In a way not seen since Gutenberg's printing press that ended the Dark Ages and ignited the Renaissance, the microchip is an epochal technology with unimaginably far-reaching economic, social, and political consequences.*
>
> —Michael Rothschild[1]

In 1804, Meriwether Lewis and William Clark set out on a two-and-a-half-year voyage to explore what is now the western United States. Many more years passed before their journals were published, and many later explorers did not know that Lewis and Clark had been there before them. In his book about the Lewis and Clark expedition, *Undaunted Courage*, Stephen Ambrose points out that information, people, and goods moved no faster than a horse—and this limitation had not changed in thousands of years.[2] In 1997, millions of people went to the World Wide Web to watch a robot cart called Sojourner roll across the surface of Mars. We chat with people thousands of miles away, instantly view Web pages from around the world, and tweet from airplanes flying more than 500 miles per hour.

Telephones, automobiles, airplanes, radio, household electrical appliances, and many other marvels we take for granted were invented in the late 19th and early 20th centuries. They led to profound changes in how we work and play, how we get information, how we communicate, and how we organize our family lives. Our entry into space was one of the most dramatic feats of technology in the 20th century. Sputnik, the first man-made satellite, launched in 1957 and Neil Armstrong walked on the moon in 1969. We still do not have personal spacecraft, vacation trips to the moon, or a large amount of commercial or research activity in space, and space tourism for the very rich is in an early stage. Space exploration has had little direct effect on our daily lives, but cars park themselves, and experimental cars drive themselves. Computer programs beat human experts at chess, *Jeopardy!*, and Go, and our smartphones answer our questions. Elderly people have robot companions. Texters send trillions of texts in a year; Facebook has more than 1.7 billion members; Twitter users tweet hundreds of millions of times a day; and these numbers will be out of date when you read them. A day without using an appliance or device containing a microchip is as rare as a day without turning on an electric light.

The first electronic computers were built in the 1940s. Scientists at Bell Laboratories invented the transistor—a basic component of microprocessors—in 1947. The first hard-disk drive, made by IBM in 1956, weighed more than a ton and stored only five megabytes of data, less than the amount of space we use for one photo. Now, we can walk around with hundreds of hours of video in a pocket. A disk with a terabyte (one thousand gigabytes, or one trillion bytes) of storage— enough for 250 hours of high-definition video—is inexpensive. Indeed, the cost per bit of memory is now about one-billionth of the cost per bit on the first solid-state memory chip in 1970. There are trillions of gigabytes in cyberspace now. Researchers are developing methods to store digital data encoded in DNA molecules and in atomic-level memory chips. With the DNA technique, a million gigabits can potentially be stored in one cubic millimeter. Both methods are still experimental but have potential for reducing the cost, space, and power requirements of today's huge data centers.

The 1991 space shuttle had a 1-megahertz[*] computer onboard. Ten years later, some luxury automobiles had 100-megahertz computers. Speeds of several gigahertz are now common. When we, the authors of this book, started our careers, personal computers had not yet been invented. Computers were large machines in air-conditioned rooms and we typed computer programs onto punched cards. Our phones had dials, they all looked the same, and the phone company owned them. If we wanted to do research, we went to a library, where the library catalog filled racks of trays containing 3 × 5 index cards. Social-networking sites were neighborhood pizza places and bars. The point is not that we are old; it is the speed and magnitude of the changes. Few current college students remember a time before smartphones existed. The way you use computer systems and mobile and wearable devices, personally and professionally, will change substantially in two years,

---

[*]This is a measure of processing speed. One megahertz is 1 million cycles per second; 1 gigahertz is 1 billion cycles per second. "Hertz" is named after the 19th-century physicist Heinrich Rudolf Hertz.

in five, and in ten, and almost unrecognizably over the course of your career. The ubiquity of computers, the rapid pace of change, and their myriad applications and impacts on daily life characterize the last few decades of the 20th century and the beginning of the 21st.

It is not just the technology that changes so fast. Social impacts and controversies morph constantly. With PCs and floppy disks came computer viruses and the beginnings of a huge challenge to the concept of copyright. With email came spam. With increased storage and speed came databases with details about our personal and financial lives. With the Web, Web browsers, and search engines came easy access by children to pornography, more threats to privacy, and more challenges to copyright. Online commerce brought bargains to consumers, opportunities to entrepreneurs, and identity theft and scams. The connection of infrastructure systems such as the electric grid to the Web brought risk of sabotage by foreign governments. Mobile phones have had so many impacts that we discuss them in more detail later in this chapter and in Chapter 2. With hindsight, it might seem odd that people worried so much about antisocial, anticommunity effects of computers and the early Internet. Now, with the popularity of social networking, texting, and sharing video, photos, and information, the Net is a very social place. In 2008, "experts" worried the Internet would collapse within two years because of the demands of online video. It did not. Privacy threats of concern several years ago seem minor compared to new ones. People worried about how intimidating computers and the Internet were; now toddlers operate apps on tablets and phones.

Discussions of social issues related to computers often focus on problems, and indeed, throughout this book we examine problems created or intensified by computer technologies. Recognizing the benefits is important too and is necessary for forming a reasonable, balanced view of the impact and value of the technology. Analyzing and evaluating the impact of new technologies can be difficult as some changes are obvious while others are more subtle. Even when benefits are obvious, the costs and side effects might not be, and vice versa. Both the technological advances brought about by computer technology and the extraordinary pace of development have dramatic, sometimes unsettling, impacts on people's lives. To some, this is frightening and disruptive. They see these changes as dehumanizing, reducing the quality of life, or as threats to the status quo and their well-being. Others see challenging and exciting opportunities. To this group, the development of technology is a thrilling and inspiring example of human progress.

When we speak of computers in this book, we include mobile devices such as smartphones and tablets, desktop computers and mainframes, embedded chips that control machines and devices (from sewing machines to oil refineries to smart watches), entertainment systems (such as video recorders and game machines), and the "Net," or "cyberspace." Cyberspace is built on computers (e.g., Web servers), communication devices (wired and wireless), and storage media, but its real meaning is the vast web of communications and information that includes the Internet and more.

In the next section, we look at phenomena, often unplanned and spontaneous, that computer and communication technology made possible. Some deeply change how we interact with other people and what we can accomplish. In the rest of the chapter, we introduce themes that show up often, and we present an introduction to some ethical theories that can help guide our thinking about controversies throughout the rest of the book. The next seven chapters look at ethical, social, and legal issues primarily from the perspective of any person who lives and works in a modern computerized society and is interested in the impact of the technology. The final chapter takes the perspective of someone who works as a computer professional who designs or programs computer systems or as a professional in any area who must make decisions and/or set policy about the use of computer systems. It explores the ethical responsibilities of the professional. The Software Engineering Code of Ethics and Professional Practice and the ACM Code of Ethics and Professional Conduct, in Appendix A, provide guidelines for professionals.

1.2 Change and Unexpected Developments

No one would design a bridge or a large building today without using computers, but the Brooklyn Bridge, built in the 1870s and 1880s, is both a work of art and a marvelous feat of engineering. The builders of the Statue of Liberty, the Pyramids, the Roman aqueducts, magnificent cathedrals, and countless other complex structures did not wait for computers. People communicated over long distances by letters and then telephone. People socialized in person before social-networking sites. Yet, we can identify several phenomena resulting from computer and communication technology that are far different from what preceded them (in degree, if not entirely in kind), several areas where the impacts are dramatic, and many that were unanticipated. In this section, we consider a sampling of such phenomena. In Section 1.2.1, we look to the future and speculate about impacts of self-driving cars. Some of the other topics we consider are routine parts of our lives now but did not exist a generation or so ago. They illustrate the amazingly varied uses people find for new tools and technologies. Most of these developments have clear benefits; we include questions that raise concerns about potential problems.

> *It is precisely this unique human capacity to transcend the present, to live one's life by purposes stretching into the future—to live not at the mercy of the world, but as a builder and designer of that world—that is the distinction between human and animal behavior, or between the human being and the machine.*
>
> —Betty Friedan[3]

1.2.1 SELF-DRIVING VEHICLES

Social scientists have credited and blamed the automobile for huge changes in our environment and lifestyles: suburbs, pollution, freedom, family vacations, ending lives, and saving lives. Will self-driving cars have similarly broad impacts? We briefly run through some possible results and some ethical, legal, and social issues. Our purpose is not only to learn about self-driving cars but also to "warm up" our thinking about potential consequences of technology throughout this book.

Perhaps the biggest benefit of self-driving cars is that they will save lives. Currently, roughly 35,000 people die in vehicle crashes each year in the United States. Human error is a cause or *the* cause of roughly 95% of crashes. Undoubtedly, there will be some fatal crashes of self-driving cars because of unanticipated situations, software bugs, or design errors, but the total number is likely to be far lower than for human drivers.

It is likely that in many situations people will summon a car when needed from a service, perhaps provided by a joint venture between a car manufacturer and a car-sharing app. (Journalist Christopher Mims suggested a few names: Applewagen, Tyft, and Goober.[4]) A trip in a self-driving car will be cheaper than a ride-sharing trip with a driver. An even less expensive car-pooling service might pick up other passengers nearby, especially at rush hour. Software can quickly determine which nearby customers are going to similar destinations, and the car-sharing service can screen members for safety when riding with strangers. How will self-driving-car services affect mass transit?

With the availability of convenient, inexpensive rides, families will probably choose to own fewer cars than they do now. Currently, a car is parked about 95% of the time, on average.[5] Depending on how the pricing works out, many people may choose not to own a car at all. (A construction worker who drives a pickup truck

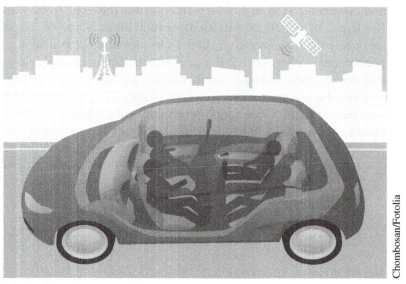

FIGURE 1.1   An idea for a self-driving car interior.

full of tools and materials will probably want to continue to own a truck, whether or not it drives itself. Who else would likely want to own his or her own vehicle?) Overall, we will need fewer cars. Will future home builders build most houses with a one-car garage or no garage at all?

Blind people, elderly people, and people with diseases that prevent driving will have a less expensive, more convenient option giving them increased autonomy. Fewer teenagers will learn to drive.

The design of cities, suburbs, and roads may change significantly. We will need less space for parking in crowded areas. When we reach our destination, a shared car will go off to give someone else a ride, and we will call another one to go home or elsewhere later. If we own the car, it can go park in a less crowded area and come back when we want it.

Will traffic increase because cars drive empty to get passengers, or will it decrease because we will spend no time looking for a parking space, people will share rides, and traffic will flow better because software will do a better job of driving than humans? Self-driving cars can coordinate their speeds and routes to reduce waiting time at traffic lights—or remove the need for traffic lights altogether in some areas. Some city planners expect traffic flow to improve so much that people will be willing to live farther from work than they do now, thus extending suburbs.

Will we need new roads specially equipped with sensors and markers to aid fully automated vehicles? Would constructing such roads be too big an expense or burden? Is it comparable to the 20th-century transition from dirt roads for horses to paved roads for cars?

Will cars with human drivers be banned from highways and major roads? Would that be an unreasonable restriction on our freedom or a reasonable transition, similar to the ban on horses or bikes on highways? Will people who like to drive for pleasure have to go to specialized parks to do so, as horse riders do now?

The software that controls a self-driving car must make critical ethical decisions such as whom to hit when a collision is unavoidable. Suppose, for example, that a child runs out into the road, the car knows it cannot stop in time to avoid hitting him, and the only alternatives are to swerve into a wall or another vehicle. It will not occur to most people when choosing between "Tyft" and "Goober" to inquire about the criteria their cars' software uses for such situations. What should the criteria be? If the number of fatalities drops overall by 90%, how important is this issue compared to all the other aspects of making the software drive safely?

What if we want to pull over to the side of the road to take a photo? Will a self-driving car refuse to park in an unofficial parking spot? What other laws and rules will its software implement? Will we be able to override them?

What other questions and impacts can you think of? We discuss some in Chapters 2, 5, 6, and 8.

1.2.2   CONNECTIONS: MOBILE PHONES, SOCIAL NETWORKING, AND THE INTERNET OF THINGS

The Web, social networking, mobile phones, and other electronic devices keep us connected to other people and to information all day, virtually everywhere. We look at a few connectivity applications, focusing on fast changes and unanticipated uses and side effects (good and bad).

Mobile Phones

In the 1990s, relatively few people had cellphones. Businesspeople and salespeople who often worked outside their office carried them. High-tech workers and gadget enthusiasts liked them. Others bought the phones so that they could make emergency calls if their cars broke down. We were used to being out of touch when away from home or office, so we planned ahead and arranged our activities not to need a phone when one was not available. Within a short time, however, cell service improved and prices dropped. Cellphone makers and service providers developed new features and services, adding cameras, video, Web connections, and location detection. Apple introduced the iPhone in 2007, phones got "smart," and we embraced the term *app*. There are now millions of apps for Apple and Android phones; people have downloaded hundreds of billions of copies. Millions, then hundreds of millions, then billions of people all over the world started carrying mobile phones—an astoundingly fast spread of a new technology in about 20 years.

Smartphones became a common tool for conversations, messaging, taking pictures, downloading music, checking email, playing games, banking, managing investments, finding a restaurant, tracking friends, and watching videos. Smartphones serve as electronic wallets and identification cards at store terminals or security checkpoints. Phones monitor security cameras at home or control home appliances from a distance. Professional people use smartphone apps for myriad business tasks. Smartphones with motion detectors remind obese teenagers to get moving. An app analyzes blood glucose levels for diabetics and reminds them when to exercise, take medication, or eat. If someone calls 911 to report a person having a heart attack, an app alerts people trained in CPR who are nearby and tells them where to find a nearby defibrillator. Military personnel on the front lines use specialized apps to download satellite surveillance video. Apps teach children the Ojibway language and other Native American languages that might be lost as the number of native speakers declines. Most of these were unanticipated uses, as were location tracking, sexting, and malicious data-stealing apps. People use mobile phones to organize flash mobs for street dances and pillow fights, or for attacking pedestrians and looting stores. Terrorists use cellphones to set off bombs. Apps designed for poor countries inform people when water is available and help perform medical imaging.

FIGURE 1.2 Some of the items replaced by a smartphone.

These examples suggest the number and variety of unanticipated applications of this one, relatively new "connection" device. The examples also suggest problems. We discuss privacy invasion by data theft and location tracking in Chapter 2. In Chapter 3, we consider whether phone service should be shut down during riots. Is the security on smartphones sufficient for banking and electronic wallets? In Chapter 5, we will consider whether security on phones should be limited to aid law enforcement. Do people realize that when they sync their phone with other devices, their data become vulnerable at the level of the weakest security? What if you lose your phone?

As a side effect of mobile phone use and the sophistication of smartphones, researchers are learning an enormous amount about our behavior.[6] Laws protect the privacy of the content of our conversations, but smartphones log calls and messages and contain devices that detect location, motion, direction, light levels, and other phones nearby. Researchers analyze this trove of data. (Yes, much of it is stored.) Analysis of the data generates valuable information about traffic congestion, commuting patterns, the spread of disease, and who is most likely to pay back a loan. In an example of detecting disease, researchers studying movement and communication patterns of MIT students could detect who had the flu, sometimes before the students knew it themselves. Researchers also can determine which people influence the decisions of others; advertisers and politicians crave such information. After a large-scale emergency such as an earthquake, tornado, or terrorist attack, the volume of messages on social media such as Twitter can help emergency response agencies determine where help is needed most.[*]

Researchers who analyzed time and location data from millions of calls said that, with enough data, a mathematical model could predict where someone would be at a particular future time with more than 90% accuracy. Is that disturbing? Who will have access to that information? Who *should* have access to it? Even now, digital assistants on our phones can remind us when to leave for routine activities that are not in our calendar, such as dropping a child off at day care, because the device monitors our daily activities and sees the pattern.

The fact that so many people carry small cameras everywhere (mostly in phones, but also hidden in other small objects such as pens[†]) affects our privacy in public and nonpublic places.[7] How well do people armed with smartphone cameras distinguish news events and evidence of crimes from voyeurism, rudeness, and stalking?

Talking or texting on a phone while driving a car increases the risk of an accident. Some states prohibit use of handheld phones while driving (and many drivers ignore the ban). One app uses motion detection by smartphones to deduce that a phone is in a moving car and blocks incoming calls. A more sophisticated version

---

[*]The term *Big Data* refers to the huge sets of data generated by our digital activities and physical activities that are digitally recorded. The examples above involve Big Data. Researchers, businesses, and government agencies analyze many such large data sets looking for patterns and useful information.
[†]At least one company sells a working pen that records high-resolution video.

locates the phone well enough to block only the driver's phone, not that of a passenger. Using a phone while out walking is risky too. Between 2010 and 2014, the number of pedestrians injured while using a phone more than doubled. New Jersey and Hawaii have proposed "distracted walking" laws that fine pedestrians for crossing streets while using a smartphone.

When people began carrying cellphones and could call for help, more headed out in the wilderness or went rock climbing without appropriate preparation. In many areas of life, people take more risk when technology increases safety. This is not unreasonable if the added risk and increased safety are in balance. When rescue calls surged, some rescue services began billing for the true cost of a rescue—one way to remind people to properly weigh the risk.

Social networking

While all this razzle-dazzle connects us electronically, it disconnects us from each other, having us "interfacing" more with computers and TV screens than looking in the face of our fellow human beings. Is this progress?

—Jim Hightower, radio commentator, 1995[8]

Facebook, one of the first of the social networking sites, started at Harvard as an online version of the hard copy student directories available at many colleges. At first, these sites were wildly popular with young people, while older people did not understand the appeal or worried about safety and privacy. Adults quickly discovered benefits of personal and business social networking. Social networks are enormously popular because of the ease with which people can share so many aspects of their lives and activities with family, friends, coworkers, and the public.

As with so many other digital phenomena, people found unanticipated uses of social networking, some good, some bad. In a phenomenon called "crowdfunding," social networks and other platforms help raise money in small amounts from a large number of people for charities, political causes, artistic projects, and investment in start-up companies. Friends and ex-boyfriends and ex-girlfriends post pranks and embarrassing material. Stalkers and bullies stalk and bully. Politicians, advertisers, businesses, and organizations seek donations, volunteers, customers, and connections. Protesters organize demonstrations and revolutions. Jurors tweet about court cases during trials (causing mistrials, overturned convictions, and jail time for offending jurors). Social networking brought us more threats to privacy and a steady stream of updates on the trivial details of people's lives. Gradually, social network companies developed sophisticated privacy controls and feedback systems to reduce problems, though they certainly have not eliminated them. Overall, to most people, the benefits far outweigh the problems.

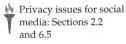 Privacy issues for social media: Sections 2.2 and 6.5

How do social networking sites affect people and relationships? People can have hundreds of friends and contacts, but have they traded quality of in-person relationships for quantity of superficial digital relationships? Does the time spent online reduce the time spent on physical activity and staying healthy? It appears that the many critics who anticipated a serious problem of social isolation were mistaken. Researchers find that people use social networks mostly to keep in touch with friends and family and that the easy, frequent contact enhances relationships, empathy, and a sense of community. On the other hand, young people who spend an excessive amount of time on a social network do poorly in school and have behavioral problems. (Are these people who would have problems in any case? Does the access to the networks exacerbate preexisting emotional problems?)

Just as researchers study social phenomena using the masses of data that smartphone systems collect, they also mine the masses of data in social networks. For example, social scientists and computer scientists analyze billions of connections to find patterns that could help identify terrorist groups.[9]

A person you follow in social media might not be a person at all. A *socialbot* is an artificial intelligence program that simulates a human being in social media. Researchers tricked Twitter users into building relationships with artificial tweeting personalities, some of which gained large followings. Political activists launch socialbots to influence voters and legislators, and advertising bots are common. The U.S. military raised concerns about automated disinformation campaigns by enemies. When the Internet was new, someone commented (and many repeated) that "on the Internet, no one knows you're a dog." It meant that we could develop relationships with others based on common interests without knowing or caring about age, race, nationality, gender, or physical attractiveness. Some of those others might not even be people, and we might not know it. Should we be comfortable with that?

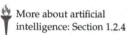
More about artificial
intelligence: Section 1.2.4

Communication and the Web

Email was first used mostly by computer scientists. In the 1980s, messages were short and contained only text. As limits on length disappeared, we began attaching digitized photos and documents. Even though texting, tweeting, and other social media have replaced email as the favored communication method in many contexts, people still send more than two hundred billion emails per day worldwide.[10]

High-energy physicists established the World Wide Web in Europe in 1990 to share their work with colleagues and researchers in other countries. In the mid- and late 1990s, with the development of Web browsers and search engines, the Web became an environment for ordinary users and for electronic commerce. The Web grew to a huge library and news source, an enormous shopping mall, an entertainment center, and a multimedia, global forum with billions of pages in less than one generation. It gives us access to information and audiences unimaginable a generation ago, empowering us to do things that we used to rely on experts for. Ordinary people make better decisions about everything from selecting a bicycle to selecting medical treatments. Software tools, many available for free, help us analyze the healthiness of our diet or plan a budget. We can find references and forms for legal processes. We can read frank reviews of smartphones, clothing, cars, books, and other products written by other buyers, not marketing departments. We can select our entertainment and watch it when we want to and where we want to. We can fight back against powerful institutions by shaming them with videos that go viral* or by posting legal documents intended to intimidate us. Businesses and organizations use "viral marketing"—that is, relying on large numbers of people to view and spread marketing messages in clever videos. A college student with a good idea and some well-implemented software can start a business that quickly grows to be worth millions or billions of dollars; several have. The openness of the Internet enables "innovation without permission," in the words of Vinton Cerf, one of the key people who has worked on Internet development since it began.[11]

Blogs (a word made up from "Web log") and videos are two examples of the many forms of creativity that flourish because Web technology and software make them so easy and inexpensive. They created new paths for jobs—with news media, publishers, and advertising and entertainment companies. Of course, some amateur blogs and videos are dull, silly, and poorly written or made, but many are gems, and people find them. Blogs provide varied, sometimes quirky perspectives. The independence of bloggers attracts readers; it suggests a genuine connection with what ordinary people are thinking and doing, not filtered through major news companies or governments. Businesses were quick to recognize the value of blogs, and many provide their own as part of their public relations and marketing programs. Inexpensive video cameras and video-manipulation tools powered a burst of short amateur videos—often humorous, sometimes worthless, and some quite serious. We can see a soldier's view of war, someone's encounter with aggressive whales, or an arrest by police. Video sites also made it easy to post and trade professional videos, infringing copyrights owned by entertainment companies and individuals. We explore copyright issues in Chapter 4.

Okay, you know about all these things. Our point, again, is how new and transformative these tools are. Before blogging got so easy, if an ordinary person wanted to express an opinion about something, he or she might have sent a letter to a newspaper—which the newspaper might have published, but the editors could have decided not to. A technical person might have posted to an early online group such as Usenet or sent a message to a small email list. If you had made a clever video, how would you have shown it to others?

The Web connects students and teachers. At first, universities offered online courses to students within their area, benefitting people who work full-time, have varying work schedules that conflict with normal class schedules, have small children at home, or cannot travel easily because of disabilities. Gradually, a potential

---

*"Going viral" describes the phenomenon where something posted in cyberspace catches the attention of people who view, copy, and spread it (or links to it) to millions more people.

"I've got pressure"

When asked by a young man to speak more quietly on his cellphone, a Hong Kong bus rider berated the man for nearly six minutes with angry insults and obscenities. In the past, a few other riders might have described the incident to friends, and then soon forgotten it. But in this instance, another rider captured the scene on his cellphone. The video soon appeared on the Internet, and millions of people saw it. People provided subtitles in different languages, set the video to music, used clips as mobile phone ringtones, and produced T-shirts with pictures and quotes. "I've got pressure" and other phrases from the rant slipped into conversations.

This incident reminds us that anything we do in a public place can be captured and preserved on video. But more, it illustrates how the Internet facilitates and encourages creativity and the quick creation and distribution of cultural artifacts and entertainment, with the contribution of ideas, modifications, variations, improvements, and new works from thousands of people.

---

to revolutionize advanced education became clear.* Hundreds of millions of people have viewed the thousands of free lessons on sciences, economics, and other subjects at the online Khan Academy, and millions more have taken university courses through Coursera. When two artificial intelligence experts offered a Stanford University graduate course for free online, they expected 500–1000 students to sign up. They got 160,000 people from around the world, and more than 20,000 completed the course, which included automatically graded homework assignments and exams.[12]

The impact of the connections provided by the Web and mobile phones is more dramatic in remote or less developed areas of the world, many of which do not have landline telephones. Mountains, thick jungle, and lack of roads separate villagers in one town in Malaysia from the next, but the villagers order supplies, check the market price of rice to get a good deal when selling their crop, and email family photos to distant relatives. Farmers in Africa get weather forecasts and instructions in improved farming methods. An Inuit man operates an Internet service provider for a village in the Northwest Territories of Canada, where temperatures drop to –40°F. Villagers in Nepal sell handicrafts worldwide via a website based in Seattle. Sales have boomed, more villagers have regular work, dying local arts are reviving, and some villagers can now afford to send their children to school. The Web abounds with examples of collaborative projects, some organized, such as Wikipedia† (the online encyclopedia written by volunteers), some spontaneous. Scientists collaborate on research with scientists in other countries much more easily and more often than they could without the Internet. Informal communities of programmers, scattered around the world, create and maintain free software. Informal, decentralized groups of people help investigate online auction

---

*For elementary education, it appears that regular classes and in-person teachers still have the advantage.
†A *wiki* is a website that allows people to add content and edit content that others provide. Wikis are tools for collaborative projects within a business or organization or among the public.

Telemedicine

Telemedicine, or long-distance medicine, refers to remote performance of medical exams, consultations, monitoring, analyses, and procedures using specialized equipment and computer networks. Doctors and nurses in one location can provide remote support for a few dozen small hospitals in several states. Doctors working with Doctors Without Borders in underdeveloped countries consult daily with a network of experts. Prisons use telemedicine to reduce the risk of escape by dangerous criminals. Many clinics and hospitals use video systems to consult with specialists at large medical centers in real time during a patient's visit. A variety of health-monitoring devices send their readings from a patient's home to a nurse over the Internet. These technologies eliminate the expense, time, inconvenience, and possible health risk of transporting sick patients, while enabling access to distant experts, more regular monitoring of patients, and earlier detection of dangerous conditions.[13]

Telemedicine goes well beyond transmission of information. Surgeons in New York used video, robotic devices, and high-speed communication links to remotely remove a gall bladder from a patient in France. Such systems can save lives in emergencies and bring a high level of surgical skills to small communities that have no surgeons.

fraud, a murder, stolen research, and other crimes. People who have never met collaborate on creating entertainment.

Some collaborative projects can have dangerous results:

- To reduce the flow of people entering the United States illegally, a governor of Texas proposed setting up night-vision webcams along the Mexican border that volunteers would monitor on the Internet. Will people monitoring a border webcam go out and attack those they see coming across the border? What training or selection process is appropriate for volunteers who monitor such security cameras?

- In China, a man posted the online name of another man he believed was having an affair with his wife. Thousands of people participated in tracking down the man's real name and address and encouraging public action against him.

- Thousands of Twitterers in Saudi Arabia called for the execution of a young writer who they believed insulted the Prophet Muhammad.

Mobs and individuals emotionally involved in a political, religious, or moral cause do not always pause for the details of due process and do not carefully determine whether they identified the correct person, whether the person is guilty of a crime, and what the appropriate punishment is. On the other hand, police departments in cities in several countries effectively use instant messaging to alert residents who help find missing children, crime suspects, or stolen cars in their neighborhoods. Enlisting volunteers is a useful collaborative tool for crime fighting and possibly antiterrorism programs. How can we guide the efforts of thousands of individuals toward useful ends while protecting against mistakes, instant vigilantism, and other abuses?

The Internet of Things

The Internet began and grew as a collection of interconnected computers: big business and government computers, then supercomputers, personal computers, laptop computers, web servers, distributed cloud computer systems, tablets, cable modems, routers, and so on—almost all devices that we would recognize as some form of computer. As miniaturization and other technology permitted, more and more devices, not traditionally considered computers, connected to the Net: mobile phones, televisions, digital TV recorders, webcams, medical devices, cars, refrigerators, egg trays within refrigerators, thermostats, light bulbs, drones, garage door openers, baby cams, dog collars, cat feeders, umbrellas (so we do not lose them), water pitchers (that automatically order new filters when needed), diapers, and more. This web of items embedded with software and connected through the Internet is called the Internet of Things, or IoT. Tech companies and analysts estimate there were 15 billion

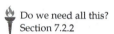
Do we need all this?
Section 7.2.2

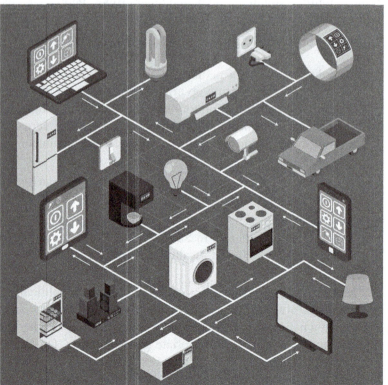

Macrovector/Fotolia

FIGURE 1.3 We can control home appliances remotely over the Internet.

devices connected to the Internet in 2015 and there will be 50–70 billion by 2020. From a distance we can turn on appliances before we arrive home or regulate the flow of water through a dam.

Our clothing is going online. Sensors in baby clothes detect when a baby is sleeping face down, at risk for sudden infant death syndrome, and warn parents on their smartphone. Sensors in diapers send a message to a parent's phone when the diaper needs changing. A heart monitor in a firefighter's shirt alerts supervisors if the firefighter is too stressed and needs a break. Athletes wear clothing that measures heart rate, respiration, muscle action, foot impact, and so on. Smart watches monitor our daily activities and our progress on physical fitness, dietary, and other goals. What other applications will we find for *wearware*?

We are only beginning to see and understand the impact the IoT has on our individual lives and communities as we gain the ability to monitor and control nearly every device at home and work from our smartphones or smartwatches. With each new advance, there is more "noise" in our lives as appliances communicate with us to update their status or notify us of a service need. These alerts and notifications can be sent to our social media account and shared with friends and family. Many people are overwhelmed by the number of text messages they receive from friends. What will be the response when our appliances join the fray? To better serve us, many of these devices collect information on our smallest preferences and our daily routines and habits. Where is this information stored, who views the data, and how does this impact our privacy and safety? Many of these devices are rushed to market without much thought to security. In Chapter 5, we consider vulnerabilities of the IoT. In Chapter 7, we consider whether we really need chips in all these products.

1.2.3 E-commerce and Free Stuff

In the early 1990s, the idea of commercial websites horrified Web users, and, indeed, commercial use of the Internet was illegal before 1992. The Web was for research, information, and online communities. A few brick-and-mortar businesses and a few young entrepreneurs recognized the potential and benefits of online commerce. Among the earliest traditional businesses on the Web, United Parcel Service and Federal Express let customers check the status of packages they sent. This was both a novelty and a helpful service. Amazon.com, founded in 1994, started selling books on the Web and became one of the most popular, reliable, and user-friendly commercial sites. Many, many Web-based businesses followed, creating new business models—such as eBay with its online auctions. Traditional businesses established websites. The Web changed from a mostly academic community to a world market in little more than a decade. Online sales in the United States total hundreds of billions of dollars a year.

Some of the benefits of e-commerce are fairly obvious: we can consider more products and sellers, some quite far away, in less time and without burning gasoline.

Some benefits are less obvious or were not obvious before they appeared. Auction sites gave people access to customers they could not have found efficiently before. The lower overhead and the ease of comparison shopping on the Web brought down prices of a variety of products. Consumers save, for example, by buying contact lenses online, according to a Progressive Policy Institute report. Consumers who do price-comparison research on the Web before buying a new car typically save hundreds of dollars.[14] Small businesses and individual artists sell on the Web without paying big fees to middlemen and distributors. The Web enabled a peer-to-peer economy (also called the sharing economy) with websites and apps where ordinary people sell or trade their skills, make small loans, and trade their homes or rent rooms for vacations.

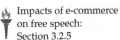
More on the sharing economy: Section 6.3.2

Growth of commerce on the Web required solutions to several problems. One was trust. People were reluctant to give their credit card numbers on the Web to companies they had not dealt with or even heard of before. Enter PayPal, a company built on the idea of having a trusted intermediary handle payment. Encryption and secure servers also made payments safer.* The Better Business Bureau established a website where we can find out whether consumers have complained about a company. Auction sites implemented rating and comment systems to help buyers and sellers determine whom to trust. Email confirmations of orders, consumer-friendly return policies, and easy packaging for returns all contributed to consumer comfort and more online sales. Indeed, as online sales increased, competition led many traditional stores to adopt e-commerce practices such as consumer-friendly return policies.

Impacts of e-commerce on free speech: Section 3.2.5

Free stuff

Libraries have provided free access to books, newspapers, and journals for generations, and radio and television provided free news and entertainment before the Internet. But there is so much more free stuff now—a truly astounding amount.

Social networks are free, as are the majority of apps for smartphones. We can get free email programs and email accounts, browsers, filters, firewalls, encryption software, word processors, spreadsheets, software for viewing documents, software to manipulate photos and video, home inventory software, antispam software, antivirus software, antispyware software, and software for many other specialized purposes, and this is a small sampling of software available for free. In addition:

- We can read news from all over the world for free.
- We can find free game-playing programs for old board games and card games such as chess and bridge, as well as for new games.

---

*The ease and security of payment on the Web has a pleasant side effect: Many people contribute more to charitable organizations, which has the unpleasant side effect of spawning scam charity sites.

- If two people have Skype accounts, phone calls and messages between them are free.

- There are free dating services on the Web.

- Major music festivals offer their concerts for free on the Internet, a nice alternative to paying $30 to $500 for a ticket.

- Major (expensive) universities such as Stanford, Yale, and MIT provide video of lectures, lecture notes, and exams for thousands of their courses on the Web for free.

- We can download whole books from Google, Project Gutenberg, and other sources for free.[*]

- We can store our personal photographs, videos, and other files in the cloud for free.

- We use search engines for free.

- Specialized, scholarly encyclopedias (e.g., the Stanford Encyclopedia of Philosophy) and thousands of other references are free.

We pay for libraries with taxes, and advertisers pay for the broadcasts of radio and television programs. On the Web, advertising pays for many, many free sites and services, but far from all. Wikipedia carries no advertising—donations pay for its hardware, bandwidth, and small paid staff. Craigslist charges fees of some businesses that post job announcements and brokers who post apartment listings in a few cities; that keeps the site free to everyone else and free of other paid ads. Businesses provide free information and services for good public relations and as a marketing tool. (Some free programs and services do not have all the features of the paid versions.) Nonprofit organizations provide information as a public service; donations or grants fund them. One of the distinct and delightful features of the Internet is that individuals provide a huge amount of free stuff simply because it pleases them to do so. They are professionals or hobbyists or just ordinary people who enjoy sharing their expertise and enthusiasm. Generosity and public service flourish in the Web environment.

It is often (though not always) obvious when we are viewing advertisements. Ads annoy some people, but their presence on a screen is often not an unreasonable price to pay for free services—and we can block some. However, to earn ad revenue to fund multimillion-dollar services, many free sites collect information about our online activities and sell it to advertisers. This tracking is often not obvious; we consider it in Chapter 2.

Ethics of ad blocking:
Section 2.5.3

---

[*]Books available for free downloading are in the public domain (that is, out of copyright).

1.2.4 ARTIFICIAL INTELLIGENCE, ROBOTICS, SENSORS, AND MOTION

Artificial intelligence

Artificial intelligence (AI) is a branch of computer science that makes computers perform tasks we normally (or used to) think of as requiring human intelligence. It includes playing complex strategy games such as chess and Go (a far more difficult game than chess), language translation, making decisions based on large amounts of data (such as approving loan applications), and understanding speech (where the appropriateness of the response might be the measure of "understanding"). AI also includes tasks performed automatically by the human brain and nervous system—for example, vision (the capture and interpretation of images by cameras and software). Learning is a characteristic of many AI programs. That is, the output of the program improves over time as it "learns" by evaluating results of its decisions on the inputs it encounters. Many AI applications involve *pattern recognition*, that is, recognizing similarities among different things. Applications include reading handwriting (for automatic sorting of mail and input on tablet computers, for example), matching fingerprints, and identifying faces in photos.

Early in the development of AI, researchers thought the hard problems for computers were tasks that required high intelligence and advanced training for humans, such as winning at chess and doing mathematical proofs. In 1997, IBM's chess computer, Deep Blue, beat World Champion Garry Kasparov in a tournament. AI researchers realized that narrow, specialized skills were easier for computers than what a five-year-old does: recognize people, carry on a conversation, and respond intelligently to the environment. In 2011, another specially designed computer system called Watson (also built by IBM) defeated human *Jeopardy!* champions. Watson processed language (including puns, analogies, and so on) and general knowledge. It searched and analyzed 200 million pages of information in less than three seconds. Practical applications of the Watson technology include medical diagnosis, searching through millions of documents for information relevant to a legal case, and various business decision-making applications. In 2016, a program called AlphaGo, developed by Google's parent company Alphabet, won a tournament against Go grandmaster Lee Sedol.

We briefly describe a few more examples of AI applications. These were astonishing advances not long ago, but are now becoming common and used by many businesses, governments, and consumers.

When a man had a heart attack in a swimming pool in Germany, lifeguards did not see him sink to the bottom of the pool, but an underwater surveillance system, using cameras and sophisticated software, detected him and alerted the lifeguards who rescued him. The software distinguishes a swimmer in distress from normal swimming, shadows, and reflections and is now installed in many large pools in Europe and the United States. Just as AI software can distinguish a swimmer in trouble from other swimmers, AI software in video surveillance systems can distinguish suspicious behavior by a customer in a store that might indicate shoplifting or other crimes. Similar systems at national monuments such as the Statue of Liberty can determine if someone leaves a package—which might be a bomb—unattended and alert security officials. Thus, without constant human monitoring, AI-equipped video systems can help prevent crimes, rather than simply identify the culprits afterward.

Search engines use AI techniques to select search results and can determine what the user meant even if the search phrase contains typos. They use context to determine the intended meaning of words that have multiple meanings. (Is "juno" a spacecraft, a movie, a goddess, a ride-sharing service, or an Internet provider?) Speech recognition is a common tool for hundreds of applications. We talk to our smartphones that use AI to figure out what a question means and find answers. Phones can use AI techniques to figure out when the owner is bored. (Repeatedly checking email and social network sites is a clue.) Computer programs that teach foreign languages give instruction in correct pronunciation if they do not recognize what the user says. Air traffic controllers train in a mockup tower whose "windows" are computer screens. The computer system responds when the trainee speaks to the simulated pilots. Such simulation allows more intensive training in a safe environment. If the trainee mistakenly directs two airplanes to land on the same runway at the same time, no one gets hurt.

People continue to debate the philosophical nature and social implications of artificial intelligence. What does it mean for a computer system to be intelligent? Alan Turing, who developed fundamental concepts underlying computer science before there were computers, proposed a test, now called the Turing test, for human-level intelligence. Let a person converse (over a network) with the system on any topic the person chooses. If the computer convinces the person that it is human, the computer passes the test. Is that enough? Many technologists think so (assuming the actual test is well designed). But is the computer intelligent?

Philosopher John Searle argues that computers are not and cannot be intelligent. They do not think; they instead manipulate symbols and do so at very high speed. They can store (or access) and manipulate a huge quantity of data, but they are not conscious. They do not understand; they simulate understanding. Searle uses the following example to illustrate the difference: Suppose you do not know the Chinese language. You are in a room with lots of boxes of Chinese symbols and a large instruction book written in English. People submit to you sequences of Chinese symbols. The instructions in your instruction book tell you how to manipulate the symbols you are given and the ones in the boxes to produce a new sequence of symbols to give back. You are very careful, and you do not get bored; you follow the instructions in the book exactly. Unknown to you, the sequences you receive are questions in Chinese. The sequences that you give back by following the instructions (just as a computer follows the instructions of a program) are the correct answers in Chinese. Everyone outside the room thinks you understand Chinese very well. Do you? Searle might say that although Watson won at *Jeopardy!*, Watson does not know it won.[15]

Whether we characterize machines as intelligent, or use the word metaphorically, or say that machines simulate intelligence, researchers and organizations are pushing AI to emulate human intelligence at an increasing rate. When Google's self-driving cars first went on public roads, they were overcautious, braked often, and would not cross double yellow lines even if a double-parked car blocked the way. Google reprogramed the cars to drive more like humans, breaking rules when it makes sense.

The goal of 17th- and 18th-century calculators was modest: to automate basic arithmetic operations. People found it disconcerting that a mindless machine could perform tasks associated with human intellectual abilities. Centuries later, Garry Kasparov's loss to a computer chess program generated worried articles about the value—or loss of value—of human intelligence. Watson generated more. Each new AI breakthrough is met with concern and fear at first. Then, a few years later, we

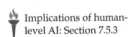 Implications of human-level AI: Section 7.5.3

take it for granted. How will we react when *Jeopardy!* is so trivial that anyone can do well at it? How will we react when we can go into a hospital for surgery performed entirely by a machine? Will it be scarier than riding in the first airplanes or automatic elevators? How will we react when we can have a conversation over the Net about any topic at all—and not know if we are conversing with a human or a machine? How will we react when chips implanted in our brains enhance our memory with gigabytes of data and a search engine? Will we still be human?

Robots

Robots are mechanical devices that perform tasks traditionally done by humans or tasks that we think of as humanlike activities. Robotic machines have been assembling products in factories for decades, working faster and more accurately than people can. AI software controls most robotic devices now. Robotic milking machines milk hundreds of thousands of cows at dairy farms while the farmhands sleep or do other chores. Fast-food sellers use robotic food preparation systems to reduce costs and speed service. A robot pharmacist machine, connected to a patient database, plucks the appropriate medications from pharmacy shelves by reading bar codes, checks for drug interactions, and handles billing. One of this robot's main goals is reduction of human error. Robots deliver medications and carry linens in hospitals, navigate around obstacles, and "push" elevator buttons with wireless signals. Physicians do complex and delicate surgery from a console with a 3D monitor and joysticks that control robotic instruments that use software to filter out the physician's shaky movements. Robots perform tasks in environments that are hazardous to people, such as:

- inspecting undersea structures and communication cables,
- searching for survivors in buildings collapsed by bombs or earthquakes,
- exploring volcanoes and other planets, and
- processing nuclear and other hazardous wastes.

For several years, Sony sold a robotic pet dog, Aibo, that walked (with a camera system providing vision), responded to commands, and learned. Several companies make robots with a more-or-less human shape that can walk up and down stairs, dance, and make facial expressions to convey emotions. However, just as general intelligence is a hard problem for AI, general movement and functioning is a hard problem for robots. Most robotic devices are special-purpose devices with a relatively limited set of operations; various companies and researchers are developing robots that can act intelligently and perform a variety of operations. Robots (doglike or humanlike) serve as companions and assistants to elderly people and childless couples. Is an emotional connection with a machine dehumanizing, or is it an improvement over living alone or in a nursing home where the staff cannot provide regular companionship? Will knowing that Grandma has a robot companion ease the guilt of family members and lead them to visit less often? Will we come to view robot companions as warmly as we do pets?

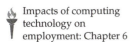
Impacts of computing technology on employment: Chapter 6

Perhaps the biggest worry about robots and AI systems is that they will eliminate a huge number of jobs, leaving most people unemployed and poor. And some worry that as AI improves and robots become smarter, they will eliminate people.

Smart sensors, motion, and control

How do robots walk, climb stairs, and dance? Tiny motion-sensing and gravity-sensing devices collect status data. Complex software interprets the data and determines the necessary motions, and then sends signals to motors. These devices—accelerometers, or *mems* (for microelectromechanical systems)—help robots, and Segway's motorized scooters, stay upright. Smartphone apps use motion detectors in phones, and millions of people play games whose controllers detect the user's motion. Mems provide image stabilization in digital cameras. They detect when a car has crashed, when someone has dropped a laptop, or when an elderly person has fallen. In those applications, the system deploys an airbag, triggers a lock on the disk drive to reduce damage, or calls for help.

Tiny microprocessors with sensors and radio transmitters are finding all sorts of applications. We mentioned a few when we introduced the Internet of Things in Section 1.2.2. Here are more examples, some in use, some in development. These examples have many obvious benefits, but what are some potential problems?

- Oil refineries and fuel storage systems use thousands of sensors to detect leaks and other malfunctions. Sandia National Laboratory developed a "chemical lab on a chip" that can detect emissions from automobiles, chemical leaks, dangerous gases in fires (reducing risk for firefighters), and many other hazards. Similar chips detect chemical warfare agents.

- Sensors detect temperature, acceleration, and stress in materials (such as airplane parts). Sensors distributed throughout bridges (such as the San Francisco

Bay Bridge) and very tall buildings can detect structural problems and report on damage from wind or earthquakes. These applications increase safety while reducing maintenance costs.

- Sensors in agricultural fields report on moisture, acidity, and so on, helping farmers to avoid waste and to use no more fertilizer than needed. Sensors detect molds or insects that might destroy crops. Sensors implanted in chickens monitor the birds' body temperature and a computer automatically reduces the temperature in the chicken coop if the birds get too hot, thus reducing disease and death from overheating.

- Sensors in food products monitor temperature, humidity, and other factors to detect potential health problems while the food is in transit to stores.

- Sensors you can scatter in your basement or bathroom detect leaks and notify you so that you can turn off the water remotely.

- Sensors in bracelet-like devices or small devices that stick to skin detect the wearer's blood-alcohol level and report to a cellphone—perhaps the wearer's, a family member's, or a probation officer's.

Several organizations have developed sensor systems that allow users to manipulate 3D images with hand movements, without touching a screen or any control device. Designers of buildings, machines, clothing, and so on use these to examine designs before implementing them. Someone with dirty (or sterile) hands (e.g., mechanics, cooks, and surgeons) could examine reference materials while working. What other applications will people think of?

Already we implant or attach microprocessor-controlled devices in or on human bodies: heart pacemakers and defibrillators and devices that restore motion to paralyzed people (which we describe in Section 1.2.5). Soon there will be implants to enhance performance of healthy people. At first, it might be physical performance for athletes—for example, to help a competitive swimmer swim more smoothly. Then what? What ethical, social, and legal issues do you think will arise as biological sciences and computer sciences combine in new ways?

1.2.5   TOOLS FOR DISABLED PEOPLE

One of the most heartwarming applications of computer technology is the restoration of abilities, productivity, and independence to people with physical disabilities. Some computer-based devices assist disabled people in using ordinary computer applications that other people use, such as Web browsers and word processors. Others improve a disabled person's mobility or enable a person to control household and workplace appliances that most of us operate by hand. Some technologies that are simply conveniences for most of us provide significantly more benefit for disabled people. For example, navigation systems that help us find our way when driving also help blind people find their way when walking in unfamiliar

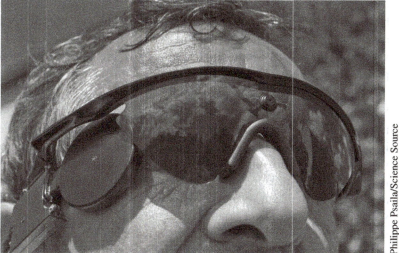

Philippe Psaila/Science Source

FIGURE 1.4 Images from the camera on the dark glasses are processed and sent via the attached antenna to a chip implanted on the man's retina—enabling a blind person to see light and dark shapes.

neighborhoods. Text messaging was very popular among deaf people before it was popular with the general population.

For people who are blind, a variety of applications help avoid collisions and help with reading. An attachment for canes uses ultrasound sensors to detect objects above the level of the cane tip, thereby helping blind people avoid objects that would hit them in the head or knees. Software reads information embedded in Web pages that sighted visitors do not need, for example, descriptions of images. Google offers search tools that rank websites based on how accessible they are for blind users. For materials not in electronic form, a scanner or camera, optical-character-recognition software, and a speech synthesizer combine to read aloud to a blind person. Handheld versions can read menus, bills, and receipts in restaurants, as well as magazines and mail at home. Where noise is a problem (or for a person both blind and deaf), a grid of buttons raised and lowered by the computer to form Braille characters can replace speech output. Braille printers provide hard copy. (Books have long been available in Braille or on tape, but the expense of production for a small market kept the selection limited.)

Some people with Parkinson's disease and other conditions causing tremors cannot control eating utensils well enough to eat without dropping or spilling a lot of food, so a company developed a spoon whose handle detects the user's tremors and uses motion stabilization technology to counteract the motion so that the spoon is more stable.[16]

Speech recognition systems are an extremely valuable tool for people who suffer from loss of limbs, quadriplegia (paralysis in both arms and legs, often resulting from an accident), and certain diseases that eliminate all or almost all use of the hands. Speech recognition systems give these people the ability to dictate documents, search the Web, and control household appliances. Deaf people can use speech recognition systems to "hear" another speaker as their tablet or phone displays the spoken words.

Prosthetic devices, such as artificial arms and legs, have improved from heavy, "dumb" wood to lighter materials with analog motors, and now to highly sensitive and flexible, digitally controlled devices that enable amputees to participate in sports and fly airplanes. A person whose leg was amputated above the knee can walk, sit, and climb stairs with an artificial "smart" knee. Sensors attached to the natural leg measure pressure and motion more than a thousand times a second and transmit the data to a processor in the prosthetic leg. Artificial intelligence software recognizes and adapts to changes in speed and slope and the person's walking style. The processor controls motors that bend and straighten the knee and support the body's movement, replacing the normal complex interplay of nerves, muscles, tendons, and ligaments. Similarly, sensors, motors, and software in leg braces enable people to walk although their legs are paralyzed. Stacey Kozel, who lost leg function because of lupus, demonstrated the power of such smart braces by hiking the Appalachian Trail.

For people with various injuries and diseases that prevent walking, there are wheelchairs that climb stairs and support and transport a person in an upright position, and there are motorized leg braces that enable a person to walk. Artificial arms use electrodes to pick up tiny electrical fields generated by contractions of muscles in the remaining upper (natural) arm. Microprocessors control tiny motors that move the artificial arm, open and close fingers, and so on. To restore control and motion to people paralyzed by spinal injuries, researchers are developing brain–computer interfaces that convert brain signals to controls for prostheses or for leg and arm muscles.[17] The impact of all these devices on the morale of the user is immense.

1.3 Themes

Here, we introduce several themes and approaches to issue analysis that appear throughout this book.

Old problems in a new context

Cyberspace has many of the problems, annoyances, and controversies of non-cyber life, among them crime, pornography, violent fiction and games, advertising, copyright infringement, gambling, and products that do not work right.

Throughout this book, we often draw analogies from other technologies and other aspects of life. Sometimes, we can find a helpful perspective for analysis and even ideas for solutions to new problems by looking at older technologies and established legal and social principles. The emphasis on the fact that similar problems occur in other areas is not meant to excuse the new problems. It suggests, however, that the cause is not always the new technology but human nature, ethics, politics, or other factors. We sometimes analyze how the new technologies change the context and impact of old problems.

Adapting to new technology

Changes in technology usually require adaptive changes in laws and regulations, social institutions, business policies, and personal skills, attitudes, and behavior.

It is easy to find many examples of laws that need to be updated. Here are a few:

- Federal rules for automobiles specify details, such as the location of turn-signal controls, that are inappropriate for self-driving cars.
- A Federal Aviation Administration regulation requires that aircraft have copies of manuals onboard; there was no exception for drones.
- A financial technology start-up that provides student loans, mortgages, and personal loans via a smartphone app can do so in 49 states—Nevada requires a physical office in the state.
- A federal regulation requiring medical x-rays on film, rather than digital formats, was still in effect in 2011.
- During Japanese election campaigns in 2005, candidates were afraid to use email and blogs and to update their websites to communicate with voters, because a 1955 law that specified the legal means of communicating with voters did not, of course, include these methods. It allowed postcards and pamphlets.

We might think some actions are obviously criminal, and others obviously should be legal, but legislators did not consider them when writing older laws. The older law, when applied to a new technology, might have a result opposite of what we consider appropriate.

In the personal realm, we have to relearn standards for deciding when to trust what we read. We have to think in new ways about how to protect our privacy. We have to decide when privacy is important and when we are willing to put it at risk for some other benefit.

Resistance from established interests

New technologies threaten the status quo. Often businesses, organizations, unions, and government agencies that stand to lose income or power attempt to block the new methods.

The advent of ride-sharing services such as Lyft and Uber raised reasonable questions concerning rules about, say, insurance for passengers. However, a law requiring a 15-minute wait before a driver can pick up a passenger (as proposed in France) has no ethical basis or social value and is intended only to make the new service less efficient and less desirable to customers than existing taxi services. To protect bookstores in France, the French government prohibited free shipping by online sellers of discounted books.

In Chapter 3, we will see examples that impact freedom of speech. In Chapter 4, we will see how the music and entertainment industries reacted to digital technologies that made copying and distribution of their products easier. In Chapter 6, we will see opposition to ride-sharing services and other new forms of work enabled by the Web and mobile apps.

Varied sources of solutions to problems

> Solutions for problems that result from new technology come from more or improved technology, the market, management policies, education and public awareness, volunteer efforts, and law.

The cycle of problems and solutions, more problems and more solutions, is a natural part of change and of life in general. Throughout this book, when we consider problems, we consider solutions from several categories. Technical solutions include hardware and software. "Hardware" might mean something other than part of a computer system, for example, improved lighting near ATMs to reduce robberies. Market mechanisms, such as competition and consumer demand, generate many improvements. Financial institutions implemented user authentication technology to help keep identity thieves out of people's online accounts. We all must become educated about the risks of the high-tech tools we use and learn how to use them safely. Legal solutions to digital problems include lawsuits, updating law enforcement techniques, and new or revised legislation and regulation. For example, there must be appropriate penalties for people who commit fraud online, and there must be appropriate liability laws for cases where system failures occur.

The global reach of the Net

> The ease of communication with distant countries has profound social, economic, and political effects—some beneficial, some not.

The Internet makes information and opportunities more easily available to people isolated by geography or by political system. Crime fighting and law enforcement are more difficult because criminals can steal and disrupt services from outside the victim's country. Laws in one country prohibiting certain content on the Web or certain kinds of Web services restrict people and businesses in other countries because the Web is accessible worldwide.

Trade-offs and controversy

> Increasing privacy and security often means reducing convenience. Protecting privacy makes law enforcement more difficult. Unpleasant, offensive, or inaccurate information accompanies our access to the Web's vast amounts of useful information.

Some of the topics we discuss are not particularly controversial. We will sometimes address an issue more as a problem-solving exercise than as a controversy. On the other hand, many of the issues are controversial: leaking confidential information on the Internet, proper policies for privacy protection, how strict copyright law should be, and the impact of computer systems on jobs.

We consider various viewpoints and arguments. Even if you have a strong position on one side of a controversy, it is important to know the arguments on the other side. Knowing there are reasonable arguments for a different point of view, even if you do not think they are strong enough to win overall, helps make a debate more civilized. We see that the people on the other side are not necessarily evil, stupid, or ignorant; they may just put more weight on different factors. To convince others of your own viewpoint, you must counter the strongest arguments of the other side, so, of course, you first must know and understand them. Finally, you might change your own mind after considering arguments you had not thought of before.

Perfection is a direction, not an option

In general, when evaluating new technologies and applications, we should not compare them to some ideal of perfect service or zero side effects and zero risk. That is impossible to achieve in most aspects of life. Instead, we should compare them to the alternatives and weigh the problems against the benefits. The ideal shows us the direction to go as we endeavor to seek improvements and solutions to problems.

Another reason that we cannot expect perfection is that we all have different ideas of what perfection is. This does not excuse sloppiness as it is often possible to meet extremely high standards.

Differences between personal choices, business policies, and law

> The criteria for making personal choices, for making policies for businesses and organizations, and for writing laws are fundamentally different.

We can make a personal choice—for example, about what social networks to join, what apps to put on our phones, or what ebooks to buy—according to our individual values and situation. A business bases its policies on many factors, including the manager's perception of consumer preferences, what competitors are doing, responsibilities to stockholders, the ethics of the business owners or managers, and relevant laws.

Laws are fundamentally different from personal choices and organizational policies because they impose decisions by force on people who did not make them. Arguments for passing a law should be qualitatively different from reasons for adopting a personal or organizational policy. It might seem odd at first, but arguments on the merits of the proposal—for example, that it is a good idea, or is efficient, or is good for business, or is helpful to consumers—are not good arguments for a law. We can use these arguments to try to convince a person or organization to adopt a particular policy voluntarily. Arguments for a law must show why the decision should be enforced against someone who *does not agree* that it is a good idea. It is better to base laws on the notion of rights rather than on personal views about their benefits or how we want people to behave.

1.4 Ethics

Honesty is the best policy.

—English proverb, pre-1600

1.4.1 What is Ethics, Anyway?

Sometimes, we discuss issues and problems related to computer technology from a somewhat detached perspective. We see how a new technology can create new risks and how social and legal institutions continually adapt, but technology is not an immutable force, outside of human control. People make decisions about what technologies and products to develop and how to use them. People make decisions about when a product is safe to release. People make decisions about access to and use of personal information. People make laws and set rules and standards.

Should you download movies from unauthorized websites? Should you talk on your cellphone while driving on a freeway? Should you install robotic equipment in your new factory instead of hiring human workers? Should you warn potential customers that the smartphone app you sell needs to access their contact list? Should you fire an employee who is criticizing your business in social media? What information should you allow advertisers and other trackers to collect from visitors to the website you run? Someone sent you the contents of a friend's (a teacher's, a city council candidate's) email account; should you post it on the Web? In these examples, you are confronting practical and legal issues—and ethical ones. In each case, you can restate the problem as a question in the form "Is it right to. . .?" Is it right to make a significant change in your company's privacy policy without giving customers or members advance notice?

Ethics is the study of what it means to "do the right thing." It is a complex subject that has occupied philosophers for thousands of years. In this section, we introduce several ethical theories and discuss some distinctions (e.g., between ethics and law) that are important to understand when tackling ethical issues. This presentation is necessarily simplified.

Ethical theory assumes that people are rational and make free choices. Neither of these conditions is always and absolutely true. People act emotionally, and they make mistakes. A person is not making a free choice when someone else is pointing a gun at him or her. Some argue that a person is not making a free choice in a situation where he or she might lose a job. However, free choice and use of rational judgment are capacities and characteristics of human beings, and they are reasonably assumed as the basis of ethical theory. We take the view that the individual is, in most circumstances, responsible for his or her actions.

Ethical rules are rules to follow in our interactions with other people and in our actions that affect other people. Most ethical theories attempt to achieve the same goal: to enhance human dignity, peace, happiness, and well-being. Ethical rules apply to all of us and are intended to achieve good results for people in general, and for situations in general—not just for ourselves, not just for one situation. A set of rules that does this well respects the fact that we are each unique and have our own values and goals, that we have judgment and will, and that we act according to our judgment to achieve our goals. The rules should clarify our obligations and responsibilities, and our areas of choice and personal preference.*

We could view ethical rules as fundamental and universal, like laws of science. Or we could view them as rules we make up, like the rules of soccer, to provide a framework in which to interact with other people in a peaceful, productive way. The titles of two books illustrate these different viewpoints. One is *Ethics:* Discovering *Right and Wrong*; the other is *Ethics*: Inventing *Right and Wrong*.[18] We do not have to decide which view is correct to find good ethical rules. In either case, our tools include reason, introspection, and knowledge of human nature, values, and behavior.

Behaving ethically, in a personal or professional sphere, is usually not a burden. Most of the time we are honest, we keep our promises, we do not steal, and we do our jobs. This should not be surprising. If ethical rules are good ones, they work for people. That is, they make our lives better. Behaving ethically is usually practical. Honesty makes interactions among people work more smoothly and reliably, for example. We might lose friends if we often lie or break promises. Social institutions encourage us to do right: We might land in jail if caught stealing, or we might lose our job if we perform it carelessly. In a professional context, doing good ethically often corresponds closely with doing a good job in the sense of professional quality and competence. Doing well in business often corresponds closely with doing good ethically in the sense that ethically developed products and ethical policies are more likely to please consumers. Sometimes, however, it is difficult

---

*Not all ethical theories fit this description. Ethical relativism and some types of ethical egoism do not. In this book, however, we assume these goals and requirements for ethical theories.

to do the right thing. It takes courage in situations where we could suffer negative consequences or we do not have the support of friends or coworkers. Courage is often associated with heroic acts, where one risks one's life to save someone in a dangerous situation—the kind of act that makes news. Most of us do not have those opportunities to display courage, but we do have many opportunities to make courageous ethical decisions in day-to-day life.

1.4.2   A VARIETY OF ETHICAL VIEWS[19]

Although there is much agreement about general ethical rules, there are many different theories about how to establish a firm justification for the rules and how to decide what is ethical in specific cases. We give very brief descriptions of a few approaches to ethics. Some ethicists[*] make a distinction between ethical theories that view certain acts as good or bad because of some intrinsic aspect of the action and ethical theories that view acts as good or bad because of their consequences. They call these deontological (or nonconsequentialist) and consequentialist theories, respectively, though the distinction is often emphasized more than necessary. If the criteria that deontologists use to determine the intrinsic goodness or badness of an act do not consider its consequences for people—at least for most people, most of the time—their criteria would seem to have little ethical merit.

Deontological theories

Deontologists tend to emphasize duty and absolute rules, to be followed whether they lead to good or ill consequences in particular cases. One example is: do not lie. An act is ethical if it complies with ethical rules and you chose it for that reason.

Immanuel Kant, the philosopher often presented as the prime example of a deontologist, contributed many important ideas to ethical theory and we mention three of them here. First is the principle of universality: We should follow rules of behavior that we can universally apply to everyone. This principle is so fundamental to ethical theory that we already accepted it in our explanation of ethics.

Second, deontologists argue that logic or reason determines rules of ethical behavior, that actions are intrinsically good because they follow from logic. Kant believed that rationality is the standard for what is good. We can reason about what makes sense and act accordingly, or we can act irrationally, which is evil. The view that something is evil because it is illogical might seem unconvincing, but Kant's instruction to "Respect the reason in you"—that is, to use your reason, rationality, and judgment, rather than emotions, when making a decision in an ethical context—is a wise one.

Third, Kant stated a principle about interacting with other people: One must never treat people as merely means to ends, but rather as ends in themselves.

---

[*]Ethicists are philosophers (and others) who study ethics.

Kant took an extreme position on the absolutism of ethical rules. He argued, for instance, that it is always wrong to lie. For example, if a person is looking for someone he intends to murder, and he asks you where the intended victim is, it is wrong for you to lie to protect the victim. Most people would agree that there are cases in which even very good, universal rules should be broken—because of the consequences.

Utilitarianism

Utilitarianism is the main example of a consequentialist theory. Its guiding principle, as expressed by John Stuart Mill,[20] is to increase happiness, or "utility." A person's utility is what satisfies the person's needs and values. An action might decrease utility for some people and increase it for others. We should consider the consequences—the benefits and damages to all affected people—and "calculate" the change in aggregate utility. An act is right if it tends to increase aggregate utility and wrong if it tends to decrease it.

Utilitarianism is a very influential theory, and it has many variations. As stated above, the utilitarian principle applies to individual actions. For each action, we consider the impact on utility and judge the action by its net impact. This is sometimes called "act utilitarianism." One variant of utilitarianism, called "rule utilitarianism," applies the utility principle not to individual actions but to general ethical rules. Thus, a rule utilitarian might argue that the rule "Do not lie" will increase total utility, and for that reason it is a good rule. Rule utilitarians do not do a utility calculation for each instance where they consider lying. Generally, a utilitarian would be more comfortable than a deontologist breaking a rule in circumstances where doing so would have good consequences.

There are numerous problems with act utilitarianism. For example, it might be difficult or impossible to determine all the consequences of an act. If we can do so, do we count what *we* believe will, or should, contribute to the happiness of the people affected, or what *they* choose themselves? How do we know what they would choose? How do we quantify happiness in order to make comparisons among many people? Should some people's utility carry more weight than that of others? Should we weigh a thief's gain of utility equal to the victim's loss? Is a dollar worth the same to a person who worked for it and a person who received it as a gift? Or to a rich person and a poor person? How can we measure the utility of freedom?

A more fundamental (and ethical) objection to act utilitarianism is that it does not recognize or respect individual rights. It has no absolute prohibitions and so could allow actions that many people consider always wrong. For example, if there is a convincing case that killing one innocent person (perhaps to distribute his or her organs to several people who will die without transplants) or taking all of a person's property and redistributing it to other community members would maximize utility in a community, utilitarianism could justify these acts. A person has no protected set of rights.

Rule utilitarianism suffers far less than does act utilitarianism from these problems. Recognizing that widespread killing and stealing decrease the security and happiness of all, a rule utilitarian can derive rules against these acts. We can state these particular rules in terms of rights to life and property.

Natural rights

Suppose we wish to treat people as ends rather than merely means and we wish to increase people's happiness. These goals are somewhat vague and open to many interpretations in specific circumstances. One approach we might follow is to let people make their own decisions. That is, we try to define a sphere of freedom in which people can act according to their own judgment, without coercive interference by others, even others (including us) who think they are doing what is best for the people involved or for humanity in general. This approach views ethical behavior as acting in such a way that respects a set of fundamental rights of others, including the rights to life, liberty, and property.

These rights are sometimes called natural rights because, in the opinion of some philosophers, they come from nature or we can derive them from the nature of humanity. John Locke[21] argued that we each have an exclusive right to ourselves, our labor, and to what we produce with our labor. Thus, he argued for a natural right to property that we create or obtain by mixing our labor with natural resources. He saw protection of private property as a moral rule. If there is no protection for property, then the person who invents a new tool would be loath to show it to others or use it in their view, as they might take it. Clearing land and planting food would be pointless, as one could not be present at all times to prevent others from picking all the crop. Thus, a right of private property increases overall wealth (utility) as well; the toolmaker or farmer has more to give to or trade with others. Respect for the rights to life, liberty, and property implies ethical rules against killing, stealing, deception, and coercion.

Some see freedom of speech as a natural right because the freedom to express oneself and to say what one thinks or feels is such a natural extension of our humanity and autonomy.

Those who emphasize natural rights tend to emphasize the ethical character of the *process* by which people interact, seeing acts generally as likely to be ethical if they involve voluntary interactions and freely made exchanges where the parties are not coerced or deceived. This contrasts with other ethical standards or approaches that tend to focus on the *result* or state achieved by the interaction, for example, seeing an action as likely to be unethical if it leaves some people poor.

Negative and positive rights, or liberties and claim rights

When people speak of rights, they are often speaking about two quite different kinds of rights. In philosophy books, these rights are usually called negative and positive rights, but the terms liberties and claim rights are more descriptive of the distinction.[22]

Negative rights, or liberties, are rights to act without interference. The only obligation negative rights impose on other people is that they may not prevent you from acting. These rights include the right to life (in the sense that no one may kill you), the right to be free from assault, the right to use your property, and the right to use your labor, skills, and mind to create goods and services and to trade with other people in voluntary exchanges. The rights to "life, liberty, and the pursuit of happiness" described in the U.S. Declaration of Independence are liberties, or negative rights. Freedom of speech and religion, as guaranteed in the First Amendment of the U.S. Constitution, are negative rights: the government may not interfere with you, jail you, or kill you because of what you say or what your religious beliefs are. The right to work, as a liberty, or negative right, means that no one may prohibit you from working or, for example, punish you for working without getting a government permit. The (negative) right to access the Internet is so obvious in free countries that we do not even think of it; however, authoritarian governments restrict or deny it.

Claim rights, or positive rights, impose an obligation on some people to provide certain things for others. A positive right to a job means that someone must hire you regardless of whether anyone voluntarily chooses to do so, or that it is obligatory for the government to set up job programs for people who are out of work. A positive right to life means that some people are obligated to pay for food or medical care for others who cannot pay for them. When we interpret freedom of speech as a claim right, or positive right, it means that we may require owners of shopping malls, radio stations, and online services to provide space or time for content they do not wish to include. Access to the Internet, as a claim right, could require such things as taxes to provide subsidized access for poor people or foreign aid to provide access in poor countries. The last example suggests the following question: How far does the obligation to provide a positive right extend? Also, when thinking about what might be a positive, or claim, right, it is helpful to consider whether something should be a claim right if it depends on achieving a certain level of societal wealth or a certain level of technology. For example, if telephone service is a positive right now, was it a positive right in 1900 when fewer than 15% of households had a telephone?[23] If access to the Internet is a positive right now, was it a positive right in the 1800s?

Here is a more fundamental problem: negative rights and positive rights often conflict. Some people think that liberties are almost worthless by themselves and that society must devise social and legal mechanisms to ensure that everyone has his or her claim rights, or positive rights, satisfied, even if that means diminishing the liberties of some. Other people think that there can be no (or very few) positive rights, because it is impossible to enforce claim rights for some people without violating the liberties of others. They see the protection of liberties, or negative rights, as ethically essential. Although we will not solve the disagreement about which kind of right is more important, we can sometimes clarify the issues in a debate by clarifying which kind of right we are discussing.

Golden rules

The Bible and Confucius tell us to treat others as we would want them to treat us. This is a valuable ethical guideline. It suggests a reciprocity, or a role reversal. We should not take the rule too literally, however; we need to apply it at the appropriate level. It tells us to consider an ethical choice we are making from the perspective of the people it affects. No matter how much you enjoy fast driving on winding roads, it might not be kind to roar around those corners with a passenger who gets carsick easily. No matter how much you like your friends to share photos of you partying, it might not be good to share a photo of friend who prefers privacy. We want people to recognize us as individuals and to respect our choices. Thus, we should respect theirs.

Contributing to society

We are focusing on how to make ethical decisions. Some ethical theories take a wider goal: how to live a virtuous life. Discussion of how to achieve that goal is beyond the scope of this book, but we can make a few comments related to ethical choices. Aristotle says that one lives a virtuous life by doing virtuous acts. This leaves us with a question: What is a virtuous act? Most people would agree that helping to serve meals at a homeless shelter is a virtuous act, but doing unpaid charitable work is not the only kind of virtuous act. Suppose a nurse is choosing between spending one evening a week taking a course to learn new nursing skills or spending one evening a week helping at the homeless shelter. Or a programmer at a bank is choosing between a course on new computer security techniques and helping at the homeless shelter. There is nothing wrong with either choice. Is either one more virtuous than the other? The first choice increases the person's professional status and possibly the person's salary; you could see it as a selfish choice. The second choice is charitable work, helping unfortunate people. But the analysis should not stop there. A professional person, well trained and up to date in his or her profession, often can do far more to help a large number of people than the same person can accomplish performing low-skill tasks outside the person's professional area. (Would it be more beneficial for the nurse to take the extra training, but the programmer to assist at the shelter because programming does not directly help others? How can we compare the long-term, indirect effects of improving online security with serving food?) Whether or not a person is paid for his or her work is not significant in evaluating its contribution. There are many powerful ethical and personal reasons for contributing time or money to charitable endeavors. Doing one's work (whether it is collecting garbage or performing brain surgery) honestly, responsibly, ethically, creatively, and well is also a virtuous activity.

> *His philanthropy was in his work.*
> —Mike Godwin, writing about Apple cofounder Steve Jobs[24]

Social contracts and a theory of political justice[25]

> *Justice in a free society means treating individuals according to identical rules of conduct.*
> —Benn Steil and Manuel Hinds[26]

Many topics we consider in this book go beyond individual ethical choices. They are social and legal policies. Thus, we introduce (quite briefly) philosophical ideas about forming social and political systems.

The early foundations of social contract theory, the idea that people willingly submit to a basic set of laws in order to live in a civil society, are in the writings of Socrates and Plato but were not fully formed until the 1600s. Thomas Hobbes developed ideas of social contract theory in his book *Leviathan* (1651). Hobbes describes a starting point called the State of Nature, a dismal place where each man acts according to his own interests, no one is safe from physical harm, and there is no ability to ensure the satisfaction of one's needs. Hobbes believed that man is rational and will seek a better situation, even at the cost of giving up some independence in favor of a set of laws and accepting some authority to enforce this "social contract." John Locke thought people could enforce moral rules, such as the rights to life, liberty, and property, in a state of nature but that it was better to delegate this function to a government instituted by an implicit social contract.

The modern philosopher John Rawls[27] took social contract theory further, developing provisions of the "contract" based on his view of justice as fairness.[*] We criticize parts of his work, but some of his points provide useful ethical guidelines. Rawls sought to establish principles for proper political power in a society with people of varying religions, viewpoints, lifestyles, and so on. Rawls, like other social contract theorists, said that reasonable people, recognizing that a legal (or political) structure is necessary for social order, will want to cooperate on terms that all accept, and they will abide by the rules of society, even those they do not like. He argued that political power is proper only if we would expect all citizens to reasonably endorse its basic, or constitutional, principles. Tolerance is essential because deep questions are difficult, we answer them differently based on our life

---

[*]The meaning of "fairness" is not obvious. In different contexts and to different people, it can mean being judged on one's merits rather than irrelevant factors, getting an equal share, or getting what one deserves.

experiences, and people of good will can disagree. Thus, a proper political system protects basic civil liberties such as freedom of speech and free choice of occupation. It will not impose the views of some on the others.

To this point, Rawls' foundation is consistent with an emphasis on liberties (negative rights). Rawls distinguishes his system of justice by adding a strong requirement for claim rights (positive rights): a just and fair political system will ensure that all citizens have sufficient means to make effective use of their freedoms. To Rawls, government financing of election campaigns is an essential feature of the system. The fairness and practical consequences of this very specific political policy are hotly debated. Rawls has made a leap that appears inconsistent with his emphasis that people of good will disagree on important issues and that a proper political system does not impose the views of one group on another.

In Rawls' view, an action or a social or political structure is not ethical if it has the effect of leaving the least-advantaged people worse than they were before (or would be in some alternative system). Thus, in a sense, Rawls gives far more weight (indeed, infinite weight) to the utility of the least-advantaged people than to anyone else, and this rule's fairness may not seem obvious. Two more challenging issues are the decisions of how many least-advantaged people must not be made worse off (the single least-advantaged individual, or the lowest 1%, or the lowest 49%) and how to deal with policies that might make someone worse off in the short term but better off in the long term. Rawls' emphasis on concern for the least well off, however, is a reminder to consider impacts on such people; a loss or harm to them can be more devastating than to someone in a better position.

Rawls proposed a conceptual formulation termed the "veil of ignorance" for deriving the proper principles or policies of a just social or political system. By extension, we can use it as a tool for considering ethical and social issues. We imagine that each person behind the veil of ignorance does not know his or her gender, age, race, talents, wealth, and so on in the real world. Behind the veil of ignorance, we choose policies that would be fair for all, protecting the most vulnerable and least-advantaged members of society. Many writers use this tool to derive what they conclude to be the correct ethical positions on social policy issues. We (the authors of this book) find that sometimes, when going behind the veil of ignorance, we come to different conclusions than those of other writers. The tool is useful, like the principles of the ethical theories we described earlier, but, like them, it is not absolute. Even ignoring our status in society, people of good will will come to different conclusions because of their knowledge of human behavior and economics and their understanding of how the world works.*

---

*Rawls specifies that we assume people behind the veil of ignorance have knowledge of accepted economic principles, but in fact many philosophers and ordinary people do not—and of course, even well-informed people will disagree.

No simple answers

We cannot solve ethical problems by applying a formula or an algorithm. Human behavior and real human situations are complex and there are many trade-offs to consider. Ethical theories do not provide clear, incontrovertibly correct positions on most issues; indeed, we can use the approaches we described to support opposite sides of many an issue. For example, consider Kant's imperative that one must never treat people as merely means to ends, but rather as ends in themselves. We could argue that an employer who pays an employee a very low wage, say, a wage too low to support a family, is wrongly treating the employee as merely a means for the employer to make money. But we could also argue that expecting the employer to pay more than he or she considers reasonable is treating the employer merely as a means of providing income for the employee. Similarly, it is easy for two utilitarians to come to different conclusions on a particular issue by measuring happiness or utility differently. A small set of basic natural rights might provide no guidance for many situations in which you must make ethical decisions; however, if we try to define rights to cover more situations, there will be fierce disagreement about just what those rights should be.

Although ethical theories do not completely settle difficult, controversial issues, they help to identify important principles or guidelines by reminding us of

Do organizations have ethics?

Some philosophers argue that it is meaningless to speak of a business or an organization as having ethics. Individual people make all decisions and take all actions, and those people must have ethical responsibility for everything they do. Others argue that an organization that acts with intention and a formal decision structure, such as a business, is a moral entity.[28] However, viewing a business as a moral entity does not diminish the responsibility of the individual people. Ultimately, it is individuals who are making decisions and taking actions. We can hold both the individuals and the company or organization responsible for their acts.*

Whether one accepts or rejects the idea that a business can have ethical rights and responsibilities, it is clear that organizational structure and policies lead to a pattern of actions and decisions that have ethical character. Businesses have a "corporate culture," or a "personality," or simply a reputation for treating employees and customers in respectful and honest— or careless and deceptive—ways. People in management positions shape the culture or ethics of a business or organization. Thus, decisions by managers have an impact beyond the particular product, contract, or action a decision involves. A manager who is dishonest with customers or who cuts corners on testing, for example, is setting an example that encourages other employees to be dishonest and careless. A manager's ethical responsibility includes his or her contribution to the company's ethical personality.

*Regardless of whether or not we view businesses and organizations as moral agents, they are legal entities and can be held legally responsible for their acts.

things to consider, and by clarifying values and reasoning. There is much merit in Kant's principle of universalism and his emphasis on treating people as intrinsically valuable "ends." "Do not lie, manipulate, or deceive" is a good ethical principle. There is much merit in utilitarianism's consideration of consequences and its standard of increasing achievement of people's happiness. There is much merit in the natural rights approach of setting minimal rules in a rights framework to guarantee people a sphere in which they can act according to their own values and judgment. The Golden Rule reminds us to consider the perspective of the people our actions affect. Rawls reminds us that it is especially important to consider the impact of our choices on the least-advantaged people.

1.4.3   SOME IMPORTANT DISTINCTIONS

A number of important distinctions affect our ethical judgments, but they are often not clearly expressed or understood. In this section, we identify a few of these. Just being aware of these distinctions can help clarify issues in ethical debates.

Right, wrong, and okay

In situations with ethical dilemmas, there are often many options that are ethically acceptable, with no specific one ethically required. Thus, it is misleading to divide all acts into two categories, ethically right and ethically wrong. Rather, it is better to think of acts as ethically obligatory, ethically prohibited, or ethically acceptable. Many actions might be virtuous and desirable but not obligatory.

Distinguishing wrong and harm

Carelessly and needlessly causing harm is wrong, but it is important to remember that harm alone is not a sufficient criterion to determine that an act is unethical. Many ethical, even admirable, acts can make other people worse off. For example, you may accept a job offer knowing someone else wanted the job and needed it more than you do. You may reduce the income of other people by producing a better product that consumers prefer. If your product is really good, you might put a competitor out of business completely and cause many people to lose their jobs. Yet there is nothing wrong with doing honest, productive work.

Declining to give something (say, $100) to someone is not the same ethically as taking the thing away from the person, yet both actions leave the person less well off by $100 than they would be otherwise. If we took that simplistic view of harm, the harm would be essentially the same. To identify harm as wrong, we must identify what the person is due, what his or her rights are, and what our rights and obligations are.

On the other hand, there can be wrong when there is no (obvious or immediate) harm. Doing something risky that endangers other people without their consent is usually wrong even if in a particular instance no harm results.

Separating goals from constraints

A prominent economist wrote that the goal or responsibility of a business is to make a profit for its shareholders. This statement appalls some ethicists, as they believe it justifies, or is used to justify, irresponsible and unethical actions. Arguments on this point miss the distinction between goals, on the one hand, and constraints on actions that may be taken to achieve the goals, on the other hand—or the distinction between ends and means. Our personal goals might include financial success and finding an attractive mate. Working hard, investing wisely, and being an interesting and decent person can achieve these goals. Ethically unacceptable actions, such as stealing and lying, might achieve them too. Ethics tells us what actions are acceptable or unacceptable in our attempts to achieve the goals. There is nothing unethical about a business having the goal of making a profit, but the ethical character of the company depends on whether the actions taken to achieve the goal are consistent with ethical constraints.[29]

Personal preference and ethics

Most of us have strong feelings about a lot of issues. It might be difficult to draw a line between what we consider ethically right or wrong and what we personally approve or disapprove of.

Suppose you get a job offer from a company whose products you do not like. You may decline the job and say you are doing so on ethical grounds. Are you? Can you convincingly argue that anyone who takes the job is acting unethically? Most likely you cannot, and that is not what you actually think. *You* do not want to work for a company you do not like. This is a personal preference. There is nothing ethically wrong with declining the job, of course. The company's freedom to produce its products does not impose an ethical obligation on you to assist it.

When discussing political or social issues, people frequently argue that their position is right in a moral or an ethical sense or that an opponent's position is morally wrong or unethical. People tend to want to be on the "moral high ground" and avoid the stigma of an accusation that their view is ethically wrong. Thus, arguments based on ethics can be, and often are, used to intimidate people with different views. It is a good idea to try to distinguish between actions we find distasteful, rude, risky, or ill-advised and actions that we can argue convincingly are ethically wrong.

Law and ethics

Between 'can do' and 'may do' ought to exist the whole realm which recognizes the sway of duty, fairness, sympathy, taste, and all the other things that make life beautiful and society possible.

—John Fletcher Moulton (Lord Moulton),
British judge and member of Parliament, 1912[30]

What is the connection between law and ethics? Sometimes very little. Is it ethical for the government or a state university to give preference in contracts, hiring, or admissions to people in one ethnic group? Is it ethical for a bank loan officer to carry customer records on a laptop to work at the beach? Current laws, whatever they happen to be at a particular time, do not answer these questions. In addition, history provides numerous examples of laws most of us consider profoundly wrong by ethical standards; slavery is perhaps the most obvious example. Ethics precedes law in the sense that ethical principles help determine whether or not we should pass specific laws.

Some laws enforce ethical rules (e.g., against murder and theft). By definition, we are ethically obligated to obey such laws—not because they are laws, but because the laws implement the obligations and prohibitions of ethical rules.

Another category of laws establishes conventions for business or other activities. Commercial law, such as the Uniform Commercial Code, defines rules for economic transactions and contracts. Such rules provide a framework in which we can interact smoothly and confidently with strangers and include provisions for how to interpret a contract if a court must resolve a dispute. These laws are extremely important to any society and they should be consistent with ethics. Beyond basic ethical considerations, however, details could depend on historic conventions, practicality, and other nonethical criteria. In the United States, drivers must drive on the right side of the road; in England, drivers must drive on the left side. There is obviously nothing intrinsically right or wrong about either choice. However, once the convention is established, it is wrong to drive on the incorrect side of the road because it needlessly endangers other people.

Unfortunately, many laws fall into a category that is not intended to implement ethical rules—or even be consistent with them. The political process is subject to pressure from special interest groups of all sorts that seek to pass laws favoring their groups or businesses. Examples include the laws (promoted by television networks) that delayed the introduction of cable television and, later, laws (promoted by some cable television companies) to restrict satellite dishes. Wisconsin prohibits selling homemade baked goods. Since the state allows sale of homemade jams, raw apple cider, and other foods, the ban likely has less to do with protecting public health and more to do with lobbying efforts by the bakers' association to outlaw competitors. Many prominent people in the financial industry reported receiving a large number of fundraising letters from members of Congress—in the week that Congress took up new regulations for their industry. Many political, religious, or ideological organizations promote laws to require (or prohibit) certain kinds of behavior that the group considers desirable (or objectionable). Examples include prohibitions on teaching foreign languages in schools (in the early 20th century),[31] prohibitions on gambling or alcohol, requirements for recycling, and requirements that stores close on Sundays. At an extreme, in some countries, this category includes restrictions on the practice of certain religions. Some politicians or political parties pass laws, no matter how public-spirited they sound, purely to give advantages to themselves or their friends or donors.

Copyright law has elements of all three categories we have described. Copyright defines a property right, violation of which is a form of theft. Because of the intangible nature of intellectual property, some of the rules about what constitutes copyright infringement are more like the second category, pragmatic rules devised to be workable. Powerful groups (e.g., the publishing, music, and movie industries) lobby for specific rules to benefit themselves. These multiple aspects of copyright law are why some violations are clearly unethical (if one accepts the concept of intellectual property), yet others seem to be entirely acceptable, even noble.

Legislators, regulators, and their staffs draft some laws and regulations in haste, and they make little sense. Some have hundreds or thousands of pages and are full of specific details that make many ethical choices illegal. When members of Congress debate whether pizza is a vegetable,[32] they are not debating an ethical issue.

Do we have an ethical obligation to obey a law just because it is a law? Some argue that we do: as members of society, we must obey the laws so long as they are not clearly and utterly ethically wrong. For civil society to function, we must accept the rules endorsed by our legislative and judicial processes. Others argue that, whereas this might often be a good policy in most cases, it is not an ethical obligation. Legislators are just a group of people, subject to errors and political influences; there is no reason to feel an ethical obligation to do something just because they say so.

Is it always ethically right to do something that is legal? No. Laws must be uniform and stated in a way that clearly indicates what actions are punishable. Ethical situations are complex and variable; the people involved might know the relevant factors, but it might not be possible to prove them in court. There are widely accepted ethical rules that would be difficult and probably unwise to enforce absolutely with laws—for example, do not lie.

New law lags behind new technology for good reasons. It takes time to recognize new problems associated with the technology, consider possible solutions, think and debate about the consequences and fairness of various proposals, and so on. A good law will set minimal standards that can apply to all situations, leaving a large range of voluntary choices. Ethics fills the gap between the time when technology creates new problems and the time when legislatures pass reasonable laws. Ethics fills the gap between general legal standards that apply to all cases and the particular choices made in a specific case. While it is not ethically obligatory to obey all laws, that is not an excuse to ignore laws, nor is a law (or lack of a law) an excuse to ignore ethics.

Exercises

Review Exercises

1.1   What is one likely effect of self-driving cars on the design of cities?

1.2   What were two unexpected uses of social networking?

1.3   What are two ways free services on the Web are paid for?

1.4   Describe two applications of speech recognition.

1.5   List two applications mentioned in this chapter that help ordinary people to do things for which we used to rely on experts.

1.6   What are two of Kant's important ideas about ethics?

1.7   What is the difference between act utilitarianism and rule utilitarianism?

1.8   Give an example of a law that implements an ethical principle. Give an example of a law that enforces a particular group's idea of how people should behave.

1.9   Explain the distinction between the negative and positive rights to freedom of speech.

1.10   When one goes behind Rawls' veil of ignorance, what is one ignorant of?

General Exercises

1.11   Write a short essay (roughly 300 words) about some topic related to computing technology or the Internet that interests you and has social or ethical implications. Describe the background; then identify the issues, problems, or questions that you think are important.

1.12   Christie's (www.christies.com), an international auction house, was founded in 1766. So why was eBay a big deal?

1.13   Some high schools ban use of cellphones during classes. Some require that students turn in their phones at the beginning of class and retrieve them afterward. What are some reasons for these policies? Do you think they are good policies? Explain.

1.14   (a)   It has become popular to post video showing people being rude, arguing, littering, and singing or dancing poorly. Is public shaming appropriate for these actions? Discuss some social and ethical considerations.

    (b)   Some parents post embarrassing videos and photos of their children as punishment for disobedience or for finding drugs in the child's room. Is public shaming appropriate for these actions? How does this differ from the situation in (a)?

1.15   Describe a useful application, other than those mentioned near the end of Section 1.2.4, for a system with which the user controls a display with hand movements, without touching a screen or controls.

1.16   Think up some computerized device, software, or online service that does not yet exist, but that you would be very proud to help develop. Describe it.

1.17   List three applications of computing and communication technology that reduce the need for transportation. What are some advantages of doing so?

1.18   For each of the following tasks, describe how it was probably done before the World Wide Web was available. Briefly tell what the main difficulties or disadvantages of the older ways were. Tell if you think there were advantages.

    (a)   Getting a copy of a bill being debated in Congress (or your country's legislature).

    (b)   Finding out if there are new treatments for lung cancer and how good they are.

    (c)   Selling a poster advertising a Beatles concert from the 1960s.

1.19   An online course in artificial intelligence at a major university had 300 students and nine teaching assistants who answered questions and conversed with students online.

The students were not told, and most did not guess, that one of the teaching assistants was an AI program. If you were in the class, would you want to be told that you were conversing with a program? Give your reasons. Explain whether you think there is an ethical issue involved.

1.20 Which kind of ethical theory, deontologist or consequentialist, works better for arguing that it is wrong to drive one's car on the left side of a road in a country where people normally drive on the right? Explain.

1.21 Develop a code of ethics and etiquette for use of smartphones at concerts.

1.22 In the following (actual) cases, tell whether the people are interpreting the right they claim as a negative right (liberty) or as a positive right (claim right). Explain. In each case, which kind of right should it be, and why?

   (a) A man sued his health insurance company because it would not pay for Viagra, the drug for treating male impotence. He argued that the insurer's refusal to pay denied his right to a happy sex life.

   (b) Two legislators who ran for reelection lost. They sued an organization that sponsored ads criticizing their voting records. The former legislators argued that the organization interfered with their right to hold office.

1.23 If John Rawls were writing now, do you think he would include providing Internet access and cellphones for all citizens as an essential requirement of a just political system? Explain.

1.24 Following a debate among political candidates during a campaign, you quietly record video of candidates talking with individuals from the audience. One candidate, responding sympathetically to a person complaining about how an insurance company handled his insurance claim, says, "All insurance company executives ought to be shot." Another candidate, talking with a person who is angry about illegal immigration, says, "Anyone sneaking across the border illegally ought to be shot." Another candidate, sprawled on a chair in the back of the room, is snoring. And a fourth, a man, invites an attractive woman back to his hotel to continue their conversation over drinks.

   Discuss the ethics of posting videos of the candidates' comments (or snoring) on the Web. Give reasons in favor of posting and reasons not to post.

   Which, if any, would you post? To what extent would, or should, your support of or opposition to the candidate affect the decision?

1.25 **(a)** Thinking ahead to Chapter 2, identify an example, application, or service mentioned in this chapter that could have a major impact on our level of privacy. Briefly explain how.

   (b) Thinking ahead to Chapter 6, identify an example mentioned in this chapter that could eliminate a large number of jobs.

   (c) Thinking ahead to Chapter 8, identify an example, application, or service mentioned in this chapter where an error in the system could pose a serious danger to people's lives. Briefly explain how.

Assignments

These exercises require some research or activity.

1.26 Go around your home or dorm and make a list of all the appliances and devices that contain a computer chip.

1.27 Arrange an interview with a disabled student on your campus. Ask the student to describe or demonstrate some of the computer tools he or she uses. (If your campus has a Disabled Student Center, its staff may be able to help you find an interview subject.) Write a report of the interview and/or demonstration.

1.28 Computing technology has had a huge impact on farming. We mentioned cow-milking machines and a few other applications in Section 1.2.4. Research a farming application and write a short report on it. (You may choose one in this book or something else.)

1.29 Research any one application of computing technology in health care and write a short report on it.

1.30 A variety of remote health services, such as online monitoring of devices worn by patients and answering patient questions over the Internet, improve health care and reduce expense and travel. However, nurses and doctors, like most professionals, are licensed by state and can practice their profession only within the state where they are licensed. To allow flexibility in remote health services, there are proposals for agreements among states to let licensed nurses work in states other than the one where they obtained their license. Find arguments that have been made by proponents and opponents of such a proposal and evaluate the arguments.

Class Discussion Exercises

These exercises are for class discussion, perhaps with short presentations prepared in advance by small groups of students.

1.31 The Encyclopædia Britannica first appeared in print in 1768. It went online in 1994. In 2012, the publisher stopped printing the hardcopy version. Was this a sad event, a positive step, or an unimportant one? Are there risks in having major stores of historic knowledge only in electronic form?

1.32 Artists, designers, and other creative people have raised money for small ($100) and large (multimillion-dollar) projects via Kickstarter, a crowdfunding site. The prospect (perhaps already achieved) that Kickstarter will generate more funding for the arts than the National Endowment for the Arts (NEA), a federal agency, disturbs some people. In what ways is Kickstarter (or sites like it) a better method to raise funds for creative projects than is the NEA? In what ways is the NEA a better method than nongovernmental crowdfunding sites? Some worry that the success of Kickstarter could lead to arguments to abolish government funding of the arts. Is this likely? Describe positive and negative impacts. Overall, would such results be good or bad?

1.33 Is it ethically acceptable or ethically prohibited for an advocacy group to launch a socialbot on a social media system that pretends to be a person and subtly promotes the group's viewpoint? Consider the same question for a socialbot that promotes a particular company's products.

1.34 A navigation app used by millions of people in a large city directs drivers through a residential neighborhood during morning rush hour when the nearby freeway is crowded. Residents complain about the extra traffic and the noise of loud car radios early in the morning. Using some of the ethical theories we described, analyze the ethics of allowing the app to route heavy traffic through residential neighborhoods. Independent of your views on whether this routing is ethical, suggest some solutions for the problems faced by the residents and the drivers.

1.35 A car company offers as an option a system that will detect a pedestrian in the path of the car, warn the driver, and brake the car if the driver does not respond. The option costs $2000. If someone buys the car, does the person have an ethical obligation to buy the optional system to protect pedestrians? Why or why not?

1.36 Is it unethical to go to a store to examine a product, and then order it on the Internet for a lower price? Give arguments for a yes answer and for a no answer. Then take a position and explain why you think it is the correct one.

 # Notes

1. Michael Rothschild, "Beyond Repair: The Politics of the Machine Age Are Hopelessly Obsolete," *The New Democrat*, July/Aug. 1995, pp. 8–11.

2. Stephen E. Ambrose, *Undaunted Courage: Meriwether Lewis, Thomas Jefferson and the Opening of the American West*, Simon & Schuster, 1996, p. 53.

3. Betty Friedan, *The Feminine Mystique*, W. W. Norton, 1963, p. 312.

4. Christopher Mims, "Driverless Cars to Fuel Suburban Sprawl," *Wall Street Journal*, June 20, 2016, www.wsj.com/articles/driverless-cars-to-fuel-suburban-sprawl-14663 95201.

5. Paul Barter, "'Cars Are Parked 95% of the time.' Let's Check!" *Reinventing Parking*, Feb. 22, 2013, www.reinventingparking.org/2013/02/cars-are-parked-95-of-time-lets-check.html.

6. Research centers doing this kind of research include the MIT Human Dynamics Laboratory, Harvard University, AT&T Labs, the London School of Economics, and others. For an overview of some of the research, see Robert Lee Hotz, "The Really Smart Phone," *Wall Street Journal*, Apr. 22, 2011, www.wsj.com/articles/SB1000142405274 8704547604576263261679848814, and Elizabeth Dwoskin, "Lending Startups Look at Borrowers' Phone Usage to Assess Creditworthiness," *Wall Street Journal*, Nov. 30, 2015, www.wsj.com/articles/lending-startups-look-at-borrowers-phone-usage-to-assess-creditworthiness-1448933308.

7. Photos appear on the Web showing religious Muslim women with uncovered faces and other people in bathrooms or locker rooms or other embarrassing or awkward situations. This problem was more acute when cameras first appeared in cellphones and most people were unaware of them.

8. Quoted in Robert Fox, "Newstrack," *Communications of the ACM*, Aug. 1995, 38:8, pp. 11–12.

9. For a good overview, see Eric Beidel, "Social Scientists and Mathematicians Join the Hunt for Terrorists," *National Defense*, Sept. 2010, www.nationaldefensemagazine. org/archive/2010/September/Pages/SocialScientistsandMathematiciansJoinTheHunt forTerrorists.aspx.

10. "Email Statistics Report, 2015–2019," The Radicati Group, Inc., Mar. 2015, www. radicati.com.

11. Statement of Vinton G. Cerf, U.S. Senate Committee on the Judiciary Hearing on Reconsidering our Communications Laws, June 14, 2006, www.judiciary.senate.gov/ download/2006/06/14/vinton-cerf-testimony-061406.

12. Steven Leckart, "The Stanford Education Experiment," *Wired*, Apr. 2012, pp. 68–77.

13. Some of these examples are described in Melinda Beck, "How Telemedicine Is Transforming Health Care," *Wall Street Journal*, June 26, 2016, www.wsj.com/articles/how-telemedicine-is-transforming-health-care-1466993402.

14. Robert D. Atkinson, "Leveling the E-Commerce Playing Field: Ensuring Tax and Regulatory Fairness for Online and Offline Businesses," Progressive Policy Institute Policy Report, June 30, 2003, www.ppionline.org. Jennifer Saranow, "Savvy Car Buyers Drive Bargains with Pricing Data from the Web," *Wall Street Journal*, Oct. 24, 2006, p. D5.

15. The last line of the paragraph is a paraphrase of the headline on an article Searle wrote, "Watson Doesn't Know It Won on 'Jeopardy!,'" *Wall Street Journal*, Feb. 17, 2011, www.wsj.com/articles/SB100014240527487034073045761543131269877674. The original Chinese room argument is in John Searle, "Minds, Brains and Programs," *Behavioral and Brain Sciences*, Cambridge University Press, 1980, pp. 417–424.

16. Liftware, now part of Alphabet, Inc., makes the tremor-canceling utensil.

17. Evan Ratliff, "Born to Run," *Wired*, July 2001, pp. 86–97. Rheo and Power Knees by Ossur, www.ossur.com. John Hockenberry, "The Human Brain," *Wired*, Aug. 2001, pp. 94–105. Aaron Saenz, "Ekso Bionics Sells its First Set of Robot Legs Allowing Paraplegics to Walk," Singularity Hub, Feb. 27, 2012, singularity-hub.com/2012/02/27/ekso-bionics-sells-its-first-set-of-robot-legs-allowing-paraplegics-to-walk.

18. By Louis P. Pojman (Wadsworth, 1990) and J. L. Mackie (Penguin Books, 1977), respectively.

19. Sources for this section include: Joseph Ellin, *Morality and the Meaning of Life: An Introduction to Ethical Theory*, Harcourt Brace Jovanovich, 1995; Deborah G. Johnson, *Computer Ethics*, Prentice Hall, 2nd ed., 1994; Louis Pojman, *Ethical Theory: Classical and Contemporary Readings*, 2nd ed., Wadsworth, 1995 (which includes John Stuart Mill's "Utilitarianism," Kant's "The Foundations of the Metaphysic of Morals," and John Locke's "Natural Rights"); and James Rachels, *The Elements of Moral Philosophy*, McGraw Hill, 1993; "John Locke (1632–1704)," *Internet Encyclopedia of Philosophy*, Apr. 17, 2001, www.iep.utm.edu/locke; Celeste Friend, "Social Contract Theory," *Internet Encyclopedia of Philosophy*, Oct. 15, 2004, www.iep.utm.edu/soc-cont; Sharon A. Lloyd and Susanne Sreedhar, "Hobbes's Moral and Political Philosophy," *The Stanford Encyclopedia of Philosophy* (Spring 2011 Edition), Edward N. Zalta (ed.), plato.stanford.edu/archives/spr2011/entries/hobbesmoral; Leif Wenar, "John Rawls," *The Stanford Encyclopedia of Philosophy* (Fall 2008 Edition), Edward N. Zalta, ed., plato.stanford.edu/archives/fall2008/entries/rawls.

20. John Stuart Mill, *Utilitarianism*, 1863.

21. John Locke, *Two Treatises of Government*, 1690.

22. J. L. Mackie uses the term *claim rights* in *Ethics: Inventing Right and Wrong*. Another term for positive rights is entitlements.

23. Claude S. Fischer, *America Calling: A Social History of the Telephone to 1940*, University of California Press, 1992, Fig. 4, p. 93.

24. Slightly paraphrased from Mike Godwin, "Steve Jobs, the Inhumane Humanist," *Reason*, Jan. 10, 2012, reason.com/archives/2012/01/10/steve-jobs-the-inhumane-humanist.

25. Julie Johnson assisted with the background for this section.
26. *Money, Markets, and Sovereignty*, Yale University Press, 2009, p. 53.
27. *A Theory of Justice*, 1971, and *Justice as Fairness*, 2001.
28. Kenneth C. Laudon, "Ethical Concepts and Information Technology," *Communications of the ACM*, Dec. 1995, 38:12, p. 38.
29. Some goals appear to be ethically wrong in themselves—for example, genocide—although often it is because the only way to achieve the goal is by methods that are ethically unacceptable (killing innocent people).
30. From a speech titled "Law and Manners," reprinted in *The Atlantic Monthly*, July 1924, pp. 1–4, www2.econ.iastate.edu/classes/econ362/hallam/NewspaperArticles/LawandManners.pdf.
31. Nebraska, for example, banned teaching foreign languages in public or private schools below ninth grade.
32. Specifically, whether the tomato sauce should be counted as a vegetable to satisfy health requirements for school lunches.

Privacy

2.1 Privacy Risks and Principles

2.1.1 WHAT IS PRIVACY?

After the fall of the communist government in East Germany, people examined the files of Stasi, the secret police. They found that the government had used spies and informants to build detailed dossiers on the opinions and activities of roughly six million people—a third of the population. The informers were neighbors, coworkers, friends, and even family members of the people they reported on. The paper files filled an estimated 125 miles of shelf space.[1]

Before the digital age, surveillance cameras watched shoppers in banks and stores. Well into the era of computers and the Internet, some pharmacies disposed of prescriptions, receipts, and order forms for medicines by tossing them into open dumpsters. Private investigators search household and commercial garbage for medical and financial information, details of purchases, evidence of romantic affairs, and journalists' notes. Digital technology is not necessary for the invasion of privacy; however, we discuss privacy at length in this book because the technology continually makes new threats possible and old threats more potent. Digital technologies—databases, digital cameras, the Web, smartphones, and global positioning system (GPS) devices, among others—have profoundly changed what people can know about us and how they use that information. Understanding the risks and problems is a first step toward protecting privacy. For computer professionals, understanding the risks and problems is a step toward designing systems with built-in privacy protections and less risk.

There are three key aspects of privacy:

- Freedom from intrusion—being left alone
- Control of information about oneself
- Freedom from surveillance (from being followed, tracked, watched, and eavesdropped upon)

We cannot expect complete privacy. We usually do not accuse someone who initiates a conversation of intruding and invading our privacy. Many friends and slight acquaintances know what you look like, where you work, what kind of car you drive, and whether you are a nice person. They need not get your permission to observe and talk about you. Control of information about oneself means control of what is in other people's minds, phones, and data storage systems and is necessarily limited by basic human rights, particularly freedom of speech. We cannot expect to be totally free from surveillance either. People see us and hear us when we move about in public—physically or in cyberspace.

If you live in a small town, you have little privacy; everyone knows everything about you. In a big city, you are more nearly anonymous. But if people know nothing about you, they might be taking a big risk if they rent you a place to live, hire you, lend you money, sell you automobile insurance, accept your credit card, and so on. We give up some privacy for the benefits of dealing with strangers. We can choose to give up more in exchange for other benefits such as convenience, personalized service, and easy communication with many friends.

For the most part, in this book, we view privacy as a good thing. Critics of privacy argue that it gives cover to deception, hypocrisy, and wrongdoing. Privacy allows fraud and protects the guilty. Concern for privacy may be regarded with a suspicious "What do you have to hide?" The desire to keep things private does not imply we are doing anything wrong. We may wish to keep health, relationship, and family issues private. We may choose not to share our religious beliefs and political views with everyone we know, perhaps to avoid distracting arguments. We may not want others to know how much junk food we eat or how many hours we spend watching silly videos. Privacy of information can be important to safety and security as well. Examples include travel plans, financial data, and for some people, simply a home address.

Privacy threats come in several categories:

- Intentional, institutional uses of personal information (in the government sector primarily for law enforcement and tax collection, and in the private sector primarily for marketing and decision making)
- Unauthorized use or release by "insiders," the people who maintain the information
- Theft of information
- Inadvertent leakage of information through negligence or carelessness
- Our own actions (sometimes intentional trade-offs and sometimes when we are unaware of the risks)

Privacy issues arise in many contexts, and more topics with privacy implications appear in later chapters. We discuss spam—the intrusion of junk email, text messages, and phone calls—in Chapter 3. We address hacking and identity theft in Chapter 5. We discuss monitoring of social media and workplace communications and other issues of privacy for employees in Chapter 6. Some privacy risks result from the fact that so much of the data stored about us is incorrect or out-of-date. Chapter 8 discusses some of these problems. Privacy comes up again in Chapter 9, where we focus on the responsibilities of computer professionals.

Throughout this chapter, we use many real incidents, businesses, products, and services as examples. In most cases, we are not singling them out for special endorsement or criticism. They are just some of the many examples we can use to illustrate problems, issues, and possible solutions.

The quotes with which we end this section comment on privacy from three perspectives: philosophical, personal, and political.

The man who is compelled to live every minute of his life among others and whose every need, thought, desire, fancy or gratification is subject to public scrutiny, has been deprived of his individuality and human dignity. [He] merges with the mass. . . . Such a being, although sentient, is fungible; he is not an individual.

—Edward J. Bloustein[2]

It's important to realize that privacy preserves not personal secrets, but a sense of safety within a circle of friends so that the individual can be more candid, more expressive, more open with "secrets."

—Robert Ellis Smith[3]

Privacy in group association may . . . be indispensable to preservation of freedom of association, particularly where a group espouses dissident beliefs.

—The Supreme Court, ruling against the state of Alabama's attempt to get the membership list of the National Association for the Advancement of Colored People (NAACP) in the 1950s[4]

2.1.2 NEW TECHNOLOGY, NEW RISKS

Today there are thousands (probably millions) of databases, both government and private, containing personal information about us. In the past, there was simply no record of some of this information, such as our specific purchases of groceries and books. When we browsed in a library or store, no one knew what we read or looked at. Certain government documents were available to the public, but accessing them took time and effort. It was not easy to link together our financial, work, and family records.

Now, large companies that operate video, social network, email, and search services can combine information from a member's use of all of them to obtain a detailed picture of the person's interests, opinions, relationships, habits, and activities. Even if we do not log in as members, software tracks our activity on the Web. In the past, conversations disappeared when people finished speaking, and, normally, only the sender and the recipient read personal communications. When we communicate by texting, email, social media, and so on, there is a record of our words that others can copy, forward, distribute widely, and read years later. We use spoken commands to talk to digital personal assistants and devices in our homes that are connected to the Internet; thus microphones are listening to us at all times.

We store our photos, videos, documents, and financial statements in a cloud of remote servers. Power and water providers will soon have metering and analysis systems sophisticated enough to determine what appliances we are using, when we shower (and for how long), and when we sleep. Cameras in some 3D television sets warn children if they are sitting too close. What else might such cameras record, and who might see it? The wireless appliances we carry enable others to determine our location and track our movements. Law enforcement agencies have very sophisticated tools for eavesdropping, surveillance, and collecting and analyzing data about people's activities, tools that can help reduce crime and increase security—or threaten privacy and liberty.

Combining powerful new tools and applications can have astonishing results. It is possible to snap a photo of someone on the street, match the photo to one on a social network, and use a trove of publicly accessible information to guess, with high probability of accuracy, the person's name, birth date, and most of his or her Social Security number. This does not require a supercomputer; it is done with a smartphone app. We see such systems in television shows and movies, but to many people these capabilities may seem exaggerated or way off in the future.

All these gadgets, services, and activities have benefits, of course, but they expose us to new risks. The implications for privacy are profound.

> *Patient medical information is confidential. It should not be discussed in a public place.*
>
> —A sign, aimed at doctors and staff, in an elevator in a medical office building, a reminder to prevent low-tech privacy leaks

Example: Search query data

Search engines collect and store terabytes of data daily. A terabyte is a trillion bytes. It would have been absurdly expensive to store that much data in the recent past, but no longer. Why do search engine companies store search queries? While it is tempting to say "because they can," there are many uses for the data. Search engine companies want to know how many pages of search results users actually look at, how many they click on, how they refine their search queries, and what spelling errors they commonly make. The companies analyze the data to improve search services, to target advertising better, and to develop new services. The database of past queries provides realistic input for testing and evaluating modifications in the algorithms search engines use to select and rank results. Search query data are also valuable to many companies besides search engine companies. For example, by analyzing search queries, companies learn what kinds of products and features people are looking for; they modify their products to meet consumer preferences.

But who else gets to see this mass of data? And why should we care? If your own Web searches have been on innocuous topics, and you do not care who sees your queries, consider a few topics people might search for and think about why they might want to keep them private: health and psychological problems, bankruptcy, uncontrolled gambling, right-wing conspiracies, left-wing conspiracies, alcoholism, antiabortion information, pro-abortion information, erotica, illegal drugs. What are some possible consequences for a person doing extensive research on the Web for a suspense novel about terrorists who plan to blow up chemical factories?

When the federal government presented Google with a subpoena* for two months of user search queries, without names of users, Google and privacy advocates opposed the precedent of government access to large masses of such data because they believed it threatened privacy. A court reduced the scope of the subpoena, and not long afterward, the risks of releasing search queries, even without names, were made clear. An AOL employee, against company policy, released a huge database of search queries on a website for search technology researchers. The data included more than 20 million search queries by more than 650,000 people from a three-month period. The data identified people by coded ID numbers, not by name. However, it is not difficult to deduce the identity of some people, especially those who searched on their own name or address. Others were identified using *reidentification*—identifying an individual from a set of anonymous data. Journalists and acquaintances identified people in small communities who searched on numerous specific topics, such as the cars they own, the sports teams they follow, their health problems, and their hobbies. Once identified, a person is linked to all his or her other searches. AOL quickly removed the data, but journalists, researchers, and others had already copied it. Some made the whole data set available on the Web again.[5†]

Example: Smartphone apps

With so many clever, useful, and free smartphone apps available, who thinks twice about downloading them? Researchers and journalists took a close look at smartphone software and apps and found some surprises.

Some Android phones and iPhones send location data (essentially the location of nearby cell towers) to Google and Apple, respectively. Companies use the data to build location-based services that can be quite valuable for the public and for the companies. (Industry researchers estimate the market for location services to be in the billions of dollars.) The location data are supposed to be anonymous, but researchers found, in some cases, that they included the phone ID.

Roughly half the apps in one test sent the phone's ID number or location to other companies (in addition to the one that provided the app). A few apps also sent age and gender information to advertising companies—without the user's knowledge or consent. Various apps copied the user's contact list to remote servers. Android phones and iPhones allowed apps to copy photos (and, for example, post them on the Internet) if the user permits the app to do other actions that have nothing to do with photos. (Google said this capability dated from when photos were on removable memory cards and thus less vulnerable.[6] This is a reminder that designers must regularly review and update security design decisions.) Leaking personal data via phone apps is a continuing issue.

---

*A subpoena is a court order for someone to give testimony or provide documents or other information for an investigation or a trial.

†Members of AOL sued the company for releasing their search queries, claiming the release violated roughly 10 federal and state laws.

Why does this matter? The data are vulnerable to loss, hacking, and misuse. If you do not know the phone stores or transmits the information, you do not know to erase it. Apps use features on phones that indicate the phone's location, the light level, movement of the phone, the presence of other phones nearby, and so on. Knowing where we have been over a period of time (combined with other information from a phone) can tell a lot about our activities and interests, as well as with whom we associate (and whether the lights were on). As we mentioned in Section 1.2.2, it can also indicate where we are likely to be at a particular time in the future.

Stolen and lost data

Criminals steal personal data by hacking into computer systems; by stealing computers, memory cards, and drives; by buying or requesting records under false pretenses; and by bribing employees of companies that store the data. Shady information brokers sell data (including mobile phone records, credit reports, credit card statements, medical and work records, and location of relatives, as well as information about financial and investment accounts) that they obtain illegally or by questionable means. Criminals, lawyers, private investigators, spouses, ex-spouses, and law enforcement agents are among the buyers. A private investigator could have obtained some of this information in the past, but not nearly so much, so easily, cheaply, and quickly.

Another risk is accidental (sometimes quite careless) loss. Businesses, government agencies, and other institutions lose computers, phones, disks, memory cards, laptops, and other devices containing sensitive personal data (such as Social Security numbers and credit card numbers) on millions of people, exposing people to potential misuse of their information and lingering uncertainty. Businesses, government agencies, and other institutions inadvertently allow sensitive files to be public on the Web; researchers have found medical information and other sensitive personal or confidential information about thousands of people in files mistakenly made accessible on the Web.

Data thieves get sensitive information by telephone by pretending to be the person whose records they seek. They provide some personal, but possibly public or innocuous, information about the target to make the request seem legitimate. That is one reason why it is important to be cautious even with data that is not particularly sensitive by itself.

Here is a small sample of stolen, lost, or leaked personal information.[7] In many incidents, the goal of thieves is to collect data for use in identity theft and fraud, crimes we discuss in Chapter 5.

- Files on hundreds of thousands of students, applicants, faculty, and/or alumni from the University of California, Harvard, Georgia Tech, Kent State, and several other universities, some with Social Security numbers and birth dates (stolen by hackers).

- Names, birth dates, and possibly credit card numbers of 77 million people who play video games online using Sony's PlayStation (stolen by hackers). Another 24 million accounts were exposed when hackers broke into a Sony online game service
- Bank of America disks with account information (lost or stolen in transit)
- Credit histories and other personal data for 163,000 people (purchased from a huge database company by a fraud ring posing as legitimate businesses)
- Patient names, Social Security numbers, addresses, dates of birth, and medical billing information for perhaps 400,000 patients at a hospital (on a laptop stolen from a hospital employee's car)
- Confidential contact information for more than one million job seekers (stolen from Monster.com by hackers using servers in Ukraine)
- The passport numbers and other personal information about the heads of approximately 30 major countries, including the United States, Russia, England, China, and Germany (accidently emailed to a sports organization by the Australian immigration agency)

A summary of sources of risks

The examples we described illustrate numerous points about personal data. We summarize here:

- Anything we do in cyberspace, even briefly, can be recorded and linked to our computer, phone, and possibly our name. This includes use of household Internet-connected appliances.
- With the huge amount of storage space available, companies, organizations, and governments save huge amounts of data that no one would have imagined saving in the recent past.
- People often are not aware of the collection of information about them and their activities.
- Software is extremely complex. Sometimes businesses, organizations, and website managers do not even know what the software they use collects and stores.[8]
- Leaks happen. The existence of the data presents a risk.
- A collection of many small items of information can give a fairly detailed picture of a person's life.
- Direct association with a person's name is not essential for compromising privacy. Reidentification has become much easier due to the quantity of personal information stored and the power of data search and analysis tools.
- Information on a public website is available to everyone; people other than those for whom it was intended will find it.

- Once information goes on the Internet or into a database, it is almost impossible to remove it from circulation since people and automated software may quickly make and distribute copies.

- It is extremely likely that data collected for one purpose (such as making a phone call or responding to a search query) will find other uses (such as business planning, tracking, marketing, or criminal investigations).

- The government sometimes requests or demands sensitive personal data held by businesses and organizations.

- We often cannot directly protect information about ourselves, so we depend on the businesses and organizations that manage it to protect it from thieves, accidental collection, leaks, and government prying.

The fact that something has risks does not mean that we should not use it. Every time we get in a car, we risk being in a crash. We are safer if we buckle the seatbelt and do not text while driving. Throughout this book, we will emphasize the importance of being aware of risks and of employing the data equivalents of seatbelts and good driving practices.

2.1.3 TERMINOLOGY AND PRINCIPLES FOR MANAGING PERSONAL DATA

We use the term *personal information* often in this chapter. In the context of privacy issues, it includes any information relating to, or traceable to, an individual person. The term applies to what we commonly think of as sensitive information but includes much else as well. It also includes information associated with a particular person's "handle," user name, online nickname, identification number, email address, or phone number. Personal information extends beyond textual data to any information, including images, from which someone can identify an individual.

Informed consent and invisible information gathering

There is an extraordinary range to the amount of privacy individuals desire. Some people blog about their divorce or illnesses and pour out details of their romantic relationships on television shows or to hundreds of social network friends. Yet, other individuals use cash to avoid leaving a record of their purchases, encrypt all their email,* and are angry when someone collects information about them. A key principle for ethical treatment of personal information is *informed consent*. When a business or an organization informs people about its data collection and use policies or about the data that a particular device or application collects, each person can decide, according to his or her own values, whether to interact with that business or organization or whether to use the device or application.

Invisible information gathering describes the collection of personal information without the person's knowledge. The important ethical issue is that if someone

---

*Encrypting data means putting it in a coded form so that others cannot read it.

is not aware of the collection and use, he or she has no opportunity to consent or withhold consent. We gave examples involving smartphones and their apps in the previous section. Here are examples from other contexts.

- A company offered a free program that changed a Web browser's cursor into a cartoon character. Millions of people installed the program but later discovered that the program sent to the company a report of the websites its users visited, along with a customer identification number in the software.[9]

- "Event data recorders" in cars record information, such as driving speed and whether or not the driver is wearing a seatbelt, for use in investigating crashes.

- "History sniffers" are programs that collect information about a person's online activity based on the different colors a browser uses to display sites recently visited.

- Software called *spyware*, often downloaded from a website without the user's knowledge, surreptitiously collects information about a person's activity and data on his or her device and then sends the information over the Internet to the person or company that planted the spyware. Spyware can track someone's Web surfing for an advertising company or collect passwords and credit card numbers typed by the user. (Some of these activities are illegal, of course.)

Sophisticated snooping technologies: Section 2.3.3

When our computers, phones, and other devices communicate with websites, they must provide information about their configuration (e.g., the Web browser used). For a high percentage of devices, there is enough variation and detail in configurations and activities to create a profile or "fingerprint" for each device. Companies provide device profiling software for combating fraud and intellectual property theft and for tracking people's online activity in order to target advertising. Financial firms that use device fingerprinting for security of customer accounts may say so in a privacy policy. Both collection of configuration information and building of activity profiles are invisible, so we are unlikely to know when someone is using these techniques to build marketing profiles. (Often information about our configuration, activity at a particular website, and so on is stored on our own machines, in *cookies*—small files maintained by the Web browser on our computer and accessed by the entity that put them there or by others.[10])

Whether or not a particular example of data collection is invisible information gathering can depend on the level of public awareness. Some people know what data their cars collect, store, and/or transmit; most do not.[11] Many businesses and organizations have policy statements or customer agreements that inform customers, members, and subscribers of their policy on collecting and using personal data, but many people simply do not read them, and if they read the policies, they forget. Thus, there is a significant privacy impact from the many automated systems that collect information in unobvious ways, even when people have been informed. However, there is an important distinction between situations where people are informed but not aware and situations where the information gathering is truly covert.

Secondary use, data mining, matching, and profiling

> *My most private thoughts, my personal tragedies, secrets about other people, are mere data of a transaction, like a grocery receipt.*
>
> —A woman whose psychologist's notes were read by an insurer[12]

Secondary use is the use of personal information for a purpose other than the one for which the person supplied it. Examples of secondary use include:

- sale of consumer information to marketers or other businesses,
- use of information in various databases to deny someone a job or to tailor a political pitch,
- the Internal Revenue Service searching vehicle registration records for people who own expensive cars and boats (to find people with high incomes),
- use of a person's text messages by police to prosecute that person for a crime,
- use of a supermarket's customer database to show alcohol purchases by a man who sued the store because he fell down.

We see more examples of secondary use throughout this chapter. One key controversial issue of personal information is the degree of control people should have over secondary uses of information about them. The variety of uses illustrated by the few examples we gave above suggests that quite different answers are appropriate for different users and different uses.

After informing people about what personal information an organization collects and what it does with that information, the next simplest and most desirable privacy policy is to give people some control over secondary uses. The two most common forms for providing such control are *opt out* and *opt in*. Under an opt-out policy, one must check or click a box on a contract, membership form, or agreement or possibly contact the organization to request that the organization not use one's information in a particular way. If the person does not take action, the presumption is that the organization may use the information. Under an opt-in policy, the collector of the information may not use it for certain secondary uses unless the person explicitly checks or clicks a box or signs a form permitting the use. (Be careful not to confuse the two. Under an opt-out policy, more people are likely to be "in," and under an opt-in policy, more people are likely to be "out," because the default presumption is the opposite of the policy name.) Responsible, consumer-friendly companies and organizations often set the default so that they do not share personal information and do not send marketing emails unless the person explicitly allows it—that is, they have an opt-in policy. On the other hand, many websites inform visitors that using the site is considered to be acceptance of its privacy policy—which most visitors do not read and which may allow tracking and sharing of data about the visitor's activity. Particularly in situations where disclosing personal information can have negative consequences and it is not obvious to a customer that the organization might disclose it, a default of nondisclosure without explicit permission (that is, an opt-in policy) is the responsible policy.

Data mining means searching and analyzing masses of data to find patterns and develop new information or knowledge. The research using social network data and smartphone data that we described in Section 1.2.2 are examples. *Matching* means combining and comparing information from different databases, often using an identifier such as a person's Social Security number or his or her computer's Internet address to match records. *Profiling* means analyzing data to determine characteristics of people most likely to engage in certain behavior. Businesses use these techniques to find likely new customers, and government agencies use them to detect fraud, to enforce other laws, and to find terrorists. Data mining, computer matching, and profiling are, in most cases, examples of secondary use of personal information.

Fair information principles

Privacy advocates have developed various sets of principles for protection of personal data. They are often called Fair Information Principles or Fair Information Practices.[13] Figure 2.1 presents such a list of principles. Informed consent and restrictions on secondary uses show up in the first and third principles. Many businesses and organizations have adopted some version of Fair Information Practices. Laws in the United States, Canada, and European countries (among others) require them in many situations. These principles are reasonable ethical guidelines; however, there is wide variation in interpretation of the principles. For example, businesses and privacy advocates disagree about what information businesses "need" and for how long.

- Inform people when you collect information about them, what you collect, and how you use it.
- Collect only the data needed.
- Offer a way for people to opt out from mailing lists, advertising, and other secondary uses. Offer a way for people to opt out from features and services that expose personal information.
- Keep data only as long as needed.
- Maintain accuracy of data. Where appropriate and reasonable, provide a way for people to access and correct data stored about them.
- Protect security of data (from theft and from accidental leaks). Provide strong protection for sensitive data.
- Develop and publish policies for responding to law enforcement requests for data.

FIGURE 2.1 Privacy principles for personal information.

It can be difficult to apply the fair information principles to new technologies and applications such as cameras in public places (for example, police camera systems and Google's Street View), the enormous amount of personal information people share in social media, and all the many Internet-connected devices we use. For example, when someone puts personal information in a tweet to tens or thousands of people, how do we determine the purpose for which he or she supplied the information? Can any recipient use the information in any way? How widely distributed must information be before it is public in the sense that anyone can see or use it? Even when people have agreed to share information, consequences of new ways of sharing or new categories of information can be unexpected and problematic. For example, in Section 2.2.2 we discuss default settings for features in social networks that have significant consequences.

When responding to requests from law enforcement agents or government agencies, many companies and organizations turn over personal data, while others do so only if presented with a subpoena or other court order. Some challenge subpoenas and inform their customers or members when they give personal data to the government; others do not. The individual whose data the entity might release is rarely aware of the government request as the government may mandate the secondary use be kept secret so that an individual under suspicion does not change online activities or attempt to hide data. For a business or an organization, planning ahead for various possible scenarios, developing a policy, and announcing it (and following it) are all part of responsible management of other people's personal data.

2.2 The Business and Social Sectors

2.2.1 MARKETING AND PERSONALIZATION

Acxiom provides complete and accurate pictures of customers and prospects, powering all marketing and relationship efforts.

—Acxiom website[14]

Marketing is an essential task for most businesses and organizations. It is one of the biggest uses of personal information—by businesses, political parties, nonprofit organizations, and advocacy groups. Marketing includes finding new customers, members, or voters and encouraging old ones to continue. It includes advertising and policies about how to price products and when and to whom to offer discounts.

Through most of the 20th century, businesses sent out catalogs and advertisements based on a small number of criteria (age, gender, and neighborhood, for example). Computers and increased storage capacity generated a revolution in targeted marketing. As the technology became more sophisticated, so did the collection and analysis of consumer data. Businesses of all sorts store and analyze terabytes of data, including consumer purchases, financial information, online activity, opinions, preferences, government records, and any other useful information to determine who might be a new customer and what new products and services an old customer might buy. Businesses now analyze thousands of criteria to target ads both online and offline. Online retailers greet us by name and make recommendations based on our prior purchases and on those of other people with similar buying patterns. These merchant activities impinge on a key aspect of privacy: control of information about oneself. Privacy advocates and some consumers object to advertising based on consumer purchase histories and online activity. Marketers argue that targeting ads via personal consumer information reduces the number of ads overall that people will see, provides ads that people are more likely to want, and reduces overhead and, ultimately, the cost of products. For example, L.L.Bean, a big mail-order business, says it sends out fewer catalogs as it does a better job of targeting customers, and another firm reported that 20–50% of people used the personalized coupons it provided on screen or by email, compared with the roughly 1% response rate for ads in general. Many people like the personalization of ads and recommendations. Targeting is so popular with some people that Google advertised that its Gmail displays no *untargeted* banner ads.

Some kinds of less obvious personalization trouble people more (when they learn of them). The displays, ads, prices, and discounts you see when shopping online might be different from those that other people see. Some such targeting is quite reasonable: A clothing site does not display winter parkas on its home page for a shopper from Florida. Some sites offer discounts to first-time visitors. Some display any of hundreds of variations of a page depending on time of day, gender, location, and dozens of other attributes of a person's session. (Some sites guess a visitor's gender based on clicking behavior.[15]) If a person hesitates over a product, a site might offer something extra, perhaps free shipping. A hotel reservation website discovered that people who use Macintosh computers, on average, select higher priced hotel rooms than people who use Windows, so it began showing more expensive options to visitors who use Macs. Is this collection and use of behavioral information an example of inappropriate invisible information gathering? Is it reasonable? Is it manipulative? Are these tactics different from what a salesperson might do in person in a store to win a customer over and make a sale?

When we shop in stores, salesclerks can see our gender and our approximate age. They can form other conclusions about us from our clothing, conversation, and behavior. Good salespeople in expensive specialty stores, car dealerships, flea markets, and third-world street markets make judgments about how much a potential customer will pay. They modify their price or offer extras accordingly. Is the complex software that personalizes shopping online merely making up for the loss of information that would be available to sellers if we were shopping in person? Are some people uneasy mainly because they did not realize that their behavior affects what appears on their screen? Or are there privacy threats lurking in these practices? A salesclerk in a store does not have a list of our online search queries. Who does? Who should?

Data mining and clever marketing[16]

Are these examples of desirable competition or scary intrusiveness and manipulation of consumers?

- The Target retail chain had its data miners analyze purchases by women who signed up for baby registries. Target discovered that pregnant women tend to increase their purchases of a group of 25 products. So when a woman began to purchase more of those products (e.g., unscented lotions and mineral supplements), Target sent coupons and ads for pregnancy and baby products—even timing the coupons for stages of the pregnancy.

- Customers of the British retailing firm Tesco, like customers of many grocery chains, permit the company to collect information on their buying habits in exchange for discounts. The company identifies young adult males who buy diapers and sends them coupons for beer—assuming that, with a new baby, they have less time to go to a pub.

- To compete with Walmart, Tesco aimed to identify customers who were most price conscious and hence most likely to be attracted to Walmart's low prices. By analyzing purchase data, the company determined which customers regularly buy the cheapest version of products that are available at more than one price level. Then the company determined what products those customers buy most often, and set prices on those products below Walmart's.

Companies can use face recognition systems in video game consoles and televisions to target ads to the individual person who is playing a game or watching TV. What risks to privacy does this entail? Is it unethical to include such features? Will most people like the customization? Do they understand that if they see ads targeted to their interests, someone somewhere is storing information about them? Does it matter if a human ever views the data or if it is processed and acted on only by software?

Our examples so far have been commercial situations. The Democratic and Republican parties collect and analyze extensive information—from consumer databases, social media, cookies from their websites, and other sources—on tens of millions of people to determine who might vote for their candidates, what to emphasize in ads and when asking for contributions, how much to ask for, and even what day of the week to send the request. A presidential campaign emailed at least six different versions of invitations to a $40,000-per-ticket fundraising dinner, each targeted to the particular people who received it.[17]

The issue is informed consent

Technological and social changes make people uncomfortable, but that does not mean the changes are unethical. It should be clear that targeted or personalized marketing is not, in itself, unethical. Most of the legitimate concerns have to do with how marketers get the data they use and with how the huge amount of data that they can collect or buy gives them more personal and sensitive information than we want them to have. In some cases, there is consent, in some there is not, and in many cases the complexity of the situation makes consent unclear.

Collection of consumer data for marketing without informing people or obtaining their consent used to be widespread, essentially standard practice. Sometimes, small print informed consumers, but often they did not see it, did not understand the implications, or ignored it. Gradually, public awareness and pressure for improvement increased, and data collection and distribution policies improved. Now responsible websites, businesses, and organizations commonly provide explicit, multipage statements about what information they collect and how they use the information. They provide opt-out and opt-in options. There are still many companies that get it wrong, whether out of lack of concern for people's privacy or by misjudging what people want. There is also a vast world of data collection over which we have little or no direct control. When someone consents to a company's use of his or her consumer information, the person probably has no idea how extensive the company is and how far the data could travel. Firms such as Acxiom, a large international database and direct-marketing company quoted at the beginning of this section, collect personal data from a huge number of online and offline sources. Companies that maintain huge consumer databases buy (or merge with) others, combining data to build more detailed databases and dossiers. They sell data and consumer profiles to businesses for marketing and "customer management." Many people do not know such firms exist.

Awareness of online tracking varies among consumers. Does a person's decision to interact with a business or visit a website constitute implicit consent to its posted data collection, marketing, and tracking policies? We know that many people do not read privacy policies. How often should a site that runs (or allows third parties to run) tracking software remind users? Some people who allow extensive tracking and information collection might later regret the decision, but potentially negative future consequences of choices we make now (such as not getting enough exercise) are common in life. Whose responsibility is it to protect us in cyberspace? Can we protect people without eliminating options for those who want them?

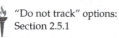
"Do not track" options: Section 2.5.1

Many nonprofit organizations, such as the Privacy Rights Clearinghouse, help to educate consumers and encourage responsible choices. Federal laws and regulations require specific privacy protections for financial and medical information[18] and set specific opt-in and opt-out requirements for certain kinds of data. (For example, the Federal Communications Commission created a rule that broadband Internet service providers cannot sell certain customer information to third parties unless the customer opts in.) Designing systems ethically and responsibly means including ways to inform and remind users of unobvious data collection, of changes in policies or features, and of risks.

Paying for consumer information

When businesses first began building extensive consumer databases, some privacy advocates argued that the businesses should pay consumers for use of their information. In many circumstances, they did (and do) pay us indirectly. For example, when we fill out a contest entry form, we trade data for the opportunity to win prizes. Many businesses give discounts to shoppers who use cards that enable tracking of their purchases. Others offer to trade free products and services for permission to send advertising messages or to collect information. Some Internet service providers offer service at two different price levels depending on whether the customer allows certain uses of the data the company collects about the customer. But some privacy advocates criticize such programs. Lauren Weinstein, founder of Privacy Forum, argues that among less affluent people the attraction of free services may be especially strong, and it "coerces" them into giving up their privacy.[19] People do not understand all the potential uses of their information and the long-term consequences of the agreements. On the other hand, such programs offer an opportunity for people with little money to trade something else of value (information) for goods and services they desire. Free-PC was early with the trend when, in 1999, it offered 10,000 free personal computers in exchange for providing personal information and watching advertising messages. Hundreds of thousands of people swamped the company with applications on the first day, and such offers continue to be popular. A consumer products company in India, for example, offers a chance to win a free smartphone in exchange for listening to ads.[20]

In any case, these programs are dwarfed by the development of social media, free video sites, and a huge number of other websites that provide information and services for free. People understand that advertising funds them. Gmail targets ads to individual users by analyzing the user's email messages. Some privacy advocates were horrified when Google introduced Gmail: it reads people's email! In exchange for permission to do so, Gmail provides free email and other services. Millions of people signed up. The success of these businesses and services shows that many people do not object to businesses using their purchase history or email

Blocking ads: Section 2.5.3

and do not consider the intrusion of some number and type of ads to be extremely bothersome, nor their Web surfing to be particularly sensitive—especially when considering the trade-off for obtaining so much for free. Do they understand the potential risks? Are they making reasonable choices?

2.2.2   Our Social and Personal Activity

Social networks—what *we* do

There are two aspects of social networks to consider: our own responsibility for what we share (how we risk our privacy and that of our friends) and the responsibilities of the companies that host our information.

A woman enjoyed the feature on a social network site that told her which members read her profile, but she was surprised and upset to find that people whose profiles she read knew that she read them. This incident illustrates a common phenomenon: people often want information about others, but they do not want others to have access to the same kinds of information about themselves. In another incident, a high school senior put a photo of herself in a bikini on Facebook. A district school system used the photo and the student's name in a community seminar urging people to be careful about what they post. The student was upset; she said she believed that only friends and friends of friends could see the photo. Both of these incidents remind us that some people do not know or understand or think enough about information sharing policies to make good decisions about what to do in cyberspace.

Many young people post opinions, gossip, and pictures that their friends enjoy. Their posts might cause trouble if parents, potential employers, law enforcement agents, or various others see them. A 17-year-old who posts photos of herself in bathing suits is thinking about her friends viewing them, not potential stalkers, rapists, or school administrators. People who try to clean up their online personas before starting a job search find that it is hard to eliminate embarrassing material. Some social network apps ask for personal information—such as religion, political views, and sexual orientation—about one's friends as well as oneself. Do people think about how the information might be used and whether their friends would like it disclosed?

Why was it for so long standard practice to stop mail and newspaper delivery when going away on a trip? This one detail about location ("away from home") was important to protect from potential burglars. Yet, now, a great many people post their location (and that of their friends) to social networks. Is this less risky?

After many incidents exposing embarrassing messages, we continue to see individuals, politicians, lawyers, celebrities, and businesspeople posting and tweeting offensive, illegal, or otherwise compromising things with the apparent belief that no one but the intended recipients will ever see them.

Government agencies and businesses do many things wrong with respect to privacy, but individuals also do not always exercise appropriate thought and care for their own privacy, future, and safety.

> *Polls show that people care about privacy.*
> *Why don't they act that way?*
>
> —Ian Kerr[21]

Social networks—what *they* do

We use Facebook for our examples here because it has many features and a large number of members, and because it has made instructive mistakes. The principles apply to other social media and other websites.

Facebook regularly introduces new services, new ways to share with friends and stay up to date on their activities. Several times, Facebook seriously misjudged how members would react; it made poor choices. Some of the examples we describe quickly generated storms of criticism from tens of thousands to hundreds of thousands of members as well as from privacy advocates.

News feeds send recent changes in a member's personal information, friends list, and activities to that member's friends.[22] When Facebook introduced the feeds, it said it did not change any privacy settings. It sends the information only to people the members had already approved and who could already see the information if they looked for it. Within a day or two, hundreds of thousands of Facebook members protested vehemently. Why? The ease of accessing information can sometimes be more important than the fact that it is available somewhere. Many people do not check on their hundreds of friends regularly. The feeds, however, spread information to everyone instantly. Here is one instance where immediate distribution makes a difference: We might share information about the end of a relationship, a serious illness, or a family problem with a few, chosen, close friends. Gradually, as we adjust to the new situation, others might learn of it. The feeds removed the emotionally protective delay.

When Facebook began telling members about purchases their friends made, problems ranged from spoiling surprise gifts to embarrassing and worrisome disclosures. Facebook's Places feature lets users tag friends who are at their location (whether or not the friend is actually there). When Facebook introduced a face recognition tool to help members tag friends in photos, the default was that the tool was on for all members. There was a way to opt out, but many users were not aware of the new feature, so they did not know to opt out. One argument for introducing new features in a turned-on mode is that all users are exposed to the feature and have a chance to evaluate the benefits; if the feature is initially turned off, many users may never know it exists. Should a social network company introduce such features turned on for everyone? Or should the company announce them and let members opt in if they choose to?

Angry members are not good for business, and several incidents demonstrated the importance, from both an ethical perspective and a business perspective, of giving careful thought to the implications and risks of new features and the selection of default settings. Changes that might seem small and subtle can have big impacts on people's perceptions of privacy, on risk, and on feelings of comfort. People might be happy if a few friends tag them in a few photos, but they might be very uneasy if an automated system tags every photo they appear in. Quantity can make a difference in perceived quality (in particular, in one's feeling of control of information about oneself). In complex environments, such as social networks with their many features and members, an opt-in policy is preferable—that is, a policy where members must explicitly turn the feature on, or else it remains off. It is also valuable to have a range of options. For example, for a tagging feature (for location or photos), options can include informing the person and allowing removal of the tag, requesting permission for each tag before it goes live, and allowing a member to completely opt out of being tagged. (Facebook modified Places to include a range of levels of protection.)

According to the Federal Trade Commission, Facebook violated its stated policies in several instances: by giving users' IDs to advertisers along with data on user activity, by allowing third-party apps full access to member personal data, and by failing to delete some of a member's data when the member deleted the account. Such actions, in violation of a company's own statements about its practices, are deceptive; they thwart informed decisions and agreements. We might dislike, denounce, debate, and disagree about the ethics of some data practices, but deceptive practices are clearly unethical.

Responsibility of free services

We should appreciate the astounding number of free services available to us from social media, search engines, free mobile apps, websites full of expert information, and so on. We can choose to use them or not. At the same time, the businesses that offer free services have a responsibility to their users. As an analogy, if you invite your neighbors to use your car anytime they wish without asking, you have an ethical responsibility not to leave the keys in the car when the brakes are not working, whether you charge a fee or not. Companies may not, ethically, offer attractive services and then cause a significant risk of harm, especially when the risk is hidden or unexpected.

Life in the clouds

As people began to own multiple devices—desktop computer, laptop or tablet, ebook reader, smartphone, fitness monitors, and more—the benefits of syncing became clear. It is convenient that our photos are available on whatever device we happen to have with us, that our calendar is up to date everywhere, and that our phone knows what page we are up to in the book we are reading on our ebook reader. To accomplish this, our data are stored on computers that do not belong to us, that we do not control. All our data are vulnerable at the level of the weakest security of our devices and the cloud services that host the data.

How else do we spread sensitive personal data through cyberspace, and what are the risks?

Millions of people prepare their tax returns online. Do they think about where their income and expenditure data are going, how long the data will remain online, or how well secured the data are? Small businesses store all their accounting information on websites that provide accounting services and access from anywhere. Several medical websites provide an easy place for people to store their medical records. You can store an inventory of your valuable property on the Web (for free) to help with insurance claims after a fire or tornado.

Some people include their birth date in online profiles or in résumés they post on job-hunting sites. On genealogy sites, people create family trees with complete profiles of family members, including birth dates and mother's maiden name. Often, medical and financial institutions used this same information (birth dates and mother's maiden name) to verify a customer's identity, either online or over the phone. While we can change a disclosed password, we cannot change our birth date or mother's maiden name.

There are big advantages to services in the cloud. They manage our data and backups for us, our data can be accessed from anywhere with Internet access, and we can easily share files and collaborate with others on projects. There are disadvantages too: increased risk to privacy and security as we lose control over our data. When our files were only on our desktop, we faced the risks of loss and theft while files stored outside our home are at risk of loss, theft, misuse by employees, accidental exposure, seizure by government agencies, uses by the service provider described in an agreement or privacy policy we did not read, uses we ignored when signing up for the service, and later uses that no one anticipated.

Years ago, when many homes had answering machines connected to telephones, some people, instead, used answering services. Messages left for them resided on recording machines at the service's business site. I (SB) recall my surprise that people were comfortable having their personal messages on machines outside their control. How quaint and old-fashioned that concern seems now. Attitudes about protecting our own personal data have changed dramatically. Even though most people do not know or think a lot about the risks in cyberspace, they recognize the benefits and value them highly, especially convenience. Few people who own a phone and a desktop computer or tablet would want the trouble of manually keeping their contacts or calendar in sync when it is so easy to let the cloud do it. We might decide the convenience of filling out tax forms online or storing our medical records online outweighs the risks. As users of all these services, we should be aware and make decisions consciously. For computer professionals, awareness of the risks should encourage care and responsibility in developing secure systems to protect the sensitive information people store in the clouds.

2.2.3 LOCATION TRACKING

It is because Humanity has never known where it was going that it has been able to find its way.
> —Oscar Wilde, in "The Critic as Artist"

Global positioning systems (GPS), mobile phones, radio frequency identification (RFID) tags,[*] and other technologies and devices enable a variety of location-based applications—that is, computer and communications services that depend on knowing exactly where a person or object is at a particular time. Since the introduction of smartphones, there has been an explosion of extraordinarily diverse applications with significant benefits and new risks.

To analyze risks, we should always consider unintended, as well as intended, uses. We will see in Section 2.3.3 that law enforcement agencies locate people

---

[*]RFID tags are small devices that contain an electronic chip and an antenna. The chip stores identification data (and possibly other data) and controls operation of the tag. The antenna transmits and receives radio signals for communicating with devices that read the tag.

by locating their phone. Though they have tried to keep details of the technology secret and the devices they use are expensive, eventually there will be an app for that. Suppose in the near future anyone can enter another person's ID number (perhaps a phone number) on their own mobile device and ask for that person's current location. Or, perhaps the reverse—a device could sweep a particular location and identify individuals by their devices or by face recognition. Who might a person *not* want to get this information? There are many possibilities: thieves, a violent spouse or an ex-spouse, a divorce lawyer, an annoying or nosy neighbor, a stalker, coworkers or business associates, the government, or anyone else who might object to your religion, politics, or sexual behavior.

Extensive records of where we have gone provide more details to the ever-growing profiles and dossiers businesses and governments build about us. With fast search, matching, and analysis tools, they can add more detail about who we spend time with and what we are doing. In Chapter 1, we mentioned that researchers learn about social organization and the spread of disease (among other things) by studying huge amounts of mobile phone data. Such statistical data can be extremely valuable to us all, but a mobile phone identifies a person, and, thus, the tracking information (if associated with the phone's number or ID) is personal information and raises the usual issues of consent, potential secondary uses, risks

Tracking employees at work: Section 6.5.3

of misuse, and so on. Care must be taken to ensure that such data are protected. If accessed surreptitiously, stolen, disclosed accidentally, or acquired by government agencies, records of our location and movements pose threats to privacy, safety, and liberty. Privacy and industry organizations have developed guidelines for mobile and location-tracking applications to implement principles in Figure 2.1 and protect against some of the risks.[23]

Let's consider an application of location tracking—studying the behavior of customers in a store or other facility—and how various implementations impact privacy. A supermarket or an amusement park might want to analyze customer traffic patterns within the facility to plan a better layout, to determine how much time people spend inside, or to analyze waiting times. Disney World tracks the movements and activities of entire families using a wristband called a MagicBand. In exchange for discounts, conveniences (opening their hotel room door, charging food directly to the room account), and special privileges (shorter lines for rides), each member of the family wears a MagicBand, equipped with a radio frequency device, that tracks them throughout the park. Disney can analyze the data it collects and use the results to improve the experience of future visitors. Alternatively, an amusement park or large store that wants to learn about customer behavior could give people a tracking ticket when they enter that they discard when they leave. It does not need to have any information connected to the person or family. For such a system, privacy is not an issue, but it would likely come with fewer discounts or other direct benefits to the customer. Thousands of families do not object to sharing detailed

---

Who's at the bar?

Hundreds of bars installed cameras with a face recognition system to provide data to a website and smartphone app. The app told users the number of people at a particular bar, the male/female ratio, and the approximate age range. Each bar received summary statistics on its patrons that could be useful for advertising or other business planning. The system did not identify individual people and did not store the video. So this is not a privacy issue. Or is it?

Such an application can remain utterly unthreatening, or it can drift over the boundary into location tracking and privacy infringement. The bar owners do not control the system, so they cannot be certain that what they tell their customers about it is true. (There are many examples of systems collecting and storing data without the knowledge of the businesses that use the system.) The developer and operator of the system might exercise great care to protect patrons' privacy, or they might succumb to temptation to add new features that require storing video or identifying individuals. Awareness of potential risks and understanding of good privacy practices are essential for both the software developers who invent and upgrade such systems and the managers who make decisions about what features to implement.

The market (that is, a lot of bar patrons) decided they were uncomfortable with this app, and it is no longer available. In five or ten years, will our tolerance have changed enough that a new, similar app could be successful?

---

personally-identified location and activity information with Disney World. In what situations is the anonymous approach more appropriate than something like Disney's MagicBand?

Tools for parents

Many technologies help parents track their children's physical location. Mobile phone services enable parents to check a child's location from the parent's phone, and devices installed in a car tell parents where their teens are and how fast they are driving. Parents can give their young children wireless watchband transmitters or other devices to locate them if they wander off in a crowded place.

Tracking children can increase safety, but there are parenting issues and risks involved in using tracking tools. At what age does tracking become an invasion of the child's privacy? Should parents tell children about the tracking devices and services they are using? Informed consent is a basic principle for adults. At what age does it apply to children? Will intense tracking and monitoring slow the development of a child's responsible independence?

A monitoring system that sends signals that can be easily intercepted and read could decrease rather than increase the safety of a child by allowing child molesters and identity thieves to collect personal data. Parents need to be aware of potential for false alarms and a false sense of security. For example, a child might lose a phone or leave a tagged article of clothing somewhere, and older kids might figure out how to thwart tracking systems. Clearly, how and when to use surveillance tools should involve thoughtful decisions for families.

After heavy opposition from parents, a school dropped its proposal to require that all students wear an RFID-equipped device while on school grounds. In this example, the decision was made by school officials, not individual parents, and monitoring of the students would have been done by the school, not the parents. The example illustrates two critical questions about technologies with potential for misuse: Who makes the decision about using the technology, and who gets to control it or access the data it collects?

Implanting tracking chips

Prisoners, children, and people with Alzheimer's disease can wear devices that locate them if they wander off. There have been several proposals for implanting identification and tracking chips in people. In the United States at this time, it appears the purpose of most implanted chips is to identify implanted medical devices or patients. One country's government considered implanting tracking chips in people who are HIV-positive. Various people have suggested other target groups, including foreign workers. Privacy advocates worry about the potential for tracking journalists and dissidents, as well as any particular individual.

Suppose, about 20 years ago, people were asked if they would carry a device with them everywhere, all day, that transmitted their location continually and allowed a record of their movements to be stored. Most people would likely have said, resoundingly, no. But the question would have been considered in isolation without consideration of the applications and benefits of smartphones—unimaginable a generation ago. Currently, a lot of people do not like the idea of implanting chips. What might the benefits be? Implanted chips can open smart locks and replace various kinds of tickets.[*] We will likely be able to tap a finger instead of a phone to make payments. (Some people have voluntarily had chips implanted for such purposes.) How else might the chips be used? How might they be misused? Will we get used to a society where it is common for people to have implanted chips, as we have become used to the privacy intrusions and risks we routinely experience or accept now?

2.2.4 A RIGHT TO BE FORGOTTEN

People sometimes want to remove information about themselves from the Internet or from a company's records. Some examples are:

- an offensive comment made in anger
- a photo on one's own social network page or a photo-sharing site

---

[*] A Londoner created false fingernails with integrated RFID technology that can be used instead of the usual prepaid card to travel the commuter rail system.

- photos of a prominent person at a sex party posted on a news organization's site or a search engine's links to such material
- a news article about an arrest or financial problems
- information in online directories
- personal data posted by others (e.g., on a genealogy site)
- the profile an advertising company developed by tracking the person's Web activity
- a collection of data gleaned from the person's smartphone use
- the collection of the person's search queries that a search engine stores

Legislators and privacy advocates in several countries have been promoting a legal right for a person to demand that websites remove material about the person and/ or that search engines remove links to it. The right to have material removed, as a legal or ethical right, has come to be called a "right to be forgotten." The wide range of material a person might want to remove suggests many practical, ethical, social, and legal questions about such a right.[24]

The policies of various websites about removing material vary. Sites with members, such as social networks, typically respond to a member's request to delete material the user posted and to delete a member's material when the member closes the account. When the material is not in a user's account, the situation is more complicated. Some sites, such as directories, collect information automatically; thus, deleted information can reappear. A filter system to prevent reposting of data about a particular person has the problem of correctly distinguishing that person from others with the same or similar names.

Should a company or website always comply with a request to delete a particular item or a person's record any time a person makes such a request? We understand that people do foolish things and regret them later, and in certain contexts it is reasonable to let many of them be forgotten. If a person wants to delete something he or she posted on a website, it is reasonable, courteous, good-spirited, and perhaps a good business policy to comply. If someone wants to remove outdated or embarrassing information posted by others, if the person is not a public figure, and if the information has no broad social value, then removing it, or removing links to it in searches, might be the reasonable, courteous thing to do. Complying with the request could be ethically acceptable and admirable but not ethically obligatory. In some cases, it could be a bad idea as the information may be important to people in a particular community, or the person who posted it may have a good reason for doing so.

What about the data that advertisers and search engines collect about us? Must they, from an ethical standpoint, comply with a request from a person who wants his or her record deleted? If the companies collected the data secretly, without permission, or in violation of their stated privacy policies and terms of use, then these are good reasons to require its deletion independent of any right to be forgotten. Suppose the information is the set of a person's search queries or something similar that a free website collects, and suppose the site makes its collection and use of the data clear in its terms of use. The company's use of the data is, in part, our payment for the free service it provides. As a business "transaction" that data belongs as much to the company as to the individual. If the company agrees to delete people's records upon request, it is providing its service to those people for free (or at a "discount" if they continue to view ads on the site). If a relatively small number of individuals request deletion of their data, a large company can probably afford to comply without significant inconvenience or reduction in the value it gets from analysis of user data. Again, complying with deletion requests could be ethically and socially admirable, good-spirited, and perhaps a good business policy. On the other hand, a person might make a deletion request to hide some illegal or offensive behavior or to remove evidence in a dispute of some kind.

If the right to be forgotten is a negative right (a liberty), it could mean that we may choose to stay off the Internet and become a recluse, but we cannot force someone else to remove information about us. As a positive right (a claim right), it allows a person to restrict sharing of information by others. This can infringe freedom of speech and restrict access to truthful information. In some applications, the right would mean that a person may break agreements (e.g., terms of use for an app or Web service) at will.

The right to be forgotten in the EU and Russia: Section 2.7

We can well understand that a person would not want a search by a prospective employer, a neighbor, or a date to turn up an article about an arrest on a charge for which the person was later cleared. Someone applying for a loan or raising money for a start-up might not want a banker's or prospective investor's search to turn up outdated or misleading information about previous defaults, bankruptcies, or other financial problems. Busy people might be unlikely to ask for an explanation of the negative information; they might just go on to another applicant. The eternal life of anything on the Web, including wrong and misleading information, can cause serious problems for some people. However, depending on the type of information, it can be a challenge to find a basis for an ethical right requiring the information not be found.

Are there contexts in which it makes sense to enforce a legal requirement to remove material when a person requests it? Perhaps for special populations, such as children (where parents might make the request or a young adult might want to remove sexting photos sent to friends while in high school), or in other special situations. Legislators must carefully craft any such legal requirement to avoid conflict with free speech, free flow of information, and contractual agreements. A legal requirement to honor removal requests will be more of a burden to small sites than to large ones, which can develop software to help automate the process and have legal staffs to defend against complaints.

Sexting: Section 3.2.3

2.3 The Fourth Amendment and Changing Technology

2.3.1 THE FOURTH AMENDMENT

> *The right of the people to be secure in their persons, houses, papers, and effects, against unreasonable searches and seizures, shall not be violated, and no Warrants shall issue, but upon probable cause, supported by Oath or affirmation, and particularly describing the place to be searched, and the persons or things to be seized.*
>
> —Fourth Amendment, U.S. Constitution

Law enforcement agencies intercept communications and search homes and businesses to collect evidence of criminal activities. Intelligence agencies do the same to collect information about the activities and plans of hostile governments and terrorists. The Fourth Amendment to the U.S. Constitution and various laws put restraints on their activities to protect innocent people and reduce the opportunity for abuses. England has a similar tradition, as expressed in William Pitt's colorful statement in 1763:

> The poorest man may in his cottage bid defiance to all the force of the Crown. It may be frail; its roof may shake; the wind may blow through it; the storms may enter; the rain may enter—but the King of England cannot enter.[25]

In this section, we consider how changing technologies (communications, surveillance technology, mobile devices, and massive databases), government policies, and court decisions affect the ability of law enforcement agencies to obtain information. We consider new threats to privacy from government intrusion and whether and how the Fourth Amendment protects against them.

The Fourth Amendment sets limits on the government's rights to search our homes and businesses and to seize documents and other personal effects. It requires that the government have good evidence to support a specific search and that a judge approve a search warrant. But with new technologies, much of our personal information is no longer safe in our homes or the individual offices of our doctors and financial advisors. It is in huge databases outside of our control, often copied to the cloud. New technologies allow the government to search our homes without entering them, to search our persons from a distance without our knowledge, and to extract the data on a smartphone in less than two minutes at a traffic stop. With each new technology, law enforcement agencies search, seize, and intercept without search warrants, arguing that the Fourth Amendment does not apply. In many but not all cases, the Supreme Court eventually says the Fourth Amendment does apply, though years, and sometimes decades, go by before the Supreme Court rules on a particular technology.

As we consider all the personal information available to government agencies now, we can reflect on the worries of Supreme Court Justice William O. Douglas about the potential abuse from government access to only the records of someone's checking account. In 1974, he said:

> In a sense a person is defined by the checks he writes. By examining them agents get to know his doctors, lawyers, creditors, political allies, social connections, religious affiliation, educational interests, the papers and magazines he reads, and so on ad infinitum. These are all tied in to one's social security number, and now that we have the data banks, these other items will enrich that storehouse and make it possible for a bureaucrat—by pushing one button—to get in an instant the names of the 190 million Americans who are subversives or potential and likely candidates.[26]

Today's readers should not miss the irony of the last sentence: 190 million was almost the entire population of the United States at the time.

> *When the American Republic was founded, the framers established a libertarian equilibrium among the competing values of privacy, disclosure, and surveillance. This balance was based on technological realities of eighteenth-century life. Since torture and inquisition were the only known means of penetrating the mind, all such measures by government were forbidden by law. Physical entry and eavesdropping were the only means of penetrating private homes and meeting rooms; the framers therefore made eavesdropping by private persons a crime and allowed government to enter private premises only for reasonable searches, under strict warrant controls. Since registration procedures and police dossiers were the means used to control the free movement of "controversial" persons, this European police practice was precluded by American governmental practice and the realities of mobile frontier life.*
>
> —Alan F. Westin, *Privacy and Freedom*[27]

2.3.2 BACKGROUND, LAW, AND COURT DECISIONS

> *The principles laid down in this opinion . . . apply to all invasions on the part of government and its employees of the sanctity of a man's home and the privacies of life. It is not the breaking of his doors, and the rummaging in his drawers, that constitutes the essence of the offense; but it is the invasion of his indefeasible right of personal security, personal liberty and private property.*
>
> —Supreme Court Justice Joseph Bradley, *Boyd* v. *United States*, 1886

Telephone conversations and wiretapping

Within 10 years of the invention of the telephone, people (in and out of government) were wiretapping them.[28] The legal status of wiretapping was debated throughout most of the 20th century. In the years when human operators made telephone connections and most people had party lines (one telephone line shared by several households), operators and nosy neighbors sometimes listened in on telephone conversations. Over time, increased wealth and new technology eliminated party lines and human operators, but telephones were still vulnerable to wiretapping.

Federal and state law enforcement agencies, businesses, private detectives, political candidates, and others widely used wiretapping. In *Olmstead* v. *United States* (1928)[29], the Supreme Court ruled that wiretapping by law enforcement agencies was not unconstitutional, although Congress could ban it. In *Olmstead*, the government had used wiretaps on telephone lines without a court order. The Supreme Court interpreted the Fourth Amendment to apply only to physical intrusion and only to the search or seizure of material things, not conversations. Justice Louis Brandeis dissented, arguing that the authors of the Fourth Amendment did all they could to protect liberty and privacy—including privacy of conversations—from intrusions by government based on the technology available at the time. He believed that the court should interpret the Fourth Amendment as requiring a court order even when new technologies give the government access to our personal papers and conversations without entering our homes.

In the Communications Act of 1934, Congress stated that, unless authorized by the sender, no person could legally intercept and divulge a message; there is no exception for law enforcement agencies. In 1937, a Supreme Court decision ruled that wiretapping violated this law.[30] Following this, federal and state law enforcement agencies and local police continued to wiretap with and without warrants for decades. The FBI bugged and wiretapped members of Congress and the Supreme Court, and in one well-publicized case, the FBI monitored the telephone calls between a defendant and her attorneys during her trial. In many cases, law enforcement agencies were wiretapping people suspected of crimes, but at times, they tapped people with unconventional views, members of civil rights groups, and political opponents of powerful government officials. Although there was publicity about extensive use of wiretapping by police, no prosecutions for it resulted.

In *Katz* v. *United States*, in 1967, the Supreme Court reversed *Olmstead* and ruled that the Fourth Amendment does apply to conversations* and that it applies in public places in some situations. In this case, law enforcement agents had attached an electronic listening and recording device on the outside of a telephone booth to record a suspect's conversation. The court said that the Fourth Amendment "protects people, not places," and that what a person "seeks to preserve as private, even in an area accessible to the public, may be constitutionally protected." To intrude in places where a reasonable person has a reasonable expectation of privacy, government agents need a court order. Even after Katz, wiretapping by government and politicians that was illegal or of questionable legality continued, most notably during the Vietnam War, when journalists, criminal suspects, and others continued to be victims of illegal wiretaps.

---

*Government agents may determine the telephone numbers called from a particular telephone and the number from which someone made a call with less court scrutiny and justification than is required for intercepting the content of the call.

Email and mobile phone conversations

When email and cellphones were new, interception by government agents and others was common. Driving around Silicon Valley eavesdropping on cellphone conversations was, reportedly, a popular form of industrial spying in the 1980s. Snoops intercepted cellphone conversations of politicians and celebrities. The Electronic Communications Privacy Act of 1986 (ECPA) extended the 1967 wiretapping restrictions in *Katz* v. *United States* to electronic communications, including electronic mail and cordless and cellular telephones. The ECPA prohibits interception of the content of electronic communications and data while in transmission, except by government agents with a search warrant. The ECPA set weaker standards for law enforcement agencies to obtain copies of stored email and to collect information about communications such as numbers called, time and date of calls or email, and other header information. The government argued that people give up their expectation of privacy by allowing ISPs to store their email on the ISP's computers; thus, the strict requirements of the Fourth Amendment would not apply. Two decades after the ECPA was passed, a federal appeals court ruled that people *do* have an expectation of privacy for email stored at their ISP and that police need a search warrant to get it.[31] The concept of expectation of privacy continues to be central to many court decisions; thus, we explore it further.

Expectation of privacy

Although the Supreme Court's decision in *Katz* v. *United States* strengthened Fourth Amendment protection in some ways, its reliance on the concept of reasonable "expectation of privacy" to define the areas where law enforcement agents need a court order has had some surprising and negative results for privacy.

As well-informed people come to understand the capabilities of modern surveillance tools, we might no longer expect privacy from government, in a practical sense. Does that mean we should not have it? The Supreme Court recognized this problem in *Smith* v. *Maryland*, in which it noted that, if law enforcement reduces actual expectation of privacy by actions "alien to well-recognized Fourth Amendment freedoms," this should *not* reduce our Fourth Amendment protection. However, the Court has interpreted "expectation of privacy" in a very restrictive way. It ruled that if we share information with businesses such as our bank, then we have no reasonable expectation of privacy for that information (*United States* v. *Miller*, 1976), and law enforcement agents do not need a court order to get it. This interpretation seems odd. We do expect privacy of the financial information we supply to a bank or other financial institution. We expect confidentiality in many kinds of information we share with a few, sometimes carefully selected, others, but many laws and court decisions allow law enforcement agencies to get information from nongovernment databases without a court order. Federal privacy rules allow law enforcement agencies to access medical records without court orders. The USA

Hotel records, or any consumer–business transactions

A law in Los Angeles requires hotels to collect and store information about all guests, and it allowed any Los Angeles police officer to inspect the records on demand, without a search warrant. The government argued that people have no claim to privacy because they have already "shared" the information with the hotel. This argument can be applied to eliminate virtually all privacy concerning transactions with others. A federal appeals court ruled that the provision of the Los Angeles law allowing police to inspect hotel records without a warrant violates the Fourth Amendment because the guest records are the property of the hotels and hotels have an interest in keeping them private.[32] Although this approach does not recognize the privacy interest of the customer, it provides at least some protection for records about people that are stored by businesses. Will law enforcement agencies argue that businesses lose their claim to privacy if they "share" the information with another business that manages some aspect of the transaction (for example, a hotel reservation website)?

PATRIOT Act (passed after the terrorist attacks in 2001) eased government access to many kinds of personal information, including library and financial records, without a court order.

We share our online activity with ISPs, websites, telecommunications companies, and search engine companies merely by typing, tapping, and speaking. We share information about our locations when we find a ride via a ride-sharing app— or just carry a mobile phone. Everything we buy online, every video we watch via a membership service becomes part of a company's business records. We back up our photos and data in the cloud. What can police get from a cloud storage company that is protected by the Fourth Amendment in our homes? The *U.S.* v. *Miller* decision predates the Internet, but courts continue to apply its ruling that the Fourth Amendment does not protect information we have shared. How should expectation of privacy apply to these technologies and services? Should the Supreme Court refine and update its position?

2.3.3 APPLYING THE FOURTH AMENDMENT IN NEW AREAS

Our use of these new technologies doesn't signal that we're less interested in privacy. The idea of the government monitoring our whereabouts, our habits, our acquaintances, and our interests still creeps us out. We often just don't know it's going on until it's too late.

—Judge Alex Kozinski[33]

Searching and tracking mobile devices

Police may legally search an arrested person without a search warrant and examine personal property on the person (in pockets, for example) or within his or her reach. The reason for this is to find and take weapons and to prevent the person from hiding or destroying evidence. But should a search warrant be required before the police can search the *contents* of the person's cellphone?

A mobile phone typically contains contacts, information on recent calls, content of messages, documents, personal calendars, photos, a history of Web browsing, and a record of where the phone has been. It may also contain books, health information, and religious apps. For many people, the phone is a traveling office, containing proprietary and confidential information. For example, a lawyer's phone might contain information about clients and cases—legally protected from access by police. The vast collection of information on a smartphone is the kind of information the Fourth Amendment is intended to protect. On the other hand, a federal government attorney arguing against a requirement for a search warrant said that during the time required to get the search warrant, confederates of a criminal could remotely delete incriminating evidence from a phone in police custody. In cases that reached state supreme courts, courts in different states ruled differently on the question of whether a search warrant is required.[34] In 2014, seven years after introduction of the iPhone, the Supreme Court ruled unanimously, in *Riley* v. *California*, that police may not search the contents of a person's cellphone without a warrant.

Law enforcement agents track thousands of people's locations each year. Sometimes they have a court order to do so, and sometimes they do not. Do they need one? We consider two technologies: one tracks private actions in public view; the other tracks people in private places.

Without a search warrant, police secretly attached a GPS tracking device to a vehicle owned by the wife of a suspect. The police said a warrant was not needed because they could have observed the car as it moved about on public streets; they characterized the GPS tracker as a labor-saving device. The Supreme Court decided the case, *U.S.* v. *Jones*, in 2012, ruling in favor of Fourth Amendment protection. The Court unanimously agreed that a vehicle is one of a person's "effects" that the Fourth Amendment explicitly protects. Therefore, police need a search warrant to attach a surveillance device to a private vehicle. A second argument was that tracking a person's location for a month, 24 hours a day, as in this case, goes beyond observing the car pass by in public; it violates a person's expectation of privacy. The justices recognized that the expectation of privacy would be a key issue in tracking cases where directly attaching a device is not necessary, but the majority chose to leave a decision about that for the future.[35]

Suppose a person is at home, at a friend's or lover's home, inside a church or a health facility, or in any private space. State, local, and federal law enforcement agencies use devices, typically called stingrays, to locate a person by locating the person's mobile phone, even when the phone is not actively in use. The stingray simulates a cell tower and agents drive or fly with it in the area where they believe the person to be. The target phone connects to the stingray at several locations as the agents move. They then use the stingray data to triangulate the exact location of the phone. With this technology, police do not need to enter private premises or physically attach anything to a person's property. Federal officials made strong efforts to keep secret the use of stingrays and the details about how they work. The American Civil Liberties Union obtained documents showing that, as far back as 2009, federal officials encouraged police to hide the fact that they were using the devices; instead they were to say that the tracking information came from confidential sources. When news reports began to appear, law enforcement agencies argued that mobile phone tracking does not require a search warrant because a person who uses a cellphone service has no expectation of privacy about the location data the phone transmits to cell towers. More likely, most people do not realize their phone regularly sends signals to nearby cell towers, or do not think about the implications of doing so, and are not aware that they can be tracked by portable cell-tower simulators just because they are carrying a phone.

After publicity and criticism about stingrays, the U.S. Department of Justice announced new policies for tracking mobile phones. The most important change is that federal agents have to get a warrant from a judge to use stingray-type devices. The federal policies do not apply to local and state police, but some states also adopted requirements for search warrants. As of this writing, the Supreme Court has not heard a case about this technology, though several state and federal courts have ruled that warrantless use of stingrays and similar devices violates the Fourth Amendment.

Alexeyboldin/Fotolia

FIGURE 2.2 Should police have access to records of all your phone's locations without a search warrant?

Although the trend seems to be toward requiring a search warrant to track a person's phone in real-time, several federal appeals courts have ruled otherwise in cases involving access to the location history data that a phone service provider stores. The phone company has a record of the cell towers a phone connects to, including dates and times. Thus, this information gives a map and timeline of a person's movements, though location is imprecise because the person is in the vicinity of the tower, not directly at it. So far, courts have ruled that this information is in the same category as other business records that police may access without a search warrant because we have shared the information with the company and thus do not have an expectation of privacy.

> *Absent a search warrant, the Government may not turn a citizen's cell phone into a tracking device.*
>
> —U.S. District Judge William Pauley, 2016[36]

"Noninvasive but deeply revealing" searches

The title above is from Julian Sanchez's description of a variety of search and detection technologies.[37] Many sound like science fiction; they are not. These technologies can search our homes and vehicles but do not require police to physically enter or open them. They can search our bodies beneath our clothes from a distance without our knowledge. Noninvasive but deeply revealing search tools (some in use and some in development) include particle sniffers that detect many specific drugs and explosives, devices that analyze the molecular composition of truck cargo without opening the truck, thermal-imaging devices (to find heat lamps for growing marijuana, for example), drones hovering over our backyards or outside our windows, and algorithms to recreate conversations and identify speakers by their voices using only video images that record the minuscule movement of plant leaves or chip bags caused by sound waves in a room where people are speaking.[38] These tools have obvious valuable security and law enforcement applications, but the technologies can be used for random searches, without search warrants or probable cause, on unsuspecting people. As Sanchez points out, we live "in a nation whose reams of regulations make almost everyone guilty of some violation at some point."[39] Before the government begins using these tools on, say, ordinary people bringing medications home from Canada, making their own beer, or keeping a banned sweetener or saturated fat in their home (or whatever might be illegal in the future), it is critical for privacy protection and liberty that we have clear guidelines for their use—and, in particular, clarification of when such use constitutes a search requiring a search warrant.

In *Kyllo* v. *United States*, in 2001, the Supreme Court ruled that police could not use thermal-imaging devices to search a home from the outside without a search warrant. The Court stated that where "government uses a device that is not in general public use, to explore details of the home that would previously have been unknowable without physical intrusion, the surveillance is a 'search.'" This reasoning suggests that when a technology becomes more widely used, the government may use it for surveillance without a warrant. This standard may allow time for markets, public awareness, and technologies to develop to provide privacy protection against the new technology. Is it a reasonable standard—a reasonable adaptation of law to new technology? Or should the court have permitted such searches without warrants? Or should the government have to satisfy the requirements of the Fourth Amendment for every search of a home where a warrant would have been necessary before the technology existed?

More than a decade after the *Kyllo* decision, law enforcement agencies were secretly using, without a search warrant, radar devices from outside buildings that detect human breathing and movement inside the buildings.[40]

Will Big Brother be listening?*

We are using more and more devices in our homes (and elsewhere) that respond to spoken commands. Many companies are selling conversation-based interfaces for appliances and the Internet, more sophisticated than what we have had on phones. We will speak to these systems as we speak to another person, and indeed, some companies develop the systems to have a personality. For such systems to operate, the microphone must be always on. What principles or guidelines will develop for use or protection of our conversations? What rules will control access to the microphone by law enforcement agencies?

An observation

Court cases we have discussed involved suspects in armed robbery, murder, and sale of illegal drugs. We want police and prosecutors to have reasonable tools to catch and prosecute violent criminals. When discussing Fourth Amendment principles and cases, it is perhaps useful to remember that rulings against use of stingrays and searching mobile phones, for example, do not mean that police may not do such things. It means they must present evidence to convince a judge to issue a search warrant before doing so. For information that courts have ruled is not protected by the Fourth Amendment (for example, the records your mobile phone service provider has about your use of your phone), law enforcement agencies obtain the information at their own discretion or with a court order that has a lower standard than a search warrant. Even if an agency has strong policies that protect privacy, an individual employee might access or use data in abusive or illegal ways. The authors of the Fourth Amendment were well aware of abuse of government power and wrote the Bill of Rights to protect against it.

---

*In George Orwell's dystopian novel *1984*, Big Brother (the government) watched everyone via "tele-screens" in all homes and public places.

2.4 Government Systems

Quis custodiet ipsos custodes? (Who will guard the guards themselves?)

—Juvenal, *Satires* (1st/2nd century Roman)

2.4.1 Video Surveillance and Face Recognition

When surveillance cameras began appearing all over in public places, many people saw them as a threat to privacy, something out of dystopian science fiction. Then, photos taken by surveillance cameras helped identify terrorists who set off bombs in the London subway. After rioters burned and looted neighborhoods in England, police used recordings from street cameras and face recognition systems to identify rioters. After the bombings at the Boston Marathon, surveillance cameras provided images of the bombers, and they were quickly identified. Surveillance video helped identify attackers or provide other information useful to investigations of terrorist attacks in Brussels, Paris, and Nice. Are the now omnipresent cameras a valuable protection or a profound threat—or are they both? We will discuss here some applications of cameras and face recognition and relevant privacy and civil liberties issues.

England was the first country to set up a large number of cameras in public places, long before the wave of terrorist attacks of the past dozen years; the purpose was to deter crime. A study by a British university found a number of abuses by operators of surveillance cameras, including collecting salacious footage, such as people having sex in a car, and showing it to colleagues. Defense lawyers complained that prosecutors sometimes destroyed footage that might clear a suspect.[41] The British government released a report saying Britain's closed-circuit TV systems were of little use in fighting crime. The only successful use of the cameras was in parking lots where they helped reduce vehicle crime.[42]

In the first large-scale, public application of face recognition, police in Tampa, Florida, without notifying attendees, scanned the faces of all 100,000 fans and employees who entered the 2001 Super Bowl (causing some reporters to dub it Snooper Bowl). The system searched computer files of criminals for matches, giving results within seconds. The American Civil Liberties Union compared the use of the face recognition system at the Super Bowl to a computerized police lineup to which innocent people were subject without their knowledge or consent. Tampa installed a similar system in a neighborhood of popular restaurants and nightclubs. Police in a control room zoomed in on individual faces and checked for matches in their database of suspects.[43] In two years of use, the system did not recognize anyone that the police wanted, but it did occasionally identify innocent people as wanted felons.

Face recognition systems had a poor accuracy rate in the early 2000s,[44] but the technology improved, along with the availability of photos to match against (tagged photos in social networks, for example). A police officer, or anyone else, can now snap a photo of a person on the street and run a smartphone app that searches profile images on popular social media sites to identify the person.

Cameras alone raise privacy issues, but when combined with face recognition systems they seriously erode our anonymity in public. Enforcing a curfew for young people was one of the uses of public cameras in England. This application suggests the kind of monitoring and control of special populations the cameras make easy. Will police use face recognition systems to track political dissidents, journalists, and political opponents of powerful people—the kinds of people targeted for illegal or questionable surveillance in the past?

Some cities have increased their camera surveillance programs, while others gave up their systems because they did not significantly reduce crime or because they were too expensive to monitor or maintain. (Some favor better lighting and more police patrols—low tech and less invasive of privacy.) Toronto city officials refused to let police take over their traffic cameras to monitor a protest march and identify its organizers. The Privacy Commissioner of Canada argued that the country's Privacy Act required a "demonstrable need for each piece of personal information collected" to carry out government programs and therefore recording activities of large numbers of the general public was not a permissible means of crime prevention.[45]

The California Department of Transportation photographed the license plates on cars driving in a particular area and then contacted the car owners for a survey about traffic in the area. Hundreds of drivers complained, objecting vehemently to what they considered unacceptable surveillance by a government agency even when the agency photographed only their license plates, not their faces—for a survey, not a police action. Many ordinary people do not like being tracked and photographed by the government without their knowledge.

Clearly, some applications of cameras and face recognition systems are reasonable, beneficial uses of the technology for security and crime prevention, and, clearly, there is a need for controls and guidelines. How should we distinguish appropriate from inappropriate uses? Should we restrict technologies such as face recognition systems to catching terrorists and suspects in serious crimes, or should we allow their use to screen people in public places to find those with unpaid parking tickets? Some cameras are hidden. Do people have a right to know when and where cameras are in use? Can we design privacy-protecting features into the technology, establish well-thought-out policies for its use, and pass appropriate privacy-protecting legislation before, as the Supreme Court of Canada worries in the quote below, "privacy is annihilated"? Or, with more than 30 million surveillance cameras in the United States, is it already too late? What trade-offs between privacy and identifying criminals and terrorists are we willing to make?

To permit unrestricted video surveillance by agents of the state would seriously diminish the degree of privacy we can reasonably expect to enjoy in a free society. . . . We must always be alert to the fact that modern methods of electronic surveillance have the potential, if uncontrolled, to annihilate privacy.

—Supreme Court of Canada[46]

This is a public meeting!

—Reporter Pete Tucker, upon his arrest for taking a photo with his mobile phone at an open meeting of a U.S. government agency. Newsman Jim Epstein was then arrested for recording the arrest of Tucker on his own phone.[47]

2.4.2 DATABASES

Protections and violations

Federal and local government agencies maintain thousands of databases containing personal information. Examples include tax returns, property ownership, medical records, divorce records, voter registration, bankruptcy, prescriptions for drugs such as pain killers, and arrest records. Others include applications for government grant and loan programs, professional and trade licenses, and school records (including psychological testing of children), and there are many, many more. Government databases help government agencies perform their functions, determine eligibility for government benefits programs, detect fraud in government programs, collect taxes, and catch people who are breaking laws. The scope of government activities is enormous, ranging from catching violent criminals to licensing hair braiders. Governments can arrest people, jail them, and seize assets from them. Thus, the use and misuse of personal data by government agencies pose special threats to liberty and personal privacy. It seems reasonable to expect governments to meet an especially high standard for privacy protection and adherence to laws.

The Privacy Act of 1974 and the E-Government Act of 2002 are the main laws concerning the federal government's use of personal data. Figure 2.3 summarizes the provisions of the Privacy Act. Although this law was an important step in attempting to protect our privacy with respect to federal databases, it has problems.

- Restricts the data in federal government records to what is "relevant and necessary" to the legal purpose for which the government collects it.
- Requires federal agencies to publish a notice of their record systems in the Federal Register so that the public may learn about what databases exist.
- Allows people to access their records and correct inaccurate information.
- Requires procedures to protect the security of the information in databases.
- Prohibits disclosure of information about a person without his or her consent (with several exceptions).

FIGURE 2.3 Provisions of the Privacy Act of 1974.

The Privacy Act, to quote one expert on privacy laws, has "many loopholes, weak enforcement, and only sporadic oversight."[48] The E-Government Act added privacy regulations for electronic data and services—for example, requiring agencies to conduct privacy impact assessments for electronic information systems and to post privacy policies on agency websites used by the public.

The Government Accountability Office (GAO) is Congress's "watchdog agency." Over the past few decades, the GAO has released numerous studies showing privacy risks and breaches and lack of compliance with privacy laws. The GAO reported in 1996 that White House staffers used a "secret" database with records on 200,000 people (including ethnic and political information) without adequate access controls. In 2006, a GAO study of 65 government websites found that only 3% of the sites fully complied with the fair information standards for notice, choice, access, and security established by the Federal Trade Commission (FTC) for commercial websites. (The FTC's site was one that did not comply.) The GAO reported that the Internal Revenue Service (IRS), the Federal Bureau of Investigation (FBI), the State Department, and other agencies that use data mining to detect fraud or terrorism did not comply with all rules for collecting information on citizens. The GAO found dozens of weaknesses in the operation of the government's communication network for transmitting medical data in the Medicare and Medicaid programs—weaknesses that could allow unauthorized access to people's medical records.[49]

The IRS is one of several federal government agencies that collects and stores information on almost everyone in the country and is a major secondary user of personal information. Year after year, hundreds of IRS employees are investigated for unauthorized snooping in people's tax files. (In one incident, an IRS employee who was a Ku Klux Klan member read tax records of members of his Klan group looking for income information that would indicate that someone was an undercover agent.) These abuses led to a law with tough penalties for government employees who snoop through people's tax information without authorization. However, a GAO report a few years later found that while the IRS had made significant improvements, the tax agency still failed to adequately protect people's financial and tax information. IRS employees were able to alter and delete data without authorization, they disposed of disks with sensitive taxpayer information without erasing files, and hundreds of tapes and diskettes were missing. A report by the Treasury's Inspector General said that the IRS did not adequately protect taxpayer information on more than 50,000 laptops and other storage media. In 2015, hackers were able to access taxpayer information by creating new accounts for taxpayers on an IRS website. This site required minimal information about a taxpayer to create an account, and once the account was created, the hacker could view past tax returns and tax payments. The IRS had to shut down the service and notify hundreds of thousands of taxpayers that their information was at risk. In this case, taxpayer information was exposed not because of a direct hack of an IRS system, but because of weak account creation policies.

Various reviews of compliance with the Privacy Act and the E-Government Act have highlighted weaknesses in these laws. For example, recognizing that most people do not read the *Federal Register*, the GAO suggested better ways to inform the public about government databases and privacy policies. The GAO continues to advocate stricter limits on use of personal information and modification of the Privacy Act to cover all personally identifiable information collected and used by the federal government, thus closing gaping loopholes that exempt much government use of personal information from the law's provisions.

Government use of private sector sources

As the Information Security and Privacy Advisory Board (a government advisory board) pointed out, "The Privacy Act does not adequately cover government use of commercially-compiled databases of personal information. The rules about the federal government's use of commercial databases, and even use of information gleaned from commercial search engines, have been vague and sometimes nonexistent." Thus, agencies can bypass the protections of the Privacy Act by using private-sector databases and searches, rather than collecting information itself.[50]

In one example, the New York City Police Department pays a private company to access the company's database that collects data from license plate readers all over the country. The readers are installed in apartment complexes, office parks, and other private areas, as well as on public streets. The system can provide lists of vehicles often seen at particular locations or often seen together. It can also provide predictions of where a vehicle is likely to be at a particular time. The system helped locate a murderer and has obvious advantages for finding criminals, but should police be able to access such data as they choose, without legal or court oversight? Should the data, mostly on innocent people, be available to the NYPD for five years?[51]

Proposals for data mining nongovernment databases to find terrorists and terrorist plots continue to appear. We summarize an interesting point Jeff Jonas and Jim Harper present about the suitability of data mining for this purpose.[52] Marketers make heavy use of data mining, spending millions of dollars analyzing data to find people who are likely to be customers. How likely? In marketing, a response rate of a few percent is considered quite good. In other words, expensive, sophisticated data mining has a high rate of false positives; most people whom data mining identifies as potential customers are not. Many people who receive targeted ads, catalogs, and sales pitches do not respond. Junk mail and pop-up ads annoy people, but they do not significantly threaten civil liberties. But, a high rate of false positives in data mining for finding terrorist suspects does. Data mining might be helpful for picking terrorists out of masses of consumer data, but appropriate procedures are essential to protect innocent but mistakenly selected people. Jonas and Harper argue for use of methods for finding terrorists that are less threatening to the privacy and civil liberties of large numbers of people and are more cost-effective.

Database example: Tracking college students

The U.S. Department of Education proposed establishing a database to contain the records of every student enrolled in a college or university in the United States. Colleges and universities would provide and regularly update the records including each student's name, gender, Social Security number, major, courses taken, courses passed, degrees, loans, and scholarships (public and private). The government would keep the data indefinitely. Intense opposition has prevented the implementation of this proposal. We discuss it as an example for analysis; the issues and questions we raise here apply in many other situations.

The federal government spends billions of dollars each year on federal grants and loans to students but does not have a comprehensive way to measure the success of these programs. Do students who get aid graduate? What majors do they pursue? The database would help evaluate federal student aid programs and perhaps lead to improvements in the programs and provide more accurate data on graduation rates and actual college costs. The ability to track the number of future nurses, engineers, teachers, and so on, in the educational pipeline can help shape better immigration policy and business and economic planning.

On the other hand, the collection of so much detail about each student in one place illustrates many of the privacy risks we described in Section 2.1.2. It is very likely that the government would find new uses for the data that are not part of the original proposal. Such a database could be an ideal target for identity thieves. Information leaks of many sorts are possible and likely. There is potential for abuse by staff members who maintain the data; for example, someone might release college records of a political candidate. And there would undoubtedly be errors in the database. If the department limits the data's use to generalized statistical analysis, errors might not have a big impact, but for some potential uses, the errors could cause significant harm.

The planned uses of the database do not include finding or investigating students who are breaking laws, but it would be a tempting resource for law enforcement agencies. A Virginia state law requires colleges to provide the names and other identifying information for all students they accept. State police then check if 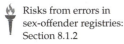 Risks from errors in sex-offender registries: Section 8.1.2   any are in sex-offender registries. What else might they check for? What other government agencies might want access to a federal student database? Would the Defense Department use the database for military recruiting? What potential risks arise if employers get access? All such uses would be secondary uses, without the consent of the students.

Some educators worry that an eventual link between this database and public school databases (on children in kindergarten through high school) would create "cradle-to-grave" tracking of childhood behavior problems, health and family issues, and so on. Such data are already at risk: In a lawsuit against the California Department of Education, a judge granted the organization that filed the suit access to a huge amount of sensitive data the department maintains on millions of school children. Although the judge set restrictions on the handling of the data, such access was probably not imagined by parents when the data collection began.[53]

It makes sense for the government to monitor the effectiveness of the grants and loans it gives to college students, and it is therefore reasonable to require data on academic progress and graduation from students who receive federal money or loan guarantees. But what justifies requiring the data on all other students? For statistics and planning, the government may do voluntary surveys, just as businesses and organizations, without the government's power of coercion, must do. Are the benefits of the database central enough to the fundamental responsibilities of government to outweigh the risks and to justify a mandatory reporting program of so much personal data on every student?*

When considering each new system or policy for personal data use or data mining by government, we should ask many questions: Is the information it uses or collects accurate and useful? Will less intrusive means accomplish a similar result? Will the system inconvenience ordinary people while being easy for criminals and terrorists to thwart? How significant are the risks to innocent people? Are privacy protections built into the technology and into the rules controlling usage?

2.4.3 PUBLIC RECORDS: ACCESS VERSUS PRIVACY

Some of the many federal and state databases contain "public records," that is, records that are available to the general public. Examples include bankruptcy records, arrest records, marriage license applications, divorce proceedings, property-ownership records (including mortgage information), salaries of government employees, and wills. These have long been public but were available only on paper in government offices. Lawyers, private investigators, journalists, real estate brokers, neighbors, and others use the records. Now that it is so easy to search and browse through files on the Web, more people access public records for fun, for research, for valid personal purposes—and for purposes that can threaten the peace, safety, personal secrets, and property of others.

Public records can include sensitive information such as Social Security numbers, birth dates, and home addresses. Maricopa County in Arizona, the first county to put numerous and complete public records on the Web, had the highest rate of identity theft in the United States.[54] Obviously, certain sensitive information should be withheld from public record websites.

 More about identity theft: Section 5.3.1

Doing so requires decisions about exactly what types of data to protect and may require expensive revisions to government software. Some local governments have adopted policies to block display of sensitive data in files posted online, and some states have laws requiring it.

---

*Critics of the proposal, including many universities, point out other risks and costs besides privacy. Colleges fear that collection of the data would lead to increased federal control and interference in management of colleges. The reporting requirements would impose a high cost on the schools. The whole project would have high costs to taxpayers.

To illustrate more issues about public records and ways to reduce risks, we describe a few kinds of specialized information—flight information for private airplanes, political contributions, and the financial statements of judges—and then raise some questions.

The pilots of the roughly 12,000 company airplanes in the United States file a flight plan when they fly. A few businesses combined this flight information, obtained from government databases, with aircraft registration records (also public government records) to provide a service telling where a particular plane is, where it is going, when it will arrive, and so on. Companies report resulting problems ranging from sports fans seeking autographs to death threats against company executives. Who else might want this information? Public interest groups and journalists—to publicize personal use of government or corporate jets; competitors—to determine with whom top executives of another company are meeting; and terrorists—to track movements of a high-profile target. Because of the security and privacy concerns, the Federal Aviation Administration now allows private jet owners to block their flight information from the public.

Political campaign committees must request and report the name, address, occupation, employer, and donation amount for donors to a candidate for president.* This information is available to the public. In the past, primarily journalists and rival campaigns examined it. Now that it is on the Web and easy to search, anyone can find out what candidate their neighbors, friends, employees, and employers support. We can also find the addresses of prominent people who might prefer to keep their address secret to protect their peace and privacy.

Federal law requires federal judges to file financial disclosure reports.[55] The reports are available to the public for purposes such as to determine whether a particular judge might have a conflict of interest in a particular case. When an online news agency sued to make the reports available online, judges objected that information in the reports can disclose where family members work or go to school, putting them at risk from defendants who are angry at a judge. Ultimately, the reports went online, with some sensitive information removed.[56]

The change in ease of access to information changes the balance between the advantages and disadvantages of making some kinds of data public. Whenever access changes significantly, we should reconsider old decisions, policies, and laws. Do the benefits of making all property-ownership records public outweigh the privacy risks and the theft risks we describe in Exercise 2.36? Do the benefits of reporting of small political contributions outweigh the privacy risks? Maybe. The point is that such questions should regularly be raised and addressed.

How should we control access to sensitive public records? Under the old rules for the financial statements of judges, when they were on paper, people requesting access had to sign a form disclosing their identity. The judges' reports were

---

*There are exceptions for very small donations.

available to the public, but the record of who accessed them could deter people intent on doing harm. This is a sensible rule, but can we implement a similar system online? Technologies for identifying and authenticating people online are developing, but they are not yet widespread enough for use by everyone accessing sensitive public data on the Web. We might routinely use such tools in the future, but that raises another question: How will we distinguish data that requires identification and a signature for access from data the public should be free to view anonymously, to protect the viewer's privacy?[57]

2.4.4 NATIONAL ID SYSTEMS

In the United States, national identification systems began with the Social Security card in 1936. In recent decades, problems with Social Security numbers and concerns about illegal immigration and terrorism generated increased support for a more sophisticated and secure national ID system. Opposition to some of these proposals is based on concerns about privacy and potential abuse (and cost and practical problems). In this section, we review Social Security numbers, various issues about national ID systems, and the REAL ID Act, a major step toward turning driver's licenses into national ID cards.

Social Security numbers[58]

The history of the Social Security number (SSN) illustrates how the use of a national identification system grows. When SSNs first appeared in 1936, they were for the exclusive use of the Social Security program. The government assured the public at the time that it would not use the numbers for other purposes. Only a few years later, in 1943, President Roosevelt signed an executive order requiring federal agencies to use the SSN for new record systems. In 1961, the IRS began using it as the taxpayer identification number, so employers and businesses that must report financial transactions to the IRS require it. In 1976, state and local tax, welfare, and motor vehicle departments received authority to use the SSN. A 1988 federal law requires that parents provide their SSN to get a birth certificate for a child. In the 1990s, the Federal Trade Commission encouraged credit bureaus to use SSNs. A 1996 law required that states collect SSNs for occupational licenses, marriage licenses, and other kinds of licenses. Although the government promised otherwise, the SSN has become a general identification number.

Few, if any, government agencies and other organizations seemed to recognize the importance of security for an identification number used for so many purposes. SSNs often appear on documents such as property deeds, which are public records (and available online). For decades, many universities used SSNs as the ID numbers for students and faculty; the numbers appeared on the face of ID cards and on class rosters. A university where I (TH) taught used my name and the last four digits of my SSN as my public email address. (It has ended that practice.) The SSN is printed on the Medicare cards of the millions of people in the Medicare program.

The state of Virginia included SSNs on published lists of voters until a federal court ruled that requiring the SSN for voter registration was unconstitutional. Congress required that all driver's licenses display the driver's SSN, but it repealed that law a few years later due to strong protests. Some employers used the SSN as an identifier and put it on badges or gave it out on request. The U.S. Department of Agriculture inadvertently included the SSNs of more than 35,000 farmers on a website where it posted details about loans and grants to farmers.

Businesses ranging from financial institutions to local cable companies ask for your SSN, or the last four digits, when you call them. That means they store the number in their records. In Section 2.1.2 and in Chapter 5, we list numerous incidents where hackers stole millions of such consumer records containing SSNs. Someone who knows your name and has your SSN can, with varying degrees of ease, get access to your work and earnings history, credit report, driving record, and other personal data. The widespread use of SSNs exposes us to fraud and identity theft. A part-time English teacher at a California junior college used the SSNs of some of her students, provided on her class lists, to open fraudulent credit card accounts. Hackers who steal the SSNs of millions of people use or sell the numbers for financial fraud on a large scale.

SSNs are too widely available to securely identify someone. Social Security cards are easy to forge, but that hardly matters, because those who request the number rarely ask for the card and almost never verify the number. The Social Security Administration itself used to issue cards without verification of the information provided by the applicant. Criminals have little trouble creating false identities, while innocent, honest people suffer disclosure of personal information, arrest, fraud, destruction of their credit rating, and so on, because of problems with the SSN.

Gradually, governments and businesses recognized the risks of careless use of the SSN and reasons why we should not use it so widely. Various state laws now prohibit businesses and organizations from requiring the SSN if they do not need it.

The SSN was not intended as a general, secure identification number, and attempts to use it as one have not only failed but have also damaged privacy and financial security. We next look at plans for more extensive, secure, digitally-connected national ID systems.

A new U.S. national ID system

It is clear that a secure ID system is needed to replace the Social Security number and for a variety of government purposes where identifying people is essential. In recent years, various government agencies have proposed new national ID card systems. The cards would have a large number of applications and would include citizenship, employment, health, tax, financial, or other data, as well as biometric information such as fingerprints or a retina scan, depending on the specific proposal and the government agency

More about biometrics: Section 5.5.1

advocating it. In many proposals, ID cards would also access a variety of databases for additional information.

Advocates of national ID systems describe many benefits, some of which depend on the card being used for a very large number of government and private applications:

- You would need the actual card, not just a number, to verify identity.
- The cards would be harder to forge than Social Security cards.
- If the ID card replaces all other forms of ID, a person would need to carry only one card, rather than separate cards for various services as we do now.
- Authentication of identity would help reduce fraud both in private credit card transactions and in government benefit programs.
- Use of ID cards for verifying work eligibility would prevent people from working in the United States illegally.
- Criminals and terrorists would be easier to track and identify.
- Citizens who are harassed or detained by police under suspicion of being in the United States illegally—a frequent problem for people in some ethnic groups—would be able to show their ID card to confirm their citizenship.

Those who are wary of multipurpose national ID systems argue that they are profound threats to freedom and privacy and that errors in the ID system can have devastating effects. "Your papers, please" is a demand associated with police states and dictatorships. Under the infamous pass laws of South Africa, people carried passes, or identification papers, that categorized them by race and controlled where they could live and work. In Germany and France during World War II, identification papers included the person's religion, making it easy for the Nazis to capture and remove Jews. In the United States, government agencies obtained from the Census Bureau data on the location of Japanese-Americans (for internment during World War II) and data on the number of people of Arab ancestry in various zip codes (after the terrorist attacks in 2001), suggesting the kinds of group targeting that can occur in a free country. Peter Neumann and Lauren Weinstein warned of risks that arise from the databases and communication complexes that would support a national ID card system: "The opportunities for overzealous surveillance and serious privacy abuses are almost limitless, as are opportunities for masquerading, identity theft, and draconian social engineering on a grand scale."[59]

The goal of some ID card systems is a "one-card society," and the convenience of carrying only one card appeals to many people. Now, however, if you lose, say, your student ID card, you can still shop with your credit card, go to a doctor, and drive your car. Loss or theft of the one-card ID would prevent many activities. Similarly, errors in the system could be devastating. Consider, for example, that over a five-year period, the U.S. Department of Veterans Affairs mistakenly classified as dead more than

Accuracy of worker verification database: Section 8.1.2

4200 people receiving veteran's benefits; it stopped sending their checks. Although the number of people affected is small as a percentage of veterans who die each year, the impact was serious, leaving some people unable to pay rent, for example. If a person is mistakenly classified as dead in a one-card system, the impact would be far more severe. Is such a card, as in the words of one critic, a "license to exist"?[60]

Some forms of identification, such as passports and ID cards for members of the military, have a high degree of security. (That is, getting one requires authenticating the applicant, and they are difficult to forge.) It is important that ID cards for such applications reliably identify the user. It is less important that supermarket club cards do so. Clearly, we need to ask what roles a national ID card should play. Some basic applications would include tax purposes, voter identification, Social Security and Medicare, and identification for government benefits. What else? If we use a new national ID number for too many purposes, including online and phone identification for a variety of businesses, we will soon have some of the same problems as with the SSN: Hackers will steal the numbers and gain access to the many systems where the number but not the card is required.

Another issue is whether or not citizens should be required by law to carry their ID card at all times. If the card connects to many databases, as it would in some proposals, what information would a police officer be able to access when he or she stops someone on the street? Plans for a national ID system with a large number of uses and connections should be approached with caution.

[W]e need to think more in terms of diversification of identification systems.
—Jim Harper[61]

Real ID

The REAL ID Act attempts to develop a secure national identification card by setting federal standards for driver's licenses (and state-issued ID cards, for people without driver's licenses). Licenses must meet these standards to be used for identification by federal agencies. Such uses include airport security and entering federal facilities. By implication, they include working for the federal government and obtaining federal benefits. It is likely the government will add many new uses, as it did with the Social Security number. Businesses and state and local governments already require the federally approved card for many transactions and services. The federal government pays for approximately half the medical care in the United States (for example, Medicaid, Medicare, benefits for veterans, and numerous federally funded programs), so it is not hard to envision requiring the driver's license for federal medical services and eventually it becoming a de facto national medical ID card.

The REAL ID Act requires that, to get a federally approved driver's license or ID card, each person must provide documentation of address, birth date, Social Security number, and legal status in the United States. Motor vehicle departments must verify each person's information, in part by accessing federal databases such as the Social Security database. The departments must scan documents submitted by applicants and store them in transferable form for at least 10 years (making motor vehicle records a desirable target for identity thieves). The licenses must satisfy various requirements to reduce tampering and counterfeiting, they must include the person's photo, and the information must be in machine-readable form.

The REAL ID Act puts the burden of verifying identity on individuals and the state motor vehicle departments. Many states object to the mandate and its high costs (estimated in billions of dollars) and more than 20 states initially passed resolutions refusing to participate. Residents in states without a federally approved driver's license could experience serious inconvenience. When Congress passed REAL ID in 2005, it was to take effect in 2008. The Department of Homeland Security extended the deadline several times. By October 2020, everyone who travels by commercial airliner within the United States will be required to have a REAL ID identification card or other identification acceptable to the Transportation Security Administration.[62]

Examples from other countries

About half the countries in the world have instituted a national ID card system in some form. In many of these countries, citizens over the age of 18 must carry the card (or produce it when asked), and they must show a valid ID card to vote.

Japan's national computerized registry system, introduced in 2002, assigned an ID number to every citizen and was intended to simplify administration procedures for government programs and make them more efficient. The system met very heavy protest: People complained of insufficient privacy protection, potential abuse by government, and vulnerability to hackers. Several cities declined to participate. In 2015–2016, Japan introduced a new system, My Number. The number and associated ID card are intended to link tax, pension, medical, employment, and marital status records. Connection to bank records may be added, so that the My Number card replaces credit and debit cards.[63]

The Indian government is building a national ID database for its 1.2 billion people that includes each person's photo, fingerprints and other biometric data, birth date, and other information. Its purposes include providing proof of identification, improving provision of government services, and catching people in the country illegally. Civil liberties groups have raised privacy objections, and India's Supreme Court has limited applications of the ID number and ordered that it not be made mandatory.[64]

An unpopular plan for an expensive mandatory national ID card in the United Kingdom stalled when emails about weaknesses of the plan leaked from government offices.

Estonia, with population of approximately 1.3 million, has a successful modern national ID system. Its ID smart cards authenticate identity for online voting, are used for medical care and online banking, and include cryptographic keys that enable people to sign digital documents. Is the size of the country an important factor in the success of the Estonian system?

Places like Nazi Germany, the Soviet Union, and apartheid South Africa all had very robust identification systems. True, identification systems do not cause tyranny, but identification systems are very good administrative systems that tyrannies often use.

—Jim Harper[65]

2.4.5 THE NSA AND SECRET INTELLIGENCE GATHERING[66]

The purpose of the National Security Agency (NSA) is to collect and analyze foreign intelligence information related to national security and to protect U.S. government communications and sensitive information related to national security. A secret presidential order formed the NSA in 1952. Its budget is still secret, although its website says the NSA/CSS (NSA and Central Security Service) is about the size of one of the larger Fortune 500 companies. The NSA builds and uses enormously powerful supercomputers to process the huge masses of information it collects and stores. Because governments encrypt their sensitive material, the NSA has long devoted a huge amount of resources to cryptology and has very advanced code-breaking capabilities.

Because the NSA uses methods that do not satisfy the Fourth Amendment, it was legally restricted to intercepting communications outside the United States (with some exceptions). Through its history, the agency generated much controversy by secretly violating restrictions on surveillance of people within the United States. In the 1960s and 1970s, the NSA monitored communications of specific American citizens (including civil rights leader Martin Luther King Jr. and entertainers who opposed the Vietnam War). A Congressional committee (the Church Committee, chaired by Senator Frank Church) found that since the 1950s, the NSA had been secretly and illegally collecting international telegrams, including telegrams sent by American citizens, and searching them for foreign intelligence information. As a result, Congress passed the Foreign Intelligence Surveillance Act of 1978 (FISA) establishing oversight rules for the NSA. The law prohibited the agency from collecting masses of telegrams without a warrant and from compiling lists of Americans to watch without a court order. The law set up a secret federal court, the Foreign Intelligence Surveillance Court, to issue warrants to the NSA to intercept communications of people it could show were agents of foreign powers or involved in terrorism or espionage.

Increased wealth, travel, and trade generated more international communication—cluttering communications channels and potentially making it harder for the NSA to detect messages of interest. Then, vastly increased processing power of computer systems enabled the NSA to filter and analyze huge quantities of communications of innocent people instead of targeting only specific suspects. In cyberspace, our email, phone conversations, tweets, searches, purchases, financial information, legal documents, and so on mix with military, diplomatic, and terrorist communications. The NSA sifts through it all, analyzing the packets of information traveling through the Internet, and collects whatever is of interest. This interception activity is extremely controversial because the NSA processes and collects data on Americans with no court order and no approval from the FISA court.

In 2006, an AT&T employee described (under oath) a secret secure room the NSA set up at an AT&T switching facility. From this room, the NSA had access to email, telephone, and Web communications of AT&T users.[67] The NSA built a database of telephone and email records that included millions of Americans. The government argued that the NSA was not intercepting or listening to telephone calls and was not collecting personal identifying information. It used sophisticated data mining technology to analyze calling patterns to learn how to detect communications of terrorist cells. Opponents of the monitoring program said the warrantless collection of the records by the NSA was illegal, and it was illegal for a telephone company to provide them. Congress passed the FISA Amendments Act in 2008 retroactively protecting AT&T (and other entities that assist the NSA) from lawsuits. Some lawsuits against the NSA for this monitoring program are still working through the courts.[68] The FISA Amendments Act includes provisions to restrict domestic surveillance, but overall it reduces previous protections.

In 2013, a security contractor working for the NSA, Edward Snowden, downloaded a huge collection of documents* about the NSA's activities.[69] Many were eventually released publicly. These documents showed, among other things, that the NSA can search through most activities any person does on the Internet; it collects data directly from the servers of several major American tech companies such as Yahoo, Facebook, Google, and Microsoft; it demanded phone record data from Verizon on all its American customers (with a gag order that prevented Verizon from discussing the release of information with its customers); it spied on leaders of major European countries; and it monitors communications of millions of foreign individuals who were not accused of terrorism or linked to terrorist activities. Although journalists had reported some of these activities previously, this documentation of the details and extent of NSA surveillance programs shocked many Americans and foreigners.

The NSA has built enormous data centers to store, decrypt, and analyze billions of gigabytes of communications and files.[70] What it cannot decrypt now, it stores to decrypt later when it develops faster computers or better algorithms. Civil libertarians are concerned that the NSA is collecting huge quantities of ordinary business and personal encrypted data that have nothing to do with terrorism or foreign intelligence.

---

*Estimates ranged from "thousands" to roughly 1.7 million documents.

How can we evaluate the NSA's programs of massive collection of communication data and online activity? As we have seen often in the past, secret programs to monitor and collect surveillance data present a huge potential for abuse, and they threaten the reputation, safety, and freedom of innocent people when investigators mistakenly decide someone's transactions look suspicious. When our government knows the details of all our actions, movements, and preferences, it becomes easier for official oppression against dissidents, political opponents, or minority groups. When individual employees can record a person's online activity with little oversight, they can spy on acquaintances, and indeed, the released documents showed that some NSA employees spied on their "love interests." But are such individual abuses, possible in any large organization, a small trade-off for the necessity of collecting information to protect the country? Is the NSA doing what a national security agency must do? We have experienced the hideous effects of terrorism, including attacks from within the United States. There used to be a clear distinction between foreign and domestic threats to security, and the NSA and FBI had clearly different roles with different legal restrictions. Preventing terrorist attacks requires tools that go beyond collecting information about suspects after a crime has been committed. We do not know who is planning an attack, and it is essential to find out. What should our laws allow the NSA to do? How should we react when it breaks existing laws?

2.5   Protecting Privacy: Technology and Markets

2.5.1   DEVELOPING PRIVACY TOOLS

Many individuals, organizations, and businesses help meet the demand for privacy to some degree:

- Individual programmers post free privacy-protecting software on the Web.
- Entrepreneurs build new companies to provide technology-based privacy protections.
- Large businesses respond to consumer demand and improve policies and services.
- Organizations such as the Privacy Rights Clearinghouse provide excellent information resources.
- Activist organizations such as the Electronic Privacy Information Center inform the public, file lawsuits, and advocate for better privacy protection.

New applications of technology can often solve problems that arise as side effects of other technologies. Soon after "techies" became aware of the use of cookies by websites, they wrote cookie disablers and made them available on the Web. Software to block pop-up ads appeared soon after the advent of such ads.

Companies sell software to scan for spyware; some versions are free. Several companies provide services, called anonymizers, with which people can surf the Web anonymously, leaving no record that identifies them or their computers. Some search engines do not store user search queries in a way that allows linking them together to one person.[71] Companies offer products and services to prevent forwarding, copying, or printing email. (Lawyers are among the major customers.)

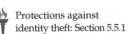 More about anonymizers: Section 3.5

There are services that fully erase email or text messages (on both the sender's and recipient's phones) after a user-specified time period; a popular messaging app deletes photos within seconds of viewing by the recipient. If our laptop, tablet, or phone is stolen or lost, we can remotely encrypt, retrieve, and/or erase files.

Extensive and hidden tracking of online activity led to calls for a "Do Not Track" (DNT) setting in browsers. A browser sends the DNT setting to websites the user visits. What should the default value be? It might seem that the privacy-protecting default is to have DNT turned on. However, the Digital Advertising Alliance and other business groups made an agreement with the U.S. government to respect the DNT setting *if* it is turned on by the user. When some browsers set DNT on by default, some advertisers chose to ignore it completely. Thus a common default, at this point, is that DNT is "unset" and may be turned on or off by each user. For sites that ignore the DNT setting, we can install free add-ons to our browsers that block Web activity trackers.

These are a very few examples of products and technology applications that protect privacy, but they do not solve all problems. Learning about, installing, and using privacy tools might be daunting to nontechnical, less educated users—a large part of the public—hence the importance of designing systems

Protections against identity theft: Section 5.5.1

with privacy protection in mind, building in protective features, and having privacy-protecting policies.

2.5.2 ENCRYPTION

Cryptography is the art and science of hiding data in plain sight.

—Larry Loen[72]

Freely available tools enable interception of data in transit and a thief or hacker can read data on a stolen or hacked computer if they are not protected. The law provides punishment for these actions if the perpetrator is caught and convicted, but we can also use technology to protect ourselves. Encryption is a technology, often implemented in software, that transforms data into a form that is meaningless to anyone who might intercept or view it. The data could be email, business plans, credit card numbers, images, medical records, mobile phone location history, and so on. Software at the recipient's site (or on one's own computer) decodes encrypted data so that the recipient (or owner) can view the messages or files. People are often not even aware that they are using encryption since software handles it automatically. For example, software encrypts credit card numbers when we send them to online merchants. Phone apps such as WhatsApp automatically encrypt calls and messages.

Privacy and security professionals view encryption as the most important technical method for ensuring the privacy of messages and data sent through computer networks. Encryption can also protect stored information from intruders and abuses by employees. It can protect data on laptops and other small data storage devices carried outside an office.

Encryption generally includes a coding scheme, or cryptographic algorithm, and specific sequences of characters (e.g., digits or letters), called *keys*, used by the algorithm to encode or decode data. Using mathematical tools and powerful computers, it is sometimes possible to "break" an older or weak encryption algorithm—that is, to decode an encrypted message or file without the secret key.

Modern encryption technology is very secure and has a flexibility and variety of applications beyond protecting data. For example, it is used to create digital signatures, authentication methods, and digital cash. Digital signature technology allows us to "sign" documents online, saving time and paper for loan applications, business contracts, and so on. Other applications provide authentication; for example, the American Medical Association issues digital credentials to doctors that a laboratory website can verify when a doctor visits to get patient test results.

Digital cash systems and other encryption-based privacy-protected transaction methods, such as BitCoin, LiteCoin, and Ripple, can let us do secure financial transactions electronically without the seller acquiring a credit card or checking account number from the buyer. They combine the convenience of credit card purchases with the anonymity of cash. With such schemes, it is extremely difficult to link records of different transactions to form a consumer profile or dossier. These techniques can provide both privacy protection for the consumer with respect to the organizations he or she interacts with and protection for organizations against forgery, bad checks, and credit card fraud. However, cash transactions make it harder for governments to detect and prosecute people who are "laundering" money earned in illegal activities, earning money they are not reporting to tax

⬥ Encryption backdoors
for law enforcement:
Section 5.5.4

authorities, or transferring or spending money for criminal purposes. Thus, many governments oppose truly anonymous digital cash systems. Some systems include provisions for law enforcement and tax collection. The potential illegal uses of digital cash have long been possible with real cash. It has been only in recent decades, with increased use of checks and credit cards, that we lost the privacy we had from marketers and the government when we used cash for most transactions.

The technologies of anonymity and cryptography may be the only way to protect privacy.

—Nadine Strossen, former president of the American Civil Liberties Union[73]

2.5.3   BLOCKING ADS

We explore problems with online ads, the ethics of blocking ads, and responses to ad blocking because ad blocking raises several issues, serves as an exercise in applying the ethical theories introduced in Chapter 1, and illustrates a variety of approaches to solving a problem.

The ethics of blocking ads

Bouncing, blaring, annoying, intrusive ads show up on our phones, computer screens, and other devices. Some of them slow the downloading of the content we want; some use up battery power. Some track online activity and collect personal information that can be misused. Some ads install malicious software.

An ad industry group estimates that 26% of Internet users in the United States have installed ad blockers on their desktop computers.[74] When Apple released a version of its mobile operating system that enabled apps to block ads, within a week hundreds of thousands of users installed ad-blocking apps. In response, some software developers and Web publishers began to question the ethics of blocking ads or selling the tools for millions of users to do so. Why? Ads pay for free video and photo sites, free social networking, and a lot of free content on the Web. Ads help support small online publishers and bring them to the attention of the public. Those who question the ethics of blocking ads (or providing tools to do so) look long term, concerned that if too many people block ads, a lot of free content may disappear and jobs could be lost—negative impacts for society as a whole. Is it ethical to create, sell, or use ad blockers?

Ignoring or blocking ads is not new. When people watched broadcast television before they had the Internet and video recorders, an ad signaled time for a bathroom break or time to go to the kitchen for a snack. When video recorders became available, people fast-forwarded over the commercials. Was it unethical to skip the commercials that paid for free television content? As we continue this discussion, think about whether your responses are consistent for TV and Internet or mobile ads, and if not, identify the characteristics that lead to different positions.

A deontologist perspective: Blocking ads does not violate the ethical prohibition against lying. Are we stealing free content if we block ads? Advertisers and Web publishers do not believe that. They offer their material to the viewer freely; they understand that not all people will view or respond to the ads.

Kant emphasized using reason—ethical action should be rational—and that ethical rules should apply universally to all people. Let's consider implications of the position that ad blocking is unethical. Is it enough not to block the ads? Suppose we do not block ads, but we ignore them. For many ads, sites hosting the ads are paid only if people click or tap an ad. Must we click on every ad? Even clicking on an ad, ultimately, is not enough. Advertisers will not continue to pay for ads unless they generate a sufficient number of sales, members, signatures—or whatever the advertiser is seeking. Must everyone buy everything we see advertised? Of course not. Continuation of ad-supported content requires that a certain number of people buy the advertised products or services. This does not seem to justify a universal ethical ban on blocking ads on one's own devices.

Other ethical approaches are more useful for considering wider social consequences of ad blocking and of creating and promoting tools to do so. We consider them next.

A utilitarian analysis: Utilitarians evaluate the negative and positive utilities of consequences. Some negatives of ad blockers are:

- Small Web publishers might lose income from ads.
- Once-free content becomes unavailable or costly.
- People (writers, advertisers, etc.) might lose their jobs.
- The person using an ad blocker might miss an opportunity to know of and purchase a product he or she would want.

Some positives are:

- Increased privacy: freedom from intrusion is one aspect of privacy.
- Reduced intrusion of commercialism.
- Improved system performance.
- A more pleasant online experience.

How do we quantify these? Most of the negatives of ad blocking depend on the hypothesis that the response to ads will drop significantly enough to negatively affect the ad industry itself and to reduce the availability of valuable content. Reports and projections for losses to publishers because of ad blocking are in billions of dollars but vary widely.[75] How do we determine how likely it is that content will disappear, how much will disappear, and how much the lost content is worth? Some publishers might find other sources of income to keep them online, for example, support from a philanthropic organization or crowdfunding. Some might devote their energy and skills to other projects that have more utility for them and for the public than their projects that failed.

How do we weigh the negative utility for those who lose jobs in advertising or publishing against the dynamism of a society that continually comes up with innovations? Is there ever a point in time when all the websites and jobs that exist should exist forever? Or for another year or month?

How do we quantify the positive utility of being free of the ads? The large number of people who were quick to install ad blockers might perceive that utility as very high. Some positive utilities of ad blocking are difficult to identify and measure because they come from future alternatives that do not exist until later. For example, in response to the issues raised about ad blocking, software developers created apps that block some ads but allow ads that meet standards for being less intrusive. This might lead advertisers to adopt new standards to eliminate the most irritating ads. Thus, we should go back to the list of positives of ad blocking above and add

- Improvements in quality of ads

Applying John Rawls's ideas: In Rawls's view, an action is not ethical if it has the effect of leaving the least advantaged people worse off. If we take a global perspective, the least advantaged people do not use the Internet or work for publishers or advertisers. The use of ad blockers is irrelevant to them, or nearly so. If we are to consider the least advantaged of a subpopulation, how do we decide which? People who might lose their jobs at publishing or advertising businesses are not the least advantaged; they are likely educated. If too many people block ads and a significant amount of formerly free content disappears or requires fees, low-income people who use the Internet will be worse off.

Coming to a decision: In Chapter 1, we also discussed natural rights, positive and negative rights, and a few other approaches to thinking about ethics. We leave applying those to ad blocking for an exercise.

The brief analysis here illustrates the problems with making a universal ethical rule against an activity based on long-term, indirect, often unpredictable consequences. There is too much diversity among people and situations. There is too much unknown about consequences in a dynamic society and economy. It seems a good idea not to conclude that a voluntary activity is unethical when there is so much uncertainty about the effects.

Does this help you decide whether to install an ad blocker or to create and sell one? It might not be unethical to do so, but we can evaluate the arguments and come to a personal conclusion about what we prefer to do. There is certainly nothing wrong with refraining from doing something that is ethically okay because of the impact we think it will have and the impact we would like to make.

Responses from ad blockers and publishers

As we mentioned above, developers of some ad blockers established standards for acceptable ads that they would not block. Others charge advertisers a fee to allow their ads through the block. Firefox and Google's Chrome browser block Adobe Flash ads. Like filters for Internet content (that we discuss in Chapter 3), these products can compete for users who like their particular policies.

The *New York Times* tested a message telling people about the need for ads to pay for content. It found that 40% of people set their ad blocker to allow ads from the *Times*.

Facebook chose not to pay ad blockers to allow ads through. Instead it chose to use technology: it announced that it would use techniques to make it more difficult for ad blockers to block ads on its desktop service (though not on mobile devices).[76] Is it wrong for Facebook to thwart the desires of those who install ad blockers? We began this section with the concern that it might be wrong to block ads because ads pay for free content. Facebook is free; ads pay for it.

Some podcast apps allow the user to skip ahead, and of course, some users skip ads. According to a news report, podcast companies say the best way to reduce ad skipping is to make ads entertaining.

This sampling of responses indicates that there are roles for technology, markets, education, and creativity in improving the online experience with respect to ads.

2.5.4   POLICIES FOR PROTECTING PERSONAL DATA

The businesses, organizations, and government agencies that collect and store personal data have ethical responsibilities (and in many cases legal ones) to protect the data from misuse, and to anticipate risks and prepare for them. These groups must continually update security policies to cover new technologies and new potential threats, and employers must train those who carry around personal data about the risks and proper security measures.

A well-designed database for sensitive information includes several features to protect against leaks, intruders, and unauthorized employee access. Each person with authorized access to the system should have a unique identifier and a password. The system can restrict users from performing certain operations, such as changing, creating or deleting, by coding user IDs to give access to only specific information and operations. For example, a billing clerk in a hospital does not need access to the results of a patient's lab tests. The computer system creates an *audit trail* by tracking information about each data access, including the ID of the person looking at a record and the particular information viewed or modified. An audit trail can later help trace unauthorized activity and thus discourage many privacy violations.

Databases with consumer information, Web-activity records, or mobile phone location data are valuable assets that give businesses a competitive advantage, so the owners of such databases have an interest in preventing leaks and unlimited distribution. That includes providing security for the data and developing modes of operation that reduce loss. Thus, for example, mailing lists are usually not sold; they are "rented." The renter does not receive a copy (electronic or otherwise) of the addresses, but instead supplies the materials to be mailed. A specialized firm then does the mailing. This reduces the risk of unauthorized copying to a small number of firms whose reputation for honesty and security is important to their business. Other applications also use this idea of trusted third parties to process confidential data. For example, car rental agencies can access a third-party service to check the driving record of potential customers. The service examines the motor vehicle department records and reports relevant information; the car rental company does not see the driver's record.

Website operators pay thousands, sometimes millions, of dollars to companies that do *privacy audits*. Privacy auditors check for leaks of information, review the company's privacy policy and its compliance with that policy, and evaluate warnings and explanations on its website that alert visitors when the site requests sensitive data, and so forth. Hundreds of large businesses have a position called *chief privacy officer* or *compliance officer* to guide and oversee the company privacy policy. Just as the Automobile Association of America rates hotels, various organizations offer a seal of approval, an icon companies that comply with their privacy standards can post on websites.

Large companies use their economic influence to improve consumer privacy. IBM and Microsoft stopped advertising on websites that do not post clear privacy policies. Walt Disney Company and InfoSeek Corporation did the same and, in addition, stopped accepting advertising on their own websites from sites that do not post privacy policies. The Direct Marketing Association adopted a policy requiring its member companies to inform consumers when they will share personal information with other marketers and to give people an opt-out option. Many companies agreed to limit the availability of sensitive consumer information, including unlisted telephone numbers and all information about children.

There continue, of course, to be many businesses without strong privacy policies, as well as many that do not follow their own stated policies. The examples described here represent a trend, not a privacy utopia, and suggest actions responsible companies can take.

2.6 Protecting Privacy: Theory, Rights, and Laws

In Section 2.3, we considered some aspects of law and Fourth Amendment principles related to protection of privacy. The Fourth Amendment protects the negative right to privacy (a liberty) against intrusion and interference by government. This section focuses mainly on discussion of principles related to rights and legal protections for personal data collected or used by other people, businesses, and organizations.

We separate legal remedies from technical, management, and market solutions because they are fundamentally different. The latter are voluntary and varied, and different people or businesses can choose from among them. Law, on the other hand, is enforced by fines, imprisonment, and other penalties; thus, we should examine the basis for law more carefully. Privacy is a condition or state we can be in, like good health or financial security. To what extent should we have a legal right to it? Is it solely a negative right or also a positive right (in the sense of Section 1.4.2)? How far should law go, and what should be left to the voluntary interplay of markets, educational efforts of public interest groups, consumer choices and responsibilities, and so forth?

2.6.1 A RIGHT TO PRIVACY

Until the late 19th century, courts based legal decisions supporting privacy in social and business activities on property rights and contracts. There was no recognition of an independent right to privacy. In 1890, a crucial article called "The Right of Privacy," by Samuel Warren and Louis Brandeis[77] (later a Supreme Court Justice), argued that privacy was distinct from other rights and needed more protection. Judith Jarvis Thomson, an MIT philosopher, argued that the old view was more accurate, that in all cases where infringement of privacy is a violation of someone's rights, that violation is of a right distinct from privacy.[78] We present some of the claims and arguments of these papers, and then we consider a variety of other ideas and perspectives about laws to protect privacy.

One purpose of this section is to show the kinds of analyses that philosophers, legal scholars, and economists perform in trying to elucidate underlying principles. Another is to emphasize the importance of principles, of working out a theoretical framework in which to make decisions about particular issues and cases.

Warren and Brandeis: The inviolate personality

The main target of criticism in the 1890 Warren and Brandeis article is newspapers, especially the gossip columns. Warren and Brandeis vehemently criticize the press for "overstepping . . . obvious bounds of propriety and decency." The kinds of information of most concern to them are personal appearance, statements, and acts and interpersonal relationships (marital, family, and others).[79] Warren and Brandeis take the position that people have the right to prohibit publication of facts about themselves and photographs of themselves. Warren and Brandeis argue that, for example, if someone writes a letter in which he says he had a fierce argument with his wife, the recipient of the letter cannot publish that information. They base this claim on no property right or other right except privacy. It is part of the right to be let alone. Warren and Brandeis base their defense of privacy rights on, in their often-quoted phrase, the principle of "an inviolate personality."

Laws against other wrongs—such as slander, libel, defamation, copyright infringement, violation of property rights, and breach of contract—can address some privacy violations, but Warren and Brandeis argue that there remain many privacy violations that those other laws do not cover. For example, publication of personal or business information could constitute a violation of a contract (explicit or implied), but there are many cases in which the person who discloses the information has no contract with the victim. The person, then, is not violating a contract but is violating the victim's privacy. Libel, slander, and defamation laws protect us when someone spreads false and damaging rumors about us, but they do not apply to true personal information whose exposure makes us uncomfortable. Warren and Brandeis believed the latter should be protected. They allow exceptions for publication of information of general interest (news), use in limited situations when the information concerns another person's interests, and oral publication. (They were writing before radio and television, so oral publication meant a quite limited audience.)

Judith Jarvis Thomson: Questioning a right to privacy

Judith Jarvis Thomson argues the opposite point of view. She gets to her point after examining a few scenarios.

Suppose you own a copy of a magazine. Your property rights include the right to refuse to allow others to read, destroy, or even see your magazine. If someone does anything to your magazine that you did not allow, that person is violating your property rights. For example, if someone uses binoculars to see your magazine from a neighboring building, that person is violating your right to exclude others from seeing it. It does not matter whether the magazine is an ordinary news magazine (not a sensitive privacy issue) or some other magazine you do not want people to know you read. The right violated is your property right.

You may waive your property rights, intentionally or inadvertently. If you absentmindedly leave the magazine on a park bench, someone could take it. If you leave it on the coffee table when you have guests at your home, someone could see it. If you read a pornographic magazine on a bus, and someone sees you and tells other people that you read dirty magazines, that person is not violating your rights. The person might be doing something impolite, unfriendly, or cruel, but not something that violates a right.

Our rights to our person and our bodies include the right to decide to whom we show various parts of our bodies. By walking around in public, most of us waive our right to prevent others from seeing our faces. When a Muslim woman covers her face, she is exercising her right to keep others from viewing it. If someone uses binoculars to spy on us at home in the shower, they are violating our right to our person.

If someone beats on you to get some information, the beater is violating your right to be free from physical attack. If the information is the time of day, privacy is not at issue. If the information is more personal, then the beater has compromised your privacy, but the right violated is your right to be free from attack. On the other hand, if a person peacefully asks whom you live with or what your political views are, the person has violated no rights. If you choose to answer and do not make a confidentiality agreement, the person is not violating your rights by repeating the information to someone else, though it could be inconsiderate to do so. However, if the person agreed not to repeat the information, but then does, it does not matter whether or not the information was sensitive; the person is violating the confidentiality agreement.

In these examples, there is no violation of privacy without violation of some other right such as the right to control our property or our person, the right to be free from violent attack, or the right to form contracts (and expect them to be enforced). Thomson concludes, "I suggest it is a useful heuristic device in the case of any purported violation of the right to privacy to ask whether or not the act is a violation of any other right, and if not whether the act really violates a right at all."[80]

Criticisms of Warren and Brandeis and of Thomson

Critics of the Warren and Brandeis position[81] argue that their notion of privacy is too broad to provide a workable principle or definition from which to conclude that a privacy right violation occurs. Their view of privacy conflicts with freedom of the press and appears to make almost any unauthorized mention of a person a violation of the person's right.

Critics of Thomson present examples of violations of a right to privacy (not just a desire for privacy), but of no other right. Some view Thomson's notion of the right to our person as vague or too broad. Her examples might (or might not) be a convincing argument for the thesis that considering other rights can resolve privacy questions, but no finite number of examples can prove such a thesis.

Neither article directly refutes the other. Their emphases are different. Warren and Brandeis focus on the use of the information (publication). Thomson focuses on how it is obtained.

Applying the theories

How do the theoretical arguments apply to privacy and personal data today?

Throughout Warren and Brandeis, the objectionable action is publication of personal information—its widespread, public distribution. Many court decisions since the appearance of their article have taken this point of view.[82] If someone published the list of all the movies you have watched (in print or by making it public on the Web), that would violate the Warren and Brandeis notion of privacy. A person might win a case if someone published his or her consumer profile. But intentional publication is not the main concern in the current context of consumer databases, monitoring of Web activity, location tracking, and so on. The amount of personal information collected nowadays might appall Warren and Brandeis, but their article allows disclosure of personal information to people who have an interest in it. By implication, they do not preclude, for example, disclosure of a person's driving record to a car rental company from which the person wants to rent a car. Similarly, it seems Warren and Brandeis would not oppose disclosure of information about whether someone smokes cigarettes to a life insurance company from which the person is trying to buy insurance. Their view does not rule out use of (unpublished) consumer information for targeted marketing, though they probably would disapprove of it.

The content of social networks would probably shock and appall Warren and Brandeis, as well. Their position would severely restrict the sharing of photos that include other people and of the location and activities of friends.

An important aspect of both the Warren and Brandeis paper and the Thomson paper is that of consent. They see no privacy violation if a person consented to the collection and use of the information.

Transactions

We have another puzzle to consider: how to apply philosophical and legal notions of privacy to transactions, which automatically involve more than one person. The following scenario will illustrate the problem.

One day in the small farm community of Friendlyville, Joe buys five pounds of potatoes from Maria, who sells him the five pounds of potatoes. (We describe the transaction in this repetitious manner to emphasize that there are two people involved and two sides to the transaction.)

Either Joe or Maria might prefer the transaction to remain secret. The failure of his own potato crop might embarrass Joe. Or Joe might be unpopular in Friendlyville, and Maria fears the townspeople will be angry at her for selling to him. Either way, we are not likely to consider it a violation of the other's rights if Maria or Joe talks about the purchase or sale of the potatoes to other people in town. But suppose Joe asks for confidentiality as part of the transaction. Maria has three options:

1. She can agree.
2. She can say no; she might want to tell people she sold potatoes to Joe.
3. She can agree to keep the sale confidential if Joe pays a higher price.

In the latter two cases, Joe can decide whether to buy the potatoes. On the other hand, if Maria asks for confidentiality as part of the transaction, Joe has three options:

1. He can agree.
2. He can say no; he might want to tell people he bought potatoes from Maria.
3. He can agree to keep the purchase confidential if Maria charges a lower price.

In the latter two cases, Maria can decide whether to sell the potatoes.

Privacy includes control of information about oneself. Is the transaction a fact about Maria or a fact about Joe? There does not appear to be a convincing reason for either party to have more right than the other to control information about the transaction. Yet this problem is critical to legal policy decisions about use of consumer information. If we are to assign control of the information about a transaction to one of the parties, we need a firm philosophical foundation for choosing which party gets it. (If the parties make a confidentiality agreement, then they have an ethical obligation to respect it. If the agreement is a legal contract, then they have a legal obligation to respect it.)

Philosophers and economists often use simple two-person transactions or relationships, like the Maria–Joe scenario, to try to clarify the principles involved in an issue. Do the observations and conclusions about Maria and Joe generalize to large, complex societies and a global economy, where, often, one party to a transaction is a business? All transactions are really between people, even if indirectly. So, if a property right or a privacy right in the information about a transaction goes to one of the parties, we need an argument showing how the transaction in a modern economy is different from the one in Friendlyville. Later in this section, we describe two viewpoints on the regulation of information about consumer transactions: the free market view and the consumer protection view. The consumer protection view suggests treating the parties differently.

Ownership of personal data

Some economists, legal scholars, and privacy advocates propose giving people property rights for information about themselves. The concept of property rights can be useful even when applied to intangible property (intellectual property, for example), but there are problems in using this concept for personal information. First, as we have just seen, activities and transactions often involve at least two people, each of whom would have reasonable but conflicting claims to own the information about the transaction. Some personal information does not appear to be about a transaction, but there still can be problems in assigning ownership. Do you own your birthday? Or does your mother own it? After all, she was a more active participant in the event.

The second problem with assigning ownership of personal information arises from the notion of owning facts. (Copyright protects intellectual property such as computer programs and music, but we cannot copyright facts.) Ownership of facts would severely impair the flow of information in society. We store information on electronic devices, but we also store it in our minds. Can we own facts about ourselves without violating the freedom of thought and freedom of speech of others?

Although there are difficulties with assigning ownership of individual facts, another issue is whether we can own our "profiles," that is, a collection of data describing our activities, purchases, interests, and so on. We cannot own the fact that our eyes are blue, but we do have the legal right to control some uses of our photographic image. In almost all states, we need a person's consent to use his or her image for commercial purposes. Should the law treat our consumer profiles the same way? Should the law treat the collection of our search queries the same way since they may be used to identify us? How can we distinguish between a few facts about a person and a "profile"?

Judge Richard Posner: Economic arguments for property rights to information

Judge Richard Posner, a legal scholar who has extensively studied the interactions between law and economics, gives economic arguments about how to allocate property rights to information.[83] Information has both economic and personal value, he points out. It is valuable to us to determine if a business, customer, client, employer, or employee is reliable, honest, and so on. Personal and business interactions have many opportunities for misrepresentation and therefore exploitation of others. Posner's analysis leads to the conclusion that, in some cases, individuals or organizations should have a property right to information, while in other cases, they should not. That is, some information should be in the public domain. A property right for information is appropriate where the information has value to society and is expensive to discover, create, or collect. Without property rights to such information, the people or businesses that make investments in discovering or collecting the information will not profit from it. The result is that people will produce less of this kind of information, to the detriment of society. Thus, the law should protect, for example, trade secrets, the result of much expenditure and effort by a business. A second example is personal information such as the appearance of one's naked body. It is not expensive for a person to obtain, but virtually all of us place value on protecting it, and concealment is not costly to society. So, it makes sense to assign the property right for this information to the individual.

Some privacy advocates want to protect information that can lead to denial of a job or denial of some kind of service or contract (e.g., a loan). They advocate restrictions on sharing of information that might facilitate negative decisions about people—for example, landlords sharing a database with information about tenant payment histories. Posner argues that a person should not have a property right to negative personal information or other information whose concealment aids people in misrepresentation, fraud, or manipulation. Such information should be in the public domain. That means a person should not have the right to prohibit others from collecting it, using it, and passing it on, as long as they are not violating a contract or confidentiality agreement and do not obtain the information by eavesdropping on private communications or by other prohibited means.

In recent decades, the trend in legislation has not followed Posner's position. Some critics of Posner's point of view believe that moral theory, not economic principles, should be the source of property rights.

2.6.2   LAW AND REGULATION

A basic legal framework

A good basic legal framework that defines and enforces legal rights and responsibilities is essential to a complex, robust society and economy. One of its tasks is enforcement of agreements and contracts. Contracts—including freedom to form them and enforcement of their terms by the legal system—are a mechanism for implementing flexible and diverse economic transactions that take place over time and between people who do not know each other well or at all.

We can apply the idea of contract enforcement to the published privacy policies of businesses and organizations. For example, Toysmart, a Web-based seller of educational toys, collected extensive information on about 250,000 visitors to its website, including family profiles, shopping preferences, and names and ages of children. Toysmart had promised not to release this personal information, but when the company filed for bankruptcy, it had a large amount of debt and virtually no assets—except its customer database, which had a high value. Toysmart's creditors wanted the database sold to raise funds to repay them, so Toysmart offered the database for sale, causing a storm of protest. Consistent with the interpretation that Toysmart's policy was a contract with the people in the database, the bankruptcy-court settlement included destruction of the database.[84]

A second task of a legal system is to set defaults for situations that contracts do not explicitly cover. Suppose a website posts no policy about what it does with the information it collects. What legal rights should the operator of the site have regarding the information? Many sites and offline businesses act as though the default is that they can do anything they choose. A strong privacy-protecting default would be that they can use the information only for the direct and obvious purpose for which they collected it. The legal system can (and does) set special confidentiality defaults for sensitive information that tradition and most people consider private, such as medical and financial information. If a business or organization wants to use information for purposes beyond the default, it would have to specify those uses in its policies, agreements, or contracts or request consent. Many business interactions do not have written contracts, so the default provisions established by law can have a big impact.

A third task of a basic legal structure is to specify penalties for criminal offenses and breach of contracts. Thus, law can specify penalties for violation of privacy policies and negligent loss or disclosure of personal data that businesses and others

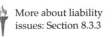
More about liability issues: Section 8.3.3

hold. Writers of liability laws must strike a balance between being too strict and too lenient. If too strict, they make some valuable products and services too expensive to provide. If too weak, they provide insufficient incentive for businesses and government agencies to provide reasonable security for our personal data.

Regulation

Technical tools, market mechanisms, and business policies for privacy protection are not perfect. Is that a strong argument for regulatory laws? Regulation is not perfect either. We must evaluate regulatory solutions by considering effectiveness, costs and benefits, and side effects, just as we evaluate other kinds of potential solutions to problems caused by technology. We briefly make a few points here.

(We will see similar issues in Section 8.3.3 when we consider responses to computer errors and failures.)

There are hundreds of privacy laws. When Congress passes laws for complex areas like privacy, the laws usually state general goals and leave the details to government agencies that write hundreds or thousands of pages of regulations, sometimes over many years. It is extremely difficult to write reasonable regulations for complex situations, and so laws and regulations often have unintended effects or interpretations. Regulations are sometimes applied where they do not make sense or where people simply do not want them.

The Children's Online Privacy Protection Act (COPPA) illustrates a problem of unintended consequences. COPPA requires that websites get parental permission before collecting personal information from children under 13—a very reasonable idea. After COPPA passed, because of the expense of complying with its requirements and the potential liability, some companies deleted online profiles of all children under 13, some canceled their free email and home pages for kids, and some banned children under 13 entirely. Facebook's terms of use prohibit children under 13 from joining, but *Consumer Reports* estimated that millions of children under 13 ignored the rule and joined.[85] The fiction that there are no members under 13 implies there is no need to provide mechanisms to protect them.

Regulations often have high costs, both direct dollar costs to businesses (and, ultimately, consumers) and hidden or unexpected costs, such as loss of services or increased inconvenience. For example, regulations that prohibit broad consent agreements and instead require explicit consent for each secondary use of personal information have an attribute economists call "high transaction cost." The consent requirement could be so expensive and difficult to implement that it eliminates most secondary uses of information, including those that consumers find desirable.

2.6.3 CONTRASTING VIEWPOINTS

> *When asked "If someone sues you and loses, should they have to pay your legal expenses?" more than 80% of people surveyed said "yes." When asked the same question from the opposite perspective: "If you sue someone and lose, should you have to pay their legal expenses?" about 40% said "yes."*

The political, philosophical, and economic views of many scholars and advocates who write about privacy differ. As a result, their interpretations of various privacy problems and their approaches to solutions often differ, particularly when they are considering laws and regulation to control collection and use of personal information by businesses.[*] We contrast two perspectives. We call them the free market view and the consumer protection view.

---

[*]There tends to be more agreement among privacy advocates when considering privacy threats and intrusions by government.

The free market view

People who prefer market-oriented solutions for privacy problems tend to emphasize:

- the freedom of individuals, as consumers or in businesses, to make voluntary agreements;
- the diversity of individual tastes and values;
- the flexibility of technological and market solutions;
- the response of markets to consumer preferences;
- the usefulness and importance of contracts; and
- the flaws of detailed or restrictive legislation and regulatory solutions.

Market-oriented solution advocates emphasize the many voluntary organizations that provide consumer education, develop guidelines, monitor the activities of business and government, and pressure businesses to improve policies. These advocates may take strong ethical positions but emphasize the distinction between the role of ethics and the role of law.

A free market view for collection and use of personal information emphasizes informed consent: Organizations collecting personal data (including government agencies and businesses) should clearly inform the person providing the information whether they will not keep it confidential (from other businesses, individuals, and government agencies) and how they will use it. The organizations should be legally liable for violations of their stated policies. This viewpoint could consider invisible information gathering to be theft or intrusion.

A free market view emphasizes freedom of contract: People should be free to enter agreements (or not enter agreements) to disclose personal information in exchange for a fee, services, or other benefits according to their own judgment. Businesses should be free to offer such agreements. This viewpoint respects the right and ability of consumers to make choices for themselves based on their own values. Market supporters expect consumers to take the responsibility that goes with freedom—for example, to read contracts or to understand that desirable services have costs. A free market view includes free flow of information: The law should not prevent people (or businesses and organizations) from using and disclosing facts they independently or unintrusively discover without violating rights (e.g., without theft, trespass, or violation of contractual obligations).

We cannot always expect to get exactly the mix of attributes we want in any product, service, or job. Just as we might not get cheeseless pizza in every pizza restaurant or find a car with the exact set of features we want, we might not always be able to get both privacy and special discounts or free services. We might not be able to get certain websites without advertising, or a specific job without agreeing to provide certain personal information to the employer. These compromises are not unusual or unreasonable when interacting with other people.

Market supporters prefer to avoid restrictive legislation and detailed regulation for several reasons. Overly broad, poorly designed, and vague regulations stifle innovation. The political system is a worse system than the market for determining what consumers want in the real world of trade-offs and costs. It is impossible for legislators to know in advance how much money, convenience, or other benefits people will want to trade for more or for less privacy. Businesses respond over time to the preferences of millions of consumers expressed through their purchases. In response to the desire for privacy many people express, the market provides a variety of privacy protection tools. Market supporters argue that laws requiring specific policies or prohibiting certain kinds of contracts violate the freedom of choice of both consumers and business owners.

This viewpoint includes legal sanctions for those who steal data and those who violate confidentiality agreements. It holds businesses, organizations, and government agents responsible for loss of personal data due to poor or negligent security practices. To encourage innovation and improvement, advocates of this viewpoint are more likely to prefer penalties when a company loses, inappropriately discloses, or abuses the data, rather than regulations that specify detailed procedures that holders of personal information must follow.

The free market viewpoint sees privacy as a "good," both in the sense that it is desirable and that it is something we can obtain varying amounts of by buying or trading in the economy, like food, entertainment, and safety. Just as some people choose to trade some safety for excitement (bungee jumping, motorcycle riding), money (buying a cheaper but less safe product), or convenience, some choose different levels of privacy. As with safety, law can provide minimum standards, but it should allow the market to provide a wide range of options to meet the range of personal preferences.

The consumer protection view

Advocates of strong privacy regulation emphasize the unsettling uses of personal information we have mentioned throughout this chapter, the costly and disruptive results of errors in databases (which we discuss in Chapter 8), and the ease with which personal information leaks out, via loss, theft, and carelessness. They argue for more stringent consent requirements, legal restrictions on consumer profiling, prohibitions of certain types of contracts or agreements to disclose data, and prohibitions on businesses collecting or storing certain kinds of data. They urge, for example, that the law require companies to have opt-in policies for secondary uses of personal information, because the opt-out option might not be obvious or easy enough for consumers who would prefer it. The consumer protection view would prohibit waivers and broad consent agreements for secondary uses.

The focus of this viewpoint is to protect consumers against abuses and carelessness by businesses and against their own lack of knowledge, judgment, or interest. Advocates of the consumer protection view emphasize that people do not realize all the ways others may use information about them and do not understand the risks of agreeing to disclose personal data. Those who emphasize consumer protection are critical of programs to trade free devices and services for personal information or consent for monitoring or tracking. Many of these advocates support laws prohibiting collection or storage of personal data that could have negative consequences in contexts where the advocates believe the risks are more important than the value of the information to the businesses that want to collect the data. Consumer advocate and privacy "absolutist" Mary Gardiner Jones objected to the idea of consumers consenting to dissemination of personal data. More than 20 years ago, she said, "You can't expect an ordinary consumer who is very busy trying to earn a living to sit down and understand what [consent] means. They don't understand the implications of what use of their data can mean to them."[86] Understanding the implications of the ways data are collected and used now is even more difficult. A former director of the American Civil Liberties Union's privacy and technology project expressed the view that informed consent is not sufficient protection. She urged a Senate committee studying confidentiality of health records to "re-examine the traditional reliance on individual consent as the linchpin of privacy laws."[87]

Those who emphasize the consumer protection point of view would argue that the Joe–Maria scenario in Friendlyville, described in Section 2.6.1, is not relevant in a complex society. The imbalance of power between the individual and a large corporation is one reason. Another is that in Friendlyville the information about the transaction circulates to only a small group of people, whom Joe and Maria know. If someone draws inaccurate or unfair conclusions, Joe or Maria can talk to the person and present his or her explanations. In a larger society, information circulates among many strangers, and we often do not know who has it and what decisions about us they base on it.

Most consumers cannot realistically negotiate contract terms with a business. At any specific time, the consumer can only accept or reject what the business offers, and rejecting the business's terms means not getting the desired product or service. If we want a loan for a house or car, we have to accept whatever terms lenders currently offer. If we need a job, we are likely to agree to disclose personal information against our true preference because of the economic necessity of working. Individuals have no meaningful power against large companies that provide search engines, for example, whether or not they know or accept a company's policy about use of their search queries.

In the consumer protection view, self-regulation by business does not work. Business privacy policies are weak, vague, or difficult to understand, and businesses sometimes do not follow their stated policies. Consumer pressure is sometimes effective, but some companies ignore it. Instead, we must require all businesses to adopt pro-privacy policies. Software and other technological privacy-protecting tools for consumers cost money, and many people cannot afford them. These tools are far from perfect anyway and hence not good enough to protect privacy.

The consumer protection viewpoint sees privacy as a right rather than something we bargain about. For example, a website jointly sponsored by the Electronic Privacy Information Center and Privacy International flashes the slogans "Privacy is a right, not a preference" and "Notice is not enough."[88] The latter indicates that they see privacy as a positive right, or claim right (in the terminology of Section 1.4.2). As a negative right, privacy allows us to use anonymizing technologies and to refrain from interacting with those who request information we do not wish to supply. As a positive right, it means we can stop others from communicating about us. A spokesperson for the Center for Democracy and Technology expressed that view in a statement to Congress, saying that we must incorporate into law the principle that people should be able to "determine for themselves when, how, and to what extent information about them is shared."[89]

2.7 Privacy Regulations in the European Union

The European Union (EU) has a comprehensive Data Protection Directive (passed in 1995).[90*] It covers processing of personal data, including collection, use, storage, retrieval, transmission, destruction, and other actions. The directive sets forth Fair Information Principles that EU member nations must implement in their own laws. Several are similar to the first five principles in Figure 2.1 (in Section 2.1.3). The EU has some additional or stronger rules. Processing of data is permitted only if the person has consented unambiguously or if the processing is necessary to fulfill contractual or legal obligations or is needed for tasks in the public interest or by official authorities to accomplish their tasks (or a few other reasons). Special categories of data—including ethnic and racial origin, political and religious beliefs, health and sex life, and union membership—must not be processed without the person's explicit consent. Member nations may outlaw processing of such data even if the person does consent. Processing of data about criminal convictions is severely restricted.

These examples illustrate the stricter rules and laws of the EU and of some member countries.

- Google modified its privacy policy in 2012 to allow the company to combine information it collects on members from its various services. The EU argued that average users could not understand how Google uses their data under the new policy and that violates the EU's privacy regulations.

---

*An updated version, the General Data Protection Regulation, is expected to take effect in 2018.

- A court in Germany said that some of Facebook's policies in its member agreement (for example, granting Facebook a license to use material a member posts or stores at Facebook) are illegal there.

- The German government told Facebook to stop running face recognition applications on German users; it violates German privacy laws.

- Google has shut down or no longer updates Street View in a few European countries because of strict privacy laws.[91]

- The EU devised legal guidelines for social networking sites recommending that sites should set default privacy settings at a high level, tell users to upload a picture of a person only if the person consents, allow the use of pseudonyms, set limits on the time they retain data on inactive users, and delete accounts that are inactive for a long time.

While the EU has much stricter regulations than the United States on collection and use of personal information by the private sector, some civil libertarians believe that the regulations do not provide enough protection from use of personal data by government agencies. Although the directive says that data should not be kept longer than necessary, European countries require that ISPs and telephone companies retain records of customer communications (date, destination, duration, and so on) for up to two years and make them available to law enforcement agencies. The EU said it needs this requirement to fight terrorism and organized crime.[92]

The EU's strict privacy directive does not prevent some of the same abuses of personal data that occur in the United States. In Britain, for example, the Information Commissioner reported that data brokers use fraud and corrupt insiders to get personal information. As in the United States, customers of illegal data services include journalists, private investigators, debt collectors, government agencies, stalkers, and criminals seeking data to use for fraud.[93]

The EU Data Privacy Directive prohibits transfer of personal data to countries outside the European Union that do not have what it considers an adequate system of privacy protection. This part of the directive caused significant problems for companies that do business both in and outside Europe. Thousands of international companies process and/or store data for European customers, employees, or members on servers in the United States. Cross-border business, valued at billions of dollars, was in jeopardy. The EU established a Safe Harbor plan under which companies outside the EU that abide by a set of privacy requirements similar to the principles in the Data Protection Directive could receive personal data from the EU. An EU court ended the Safe Harbor program after disclosures of extensive surveillance and collection of private data systems by the U.S. National Security Agency (see Section 2.4.5), replacing it in 2016 with a new plan called Privacy Shield that has stricter rules.

Many privacy advocates describe U.S. privacy policy as "behind Europe" because, although the United States has privacy laws covering specific areas such as medical information, video rentals, driver's license records, and so on, it does not have comprehensive federal legislation regulating personal data collection and use in all areas. This results from the different cultures and traditions in the United States and Europe. For example, European countries tend to put more emphasis on legal protection for reputation, while the U.S. Constitution gives great weight to freedom of speech. Generally, Europe puts more emphasis on regulation and centralization, especially concerning commerce, whereas U.S. tradition puts more emphasis on contracts, consumer pressure, market flexibility, and penalties for abuses by enforcement of laws such as those against deceptive and unfair business practices.

The EU's right to be forgotten

In a case in which a Spanish man sued to require Google to remove links to certain documents that showed up in search results, the EU Court of Justice ruled, in 2014, that the Data Protection Directive included a "right to be forgotten": A person can require search engine companies to prevent links to certain kinds of information from appearing in some search results (for example, searches on the person's name). There is an exception for information of sufficient public interest. The criteria and exceptions are vague and subjective. In the first year after the ruling, Google received requests for removal of almost a million links and granted about

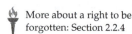
More about a right to be forgotten: Section 2.2.4

35%. (If a request is denied, a person can appeal to a government agency.) Google's advisory board that handles the requests said that many of the cases are easy (for example, certain items concerning children or a seminude photo published without a person's permission), but some are extremely difficult to decide.

The right to be forgotten can have a cascading effect: A newspaper wrote about a case in which Google agreed to a request to remove links to an article the paper had published. The person who made the original request then requested removal of links to the article discussing the first removal.

At first, when Google blocked links in response to a request in Europe, it did so only from European versions of its search engine, not from google.com. The French government ordered Google to block searches not only on google.fr but also on google.com, which people in Europe can use. Blocking on google.com would enforce an EU citizen's right to be forgotten worldwide, in countries that do not recognize such a right. Google compromised by blocking links on all of

Enforcing one country's laws in another: Section 5.7

its global search engines but only for searches originating in the country of the person requesting the block. Thus, a person in the United States or Germany, for example, could still use google. com to find information about a French person that is blocked in France. French regulators rejected this compromise, continuing to insist that Google block the links globally.

Governments that do not have strong protections for freedom of speech, political freedom, and democracy often use censorship laws in free countries as excuses for some of their own. Russia, citing the EU's precedent, passed a right-to-be-forgotten law, but it lacks key safeguards, including certain exceptions for information in the public interest or about public figures.[94]

The EU is working on applying its right to be forgotten to databases and other areas besides Web search.

 # Exercises

Review Exercises

2.1 What does the term *personal information* mean?

2.2 What does the term *secondary use* mean? Give an example.

2.3 What does the term *reidentification* mean? Give an example.

2.4 Explain the difference between *opt-in* and *opt-out* policies for secondary uses of personal information.

2.5 What did the U. S. Supreme Court decide about whether police could search cellphones?

2.6 Describe one application of face recognition that infringes privacy.

2.7 Describe two tools people can use to protect their privacy on the Web.

2.8 Describe two methods a business or agency can use to reduce the risk of unauthorized release of personal information by employees.

General Exercises

2.9 A company in the Netherlands that makes navigation devices collects location data from the devices to provide real-time services to its customers. It also provides anonymous statistical data to government agencies to improve roads and traffic flow. Unknown to the company and its customers, the police used the data to choose sites for traffic cameras to catch speeders. Was this a privacy violation? Why or why not?[95]

2.10 "Caller ID" is the feature that displays the telephone number of the caller on the telephone of the person receiving a call. With Caller ID now routine and widely used, it might be surprising that when the service was first available, it was very controversial because of privacy implications.

    (a) What aspect of privacy (in the sense of Section 2.1.1) does Caller ID protect for the recipient of the call? What aspect of privacy does Caller ID violate for the caller?

    (b) What are some good reasons why a nonbusiness, noncriminal caller might not want his or her number displayed?

2.11 In jury trials, attorneys receive the list of people in the jury pool shortly before the jury selection process begins. Some attorneys search for information about prospective jurors on social networks. The attorneys use this information in deciding which potential jurors to accept, and they could use the information to slant their arguments in ways that would appeal to specific jurors.

    (a) Which of the risks at the end of Section 2.1.2 does this use of personal information illustrate?

    (b) What are some pros and cons of prohibiting attorneys from searching social media for information about prospective jurors?

(c) A judge gave attorneys the option of agreeing not to perform such searches or of informing the prospective jurors of the searches they did. Is this a good compromise? Give some reasons.

2.12 Power and water providers have smart metering and analysis systems sophisticated enough to deduce what appliances we are using at various times of day (e.g., cellphones charging and an air conditioner running), when we shower (and for how long), and when we sleep. List several ways you can think of that this information could embarrass or cause problems for a person if leaked, stolen, or acquired by law enforcement agents.

2.13 Which of the guidelines in Figure 2.1, if any, did AOL's release of user search queries (Section 2.1.2) violate?

2.14 The AOL search-query database released on the Web included the search query "How to kill your wife" and other related queries by the same person. Give arguments for and against allowing law enforcement agents to search the query databases of search engine companies periodically to detect plans for murders, terrorist attacks, or other serious crimes so that they can try to prevent them.

2.15 One of the risks associated with databases of personal information is that criminals steal and use the information. How is this statement similar to and how does it differ from saying, "One of the risks associated with buying an expensive car is that criminals steal them"? Can you draw any useful insights from the analogy?

2.16 Customer service centers of some companies use software to analyze a customer's words, categorize the customer's personality type, and help determine how the service agent can best respond to the customer. The system saves information associated with the customer's phone number so that on subsequent calls, the system can route the call to a service agent with a compatible personality. The system, according to one company, helps shorten calls and increase positive resolutions for the customer.[96] Is this analysis of the caller an unreasonable privacy intrusion? When we call a customer service number, we are often told that the call is recorded to improve customer service. Is "to improve customer service" enough to inform customers about this use of data about them? How much detail do you want to be told each time you call?

2.17 Choose one of the marketing practices described in Section 2.2.1 that you consider unethical. (If there are none, choose one for which you think there are at least some good arguments against it on ethical grounds.) Give arguments why it is unethical.

2.18 Life insurance companies are experimenting with analysis of consumer profiles, to determine whether a person eats healthy food, exercises, smokes or drinks too much, has high-risk hobbies, and so on, to estimate life expectancy. Companies might use the analysis to find populations to market policies to. From the perspective of privacy, what are some of the key ethical or social issues raised? Evaluate some of them.

2.19 A children's hospital collected and analyzed DNA from 100,000 children for a DNA database. The database is anonymous; the hospital does not store the DNA information with other information that identifies the individual it came from. Discuss potential valuable uses of such a database. Discuss potential risks and problems. If you were the head of a hospital, would you have approved the project? As an individual, if you and your family were asked to provide DNA for the database, would you agree? Give reasons.

2.20 Under what circumstances, if any, do you think a person should ask for another person's permission before posting a photo or video that the other person is in? When is it simply a courtesy, and when is it an ethical obligation? Explain your reasons.

2.21 Consider Exercise 2.20, but suppose instead of posting a photo or video, you write an article that describes what a person is doing in the photo or video. Would you give the same responses to the questions in Exercise 2.20 about asking for permission? Why or why not?

2.22 A very large social network company analyzes all data it gathers through its service on its members' activities to develop statistical information for marketers and to plan new services. The information is very valuable. Should the company pay its members for its use of their information? Why, or why not?

2.23 Suppose you regularly shop at a particular store chain. Compare what a salesclerk knows about you when you ask for help in a store with what the system knows about you when you log in to the store's website. Considering just this aspect—what is known about you—which experience do you prefer? Why?

2.24 **(a)** Some businesses (a supermarket, a dry cleaner, or a theater, for example) use telephone numbers to access customer or subscriber accounts. Assuming the records are not available to the public online and do not include credit card numbers, is the use of the telephone number in such situations secure enough to protect privacy? Why?

(b) Some mobile phone service providers let customers retrieve voice mail messages without entering a PIN (personal identification number) when they call from their own phone. But someone else can fake the calling number with a Caller ID spoofing service and retrieve a person's messages. Is PIN-less retrieval a reasonable trade-off between convenience and privacy? Give your reasons.

2.25 Bills introduced in the U.S. Congress (and proposed in other countries) would require that anyone buying a prepaid mobile phone must show identification and/or register the phone. Give arguments for and against passage of such a law.

2.26 A court ordered a social media company and a search engine company to remove racy photos of a pop star and links to the photos. The companies removed *all* references to the person. What do you think of this incident?

2.27 A newspaper reported, 20 years ago, about a malpractice lawsuit filed against a surgeon. The surgeon later won the lawsuit. Suppose, currently, a Google search on the surgeon's name brings up a link to the original article, which does not mention the result of the lawsuit. The surgeon asks Google to remove the link from results for searches on his name. Give arguments for and against Google doing so.

2.28 Federal agents installed a camera on a utility pole and collected 10 weeks of video of a suspect's farm without a search warrant. Prosecutors argued that a warrant was not needed because passersby on public roads could have seen what the camera saw. Suppose you are a judge making a decision on whether to admit evidence from the video. What questions, if any, would you ask, and what would your decision be? Explain.

2.29 Do you think law enforcement agents should be required to get a search warrant before flying a drone equipped with a camera and recording device over someone's backyard? Give reasons.

2.30 A bill introduced in the New York legislature would require that drivers involved in a car crash give their phone to police so that the police can check whether the driver was using the phone at the time of the crash. Give arguments for and against passage of the bill.

2.31 A member of the Tampa, Florida, City Council described the camera and face recognition system installed in a Tampa neighborhood (Section 2.4.1) as "a public safety tool, no different from having a cop walking around with a mug shot."[97] Is he right? What are some similarities and differences, relevant to privacy, between the camera system and a cop walking around?

2.32 A company planned to sell a laser device a person can wear around his or her neck that makes photographs taken of the person come out streaked and useless. The company marketed it to celebrities hounded by photographers. Suppose the device works well against surveillance cameras commonly used in public places and in many businesses. Suppose many people begin to use the device routinely when outside their homes. Suppose law enforcement agencies propose making its use illegal. Give arguments for and against such a proposal.

2.33 The quotation at the end of Section 2.4.1 from reporter Pete Tucker is not about surveillance cameras or the Fourth Amendment. Why is it there? What point does it make?

2.34 A college student set up a hidden webcam to record his roommate having sex in their dorm room. The student gave a password to several friends so that they could watch on the Web. This is clearly an unethical, crude, cruel, and boorish invasion of privacy. How should the university respond?

2.35 People who flee severe hurricanes and other destructive events leave behind and lose important documents and records such as birth certificates, credit cards, property records, and employment records. A U.S. government agency proposed a new database where people could voluntarily store essential personal records in case of similar natural disasters. Discuss pros and cons of this proposal.

2.36 With deeds, mortgage records, and so forth, online, some cities have seen a significant increase in fraudulent sales of houses by people who use online information to forge deeds, impersonate the owners, and sell the houses to unsuspecting buyers. What are some benefits of having such information online? Considering thefts and privacy issues, do you think the records should be online? If so, why? If not, why not, and what alternative access would you suggest?

2.37 Consider the list of advantages of a secure national ID card in Section 2.4.4. For which of these advantages is it necessary to require that people carry their ID cards with them at all times?

2.38 Read Exercise 1.36 in Chapter 1. What are the similarities and differences between the ethical question in that exercise and the ethical question in Section 2.5.3 about blocking ads?

2.39 Write a paragraph discussing the application of natural rights and/or positive and negative rights (see Section 1.4.2) to the ethics of ad blocking.

2.40 A popular Web browser includes an option to tell websites that you do not want to be tracked. By default, when someone installs the browser, should the do-not-track option be on or off? Give a reason for each choice.

2.41 A disgruntled employee of a county health department sent a confidential file containing the names of about 4000 AIDS patients to a newspaper. What are some ways to prevent such a leakage of sensitive data?

2.42 Give an explanation, with examples and/or analogies, to describe what it means for privacy to be a negative right (liberty). Do the same for privacy as a positive right (claim right). (See Section 1.4.2 for explanations of negative and positive rights.) Which kind of right, if either, seems more appropriate for privacy? Why?

2.43   Implementations of digital cash can allow secure and anonymous transactions. Do people have a negative right (in the sense of Section 1.4.2) to use anonymous digital cash? Considering the privacy benefits and the potential for use by tax evaders, criminals, and terrorists, do you think fully anonymous digital cash should be outlawed? Give your reasons.

2.44   Section 2.5.4 gave two examples of uses of trusted third parties to reduce access to personal information. Give another example, either a real one you know of or an application you think would be useful.

2.45   A business maintains a database containing the names of shoplifters. Managers of retail stores can subscribe to access the database.

    (a)   Should such a service be illegal to protect privacy? (Give reasons.)

    (b)   Describe the likely position of each of Warren and Brandeis, Judith Thomson, and Richard Posner (Section 2.6.1), with their reasons, on the question in part (a).

    (c)   Would your answer to part (a) differ if the question were about a database of tenant history available to landlords? Or a database available to the public with comments from tenants about landlords? How and why?

2.46   One writer defines privacy as "freedom from the inappropriate judgement of others."[98] Is this a good definition of privacy? Why or why not?

2.47   A health-information website has many articles on health and medical issues, a chat room where people can discuss health issues with other users, and provisions for people to send questions by email for doctors to answer. You work as an intern for a company hired to do a privacy audit. The audit team will examine the site, find privacy risks (or good privacy protection practices), and make recommendations for changes as needed. Describe at least three things you would look for, explain their significance, and tell what your recommendations would be if you do or do not find them.

2.48   An Ivy League university set up a website that student applicants could access, using their Social Security number and other personal information, to find out if the school had accepted them for admission. Officials at the university determined that computers in the admissions office of another Ivy League university accessed some student accounts. Many students apply to both schools. People suspected that the university that accessed the accounts wanted to determine which students the other school had accepted before making its own decisions. The personal information needed to access the site was in the students' applications, available to both universities.

    Analyze this incident. Identify the things done wrong (assuming the suspicions about the snooping are accurate). What actions should the administrations of both universities take?

2.49   Suppose each of the following is a proposed law. For each one, choose a side, either supporting or opposing it, and defend your position.

    (a)   To protect the public, companies that provide Web searching services to members or to the public must maintain user search query records (in a way that links the queries to the person doing the search) for two years in case law enforcement agencies or terrorism investigators need them.

    (b)   To protect privacy, companies that provide Web searching services to members or to the public must not store user search queries in a way that links the queries of any one person together for more than one week.

2.50 When applying the right to be forgotten in the European Union, Google informs news organizations when it removes links to their content in response to a person's request. It specifies the article but not the person who made the request. Some privacy advocates criticize Google for doing so. Why do you think privacy advocates oppose this disclosure? Why do you think Google does it? Should Google continue? Why or why not?

2.51 Consider the guidelines developed in the European Union for social network sites (Section 2.7). Evaluate these simply as guidelines, not legal requirements. Evaluate them as legal requirements. (Consider, among other issues, how to define the sites to which the rules would apply.)

2.52 Assume you are a professional working in your chosen field. Describe specific things you can do to reduce the impact of any two problems we discussed in this chapter. (If you cannot think of anything related to your professional field, choose another field that might interest you.)

Assignments

These exercises require some research or activity.

2.53 (a) Read the privacy policy of a large, popular website. Write a brief summary. Identify the site (name, Web address, and type of site). Give examples of parts of the policy that are, or are not, clear or reasonable.

    (b) Choose any smartphone app that includes a privacy statement or policy. Summarize and evaluate it. Can you think of any important things that are missing?

2.54 Google Street View's cameras occasionally capture people in embarrassing behavior and in places they would prefer the whole world not see them. How, and how well, does Google address these and other privacy concerns?

Class Discussion Exercises

These exercises are for class discussion, perhaps with short presentations prepared in advance by small groups of students.

2.55 Researchers are developing a system to detect a person's emotions while the person is talking on a smartphone or other device.

    (a) You are the researchers. Describe all the wonderful potential applications for your project.

    (b) You are social scientists and privacy watchdogs. Describe potential annoying, manipulative, or abusive uses.

    (c) You are a team of technical experts and ethicists. Propose guidelines for the use of the technology.

2.56 Discuss Facebook's policies from a privacy perspective. What does it do well? What does it do poorly? How could it improve?

2.57 (a) A large retailer mines its customer database to determine whether a customer is likely to be pregnant. (See the box in Section 2.2.1.) It sends ads or coupons for products she might buy. Is this ethically acceptable or ethically prohibited?

(b) The retailer knows that customers are uncomfortable with the idea that the retailer can determine that they are pregnant. The retailer sends ad and coupon booklets or email that includes many pregnancy and baby products along with unrelated products. The customers who receive them do not realize that the ads are targeted for them. Is this ethically acceptable or ethically prohibited?

2.58 Veterinarians implant computer chips into pets and farm animals to identify them if they get lost. Discuss some benefits and risks of doing so with children.

2.59 Several men contracted syphilis, a serious sexually transmitted disease, after arranging to meet partners through an online chat room used mostly by gay men. The public health department asked the company that hosted the site for the names and addresses of all people who used the chat room so that it could inform them about possible exposure to the disease. The public health department did not have a court order. The site's policy says it will not release information that links screen names with real names. Should it make an exception in this case? Give arguments on both sides. How do you weigh the trade-off between the possibility of an infected person remaining uninformed and the loss of privacy to visitors to the chat room? How important is it that the company abide by its posted privacy policy?

2.60 Are businesses that provide free Internet services or other benefits in exchange for tracking Web activity offering a fair option for consumers, or are they unfairly taking advantage of low-income people who must give up some privacy for these services?

2.61 Do young people today view privacy differently from the previous generation?

2.62 In one of Vernor Vinge's science fiction novels,[99] an organization scatters false information about people on the Web. Does that sound nasty? The name of the organization is Friends of Privacy. Is it? In what way could the organization see itself as protecting privacy?

2.63 The head of an international sports organization was photographed performing sex acts at a party. He won lawsuits in Germany and France requiring Google not to show links to the photos on its search engines in those countries. Give arguments for and against removing links in such a case. Indicate what other information, if any, would be relevant to your making a decision about whether the links should be removed. Suppose the EU required Google to remove the links from searches on google.com as well as google.de and google.fr. Would this be a serious restriction on access to information by people in other countries?

2.64 Develop a policy for a large social network company on how to respond to requests from members to remove items they posted and items other members posted about them (including photos and videos they are in).

2.65 Which do you think should have larger data storage capacity: Google or the National Security Agency? Why? (Try to find recent estimates of the storage capacity of each.)

 # Notes

1. James O. Jackson, "Fear and Betrayal in the Stasi State," *Time*, Feb. 3, 1992, pp. 32–33.
2. "Privacy as an Aspect of Human Dignity," in Ferdinand David Schoeman, ed., *Philosophical Dimensions of Privacy: An Anthology*, Cambridge University Press, 1984, pp. 156–203, quote on p. 188.
3. "Reading *Privacy Journal's* Mail," *Privacy Journal*, May 2001, p. 2.

4. *NAACP* v. *Alabama*, 357 U.S. 449 (1958).

5. Michael Barbaro and Tom Zeller Jr., "A Face Is Exposed for AOL Searcher No. 4417749," *New York Times*, Aug. 9, 2006, www.nytimes.com. AOL acknowledged that the release was a bad mistake, fired the employees responsible, and considered improvements in internal policies to reduce the chance of similar errors in the future.

6. Brian X. Chen and Nick Bilton, "Et Tu, Google? Android Apps Can Also Secretly Copy Photos," *New York Times*, Mar. 1, 2012, bits.blogs.nytimes.com/2012/03/01/android-photos.

7. Many of these examples come from news reports. The Privacy Rights Clearinghouse lists such incidents on its website.

8. For an excellent, readable, overview of data breaches, see Verizon, "2016 Data Breach Investigations Report," www.verizonenterprise.com/resources/reports/rp_DBIR_2016_Report_en_xg.pdf. Offending software is sometimes buried in ads or other content provided by third parties. Some retailers do not know that the software they use stores credit card numbers. (It is not supposed to.) For example, see Verizon Business Investigative Response team, "2008 Data Breach Investigations Report," www.verizonenterprise.com/resources/security/databreachreport.pdf.

9. Associated Press, "Popular Software for Computer Cursors Logs Web Visits, Raising Privacy Issue," *Wall Street Journal*, Nov. 30, 1999, p. B6.

10. For an early history of cookies, see John Schwartz, "Giving Web a Memory Cost Its Users Privacy," *New York Times*, Sept. 4, 2001, www.nytimes.com/2001/09/04/business/giving-web-a-memory-cost-its-users-privacy.html.

11. The National Highway Traffic Safety Administration requires that car makers inform owners if a car is equipped with a data recorder and specifies that the owner's consent is needed to collect data from the recorder.

12. Quoted in Theo Francis, "Spread of Records Stirs Patient Fears of Privacy Erosion," *Wall Street Journal*, Dec. 26, 2006, p. A1.

13. The Privacy Rights Clearinghouse shows several specific sets of Fair Information Principles in "A Review of the Fair Information Principles," www.privacyrights.org/content/review-fair-information-principles-foundation-privacy-public-policy.

14. Acxiom Latin America website, "Customer Information Management Solutions," www.acxiom.com.

15. Jessica E. Vascellaro, "Online Retailers Are Watching You," *Wall Street Journal*, Nov. 28, 2006, pp. D1, D3.

16. Cecilie Rohwedder, "No. 1 Retailer in Britain Uses 'Clubcard' to Thwart Wal-Mart," *Wall Street Journal*, June 6, 2006, p. A1. Charles Duhigg, "How Companies Learn Your Secrets," *New York Times*, Feb. 16, 2012, www.nytimes.com/2012/02/19/magazine/shopping-habits.html.

17. Lois Beckett, "Obama's Microtargeting 'Nuclear Codes'," ProPublica, Nov. 7, 2012, www.propublica.org/article/obamas-microtargeting-nuclear-codes; Michael Sherer, "Inside the Secret World of the Data Crunchers Who Helped Obama Win," *Time*, Nov. 7, 2012, swampland.time.com/2012/11/07/inside-the-secret-world-of-quants-and-data-crunchers-who-helped-obama-win/. One way the fund-raiser invitations varied was in emphasizing different celebrities who would attend, based on who the campaign thought would appeal most to the person invited.

18. For example, regulations established under the Gramm–Leach–Bliley Act of 1999, which are responsible for the millions of privacy notices and opt-out forms mailed out by credit card companies.

19. Julia Angwin, "A Plan to Track Web Use Stirs Privacy Concern," *Wall Street Journal*, May 1, 2000, pp. B1, B18.

20. Preetika Rana, "Indians Spurn Snacks, Shampoo to Load Their Smartphones," *Wall Street Journal*, Aug. 15, 2016, www.wsj.com/articles/indians-spurn-snacks-shampoo-to-load-their-smartphones-1471163223.

21. Quoted in *Privacy Journal*, Apr. 2006, p. 2.

22. Ruchi Sanghvi, "Facebook Gets a Facelift," Sept. 5, 2006, blog.facebook.com/blog.php?post=2207967130. "An Open Letter from Mark Zuckerberg," Sept. 8, 2006, blog.facebook.com/blog.php?post=2208562130; and many news stories.

23. See, for example, Center for Democracy and Technology, "Best Practices for Mobile Applications Developers," www.cdt.org/files/pdfs/Best-Practices-Mobile-App-Developers.pdf, and CTIA—The Wireless Association, "Best Practices and Guidelines for Location Based Services," www.ctia.org/policy-initiatives/voluntary-guidelines/best-practices-and-guidelines-for-location-based-services.

24. Jeffrey Rosen covers many in his article "The Right to Be Forgotten," *Stanford Law Review*, Feb. 13, 2012, www.stanfordlawreview.org/online/privacy-paradox-the-right-to-be-forgotten/. See also Eugene Volokh, "Freedom of Speech and Information Privacy: The Troubling Implications of a Right to Stop People from Speaking about You," *Stanford Law Review* (52 Stanford L. Rev. 1049), 2000, www2.law.ucla.edu/volokh/privacy.htm.

25. Quoted in David Banisar, *Privacy and Human Rights 2000: An International Survey of Privacy Laws and Developments*, EPIC and Privacy International, 2000.

26. *California Bankers Assn.* v. *Shultz*, 416 U.S. 21 (1974).

27. Alan F. Westin, *Privacy and Freedom*, Atheneum, 1968, p. 67.

28. The historic information in this section is from Alan F. Westin, *Privacy and Freedom*; Alexander Charns, *Cloak and Gavel: FBI Wiretaps, Bugs, Informers, and the Supreme Court,* University of Illinois Press, 1992 (Chapter 8); Edith Lapidus, *Eavesdropping on Trial*, Hayden Book Co., 1974; and Walter Isaacson, *Kissinger: A Biography*, Simon and Schuster, 1992.

29. The citations for the cases mentioned in this section are *Olmstead* v. *United States*, 277 U.S. 438(1928); *Katz* v. *United States*, 389 U.S. 347(1967); *Smith* v. *Maryland*, 442 U.S. 735(1979); and *United States* v. *Miller*, 425 U.S. 435(1976).

30. *Nardone* v. *U.S.* 302 U.S. 379(1937).

31. *Warshak* v. *U.S.*, Case 06-492, Sixth Circuit Court of Appeals, 2008.

32. *Patel* v. *City of Los Angeles*, Dec. 2013.

33. Alex Kozinski, "On Privacy: Did Technology Kill the Fourth Amendment?" *Cato Policy Report*, Nov./Dec. 2011, www.cato.org/policy-report/novemberdecember-2011/privacy-did-technology-kill-fourth-amendment.

34. Mark Walsh, "Low-tech High Court to Weigh Police Search of Smartphones," *ABA Journal*, Apr. 1, 2014. Stephanie Francis Ward, "States Split Over Warrantless Searches of Cellphone Data," *ABA Journal*, Apr. 1, 2011.

35. *U.S.* v. *Jones*, Jan. 23, 2012, www.supremecourt.gov/opinions/11pdf/10-1259.pdf. The case began in 2004.

36. *United States* v. *Raymond Lambis*, July 12, 2016.

37. Julian Sanchez, "The Pinpoint Search," *Reason*, Jan. 2007, pp. 21–28.

38. Larry Hardesty, "Extracting Audio from Video Information," *MIT News*, Aug. 4, 2014, news.mit.edu/2014/algorithm-recovers-speech-from-vibrations-0804.

39. Sanchez, "The Pinpoint Search," p. 21.

40. Brad Heath, "New Police Radars Can 'See' Inside Homes," *USA Today*, Jan. 20, 2015, www.usatoday.com/story/news/2015/01/19/police-radar-see-through-walls/22007615.

41. Marc Champion and others, "Tuesday's Attack Forces an Agonizing Decision on Americans," *Wall Street Journal*, Sept. 14, 2001, p. A8.

42. "Cameras in U.K. Found Useless," *Privacy Journal*, Mar. 2005, pp. 6–7.

43. Dana Canedy, "TV Cameras Seek Criminals in Tampa's Crowds," *New York Times*, July 4, 2001, pp. A1, A11.

44. The National Institute of Standards and Technology, a federal government agency, reported an accuracy rate of 57%. Jesse Drucker and Nancy Keates, "The Airport of the Future," *Wall Street Journal*, Nov. 23, 2001, pp. W1, W12. David Banisar raised issues about accuracy in "A Review of New Surveillance Technologies," *Privacy Journal*, Nov. 2001, p. 1.

45. Ross Kerber, "Privacy Concerns Are Roadblocks on 'Smart' Highways," *Wall Street Journal*, Dec. 4, 1996, pp. B1, B7. Banisar, "A Review of New Surveillance Technologies." Michael Spencer, "One Major City's Restrictions on TV Surveillance," *Privacy Journal*, Mar. 2001, p. 3. Murray Long, "Canadian Commissioner Puts a Hold on Video Cameras," *Privacy Journal*, Nov. 2001, pp. 3–4.

46. Quoted in Long, "Canadian Commissioner Puts a Hold on Video Cameras."

47. Jim Epstein, "Why I Was Arrested Yesterday at a D.C. Taxi Commission Meeting," June 23, 2011, reason.com/reasontv/2011/06/23/taxi-commission-arrest.

48. Steven A. Bercu, "Smart Card Privacy Issues: An Overview," *BOD-T-001*, July 1994, Smart Card Forum.

49. "Information Security: The Centers for Medicare & Medicaid Services Needs to Improve Controls over Key Communication Network," Government Accountability Office, Aug. 2006, www.gao.gov/new.items/d06750.pdf. *Computers and Privacy: How the Government Obtains, Verifies, Uses, and Protects Personal Data*, U.S. General Accounting Office, 1990 (GAO/IMTEC-9070BR). "House Panel Probes White House Database," *EPIC Alert*, Sept. 12, 1996. OMB Watch study, reported in "U.S. Government Web Sites Fail to Protect Privacy," *EPIC Alert*, Sept. 4, 1997. *Internet Privacy: Comparison of Federal Agency Practices with FTC's Fair Information Principles*, U.S. General Accounting Office, Sept. 11, 2000 (GAO/AIMD00-296R). U.S. Government Accountability Office, *Data Mining* (GAO 05-866), Aug. 2005, www.gao.gov/new.items/d05866.pdf. The GAO was called the General Accounting Office until 2004.

50. The Information Security and Privacy Advisory Board, *Toward A 21st Century Framework for Federal Government Privacy Policy*, May 2009, csrc.nist.gov/groups/SMA/ispab/documents/correspondence/ispab-report-may2009.pdf. U.S. Government Accountability Office, *Privacy: Congress Should Consider Alternatives for Strengthening Protection of Personally Identifiable Information* (GAO-08-795T), June 18, 2008, www.gao.gov/products/GAO-08-795T.

51. Nathan Tempey, "The NYPD Is Tracking Drivers Across the Country Using License Plate Readers," *Gothamist*, Jan. 26, 2016, gothamist.com/2016/01/26/license_plate_readers_nypd.php.

52. Jeff Jonas and Jim Harper, "Effective Counterterrorism and Limited Role of Predictive Data Mining," Cato Institute Policy Analysis No. 584, Dec. 11, 2006.

53. Robert Ellis Smith, "Ominous Tracking of University Students," *Privacy Journal*, Aug. 2006, p. 1. Sharon Noguchi, "10 Million California Student Records About To Be Released to Attorneys," *The Mercury News*, Feb. 16, 2016, www.mercurynews.com/crime-courts/ci_29524376/10-million-calif-student-records-about-be-released.

54. Federal Trade Commission, "Identity theft," www.consumer.gov/idtheft. "Second Thoughts on Posting Court Records Online," *Privacy Journal*, Feb. 2006, pp. 1, 4.

55. The law is The Ethics in Government Act.

56. Tony Mauro, "Judicial Conference Votes to Release Federal Judges' Financial Records," Freedom Forum, Mar. 15, 2000, www.firstamendmentcenter.org/judicial-conference-votes-to-release-federal-judges-financial-records.

57. The article "Can Privacy and Open Access to Records Be Reconciled?" *Privacy Journal*, May 2000, p. 6, outlines principles and guidelines devised by Robert Ellis Smith for access to public records.

58. Sources for this section include: Chris Hibbert, "Frequently Asked Questions on Social Security Numbers and Privacy," cpsr.org/issues/privacy/ssn-faq/; "ID Cards to Cost $10 Billion," *EPIC Alert*, Sept. 26, 1997; Glenn Garvin, "Bringing the Border War Home," *Reason*, Oct. 1995, pp. 18–28; Simson Garfinkel, *Database Nation: The Death of Privacy in the 21st Century*, O'Reilly, 2000, pp. 33–34; "A Turnaround on Social Security Numbers," *Privacy Journal*, Dec. 2006, p. 2; *Greidinger* v. *Davis*, U.S. Court of Appeals, Fourth Circuit; Ellen Nakashima, "U.S. Exposed Personal Data," *Washington Post*, Apr. 21, 2007, p. A05; "USDA Offers Free Credit Monitoring to Farm Services Agency and Rural Development Funding Recipients," www.usda.gov/wps/portal/usda/usdamediafb?contentid=2007/04/0105.xml&printable=true&contentidonly=true.

59. Peter G. Neumann and Lauren Weinstein, "Inside Risks," *Communications of the ACM*, Dec. 2001, p. 176.

60. Quoted in Jane Howard, "ID Card Signals 'End of Democracy'," *The Australian*, Sept. 7, 1987, p. 3.

61. Jim Harper, "Understanding and Responding to the Threat of Terrorism," *Cato Policy Report*, Cato Institute, Mar./Apr. 2007, pp. 13–15, 19.

62. Department of Homeland Security, "Real ID and You: Rumor Control," www.dhs.gov/real-id-and-you-rumor-control.

63. James Brooke, "Japan in an Uproar as 'Big Brother' Computer File Kicks In," *New York Times*, Aug. 6, 2002, www.nytimes.com/2002/08/06/international/asia/06JAPA.html; Eiichiro Okuyama, "Japan's National ID System Poses Risks and Advantages," Keio University, International Center for the Internet and Society, Jan. 31, 2015, kipis.sfc.keio.ac.jp/japans-national-id-system-poses-risks-advantages/.

64. Utkarsh Anand, "Supreme Court Allows Aadhaar Card Use on Voluntary Basis for Government Schemes," *The Indian Express*, indianexpress.com/article/india/india-news-india/sc-allows-aadhaar-use-for-other-government-schemes-on-voluntary-basis/.

65. Jim Harper, "Understanding and Responding to the Threat of Terrorism," *Cato Policy Report*, Mar./Apr. 2007, pp. 13–15, 19.

66. Background sources for this section include: James Bamford, *The Puzzle Palace: A Report on NSA, America's Most Secret Agency*, Houghton Mifflin, 1982; NSA FAQ: www.nsa.gov/about/faqs/about-nsa-faqs.shtml; Statement for the Record

of NSA Director Lt. General Michael V. Hayden, USAF, House Permanent Select Committee on Intelligence, Apr. 12, 2000, www.nsa.gov/public_info/speeches_testimonies/12apr00_dirnsa.shtml; James Bamford, *Body of Secrets: Anatomy of the Ultra-Secret National Security Agency, from the Cold War Through the Dawn of a New Century*, Doubleday, 2001; James Bamford, "The Black Box," *Wired*, Apr. 2012, pp. 78–85, 122–124 (online at www.wired.com/threatlevel/2012/03/ff_nsa-datacenter). Bamford has written extensively about the NSA over several decades. His sources include former long-time NSA employees.

67. Declaration of Mark Klein, June 8, 2006, www.eff.org/document/klein-declaration-redacted.

68. For example, *Jewel* v. *NSA*, filed by the Electronic Frontier Foundation.

69. The documents that have been published are collected at the Snowden Surveillance Archive, Canadian Journalists for Free Expression, snowdenarchive.cjfe.org/greenstone/cgi-bin/library.cgi. Many news articles described the documents, for example, Cyrus Farivar, "The Top 5 Things We've Learned about the NSA Thanks to Edward Snowden," *Ars Technica*, Oct. 18, 2013, arstechnica.com/tech-policy/2013/10/the-top-5-things-weve-learned-about-the-nsa-thanks-to-edward-snowden/.

70. Bamford, "The Black Box."

71. Ixquick, www.ixquick.com, is one example. It is a metasearch engine; that is, it uses several other search engines to find results and provides what it considers the best results to the user.

72. Larry Loen, "Hiding Data in Plain Sight," *EFFector Online*, Jan. 7, 1993, www.eff.org/effector/4/5.

73. Quoted in Steve Lohr, "Privacy on Internet Poses Legal Puzzle," *New York Times*, Apr. 19, 1999, p. C4.

74. Interactive Advertising Bureau, as reported in Jack Marshall, "Facebook Will Force Advertising on Ad-Blocking Users," *Wall Street Journal*, Aug. 9, 2016, www.wsj.com/articles/facebook-will-force-advertising-on-ad-blocking-users-1470751204.

75. Research firms Ovum and Juniper Research estimate reduced global revenue in the range $16–78 billion by 2020, depending on how publishers respond.

76. Marshall, "Facebook Will Force Advertising . . ."

77. Samuel D. Warren and Louis D. Brandeis, "The Right to Privacy," *Harvard Law Review*, 1890, v. 4, p. 193.

78. Judith Jarvis Thomson, "The Right to Privacy," in David Schoeman, *Philosophical Dimensions of Privacy: An Anthology*, Cambridge University Press, 1984, pp. 272–289.

79. The inspiration for the Warren and Brandeis article, not mentioned in it, was that gossip columnists wrote about extravagant parties in Warren's home and newspapers covered his daughter's wedding. The background of the article is described in a biography of Brandeis and summarized in the critical response to the Warren and Brandeis article by William L. Prosser ("Privacy," in Schoeman, *Philosophical Dimensions of Privacy: An Anthology*, pp. 104–155).

80. Thomson, "The Right to Privacy," p. 287.

81. See, for example, Schoeman, *Philosophical Dimensions of Privacy: An Anthology*, p. 15, and Prosser, "Privacy," pp. 104–155.

82. Prosser, "Privacy," cites cases.

83. Richard Posner, "An Economic Theory of Privacy," appears in several anthologies including Schoeman, *Philosophical Dimensions of Privacy*, pp. 333–345, and Johnson and Nissenbaum, *Computers, Ethics & Social Values,* Prentice Hall, 1995.

84. New York State Office of the Attorney General, "Toysmart Bankruptcy Settlement Ensures Consumer Privacy Protection," Jan. 11, 2001, www.ag.ny.gov/press-release/toysmart-bankruptcy-settlement-ensures-consumer-privacy-protection.

85. "That Facebook Friend Might Be 10 Years Old, and Other Troubling News," *Consumer Reports*, June 2011, www.consumerreports.org/cro/magazine-archive/2011/june/electronics-computers/state-of-the-net/facebook-concerns/index.htm.

86. Dan Freedman, "Privacy Profile: Mary Gardiner Jones," *Privacy and American Business* 1(4), 1994, pp. 15, 17.

87. Janlori Goldman, statement to the Senate Judiciary Subcommittee on Technology and the Law, Jan. 27, 1994.

88. www.privacy.org.

89. Deirdre Mulligan, statement to U.S. House of Representatives Committee on the Judiciary hearing on "Privacy and Electronic Communications," May 18, 2000, www.cdt.org/testimony/000518mulligan.shtml. The quotation in her statement is from Alan F. Westin, *Privacy and Freedom*, Atheneum, 1968.

90. "Directive 95/46/EC of the European Parliament and of the Council of 24 October 1995 on the Protection of Individuals with Regard to the Processing of Personal Data and on the Free Movement of Such Data," available at European Commission, Justice and Home Affairs, ec.europa.eu/justice_home/fsj/privacy/law/index_ en.htm.

91. Caroline McCarthy, "German Court Rules Google Street View is Legal," CNet News, Mar. 21, 2011, news.cnet.com/8301-13577_3-20045595-36.html. David Meyer, "Google's Cars Return to German Roads, but not for Street View," GigaOM Media, Dec. 5, 2014, gigaom.com/2014/12/05/googles-cars-return-to-german-roads-but-not-for-street-view/.

92. Jo Best, "EU Data Retention Directive Gets Final Nod," CNET News, Feb. 22, 2006, www.cnet.com/news/eu-data-retention-directive-gets-final-nod/.

93. "Just Published," *Privacy Journal*, Aug. 2006, p. 6. Information Commissioner's Office, *What Price Privacy? The Unlawful Trade in Confidential Personal Information*, May 10, 2006, ico.org.uk/media/about-the-ico/documents/1042393/what-price-privacy.pdf.

94. "Legal Analysis: Russia's Right to Be Forgotten," Article 19, Sept. 16, 2016, www.article19.org/resources.php/resource/38099/en/legal-analysis:-russia's-right-to-be-forgotten. (Article 19 is a British human rights organization.)

95. The company is TomTom. It revised its contracts to prohibit police use of its speed data.

96. Christopher Steiner, *Automate This: How Algorithms Came to Rule Our World*, Penguin Group, 2012.

97. Robert F. Buckhorn Jr., quoted in Dana Canedy, "TV Cameras Seek Criminals . . ."

98. L. D. Introna, "Workplace Surveillance, Privacy and Distributive Justice," *Proceedings for Computer Ethics: Philosophical Enquiry (CEPE2000)*, Dartmouth College, July 14–16, 2000, pp. 188–199.

99. Vernor Vinge, *Rainbows End*, Tor, 2006.

Freedom of Speech

3.1 The First Amendment and Communications Paradigms

Congress shall make no law. . . abridging the freedom of speech, or of the press. . . .

—First Amendment to the U.S. Constitution (ratified in 1791)

The press in its historic connotation comprehends every sort of publication which affords a vehicle of information and opinion.

—U.S. Supreme Court, 1938[1]

For the first time in history, we have a many-to-many medium, in which you don't have to be rich to have access, and in which you don't have to win the approval of an editor or publisher to speak your mind. Usenet* and the Internet, as part of this new medium, hold the promise of guaranteeing, for the first time in history, that the First Amendment's protection of freedom of the press means as much to each individual as it does to Time Warner, or to Gannett, or to the New York Times.

—Mike Godwin, 1994[2]

In this section, we examine principles of freedom of speech, the regulatory structure that controlled earlier communications media, and changes brought about by digital media.† In later sections, we consider attempts to restrict information on the Internet, protect children from inappropriate material, control spam (mass, unsolicited email), and limit anonymity (a protection for speakers). The First Amendment prohibits the government from jailing or fining people for what they say. It is an extremely important protection for liberty, as governments tend to abuse their power to prohibit speech, for example, silencing political opposition by prohibiting speech that disturbs vaguely defined "social order." Freedom of speech allows a very large amount of controversial, dangerous, and offensive speech. It does not require that we listen to, publish, or allow such speech on our websites. We, and publishers of all sorts, have responsibility for ethical and social standards. In Sections 3.3 and 3.4, we discuss some quandaries and trade-offs in setting such standards. In Section 3.6, we examine how communications and surveillance technologies affect freedom of speech in different countries, especially some that have a long tradition of censorship. In Section 3.7, we return to regulatory issues and discuss the controversy over whether net neutrality rules help or hinder free speech and access to information.

3.1.1 FREE SPEECH PRINCIPLES

Telephone, movies, radio, television, cable, satellites, and, of course, the Internet and cellphones did not exist when the Constitution was written. Freedom of the press applied to publishers who printed newspapers and books and to "the lonely

---

*An early (pre-Web) collection of Internet discussion groups.

†Although much of our discussion is in the context of the U.S. Constitution's First Amendment, the arguments and principles about the human right of freedom of speech and the impact of digital media apply globally.

pamphleteer"[3] who printed and distributed pamphlets expressing unconventional ideas. One might think the First Amendment should apply to each new communications technology according to its spirit and intention: to protect our freedom to say what we wish and to encourage open debate. Politically powerful people, however, continually try to restrict speech that threatens them. From the Alien and Sedition Acts of 1798 to regulation of political action committees, such laws have been used against newspaper editors who disagreed with the political party in power and against ad hoc groups of people speaking out on issues. Attempts to restrict freedom of speech and of the press flourish with new technologies. Law professor Eric M. Freedman sums up: "Historical experience—with the printing press, secular dramatic troupes, photographs, movies, rock music, broadcasting, sexually explicit telephone services, video games, and other media—shows that each new medium is viewed at first by governments as uniquely threatening, because it is uniquely influential, and therefore a uniquely appropriate target of censorship."[4]

As we proceed with our discussion of free speech issues, it is helpful to remember several important points.

- The First Amendment was written for the protection of offensive and/ or controversial speech and ideas—there is no need to protect speech and publication that no one objects to.

- The First Amendment covers spoken and written words, pictures, art, and other forms of expression of ideas and opinions.

- The First Amendment is a restriction on the power of government, not individuals or private businesses. Publishers do not have to publish material they consider offensive, poorly written, or unlikely to appeal to their customers for any reason. Rejection or editing by a publisher is not a violation of a writer's First Amendment rights. Websites, search engine companies, and magazines may decline specific advertisements if they so choose. That does not violate the advertiser's freedom of speech.

Over the course of many years and many cases, the U.S. Supreme Court has developed principles and guidelines about protected expression.[*]

- When a government action or law causes people to avoid legal speech and publication out of fear of prosecution—perhaps because a law is vague—the action or law is said to have a "chilling effect" on First Amendment rights. Laws with a significant chilling effect are unconstitutional.

- Restrictions on speech such as noise regulations or permit requirements for parades or rallies must be content neutral. That is, the rules must be independent of the opinions expressed.

---

[*]The specific laws, court decisions, and guidelines are complex in some cases. The discussion here is general and simplified.

- Advocating illegal acts is (usually) legal; a listener has the opportunity and responsibility to weigh the arguments and decide whether or not to commit the illegal act.

- The First Amendment does not protect libel and direct, specific threats. Inciting violence, in certain circumstances, is illegal.

- Although the First Amendment makes no distinctions among categories of speech, courts have treated advertising as "second class" speech and allowed restrictions that would not be acceptable for other kinds of speech. In recent years, courts have begun to rule that restrictions on truthful advertising do indeed violate the First Amendment.[5] Similarly, since the 1970s, the government has severely regulated political campaign speech, but recent Supreme Court decisions have slowed or reversed this trend.

There is a censorship issue whenever the government owns or substantially subsidizes communications systems or networks (or controversial services). For example, at times while abortion has been legal, federally subsidized family planning clinics were not permitted to discuss it. At various times, the government has made it illegal to send information through the mail that the First Amendment otherwise protects. A federal agency that provides funds for public radio stations rejected the application of a university because it broadcasts one hour a week of religious programming. In Section 3.2.2, we will see that Congress used its funding power to require censorship of the Internet in public libraries and public schools. No matter what side of these issues you are on, no matter how the policy changes with different presidents or Congresses, the point is that, in many circumstances, when the government pays, it can choose to restrict speech that the Constitution would otherwise protect.

3.1.2 REGULATING COMMUNICATIONS MEDIA

In this section, we introduce the traditional three-part framework for First Amendment protection and government regulation of communications media that developed in the United States in the 20th century. Then we discuss how modern communications technology and the Internet strained that framework and required updating.

The three categories are:

- print media (newspapers, books, magazines, and pamphlets),
- broadcast (television and radio), and
- common carriers (telephone, telegraph, and the postal system).

The first category has the strongest First Amendment protection because it existed when the Bill of Rights was written and so there was no question about whether the First Amendment applied. Although some books have been banned in the United States and people have been arrested for publishing information on certain topics (such as contraception), the trend has been toward fewer government restraints on the printed word.

Television and radio are similar to newspapers in their role of providing news and entertainment, but the government regulates both the structure of the broadcasting industry and the content of programs. The government grants broadcasting licenses, and licensees must meet government standards of merit—a requirement that would not be tolerated for print publishers because of the obvious threat to freedom of expression. The government has used threats of license revocation to get stations to cancel or censor sexually oriented talk shows. The government banned cigarette ads from radio, television, and electronic media under the control of the Federal Communications Commission (FCC), but the ads continued to be legal in magazines and newspapers. In a case challenging the constitutionality of a ban on broadcast "indecency," the Supreme Court upheld the ban.* The federal government frequently proposed requirements to reduce violence on television or increase programming for children, but the government cannot impose such requirements on print publishers. Whether you favor or oppose any of these particular policies, the point is that the government has more control over television and radio content than it has over communication methods that existed at the time the Bill of Rights was written.

The main argument used to deny full First Amendment protection to broadcasters was scarcity of broadcast frequencies. There were only a handful of television channels and few radio frequencies in the early days of broadcasting. In exchange for the "monopoly" privilege of using the scarce, publicly owned spectrum, broadcasters were tightly regulated. With cable, satellites, hundreds of channels, and eventually the Internet, the argument based on scarcity and monopoly is irrelevant, but the precedent of government control remains. A second argument for government-imposed restrictions on content was that broadcast material comes into the home and is difficult to keep from children. This argument applies to the Web as well.

Common carriers, the third category of communications companies and regulation, provided a medium of communication (not content) and were required to make their service available to everyone. In some cases, as with telephone service, the government required them to provide "universal access," that is, to subsidize service for people with low incomes. Based on the argument that common carriers are a monopoly, the law prohibited them from controlling the content of material that passed through their system. Telephone companies were prohibited from providing content or information services on the grounds that they might discriminate against competing content providers who must also use their telephone lines.

---

*The FCC had fined comedian George Carlin for a radio program about the seven dirty words one could not say on the radio.

Common carriers had no control over content, so they had no responsibility for illegal content passing through. As you are probably aware, many companies that now provide communications infrastructure also provide content; the common-carrier category has changed dramatically.

Beginning in the 1980s, computer bulletin board systems (BBS), commercial services like CompuServe, Prodigy, and America Online (AOL), and ultimately the World Wide Web became major arenas for distribution of news, information, and opinion. Because of the immense flexibility of computer communications systems, they do not fit neatly into the publishing, broadcasting, and common carriage paradigms. Cable television had strained this framework previously; in commenting on a law requiring cable stations to carry certain broadcasts, the Supreme Court said cable operators have more freedom of speech than television and radio broadcasters, but less than print publishers.[6] But the Web does not fit between the traditional categories any better than it fits within any one of them. It has similarities to all three, as well as additional similarities to bookstores, libraries, and rented meeting rooms—all of which the law treats differently.

As new technologies blurred the technical boundaries between cable, telephone, computer networks, and content providers, Congress passed the Telecommunications Act of 1996. This law significantly revised the Communications Act of 1934, the main law at the time for regulation of communications. The Telecommunications Act changed the regulatory structure by removing many artificial legal divisions of service areas and many restrictions on services that telecommunications companies may provide. The law also significantly clarified the question of the liability of Internet Service Providers (ISPs) and other online services for content posted by third parties such as members and subscribers. Print publishers and broadcasters select and edit the material they publish or broadcast, and they are legally liable for it. They can be sued for libel (making false and damaging statements) and for copyright infringement and are legally responsible for obscene material in their publications and programs. Before passage of the Telecommunications Act, several people brought suits against BBS operators, ISPs, AOL, and other service providers for content that others put on their systems. To protect themselves from lawsuits and possible criminal charges, many service providers erred on the side of caution and removed a lot of content that was legal—seriously restricting the amount of information and opinion in cyberspace. The Telecommunications Act stated that "no provider or user of an interactive computer service shall be treated as the publisher or speaker of any information provided by another information content provider."[7] This statement removed uncertainty and protected service providers, thus encouraging the vast growth of user-created content that we take for granted now.*

---

*Service providers remain at risk in many countries. For example, the head of eBay in India was arrested because someone sold pornographic videos on eBay's Indian site even though the actual videos did not appear on the site and the seller violated company policy by selling them. Some repressive governments hold service providers liable for posts criticizing government policies.

Congress passed the first major Internet censorship law, the Communications Decency Act, in 1996. The Supreme Court ruled its censorship provisions unconstitutional. However, efforts to censor the Internet continued. We investigate arguments about, as well as the impacts of, censorship and other restrictive laws in Section 3.2. In addition, we will see in Section 3.2.5 that many innovative individuals and entrepreneurs who tried to publish information, advertise products, and provide services on the Web encountered legal problems (and sometimes fines) not because of explicit censorship laws but because of long-standing laws that restricted commerce to benefit powerful organizations, businesses, and governments. In several cases, these confrontations between new technology and old laws resulted in increased freedom.

3.2 Controlling Speech in Cyberspace

> *I disapprove of what you say, but I will defend to the death your right to say it.*
> —S. G. Tallentyre (Evelyn Beatrice Hall), Voltaire's biographer, describing Voltaire's view of freedom of speech[8]

3.2.1 WHAT IS OFFENSIVE SPEECH? WHAT IS ILLEGAL?

What is offensive speech? What should the law prohibit or restrict on the Web? The answers depend on your viewpoint. It could be political or religious speech, pornography, criticism of Islam, criticism of Judaism, racist or sexist slurs, Nazi materials, libelous statements, abortion information, antiabortion information, criticism of climate change predictions, advertising of alcoholic beverages, advertising in general, depictions of violence, discussion of suicide, or information about how to build bombs. Here are just a few actions taken, attempted, or suggested to ban speech:

- The state of Georgia tried to ban pictures of marijuana from the Internet.
- A doctor argued for regulating medical discussion on the Net so that people would not get bad advice.
- The Chinese government restricts reporting of emergencies (such as major accidents or disasters) and how the government handles them.
- The French government approved a law banning anyone except professional journalists from recording or distributing video of acts of violence.

Most efforts to censor the Internet in the United States, including several laws passed by Congress, focus on pornographic and other sexually explicit material, so we begin with discussion of such material; many of the same principles apply to efforts to censor other kinds of material.

People discuss sexual activity, of conventional and unconventional sorts, in graphic detail in cyberspace. The distinctions between erotica, art, and pornography are not always clear, and different people have very different personal standards. There is much on the Net that is extremely offensive to adults. Some people want to prohibit it altogether while others seek ways to keep it away from children. The Internet began as a forum for research and scientific discussion, so the rapid proliferation of pornography shocked many people even though the same kind of material was already available in adult magazines, bookstores, and movie theaters. As a writer for *Wired* points out, sexual material quickly invades all new technologies and art forms[9]; from cave paintings to frescos in Pompeii to stone carvings at Angkor Wat, erotica have flourished. The printing press produced Bibles and porn. Photography produced *Playboy*. Hundreds of thousands of subscription websites provide adult entertainment.[10] Whether all this is good or bad, whether it is a natural part of human nature or a sign of degeneracy and evil, and whether we should tolerate it or stamp it out—are moral and social issues beyond the scope of this book. People debate pornography endlessly. In addressing the issue of pornography and of other kinds of speech that offend people, we try to focus specifically on new problems and issues related to new technology.

What was already illegal?

The Supreme Court ruled that the First Amendment does not protect obscene material. In 1973, in *Miller* v. *California*, the Court established a three-part guideline for determining whether material is obscene under the law. The criteria are that

1. it depicts sexual (or excretory) acts whose depiction is specifically prohibited by state law,
2. it depicts these acts in a patently offensive manner, appealing to prurient interest as judged by a reasonable person using community standards, and
3. it has no serious literary, artistic, social, political, or scientific value.

The second point—the application of community standards—was a compromise intended to avoid the problem of setting a national standard of obscenity in so large and diverse a country. Thus, small conservative or religious towns could restrict pornography to a greater extent than cosmopolitan urban areas. The wide accessibility of the Internet threatened this compromise. In an early Internet case, a couple who lived in California and sold sexually explicit material were prosecuted in Tennessee and found guilty of distributing obscenity under the local community standards even though legal observers agreed the couple would not be found guilty in California. A spokesman for the American Civil Liberties Union (ACLU) commented that prosecutions like this one meant that "nothing can be put on the Internet that is more racy than would be tolerated in the most conservative community in the U.S."[11] For this reason, some courts have recognized that "community standards" is no longer an appropriate tool for determining what is acceptable material.

Does the First Amendment apply to software?

Throughout the 1990s, the U.S. government battled the Internet community and privacy advocates as it attempted to restrict the availability of secure encryption (i.e., encryption that is so difficult and expensive to crack that it is not practical to do so.) The government prohibited export of powerful encryption software, and it interpreted anything posted on the Internet as effectively exported. Thus, even researchers who posted research papers containing encryption algorithms faced possible prosecution. (The government argued that the export prohibition was necessary to keep strong encryption from terrorists and enemy governments, although strong encryption schemes were already available on Internet sites all over the world.)

Privacy and security advocates raised legal challenges to the export restrictions based on the First Amendment. The question is whether cryptography algorithms, and computer programs in general, are speech and hence protected by the First Amendment. The government argued that software is not speech and that control of cryptography was a national security issue, not a freedom-of-speech issue. The federal judge who heard the case thought otherwise. She said:

This court can find no meaningful difference between computer language . . . and German or French. . . . Like music and mathematical equations, computer language is just that, language, and it communicates information either to a computer or to those who can read it. . . . For the purposes of First Amendment analysis, this court finds that source code is speech.[12]

The U.S. government removed almost all export restrictions on encryption in 2000.

It has long been illegal to create, possess, or distribute child pornography. We discuss child pornography in Section 3.2.3, where we consider sexting and unexpected applications of child pornography laws.

3.2.2   CENSORSHIP LAWS AND ALTERNATIVES

Our sole intent is to make the Internet safer for our youth.

—Department of Justice spokesman[13]

Even where the protection of children is the object, the constitutional limits on government action apply.

—Justice Antonin Scalia[14]

Major Internet censorship laws

In the first decade of the World Wide Web, Congress, responding to public outcry about pornography and other forms of offensive material on the Internet, passed several censorship laws. Ultimately, the Supreme Court ruled that most of them violated the First Amendment. We review the history of these laws because the results were critical in establishing the open Internet we see today. Attempts to censor continue to pop up periodically, so it is valuable to be familiar with the arguments.

The first and most sweeping censorship law for the Internet was the Communications Decency Act (CDA) of 1996.[15] In the CDA and the censorship laws that followed, Congress attempted to avoid an obvious conflict with the First Amendment by focusing on children. The CDA made it a crime to make available to anyone under 18 any communication that is obscene or indecent. A fundamental problem with the law is that it can be difficult to keep inappropriate material from children while allowing access for adults. The Supreme Court had ruled on this problem in *Butler* v. *Michigan*, a significant 1957 case striking down a Michigan law that made it illegal to sell material that might be damaging to children. Justice Frankfurter wrote that the state must not "reduce the adult population of Michigan to reading only what is fit for children."[16] A child can access almost anything on the Net. Thus, opponents of the CDA said, the CDA violated Justice Frankfurter's dictum, not just in Michigan but throughout the country. They gave examples of information that is legal in print but might be cause for prosecution if available online: the Bible, some of Shakespeare's plays, and serious discussions of sexual behavior and health problems like AIDS. Supporters of the CDA argued that this was overreaction. No one would be prosecuted, they said, for such material. A lack of clear standards, however, can lead to uneven and unfair prosecutions, and uncertainty can have a chilling effect on those who provide information for adults that might not be suitable for children.

The Supreme Court ruled unanimously, in *American Civil Liberties Union et al.* v. *Janet Reno*, that the censorship provisions of the CDA were unconstitutional. The courts made strong statements about the importance of protecting freedom of expression in general and on the Internet. The court decisions against the CDA established that "the Internet deserves the highest protection from government intrusion."

Figure 3.1 summarizes principles courts use to help determine if a censorship law is constitutional. When the government is pursuing a legitimate goal that might infringe on free speech (in this case, the protection of children), it must use the least restrictive means of accomplishing the goal. The courts found that filtering software was less restrictive and more desirable than censorship. The judges also commented, "The government can continue to protect children from pornography on the Internet through vigorous enforcement of existing laws criminalizing obscenity and child pornography."[17]

Congress tried again, with the Child Online Protection Act (COPA), in 1998. This law was more limited than the CDA. COPA made it a federal crime for commercial websites to make available to minors material "harmful to minors" as

---

- Distinguish speech from action. Advocating illegal acts is (usually) legal.
- Laws must not chill expression of legal speech.
- Do not reduce adults to reading only what is fit for children.
- Solve speech problems by the least restrictive means.

FIGURE 3.1 Freedom of speech guidelines.

Evolving risks to children

Parents have a responsibility to supervise their children and to teach them how to deal with inappropriate material and threats. But technology certainly has changed the risks to children and made the job of parents more difficult. If a young child tried to buy a ticket for an X-rated movie at a movie theater or to buy an adult magazine in a store, a cashier would see the child and refuse (at least, most of the time). In a supermarket or a playground, a parent or other observer might see a "stranger" talking to a child, but a potential child molester online is not visible. The home used to be a safe haven from pornography and violent or hateful materials. Parents could relax when a child was playing in his or her bedroom. With Internet connections and smartphones, that is no longer true.

The dangers a child might encounter on the street have changed too. For example,

officials in New York worried that child molesters could meet children by playing Pokémon GO (a free, augmented reality game in which players walk around outdoors searching for and "capturing" Pokémon creatures that appear on their screens[*]). They banned registered sex offenders on parole from playing the game.

Pedophiles have websites that link to sites of Cub Scouts, Brownies (the young version of Girl Scouts), junior high school soccer teams, and so on—sites with pictures of children and sometimes names and other personal information. This does not mean that such youth organizations should not put pictures on their websites; however, they should consider whether to include children's names, require registration for use of the site, or take other protective measures.

[*]It was a huge craze for a while. Is it still?

judged by community standards. Once again, First Amendment supporters argued that the law was too broad and would threaten art, news, and health sites. Courts evaluating COPA noted that the community-standards provision would restrict the entire Internet to the standards of the most conservative community. The courts also said COPA's requirements that adults provide identification to view material not appropriate for minors would have an unconstitutional chilling effect on free speech. After more than 10 years of lawsuits and appeals, the Supreme Court declined to hear the last government appeal, and COPA died in 2009.

Congress passed the Children's Internet Protection Act (CIPA) in 2000 to require libraries and schools to use filter software on Internet terminals. When public libraries first installed Internet terminals, people used the terminals to look at "X-rated" pictures within view of children or other library users who found them offensive. Children and adults accessed adult sexual material and extremist political and racist material. Librarians around the country tried to satisfy library users, parents, community organizations, civil libertarians, and their own Library Bill of Rights (which opposes restricting access to library materials because of age). Here are some of the actions they took:

- Installing polarizing filters on terminals or building walls around terminals so that the screens were visible only from directly in front (both to protect the privacy of the user and to shield other users and employees from material they found objectionable)

- Setting time limits on use of terminals
- Asking patrons to stop viewing pornography, just as they would ask someone to stop making noise
- Installing filtering software, either on all terminals or on terminals in the children's section
- Requiring direct parental supervision or written parental permission for children using the Internet

CIPA sought to override these methods and attempted to avoid the courts' objections to the CDA and COPA by using the federal government's funding power. CIPA requires that schools and libraries that participate in certain federal programs (receiving federal money for technology) install filtering software on all Internet terminals to block access to sites with child pornography, obscene material, and material "harmful to minors." Of course, many schools and libraries rely on those funds. Civil liberties organizations and the American Library Association sued to block CIPA.[18] The Supreme Court ruled that CIPA does not violate the First Amendment. CIPA does not *require* the use of filters and does not impose jail or fines on people who provide content on the Internet. Instead, it sets a condition for receipt of certain federal funds. The court made it clear that if an adult asks a librarian to disable the filter on a library Internet terminal the adult is using, the librarian must do so. Of course, some adults are unaware of the filter software, unaware that they can legally request it be turned off, or unwilling to call attention to themselves by making the request.

Outside of schools and libraries, the trend of judicial decisions is to give the Internet First Amendment protection similar to that of print media, that is, the highest degree of protection.

Alternatives to censorship

What alternatives to censorship are available to protect children from inappropriate material on the Web (and to shield adults from material that is offensive to them)? Are there solutions that do not threaten to diminish free discussion of serious subjects or deny sexually explicit material to adults who want it? As we see for many problems, there are a variety of solutions based on the market, technology, responsibility, and education, as well as law.

The development of software filters is an example of a quick market response to a problem. Many families with children use filtering software (some of which is free or built into modern operating systems). Software filters can block websites with specific words, phrases, or images or they can block sites according to various rating systems. Filters can contain long lists of specific sites to block or parents can

Talking about bombs—or farming

The terrorists who set off bombs at the Boston Marathon in 2013 learned how to make their bombs from a magazine on the Internet, as did students who carried bombs into schools. As far back as 1995, within a few weeks of the bombing of the Oklahoma City federal building, the Senate's terrorism and technology subcommittee held hearings on "The Availability of Bomb Making Information on the Internet." There are many similarities between the controversy about bomb-making information on the Web and the controversy about pornography. As with pornography, bomb-making information was already widely available in traditional media, protected by the First Amendment, and it has legitimate uses. Information about how to make bombs appeared in the print version of the *Encyclopaedia Britannica* and in books in libraries and bookstores. The U.S. Department of Agriculture distributed a booklet called the "Blasters' Handbook"—farmers use explosives to remove tree stumps.[19]

Arguing to censor information about bombs on the Internet, Senator Dianne Feinstein said, "There is a difference between free speech and teaching someone to kill."[20] Arguing against censorship, a former U.S. attorney said that "information-plus," (i.e., information used in the commission of a criminal act) is what the law should regulate. Senator Patrick Leahy emphasized an established legal principle outside of cyberspace—that it is "harmful and dangerous *conduct,* not speech, that justifies adverse legal consequences." There are, of course, existing laws against using bombs to kill people or destroy property, as well as laws against making bombs or conspiring to make them for such purposes. In the 1990s, Congress passed a law mandating long prison terms for anyone who distributes bomb-making information knowing or intending that it will be used to commit a crime, but it has not reduced the availability of such information.

Is it reasonable, in a free society, to ban bomb-making information? Is it reasonable, as a practical matter, to expect to eliminate bomb-making information from the Internet? Is the real problem, as a Salon writer suggests,[21] people with ideological obsessions or mental dysfunctions, or is it availability of the information?

choose categories to filter (e.g., sex or violence), add their own list of banned sites, and review a log of their child's activity. However, as with many of the solutions we describe for problems generated by new technologies, filters are not perfect; they can screen out both too much (sites about Middlesex and Essex) and too little (missing some obviously objectionable material). Filters sometimes block sites containing educational material and political discussion, for example, the home page of a university's biology department and the websites of a candidate for Congress containing statements about abortion and gun control.

Filters have improved with time, but it is not possible to completely eliminate errors and subjective views about what is too sexual or too violent or too critical of a religion, what medical information is appropriate for children of what age, and so on. Setting up filtering tools can be challenging to some parents who simply give up, but about half of parents of children and teen-agers use some form of parental-control tool to control or monitor their children's online activity.[22] The weaknesses of filtering tools—particularly the blocking of legal material—present a free speech issue when legislators mandate filters or when public institutions use filters.

Businesses and online communities provide a variety of other alternatives to government censorship. Here are some examples:

- Wireless carriers set "decency" standards for companies providing content for their networks. Their rules are detailed and stricter than what the government can prohibit.[23]

- Commercial services, online communities, and social networking sites develop policies to protect members. They remove offensive material and expell subscribers who distribute material banned by law or the site's policies. (Such groups also aid law enforcement with investigations of child pornography and of attempts to meet and molest children.)

- Social network sites have developed technology to trace members who post child pornography.

- Companies and organizations offer online services, websites, and cellphone services targeted at families and children. Some allow subscribers to lock children out of certain areas.

- Many websites provide information with tips on how to control what children view.

Video games

Violent video games have been the focus of criticism since they began appearing. Some are very gory; some depict murder and torture; some focus on violence against women and members of specific ethnic and religious groups. Are they bad for children? Are they more dangerous than other forms of violence and violent sexism and racism that a minor sees in books or other media? Should we ban them?

Some argue that the interactivity of video games has a more powerful impact on children than passively watching television or reading a violent story. Others point out that children have played at killing each other (cops and robbers, cowboys and Indians) for generations. Does falling down "dead" on the grass compare to the repeated, explosive gore of a video game? At what age is a child mature enough to decide to play a violent video game: 12? 18? Who should decide what games a child plays: parents or legislators? Parents are not always with their children; they worry that peer pressure overrides parental rules and guidance.

A California law banned sale or rental of violent video games to minors. In 2011, the Supreme Court ruled that the law violated the First Amendment. The Court pointed out that violence and gore are common in classic fairy tales (e.g., the grim Grimm Brothers), cartoons (Elmer Fudd always shooting at Bugs Bunny), superhero comics, and literature teenagers are required to read in high school. Many video games are extremely disgusting, but the Court said that "disgust is not a valid basis for restricting expression."[24]

The video game industry developed a rating system that provides an indication for parents about the amount of sex, profanity, and violence in a game.[25] Some online game sites restrict their offerings to nonviolent games and advertise that policy.

3.2.3 Child Pornography and Sexting

Child pornography law

Child pornography includes pictures or videos of actual minors (children under 18) engaged in sexually explicit conduct.* Laws against creating, possessing, or distributing child pornography predate the Internet and cover a broad range of images, many of which would be legal if the person depicted were an adult. Production of child pornography is illegal primarily because its production is considered abuse of the actual children, not because of the impact of the content on a viewer. The adults who produce child pornography often coerce or manipulate children into posing or performing. (The mere possession of child pornography does not directly abuse children, but the Supreme Court accepted the ban on possession on the argument that the buyers or users of the images encourage their production.) It is not automatically illegal to make or distribute sexually explicit movies or photos in which an adult actor plays a minor. In other words, the legal basis for child pornography laws is to prevent using, abusing, and exploiting children, not portraying them.

Law enforcement agents regularly make arrests for distribution of child pornography by email, chat rooms, social media, and mobile phones. They use surveillance, search warrants, sting operations, and undercover investigations to build their cases and make the arrests.

In the 1996 Child Pornography Prevention Act, Congress extended laws against child pornography to include "virtual" children, that is, computer-generated images that appear to be minors, as well as other images where real adults appear to be minors. The Supreme Court ruled in 2002 (in *Ashcroft* v. *Free Speech Coalition*) that this violated the First Amendment. Justice Anthony Kennedy commented that the extension to virtual images "proscribes the visual depiction of an idea—that of teenagers engaging in sexual activity—that is a fact of modern society and has been a theme in art and literature throughout the ages."[26]

As the quality of digital imagery improved, a potential problem loomed for enforcement of laws against child pornography: If police found someone in

---

*This is a simplification. The laws include more detail and definitions.

possession of pornographic images of minors, the person could claim the images were computer generated, not photos of real children, leaving prosecutors the burden of proving otherwise. Congress passed the Prosecutorial Remedies and Other Tools to end the Exploitation of Children Today (PROTECT) Act of 2003, which (among many other provisions) classifies as child pornography a "computer-generated image that is, or is indistinguishable from, that of a minor engaging in sexually explicit conduct." Thus, prosecutors do not have to prove that a real child was involved. However, by including virtual images that appear to be real, this expands child pornography law beyond the prevention of abuse or exploitation of real children and could ban some forms of art. The Supreme Court has not yet heard a case about whether this part of the PROTECT Act is constitutional.

Sexting

Sexting means sending sexually suggestive or explicit text or photos, usually by smartphone or social media. The phenomenon we discuss here involves children, particularly teenagers under 18, sending nude or seminude photos of themselves or their boyfriends or girlfriends to each other or to classmates.* This practice is horrifying to parents and educators, who recognize the dangers it poses to children. One common result of sexting is severe embarrassment and taunting when the pictures become widely distributed. In an extreme case, after an ex-boyfriend redistributed pictures of an 18-year-old girl, she killed herself. Many young people (like many adults) do not think about how quickly something intended for one person or a small group spreads to a large audience, nor how difficult it is to remove something from cyberspace once it is out there. They do not think about the impact on their future personal and career relationships. In addition, most teens do not know that sexting is illegal, and penalties can be severe.

Child pornography laws were intended to apply to adults who commit a repugnant abuse of children, but sexting led to application of the laws in unanticipated ways. Prosecutors have brought child pornography charges against children for sexting. Possession of child pornography is illegal, so children who have pictures of friends under 18 on their phones that prosecutors think meet the definition of child pornography are potentially in violation. Is sending nude or sexually suggestive photos of oneself a form of expression? Is it foolish and potentially damaging behavior by an immature person that parents and school officials should deal with? Should it be a criminal felony with severe penalties that can include being put in a sex-offender database for many years?

Some prosecutors may see the threat of prosecution as the only tool available to stop young people from doing something they will strongly regret in the future. Others may be imposing their moral standards on other people's children. In one case, a 14-year-old girl was prosecuted after refusing a deal that required

---

*Sexting is certainly not limited to teenagers. At least two members of Congress have resigned over sexting scandals.

she attend a counseling class and write an essay about her actions. A court ruled that using a threat of prosecution in this way was to compel speech (the essay) and, thus, violated the First Amendment. Tools that might be useful in schools trying to discourage sexting (such as counseling and essays) may not be acceptable when forced by the government.

Some states have revised their laws in a variety of ways to reduce the penalties for sexting. For example, some have made it a misdemeanor, rather than a felony, if a young person sends an illegal photo to another young person of similar age. Other states have reduced or eliminated penalties if photos are distributed (among minors) with the consent of the person in the picture. Revising child pornography laws to deal appropriately with sexting is essential, but that alone is not sufficient. Sexting should be addressed through parental involvement, reasonable school policies, and education about its consequences.

A related problem is unauthorized distribution of explicit photos of schoolmates. Often the purpose is to embarrass the person in the photos. The penalties for distribution of child pornography by adults seem too severe for school children, but what response is appropriate?

Taunting teachers

Children can be the source, as well as the target or victim, of offensive material. Children make fun of other children and teachers and can be very cruel. Parents and schools have always needed policies for dealing with such behavior. Here we look at how the legal system deals with, or should deal with, online attacks on teachers which can range from jokes and parodies to threatening comments and false accusations of serious crimes.

The Supreme Court ruled in 1969 that the First Amendment protects freedom of speech on public school grounds though some exceptions are allowed. For example, schools can punish students if they disrupt school activities. Away from school grounds, there was little dispute: The First Amendment applied, as did existing laws against threats and false accusations. As we observed in Chapter 1, the Web and social media multiply the effect of negative comments and can contribute to mob-like behavior. In recent years, schools have begun punishing students for comments in social media directed against teachers and school officials. Court rulings on challenges to such punishments have not been consistent. In one state, teachers successfully lobbied for a law making it a crime in certain circumstances to intimidate a school employee online.

Here are several questions to consider about such a law; they raise fundamental issues beyond issues of new technologies: Should children have less legal protection for freedom of speech than adults? Should one category of adults—in this case, school employees—have special legal protection from criticism or bullying not provided to others such as a school friend's parent, a local storekeeper, or a neighbor? Are the vagueness of the offense and the broad discretion teachers and prosecutors have in deciding to apply the law good things or bad things?

3.2.4 Spam

What is the problem?

The term *spam*, in the context of electronic communications, originally referred to unsolicited bulk email.[*] It now applies to text messages, tweets, and phone calls as well. Details of a precise definition, depending on how one defines "bulk" and "unsolicited," can be critical to discussions about how to deal with spam, especially when we consider laws to restrict it.

Spam has infuriated users of the Internet for decades. Most, but not all, spam is commercial advertising. Spam developed because email is extremely cheap compared to printed direct-mail advertising. Spam angers people because of the content, the way it is sent, and the sheer volume of it. The content can be ordinary commercial advertising, political advertising, solicitations for funds from nonprofit organizations, pornography and advertisements for it, fraudulent "get rich quick" scams, or scams selling fake or nonexistent products. Topics come in waves, for example, ads for Viagra, ads for low mortgage rates, promotions for various stocks, and Nigerian refugees who need help getting $30,000,000 out of Africa. ISPs filter out email from known spammers, so many spammers disguise the source of their email and use other schemes to avoid filters. Criminal spammers hijack large numbers of computers by spreading viruses that allow the spammer to send huge amounts of spam from the infected machines, called "zombies."

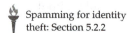
Spamming for identity theft: Section 5.2.2

How much spam travels through the Internet? The first case that created an antispam furor involved advertising messages sent by a law firm to 6000 bulletin boards or newsgroups in 1994. At that time, any advertising or postings not directly related to the topic of the group raised the ire of Net users. More recently, one man was accused of running a zombie network that sent billions of emails per day. Another spammer was arrested for clogging Facebook with 27 million spam messages.[27]

Why not just ban spam? We will see some reasons in the next few pages.

Cases and free speech issues

In 1996, about half of the email received at AOL was spam, and a lot of it came from an email advertising service called Cyber Promotions, so AOL installed filters to block mail from Cyber Promotions. Cyber Promotions obtained an injunction against AOL's use of filters, claiming AOL violated its First Amendment rights, and thus began the battle over the legal status of spam.

Cyber Promotions' case was weak, and the court soon removed the injunction. Why did AOL have the right to block incoming spam? The spam used AOL's

---

[*]Spam is the name of a spiced meat product sold in cans by Hormel Foods. The use of the word in the context of email comes from a Monty Python skit in which some characters repeatedly shouted, "Spam, spam, spam," drowning out other conversation.

computers, imposing a cost on AOL; AOL's property rights allow it to decide what it accepts on its system. AOL is a membership organization; it can implement policies to provide the kind of environment it believes its members want. Finally, AOL is a private company, not a government institution. On the other side, some civil liberties organizations were uneasy about allowing AOL to filter email because AOL decided what email to block from its members. They argued that because AOL is large, it is a lot like the U.S. Post Office, and it should not be allowed to block any mail.

Over the next few years, AOL filed several lawsuits and sought injunctions to stop spammers from sending unsolicited bulk mailings to its members. Notice the subtle shift: Cyber Promotions originally sought an injunction to stop AOL from filtering out its email and then AOL sought injunctions to stop spammers from sending email. Private filtering as done by AOL does not violate a spammer's freedom of speech, but does a government order not to send the mail violate freedom of speech? We listed several arguments why a service provider should be free to filter incoming mail—do any of the arguments support injunctions against the spammers? One does: the argument that spam uses the recipient company's property (computer system) against its wishes and imposes a cost on the recipient. AOL and other services won multimillion-dollar settlements from Cyber Promotions and other spammers. But how far does, or should, the owner's control extend? A former Intel employee, Ken Hamidi, sent six emailings critical of Intel to more than 30,000 Intel employees over a period of less than two years. He disguised his return address to make it difficult for Intel to block his email. Intel sought a court order prohibiting him from sending more email to its employees (at work). Note that in this case the spam was not commercial. Intel argued that freedom of speech gave Hamidi the right to criticize Intel on his own website, but it did not give him the right to intrude into Intel's property and use its equipment to deliver his messages; Intel argued that the email was a form of trespass. The California Supreme Court ruled in favor of Hamidi. The Court said that Hamidi's bulk emailing was not trespass, because it did not damage Intel's computers or cause economic harm to the company.[28]

Amnesty International has long used its network of thousands of volunteers to flood government officials in various countries with mail when a political prisoner is being tortured or is in imminent danger of execution. Organizations have set up Web pages where people can click on a form letter to be emailed to every member of Congress (or to a list of businesses). Is this spam or an exercise of free speech? Does our answer depend on how sympathetic we are to the specific organization's message?

Blocking spam

Freedom of speech does not require the intended listener, or message recipient, to listen. A variety of filtering products screen out spam at the recipient's site by blocking email from specified addresses, by blocking messages with particular

An issue for designers and users of filters

We saw that filters are not perfect. They block more or less than the material one wants blocked, and often they block both more and less. If the filter is intended to block sexually explicit material from young children, it might be acceptable to err on the side of blocking some inoffensive material to be sure of preventing the undesirable material from getting through. On the other hand, if the filter is for spam, most people would not mind a few spam messages getting through but would be quite unhappy if some of their nonspam messages were blocked.

words, and by more sophisticated methods. Large email service providers, such as Google, Yahoo, Microsoft, and Apple can identify likely spam when thousands (or millions) of members receive a similar email, but this filtering often means the service must scan our email. Is this an acceptable trade-off between privacy and spam elimination?

Many people now see very little spam because their service provider filters it out.

Many businesses subscribe to services that provide lists of spammers to block. Aggressive antispam services list not only spammers but also ISPs, universities, businesses, and online services that do not take sufficient action to stop members of their communities from sending spam. Such action encourages managers to do something—for example, limit the number of outbound messages from one account. How much discretion should an antispam service have in deciding whom to include on its list of spammers? Harris Interactive, which conducts public opinion surveys by email ("Harris polls"), sued the Mail Abuse Prevention System (MAPS) for including Harris on its blacklist. Harris claimed that the people receiving its email signed up to receive it. MAPS claimed Harris did not meet its standards for assuring the recipients' consent. Harris claimed inclusion on the list cut it off from about half of its survey participants and harmed its business and that a competing polling company recommended it for the spammer list.[29] This case illustrates the potential for "gaming" the system by competitors and the differences of opinion that can arise about who is a spammer.

As anyone with a phone likely knows, we receive numerous robocalls[*] daily. A company that maintains a database of numbers from which spam calls originate offers an app that hangs up on robocalls after one ring. The company also sells access to the database to phone service companies that choose to automatically block robocalls.[30]

It is interesting to review how attitudes about spam filtering have changed. We saw that when AOL began aggressively filtering to block spam, some Internet groups compared the filtering to censorship. Even though AOL was not a

---

[*]Automated phone calls with recorded messages (marketing, political, or scams).

government entity, it was large and millions of people received their mail at AOL. People worried that the precedent of a large corporation filtering email for any reason could lead to corporations filtering email because of content they did not like. Now, many advocacy groups and customers of communications services see spam filtering as valuable and essential.

Antispam laws

The impact of antispam laws and decisions about their constitutionality can be quite significant. Virginia's law prohibited anonymous, unsolicited, bulk email, and a man convicted of spamming in Virginia was sentenced to nine years in jail. The conviction was reversed when the state's Supreme Court ruled that the law violated the First Amendment.

The federal CAN-SPAM Act[31] applies to email sent to computers and email and text messages sent to mobile devices. It targets commercial spam and covers labeling of advertising messages (for easier filtering), opt-out provisions, and methods of generating email lists. Commercial messages must include valid mail header information (e.g., faking the "From" line to disguise the sender is prohibited) and a valid return address or phone number. Deceptive subject lines are prohibited. Unless you have given your consent, advertisers are not permitted to use an auto-dialer to send spam text messages to your mobile phone. Criminal penalties apply for some of the more deceptive practices and for sending spam from someone else's computer without authorization (e.g., via a virus).[32]

The law has been helpful in reducing problem spam, or just messages we do not want, from legitimate businesses. We can filter it out and we can get off mailing lists. Some telemarketers ignore the law, and many robocalls slip through exceptions in the law. People promoting fraudulent "get rich quick" schemes clearly do not care about what is legal and are not likely to obey laws to identify themselves. Laws like CAN-SPAM make it easier to fine or jail them by convicting them of violating antispam regulations in cases where there is insufficient evidence for convictions based on fraudulent content in the messages.[*] Is this a benefit or a threat to free speech and due process?

Because antispam laws must avoid conflicts with freedom of speech, and because the most abusive spammers ignore laws, laws can reduce spam but are not likely to eliminate the problem.

3.2.5 Challenging Old Regulatory Structures and Special Interests

Most people would not consider ads for wine and real estate on the Web to be offensive material. However, special interest groups tried to remove them. Such

---

[*]Prohibition-era gangster Al Capone went to jail for income-tax evasion because prosecutors could not convict him of other crimes.

groups lobby (often successfully) for laws to restrict uses of new technologies that they see as threats to their income and influence. Most of the cases we discuss here have free speech implications. Several involve regulatory laws that restrict advertising and sales on the Web. Such regulations have noble purposes, such as protecting the public from fraud. But, they also have the effect of entrenching the already powerful, keeping prices high, and making it more difficult for new and small businesses or independent voices to flourish.

Several companies sell self-help software to assist people in writing wills, premarital agreements, and many other legal documents. The software includes legal forms and instructions for filling them out. This is a typical example of the Web empowering ordinary people and reducing our dependence on expensive experts. A Texas judge banned Quicken legal software from Texas with the argument that the software amounted to practicing law without a Texas license. The Texas legislature later changed its law to exempt software publishers.

When people started publishing online newsletters about certain types of investments, they discovered that they were violating 25-year-old regulations requiring government licenses. License requirements included fees, fingerprinting, a background check, and presenting a list of subscribers on demand to the Commodity Futures Trading Commission (CFTC), the federal agency that administers the regulations. Publishers who did not register with the CFTC could be fined up to $500,000 and jailed up to five years. The stringent regulations were designed for traders who handle other people's money, but the CFTC applied them to people selling investment newsletters or software to analyze commodity futures markets. A federal judge ruled that the CFTC regulations were a prior restraint on speech and violated the First Amendment both for Internet publishers and for traditional newsletter publishers. By raising an issue of free speech on the Web, this case led to termination of a long-standing unconstitutional restraint of free speech in traditional media as well.[33] The ruling may have reduced the protection for investors against receiving poor investment advice, a worrisome result for some because people generally place faith in experts and the answers they get from computer software. In Chapter 7, we consider the problems of unreliable information on the Web and how to determine what to believe.

The Web provides the potential for reducing prices for many products by eliminating the "middleman." Small producers, who cannot afford expensive distributors or wholesalers, can sell directly to consumers nationwide. But not if the business was a small winery. Thirty states in the United States had laws restricting the shipping of out-of-state wines directly to consumers. The laws protected large wholesaling businesses that typically get 18–25% of the price and buy mostly from large wineries or those that sell expensive wines. The laws also protected state revenue; state governments cannot collect sales taxes on many out-of-state sales. State governments argued that the laws prevented sales to minors. This was a weak argument in states that permit direct shipments from in-state wineries. New York also banned *advertising* out-of-state wines directly to consumers in the state.

A winery that advertised its wines on the Web ran a risk because the website was accessible to consumers in New York. Winery operators challenged the New York wine law, arguing that it unconstitutionally restricted freedom of speech, interfered with interstate commerce, and discriminated against out-of-state businesses.[34] The Supreme Court ruled that bans on out-of-state shipments directly to consumers were unconstitutional.

If you are a business that makes a product, can you tell people where your product is sold? Can you put a list on your website of retail locations that sell the product? Many businesses do, but Texas prohibited beer makers from doing so. A judge ruled that the prohibition violated the First Amendment.[35]

The governments of California and New Hampshire attempted to require that operators of websites like ForSaleByOwner.com get state real estate licenses in those states because they list homes for sale within the states. The license requirements are irrelevant and expensive for such sites, and state laws allow newspapers to publish real estate ads, both in print and on their websites, without a real estate license. Federal courts ruled that these requirements for real estate licenses violate the First Amendment rights of website operators. The rulings protect the same First Amendment rights for websites as for older media and also reduce the powers of a special interest (in this case, real estate brokers) to restrict competition.

A law in France prohibits stores from giving big discounts on printed books. Small book sellers asked the French government for similar regulation for ebooks. Perhaps the popularity of ebooks and discounts will lead to reversal of the old law restricting discounts of printed books.

3.3 Decisions about Legal but Objectionable Content

> *Free speech is enhanced by civility.*
>
> —Tim O'Reilly[36]

Policies of large companies

Most of our discussion so far focused on issues related to censorship laws—laws prohibiting distribution of or access to certain kinds of material. In Section 3.2.4, we began to consider issues raised when large companies or organizations block messages, many of which are legal. In this section, we continue the discussion of legal content that is sensitive or objectionable. We focus on policy issues for large online companies that millions of people use daily and that thus have significant social influence. Here are examples to give an idea of the wide variety of types of content that some companies block in some way.

- Google will not take ads for firearms, tobacco, or high-interest payday loans.
- Facebook removes what it considers to be hate speech and violent or graphic images. It also closes accounts of terrorists and friends of terrorists who

appear to be supporting terrorism. Microsoft prohibits hate speech, advocacy of violence, and terrorist content on its online services.

- For a short while, Facebook blocked images of mothers breast-feeding, because some members complained the images were obscene.

- Many auction sites prohibit sales of some kinds of legal products. eBay does not allow the Confederate flag or other items bearing images of the flag.

- An online news and entertainment company refused to run ads for one of the major political parties in a presidential campaign.

- Google banned search results for an entire domain whose users were suspected of posting child pornography there.

- Some companies prohibit or decline to sell or advertise or provide search results for legal "adult" entertainment material, bomb-making information, Nazi materials and other forms of hate speech, revenge pornography,* personal information about other people, and information that might be of use to terrorists.

And here are a few examples of material that such companies allow, although some people think they should not.

- YouTube allows videos about religions that some consider offensive (for example, anti-Muslim and anti-Semitic videos) or graphic violence that would be illegal on broadcast television.

- A satellite view in Google maps shows the South Korean presidential house clearly. The South Korean government wants the site, and sites of power plants and military installations, camouflaged for security.

Whatever policy a company adopts, it will likely face much criticism. When Yahoo expanded its online store for adult material (erotica, sex videos, and so forth—all legal), many users complained. Critics objected that because Yahoo is a large, mainstream company, its action gave acceptability to pornography. Yahoo reversed policy and removed ads for adult material. This brought complaints from other people that the company had "caved in" to pressure from its mainstream advertisers and users.

Does the legal right of adults to purchase, read, or view something (a negative right, to be free from arrest) impose an ethical or social obligation on a business to allow it on their systems? As the examples above suggest, we are focusing, mostly, on very large companies like Google, Facebook, Craigslist, Amazon, or Yahoo that provide news, entertainment, Web hosting, social networking, advertising, email services, photo storage, and so on, to many millions of people. The main

---

*Revenge pornography refers to sexually explicit images uploaded to the Internet with the purpose of embarrassing or humiliating the person in the images (often an ex-partner). Some states have laws against it but not all.

justification for an affirmative answer, that is, opposition to restrictions on legal content, is the view that the effect of large, influential businesses banning any legal material is similar to government censorship. Although there are significant differences from government censorship—a government ban is universal and violators are fined or jailed—the decisions of such widely used sites, tools, and venues do have an enormous impact. On the other hand, in a free society where the government does not decide what we can read or view, it is more important for sellers and online service providers to take seriously their role and responsibility in deciding what material they will make available—in part *because* they are so influential. Recognition of antisocial or risky uses of some material might lead to ethical decisions to decline to allow it.

How broad should content bans be? Should a company ban a very small number of categories of really bad material (perhaps terrorist content, inciting violence, and hate speech), or should it ban more, perhaps material that might offend some groups of users but not a majority? Should it implement biases of the founders or leaders of the company, or strive to avoid such biases? It is reasonable that answers to these questions might differ for, say, search engines and hosted content. How should a search engine respond to a search for graphic pictures of torture by a government or by terrorists? The role of a widely used search engine is different from hosting video on a company site or hosting a social network. With a search engine, we want a wide search, sometimes to find news and unpleasant facts. We do not want search engines to discriminate against unpopular opinions and controversial material. It is reasonable that a search engine policy be less restrictive than policies for other services. Microsoft, for example, removes links to terrorist content from its Bing search engine only when the content is illegal, but it applies a stricter standard on its own online services such as cloud storage and email.

How wide should the category of banned hate speech be? Is an article in support of the death penalty for homosexuality in some Muslim countries—or an article in support of the condemnation of homosexuality in the Christian Bible—an example of hate speech or an expression of religious freedom? An organization set up two similar inflammatory Facebook pages, one anti-Palestinian and one anti-Israel. After both were reported to Facebook as objectionable content, Facebook removed one but not the other. Is that reasonable? How can bias be reduced?

Google's ban on ads for payday loans raises questions about how far such a company should go in promoting specific social policies through its ad policies. Payday loans are short term (e.g., a few weeks or months), high-interest (often more than 100% on a yearly basis) loans of small amounts (e.g., a few hundred dollars). Customers tend to be low-income people without credit cards and without home equity, people who cannot qualify for standard bank loans. Some see the loans as an option for these customers, and some see the loans as exploiting them. At the time Google imposed the ad ban, its parent company, Alphabet, was an investor in a loan company. The point here is not to decide whether these loans are good or bad. It is to recognize the broad range of content that could be banned—from terrorist content to products and services that have both advantages and disadvantages—and to think about appropriate policies for such influential companies.

We have asked more questions than we have answered. Some of the questions are intrinsically hard ones; we cannot cite a law or a clear ethical principle that produces an answer in each case. But as companies with a large online presence take responsibility for the content available to their members and the public, they must grapple with these questions.

A website with risks

Consider websites an individual or small organization might set up. To make the discussion concrete, we consider a site about suicide for terminally ill patients in constant, severe pain. The points we raise here apply to other kinds of sensitive information as well. What should the site organizers consider?* First, even if the site is not advertised, search engines will find it. Depressed teenagers and depressed adults will find it. What we put on a public website is public, available to everyone worldwide. The organizers should think about potential risks and research them. Then what? One option is to decide not to set up the site at all. Suppose the site organizers decide to proceed because they believe their plan has significant value for the intended audience. What can they do to reduce risks? Perhaps require a password to access the site. How would someone obtain a password? Would a simple waiting period reduce the risk for temporarily depressed people? Would the password requirement discourage access by intended users because of privacy concerns? Do you have an ethical responsibility to avoid helping 15-year-olds commit suicide? Can you assume they would find the information to do so somewhere else and that the responsibility to decide is theirs? Do you have an ethical responsibility to help a terminally ill person in pain to commit suicide? Or will your site offer a service some people want but with risks to others that you need to minimize?

People who post risky material have an ethical responsibility to seriously consider questions such as these. The answers are not obvious or easy. Freedom of speech is not the deciding factor.

Whether thinking about setting up a website with sensitive information or thinking about passing along a funny but embarrassing video of a friend, we sum up a few guidelines:

- Consider potential risks.
- Consider unintended readers or users.
- Consider ways to prevent access by unintended users.
- Remember that it can be difficult to withdraw material once released.

---

*Some people consider suicide itself, and any encouragement of it, to be immoral. For the sake of this discussion, we assume the people setting up the site do not.

3.4   Leaking Sensitive Material

The Web is a convenient and powerful tool for whistleblowers. People can anonymously post documents and make them available to the world. Small organizations and large news companies set up websites specifically to receive and publish leaked documents. Corruption and abuse of power in businesses and governments are common topics. Some leaks serve valuable social purposes. On the other hand, because it is easy to leak a large cache of someone else's documents, people sometimes do so carelessly. Sensitive material, leaked irresponsibly, can harm innocent people.

Throughout, we should remember that leaking begins with a strong ethical case against it. Leaked documents are often obtained by hacking into someone else's computer or by an insider who violates a confidentiality agreement. The documents belong to someone; they are being stolen or used without the owner's permission. A leak can cause serious damage to a person or organization without their doing anything wrong. Freedom of speech and of the press do not legitimize stealing files and publishing them, nor do they excuse acting irresponsibly. This does not mean that leaking is always wrong or that publishing leaked material is wrong. Instead, the reasons for leaking the material must be strong enough to overcome the ethical arguments against it, and the publisher of the leaked material must handle it responsibly.

To analyze the ethics of leaks, we consider the type of material released, the value to society, and the risks to society and innocent individuals. We also look at additional issues related to release of very large numbers of documents and some responsibilities of anyone setting up a site to accept and publish leaked material.

Documents that include significant evidence of serious wrongdoing are reasonable candidates for leaks. Wrongdoing might be corruption; political repression; mass murder by armies in international (or internal) wars; serious violations of laws or professional ethics; safety lapses in large systems that affect the public; dishonest practices by a business, scientists, or police; and cover-ups of such activities—to cite just a few categories. Another class of documents describes internal discussions and decision making in businesses, organizations, or governments, and candid reports on products and events. There is justification for leaking these if they provide evidence of wrongdoing or risk, but not merely to embarrass people or damage a competitor or organization one disapproves of.

In recent years, massive amounts of confidential or secret information have been exposed to the public through news organizations and websites, such as WikiLeaks, that are set up specifically to publish leaked or stolen information of significance. In this discussion, we present several controversial examples that are too broad and complex to fully analyze here. They help to illustrate the questions to consider when evaluating leaks, and—we hope—generate more discussion. Two of these examples involve release of thousands of emails; two involve U.S. military and national security documents; and one involves the exposure of private records from a law firm.

In the first case, an unknown hacker copied thousands of emails and other documents from the Climate Research Unit (CRU) at the University of East Anglia in England, one of the major centers of research on global warming; the incident has been called "Climategate."[37] The emails showed that researchers at the University of East Anglia pursued a variety of methods to deny access to their temperature data by scientists who question some aspects of climate change, a violation of scientific practice. The documents described efforts to stop scientific journals from publishing papers by those scientists and to attack the reputations of some of them. Some emails discussed criticisms and uncertainties related to details of the argument that human activity causes global warming. Researchers discuss such uncertainties in papers and conferences, but news reports often exclude them. Investigations by the British government and other groups concluded that the research center had broken Britain's Freedom of Information Act. The reports criticized various procedures the research group used but not its scientific conclusions. Is it important for the public to know what is in the emails? What criteria argue for or against this leak?

Chelsea (then Bradley) Manning, when a member of the U.S. Army, copied a large set of U.S. military and diplomatic documents and videos related to the wars in Iraq and Afghanistan, including videos of shooting incidents. WikiLeaks made them public. When a long, costly war is controversial, does the public have a right to see the internal reports and vivid video that can inform, but potentially enflame, the debate? Manning gave WikiLeaks a set of roughly 250,000 confidential U.S. diplomatic cables that included, among much else, discussions of the personalities of foreign leaders. Many of the cables were parts of normal discussions that happen privately and precede public policy development. Does the value of informing the public outweigh the value of confidential, frank internal discussion when developing diplomatic policies?

National Security Agency (NSA) contractor Edward Snowden passed thousands of documents to a reporter that showed the extent to which the NSA was spying on U.S. citizens, citizens of other countries, and leaders of many other countries. As we described in Section 2.4.5, the public discovered that many communications and large amounts of data previously thought private were captured and processed by the NSA. In many of these cases, the NSA overstepped its authority, pressuring telecommunications companies to hand over data on phone calls or going beyond the authority given to it by the Foreign Intelligence Surveillance Court. The range of viewpoints about Snowden's leak is illustrated by these responses: An organization founded by a retired CIA officer gave Snowden its award for integrity and ethics in intelligence work, and the U.S. government indicted Snowden for espionage. Is Snowden a hero or a traitor or—considering the amount and variety of the material he leaked—did he do some good and some bad?

A hacker obtained more than 11 million documents from the Panamanian law firm Mossack Fonseca, referred to as the "Panama Papers" or the "Mossack Fonseca papers."[38] The documents showed that the firm helped people, including more than a hundred heads-of-state and political officials or members of their families from dozens of countries, create offshore companies and other entities to store or invest large amounts of money. In many cases, the money likely came from corruption; in some it was legitimately earned or inherited. Some documents indicated laundering drug money, arms dealing, tax evasion, fraud, and so on. There are legitimate uses for offshore companies, and some documents revealed legal, private, financial transactions of people who earn a lot of money in sports, business, and other fields. Several countries began investigations based on information in the leak; others (e.g., Russia and China) reacted by suppressing news of the documents.

During the 2016 presidential election campaigns, WikiLeaks released tens of thousands of emails hacked from the Democratic National Committee (DNC) and an email account of Clinton campaign chair John Podesta.[39] The DNC is supposed to be neutral with respect to its own party candidates during the primaries; the emails show that it worked to undermine the Bernie Sanders campaign. The U.S. government blamed the DNC email hack on the Russian government and argued that the purpose was to influence the presidential election.[40] Julian Assange, head of WikiLeaks, argued that the emails were significant as news, showing that the DNC attempted to influence the primary elections.[41] The Podesta emails disclosed internal campaign discussions and planning, with some embarrassing elements (e.g., disrespect for Catholics and indications that someone leaked questions to Clinton in advance of a CNN program). Were these emails unusual or important enough for WikiLeaks to publish?

Releasing a huge mass of documents

In the spirit of the Web, leakers can let the public search through huge caches of documents for those of special interest. This can be valuable, but it can be wrong. Recall that an important ethical justification for leaking documents that belong to someone else is that the leaker knows they contain information the public should see. If a significant amount of the information does not meet the criteria for ethical leaking, then it may be hard to justify publishing the entire set of documents. The documents might be interesting to the public, but in most cases that is not sufficient justification. On the other hand, selective disclosure can distort information by presenting it without context; selection must be done carefully.

The five major leaks we are using as examples each included thousands or hundreds of thousands of documents. Did the leakers or publishers of the documents review and evaluate them to be sure they met reasonable criteria to justify the leaks and publication? It appears that some groups that publish leaks do attempt to select what to publish. For example, there were indications that names were removed from some documents WikiLeaks published; the leaker of the Climategate emails removed some personal contact information and other personal information in the emails; and the International Consortium of Investigative Journalists (ICIJ), the organization that reviewed and released some of the Mossack Fonseca documents, took more than a year to review the documents before simultaneously publishing a selected set on several news sites. Yet, still, much was published that should not have been. The published DNC and Podesta emails included many private communications.

Potentially dangerous leaks

WikiLeaks released a secret U.S. government cable listing critical sites, such as telecommunications hubs, dams, pipelines, supplies of critical minerals, manufacturing complexes, and so on, where damage or disruption would cause significant harm. Some might defend publication of the list by arguing that it encourages better protection of the sites or that terrorists already know about the sites, but the risks seem to overwhelm any public value of this leak. Other documents detailed discussions between U.S. government officials and an opposition leader in a country with a very repressive government. Some cables named whistleblowers, confidential informants, human rights activists, intelligence officers, and Chinese people (in business, academia, and the Chinese government) who provided information about social and political conditions in China. The release of these documents put those people at risk. Other documents named people who escaped from repressive countries, potentially endangering their families. Some leaks do not endanger lives, but they infringe privacy or threaten people's jobs, reputations, freedom, and other values.[42] Those who provide leaked material and those who publish it have an ethical responsibility to avoid or minimize harm to innocent people, but often the providers and publishers do not meet that responsibility sufficiently.

More ethical considerations

Privacy and confidentiality are important to individuals and to the legitimate functioning of businesses and governments. Privacy and confidentiality are not absolute rights, but they are significant values. Leakers have as much ethical responsibility to respect privacy (even for people they dislike or disagree with) as do governments and businesses. Thus, justification for overriding privacy and publishing confidential documents should be strong and reasonably specific.

Attorney–client confidentiality and attorney–client privilege are principles that protect communications between an attorney and a client and protect various documents related to the attorney's work for the client. These principles are considered important for both innocent and guilty people. Should an even stronger standard than usual be applied when considering release of documents stolen from a law firm? Does the ICIJ's desire to expose what it called a "shadowy offshore industry" in the Mossack Fonseca leak override the privacy of the attorney–client relationship, especially for those people who were doing nothing wrong?

Leaking of government documents is another special case. In some ways it is more justifiable to leak or publish government documents; in other ways it is less justifiable. The public has a reasonable claim to a right to know what is being done in its name and with its money. On the other hand, criminal investigations and national security often require secrecy. Many states and free countries have laws requiring disclosure of certain public records and laws such as the Freedom of Information Act that allow public access to government documents in many situations. The legal processes can be tedious and ineffective sometimes, but the processes should be tried, if they apply, before resorting to hacking to get files or before obtaining them from an insider. Sometimes, leaks may be the only way to expose corruption and cover-ups.

When evaluating the ethics of leaking documents on political or highly politicized issues, it can be difficult to make judgments that are independent of our views on the issues themselves. Some people believe that our judgments of the leaks should *not* be independent of the issues: If we oppose U.S. foreign policy, the Manning leaks are good. If we believe climate change is human caused and a serious threat, the climate research leaks are bad. Of course, if we hold the opposite views, we might come to the opposite conclusions. This does not help us to develop good criteria for evaluating the ethics of leaking and for guiding us if we come to have access to sensitive data. We can make a much stronger case for ethical criteria by which to evaluate leaks if we are willing to apply the same criteria to leaking similar material on both sides of a political issue.

Responsibilities of operators of websites for leaks

Suppose a person or organization decides to establish a site to publish leaked documents that serve an important public purpose. In addition to giving serious consideration to the various points we have raised, the site operators have responsibilities to avoid abuse of the site. The site must have sufficient security to protect the whistleblowers—the people who supply the documents. The operators should have a well-thought-out policy about how to handle requests or demands from law enforcement agencies (of various countries) for the identity of a person supplying documents. The intent of some leaks is to sabotage a competitor or a political opponent. Verification of the authenticity and validity of leaked documents can be difficult, but it is a responsibility of the site operators. Serious harm to innocent individuals, businesses, economies, and communities can result from publishing inaccurate or forged documents and sometimes from authentic but maliciously leaked documents.

As a German newspaper observed, "When delicate information is at stake, great prudence is demanded so that the information doesn't fall into the wrong hands and so that people are not hurt."[43] Freedom of speech and of the press leave us with the ethical responsibility for what we say and publish.

3.5 Anonymity

The Colonial press was characterized by irregular appearance, pseudony-mous invective, and a boisterous lack of respect for any form of government.

—"Science, Technology, and the First Amendment,"
U.S. Office of Technology Assessment[44]

Common Sense

From the description quoted above, the Colonial press—the press the authors of the First Amendment to the U.S. Constitution found it so important to protect—had a lot in common with the early Internet, including controversy about anonymity.

Jonathan Swift published his political satire *Gulliver's Travels* anonymously. Thomas Paine's name did not appear on the first printings of *Common Sense*, the book that roused support for the American Revolution. *The Federalist Papers*, published in newspapers in 1787 and 1788, argued for adoption of the new U.S. Constitution. The authors, Alexander Hamilton, James Madison, and John Jay, had already served the newly free confederation of states in important roles. Jay later became chief justice of the Supreme Court, Hamilton the first secretary of the Treasury, and Madison president. But when they wrote the Federalist Papers, they used a pseudonym, Publius. Opponents of the Constitution, those who believed it gave too much power to the federal government, used pseudonyms as well. In the 19th century, when it was not considered proper for women to write books, writers such as Mary Ann Evans and Amantine Lucile Aurore Dupin published under male pseudonyms, or pen names (George Eliot and George Sand). Prominent profes-sional and academic people use pseudonyms to publish murder mysteries, science fiction, or other nonscholarly work, and some writers—for example, the iconoclas-tic H. L. Mencken—used pseudonyms for the fun of it.

Positive uses of anonymity

Anonymous pamphleteering is not a pernicious, fraudulent practice, but an honorable tradition of advocacy and of dissent. Anonymity is a shield from the tyranny of the majority.

—U.S. Supreme Court[45]

Although the First Amendment provides constitutional protection for political speech, there are still many ways in which the government can retaliate against its critics. On the Internet, people talk about personal topics such as health, gambling habits, problems with teenage children, religion, and so on. Victims of rape and of other kinds of violence and abuse and users of illegal drugs who are trying to quit are among those who benefit from a forum where they can talk candidly without giving away their identity. (Traditional in-person support and counseling groups use only first names, to protect privacy.) Whistleblowers, reporting on unethical or illegal activities where they work, may choose to release information anonymously. In wartime and in countries with oppressive governments, anonymity can be a life-or-death issue. In all these situations, anonymity provides protection against retaliation or embarrassment.

Businesses provide a variety of sophisticated anonymity tools and services such as anonymous email that reporters, human rights activists, and ordinary people use. The founder of a company that provided anonymous Web-surfing services said the company developed tools to help people in Iran, China, and Saudi Arabia get around their governments' restrictions on Internet access.[46] Many people use anonymous Web browsers to thwart the efforts of businesses to collect information about their Web activity and build dossiers for marketing purposes.

We might think the main benefit of anonymizing services is protection for individuals—protecting privacy, protecting against identity theft and consumer profiling, and protecting against oppressive governments. However, businesses, law enforcement agencies, and government intelligence services also need to use the Internet anonymously. If a competitor of a company can get logs of websites that the company's employees visit, the competitor may be able to figure out what new products the company is planning. Thus, a business might route its Internet traffic through a service that encrypts and forwards web traffic to conceal identities.

Anonymous remailer services

Johan Helsingius set up the first well-known anonymous email service in Finland in 1993. (Users were not entirely anonymous; the system retained identifying information.) Helsingius originally intended his service for users in the Scandinavian countries. However, it was extremely popular and grew to an estimated 500,000 users worldwide. Helsingius became a hero to dissidents in totalitarian countries and to free speech and privacy supporters everywhere. He closed his service in 1996 after the Church of Scientology and the government of Singapore took action to obtain the names of people using it, but by then, many other similar services were available.

To send anonymous email using a "remailer" service, one sends the message to the remailer, where the return address and other identifying information is stripped off and the message is re-sent to the intended recipient. Messages can be routed through many intermediate destinations to more thoroughly obscure their origins. If someone wants to remain anonymous but receive replies, he or she can use a service where a coded ID number is attached to the message when the remailer sends it. The ID assigned by the remailer is a pseudonym for the sender, which the remailer stores. Replies go to the remailer site, which forwards them to the original person.

After leaking NSA documents (see Section 2.3.5 and Section 3.4), Edward Snowden used the encrypted email service Lavabit to hide his location. The owner and operator, Ladar Levison, shut down the site after the federal government ordered him to turn over the site's encryption keys as part of its investigation of Snowden. Releasing these keys would have exposed all Lavabit users and violated their confidentiality.

Suppose law enforcement agents suspect a site contains child pornography, terrorist information, copyright-infringing material, or anything else relevant to an investigation. If investigators visit the site from their department computers, the site may display a bland page with nothing illegal. Also, when law enforcement agents go "under cover" and pretend to be a member or potential victim of an online criminal group, they do not want their IP address to expose them. A senior CIA official explained the CIA's use of anonymity services online: "We want to operate anywhere on the Internet in a way that no one knows the CIA is looking at them."[47]

Negative uses of anonymity

Anonymity in cyberspace protects criminal and antisocial activities. People use it for fraud, harassment, and extortion, to distribute child pornography, to hack, to libel or threaten others with impunity, to steal confidential business documents or other proprietary information, and to infringe copyrights. Anonymous postings can spread false rumors that seriously damage a business, manipulate stock, or incite violence, and terrorists use anonymity to plan attacks. Anonymity makes it difficult to track wrongdoers and, thus, poses challenges to law enforcement and our security. It can also mask illegal surveillance by government agencies—or legal but repressive surveillance in unfree countries.

Because of its potential to shield criminal activity or because they consider it incompatible with politeness and netiquette (online etiquette), some services and online communities choose to discourage or prohibit anonymity.

Is anonymity protected?

For those not using true anonymity services, secrecy of our identity in cyberspace depends on both the privacy policies of service providers and those of the sites we visit—and on the laws and court decisions about granting subpoenas for disclosure. How well protected are our real identities? How strongly should they be protected?

A business or organization can try to get a subpoena ordering an ISP or website to disclose a person's real identity. In some cases, businesses seek names of people who post criticism, protected by the First Amendment, but who might be employees whom the business would fire. In some cases, businesses seek the names of people who post negative and, according to the business, fraudulent reviews on sites such as Yelp. We are not exempt from ordinary ethics and laws merely because we use the Internet or sign comments with an alias rather than a real name. How do we protect free speech and criticism while allowing a way to hold people responsible for illegal speech? Many state courts have begun to establish and follow guidelines for granting subpoenas. One guideline is that they examine the individual case to determine if the evidence is strong enough that the person or organization requesting the identity is likely to win a lawsuit (for, say, defamation)—and only then issue a subpoena for the person's real name. In a case where an anonymous commenter posted a statement implying that a local political candidate was a sexual predator who abused children, a court granted the candidate a subpoena to get identifying information from Comcast so he could sue for defamation. Free speech advocates recommend that Web companies be required to notify a member when they receive a subpoena for the member's identity so that the person has an opportunity to fight the subpoena in court.

Many legal issues about anonymity are similar to those in the law enforcement controversies we discuss in Chapters 2 and 5. Law enforcement agencies have been able to trace many criminal suspects through the Web. Should it be the responsibility of law enforcement to develop tools to find criminals who hide behind anonymity, or should the task be made easier by requiring that we identify ourselves? Does the potential for harm by criminals who use anonymity outweigh the loss of privacy and restraint on freedom of speech for honest people who use anonymity responsibly? Is anonymity an important protection against possible abuse of government power? Should people have the right to use available tools, including anonymizers, to protect their privacy?

> *An instance of the inexplicable conservatism and arrogance of the Turkish customs authorities was recently evidenced by the prohibition of the importation of typewriters into the country. The reason advanced by the authorities for this step is that typewriting affords no clew to the author, and that therefore in the event of seditious or opprobrious pamphlets or writings executed by the typewriter being circulated it would be impossible to obtain any clew by which the operator of the machine could be traced. . . . The same decree also applies to mimeograph and other similar duplicating machines and mediums.*
>
> —*Scientific American*, July 6, 1901[48]

3.6 The Global Net: Censorship and Political Freedom

> *To suppress free speech is a double wrong. It violates the rights of the hearer as well as those of the speaker.*
>
> —Frederick Douglass, 1860[49]

3.6.1 TOOLS FOR COMMUNICATION, TOOLS FOR OPPRESSION

> *As women get greater exposure to media, to technology, there is greater realization of their rights.*
>
> —Zohra Yusuf, chairwoman of the Human Rights Commission of Pakistan[50]

> *The coffee houses emerged as the primary source of news and rumor. In 1675, Charles II, suspicious as many rulers are of places where the public trades information, shut the coffee houses down.*
>
> —Peter L. Bernstein[51]

Authoritarian governments have taken steps to cut, or seriously reduce, the flow of information and opinion throughout history.* The vibrant communication made possible by the Internet threatens governments in countries that lack political and cultural freedom. For a long time, the "conventional wisdom" among users and observers of the Internet was that it is a protection against censorship and a tool for increased political freedom. Email and fax machines played a significant role during the collapse of the Soviet Union and the democracy demonstrations in China's Tiananmen Square. Websites with content that is illegal in one country can be set up in some other country. People in countries whose governments censor news can access information over the Web from elsewhere. Facebook and mobile phones were key tools in organizing the 2011 Arab Spring. Dissidents in Iran, Vietnam, various Middle Eastern countries, and elsewhere use Skype and WhatsApp to communicate because of the strong encryption in these applications.

Unfortunately, but not surprisingly, oppressive governments learned and adopted countermeasures to block the flow of information. They use sophisticated interception and surveillance technologies to spy on their citizens more thoroughly than before. In the rest of this section, we describe censorship and interception tools and policies that oppressive regimes (and some democracies) use.

In countries such as China and Saudi Arabia, where the national government owns the Internet backbone (the communications lines and computers through which people access information), the governments install their own computers between their people and the outside world and use sophisticated firewalls and filters to block what they do not want their people to see. Many countries in the Middle East limit Internet access. The government of Saudi Arabia blocks pornography and gambling, as many countries might, but it also blocks sites on the Bahai faith, the Holocaust, and religious conversion of Muslims to other faiths. And to maintain this control, it blocks sites with information about anonymizers, tools to thwart filters, and encryption.

Turkey and Pakistan banned YouTube for several years. Pakistan banned Internet telephony, and Turkey blocked Twitter after circulation of corruption charges against the Prime Minister. Burma (Myanmar) banned use of the Internet or creation of Web pages without official permission, and banned posting of material about politics, as well as posting of any material deemed by the government to be harmful to its policies. (Under an earlier law, possession of an unauthorized modem or satellite dish was punishable by a jail term of up to 15 years.) Vietnam uses filtering software to find and block anticommunist messages coming from other countries. Two songwriters received multiyear jail sentences in Vietnam for posting songs online that the government considered to be critical of the government.†

---

*In Poland, for example, before the communist government fell in 1989, it was illegal to make a photocopy without permission from government censors. Other governments have banned satellite dishes and residential telephones.

†Where the technology has not caught up, governments restrict old communications media. A rival of Zimbabwe's president Robert Mugabe in Zimbabwe's 2001 presidential election was charged with possession of an unlicensed two-way radio.

Incamerastock/Alamy Stock Photo

FIGURE 3.2 What will this search turn up?

Some countries ban Skype while others subvert it. The Egyptian government, for example, used spyware to intercept Skype communications. They planted spyware on people's computers to intercept communication before it was encrypted on the sender's computer or after it was decrypted on the recipient's computer.[52] Later, they worked with security companies to monitor Facebook, Twitter, Skype, and WhatsApp communications.

In China and other repressive countries, governments are struggling with the difficulties of modernizing their economies and technology while maintaining tight control over information. With hundreds of millions of Web users, the Chinese government strictly controls and censors what people read and post online. Chinese regulations prohibit "producing, retrieving, duplicating, and spreading information that may hinder public order." Banned or censored sites and topics have included Facebook, Google, Wikipedia, the *New York Times*, discussion of democracy, religious sites, human rights organizations, news and commentary about Taiwan and Tibet, information about censorship (and how to evade it), economic news, and reports of major accidents or natural disasters and outbreaks of diseases. When Chinese citizens began texting to communicate about banned topics, the government set up a system to filter the messages. After ethnic protests turned violent in one region, China cut communications and then blocked Internet access in the region for 10 months. China banned any reports or discussion of the Mossack Fonseca papers (see Section 3.4) from all websites since the documents showed family members of top government officials had secret bank accounts outside the country. The government employs more than two million people to monitor websites, microblogs, and social media, and in an attempt to tighten control over access to information by its citizens, the government began requiring that all online content be hosted on servers within China.[53]

The government of Iran, at various times, blocked Amazon.com, Wikipedia, the *New York Times*, YouTube, and a site advocating the end of the practice of stoning women. Reporters Without Borders said that Iran blocked access to more than five million websites in recent years. Generally, the government says it blocks websites and jams satellite TV broadcasts to keep out decadent Western culture. The Iranian government uses sophisticated online surveillance tools and trained cyber police to spy on dissidents by, among other techniques, examining individual packets of email, phone conversations, images, social network communications, and so forth.

In some countries, government agents, using social media, pretend to be dissidents and distribute information about planned protests; the police arrest anyone who comes. Some governments have intercepted communications and used spyware on sites such as Facebook and Yahoo to collect passwords, find the names of dissident bloggers, and take down pages critical of the government. Some governments (e.g., China, Iran, Russia, and Vietnam) ban or discourage email services and social networking sites based in the West and set up their own—which, of course, they control. Russia requires that foreign companies store user data for their Russian members and customers on servers within Russia.* Bloggers in Russia who have more than 3000 daily readers must register with the government and provide their home address. As we will see in Section 3.6.2, governments are increasingly using their leverage over companies that want to do business in their countries to enforce censorship requirements and other content standards.[54]

Will the Internet and related communications technologies be tools for increasing political freedom, or will they give more power to governments to spy on, control, and restrict their people?

> *The office of communications is ordered to find ways to ensure that the use of the Internet becomes impossible. The Ministry for the Promotion of Virtue and Prevention of Vice is obliged to monitor the order and punish violators.*
>
> —Excerpt from the Taliban edict banning all Internet use in Afghanistan[55]

---

*Some governments say that this requirement is a privacy protection for their citizens. However, it makes it easier for repressive governments to get information about online activities of dissidents.

3.6.2   Aiding Foreign Censors and Repressive Regimes

Freedom of expression isn't a minor principle that can be pushed aside when dealing with a dictatorship.

—Reporters Without Borders[56]

We're allowing too much, maybe, free speech in countries that haven't experienced it before.

—Adam Conner, a Facebook lobbyist[57]

Providing services, obeying local laws

Search engine companies, social media companies, and news and entertainment companies based in free countries offer services in countries with strict censorship and repressive governments. To operate within a country, companies must follow the laws of that country. What are the trade-offs between providing services to the people and complying with the government's censorship requirements? To what extent does, or should, the prospect of a huge business opportunity in a new country affect a company's decision? How do companies deal with the censorship requirements? What are their ethical responsibilities?

Google has long promoted the ideal of access to information and has usually refused to censor its search engine. In 2006, Google disappointed many free speech and human rights advocates by introducing a Chinese version in China, google.cn, that complied with Chinese law and did not show sites with banned content. The agreement to operate a censored version in China reflected the view that some access is better than no access. Google co-founder Sergey Brin, who was born in the Soviet Union and experienced totalitarian government, was uneasy with the decision. Google stopped operating the censored search engine in 2010. The main impetus for the change was a highly sophisticated hack attack originating in China on Google and about 30 other companies. A primary goal of the attack appeared to be access to Gmail accounts of Chinese human rights activists, angering Brin and others at Google. Google's initial refusal to censor, its reversal in 2006, and its reversal again in 2010 illustrate the difficulty of deciding how to deal with repressive governments.

Before Microsoft closed its MSN Web portal in China (in 2016), the company censored terms like "freedom" and "democracy" and shut down a Chinese journalist's blog that criticized the government. Yahoo's Chinese site complies with local law and omits news stories that offend the government. Yahoo provided information to the Chinese government that helped identify at least two people who were then jailed for pro-democracy writing. Yahoo said it was required to comply with Chinese law and the company had not been told the reason for the government request for the information.[58]

For Skype to operate in China, the Chinese government required Skype to work in a joint venture with a Chinese communications company (TOM), use a modified version of the Skype software, and filter out sensitive topics from text chat. According to a study by a Canadian university, the modified software allowed widespread surveillance, and TOM stored information from millions of messages.

When U.S. and other non-Chinese companies set up branches in China and comply with restrictive laws, should we view them as providing more access to information in China than would otherwise exist, albeit not as much as is technically possible? Should we view them as appropriately respecting the culture and laws of the host country? Should we view them as partners in the Chinese government's ethically unacceptable restrictions on debate and access to information by its citizens?

Mark Zuckerberg, CEO of Facebook, suggested that the advantages of social networking in China outweigh the restrictions. We can view this argument, similar to the arguments from other companies for complying with demands of authoritarian governments, as a utilitarian argument. If a company turns over the names of people who violate censorship laws, the government arrests a small number of dissidents, but a very large number of people benefit from the increased services and communications. If one considers longer-term effects, however, one must consider that the work of a small number of dissidents can have a huge impact on the freedom of the society as a whole. The arrest of a dissident might spur a protest ultimately bringing more freedom—or a brutal crackdown. A rights-based ethical system might accept providing a search or social media service that is somewhat limited. The people have the right (ethical, even if not legal) to seek and share information, but the service provider is not ethically obligated to provide it 100%. However, a rights-based view tells us it is wrong to help jail a person for expressing his views on politics or for criticizing the government. Should companies draw a line, perhaps agreeing to restrict access to information but refusing to disclose information that a government can use to jail someone for publishing his or her views? A government might need to identify a person whom it suspects of stalking, fraud, selling child pornography, or other crimes. A service provider might want to provide information in such criminal cases. If the government does not disclose the reason for a request, or is dishonest about the reason, how can a service provider make an ethical decision?

Selling surveillance tools

It is perhaps not surprising that repressive governments intercept communications and filter Internet content, but it is perhaps disturbing that companies in Western democracies (including England, Germany, France, and the United States) sell them the tools to do so. Companies sell governments sophisticated tools to filter Internet content, to hack smartphones and computers, to block text messages, to collect and analyze massive amounts of Internet data, to plant spyware and other malware (malicious software), to monitor social networks, and to track cellphone users. The companies say the tools are for criminal investigations (as well as for detecting and filtering undesirable content) and do not violate the laws of the country using them. Of course, countries with repressive governments have criminals and terrorists too. Do we trust these governments to use the tools only against the bad guys, in ways consistent with human rights? Is it ethical for companies in free countries to sell the tools to repressive governments?

> *We don't really get into asking, "Is this in the public interest?"*
>
> —An organizer of a trade show for companies selling
> hacking and interception gear to governments[59]

3.6.3 SHUTTING DOWN COMMUNICATIONS IN FREE COUNTRIES

Governments in relatively unfree countries that tightly control communications shut down access to the Internet or shut down mobile phone service now and then. These events evoke criticism in the free world, where few expected it could happen. Then the British government and some U.S. cities considered it, and the transit system in San Francisco blocked cellphone service for a few hours, raising new issues for communications in free countries. Giving governments authority to shut down communications poses obvious threats to freedom of speech, ordinary activities, and political liberty. Is it reasonable in limited situations when public safety is at risk? Does shutting communication services in free countries give excuses to dictators? Can we make a clear distinction between short-term responses to violent mobs in free countries and censorship and repression of political discussion in unfree countries? As background for thinking about these questions, we consider the incidents in Britain and the United States.

Mobs of hooligans (that old-fashioned word seems to fit) rampaged through neighborhoods in London and other British cities setting fires, looting businesses, and beating up people who tried to protect themselves or their property. They planned and coordinated their attacks using text messages, Twitter, BlackBerry Messenger, and similar tools. During the violence, people in the government (and others) argued that Research In Motion (then the name of the company that makes Blackberry devices) should shut down BlackBerry Messenger. (It did not.) After the riots, the British government considered seeking legislation authorizing it to shut down communications systems, including social media and messaging systems, in such situations. It decided, at least for the time being, not to seek this power.

Shortly after the violence in England, the Bay Area Rapid Transit system (BART) in the San Francisco Bay Area shut off wireless service in some of its subway stations after learning of a plan to "use mobile devices to coordinate. . . disruptive activities and communicate about the location and number of BART Police."[60] BART owns the communications equipment; it said its contracts with cell service companies allow it to shut off the service when it thinks necessary. The managers of a private business, expecting violence on or near their property, have the right to shut off their wireless service; refuse entry to anyone carrying, say, a baseball bat; or close up if they think it a wise measure to protect the public and the business. If BART were a private company, there would be arguments on both sides of the question of whether its action was wise, but it would not raise the First Amendment issues of a government-ordered shutdown. (Some of the arguments, and the distinction between government and private action, are similar to those concerning the right of a communications service to filter out spam; see Section 3.2.4.) BART is a government agency, but it shut down its own wireless service in its own space. Did it threaten freedom of speech, or was it a legitimate safety decision? How does this differ from Egypt shutting down Internet access during the 2011 Arab Spring uprisings?

Several U.S. cities that experienced coordinated violence considered laws to authorize government agencies to block communications, but none passed such laws. California instituted a requirement for a court order, with specific details and limitations, before police can block communications—with an exception for emergencies. Incidents such as those we described above occur with little warning and would likely be considered emergencies. Thus, laws such as California's might allow rather than prevent blocking of communications.

What can be done, short of shutting down communications, to reduce the use of social networks, mobile devices, etc., for planning mass violence? The membership policies of various social media companies ban threats of violence. Facebook, for example, monitors posts to enforce its ban, though some groups use code words to hide plans. The companies can close the accounts of those who violate the agreements, but it is unlikely that such companies would be able to act quickly enough to stop a violent event. In past riots, police have collected information from social media and phones of people they arrested, and in doing so, learned of plans for more violent attacks and were prepared to prevent them. While helpful, this also seems like weak protection. But what are the consequences of giving governments the authority to shut down communications? Police can abuse this power, preventing people from recording video of police activity, preventing legitimate protests and demonstrations, as repressive governments do. A large-scale shutdown would inconvenience (and possibly harm) innocent people. Would the U.S. Supreme Court declare unconstitutional a law that authorizes a government agency to order a private communications service to shut down?

> *It may be BART's equipment, but that doesn't mean that they have the freedom to do whatever they want to with it.*
>
> —Michael Risher, ACLU attorney[61]

3.7 Net Neutrality: Regulations or the Market?

What is net neutrality?

"Net neutrality" refers to a variety of proposals for restrictions on how telecommunications companies interact with their broadband customers (primarily for Internet services) and how they set charges for services. There are two different but related issues, sometimes blurred in the arguments: (1) whether the companies that provide the communications networks should be permitted to exclude or give different treatment to content based on the content itself, on the category of content, or on the company or organization that provides it, and (2) whether the companies that provide the communications networks should be permitted to offer content providers and individual subscribers different levels of speed and priority at different price levels. The latter is sometimes called "tiered" service—that is, different levels of service with different charges. The practice of exempting certain services or applications from mobile data charges or limits, called *zero-rating*, is an example of a nonneutral practice.

A simple statement of the net neutrality principle is that all Internet traffic should be treated the same. Advocates want governments to mandate that telecommunications companies treat all legal content that travels through their broadband lines and wireless networks the same way. Opponents want flexibility in the development of services and pricing schemes for content delivery.

Supporters of net neutrality argue that allowing communications companies to set varying rates for varying kinds of Internet access would be devastating as it would squeeze out independent voices and erode the diversity of the Internet. Only big companies and organizations would be able to afford the prices necessary to ensure that their content is included or moves fast enough to be relevant. Tiered access programs and zero-rating will give telecommunications companies too much power over content on the Internet, because communications companies could give special treatment to their own content providers or others they select. Supporters argue that tiered service is a threat to democratic participation and free speech online.

Although the debate is sometimes presented as big companies versus little voices, very large companies are on both sides of the debate, as are organizations and prominent people who want to preserve the openness and vitality of the Net. Internet content providers, individual bloggers, and companies such as eBay, Microsoft, Amazon, Netflix, Google, and Twitter support (or have supported) net neutrality rules. Major telecommunications companies, companies that offer flexible (nonneutral) services, and pro-free-market organizations oppose such rules.

Opponents of net neutrality requirements argue that such regulations slow the development of innovative services, the advance of high-speed Internet connections, and investment in infrastructure. Enforcing net neutrality is inconsistent with the Telecommunications Act of 1996, which says, "It is the policy of the United States . . . to preserve the vibrant and competitive free market that presently exists for the Internet and other interactive computer services, unfettered by Federal or State regulation."[62] Opponents see the lack of government gatekeepers and regulatory control as critical to the enormous growth in Internet services since 1996. Some who support free markets oppose mandated uniform pricing on principle, as an unethical interference in the free choices of sellers and buyers.

Offering different levels of service with different rates is not unusual and makes sense in many areas:

- We have a choice of paying standard delivery charges for products we buy online or paying extra for faster delivery.
- Power companies vary charges for electricity at different times of the day to encourage shifting use to off-peak hours.
- People pay to drive in express lanes on highways; the price may vary with the time of day and level of traffic.
- Many of us use the free but limited versions of a variety of online services such as cloud storage.
- Many businesses give large-quantity discounts.
- Some institutions and businesses—hospitals, for example—pay a higher rate for services such as electricity under contracts that guarantee higher priority for repairs or emergency service when necessary.

Do variable pricing and variable service schemes make sense for the Internet? Would it make sense for, say, medical monitoring data to have priority over other kinds of data? What about video? As of this writing, Netflix and YouTube comprise more than half of all Internet traffic. This raises a number of questions: Should video have high priority (like voice calls) because delays are annoying to the customer? Or, should video have lower priority because it uses so much bandwidth? Or should it be treated the same as all other traffic? Should Netflix and YouTube be required to pay additional fees because their high usage results in less bandwidth available to other sites and services? Or should they have the option to pay to receive higher priority transmission so that their viewers receive high-quality video?[*] This list of questions illustrates the many options possible. Should all but one of the options be prohibited by law? More fundamental questions are: Who should decide what services are provided and how they are priced—service providers and customers or Congress and the Federal Communications Commission (FCC)? Would extra charges for high-bandwidth services encourage development of more efficient delivery techniques? How, overall, would different responses to these questions affect innovation, access, the variety of content on the net, and efficient use of Internet resources?

Nonneutral Internet services

T-Mobile's Binge On feature allows subscribers to stream unlimited video from dozens of providers without incurring data charges. Video providers that are not

---

[*]For several years, Netflix reduced video streaming resolution for customers on some cellular networks so the customers would not exceed their data caps. This revelation led to criticism for hypocrisy because Netflix is a strong supporter of net neutrality.

included complained that it would be difficult for them to compete with the effectively free Binge On content. In another example, a few telecom companies have programs in which other businesses subsidize data charges for people who access their material, such as movie trailers and hotel websites. Sprint offered inexpensive plans with access to a few sites on a short list, including Facebook and Twitter but not all Internet sites. These programs violate the net neutrality principle. Are these plans analogous to other typical ways businesses try to attract customers (e.g., by offering free shipping), or do they give telecom companies too much power over content? Free Basics is a program established by Facebook to bring Internet access to poor people around the world. It includes hundreds of free apps and free but limited, low-data access to Internet sites that meet its requirements. (It does not include video, for example.) Certain telecom companies subsidize Free Basics access in the hopes that people who start using the Internet will later pay for full plans. It is controversial because it does not provide access to the entire Internet, and Facebook sets the standards for what is included. (One requirement is that apps must work on older phones with limited bandwidth.) As with Binge On, critics argue that Free Basics gives an advantage to the companies and services it includes.[*] Others critics refer to it as "digital colonialism," leading to an Internet controlled by a powerful U.S. company. Free Basics is available in more than 35 countries. It was available in India for about a year before the Indian government's Internet regulation agency banned it for violating India's net neutrality policy. The agency said that Internet companies should not "shape the users' Internet experience."[63]

Most of the examples above are examples of zero-rating. A few countries besides India have banned zero-rating programs. The controversies over zero-rating in general, and Free Basics in particular, raise many questions: Is partial free access better than none? Who benefits from free services? Who benefits from banning free services? Is the advantage that zero-rating provides to the included companies a significant one? If a publisher offered a large list of books to poor countries for free or at a reduced price, would we complain that they should not shape the people's reading experience? Will competition from the free or subsidized services push others out of business? What are the likely long-term effects on access to diverse Internet sites and apps in poor countries? Who should decide whether zero-rating services may be made available: government agencies or members of the public who can choose to use them or not?

Enforcing net neutrality

As of this writing, the U.S. Congress has not passed a law to require net neutrality or given the FCC power to do so. A federal court ruled at least twice (in 2010 and 2014) that the FCC did not have legal authority to impose net neutrality. In 2015,

---

[*]A similar argument was made when PCs were new and Apple donated many to schools in the 1980s. Critics opposed the gift, arguing that students would get used to using Apple products, giving the company an unfair advantage.

the FCC declared that broadband Internet is subject to regulation by the FCC as a utility under the Communications Act of 1934, which gave the agency very broad regulatory authority over pre-Internet telephone companies.[64] Under this act, the FCC would have the authority not only to enforce net neutrality rules (with whatever exceptions it chooses) but also to approve or reject proposals for new services and to control pricing. This time, a federal court upheld the FCC's action,[65] but the case may go to the Supreme Court.

Vinton Cerf, vice president and Chief Internet Evangelist at Google[*] and a highly respected Internet pioneer, said the neutrality of the carriers and the lack of gatekeepers and centralized control were key factors responsible for the success of the Net and innovations like blogging and Internet telephony. He argues that, while speed is important for applications such as video streaming and less so for applications such as email and file transfer, the companies that provide access to the network should not be making the decisions.[66] David Farber, another highly respected Internet pioneer, opposes neutrality regulations and the FCC's decision, saying, "We don't want to inadvertently stall innovation by imposing rules or laws the implications of which are far from clear," and that regulation is "a step toward a more rigid regime at odds with the freewheeling innovation of the Internet economy."[67]

The Internet has thrived for two decades without variable pricing and with little zero-rating but also without net neutrality requirements and regulation by the FCC. Requiring FCC approval for proposed new Internet services involves uncertainties, delays, high costs, potential for political favoritism, and some just plain poor decisions. Will the FCC's control of the Internet stifle the growth and innovation of the past few decades or protect it?

> *Washington regulating the Internet is akin to a gorilla playing a Stradivarius.*
>
> —L. Gordon Crovitz, Information Age columnist for the *Wall Street Journal*[68]

> *Zero-rating is pernicious; it's dangerous; it's malignant.*
>
> —Susan Crawford, Professor, Harvard Law School[69]

 # Exercises

Review Exercises

3.1   Briefly explain the differences between common carriers, broadcasters, and publishers with respect to freedom of speech and control of content.

3.2   What was one of the main reasons why courts ruled the censorship provisions of the Communications Decency Act in violation of the First Amendment?

---

[*]Really, that is his title.

3.3 What is one way of reducing spam?

3.4 Google will not carry ads for certain kinds of products. Name one.

3.5 Give an example of an anonymous publication from more than 100 years ago.

3.6 Mention two methods some governments use to control access to information.

3.7 Give an example of an Internet service that is inconsistent with the principle of net neutrality.

General Exercises

3.8 A large company has a policy prohibiting employees from blogging about company products. What are some possible reasons for the policy? Does it violate the First Amendment?

3.9 What policy for Internet access and use of filter software do you think is appropriate for elementary schools? For high schools? Give your reasons.

3.10 Various organizations and members of Congress suggest requiring Web sites that contain material "harmful to minors" to move to the Web domain ".xxx". Give some reasons for and against such a requirement.

3.11 A bill was introduced in Congress to require that websites with pornography get proof of age from anyone who tries to visit the site, possibly by requiring a credit card number or some other adult identification number. Discuss some arguments for and against such a law.

3.12 Library staff members in two cities filed complaints with the federal Equal Employment Opportunity Commission (EEOC) arguing that they were subjected to a "hostile work environment." The libraries where they worked did not provide filters on Internet terminals. Staffers were forced to view offensive material on the screens of library users and pornographic printouts left on library printers. Discuss the conflict between a hostile work environment and freedom of speech in this situation. Without considering the current laws, how would you resolve the conflict here?

3.13 A state legislator proposed requiring that the company that makes the game Pokémon GO (see the box on risks to children in Section 3.2.2) prevent Pokémon creatures from appearing near the homes of registered sex offenders. Would such a requirement be a violation of the First Amendment? Explain. Would it be a good idea for the company to do so voluntarily? Explain.

3.14 Suppose someone retweets a tweet that makes explicit threats against other people, threats that are not protected by the First Amendment. Consider whether the retweeter should be held legally responsible for the content to an equal degree as the original tweeter. What other information would you consider relevant in making this decision?

3.15 While developing regulations for drones, the Federal Aviation Administration banned most commercial uses of drones for several years but allowed hobbyist and other noncommercial uses. However, the agency warned hobbyist drone users that they could not post videos of their drones on YouTube, because YouTube has advertising and is hence commercial. Should posting a video of a legal activity be protected by the First Amendment?

3.16 For each of the following actions, tell whether you think a high school should punish a student. Tell whether you think the action should be a crime. Give reasons. Would it make a difference if the student is at a college?

(a) Sending sexually explicit emails about a teacher to other students.

(b) Encouraging other students via social media to call the school principal an obscene name.

(c) Sending a tweet that falsely accuses a teacher of groping a student.

3.17   Suppose you are writing an antispam law. What do you think is a reasonable definition of spam in this context? Indicate the number of messages and how the law would determine whether a message was unsolicited.

3.18   Federal regulations and laws in some states (some long-standing, some passed specifically for the Internet) prohibit or restrict many kinds of online sales. For example, at various times, laws have restricted the sale of contact lenses, caskets, and prescription medicines on the Web. Laws prohibit auto manufacturers from selling cars directly to consumers online. The Progressive Policy Institute estimated that such state laws cost consumers billions of dollars a year.[70]

For which of these laws can you think of good reasons? Which seem more like the anticompetitive laws described in Section 3.2.5?

3.19   Amateur astronomers around the world locate and track satellites—both commercial and spy satellites—and post their orbits on the Web.[71] Some intelligence officials argue that if enemies and terrorists know when U.S. spy satellites are overhead, they can hide their activities. What issues does this problem raise? Should astronomers refrain from posting satellite orbits? Why, or why not?

3.20   Consider that a large online company that provides a widely used search engine, social network, and/or news service is considering banning ads for the following products and services from its site: e-cigarettes, abortion clinics, ice cream, and sugared soft drinks. Which, if any, do you think they should ban? Give reasons. In particular, if you select some but not all, explain the criteria for distinguishing.

3.21   Someone posted a video on a popular video site showing a group of men with clubs entering a building and beating unarmed people. The site's policy prohibits posting videos with graphic violence. When a viewer complained, the site removed the video. Other viewers appealed the removal, saying the video documented abuse of prisoners in a Russian prison camp. Suppose you are a manager at the site. Develop a plan for dealing with such videos. Will you repost the video? Explain the issues you considered.

3.22   (a)   Suppose a website that publishes leaked documents posts the contents of the email account of a candidate for president during the election campaign. Describe some things that might be among the leaked documents that could hurt a campaign but do not indicate any wrongdoing.

      (b)   Devise standards for the ethics of leaking the emails of a political candidate during a campaign that you would be comfortable with no matter whether you support or oppose the candidate.

      (c)   During the 2016 presidential campaign, someone hacked into and leaked personal emails of former Secretary of State Colin Powell that were very critical of both Donald Trump and Hillary Clinton, the Republican and Democratic party candidates. Was this an ethically justified leak? Give reasons.

3.23   You are aware of a study that concludes that California's emergency systems, including hospitals, emergency supplies, police, and so forth, are not sufficient for responding to the magnitude of earthquake likely to occur in the next 30 years. The study has not been released to the public, and you are thinking of leaking it to a website that publishes leaked documents. List benefits of leaking the study and risks of doing so. List any other questions you consider relevant to making the decision. Indicate how different answers to some of the questions might affect your decision.

3.24 Give some arguments for and against Facebook allowing users to use pseudonyms.

3.25 Companies that set up offshore accounts with hidden ownership are similar to companies that operate anonymizer services for the Web in that both have legitimate uses and both are used by criminals. Suppose a hacker gave you the Mossack Fonseca papers (Section 3.4) and a large set of emails hacked (and decrypted) from an anonymizer service. What criteria would you use in choosing which documents from each set to publish? Try to be specific and tell how your criteria would apply to particular items you might find.

3.26 In many villages in India, girls under 18 and unmarried women are prohibited from owning cellphones. What are some positive and negative aspects of such a ban?

3.27 A company sells spyware that can intercept and record phone communications and email on a variety of email services. Suppose the company sells the software to government agencies in the United States (or your country, if you are outside the United States) that use the software to pursue criminals and terrorists. Using ethical criteria from Chapter 1 and legal or constitutional criteria from Chapter 2 as well as this chapter (or your country's constitution, if you are outside the United States), evaluate the decision to sell the software.

3.28 Using ethical criteria from Chapter 1, evaluate the decision to sell the software described in the previous exercise to a repressive government.

3.29 We saw in Section 3.2.4 that some people made an analogy between AOL and the U.S. Post Office and felt that AOL should not block any email, including spam. Do you think the net neutrality principle should apply to spam? Give reasons.

3.30 If the U.S. Congress enacts a net neutrality requirement, what exceptions, if any, do you think it should have?

3.31 Do you agree with the quotation from Susan Crawford at the end of Section 3.7? Give your reasons.

3.32 Assume you are a professional working in your chosen field. Describe specific things you can do to reduce the impact of any two problems we discussed in this chapter. (If you cannot think of anything related to your professional field, choose another field that might interest you.)

3.33 Think ahead to the next few years and describe a new problem, related to issues in this chapter, likely to develop from digital technology or devices.

Assignments

These exercises require some research or activity.

3.34 Find out whether your school restricts access to any websites from its computer systems. What is its policy for determining which sites to restrict? What do you think of the policy?

3.35 Why is it difficult or impossible to have material removed from WikiLeaks yet the website Gawker was successfully sued for posting a celebrity's sex video?

3.36 Glassdoor.com is a job and recruiting website that allows anonymous posts about firms by current and former employees. In 2016, a law firm, Layfield & Barrett, served a subpoena on Glassdoor to get identifying information for people who posted criticisms of the firm. The law firm was filing a defamation suit against the posters.[72] Find the current status of the case. If there has been a court decision on whether to block the subpoena, give the result and the reasons. Do you think anonymity should be protected in this case?

3.37 At the time we wrote this, Facebook, banned in China since 2009, was trying to establish a presence there. It would have to comply with China's censorship requirements and requirements to provide user information to the government. Is Facebook now in China? If so, how has it dealt with the censorship and reporting requirements?

Class Discussion Exercises

These exercises are for class discussion, perhaps with short presentations prepared in advance by small groups of students.

3.38 Under laws in Germany that protect the privacy of criminals who have served their sentence, a murderer took legal action to force Wikipedia to remove its article about his case. Discuss the conflict between privacy and freedom of speech raised by this case.

3.39 To what extent is violent material on the Web and in computer games responsible for shootings in schools? What should or could be done about it, without violating the First Amendment?

3.40 A computer system manager at a public university noticed unusually high traffic to one student's home page on the university's system. The system manager discovered that the student's home page contained several sexually oriented pictures. The pictures were similar to those published in many magazines available legally. The system manager told the student to remove the pictures. A female student who accessed the pictures before they were removed filed a grievance against the university for sexual harassment. The student who set up the home page filed a grievance against the university for violation of his First Amendment rights.

Divide the class into four groups: representatives for the female student, the male student, and the university (one group for each grievance). A spokesperson for each group presents arguments. After open discussion of the arguments, take a vote of the class on each grievance.

3.41 A licensed veterinarian in Texas with 30 years of experience gave advice over the Internet to pet owners, some in remote parts of the world, about pet health issues. The Texas government ordered him to shut his site because it is illegal in Texas for a veterinarian to give advice over the Internet without examining the animal. Present arguments for and against this law.

3.42 A hacker claimed to have broken into the private AOL account of the head of the U.S. Central Intelligence Agency and copied his contact list, emails, and various documents. The hacker posted more than 2000 email contacts. Shortly after, WikiLeaks published some of the documents. Discuss the pros and cons of releasing this information. What are the benefits? What are the risks or problems? Was it ethical to publish the material? Support your answer.

3.43 The owner of a carpet cleaning service sued seven anonymous Yelp reviewers for defamation. He claimed they were not actual customers and that their reviews were false and fraudulent, and he demanded that Yelp disclose their identities. First, discuss various motivations people might have to post false reviews. Then divide into two groups: one to argument in favor of ordering Yelp to disclose the identities and one to argument against.

3.44 Is the control that large companies such as Google have over Internet search results a threat to freedom of speech?

3.45 **(a)** In a riot situation, where rioters plan and coordinate their activities using a popular messaging system, should the company that runs the system shut it down temporarily? Assume the government does not have the legal authority to order the shut down, but law enforcement agencies and government officials have asked the company to do so to prevent more violence.

(b) Should the federal government have authority to shut down the Internet in an emergency?

 # Notes

1. *Lovell* v. *City of Griffin*.
2. From a speech at Carnegie Mellon University, Nov. 1994, quoted with permission. (The speech is excerpted, including part of the quotation used here, in Mike Godwin, "alt.sex.academic.freedom," *Wired*, Feb. 1995, p. 72.)
3. The phrase is from the Supreme Court decision in *Lovell* v. *City of Griffin*.
4. Eric M. Freedman, "Pondering Pixelized Pixies," *Communications of the ACM*, Aug. 2001, 44:8, pp. 27–29.
5. It was illegal for pharmaceutical companies to tell doctors about medical journal articles on certain topics until a federal appeals court ruled that truthful, nonmisleading information was protected by the First Amendment (*U.S.* v. *Caronia*, 2012). Advertising wine on the Internet was protected in a 2006 case in Minnesota. Earlier cases concerned advertising of tobacco, legal gambling, vitamin supplements, alcohol content of beer, prices of prescription drugs, and Nike's claim that it did not use sweatshop labor. Lee McGrath, "Sweet Nectar of Victory," *Liberty & Law*, Institute for Justice, June 2006, vol. 15, no. 3, pp. 1, 10. Robert S. Greenberger, "More Courts Are Granting Advertisements First Amendment Protection," *Wall Street Journal*, July 3, 2001, pp. B1, B3.
6. "High Court Rules Cable Industry Rights Greater Than Broadcast's," *Investor's Business Daily*, June 28, 1994.
7. Title V, Section 230.
8. In *The Life of Voltaire*, Smith, Elder & Company, 1904. See also Fred S. Shapiro, ed., *The Yale Book of Quotations*, Yale University Press, 2007. The quotation is often incorrectly attributed to Voltaire himself.
9. Gerard van der Leun, "This Is a Naked Lady," *Wired*, Premiere Issue, 1993, pp. 74, 109.
10. Dick Thornburgh and Herbert S. Lin, eds., *Youth, Pornography and the Internet*, National Academy Press, 2002, books.nap.edu/catalog/10261.html.
11. Robert Peck, quoted in Daniel Pearl, "Government Tackles a Surge of Smut on the Internet," *Wall Street Journal*, Feb. 8, 1995, p. B1.
12. Judge Marilyn Patel, quoted in Jared Sandberg, "Judge Rules Encryption Software Is Speech in Case on Export Curbs," *Wall Street Journal*, Apr. 18, 1996, p. B7. The case, *Bernstein* v. *United States*, and others continued for several more years, but in 1999 and 2000 two federal appeals courts ruled that the export restrictions violated freedom of speech. One court praised cryptography as a means of protecting privacy.

13. Brian Roehrkasse, quoted in Bloomberg News, "U.S. Need for Data Questioned," *Los Angeles Times*, Jan. 26, 2006, articles.latimes.com/2006/jan/26/business/fileahy26, viewed Nov. 22, 2011.

14. In *Brown v. Entertainment Merchants Association*, the Supreme Court decision invalidating California's ban on sale or rental of violent video games to minors, 2011.

15. Passed as Title V of the Telecommunications Act of 1996.

16. *Butler v. Michigan*, 352 U.S. 380 (1957).

17. Adjudication on Motions for Preliminary Injunction, *American Civil Liberties Union et al. v. Janet Reno* (No. 96-963) and *American Library Association et al. v. United States Dept. of Justice* (No. 96-1458).

18. *American Library Association v. United States*.

19. Brock Meeks, "Internet as Terrorist," *Cyberwire Dispatch*, May 11, 1995, www.cyberwire.com/cwd/cwd.95.05.11.html. Brock Meeks, "Target: Internet," *Communications of the ACM*, Aug. 1995, 38(8), pp. 23–25.

20. The quotations in this paragraph are from Meeks, "Internet as Terrorist."

21. Andrew Leonard, "Homemade Bombs Made Easier," *Salon*, Apr. 26, 2013, www.salon.com/2013/04/26/homemade_bombs_made_easier/; an interesting article addressing many aspects of this issue.

22. Larry Magid, "Survey: Parents Mostly Savvy on Kids' Internet Use," SafeKids.com, Sept. 14, 2011, www.safekids.com/2011/09/14/survey-parents-mostly-savvy-on-kids-internet-use/.

23. Amol Sharma, "Wireless Carriers Set Strict Decency Standards for Content," *Wall Street Journal*, Apr. 27, 2006, pp. B1, B4.

24. *Brown v. Entertainment Merchants Association*.

25. Entertainment Software Ratings Board, www.esrb.org.

26. In the decision striking down the Child Pornography Prevention Act (*Ashcroft v. Free Speech Coalition*). More arguments against the law are in Freedman, "Pondering Pixelized Pixies." Arguments on the other side appear in Foster Robberson, "'Virtual' Child Porn on Net No Less Evil Than Real Thing," *Arizona Republic*, Apr. 28, 2000, p. B11.

27. Mike Rosenberg, "Facebook 'Spam King' Indicted after FBI Investigation," *The Mercury News*, Aug. 5, 2011, www.mercurynews.com/ci_18619427.

28. Martin Samson, "*Intel Corp. v. Kourosh Kenneth Hamidi*," Internet Library of Law and Court Decisions, www.internetlibrary.com/cases/lib_case324.cfm.

29. Jayson Matthews, "Harris Interactive Continues Spam Battle with MAPS," Aug. 9, 2000, www.dotcomeon.com/harris.html.

30. The app, Nomorobo, is reviewed in M. David Stone, "Nomorobo," *PCMagazine*, Sept. 30, 2015, www.pcmag.com/article2/0,2817,2492079,00.asp.

31. The full name is the Controlling the Assault of Non-Solicited Pornography and Marketing Act.

32. Federal Trade Commission, "CAN-SPAM Act: A Compliance Guide for Business," Sept. 2009, www.ftc.gov/tips-advice/business-center/guidance/can-spam-act-compliance-guide-business.

33. John Simons, "CFTC Regulations on Publishing Are Struck Down," *Wall Street Journal*, June 22, 1999, p. A8. Scott Bullock, "CFTC Surrenders on Licensing Speech," *Liberty & Law*, Institute for Justice, Apr. 2000, 9:2, p. 2.

34. *Swedenburg v. Kelly*.

35. Texas Alcoholic Beverage Commission, "Summary of Judge's Ruling in Authentic Beverage Company Inc. v. TABC," Apr. 23, 2012, www.tabc.state.tx.us/marketing_practices/authentic_vs_TABC.asp.

36. Quoted in Brad Stone, "A Call for Manners in the World of Nasty Blogs," *New York Times*, Apr. 9, 2007, www.nytimes.com/2007/04/09/technology/09blog.html.

37. A person or organization using the name foia.org leaked the climate research emails. (FOIA is the acronym for "Freedom of Information Act.") Documents were originally found at foia2011.org/index.php?id=402 but have since been removed. The emails are quoted in numerous news articles with responses from the CRU researchers. "University of East Anglia Emails: The Most Contentious Quotes," *The Telegraph*, Nov. 23, 2009, www.telegraph.co.uk/news/earth/environment/global-warming/6636563/University-of-East-Anglia-emails-the-most-contentious-quotes.html. Antonio Regalado, "Climatic Research Unit Broke British Information Law," *Science*, Jan. 28, 2010, www.sciencepubs.com/news/2010/01/climatic-research-unit-broke-british-information-law. Larry Bell, "Climategate II: More Smoking Guns from the Global Warming Establishment," *Forbes*, Nov. 29, 2011, www.forbes.com/sites/larrybell/2011/11/29/climategate-ii-more-smoking-guns-from-the-global-warming-establishment/#1d609cc33a6b. "Cherry-Picked Phrases Explained," University of East Anglia, Nov. 23, 2011, www.uea.ac.uk/about/media-room/press-release-archive/cru-statements/rebuttals-and-corrections/phrases-explained.

38. "The Panama Papers," International Consortium of Investigative Journalists, panamapapers.icij.org/.

39. Aaron Blake, "Here Are the Latest, Most Damaging Things in the DNC's Leaked Emails," *Washington Post*, July 25, 2016, www.washingtonpost.com/news/the-fix/wp/2016/07/24/here-are-the-latest-most-damaging-things-in-the-dncs-leaked-emails/, and many other news reports.

40. David E. Sanger and Charlie Savage, "U.S. Says Russia Directed Hacks to Influence Elections," *New York Times*, Oct. 7, 2016, www.nytimes.com/2016/10/08/us/politics/us-formally-accuses-russia-of-stealing-dnc-emails.html.

41. Meg Anderson, "Julian Assange Sees 'Incredible Double Standard' in Clinton Email Case," National Public Radio, Aug. 17, 2016, www.npr.org/2016/08/17/489386392/julian-assange-sees-incredible-double-standard-in-clinton-email-case, and Judy Woodruff, "More DNC Information to Come, Says WikiLeaks Founder," PBS News Hour, Aug. 3, 2016, www.pbs.org/newshour/bb/dnc-information-come-says-wikileaks-founder/.

42. Tim Lister, "WikiLeaks Lists Sites Key to U.S. Security," CNN U.S., Dec. 6, 2010, www.cnn.com/2010/US/12/06/wikileaks/. Tim Lister and Emily Smith, "Flood of WikiLeaks Cables Includes Identities of Dozens of Informants," CNN U.S., Aug. 31, 2011, www.cnn.com/2011/US/08/31/wikileaks.sources/.

43. *Die Welt*, quoted in Floyd Abrams, "Don't Cry for Julian Assange," *Wall Street Journal*, Dec. 8, 2011, online.wsj.com/article/SB10001424052970204323904577038293325281030.html.

44. U.S. Congress, Office of Technology Assessment, *Science, Technology, and the First Amendment*, OTA-CIT-369, Jan. 1988.

45. *McIntyre* v. *Ohio Elections Commission*, 1995.

46. Jeffrey M. O'Brien, "Free Agent," *Wired*, May 2001, p. 74.

47. Neil King, "Small Start-Up Helps CIA Mask Its Moves on Web," *Wall Street Journal*, Feb. 12, 2001, pp. B1, B6.

48. Quoted in Robert Corn-Revere, "Caught in the Seamless Web: Does the Internet's Global Reach Justify Less Freedom of Speech?" chapter in Adam Thierer and Clyde Wayne Crews Jr., eds., *Who Rules the Net? Internet Governance and Jurisdiction*, Cato Institute, 2003.

49. From his speech "A Plea for Free Speech in Boston."

50. Quoted in Saeed Shah and Niharika Mandhana, "Killing in the Name: South Asia's Badge of Dishonor," *Wall Street Journal*, July 18, 2016, www.wsj.com/articles/killing-in-the-name-south-asias-badge-of-dishonor-1468861581.

51. Peter L. Bernstein, *Against the Gods: The Remarkable Story of Risk*, John Wiley & Sons, 1996, p. 89.

52. This was reported before the revolution in Egypt in 2011.

53. Louisa Lim, "China to Censor Text Messages," BBC News, July 2, 2004, news.bbc.co.uk/2/hi/asiapacific/3859403.stm. Dong Le, "China Employs Two Million Micro-blog Monitors State Media Say," BBC News, Oct. 4, 2013, www.bbc.com/news/world-asia-china-24396957.

54. "Russia Enacts 'Draconian' Law for Bloggers and Online Media," BBC, Aug. 1, 2014, www.bbc.com/news/technology-28583669. For more on how governments use the Net to thwart freedom movements, see Evgeny Morozov, *The Net Delusion: The Dark Side of Internet Freedom*, PublicAffairs, 2011.

55. Barry Bearak, "Taliban Will Allow Access to Jailed Christian Aid Workers," *New York Times*, Aug. 26, 2001, www.nytimes.com/2001/08/26/world/taliban-will-allow-access-to-jailed-christian-aid-workers.html.

56. In "Google Launches Censored Version of its Search-Engine," Jan. 25, 2006, www.rsf.org.

57. Quoted in L. Gordon Crovitz, "Facebook's Dubious New Friends," *Wall Street Journal*, May 2, 2011, online.wsj.com/article/SB10001424052748703567404576293233665299792.html.

58. Elinor Mills, "Google to Censor China Web Searches," CNET News, Jan. 24, 2006, www.cnet.com/news/google-to-censor-china-web-searches/.

59. Quoted in Jennifer Valentino-DeVries, Julia Angwin, and Steve Stecklow, "Document Trove Exposes Surveillance Methods," *Wall Street Journal*, Nov. 19, 2011, www.wsj.com/articles/SB10001424052970203611404577044192607407780.

60. "Statement on Temporary Wireless Service Interruption in Select BART Stations on Aug. 11," BART, Aug. 12, 2011, www.bart.gov/news/articles/2011/news20110812.aspx. See also Geoffrey A. Fowler, "Phone Cutoff Stirs Worry About Limit on Speech," *Wall Street Journal*, Aug. 16, 2011, www.wsj.com/articles/SB10001424053111904253204576510762318054834.

61. Quoted in Fowler, "Phone Cutoff Stirs Worry. . ."

62. Added by the Telecommunications Act of 1996 as an amendment to the Communications Act of 1934 (U.S. Code Title 47, section 230).

63. Nellie Bowles, "Facebook's 'Colonial' Free Basics Reaches 25 Million People–Despite Hiccups," *The Guardian*, Apr. 12, 2016, www.theguardian.com/technology/2016/apr/12/facebook-free-basics-program-reach-f8-developer-conference. Julie McCarthy, "Should India's Internet Be Free of Charge, Or Free of Control?" All Tech Considered, NPR, Feb. 11, 2016, www.npr.org/sections/alltechconsidered/2016/02/11/466298459/should-indias-internet-be-free-of-charge-or-free-of-control.

64. The 400-page FCC rule document is at transition.fcc.gov/Daily_Releases/Daily_ Business/2015/db0312/FCC-15-24A1.pdf.

65. *U.S. Telecom Association* v. *FCC.*

66. Alan Davidson, "Vint Cerf Speaks Out on Net Neutrality," Google Blog, googleblog. blogspot.com/2005/11/vint-cerf-speaks-out-on-net-neutrality.html. Matt McFarland, "5 Insights from Vint Cerf on Bitcoin, Net Neutrality and More," *Washington Post*, Oct. 10, 2014, www.washingtonpost.com/news/innovations/wp/2014/10/10/5-insights-from-vinton-cerf-on-bitcoin-net-neutrality-and-more/.

67. David Farber, "A note on Net Neutrality and my reaction to the current 'debate,'" quoted from the post on seclists.org/interesting-people/2006/Mar/216. Steve Lohr, "In Net Neutrality Push, F.C.C. is Expected to Propose Regulating Internet Service as a Utility," *New York Times*, Feb. 2, 2015, www.nytimes.com/2015/02/03/technology/in-net-neutrality-push-fcc-is-expected-to-propose-regulating-the-internet-as-a-utility.html.

68. L. Gordon Crovitz, "Horror Show: Hollywood vs. Silicon Valley," *Wall Street Journal*, Nov. 28, 2011, online.wsj.com/article/SB100014240529702044521045770598 94208244720.html.

69. Backchannel, Jan. 5, 2015, backchannel.com/less-than-zero-199bcb05a868.

70. Robert D. Atkinson, "Leveling the E-Commerce Playing Field: Ensuring Tax and Regulatory Fairness for Online and Offline Businesses," Progressive Policy Institute, www.ppionline.org, June 30, 2003.

71. Massimo Calabresi, "Quick, Hide the Tanks!" *Time*, May 15, 2000, p. 60.

72. Kathryn Rubino, "'Working Here Is Psychological Torture': Law Firm Sues over Anonymous Comments," *Above the Law*, May 16, 2016, abovethelaw.com/2016/05/working-here-is-psychological-torture-law-firm-sues-over-anonymous-comments/.

Intellectual Property

> *The Congress shall have Power To . . . promote the Progress of Science and useful Arts, by securing for limited Times to Authors and Inventors the exclusive Right to their respective Writings and Discoveries. . .*

—U.S. Constitution, Article I, Section 8

4.1 Principles and Laws

4.1.1 WHAT IS INTELLECTUAL PROPERTY?

Have you made a video set to a popular song and put it on the Web? Have you recorded a televised movie to watch later in the week? Have you downloaded music from the Web without paying for it? Have you watched a streaming video of a live sports event? Do you know which of these actions are legal and which are illegal, and why? Is it legal for a search engine to copy videos and books in order to display excerpts? How should intellectual property owners respond to new technologies that make it easy to copy and distribute their property without permission? How do copyright owners abuse copyright? If you are developing software for an online retail site, can you implement one-click shopping without permission of a patent holder? Will enforcement of strict notions of copyright and patent smother the creativity enabled by modern technology? We begin our exploration of these and other issues about intellectual property by explaining the concept of intellectual property and reviewing principles of intellectual property laws in the United States.[*]

Copyright is a legal concept that defines rights to certain kinds of intellectual property. Copyright protects works such as books, articles, plays, songs (both music and lyrics), works of art, movies, software, and videos. Facts, ideas, concepts, processes, and methods of operation cannot be copyrighted. Patent, another legal concept that defines rights to intellectual property, protects inventions, including some software-based inventions.

In addition to copyright and patents, various laws protect other forms of intellectual property. They include trademarks and trade secrets. This chapter concentrates more on copyright than other forms of intellectual property because digital technology and the Internet affect copyright so strongly. Patent issues for software and Web technologies are quite important and controversial, and we address those in Section 4.6.

The key to understanding intellectual property protection is to understand that the thing protected is the intangible creative work—not its particular physical form. When we buy a novel in book form, we are buying a physical collection of paper and ink. When we buy a novel as an ebook, we are buying certain rights to an electronic-book file. In both cases, we are not buying the intellectual property— that is, the plot, the organization of ideas, the presentation, the characters, and the events that form the abstraction that is the intangible "book," or the "work." The owner of a physical book may give away, lend, or resell the one book he or

---

[*]There are international agreements about intellectual property, but laws differ in different countries.

she bought but may not make copies (with some exceptions). The legal right to make copies belongs to the owner of the intangible "book"—that is, the owner of the copyright. The principle is similar for software, music, movies, and so on. The buyer of a software package is buying only a copy of it or a license to use the software. When we buy a movie on disk or via streaming video, we are buying the right to watch it, but not the right to play it in a public venue or to charge a fee.

Why does intellectual property have legal protection? The value of a book or a song or a computer program is much more than the cost of printing it, putting it on disk, or uploading it to the Web. The value of a painting is independent of, and usually higher than, the cost of the canvas and paint used to create it. The value of intellectual and artistic works comes from the creativity, ideas, research, skills, labor, and other nonmaterial efforts and attributes their creators provide. Our property rights to the physical property we create or buy include the rights to use it, to prevent others from using it, and to set the (asking) price for selling it. We would be reluctant to make the effort to buy or produce physical things if anyone else could just take them away. If anyone could copy a novel, a computer program, or a movie for the small price of the copying, the creator of the work would receive very little income from the creative effort and would lose some of the incentive for producing it. Protection of intellectual property has both individual and social benefits: It protects the right of artists, authors, and inventors to compensation for what they create, and, by so doing, it encourages production of valuable, intangible, easily copied, creative work.

The author of a particular piece of intellectual property, or his or her employer (e.g., a newspaper or a software company), may hold the copyright or may transfer it to a publisher, a music recording company, a movie studio, or some other entity. Copyrights last for a limited time—for example, the lifetime of the author plus 70 years. After that, the work is in the *public domain*: Anyone may freely copy and use it. Congress has extended the time period for copyright control several times. These extensions are controversial, as they hold more material out of the public domain for a long time. For example, the movie industry lobbied for and obtained an extension of its copyright protection period from 75 years to 95 years when the first Winnie the Pooh book and Mickey Mouse cartoon (both owned by the Walt Disney Company) were about to enter public domain.

U.S. copyright law (Title 17 of the U.S. Code[1]) gives the copyright holder the following exclusive rights, with some very important exceptions that we will describe later:

- To make copies of the work
- To produce derivative works such as translations into other languages or movies based on books
- To distribute copies
- To perform the work in public (e.g., music and plays)
- To display the work in public (e.g., artwork, movies, computer games, and video on a website)

Infringement of these rights is subject to civil and/or criminal penalties. Restaurants, bars, shopping centers, and karaoke venues pay fees for the copyrighted music they play.* Moviemakers pay for the right to base a movie on a book, even if they make significant changes to the story.

Making a copy of a copyrighted work or a patented invention does not deprive the owner or anyone else of the original work's use. Thus, taking intellectual property by copying is different from theft of physical property, and copyright law does not prohibit *all* unauthorized copying, distribution, and so on. A very important exception is the "fair use" doctrine, which we discuss in Section 4.1.4.

Most of the discussions in this chapter are within a context that accepts the legitimacy of intellectual property protection but revolve around its extent, how new technology challenges it, and how it can or should evolve. Some people reject the whole notion of intellectual property as property, and hence, they reject copyrights and patents. They see these mechanisms as providing government-granted monopolies, violating freedom of speech, and limiting productive efforts. This issue is independent of digital technology, so we do not cover it in depth in this book. However, the discussion of free software, in Section 4.5, overlaps arguments about the legitimacy of copyright in general.

4.1.2 Challenges of New Technologies

Copyright law will disintegrate.

—Nicholas Negroponte[2]

New technologies have been disrupting existing equilibria for centuries, yet balanced solutions have been found before.

—Pamela Samuelson[3]

In the past, it was generally businesses (newspapers, publishers, entertainment companies) and professionals (photographers, writers) who owned copyrights, and it was generally businesses (legal and illegal) that could afford the necessary copying and production equipment to infringe copyrights. Individuals rarely had to deal with copyright law. Digital technology and the Internet empowered us all to be publishers, and thus to become copyright owners (for our blogs and photos, for example), and they empowered us all to copy, and thus to infringe copyrights.

A few previous technologies raised challenges to intellectual property protection. For example, photocopiers made copying of printed material easy. However, such earlier technologies were not nearly as serious a challenge as digital technology. Early photocopies of complete books were bulky, sometimes of lower print quality, awkward to read, and more expensive to produce than a paperback. Figure 4.1 describes technological advances over the past few decades that made high-quality copying and high-quantity distribution extremely easy and cheap.

---

*Not all do, of course, but it is the accepted, and legal, practice.

- Storage of all sorts of information (e.g., text, sound, graphics, and video) in standard digitized formats; the ease of copying digitized material and the fact that each copy is a "perfect" copy.
- High-volume, relatively inexpensive digital storage systems, including hard disks for servers, cloud-based storage, and small portable media such as DVDs, memory sticks, flash drives.
- Compression formats (such as MP3 for music, which reduced the size of audio files by a factor of about 10–12) making music and movie files small enough to download, copy, and store.
- Search engines, which make it easy to find material, and the Web itself.
- Peer-to-peer technology, which permits easy transfer of files over the Internet by large numbers of strangers without a centralized system or service; and later, file-hosting services that enable storage and sharing of large files (e.g., movies).
- Broadband (high speed) Internet connections that make transfer of huge files quick and enable streaming video.
- Miniaturization of cameras and other equipment that enable audience members to record and transmit movies and sports events; and, before that, scanners, which simplify converting printed text, photos, and artwork to digitized electronic form.
- Software tools for manipulating video and sound, enabling and encouraging nonprofessionals to create new works using the works of others.
- Social media, where it is easy and common to share photos and videos.

FIGURE **4.1** Digital technologies that make copyright infringement easy and cheap.

The first category of intellectual property to face significant threats from digital media was computer software itself. Copying software was a common practice. As one writer said, it was "once considered a standard and acceptable practice (if it were considered at all)."[4] People gave copies of games and word processors to friends on floppy disks, and businesses copied business software. *Warez,* unauthorized copies of software, were traded on computer bulletin boards. Software publishers began using the term *software piracy* for high-volume, unauthorized copying of software. Pirated software included (and still includes) just about any consumer or business software sold. New versions of popular games often appear on unauthorized sites or for sale in other countries before their official release. The software industry estimates the value of pirated software in billions of dollars.

In the early 1990s, one could find and download from the Internet unauthorized copies of popular humor columns (copied from newspapers), lyrics of popular songs, and many images (e.g., Walt Disney Company characters, Playboy pinups, and myriad Star Trek items). Music files were too large to transfer conveniently and applications for listening to music on computers were unavailable or awkward to use. Devices for recording or copying digital music were expensive, but as often happens, technology improved and prices fell. (Compact disk recorders, for example, sold for about $1000 when first introduced and for $99 within about three years.)

By the mid-1990s, with the advent of the MP3 format, people could download an MP3 song from the Internet in a few minutes, and thousands of audio sites appeared, making millions of songs available. The MP3 format has no mechanism for preventing unlimited or unauthorized copying, and though many songwriters, singers, and bands willingly made their music available, most trading of MP3 songs was unauthorized.

As Internet access speeds and compression technologies improved through the early 2000s, sophisticated file-sharing schemes, inexpensive video cameras, video-editing tools, and video-sharing sites enabled members of the public to provide entertainment for each other—and to post and share professional videos owned by others. Copying music and movies became easy, fast, cheap, and ubiquitous. The scope of the term *piracy* expanded to include:

- high-volume, unauthorized copying of any form of intellectual property,
- individuals posting unauthorized files to legitimate file-sharing sites, and
- underground groups trading unauthorized copies.

The improved technologies gave rise to highly profitable, multimillion-dollar businesses (mostly outside the United States) that encourage members to upload and share files, knowing that most of the files are unauthorized copies.

The content industries claim that about one-quarter of Internet traffic world-wide consists of copyright-infringing material.[5] The entertainment industry, like the software industry, estimates that people copy, trade, and sell billions of dollars of its intellectual property without authorization each year. The dollar amounts from industry sources might be inflated,[*] but the amount of unauthorized copying and distribution of music, video, and other forms of intellectual property is massive. Entertainment companies and other content providers are losing significant actual and potential income for their intellectual property and this affects thousands of creative individuals who help create these works.

As we seek solutions to this problem, though, we should recognize that "the problem" looks different from different perspectives. So, what does it mean to solve the problems of technology's impact on intellectual property rights? What are the problems for which we seek solutions?

- To consumers, the problem is to get entertainment cheaply and conveniently.
- To writers, singers, artists, actors—and to the people who work in production, marketing, and management—the problem is to ensure that they are paid for the time and effort they put in to create the intangible intellectual property products we enjoy.

---

[*]Some figures seem to assume that everyone who downloads a movie or song for free illegally would buy it at full price if it were not available for free.

- To the entertainment industry, publishers, and software companies, the problem is to protect their investment and expected, or hoped-for, revenues.

- To the millions who post amateur works using the works of others, the problem is to continue to create without unreasonably burdensome requirements and threats of lawsuits.

- To scholars and various advocates, the problem is how to protect intellectual property while also protecting fair use, reasonable public access, and the opportunity to use new technologies to the fullest to provide new services and creative work.

We explore problems and solutions from several of these perspectives in this chapter.

The two quotations at the beginning of this section date from 1995, when the significant threat to copyright from digital media was becoming clear. Users and observers of digital media and of the Internet debated whether copyright would survive the enormously increased ease of copying and the habits and expectations that developed about sharing information and entertainment online. Some argued that copyright would survive, mostly because of firm enforcement of copyright law, while others said the ease of copying would win out; most content would be free or almost free. To some degree, both predicted results have occurred: Enforcement has been fierce, but much content is free or cheap, legally, due to improved technology and the many services that provide free content sponsored by advertising.

4.1.3 A BIT OF HISTORY

A brief history of copyright law will provide background and help illustrate how new technologies require changes or clarifications in law.[6]

The first U.S. copyright law, passed in 1790, covered books, maps, and charts. It protected them for 14 years. Congress later extended the law to cover photography, sound recordings, and movies. The definition of an unauthorized copy in the Copyright Act of 1909 specified that it had to be in a form that could be seen and read visually. Even with the technologies of the early 20th century, this requirement was a problem. A court applied it in a case about copying a song onto a perforated piano-music roll for automatic pianos that played such rolls (called player pianos). A person could not read the music visually from the piano roll, so the copy was not judged a violation of the song's copyright, even though it violated the spirit and purpose of copyright.[7] Later, in the 1970s, a company sued for protection of its chess-playing program, implemented on a read-only-memory (ROM) chip in its handheld computer chess game. Another company, having likely copied the ROM, sold a game with an identical program. But because the ROM could not be read visually, a court held that the copy did not infringe the program's copyright.[8] Again, this did not well serve the purpose of copyright: The programmers received no compensation from a competitor's sales of their work.

In 1976 and 1980, Congress revised copyright law to cover software in the category of literary works. Software thus protected includes computer databases that exhibit creativity or originality[9] and computer programs that exhibit "authorship," that is, contain original expression of ideas. Recognizing that technology was changing rapidly, the revised law specifies that copyright applies to literary works "regardless of the nature of the material objects . . . in which they are embodied." A copy could be in violation of a copyright if the original can be "perceived, reproduced, or otherwise communicated by or from the copy, directly or indirectly."

One significant goal in the development of copyright law, illustrated by the examples above, has been devising good definitions to extend the scope of protection to new technologies. As copying technologies improved, another problem arose: A lot of people will break a law if it is easy to do so and the penalties are weak. In the 1960s, growth in illegal sales of unauthorized copies of recorded music (then usually on magnetic tape) accompanied the growth of the music industry. In 1982, high-volume copying of records and movies became a felony. In 1992, making a small number of copies of copyrighted work "willfully and for purposes of commercial advantage or private gain" became a felony. In response to the growing phenomenon of sharing files for free on the Internet, the No Electronic Theft Act of 1997 made it a criminal offense to willfully infringe copyright (for works with total value of more than $1000 within a six-month period) even if there is no commercial advantage or private gain. After huge growth in sales of unauthorized copies of movies, Congress made it a felony offense to record a movie in a movie theater—one of the ways copies get to those who reproduce and sell them illegally. Critics of these laws argue that the small offenses covered do not merit the severe penalties.

Why did copyright laws get more restrictive and punishing? Congress often delegates the drafting of laws in complex areas to the industries involved. Generally, creators and publishers of copyrighted works, including print publishers, movie companies, music publishers, sound recording companies (record labels), and the software industry, support stronger copyright protection. For most of the 20th century, the intellectual property industries drafted laws heavily weighted toward protecting their assets. On the other side, librarians and academic and scientific organizations generally opposed strict rules reducing the public's access to information. Most people were unaware of or indifferent to copyright issues. But digital media, and especially the growth of the Web, focused attention on issues about how much control copyright owners should have. In the 1990s, cybercitizens and organizations such as the Electronic Frontier Foundation joined librarians and others to fight what they viewed as overly restrictive copyright law, while the content industries continue to be powerful lobbyists for their point of view.

4.1.4 THE FAIR USE DOCTRINE

Copyright law and court decisions attempt to define the rights of authors and publishers consistent with two goals: promoting production of useful work and encouraging the use and flow of information. The fair use doctrine allows uses of copyrighted material that contribute to the creation of new work (such as quoting part of a work in a review) and uses that are not likely to deprive authors or publishers of income for their work. Fair uses do not require the permission of the copyright holder. The notion of fair use (for literary and artistic works) grew from judicial decisions; then in 1976, U.S. copyright law explicitly included it. The 1976 copyright law predated the widespread use of personal computers, so it addressed software issues mainly pertaining to large business systems, and it did not address issues related to the Web at all. Thus, it did not take into account many situations where questions of fair use now arise.

The law identifies possible fair uses, such as "criticism, comment, news reporting, teaching (including multiple copies for classroom use), scholarship, or research."[10] It lists four factors to consider in determining whether a particular use is a "fair use":

1. The purpose and nature of the use, for example, whether it is for commercial or educational purposes (commercial use is less likely to be fair use) or whether it transforms the copied work to something new or simply reproduces it.
2. The nature of the copyrighted work. (Use of creative work, such as a novel, is less likely than use of factual work to be fair use.)
3. The size and significance of the portion used.
4. The effect of the use on the potential market for or value of the copyrighted work. (Uses that reduce sales of the original work are less likely to be considered fair.)

No single factor alone determines whether a particular use is a fair use, but the last one generally gets more weight than the others.

Court decisions about copyright must be consistent with the First Amendment. For example, courts interpret the fair use principle broadly to protect creation of parodies of other works. In many situations, it is not obvious whether a use is a fair use. Courts interpret and apply the guidelines in specific cases. Law scholars say that results of fair use cases are often notoriously difficult to predict. The uncertainty can chill free speech. Fear of an expensive legal case can reduce creation of valuable new work that makes use of other works, even when the use is likely to be determined fair.

4.1.5 ETHICAL ARGUMENTS ABOUT COPYING

There is intrinsic "fuzziness" about the ethics of copying. Many people who get their music, movies, or software from unauthorized sources realize they get "something for nothing." They benefit from the creativity and effort of others without paying for it, which, to most people, seems wrong. On the other hand, there may be situations where copying does not seem wrong. We explore some of the reasons and distinctions.

Copying or distributing a song or computer program does not decrease the use and enjoyment any other person gets from his or her copy. This fundamental distinction between intellectual property and physical property is a key reason why copying is ethical in far more circumstances than taking physical property. However, most people who create intellectual property in entertainment, software, and so on, are doing so to earn income, not for the benefit of using their product themselves. If movie theaters and websites could show or stream copies of movies without paying for them, far fewer people and companies would invest money, time, energy, and creative effort in making movies. If websites could offer free downloads of books without an agreement with the publisher, publishers would probably not sell enough copies to cover costs; they would stop publishing. The value of intellectual property includes its value as a product offered to consumers to earn money. When people widely copy intellectual property without permission, they diminish the value of the work as an asset to the owner. This is a property aspect that is stolen by copyright infringement. That is why copying is wrong in many situations.

Supporters of unauthorized file-sharing services and people who advocate loose restrictions on copying intellectual property argue that permitting copying for, say, trying out a song or computer program before buying it benefits the copyright owner because it encourages sales. Such uses seem ethical, and indeed, since a lot of the "wrong" in unauthorized copying stems from depriving owners of income from their product, the fourth of the fair use guidelines considers the impact on the market for the product. However, we should be careful not to go too far in usurping a copyright holder's decisions. Many businesses give free samples and low-priced introductory offers to encourage sales, but that is a business decision. The investors and employees of the business take the risk for such choices. A business normally makes its own decisions about how it markets its product, not consumers who want free samples.

People who copy for personal use or distribute works of others without charge usually do not profit financially. Personal use is, reasonably, more likely to be fair use (both ethically and legally) than is commercial use, but is personal use always fair? Is financial gain always relevant? In some contexts, a profit motive, or financial gain, is a factor in concluding that an activity is wrong, yet in other contexts, it is irrelevant. Vandals do not profit financially from their action, but vandalism is unethical (and a crime) because it destroys—or reduces the value of—someone's property. A profit motive is not a significant factor in determining where to protect freedom of speech. Freedom of speech is an important social, ethical, and legal principle for book, magazine, newspaper, and website publishers, most of whom are in business to make a profit. Many kinds of abusive or threatening speech are unrelated to financial gain but are unethical.

Here are some arguments people make in support of personal copying or posting content on the Web without authorization (in situations that are not clearly fair use) and some counterpoints to consider. The responses below do not mean that unauthorized copying or use of someone else's work is always wrong—in certain cases it is not. These are brief suggestions for analyzing the arguments.

- *I cannot afford to buy the software or movie or pay the royalty for use of a song in my video.* There are many things we cannot afford. Not being able to afford something does not justify taking it.

- *The company is a large, wealthy corporation.* The size and success of the company do not justify taking from it. Programmers, writers, and performing artists also lose income when works are copied.

- *I wouldn't buy it at the retail price (or pay the required fee) anyway. The company is not really losing a sale or losing revenue.* The person is taking something of value without paying for it, even if the value to that person is less than the price the copyright owner would charge. There are times when we get things of value without paying. For example, people do us favors and many people put valuable information on the Web for free. It can be easy to ignore a crucial distinction: Who makes the decision?

- *Making a copy for a friend is just an act of generosity.* Philosopher Helen Nissenbaum argued that someone who copies software for a friend has a countervailing claim against the programmer's right to prohibit making the copy: the "freedom to pursue the virtue of generosity."[11] Surely we have a liberty (i.e., a negative right) to be generous, and we can exercise it by making or buying a gift for a friend. It is less clear that we have a claim right (a positive right) to be generous. Is copying the software an act of generosity on our part or an act that compels involuntary generosity from the copyright owner?

- *This violation is insignificant compared to the billions of dollars lost to piracy by dishonest people making big profits.* Yes, large-scale commercial piracy is worse. That does not imply that individual copying is ethical. And, if the practice is widespread, the losses do become significant.

- *Everyone does it. You would be foolish not to.* The number of people doing something does not determine whether it is right. A large number of people in one peer group could share similar incentives and experiences (or lack thereof) that affect their point of view.

- *I want to use a song or video clip in my video, but I have no idea how to get permission.* This is a better argument than many others since technology has outrun the business mechanisms for easily making agreements. The "transaction costs," as economists call them, may be so high that a strict requirement for obtaining permission slows development and distribution of new intellectual property.

- *I'm posting this video (or segment of a TV program) as a public service.* If the public service is entertainment (a gift to the public), the observations above about copying as a form of generosity are relevant here. If the public service is to express an idea or make some statement about an important issue, the posting might be analogous to creating a review or a parody. In some cases, these might be reasonable fair uses with social value. Simply posting a complete program, or a substantial portion of one, is probably not a fair use.

Laws are not always good guides for ethical decisions, but the fair use guidelines do a respectable job of identifying criteria to help distinguish fair and unfair copying. Because of the complexity of the issues, there will always be uncertainty in the application of the guidelines, both ethically and legally. The guidelines might need expansion and clarification to cover new media, but they give us a good framework that corresponds to sensible ethical criteria.

Plagiarism and copyright

Plagiarism is using someone else's work (usually written work) and representing it as one's own. Among students, it typically means copying paragraphs (perhaps with small changes) from websites, books, or magazines and incorporating them, without attribution, into a paper the student submits for a class assignment. Plagiarism also includes buying a term paper and submitting it as one's own work. Some novelists, nonfiction writers, and journalists have plagiarized sections or complete works from other authors.

Social conventions can influence the determination of what is plagiarism. For example, the public and book publishers generally know that ghostwriters write books for politicians and celebrities even when only the politician's or celebrity's name appears as the author. Few call this practice plagiarism because the ghostwriter has agreed in a contract to the lack of attribution.

Most often, the author of plagiarized material does not know of or authorize the material's use, so plagiarism often includes copyright infringement. If the material is in the public domain or if someone agrees to write a paper for another, it is not copyright infringement, but it still might be plagiarism.

Plagiarism is dishonest as it misappropriates someone else's work without permission (usually) and without credit. In academia, plagiarism is a lie to the instructor, a false claim to have done an assignment oneself. In journalism or publishing, it is a lie to the employer or publisher and to the public. Plagiarism violates school rules and is considered a serious breach of professional ethics.

Thousands of high schools and colleges submit student term papers and essays to services, such as TurnItIn (turnitin.com), that check for plagiarism. TurnItIn compares the submitted student work to its database of millions of student papers and to material on the Web and in journal archives. The service builds its database of student papers by adding those submitted for checking. Several students sued the company for infringing their copyrights by adding their papers to the database. A federal appeals court ruled that TurnItIn's storage of student term papers is a fair use even though TurnItIn copied the entire paper and is a commercial entity. The facts that TurnItIn provides a service very different from writing a term paper and that its service does not reduce the market for a student's paper weighed more strongly.[12]

4.2 Significant Fair Use Cases and Precedents

The fair use doctrine is important for different reasons in different contexts. First, it helps us figure out under what circumstances we as consumers can legally copy music, movies, software, and so on. Second, developers of new software, recording devices, game players, and other products often must copy some or all of another company's software as part of the process of developing the new product, and the new product might compete with the original company's product. Is such copying a fair use? We look at cases that cover these contexts. Some of the cases also involve the degree of legal responsibility a company has for copyright violations by users of its products or services. This point is important for many Web-based services, some that implicitly or explicitly encourage unauthorized uses of the works of others.

4.2.1 *SONY* v. *UNIVERSAL CITY STUDIOS* (1984)

The Sony case was the first case about private, noncommercial copying of copyrighted work that the U.S. Supreme Court decided.[13] It concerns videotape recording machines, but it is cited in Web-based entertainment cases and in cases about new kinds of digital recording devices.

Two movie studios sued Sony for contributing to copyright infringement because some customers used its Betamax video cassette recording machines to record movies shown on television. Thus, this case raised the important issue of whether copyright owners can sue makers of copying equipment because some buyers use the equipment to infringe copyrights. First, we focus on the other issue the Supreme Court decided in the Sony case: whether recording a movie for personal use was a copyright infringement or a fair use. People copied the entire movie, and movies are creative, not factual, works. Thus, factors (2) and (3) of the fair use guidelines argue against the taping. The purpose of recording the movie was to view it at a later time. Normally the consumer reused the tape after viewing the movie, making it an "ephemeral copy." The copy was for a private, noncommercial purpose, and the movie studios could not demonstrate that they suffered any harm. The Court interpreted factor (2), the nature of the copyrighted work, to include not simply whether it was creative or factual but also the fact that the studios receive a large fee for broadcasting movies on television, and the fee depends on having a large audience of people who view the movies for free. So factors (1), (2), and (4) argue for fair use. The Court ruled that recording a movie for viewing at a later time was a fair use.

The fact that people copied the entire work did not necessitate a ruling against fair use, although many examples of fair use apply only to small excerpts. The fact that the copying was a private, noncommercial use was significant. The Court said that private, noncommercial uses should be presumed fair unless there is realistic likelihood of economic harm to the copyright holder.

On the issue of the legitimacy of the Betamax machine, the Court said makers of a device with substantial legal uses should not be penalized because some people use it to infringe copyright. This is a very important principle.

4.2.2 REVERSE ENGINEERING: GAME MACHINES

In the Sony case, the Supreme Court's decision said that noncommercial copying of an entire movie can be fair use. In several cases involving game machines, the courts ruled that copying an entire computer program for a *commercial* use was fair, largely because the purpose was to create a new product, not to sell copies of another company's product. The first case is *Sega Enterprises, Ltd.* v. *Accolade, Inc.* Accolade made video games to run on Sega machines. To make their games run properly, Accolade needed to figure out how part of Sega's game-machine software worked. Accolade copied Sega's program and decompiled it (i.e., translated it from machine code to a form in which they could read and understand it). This is an example of *reverse engineering*—figuring out how a product works, usually by taking it apart. Sega sued; Accolade won. Accolade's purpose in copying Sega's software was to produce new creative work, satisfying the first of the fair use criteria. The fact that Accolade was a commercial entity was not critical. Although Accolade's games might reduce the market for Sega's games, that was fair competition. Accolade was not selling copies of Sega's games.[14] In *Atari Games* v. *Nintendo*, the court also ruled that making copies of a program for reverse engineering was not copyright infringement. Instead, it is a fair "research" use.

The court applied similar arguments in deciding in favor of Connectix Corporation in a suit by Sony Computer Entertainment, Inc. Connectix copied Sony's PlayStation BIOS (the basic input–output system) and reverse engineered it to develop software that emulates the PlayStation console. Game players could then buy the Connectix program and play PlayStation games on their computers without buying the PlayStation console. Connectix's program did not contain any of Sony's code, and it was a new product, different from the PlayStation console. The court determined that copying the BIOS for this purpose was fair use.[15]

These decisions show how courts interpret fair use for situations not imagined when the guidelines were written. Reverse engineering is an essential process for creating new products that must interact with other companies' hardware and software.

4.2.3 SHARING MUSIC: THE NAPSTER AND GROKSTER CASES

When Big Steel and the auto industry were under pressure during the '70s from low-cost imports, their first instinct was not to change their outmoded manufacturing plants but to beseech the courts to bar the outlanders. The record industry has taken a similar tack.

—Karl Taro Greenfeld[16]

Napster opened on the Web in 1999 as a service allowing users to copy songs in MP3 formatted files from the hard disks of other users. It was wildly popular and had more than 50 million users little more than a year later. Almost 100 million MP3 files were available on the service. Webnoize found that almost 75% of college students it surveyed used Napster. It was common knowledge that Napster users copied and distributed most of the songs they traded without authorization from the copyright holders. Eighteen record companies sued for copyright infringement and asked for thousands of dollars in damages for each song traded on Napster, and the record companies won.[17]

The Napster case is important for many reasons. The fact that so many people participated in an activity that courts decided was illegal is an indication of how new technology challenges both existing law and attitudes about what is acceptable. Many people thought the success of Napster meant the end of copyright. Instead the court decision showed that the legal system can still have a powerful impact. The arguments in the case apply to many other sites and services on the Internet.

The issues in the lawsuit against Napster were the following:

- Was the copying and distribution of music by Napster users legal under the fair use guidelines?
- If not, was Napster responsible for the actions of its users?

Napster argued that the sharing of songs by its users was a legal fair use. Let's review the fair use guidelines and how they apply.

Copying songs via Napster does not fit any of the general categories of purposes covered by fair use (e.g., education, research, and news), but neither does copying movies on tapes. The *Sony* v. *Universal City Studios* case showed that the Supreme Court is willing to include entertainment as a possible fair use purpose.

Napster argued that sharing songs via its service was fair use because people were making copies for personal, not commercial, use. Copyright experts said "personal" meant very limited use—say, within a household—not trading with thousands of strangers.

Songs (lyrics and music) are creative material. Users copied complete songs. Thus, fair use guidelines (2) and (3) argue against fair use, but, as the Sony case indicated, they do not necessarily outweigh other factors.

The final, and perhaps most important, point is the impact on the market for the songs—that is, the impact on the income of the artists and music companies that hold the copyrights. Napster argued that it did not hurt record industry sales; users sampled music on Napster and bought the CDs they liked. The music industry claimed Napster severely hurt sales. Survey and sales data did not unequivocally support either side. Sales data showed sales rising significantly during most years in the 1990s and dropping or rising only slightly in 2000. For example, music sales in the United States (the largest market) dropped 1.5% in 2000. Sales of singles were down 46%.[18] We do not know if Napster was the only reason for the declines, but it is reasonable to conclude that the huge volume of copying on Napster had a negative impact on sales and that the impact would grow.

Many legal observers thought the large-scale copying by Napster users was illegal copyright infringement, not fair use, and that is how the court ruled. But was Napster responsible for copyright infringement by its users?

Napster did not keep copies of songs on its computers. It provided lists of available songs and lists of users logged on at any time. Users transferred songs from each other's hard disks using peer-to-peer software downloaded from Napster. Napster argued that it was similar to a search engine and that a new law, the Digital Millennium Copyright Act (DMCA, which we discuss at length in Sections 4.3.2 and 4.3.3), protected it from responsibility for copyright violations by its users. The record companies argued that the DMCA requires companies to make an effort to prevent copyright violations and that Napster did not take sufficient steps to eliminate unauthorized songs or users who committed violations.

Napster cited the Sony Betamax case, in which the court said the maker of devices with substantial legitimate uses is not liable for users of the device who infringe copyrights, even if the maker knows some will. Napster had substantial legitimate uses in promoting new bands and artists who were willing to let users copy their songs. The recording industry argued that Napster was not a device or new technology, and it was not asking to ban a technology or shut Napster down. The record companies objected to how Napster *used* widely available technology to aid copyright infringement. The recording industry wanted Napster to stop listing songs without permission of the copyright owners.

Sony's relationship with a customer ended when the customer bought the Betamax machine while Napster interacted with its members in providing access to songs they copied. The court said Napster was liable because it had the right and ability to supervise its system, including the copyright-infringing activities, and had a financial interest in those activities. Napster was a business and although it did not charge for copying songs, it expected the free copying to attract users so that it would make money in other ways.

The court ruled in 2001 that Napster "knowingly encourages and assists in the infringement of copyrights."[19] Napster faced civil suits that could have required payments of billions of dollars in damages. After some ineffective attempts to remove unauthorized songs from its song lists, Napster shut down. Another company bought the "Napster" name and set up a legal music streaming subscription service.

About the time of the Napster decision, numerous companies and websites (Gnutella, Morpheus, Kazaa, and others) sprang up to provide a new kind of peer-to-peer file-sharing service. These systems enabled copying of files

What consumers want from the entertainment industry

Why was Napster so popular? When I (SB) asked my college students (while the illegal version of Napster was thriving in 2000), many shouted out, "It's free!" That's the obvious reason, but it was not the only one. My students quickly generated a list of other desirable features of Napster. They could

- get individual songs without having to buy a whole CD to get the few they wanted.
- sample songs to see if they really wanted them.
- have access to a huge "inventory" that was not limited to one particular store or music label.
- get songs that were not commercially available.
- conveniently get their music online.
- download and play a song from anywhere; they did not need to have a physical CD with them.

- view information on Napster about singers and musicians.
- chat online with other users while they downloaded songs in the background.

What is impressive about this list of features is that we have them all now through legal, paid subscription services, free services supported by advertising, and other websites. Napster used a variety of then-new technologies to provide flexibility, convenience, and services, in addition to free music. The record companies did not embrace the new technologies but instead expected their customers to continue to buy CDs from stores or order on the Web and wait a few days for shipping. Record companies were used to the old paradigm of getting paid by each customer for each copy and were reluctant to experiment with new methods.

among users on the Internet without a central service, like Napster, to sue when users infringed copyrights. Within months of Gnutella's appearance, more than a million files were available. Many were unauthorized MP3 music files and unauthorized software. In *MGM* v. *Grokster*, the music and movie industry sued Grokster and StreamCast Networks (the owner of Morpheus). Although the companies did not provide a central service or list of music files available on the disks of users (as did Napster), they provided the software for sharing files. Technologists and supporters of file sharing argued that peer-to-peer file-transfer programs had potential for many productive, legal uses. (They were correct.) However, the Supreme Court ruled unanimously that intellectual property owners could sue the companies for encouraging copyright infringement. (At about the same time, an Australian court made a similar ruling against Kazaa.)

The Napster and Grokster decisions made it clear that businesses that encourage copyright infringement and provide tools to do so as a fundamental part of their business model cannot operate legally in the United States. Many file-sharing companies settled suits with the entertainment industry, paying millions of dollars. Many shut down, but many more sprouted underground and in other countries. Those who wanted to operate legal businesses providing music realized that they had to make agreements with, and payments to, music companies.

4.2.4 USER AND PROGRAMMER INTERFACES

Does copyright apply to user interfaces? The term *look and feel* of a program refers to features such as pull-down menus, windows, icons, finger taps and movements, and the specific ways one uses these to select or initiate actions. Two programs that have similar user interfaces are sometimes called "workalike" programs. The internal structure and programming could be entirely different, so one program could be faster or have other advantages. Should the look and feel of a program be copyrightable? Does a workalike program infringe the copyright of the earlier program it resembles?

In the 1980s and 1990s, some companies won copyright infringement suits against others whose software had similar look and feel. When Apple first sold the Macintosh with its windowed operating system, it strongly encouraged Mac programmers to adopt that look and feel so users would quickly know how to perform many basic application activities, from opening and printing a file to cutting and pasting text. While Apple encouraged a common look on its platform, it fiercely defended the Mac look and feel from implementations on other platforms, such as Microsoft's Windows.

An appeals court, reversing a look and feel case, ruled that menu commands are "a method of operation," explicitly excluded from copyright protection. They are, the court said, like the controls of a car.[20] The trend of court decisions has been against copyright protection for "look and feel." Courts ruled that features such as overlapping windows, pull-down menus, and common operations like cut and paste are outside the scope of copyright.

The main argument in favor of protecting a user interface is that it is a major creative effort. Thus, the usual arguments for copyright and patent apply (e.g., rewarding and encouraging innovation). On the other hand, standard user interfaces increase productivity of users and programmers since we do not have to learn new interfaces for each program, device, or operating system. Programmers do not have to "reinvent the wheel"—that is, design a new interface just to be different. They can concentrate on developing the truly new aspects of their programs. The value of similar interfaces for browsers, smartphones, and so on, is now well recognized and taken for granted.[*]

When software developers create programs, they often rely on an application programmers interface (API) that allows their code to interact with another programmer's application. An API is a "user interface" for programmers. When developing the Android operating system, Google used 37 APIs from the Java programming language (about 20% of Java APIs). Google did not design Android to replace or work with Java but instead wanted to make it easy for programmers who were familiar with Java to write Android programs; using the APIs from Java reduced the learning curve for new Android developers. Google used the APIs

---

[*]Several companies have patents on the screen technologies that enable touch commands.

without permission from Oracle, the owner of Java, and Oracle sued Google for copyright infringement asking for nearly $9 billion. The first critical legal decision in *Oracle America* v. *Google* was whether APIs were copyrightable at all. The judge in the first trial said no because systems or methods of operation are not copyrightable. However, a U.S. Federal Appeals Court decided that there was enough original creativity in the APIs to make them copyrightable. This controversial decision disturbed many programmers, because implementing APIs is a widespread practice to ensure interoperability of programs. In the trial following the appeal (in 2016), to determine whether Google's use of the Java APIs infringed on Oracle's copyright or was fair use, the jury determined it was fair use. Oracle said it would appeal, so the final result is not yet known.

4.3 Responses to Copyright Infringement

4.3.1 DEFENSIVE AND AGGRESSIVE RESPONSES FROM THE CONTENT INDUSTRIES

The entertainment and software industries employ numerous approaches in their efforts to prevent unauthorized use of their products. The methods include technology to detect and thwart copying, education about copyright law and reasons to protect intellectual property, lawsuits, lobbying for expansions of copyright law, lobbying to restrict or prohibit technologies that aid copyright infringement, and new business models to provide digital content to the public in convenient forms. Generally, these actions are reasonable, but there are instances when content industries take unreasonable actions or abuse their power and attempt to go beyond the intent of copyright law.

Thwarting copyright infringement with technology

A variety of techniques for protecting software developed early, with varying success. Diskettes containing software had "copy protection" mechanisms to prevent copying. Software companies encode an expiration date in free sample versions of software; the software destroys itself or does not function after that date. Often expensive graphics or business software includes a hardware *dongle*, a device that the user has to plug into a port on the computer so that the software runs, thus ensuring the software runs on only one machine at a time. Some software requires activation or registration with a special serial number. Most of these techniques were "cracked"—that is, hackers found ways to thwart the protection mechanisms. Many companies dropped software protection for less expensive software applications, largely because consumers dislike the inconvenience that accompanies it. Most modern software uses the Internet to check with the software company to verify that the program is licensed. A few software access controls developed into the more sophisticated digital rights management schemes for entertainment and ebooks that we discuss later in this section.

Some music companies adopted a clever tactic to discourage unauthorized file sharing: They put a large number of damaged music files, called "decoys," on file-sharing sites. The decoys might, for example, fail to download properly or be full of scratchy noises. The idea was that people would become frustrated and stop using the file-sharing sites if a large percentage of the songs they tried to download would not play properly. Movie companies adopted the tactic too, scattering many fake copies of new movies on the Internet.

Some movie theaters showing recently released movies set up special cameras that face the audience, detect recording devices, and alert security personnel. As another protection against illegal recording, some movies shown in theaters contain a digital watermark that disk players detect, alerting the device that the movie was illegally recorded in a theater. After playing the movie for 20 minutes, long enough to "hook" the viewer, the device stops and asks the viewer to pay for a legal copy.

Law enforcement

Software industry organizations, dubbed "software police," were active in offices since the early, pre-Internet days of business computing. In most cases, violations of copyright law were so clear that the business or organization agreed to big fines rather than go to trial. Software copying by businesses decreased, due in part to better understanding of the ethical issues involved and in part to fear of fines and exposure in a business climate that gradually came to view large-scale copyright violation as not acceptable.

Law enforcement agencies raided swap meets, warehouses, and other sites and prosecuted sellers of pirated software (and, later, music CDs and movie DVDs). Courts handed out severe penalties for organized, large-scale efforts. For example, the owner of iBackup received a prison sentence of more than seven years and was ordered to pay restitution of more than $5 million after pleading guilty to illegally copying and selling software worth more than $20 million. Similarly, a man who repeatedly recorded new movies on his camera in movie theaters and made pirate copies to sell received a sentence of seven years in jail.

Law enforcement efforts continue in cyberspace, tracking sites that trade or sell large volumes of copies of unauthorized software and entertainment.

Banning, suing, and taxing

Via both lawsuits and lobbying, the intellectual property industries have delayed, restricted, or prevented services, devices, technologies, and software that make copying easy and that people are likely to use widely in ways that infringe copyrights although they also have many legal uses. The technology for consumer CD-recording devices for music was available in 1988, but lawsuits filed by record companies delayed its introduction. A group of companies, including a television network and the Walt Disney Company, sued the makers of digital video recording

International piracy

Some countries traditionally have not recognized or protected intellectual property, including copyrights, patents, and trademarks. Counterfeiting of brand name products, from blue jeans to expensive watches and medicines, is common in some parts of the world. Ignoring foreign copyrights on books and other printed material has long been common practice in many countries as well. Thus, software, music, and movie piracy in these countries are variants of an old phenomenon. Websites that sell or share games, software, and entertainment files without authorization thrive in many countries.

The Business Software Alliance (BSA), a software industry organization, estimates that piracy accounts for 39% of personal computer software in use worldwide. The regions with the highest rates are Central and Eastern Europe and Latin America.[21] (Obviously, it is difficult to get accurate figures for illegal activities. BSA makes estimates by considering the number of computers sold, the expected average number of software packages on each computer, and the number of software packages sold.)

Many countries with high piracy rates do not have a significant software industry. Thus, they do not have domestic programmers and software companies to lobby for protection of software. The lack of a domestic software industry may be an effect, as well as a contributing cause, of weak legal protection for software. It is difficult for such an industry to develop when it cannot recover its investment in software development. The fact that the major software companies are from other countries may make both the people and the governments less inclined to take action to reduce unauthorized sales. In the United States, with its many legitimate sellers of entertainment and software, customers are likely to know when they are buying illegal products or sharing unauthorized files. In countries where it is common to purchase food unpackaged in outdoor markets, customers might not think there is anything unusual (or wrong) about the way unauthorized vendors sell software and music. In many countries,

it is easier for a consumer to find a street vendor selling a U.S. movie on DVD than to find an authorized DVD dealer. Another reason for piracy in some countries is that the economies are weak and the people are poor. A $20 U.S. DVD may be the equivalent of a week's wages, but a $1 pirated version is affordable. (Some U.S. movie companies sell DVDs in China at relatively low prices to attract customers away from the illegal market.) Thus, culture, politics, economic development, low incomes, and lax enforcement of intellectual property laws are all contributing factors.

The BSA calculated that the software piracy rate in China was 98% in 1994. The U.S. government repeatedly pressured China's government to improve intellectual property protection, and China repeatedly announced programs to do so, but with relatively little impact. As China's economy grew, its government made more effective efforts to reduce illegal production, sale, and use of intellectual property. Recognition that poor intellectual property protection hindered its own content industries contributed to increased copyright protection in China. For example, under pressure from a Chinese company that represents U.S. music companies and owns rights to thousands of Chinese songs, China's major search engine removed thousands of links to sites that offered pirated songs. Court decisions against infringement of foreign copyrights and jail sentences for offenders increased. In China, personal computer manufacturers used to sell their machines bare, without an operating system. This practice encouraged people to buy cheap, unauthorized copies. The Chinese government required that all PCs be sold with an authorized operating system preinstalled. Also, according to the BSA, the Chinese government significantly reduced the use of unauthorized software by its own government agencies. The BSA reports that the software piracy rate in China dropped to 70% in 2015. (A Chinese study, based on surveys, reported a 45% rate for 2010.) For comparison, the BSA gives a rate of 17% for the United States.[22]

machines that store TV programs and can skip commercials. The movie and record industries delayed introduction of DVD players by threatening to sue companies that make them if consumers could copy movies on the devices. The Recording Industry Association of America (RIAA) obtained a restraining order to stop Diamond Multimedia Systems from shipping its Rio machine, a portable device to play MP3 music files. Diamond eventually won, partly because the court interpreted the Rio as a player, not a recorder, that allowed people to play their music at different locations—just as the Sony decision (Section 4.2.1) said people could watch TV shows at different times.[23] Some observers believe that Apple's iPod would not have been possible if the RIAA's lawsuit against the Rio had succeeded.

As new companies introduced a variety of new products and services to deliver entertainment in flexible and convenient ways, the costs of fighting industry lawsuits effectively shut some of them down—with no trial to decide whether their products were legal.

The entertainment industry pushed hard for laws and industry agreements to require that makers of personal computers and digital recorders and players build copy-protection mechanisms into their products. It pressured device makers to design their systems so that files in unprotected formats do not play well—or at all. Such requirements could reduce illegal copying, of course. However, they interfere with use and sharing of homemade works, they complicate sharing of material in the public domain, and they restrict legal copying for personal use and other fair uses. Laws requiring or prohibiting specific features violate the freedom of manufacturers to develop and sell products they consider appropriate.

The entertainment industry sued or took other legal action against thousands of people for downloading or sharing unauthorized music files. Letters to college students threatened fines of thousands of dollars. Eventually, recognizing that the lawsuits angered customers and were not particularly effective in stopping copying and sharing, the industry cut back on the policy of mass lawsuits. Instead, the industry made agreements under which ISPs warn customers who transfer music or movies illegally and may close the accounts of customers who ignore the warnings.

As an alternative to banning devices that increase the likelihood of copyright infringement, several governments, including most in the European Union, tax digital media and equipment to pay copyright holders for losses expected from unauthorized copying. They introduced special taxes on photocopiers and magnetic tape in the 1960s and later added taxes on personal computers, printers, scanners, blank DVDs, recorders, iPods, and cellphones. Advocates of these taxes argue that makers of copying equipment are responsible for losses their equipment causes for intellectual property owners and that the tax schemes are a reasonable compromise in a situation where it is difficult to catch each infringer. Critics argue that the taxes make equipment more expensive, penalize equipment makers unfairly, charge honest users unfairly, and politicize the difficult job of fairly distributing the money collected.

Analogies and perspective

Should we ban or restrict software, a technology, a device, or research because it has the potential for illegal use, or should we ban only the illegal uses? This question addresses a principle covering much more than copyright infringement. Law enforcement agencies advocate banning anonymous Web browsing and email, because they can hide criminal activity. In Chapter 5, we describe the FBI's pressure for banning telephone technology that is difficult to tap and encryption schemes that are difficult for them to crack. The issue of banning or restricting tools that have criminal uses also arises in numerous areas unrelated to computer technology. Some U.S. cities prohibit sale of spray paint to minors, because they might paint graffiti on walls. Of course, they might paint a table. Some cities ban chewing gum, because some people discard the gum on the street, making a mess. Many countries prohibit ordinary people from owning guns to protect their homes or businesses, because some people misuse guns. Laws ban drug paraphernalia, because people might use it with illegal drugs. Some of these laws make prevention of specific crimes easier.

For example, it can be difficult to find the person who painted graffiti, but it is easy to reduce the sale of spray paint by threatening shop owners with fines.

In a free society, which should win: the freedom of people to develop and use tools for legal purposes, or the prevention of potential crimes? Those who reject the policy of banning a tool that has both legitimate and illegal uses argue its absurdity by taking it to its extreme: Should we ban matches because arsonists use them? Others argue that we should look at each application individually, considering the risks of harm. Proponents and lobbyists for bans on tools usually rank the damage they could cause (in general or to the interests of their clients) more highly than the loss of freedom and convenience to those who would use the tool honestly and productively. We can rarely predict all the creative and innovative (legal) uses of a new technology. Bans, delays, and expensive restrictions often cost all of society the unforeseen benefits. The technologies listed in Figure 4.1 in Section 4.1.2 as causes of problems for intellectual property protection are the foundation of incredible benefits that we enjoy.

Digital rights management

Digital rights management technologies (DRM) are a collection of techniques that control access to and uses of intellectual property in digital formats. DRM includes hardware and software schemes using encryption and other tools. DRM implementations embedded in text files, music, movies, ebooks, and so on, can prevent saving, printing, making more than a specified number of copies, distributing a file, extracting excerpts, or fast-forwarding over commercials.

More about encryption: Section 2.5.2

There are many criticisms of digital rights management. DRM prevents fair uses as well as infringing uses. For example, it can prevent extraction of small excerpts for review or for a fair use in a new work. You cannot play or view protected works on old or incompatible machines and operating systems.

We have long had the right to lend, resell, rent out, or give away a physical book, record, or CD that we owned. (These activities do not require making a copy.) If we could not lend or give a book to a friend, the friend might buy a copy, providing income to the copyright owner. But in 1908, the Supreme Court established the principle that the copyright owner has the right only to the "first sale" of a copy.[24] Publishers, especially of textbooks, which resell often, lobbied for legislation requiring a royalty to the publisher on each resale; they were unsuccessful. DRM, however, enables the content seller to prevent lending, selling, renting, or giving away a purchased copy.

The music industry fought a long battle against distribution of music in (unprotected) MP3 format, preferring to use DRM, though some in the entertainment industry argued that DRM was ineffective against piracy. Between 2007 and 2009, a major shift occurred in music sales as EMI Group, Universal Music Group, and Sony (some of the largest music companies in the world) began selling music without DRM and Apple eliminated DRM from its iTunes store for music. The debate about DRM continues within the movie and book industries, where many see it as essential to protect against piracy. They fear the industries will suffer severe economic losses if they do not include access controls on digital content.

DRM differs in a fundamental way from the banning, suing, and taxing we described earlier because it does not interfere with other people or businesses. Producers of DRM-protected content are offering their own products in a particular way that has some disadvantages to the public. Surely, a publisher should be free to offer its products in whatever form it chooses. If the car model we want to buy comes only in black, white, or green, we cannot demand that the company provide one in orange, but we can buy one and paint it orange. Can we do the equivalent with intellectual property wrapped in DRM? In the next section, we will see that a law says we often cannot.

> *The more we attempt to provide government protection to the old ways of doing business, the less motivation we provide to the entertainment industry to adapt and benefit from new technology.*
>
> —Les Vadasz, former vice president of Intel[25]

4.3.2 THE DIGITAL MILLENNIUM COPYRIGHT ACT: ANTICIRCUMVENTION

Congress passed the Digital Millennium Copyright Act (DMCA) in 1998. This very important law has two significant parts. The "anticircumvention" provisions prohibit circumventing technological access controls and copy-prevention systems implemented by copyright owners in intellectual property. The "safe harbor" provisions protect websites from lawsuits for copyright infringement by users of the site. We discuss the anticircumvention provisions in this section and safe harbor in the next one.

Circumventing access controls

Programmers and researchers regularly find ways to crack, thwart, or "circumvent" DRM, sometimes to infringe copyright on a large scale and sometimes for a variety of legal purposes. The "anticircumvention" provisions of the DMCA prohibit making, distributing, or using tools (devices, software, or services) to circumvent DRM systems used by copyright holders; the law provides for heavy penalties and fines for violators. (We mention exceptions later.) These provisions are extremely controversial. The ideal purpose of the DMCA is to reduce piracy and other illegal uses of intellectual property. However, it criminalizes actions that do not infringe copyrights. The DMCA outlaws devices and software that have legitimate purposes which court decisions protected before the DMCA. Content companies use the law in ways that threaten fair use, freedom of speech, research, competition, reverse engineering, and innovation. We give some examples.[26]

The first major legal cases based on the DMCA involved the Content Scrambling System, or CSS, a protection scheme for movies. Three programmers, including 15-year-old Jon Johansen of Norway,[*] wrote and distributed a program, called DeCSS, that defeated the scrambling.[27] Although DeCSS could be used to make unauthorized copies, it could also be used for legal purposes such as making personal back-up copies. Several Hollywood studios sued people who posted DeCSS on their websites, and a judge ruled that the program was illegal under the DMCA, no matter how it was used, and ordered its removal from the Web.[28] Soon after the decision, descriptions of DeCSS appeared on the Web in haiku, bar code, short movies, a song, a computer game, and art—demonstrating how difficult it is to distinguish between forms of expression, which the First Amendment strongly protects, and computer code, which the judge in this case said the government can regulate.[29][†] Jon Johansen was tried in Norway under a Norwegian law. The Norwegian court ruled that it was not illegal to break DVD security to view legally purchased DVDs and that the prosecutors had not proved Mr. Johansen used the program to illegally copy movies.

A team of researchers responded to a challenge by the Secure Digital Music Initiative (SDMI), an industry consortium, to test its digital watermarking schemes (a form of copyright protection) for music files. The researchers quickly found ways to thwart several of the techniques and planned to present a paper on the flaws in the protection schemes at a conference. The head of the research group, Princeton University computer science professor Edward Felten, said SDMI threatened lawsuits based on the DMCA. He decided not to present the paper.[30] The DMCA has exceptions for actions necessary for encryption research and computer security, but the scope of the exceptions is limited and unclear. This case showed that

---

[*]The others chose to remain anonymous.
[†]Recall that encryption export rules (discussed in a box in Section 3.2), like the DMCA, restricted publication of research and software, but at about the same time as the DeCSS case, courts ruled that software is a form of speech.

the DMCA and the industry's threats of lawsuits have a chilling effect on publication of research. In another example, a major book publishing company decided not to publish a planned book on security vulnerabilities in popular game consoles. Software engineering journals must make decisions about liability for some research papers they might publish. A computer science professional organization argued that fear of prosecution under the DMCA could cause researchers and conferences to leave the United States, eroding its leadership in the field. Eventually, the recording industry and the government issued statements that lawsuits under the DMCA against scientists and researchers studying access control technologies were not appropriate.[31]

Russian programmer arrested for violating the DMCA: Section 5.7.1

Smartphones, tablets, game machines, garage door openers, and myriad other devices have mechanisms to prevent installation of software or use of services and products that the maker of the device does not supply or approve. Cracking such mechanisms is sometimes called *jailbreaking*, unlocking, or *rooting*.[*] Originally, for example, Apple allowed only AT&T service contracts for iPhones; George Hotz figured out how to circumvent this limitation, as well as limitations on Sony game machines. Many uses of jailbreaking do not infringe copyright, for example, installing apps on an iPhone that are not certified by Apple. We saw in several cases in Section 4.2 that courts ruled, before the DMCA, that copying for reverse engineering to produce new products was a fair use. However, Apple threatened DMCA lawsuits against a website that hosted discussion of reverse engineering iPods so that they could work with software other than iTunes.[32] Other companies threatened suits for similar discussions for other devices. The Electronic Frontier Foundation (EFF) cites examples where companies use the anticircumvention provisions to threaten other businesses that try to sell new competing products, for example, printer toner cartridges and remote controllers for garage door openers.[33] In some cases the makers of the new products eventually win but only after long, expensive legal action. We cannot know how many new innovative products and services people would have developed but did not because of the DMCA.

Exemptions

The Library of Congress decides on exemptions to the DMCA's anticircumvention provisions. In a complex process, it considers new proposals and issues rules every three years. Exemptions previously approved must be reconsidered every three years even if there is no opposition to them. The Library of Congress now allows some circumvention of CSS for fair use purposes. In 2010, it stated that for professional educators and students, CSS could be circumvented for educational fair use such as research on security vulnerabilities in access controls on compact

---

[*]We are using the terms informally, not with technical definitions.

disks. Three years after introduction of the iPhone, it allowed altering phones to install third-party software (e.g., apps) or to use an alternate service provider, but it did not allow jailbreaking for tablets and video game consoles until 2015. It allowed a limited exemption for circumventing access controls on ebooks to use text-to-speech software (a useful function for blind people). In 2015, it allowed exemptions for security research and repairs on cars. As new devices, including fitness wearables, medical devices, smartwatches, and so forth, become available, people must apply to the Library of Congress to grant exceptions so that they can circumvent controls to perform legal actions on the devices. As new uses develop, for example, making excerpts of a movie for students in a massively open online course (MOOC) in film studies, an exemption is needed.[34]

Commercially distributed Blu-ray discs use DRM to prevent copying. At this time, it is still illegal for individuals to create software to copy protected Blu-Ray discs for personal, noninfringing use.

The exemptions the Library of Congress grants are often quite narrow and come after years of delays in legal uses of lawfully purchased products and delays in innovation of new products and services. The DMCA and its exemption process illustrate a poor way to design a law; organizations such as the EFF continue to call for Congress to repeal the DMCA's anticircumvention provisions or limit them to copyright infringement.

4.3.3 The Digital Millennium Copyright Act: Safe Harbor

The "safe harbor" provisions of the DMCA protect websites and social media companies from lawsuits and criminal charges for copyright infringement when users post infringing material. The site operators must make a good-faith attempt to keep infringing material off their sites, and they must remove such material when asked to do so by the copyright owners. Websites can lose the protection if they profit from the infringing material. Like the safe harbor provisions of the Telecommunications Act of 1996 (Section 3.1.2) for other kinds of illegal content, this was a welcome protection for website owners and the public. It recognized that sites with user content have tremendous social value, but operators could not review everything members post. The safe harbor provisions of the DMCA permitted the development of thousands of sites that host user-generated content, including blogs, photos, videos, recipes, reviews, and the myriad other creative works we share. Holding the sites legally liable for copyright-infringing material a user might post could have severely restricted this phenomenon.

On the other hand, such sites include a huge amount of unauthorized copyrighted material, from short clips of movies, TV shows, and concerts to entire movies and other shows. Also, individuals who can earn significant income from ads displayed with their videos on sites such as YouTube earn nothing when people copy and share their videos on Facebook. Copyright owners request removal of their content (and links to their content) by sending so-called takedown notices, but infringing material appears and reappears faster than content owners can find it and request its removal. The entertainment industry and other content producers are unhappy that they have to bear the responsibility and expense of continually searching sites for material that infringes their copyrights and sending the take-down notices. The content producers argue that the large advertising revenue sites such as YouTube take in depends in part on the unauthorized content. Such sites, they argue, are similar to the peer-to-peer music sites that made their money on the intellectual property of others without permission and the sites should have the responsibility of filtering out copyright-infringing material, rather than the burden being on the copyright holders. Supporters of the safe harbor provisions fear that weakening safe harbor protection would threaten the many websites that host user-generated material.

The lawsuit *Viacom International, Inc.* v. *YouTube, Inc.* could have clarified the extent of safe harbor, but after seven years in court, Viacom and Google settled the case in 2014 without disclosing the terms. (Viacom had asked for $1 billion in damages, claiming YouTube knowingly profited from Viacom videos on the site.) However, in a significant case decided in 2015, *BMG Rights Management* v. *Cox Communications*, Cox, a major cable company and Internet Service Provider, lost the safe harbor protection. BMG, which represents thousands of entertainment copyright holders, identified hundreds of thousands of illegally downloaded songs and sent takedown notices to Cox. The judge determined that Cox did not qualify for the safe harbor defense in this case; Cox had the power to close accounts of repeat offenders who used peer-to-peer file sharing to illegally upload and down-load music files, but Cox did not consistently do so. The jury found that Cox will-fully participated in copyright infringement. Cox appealed the decision, but if upheld, this case shows that some courts take seriously the requirement that com-panies using the safe harbor defense make a good-faith attempt to keep infringing material out of their systems.

For many years, the burden of finding copyright-infringing material was almost entirely on the content owners. Now, large video-sharing sites, social network-ing sites, and so on, use sophisticated tools to search user-posted content, looking for digital "fingerprints" of a company's intellectual properties. The quality of the tools varies, and the process still misses a lot. For example, some music companies say the process misses about half of their music. YouTube said the music industry submits about 2000 notices per day about videos they found manually that contain their music.[35] On the other hand, just as the filters we discussed in Chapter 3 can filter out inoffensive material, the automated tools can mistakenly flag and remove noninfringing content. Some automated search tools provide a very useful mecha-nism for paying content owners; we discuss it in the next section.

Although, overall, the safe harbor provision was a generally positive and important move, the takedown process has weaknesses for hosting sites and for the public, as well as for the copyright holders. The takedown requirement is clearly open to abuse that threatens free speech and fair competition. Copyright holders often interpret fair use principles narrowly and send takedown notices for material that might be fair use. A study of takedown notices found that for about 30% of the notices there is a significant question whether the material actually does infringe copyright. The fair use provisions protect much of it—for example, quotations from a book in an unfavorable book review. In one incident, Wendy Seltzer, a law professor, posted a video clip from a football game. YouTube removed it after the National Football League sent a takedown notice, then reposted it when Seltzer claimed it was an educational fair use (demonstrating issues about copyright—the clip included the NFL's copyright notice), and then took it down again after the NFL sent another takedown notice. At one point, more than half the notices businesses sent to Google demanding removal of links to allegedly infringing Web pages came from competitors of the targeted sites.[36]

How can search engine companies and websites evaluate all the takedown notices they receive? How should they respond when they receive a notice that they believe is intended to silence critics or undermine competitors? Since it is often not obvious how a court will interpret the fair use guidelines, website operators are likely to protect themselves by complying with requests from large content companies that have large legal staffs.

The entertainment industry and other content companies continue to lobby to curtail the safe harbor provisions of the DMCA, arguing that hosting sites should have more liability for infringing content posted by users. The entertainment industry argues that more legal tools are needed to shut down pirate sites outside the United States. As in other situations where it is difficult to find or stop the people who are doing what the government wants to stop, the content companies would put more burden of enforcement (and penalties) on legitimate companies. For example, they advocate requiring ISPs to block access to designated infringing sites, and they advocate requiring payment companies (e.g., Paypal and credit card companies) to stop processing payments to such sites. There is strong debate about how new stringent requirements would affect YouTube, search engines, Flickr, Twitter, and so on, as well as many small sites that do not have the expertise to comply nor the attorneys to fight lawsuits. Critics of such requirements warn that the standards the industry uses to identify infringing sites are too vague and broad and that blocking access and funding, once begun, tends to expand to other purposes and threatens freedom of speech. Piracy continues to be a major headache and cost for the creators and owners of intellectual property. The challenge continues to be finding effective ways to reduce it without burdening legitimate activities and businesses or thwarting innovation and development of new services.

4.3.4 Evolving Business Models

The movie industry viewed video cassette recorders as a threat in the 1980s but eventually earned billions renting and selling movies on cassettes. After what seemed a very long time, many music companies came to realize that people who share music files are people who like music—they are potential customers. The success of Apple's iTunes, which has sold more than 10 billion songs and tens of millions of videos, shows that companies can sell digital entertainment successfully, from the point of view of the customers and the rights holders. Music subscription services now operate under agreements with the music companies. Similarly, many companies offer (authorized) movie streaming services.

For many years, there was no useful mechanism for content companies to earn income when people posted their content on popular sites such as YouTube; the only option was to request its removal. Some newer automated systems that search for copyright-infringing material provide a payment mechanism. Depending on agreements between the companies, the site can block or remove an item entirely or pay the copyright owner for its appearance on the site. This creative solution allows users to post copyrighted material or include such material in their (usually noncommercial) creations without the overhead and legal liability for getting permissions. It makes sense that websites that benefit from advertising and have the assets and expertise to develop and use the sophisticated filtering tools make the payments, instead of individual users.

Tools for authorized sharing

Many authors and artists, including those who sell their work on the Web, are willing to share—to a degree. How can they easily—without a publishing company's staff of lawyers and without the overhead of explicit authorization—indicate what they are willing to let others do with their work? From the user perspective, how does someone who wants to copy, say, a photo from someone else's website, determine if he or she must get permission or pay a fee? Many people are willing to respect the preferences of an author or artist, but it is often not easy to determine what those preferences are.

Creative Commons,[37] a nonprofit organization, developed a spectrum of licensing agreements inspired by the GNU General Public License for software (Section 4.5). The licenses, which the author or artist announces to viewers by a choice of clickable icons, explicitly permit a selection of actions normally requiring authorization from the copyright owner. For example, one can allow or disallow copying for commercial uses, require a specified credit line with any use, allow copies or display of the entire work only if there are no changes, allow use of pieces of the work in new works, or put the entire work in the public domain. Like so much on the Web, the use of the licenses and associated software is free. The photo site Flickr is one of the largest users of Creative Commons licensing. Anyone who stores photos on Flickr can indicate what uses he or she permits.

Easy-to-use schemes like this eliminate confusion and expensive overhead and so facilitate and encourage sharing while protecting the wishes of intellectual property owners.

Infringing business models

Some attempts at new business models do not work. Zediva, a small start-up, bought DVDs and rented them to customers, but it did not send the physical DVD. Instead, it streamed the movie to the renter. Zediva argued that if it could rent the physical DVD without authorization from the studios, as do services such as Netflix under the first sale doctrine (Section 4.3.1), then it should be legal to rent it digitally over the Internet, streaming a movie from one DVD to only one renter at a time. The movie studios argued that streaming a movie is a public performance, which requires authorization from the copyright owner. A court agreed and Zediva shut down.[38] Does this interpretation of the law make sense? Should Zediva's variant on streaming be legal?

Another start-up, Aereo, took advantage of free television broadcast signals in the United States. The company set up warehouses throughout the country with thousands of dime-sized antennas; subscribers rented exclusive use of an antenna (one user to one antenna) to watch live broadcast television. Subscribers were also given access to a digital video recorder (DVR) in the cloud. An earlier court ruling between several networks and Cablevision determined that a remote DVR service like Aereo's did not infringe copyright. Television broadcasters fought the Aereo antenna rental concept by arguing that Aereo was retransmitting the signal and therefore is subject to the same fees that cable companies must pay. As in the Zediva case, the Supreme Court ruled that Aereo's service was a public performance. Even though the broadcast signals were free, Aereo did not have the right to retransmit programs without the consent of the content creators.[39]

Other business models appear intended to get around copyright law while helping people distribute illegally copied video. How far can they go? The Pirate Bay case (in Sweden, 2009) addressed the issue of whether the site violated Swedish copyright law by helping users find and download unauthorized copyrighted material (music, movies, computer games) even though the site itself did not host the material. Four organizers of The Pirate Bay were convicted of contributory copyright infringement. The Motion Picture Association of America has sued several other sites that do not host infringing videos but provide links to sites that do. It has won some of the suits. Do these sites differ in any fundamental way from the original Napster and Grokster? Should merely listing or linking to sites with unauthorized files be illegal?

Cyberlockers are services that provide storage of large files on the Web. Members transfer hundreds of thousands of files daily on popular sites. As with Napster about two decades ago, singers and musicians store files on cyberlockers for free downloads to promote their work. The term *cyberlocker*, however, often refers to services that either intentionally encourage sharing files (e.g., movies) without authorization or structure their business in ways that make copyright infringement on a huge scale easy. The entertainment industry cites Megaupload, a cyberlocker that did more than $100 million in business (e.g., from membership fees), as an example of this form of piracy. Megaupload operated from Hong Kong and New Zealand, with servers in several countries, and had 180 million registered users. It claimed that its terms of use prohibited copyright infringement and that it took down infringing material when notified to do so. Determining whether a particular business illegally contributes to copyright infringement depends on consideration of the factors that are required for safe harbor protection and how seriously the business complies. The U.S. government shut down Megaupload (by legally seizing its domain names), and police in New Zealand arrested its founder and several employees. A study found that online sales and rentals of movies were 6–10% higher in the weeks after Megaupload and Megavideo, a similar sharing site, were shut down, suggesting that the cyberlockers affected the market for the movies. Other cyberlocker businesses modified some of their practices to protect themselves from legal action.[40]

4.4 Search Engines and Online Libraries

Copying is essential to many of the operations and services of search engines. In response to search queries, search engines display copies of text excerpts from websites and copies from images or video. In order to respond to user queries quickly, search engines copy and cache* Web pages and sometimes display these copies to users. Search engine companies copy entire books so that they can search them and display segments in response to user queries. Besides their own copying, search engines provide links to sites that might contain copyright-infringing material. Individuals and companies have sued Google for almost every search service it provides (Web text, news, books, images, and video). Should search engines need authorization for the copying essential to search services? Should they be paying fees to copyright owners? As always, uncertainties about the legal status of industry practices can delay innovation. Google boldly introduces new services amid complaints of copyright infringement, but fear of lawsuits has deterred smaller companies that cannot estimate business costs in advance if they do not know their liability. We consider arguments related to a few of the contested practices.

The search engine practice of displaying copies of excerpts from Web pages or documents seems to fit easily under the fair use guidelines. The excerpts are short and displaying them helps people find the site with the excerpted material— usually an advantage to the site owner. In most cases, the site from which the search engine copies the excerpt is public, available to anyone who wants to read its content. Web search services are a hugely valuable innovation and a tool for the socially valuable goal of making information easily available. In *Kelly* v. *Arriba*

---

*Caching, generally in computer science, means storing data that were computed or fetched from a distant or slow source so that, when requested again, the data can be delivered quickly.

Soft, an appeals court ruled that copying images from Web pages, converting them to thumbnail images (small, low-resolution copies), and displaying the thumbnails to search engine users did not infringe copyrights. In *Field* v. *Google*, an author sued Google for copying and caching a story he had posted on his website. The court ruled that caching Web pages is a fair use.

There are, however, some reasonable arguments against caching and displaying excerpts. Most major operators of search engines are businesses and earn significant revenue from advertising. Thus, the copying accomplishes a commercial purpose. The display of short excerpts can reduce income to copyright holders, such as news organizations, if people gather enough information from the excerpt and do not click through to the news site.

European laws favor publishers more than laws in the United States. A group of Belgian newspapers claimed that they lose revenue from subscription fees when Google displays headlines, photos, and excerpts from their news archives, and they won a lawsuit in a Belgian court. Germany passed a law requiring search engines and news aggregators such as Google News to get permission from newspapers to display brief excerpts from their articles. Google would not pay for such permissions, so a group of German publishers, including Axel Springer, Germany's largest news publisher, did not allow Google to show their content. Springer found traffic to its sites from Google dropped significantly, and it reversed its policy. Spain's law went further than Germany's. Spain required that services such as Google pay a fee to a news industry organization; it does not permit individual publishers to waive the fee. Google's response was to shut down Google News Spain and remove Spanish publishers from its other news services. A year after the law went into effect, Spanish newspapers reported declines of 10% to 14% in site visitors, and several small news aggregator sites in Spain shut down.[41]

Consider the three ways we have just seen to address the question of whether the copyright of news publishers extends to use of excerpts by search and aggregator services. In the United States, the trend is to treat the use of excerpts as fair use, hence with a price of zero. In Germany and Belgium, the trend is toward copyright applying to the excerpts; then both sides weigh the likelihood and value of increased or decreased traffic to publishers' sites and determine a price (possibly zero) for displaying excerpts. The Spanish law is not based on either view of copyright. It imposed a price that was high enough to eliminate a service that consumers and many of the businesses involved would prefer to have (especially small sites that are more dependent on visitors finding them via search engines).

Books online

Project Gutenberg began converting books in the public domain into digital formats in the 1970s. Volunteers typed the entire text of the books—inexpensive scanners were not yet available. With the excellent scanning tools available in the early 2000s, Google and Microsoft began scanning millions of entire books from university (and other) research libraries, with the consent of the libraries. Microsoft scanned only books in the public domain. Google's Library Project scans books covered by copyright, gives electronic copies to the libraries that provide the books, and displays excerpts ("snippets") in response to searches—all without permission of the copyright holders.

Google's scanning millions of whole books without permission certainly seemed to be blatant, massive copyright infringement. As one might expect, Google's Library Project generated many lawsuits. The most important is *The Authors Guild et al.* v. *Google, Inc.*, filed in 2005 and finally resolved in 2016. Judge Denny Chin ruled that Google's Library Project was fair use.[42] Chin put a lot of emphasis on the first of the fair use criteria (Section 4.1.4), in particular that Google's project transformed books into something new and very valuable to society. By scanning and indexing the content of millions of books, he said, Google has provided a new set of powerful tools that increase access to information, help researchers and readers find relevant books, and enable language researchers to analyze history and use of language. The scanning preserves old and fragile books. Providing libraries with digital copies of books in their collections aids librarians in locating materials for users. Chin also observed that Google does not sell copies of the books or the snippets, and it does not display ads on Web pages about books it did not have permission to copy. For the fourth fair use criterion—impact on the market for the copied work—Chin described various techniques Google employs to prevent a user from collecting enough snippets to create a copy of a book. By helping people find books and because it includes links to places where people can buy books that turn up in response to a search, Google Books no doubt improves sales, reasoned Chin. The Authors Guild pointed out that the scale of Google's copying was unprecedented and that Google uses the content of the books to improve its search results, translations, and language analysis—thus contributing to Google's commercial success. It argued that the term *transformative use* in the fair use criteria had previously meant new creative material such as parodies and that Chin's application of the term to Google's book copying was an unprecedented expansion of fair use. The Authors Guild lost an appeal and the Supreme Court declined to take the case.

Aside from considering the arguments for and against the decision, it is interesting to speculate about how Judge Chin's ruling would have differed if he had decided the case in 2005. Was the long delay of the legal process a good thing in this case because it provided time for the benefits of a new service to become clear—or was it a bad thing because it entrenched an injustice, making it difficult to remove a service so many people have become used to using?

> *[W]e're witnessing a vast redistribution of wealth from the creative sector to the tech sector, not only with books, but across the spectrum of the arts. . .*
>
> —Roxana Robinson, Authors Guild president[43]

4.5 Free Software

In Chapter 1, we talked about all the free stuff on the Web. Individuals post information and create useful websites. Large groups of volunteers, who do not know each other, collaborate on projects. Experts share their knowledge and contribute their work. This creation of valuable information "products" is decentralized and has little or no "management" in the business sense. It flows from incentives other than profits and market pricing. This phenomenon, which some call "peer production," has a predecessor: the free software movement, begun in the 1970s.[44]

4.5.1 WHAT IS FREE SOFTWARE?

Free software is an idea, an ethic, advocated and supported by a large loose-knit group of computer programmers who allow and encourage people to copy, use, and modify their software. The *free* in free software means freedom, not necessarily lack of cost, though often there is no charge. Free software enthusiasts advocate allowing unrestricted copying of programs and making the source code (the human-readable form of a program) available to everyone. Software distributed or made public in source code is *open source*, and the open source movement is closely related to the free software movement. (Commercial software, often called "proprietary software," is normally sold in object code, the code run by the computer but not intelligible to people. The source code is kept secret.)

Richard Stallman is the best-known founder and advocate of the free software movement. Stallman began the GNU[*] project in the 1970s (though the GNU name came later). It began with a Unix-like operating system, a sophisticated text editor, and many compilers and utilities. GNU now has thousands of programs freely available and popular among computer professionals and skilled amateur programmers. In addition, hundreds of thousands of software packages are available as free software, including audio and video manipulation packages, games, educational software, and various science and business applications.[45]

With the source code available, free software has many advantages over traditional propriety software. Any of millions of programmers can find and fix bugs

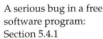
A serious bug in a free software program: Section 5.4.1

quickly, adapt and improve programs, modify a program to meet the needs of specific users, or create new and better programs based on the old ones. Stallman compares software to a recipe: We can all decide to add a little garlic or take out some salt without paying a royalty to the person who developed the recipe.

To enforce the openness and sharing of free software within the current legal framework that provides copyright protection, the GNU project developed the concept of *copyleft*.[46] Under copyleft, the developer copyrights the program and releases it under an agreement that allows people to use, modify, and distribute it,

---

[*]"GNU" is an acronym for "GNU's Not Unix." (Programmers like recursive acronyms.)

or any program developed from it, but only if they apply the same agreement to the new work. In other words, no one may develop a new program from a copylefted program and add restrictions that limit its use and free distribution. The widely used GNU General Public License (GPL) implements copyleft. Courts uphold copyleft: A federal court said a person who distributes open source software can sue someone who uses the software for commercial products without following the open source licensing agreement. The case, *Jacobsen* v. *Katzer*, involved free and open source model train software Jacobsen developed.[47]

For a long time, technically savvy programmers and hobbyists were the principal users of free software; commercial software companies were hostile to the free software idea. That view changed with the Linux operating system.[*] Linus Torvalds wrote the Linux kernel and distributed it for free on the Internet. A global network of free software enthusiasts continued development. At first, Linux was difficult to use and not well suited as a consumer or business product; businesses referred to it as "cult software." Gradually, small companies began selling a version of Linux along with manuals and technical support, and, eventually, major computer companies, including IBM, Oracle, Hewlett-Packard, and Silicon Graphics, used, supported, and marketed it. Other examples of popular free software include Firefox, the Web browser provided by Mozilla, and Apache, the most widely used program to run websites. Google's mobile operating system, Android, which is Linux based, has elements of free and open source software.

Major companies came to appreciate the benefits of open source. Several now make source code for their own products public, allowing free use in noncommercial applications. Sun Microsystems[†] licensed the Java programming language under GPL. Google, Amazon, and other companies released code for their artificial intelligence software that interprets language. Adopting the view of the free software movement, companies expected that programmers would trust the software more if they could see how it operates. IBM donates hundreds of its patents to the open source community. Free software grew to become a competitor for Microsoft, and those who are critical of Microsoft's products and influence see free software as having a considerable social benefit. Some state governments encouraged administrative offices to shift from Microsoft Office to Linux-based office software to avoid the licensing costs of Microsoft's products.

There are weaknesses to the free software model:

- Much free software is not easy for ordinary consumers to use.
- Because anyone can modify free software, there can be many versions of an application and few standards, creating a difficult and confusing environment for nontechnical consumers and businesses.

---

[*]Technically, Linux is the kernel, or core part, of the operating system. Other parts are from the GNU project, but the whole operating system is usually referred to as "Linux."
[†]Oracle acquired Sun in 2010.

- Many businesses want to deal with a specific vendor from whom they can request enhancements and assistance and are uncomfortable with the loose structure of the free software movement.

Some of these weaknesses faded as businesses learned how to work with a new paradigm and as new businesses, organizations, and collaborative communities developed to support and enhance free software (including Red Hat and Ubuntu for Linux).

The spirit behind free software and open source spread to other forms of creative work. For example, the Berkeley Art Museum provides digital artworks online with their source files and allows people to download and modify the art.

4.5.2 SHOULD ALL SOFTWARE BE FREE?

Some people in the free software movement do not believe that copyright should protect software at all. They argue that all software should be open source, free software. Thus, here we consider not the question "Is free software a good thing?" but "Should free software be the only thing?" When considering this question, we must take care to clarify the context of the question. Are we looking at it from the point of view of a programmer or business deciding how to release software? Are we developing our personal opinion about what would be good for society? Or are we advocating that we change the legal structure to eliminate copyright for software, to eliminate proprietary software? We will focus on the last two: Would it be good if all software were free software? And should we change the legal structure to require it?

Free software is undoubtedly valuable, but does it provide sufficient incentives to produce the huge quantity of consumer software available now? How are free software developers paid? Programmers donate their work because they believe in the sharing ethic. They enjoy doing what they do. Stallman believes that many good programmers would work like artists for low pay out of commitment to their craft. Contributions, some from computer manufacturers, support some free software efforts. Stallman has suggested government grants to universities as another way of funding software.

Would such funding methods for free software be sufficient? Most programmers work for a salary, even if they write free software on their own time. Would they be able to support themselves on free software alone? Would the extra services for which a business could charge bring in enough revenue to support all software development? Would the free software paradigm support the kinds of consumer software sold in millions of copies? What other funding methods could developers use?

A supporter of free software used the analogy of listener-supported radio and television. It is a good analogy for free software but not one for eliminating proprietary software, because most communities have one listener-supported station and numerous proprietary ones.

Stallman believes that proprietary software—particularly, the aspect that prohibits people from making copies and changes in programs without the software publisher's approval—is ethically wrong. He argues that copying a program does not deprive the programmer, or anyone else, of use of the program. (We saw some counterarguments to this viewpoint in Section 4.1.5.) He emphasizes the distinction between physical property and intellectual property. He also points out that the primary purpose of copyright, as stated in the U.S. Constitution, is to promote progress in arts and sciences, not to compensate writers.[48]

For those who oppose copyright and proprietary software completely, the concept of copyleft and the GNU Public License provide an excellent device for protecting the freedom of free software within the current legal framework. For those who believe there are important roles for both free and proprietary software, they are an excellent device with which the two paradigms can coexist.

4.6   Patents for Software Inventions[*]

> *Whoever invents or discovers any new and useful process, machine, manufacture, or composition of matter, or any new and useful improvement thereof, may obtain a patent therefor, subject to the conditions and requirements of this title.*
>
> —U.S. Patent Law (Title 35 U.S. Code, Section 101)

> *A smartphone might involve as many as 250,000 (largely questionable) patent claims.*[†]
>
> —David Drummond, Chief Legal Officer of Google[49]

4.6.1   PATENT TRENDS, CONFUSION, AND CONTROVERSIES

Patents protect inventions by giving the inventor a monopoly for a specified period of time.[‡] Patents differ from copyrights in that they protect the invention, not just a particular expression or implementation of it. Anyone else who wants to use the patented invention or process must get the authorization of the patent holder (usually by obtaining a license and paying a fee, or royalty), even if the other person

---

[*]Patent law is extremely complex. We use some terms informally, not in their precise legal meanings. The aim here is to present an overview of problems and controversies, not a legal analysis. Also, although we speak of software patents, some examples involve business methods implemented in software and overlap of software and hardware.

[†]For perspective, we note that since 1895, thousands of patents (with some estimates over 100,000) have been issued covering various aspects of the automobile.

[‡]Under current law, the period is 20 years from the time of application.

independently came up with the same idea or invention. Businesses routinely pay license fees to use patented inventions in their products. Laws of nature and mathematical formulas cannot be patented. Nor are patents to be granted for an invention or method that is obvious (so that anyone working in the field would have used the same method) or if it was in use by others before the filing of the patent application.

The U.S. Patent and Trademark Office (which we will call simply the Patent Office) evaluates each patent application and decides whether to grant a patent. In the early days of computing technology, the Patent Office did not issue patents for software; it declared computer programs not patentable. In 1981, the Supreme Court said that while software itself is not patentable because it is abstract, a machine or process that includes software, and in which the sole new aspect is the innovation implemented in the software, could be eligible for a patent. In the following decades, the Patent Office issued tens of thousands of software-related patents, and the Federal Circuit court (which handles patent appeals) approved many, interpreting Supreme Court guidelines loosely. Patents now cover encryption algorithms, data-compression algorithms, one-click shopping and other e-commerce techniques, copy-protection schemes, news feeds, location-based services for smartphones, privacy controls, pop-up ads, delivery of email to phones, and so on. The number of software patents continued to climb steeply, reaching more than 65,000 *in a year*. One writer commented that from a software developer's perspective, each new patent is the equivalent of a new law that he or she must obey. There are simply not enough patent attorneys to review the patents and determine if a new software product would violate an existing patent.[50]

Fierce controversies rage over whether there should be patents for software-based inventions at all, while others argue about many specific patents and about the criteria for granting them. Various organizations and companies argue that many patented techniques are not particularly new or innovative. Below are a few sample cases that illustrate some controversies and the uncertainties and costs involved.

- Amazon.com generated a lot of criticism when it sued Barnesandnoble.com for violating its patent on one-click shopping; many in the industry objected that the government should not have granted the patent in the first place.[*]

- After Amazon began recommending books to customers based on their previous purchases, IBM sued Amazon for violating several of its patents on e-commerce techniques. IBM had obtained a patent on electronic catalogues in 1994, before online retail was common, that covered a wide area, including targeted advertising and recommending specific products to a customer. Eventually, Amazon agreed to pay IBM a licensing fee.[51]

- Uniloc America sued dozens of companies, including Microsoft and the maker of the game *Minecraft*, for infringing its patent on a product activation method

---

[*]The companies settled the suit without disclosing the terms.

which requires a user to enter a code to activate software. (The purpose of the activation process is to prevent users from installing software on multiple computers.) At one point in the long-running legal battle between Uniloc and Microsoft, a jury ordered Microsoft to pay Uniloc $388 million for patent infringement. Then, in 2016, after a decade of lawsuits, a review board of the Patent Office ruled that Uniloc's patent itself was invalid.

- Apple filed several lawsuits against Samsung, the major maker of Android phones, beginning in 2011. The suits claimed Samsung infringed Apple patents for various features of smartphones and tablets, including scrolling behavior, the slide-to-unlock feature, and technology that implements operations by finger motions such as pinch-to-zoom and tapping to perform tasks such as calling a phone number that is in an email or text message. After Apple won a judgment of more than $1 billion against Samsung, the Patent Office and a court invalidated some of the Apple patents, including pinch-to-zoom and slide-to-unlock, because the techniques had been patented or used earlier. The $1 billion judgment against Samsung was reduced but the case was not yet fully resolved in 2016.[52]

Decisions about granting (or revoking) patents are complex, as are decisions about whether software, a device, or a method infringes a patent. Reasonable decisions require knowledge of details of the particular case, technical expertise in the area, and knowledge of the history of related technology. Establishing that an invention is not obvious and is not already in use is difficult in fast-developing fields such as Web and smartphone technologies. The Patent Office staff must research and process a very large number of patent applications. It has made expensive mistakes.

Patent licensing and patents as weapons

Some companies accumulate thousands of technology patents, buying most or all of their patents from individuals or other companies, but they, themselves, do not make any products. They license their acquired patents to other businesses, collect fees, and litigate against others who they see as violating patents in their portfolio. One firm had an estimated 30,000 patents and collected close to $2 billion in license fees. Critics of this phenomenon see the existence of patent-licensing firms as an indication of a serious flaw in the patent system. However, *if* the patents themselves are legitimate (an open question for many), this business model is not unreasonable. Marketing and negotiating contracts are tasks that an inventor might have neither the skills for nor the desire to do. A person, company, or university might be better at inventing and patenting new technologies than at implementing them in a successful business or finding others to do so. In a highly specialized economy, the existence of firms that buy and license patents is not in itself a negative thing. There are analogous services in other contexts. (For example, some farmers sell their crop well in advance of harvest to free themselves from risks of market fluctuation. The buyers might be firms with expertise in economics and risk analysis.)

However, some companies buy up thousands of patents not to license them but mainly (or only) to bring lawsuits for patent infringement. Critics call these companies "patent trolls." Simply put, patent trolls are companies and organizations that "misuse patents as a business strategy."[53] They sue in the hopes of getting large judgments or settlements, generating high legal costs for the victims (and ultimately the victims' customers and investors) and high social costs by threatening or discouraging innovators.

The huge number of software-related patents has contributed to another peculiar phenomenon: Large companies buy patents as defensive weapons. Sony, Apple, Microsoft, and several other companies formed a consortium and paid billions of dollars to buy thousands of wireless and smartphone patents from the wireless manufacturer Nortel when that company went out of business. This consortium did not buy all these patents because they need them for products they are developing. They bought patents so that they could sue other companies for patent infringement when those companies sue them for patent infringement. Google explicitly said it bid (billions of dollars) on the Nortel patents to "create a disincentive for others to sue Google" and to protect continued innovation in Android and other projects.[54] It is common for news articles to refer to "arsenals of patents" and to explicitly call patents "weapons."

Court decisions and attempts at solutions

Courts have made several attempts to clarify the criteria for determining what innovations based in software are patentable, often issuing decisions that reject prior criteria. Some decisions depended on whether software produced "a useful, concrete, and tangible result," whether a business method "transforms a particular article into a different state or thing," and whether the term *process* in patent law includes "methods." One decision declared a previous standard for software patentability to be only a "useful and important clue," not a determining factor. If these phrases and terms do not seem to clarify the criteria, that is the point.[55]

Supreme Court Justice Anthony Kennedy summed up the difficulties in making patent decisions:

> This [Information] Age puts the possibility of innovation in the hands of more people and raises new difficulties for the patent law. With ever more people trying to innovate and thus seeking patent protections for their inventions, the patent law faces a great challenge in striking the balance between protecting inventors and not granting monopolies over procedures that others would discover by independent, creative application of general principles. Nothing in this opinion should be read to take a position on where that balance ought to be struck.[56]

Although the number of software patents continues to grow, Congress and the courts have taken some steps to slow or reverse the trend of granting large numbers of questionable patents. A significant Supreme Court ruling in 2007 (*KSR* v. *Teleflex*) broadened the definition of "obvious" for rejecting patents. Under the America Invents Act of 2011, the Patent Office adopted new rules making it easier and cheaper to challenge the validity of previously granted patents. The Supreme Court ruled against certain software patents in a case in 2014,[57] and since that decision, federal courts have rejected patents in more cases. However, these steps are not without critics, some of whom argue that the criteria established in the 2014 decision are so vague that they could be used to invalidate any patent. Just as fear of patent infringement lawsuits creates uncertainty that can slow innovation, an easier process to invalidate previously granted patents adds uncertainty for inventors and can affect decisions about investing in an invention.

The attempt to devise rules and standards that work well for software is complicated by the fact that often the same rules must apply to patents in completely different fields. While Google and Facebook, for example, argue for stricter standards for granting patents, easier procedures for challenging and overturning patents, and limits on damage awards in patent infringement suits, businesses in industries that make huge investments to develop new products (e.g., biotech, pharmaceuticals, and medical devices) argue for stronger patent protection.

We saw that application of the fair use criteria for determining copyright infringement leads to uncertain results. The situation for patents is far more confused and unsettled.

4.6.2   TO PATENT OR NOT?

In favor of software patents

Before the digital age, inventions were physical devices and machines. But, a huge portion of the astounding number of remarkable and innovative developments in computing and communication technology consists of techniques implemented in software. These inventions have contributed enormous value to all of us and though we may take many for granted now, they were truly innovative. The main arguments in favor of patents for software-based inventions are similar to those for patents and copyright in general. By protecting rights to creative work, patents reward inventors ethically and fairly and encourage them to disclose details of their inventions so others can build upon them, thus encouraging innovation. Patent protection is necessary to encourage the large investment often required to develop innovative systems and techniques.

Businesses routinely pay royalties and license fees for use of intellectual property. It is a cost of doing business, like paying for electric power, raw materials, and so on. Software-related patents fit into this well-established context.

Copyright covers some software, but it is not sufficient for all of it. Software is a broad and varied field and can be analogous both to writing and to invention. A particular computer game, for example, might be analogous to a literary work, like a novel, and copyright would be appropriate. On the other hand, the first spreadsheet program, VisiCalc, introduced in 1979, was a remarkable innovation that had enormous impact on ways of doing business planning and on the sales of computer software and hardware. Similarly, the first hypertext system, the first peer-to-peer system, and many of the innovations that make smartphones so useful have characteristics more like new inventions. A patent might be more appropriate for such innovations.

Against software patents

Critics of software patents include those who oppose software patents in general as a matter of principle and those who conclude that the system developed so far has done a very poor job. Both see patents for software as stifling innovation, rather than encouraging it.

There are now so many software patents that it is difficult for software developers (individuals writing apps or large companies developing new technology) to know if their software infringes patents. Many software developers come up with the same techniques independently, but patent law does not allow them to use their own invention if someone else has patented it. The costs of lawyers to research patents and the risk of being sued discourage small companies from attempting to develop and market new innovations. Businesses cannot sensibly estimate costs of new products and services when lawsuits are so common and results so uncertain. Even large companies, as we indicated earlier, amass patents as defensive weapons for inevitable lawsuits.

If courts uphold patents for common software techniques, e-commerce tools, smartphone features, and so on, then prices will go up and we will see more incompatible devices and inconsistent user interfaces. In Section 4.2.4, we reviewed earlier controversies about copyrighting user interfaces (the "look and feel" of software systems). The principle that evolved in those cases—that uniformity of interfaces is valuable and that the look and feel should not be copyrightable— suggests a similar principle against patentability of user interfaces for phones and other devices.

It is difficult to determine what is truly original and to distinguish a patentable innovation from one that preempts an abstract idea, mathematical formula, or fact of nature. (Indeed, many computer scientists see all algorithms, and therefore all software, as mathematical formulas.) The very fact that there are so many controversial software patents argues against granting these kinds of patents. The Supreme Court has not been able to arrive at clear, consistent legal criteria. This legal confusion suggests that it might be better not to issue patents in these areas.

Evaluating the arguments

Some of the problems of software patents are problems of patents in general. That does not mean we should abandon patents; most things have advantages and disadvantages. (It does suggest areas for possible improvement.) Lawsuits over patents for physical inventions are common. (The holder of the 1895 patent on an automobile sued Henry Ford.) Intellectual property law is a subset of property rights law and for complex areas, it sometimes takes many years to work out reasonable principles.* Software patent holders sue others who independently develop the same techniques, but all patents allow such suits. This seems to be an unfair aspect of the patent system. Does it do significantly more damage for software-related inventions than for other inventions?

That there has been an enormous amount of innovation in the last few decades is obvious. Looking at the same facts and trends, some see patents on software as essential to this innovation, whereas others see them as threatening it. While the patent system has some big flaws, it is likely one of the important factors that contributed to the centuries of innovation in the United States. Legal scholars and software industry commentators emphasize the need for clear rules so that companies can do their work without the threat of changing criteria and unforeseen lawsuits. So, is the idea of patenting software innovations fundamentally flawed, or is it that reasonable criteria have not yet developed? If the latter, is it better to stop granting such patents in the meantime, while better criteria develop, or is it better to continue to issue software patents? Several Supreme Court justices have stated that, while certain patent criteria were useful for the industrial age, the information age and its new technologies need a new approach.[58] We do not have a good new approach yet. Billions of dollars and future technology development depend on how these controversies are resolved.

 Exercises

Review Exercises

4.1   What are the four factors to consider in deciding whether a use of copyrighted material is a fair use?

4.2   Give an example in which plagiarism is also copyright infringement, and give an example in which it is not.

4.3   Summarize the main reasons why the court in the Sony Betamax case ruled that videotaping a movie from television to watch later was not an infringement of copyright.

4.4   Give an example of a device the music or movie industry has tried to ban.

---

*Riparian law is a good example. If you own property that includes part of a river, do you have the right to build a dam, say, to produce energy or make a recreational lake? Do you have a right to a certain amount of clean water flowing by regularly? The two are incompatible; the latter implies that the owner upstream cannot build a dam.

4.5 Give two examples of uses of intellectual property that DRM controls.

4.6 What are the two main provisions of the Digital Millennium Copyright Act?

4.7 Did the courts decide that Google's copying of millions of books was fair use or copyright infringement?

4.8 List some benefits of free software (in the sense of Section 4.5).

4.9 What was one type of controversial patent for a software-related innovation?

General Exercises

4.10 Describe two things the entertainment industry has done to protect its copyrights. For each, tell whether you think the action is justified. Give reasons.

4.11 Your uncle owns a sandwich shop. He asks you to write an inventory program for him. You are glad to help him and do not charge for the program. The program works pretty well, and you discover later that your uncle has given copies to several friends who also operate small food shops. Do you believe your uncle should have asked your permission to give away your program? Do you believe the other merchants should pay you for the copies?

4.12 A political group organized a forum on its website to encourage people to post and comment on individual news articles relevant to political issues of concern to the group. Other participants added their comments, and debate and discussion of the articles continued. Two newspaper companies sued, arguing that posting the articles violated their copyrights. Analyze the case. How do the fair use guidelines apply? Who should win?[59]

4.13 During the 2008 presidential campaign, a graphic designer found a photo of Barack Obama on the Internet, modified it to look more like a graphic design, and made the very popular "Hope" campaign poster without credit to the photographer or permission from the Associated Press (AP), which owns the photo. AP argued that the designer infringed AP's copyright and that the design, on sweatshirts, etc., produced hundreds of thousands of dollars in income. The designer claimed his use was a fair use. Using the fair use criteria, evaluate the claims.[60]

4.14 You are a teacher. You would like your students to use a software package, but the school's budget does not include enough money to buy copies for all the students. Your school is in a poor neighborhood, and you know most of the parents cannot afford to buy the software for their children.

  (a) List some ways you could try to obtain the software without making unauthorized copies.

  (b) Suppose the methods you try do not work. Will you copy the software or decide not to use it? Give some arguments for and against your position. Explain why you think the arguments on your side are stronger.[61]

4.15 Which of the following activities do you think should be a fair use? Give reasons using copyright law and/or court cases. (If you think the ethically right decision differs from the result that follows from applying the fair use guidelines, explain how and why.)

  (a) Making a copy of a friend's spreadsheet software to try out for two weeks and then either deleting it or buying your own copy.

  (b) Making a copy of a computer game, playing it for two weeks, and then deleting it.

4.16   Mr. J wrote the first serious book on the problem of stuttering about 50 years ago. The book is out of print, and Mr. J has died. Mr. J's son wants to make this classic work available to speech pathologists by scanning it and putting it on the Web. The publisher held the copyright (still in effect), but another company bought out the original publishing company. The son does not know who has the copyright now.

    (a)   Analyze this situation according to the fair use guidelines. Consider each of the criteria and tell how it applies. Do you think Mr. J's son should post the book?

    (b)   Suppose Mr. J's son does put the book on the Web and that the publishing company holding the copyright asks a judge to issue an order for Mr. J to remove it. You're the judge. How would you rule? Why?

4.17   Preservationists are reluctant to transfer some very old movies on old, deteriorating film to digital formats because of difficulties in determining and locating the copyright owners. What aspect of copyright law contributes to this problem? Suggest some solutions.

4.18   Millions of people store legally purchased files, such as music, on cloud services both for backup and so that the files are available from anywhere. Is copying legally purchased files to and from the cloud a fair use? Explain how you would apply the fair use criteria.

4.19   Service Consultants, a software support company, provides software maintenance service to business customers of a software vendor. Service Consultants copied the vendor's program, not to resell the software but to provide service for clients. The vendor sued, and the service company argued that the copying was a fair use. Give arguments for each side. Which side do you think should win? Why?[62]

4.20   Describe an important benefit of the safe harbor provisions of the DMCA. Describe an important weakness of the safe harbor provisions from the perspective of the entertainment industries. Describe an important weakness from the perspective of the public.

4.21   The first Mickey Mouse cartoon appeared in 1928. Give ethical and/or social arguments (not legal arguments) both for and against each of the following uses of the cartoon or the Mickey Mouse character without authorization from the Walt Disney Company, which owns the copyright. Tell which side you think is stronger, and why.

    (a)   Post a digitized copy of the original cartoon on a video-sharing site.

    (b)   Use the Mickey Mouse character as the spokesperson in an advertisement very strongly critical of a candidate running for president.

    (c)   Edit a digitized copy of the original cartoon to improve visual and sound quality, produce copies with the dialog dubbed in various other languages, and sell thousands of copies in other countries.

4.22   Companies selling music or movies (for example) can include digital rights management tools that cause files to self-destruct after a specified amount of time. Assume the time limit is made clear to potential buyers. Give some advantages and disadvantages of this practice. Do you think it is ethical for entertainment businesses to sell content with such a limitation? Why or why not?

4.23   Do you think taxing media and devices that aid copyright infringement (as described in Section 4.3.1) is a reasonable solution for collecting fees to pay content providers? Give your reasons.

4.24   **(a)**   Suppose the movie industry asks a court to order a website to remove links to other sites that review movies and provide unauthorized (complete) copies of the movies for downloading. Give arguments for each side. What do you think the decision should be? Why?

(b) Suppose a religious organization asks a court to order a website to remove links to other sites that have copies of the organization's copyrighted religious documents and discussions of the religion's doctrines. Give arguments for each side. What do you think the decision should be? Why?

(c) If your decisions are the same for both cases, explain what similarity or principle led you to that conclusion. If your decisions differ for the two cases, explain the distinction between the cases.

4.25 Pick one of the actions mentioned in the first paragraph of this chapter and tell whether or not it is legal and why. If there is not enough information given, explain what your answer would depend on.

4.26 Compare the following statements. Are they equally valid (or invalid)? Why or why not? Is home burglary a good analogy for disabling copy protection? Why or why not?

One side effect of the DMCA's anticircumvention provision is to reduce incentive for the entertainment and publishing industries to develop truly strong protection schemes. The DMCA allows them to use weak schemes and then threaten legal action against anyone who cracks them.

One side effect of laws against burglary is to reduce incentive for homeowners to use sturdy locks. The law allows people to use weak locks and then take legal action against anyone who breaks in.

4.27 Consider the second and third criteria for fair use and explain how you would apply them to Google's Library Project (Section 4.4) in the case *The Authors Guild et al.* v. *Google, Inc.* (For the second criterion, it might be relevant that more than 90% of the copied books were nonfiction.) Overall, do you agree with Judge Chin's decision? Why, or why not?

4.28 Which arguments for free software (as in Section 4.5) apply to music? Which do not? Give reasons.

4.29 A cook can modify a recipe by adding or deleting a few ingredients without getting permission or paying a royalty to the person who developed the recipe.

(a) Give an example of modifications of a professional song or a piece of software that is analogous to a cook using the recipe.

(b) Do you think your example satisfies the fair use guidelines? That is, is it very likely courts would consider it a legal fair use? Explain why.

(c) Copyright protects cookbooks. A court would likely find that selling a cookbook in which many of the recipes are slight modifications of recipes in someone else's cookbook is copyright infringement. Give an example of modifications of a professional song or a piece of software that is analogous to selling such a cookbook.

4.30 Thomas Jefferson and several modern writers used fire as an analogy for copying intellectual property: We can light many candles from one without diminishing the light or heat obtained from the first candle. Suppose a group of people go camping in the wilderness using primitive methods. One person gets a fire started. Others want to start their fire from that one. Give ethical or practical reasons why they might be expected to trade something, perhaps some wild fruit they found, for the use of the fire?

4.31   Two professors suggested that software is a "public good" (like public schools and national defense), that we should allow anyone to copy it, and that the federal government should subsidize it.[63] Suppose this proposal, made in the 1990s, had been adopted. How well do you think it would have worked? How would it have affected the quantity and quality of software produced? Give reasons.

4.32   Describe one kind of software or technique used in software that you think is innovative, like an invention, for which patent protection might be appropriate.

4.33   Did you know, before you read this chapter, that restaurants pay fees for the music they play, community theaters pay fees for the plays they perform, and large companies routinely pay large fees to other companies for use of patented inventions and technologies? Does this long tradition of paying for intellectual property affect your view of the legitimacy of sharing entertainment on the Web without authorization? Give your reasons.

4.34   Assume you are a professional working in your chosen field. Describe specific things you can do to reduce the impact of any two problems we discussed in this chapter. (If you cannot think of anything related to your professional field, choose another field that might interest you.)

4.35   Think ahead to the next few years and describe a new problem, related to issues in this chapter, likely to develop from digital technology or devices.

Assignments

These exercises require some research or activity.

4.36   Read the member agreement or policy statement of a website that hosts user videos. Give the name and Web address of the site you chose, and briefly describe it if it is not a well-known site. What does its statement say about posting files that contain or use works of others without authorization?

4.37   Find data for the past 15 or 20 years on music industry revenue for recorded music. Describe how it has changed over that time. (Indicate whether the data are for the United States or worldwide and whether they include music subscription services and ad revenue as well as sales.)

4.38   Read these articles from *Wired*:

>   Lance Rose, "The Emperor's Clothes Still Fit Just Fine," *Wired*, Feb. 1995, www.wired.com/1995/02/rose-if/
>
>   Esther Dyson, "Intellectual Value," *Wired*, July 1995, www.wired.com/1995/07/dyson-2

Write a short essay telling which author's views about the future of intellectual property in the digital age have proved more accurate based on events in the years since they wrote the articles.

Class Discussion Exercises

These exercises are for class discussion, perhaps with short presentations prepared in advance by small groups of students.

4.39   A website hosts written works posted by authors. Some people post copyrighted work by other authors without permission. When an author asks the site to remove such material, the site complies and adds the text of the work to its filter database to prevent reposting without permission. An author sued the site claiming the site infringed her copyright by storing her work. Argue the author's case. Argue the site's defense. Evaluate the arguments and decide the case.

4.40 Some people argue that digital rights management (DRM) violates the public's right to fair uses.

    (a) Should a person or company that creates intellectual property have an ethical and/or legal right to offer it for sale (or license) in a form protected by their choice of digital rights management technology (assuming the restrictions are clear to potential customers)? Give reasons.

    (b) Should people have an ethical and/or legal right to develop, sell, buy, and use devices and software to remove digital rights management restrictions for fair uses? Give reasons.

4.41 Debate whether Congress should repeal the Digital Millennium Copyright Act's anticircumvention provisions.

4.42 Which factor is or will be more important for protection of digital intellectual property: strict copyright laws (and strict enforcement) or technology-based protections (or neither)? Why?

4.43 With respect to copyright issues for digital media and the Web, in what ways are entertainment companies the victims? In what ways are entertainment companies the villains?

4.44 Debate whether software should be copyrightable or should be freely available for copying.

4.45 Discuss to what extent the finger movements we use to navigate on a smartphone screen should be patentable.

 # Notes

1. www.copyright.gov/title17.

2. Nicholas Negroponte, "Being Digital," *Wired*, Feb. 1995, p. 182.

3. Pamela Samuelson, "Copyright and Digital Libraries," *Communications of the ACM*, Apr. 1995, 38:3, pp. 15–21, 110.

4. Laura Didio, "Crackdown on Software Bootleggers Hits Home," *LAN Times*, Nov. 1, 1993, 10:22.

5. David Price, "Sizing the Piracy Universe," NetNames, Sept. 2013, copyrightalliance. org/sites/default/files/2013-netnames-piracy.pdf.

6. We used several sources for the history in this section in addition to sources cited in individual endnotes: National Research Council, *Intellectual Property Issues in Software*, National Academy Press, 1991; Neil Boorstyn and Martin C. Fliesler, "Copyrights, Computers, and Confusion," *California State Bar Journal*, Apr. 1981, pp. 148–152; Judge Richard Stearns, *United States of America* v. *David LaMacchia*, 1994; Robert A. Spanner, "Copyright Infringement Goes Big Time," *Microtimes*, Mar. 8, 1993, p. 36.

7. The piano roll case is *White-Smith Publishing Co.* v. *Apollo*, reported in Boorstyn and Fliesler, "Copyrights, Computers, and Confusion."

8. *Data Cash Systems* v. *JS & A Group*, reported in Boorstyn and Fliesler, "Copyrights, Computers, and Confusion."

9. In *Feist Publications, Inc.* v. *Rural Telephone Service Company, Inc.*, the Supreme Court ruled that Rural Telephone Service's telephone directory did not meet the requirement for copyright protection.

10. U.S. Code Title 17, Section 107.

11. Helen Nissenbaum, "Should I Copy My Neighbor's Software?" in Deborah G. Johnson and Helen Nissenbaum, *Computers, Ethics & Social Values*, Prentice Hall, 1995, pp. 201–213.

12. *Vanderhye* v. *IParadigms LLC*, decided Apr. 16, 2009, U.S. Court of Appeals, Fourth Circuit, caselaw.findlaw.com/us-4th-circuit/1248473.html.

13. *Sony Corporation of America* v. *Universal City Studios, Inc.*, 464 U.S. 417(1984). Pamela Samuelson, "Computer Programs and Copyright's Fair Use Doctrine," *Communications of the ACM*, Sept. 1993, 36:9, pp. 19–25.

14. "9th Circuit Allows Disassembly in Sega vs. Accolade," *Computer Law Strategist*, Nov. 1992, 9:7, pp. 1, 3–5. "Can You Infringe a Copyright While Analyzing a Competitor's Program?" *Legal Bytes*, George, Donaldson & Ford, L.L.P., publisher, Winter 1992–93, 1:1, p. 3. Pamela Samuelson, "Copyright's Fair Use Doctrine and Digital Data," *Communications of the ACM*, Jan. 1994, 37:1, pp. 21–27.

15. *Sony Computer Entertainment, Inc.* v. *Connectix Corporation*, U.S. 9th Circuit Court of Appeal, No. 99-15852, Feb. 10, 2000.

16. Karl Taro Greenfeld, "The Digital Reckoning," *Time*, May 22, 2000, p. 56.

17. Stuart Luman and Jason Cook, "Knocking Off Napster," *Wired*, Jan. 2001, p. 89. Karl Taro Greenfeld, "Meet the Napster," *Time*, Oct. 2, 2000, pp. 60–68. "Napster University: From File Swapping to the Future of Entertainment," June 1, 2000, described in Mary Hillebrand, "Music Downloaders Willing to Pay," *E-Commerce Times*, June 8, 2000, www.ecommercetimes.com/story/3512.html.

18. Charles Goldsmith, "Sharp Slowdown in U.S. Singles Sales Helps to Depress Global Music Business," *Wall Street Journal*, Apr. 20, 2001, p. B8.

19. *A&M Records* v. *Napster*, No. 0016401, Feb. 12, 2001, DC No. CV-99-05183-MHP.

20. David L. Hayes, "A Comprehensive Current Analysis of Software 'Look and Feel' Protection," Fenwick & West LLP, 2000, www.fenwick.com/FenwickDocuments/Look_-_Feel.pdf.

21. 2015 data from BSA, "BSA Global Software Survey," May 2016, globalstudy.bsa.org/2016/downloads/studies/BSA_GSS_InBrief_US.pdf.

22. Ibid.

23. *RIAA* v. *Diamond Multimedia*, 1999.

24. *Bobbs-Merrill Co.* v. *Straus*, 1908. The first-sale principle became part of copyright law in 1976.

25. Les Vadasz, "A Bill that Chills," *Wall Street Journal*, July 21, 2002, p. A10.

26. Some of the examples here and many others appear in Root Jonez, "Unintended Consequences: Twelve Years under the DMCA," Electronic Frontier Foundation, Mar. 3, 2010, www.eff.org/press/archives/2010/03/03.

27. Scarlet Pruitt, "Norwegian Authorities Indict Creator of DeCSS," CNN.com, Jan. 14, 2002, www.cnn.com/2002/TECH/industry/01/14/decss.writer.idg/index.html.

28. *Universal City Studios, Inc.* v. *Reimerdes*, 111 F.Supp.2d 294 (S.D.N.Y. 2000).

29. David S. Touretzky, a computer science professor at Carnegie Mellon University, collected many forms of expressing DeCSS on his website, "Gallery of CSS Descramblers," www.cs.cmu.edu/~dst/DeCSS/Gallery/.

30. The paper leaked and appeared on the Web. It was eventually published at a computer security conference. Scott A. Craver *et al.*, "Reading Between the Lines: Lessons from the SDMI Challenge," www.usenix.org/events/sec01/craver.pdf.

31. Jonez, "Unintended Consequences." *Felten et al.* v. *RIAA, SDMI, et al.* The statement by the ACM, one of the major organizations for professional and academic computer scientists, is at cacm.acm.org/magazines/2001/10/7240-viewpoint-the-acm-declaration-in-felten-v-riaa/fulltext.

32. "Unintended Consequences: Sixteen Years Under the DMCA," Electronic Frontier Foundation, www.eff.org/files/2014/09/16/unintendedconsequences2014.pdf.

33. Ibid.

34. Copyright Office, Library of Congress, "Section 1201 Exemption to Prohibition Against Circumvention of Technological Measures Protecting Copyrighted Works," www.copyright.gov/1201/. Marcia Hofmann and Corynne McSherry, "The 2012 Rulemaking: What We Got, What We Didn't and How to Improve the Process Next Time," Electronic Frontier Foundation, Nov. 2, 2012, www.eff.org/deeplinks/2012/11/2012-dmca-rulemaking-what-we-got-what-we-didnt-and-how-to-improve. Parker Higgins *et al.*, "Victory for Users: Librarian of Congress Renews and Expands Protections for Fair Uses," Oct. 27, 2015, www.eff.org/deeplinks/2015/10/victory-users-librarian-congress-renews-and-expands-protections-fair-uses.

35. Hannah Karp, "Music Industry Out of Harmony with YouTube on Tracking of Copyrighted Music," *Wall Street Journal*, June 28, 2016, www.wsj.com/articles/industry-out-of-harmony-with-youtube-on-tracking-of-copyrighted-music-1467106213.

36. Jennifer M. Urban and Laura Quilter, "Summary Report: Efficient Process or 'Chilling Effects'? Takedown Notice under Section 512 of the Digital Millennium Copyright Act," full report in *Santa Clara Journal of High Tech Law and Technology*, Mar. 2006, digitalcommons.law.scu.edu/cgi/viewcontent.cgi?article=1413&context=chtlj.

37. www.creativecommons.org.

38. Ryan Singel, "Movie Studios Sue Streaming Movie Site Zediva," *Wired*, Apr. 4, 2011, www.wired.com/epicenter/2011/04/mpaa-sues-zediva, and Barbara Ortutay, "Movie Studios Win Lawsuit against Zediva," Oct. 31, 2011, www.yahoo.com/news/movie-studios-win-lawsuit-against-182614348.html.

39. *American Broadcasting Companies* v. *Aereo*, 2014.

40. Joe Mullin, "How 'Cyberlockers' Became the Biggest Problem in Piracy," Jan. 19, 2011, gigaom.com/2011/01/20/419-how-cyberlockers-became-the-biggest-problem-in-piracy/. Geoffrey A. Fowler, Devlin Barrett, and Sam Schechner, "U.S. Shuts Offshore File-Share 'Locker,'" *Wall Street Journal*, Jan. 20, 2012, www.wsj.com/articles/SB10001424052970204616504577171060611948408. Brett Danaher and Michael D. Smith, "Did Shutting Down Megaupload Impact Digital Movie Sales?" Initiative for Digital Entertainment Analytics, Carnegie Mellon University, idea.heinz.cmu.edu/2013/03/07/megaupload/. Brett Danaher and Michael D. Smith, "Gone in 60 Seconds: The Impact of the Megaupload Shutdown on Movie Sales," Social Science Research Network, Sept. 14, 2013, papers.ssrn.com/sol3/papers.cfm?abstract_id=2229349.

41. Harro Ten Wolde and Eric Auchard, "Germany's Top Publisher Bows to Google in News Licensing Row," Reuters, Nov. 5, 2014, www.reuters.com/article/2014/11/05/us-google-axel-sprngr-idUSKBN0IP1YT20141105. Steven Musil, "Google News

to Close Up Shop in Spain in Response to New Law," CNet, Dec. 10, 2014, www.cnet.com/news/google- news-to-close-up-shop-in-spain-in-response-to-new-law. Anna Solana, "The Google News effect: Spain Reveals the Winners and Losers from a 'Link Tax,'" ZDNet, Aug. 14, 2015, www.zdnet.com/article/the-google-news-effect-spain-reveals-the-winners-and-losers-from-a-link-tax.

42. Judge Denny Chin, *The Author's Guild et al.* v. *Google, Inc.*, Case 1:05-cv-08136-D, Nov. 14, 2013, www.nysd.uscourts.gov/cases/show.php?db=special&id=355.

43. Quoted in The Authors Guild, "Supreme Court Declines to Review Fair Use Finding in Decade-Long Book Copying Case against Google," Apr. 18, 2016, www.authorsguild.org/industry-advocacy/supreme-court-declines-review-fair-use-finding-decade-long-book-copying-case-google/.

44. See Yochai Benkler, "Coase's Penguin, or Linux and *The Nature of the Firm*," *The Yale Law Journal*, Dec. 2002, pp. 369–446, for an analysis of the phenomenon of peer production: www.yale.edu/yalelj/112/BenklerWEB.pdf.

45. The Free Software Directory, directory.fsf.org/wiki/Main_Page.

46. "What Is Copyleft?" www.gnu.org/philosophy.

47. Andy Updegrove, "A Big Victory for F/OSS: Jacobsen v. Katzen Is Settled," The Standards Blog, ConsortiumInfo.org, Feb. 19, 2010, www.consortiuminfo.org/standardsblog/article.php?story=201002190850472.

48. This is a brief summary of Stallman's views. See his article "Why Software Should Be Free" and many others at the GNU website, www.gnu.org/philosophy.

49. David Drummond, "When Patents Attack Android," *The Official Google Blog*, Aug. 3, 2011, googleblog.blogspot.com/2011/08/when-patents-attack-android.html. For a diagram illustrating this statement, see Steve Lohr, "A Bull Market in Tech Patents," *New York Times*, Aug. 16, 2011, www.nytimes.com/2011/08/17/technology/a-bull-market-in-tech-patents.html.

50. The estimated number of software patents and the analogy of each patent to a new law is from Brian Kahin, "Software Patents: Separating Rhetoric from Facts," *Science Progress*, May 15, 2013, scienceprogress.org/2013/05/software-patents-separating-rhetoric-from-facts/.

51. Charles Forelle and Suein Hwang, "IBM Hits Amazon with E-Commerce Patent Suit," *Wall Street Journal*, Oct. 24, 2006, p. A3.

52. This summary uses information from several articles by Joe Mullin in *Ars Technica*, including "A Year After Trial, USPTO Knocks Out Apple's 'Pinch to Zoom' Patent," July 29, 2013, arstechnica.com/tech-policy/2013/07/a-year-after-trial-uspto-knocks-out-apples-pinch-to-zoom-patent/, and "Apple's $120M Verdict Against Samsung Destroyed on Appeal," Feb. 26, 2016, arstechnica.com/tech-policy/2016/02/appeals-court-reverses- apple-v-samsung-ii-strips-away-apples-120m-jury-verdict/.

53. We found this definition at www.investopedia.com/terms/p/patent-troll.asp.

54. Kent Walker, "Patents and Innovation," *The Official Google Blog*, Apr. 4, 2011, googleblog.blogspot.com/2011/04/patents-and-innovation.html. The Nortel patents were sold in a bankruptcy auction.

55. Key cases are *Diamond v. Diehr*, 450 U.S. 175 (1981); *State Street Bank & Trust Co.* v. *Signature Financial Group*, 1998; *In re Bilski*, Federal Circuit, 2008; *Bilski* v. *Kappos*, June 28, 2010, www.supremecourt.gov/opinions/09pdf/08-964.pdf. See also Daniel Tysver, "Are Software and Business Methods Still Patentable after the Bilski Decisions?" *Bitlaw*, 2010, www.bitlaw.com/software-patent/bilski-and-software-patents.html.

56. *Bilski* v. *Kappos*.

57. For discussion of the case, *Alice Corp.* v. *CLS Bank*, and its implications, see www.scotusblog.com/case-files/cases/alice-corporation-pty-ltd-v-cls-bank-international/.

58. *Bilski* v. *Kappos*.

59. This exercise is based on the *Los Angeles Times* v. *Free Republic* case. The court's decision in favor of the newspapers seems inconsistent with the reasoning in the reverse engineering cases described in Section 4.2 and other fair use cases. It was criticized by some scholars.

60. The designer, Shepard Fairey, and AP settled out of court in 2011, with some details of the settlement confidential. Fairey later pleaded guilty to fabricating documents and lying during the litigation process.

61. This exercise was sparked by a brief note in Helen Nissenbaum, "Should I Copy My Neighbor's Software?" in Deborah G. Johnson and Helen Nissenbaum, *Computers, Ethics & Social Values*, Prentice Hall, 1995, p. 213.

62. In a few such cases the software support companies were found to have infringed copyright. In 2010, Oracle won a large jury award from SAP for actions of its Tomor-rowNow unit, which provided support for Oracle software.

63. Barbara R. Bergmann and Mary W. Gray, "Viewpoint: Software as a Public Good," *Communications of the ACM*, Oct. 1993, 36:10, pp. 13–14.

Crime and Security

5.1 Introduction

Con artists and crooks of many sorts have found ample opportunity to cheat unsuspecting people in cyberspace. Some scams are almost unchanged from their pre-Web forms: pyramid schemes, chain letters, sales of counterfeit luxury goods, phony business investment opportunities, and so forth. Each generation of people, whatever level of technology they use, needs a reminder that if an investment or bargain looks too good to be true, it probably is. Other scams are new or have evolved to take advantage of characteristics of online, interconnected, and mobile activities. In online dating scams, crooks use profiles and photos lifted from social media sites, then develop online relationships and convince the unwary to send money for a family emergency or some other false reason. In a particularly offensive scam, people set up websites after disasters such as terrorist attacks and hurricanes to fraudulently collect credit card donations from people who think they are contributing to the Red Cross or funds for victims.

In this chapter, we focus heavily on hacking—intentional, unauthorized access to computer systems—because it is a significant component of a variety of serious crimes such as theft (of money, information, identities, and physical property), fraud, and sabotage. We frequently see news reports of major break-ins to the computer systems of large companies and government agencies. Here are a few examples:

- The Internal Revenue Service (IRS) reported that thieves stole personal information from more than 300,000 tax returns stored in an IRS database.

- A hacker stole records of more than 100 million LinkedIn members, including IDs, email addresses, and passwords. The records were offered for sale. A website that sells stolen credentials claimed to have more than 30 million Twitter usernames and passwords for sale. Sixty-eight million usernames and passwords were stolen from DropBox. A hacker stole data from more than 500 million Yahoo accounts; the data included names, birth dates, encrypted passwords, and security questions and answers. In several of these cases, the companies were not aware of the extent of the breaches until years later.

- Hackers in Ukraine broke into news services where they had access to information about corporate earnings before the information was public. The information was used to make valuable stock trades. Most likely for the same purpose, hackers broke into the computer systems of law firms whose clients include banks and large companies. They had access to confidential data— about potential mergers, lawsuits, and so on—that affect stock prices.

- Hackers broke into computers at the federal government's Office of Personnel Management and stole records of more than 20 million federal employees. Stolen files contained fingerprints for more than five million people and information (including about psychiatric care) from background checks for personnel in sensitive jobs such as in law enforcement, the military, and foreign service. Many current and retired employees found themselves victims of identity theft. The leak potentially threatens people with security clearances and the data they can access, hence also the security of the country.

More and more frequently now, hackers break into electronically equipped devices and machines, from cars and drones to baby monitors. Crimes in cyberspace affect millions of people and cost billions of dollars. As many examples illustrate, the perpetrators of major crimes may be in another country; indeed, they may be foreign governments. Incidents of hacking the controls of cars suggest the potential for physical harm. Numerous government studies warn of vulnerabilities in critical infrastructure systems (power and transportation, for example) and of the potential for sophisticated attacks.

In this chapter, we consider social issues such as: Why is sensitive information such as background checks of federal employees and credit card numbers stored without encryption? What are the sources of the vulnerabilities of our data, devices, and physical infrastructure? What can we do, as professionals and as individual users, to reduce hacking risks? We address legal issues: What activities should be illegal? What penalties are appropriate? How can law enforcement agencies reduce cybercrimes? The ethical quality of most of the cybercrimes we consider is clear: Stealing and destroying property and information is wrong. But many ethical questions remain interesting: How should we evaluate nonmalicious hacking, including hacking to discover vulnerabilities? Who is ethically responsible for security? How can you responsibly make the appropriate people aware of a security vulnerability you discover without tipping off criminal hackers? To inform our discussion of many of these issues, we also describe how hackers do what they do and how cybersecurity professionals work to keep our systems safe.

Many of the crimes we discuss in Sections 5.1–5.6 are destructive activities that most people agree should be illegal. But there are many peaceful activities that are legal in some countries and illegal in others. Businesses and individuals are sued and arrested for violating laws of countries that their online business or writing reaches. In Section 5.7, we consider how serious this problem is and how we might deal with it.

Our first task, in Section 5.2, is to examine what "hacking" is, how its meaning has changed over time, and how hackers carry out their activities.

5.2 What is Hacking?

5.2.1 The Evolution of Hacking

The term "hacking," to many people, means an irresponsible, destructive action performed by a criminal. Hackers, individuals who perform hacking activities, break into computer systems and intentionally release computer viruses. They steal money and sensitive personal, business, and government information. They crash websites, destroy files, and disrupt businesses. Yet, other people who call themselves hackers do none of these things (both authors of this book, at times, among them). Let's organize the discussion into three eras of hacking:

- Era 1—the early years (1960s and 1970s), when hacking was a positive term
- Era 2—from the late 1970s to the late 1990s, when hacking took on its more negative meanings
- Era 3—from late 1990s to today, with the growth of the Web, e-commerce, and the number of online devices (such as medical devices and automobiles)

The boundaries are not sharp, and each era includes the kinds of hacking common in the earlier ones. In Sections 5.3 and 5.5.3 we consider hacking for special purposes (e.g., political activism, government hacking for espionage and disruption in other countries, and hacking to discover security flaws).

Hacking Era 1: The joy of programming

In the early days of computing, a "hacker" was a creative programmer who wrote very elegant or clever programs. Hackers were "computer virtuosos," and a "good hack" was an especially clever piece of code. Hackers created many of the first computer games and operating systems. Although they sometimes found ways into systems where they were not authorized users, early hackers mostly sought knowledge and intellectual challenges—and, sometimes, the thrill of going where they did not belong. Most had no intention of disrupting services; they frowned on doing damage. Some tended to be outside the social mainstream and many were high school and college students—or dropouts. Hacking in this era was usually performed on a single computer or a small network under the hacker's control or part of the hacker's typical work or academic environment.

The *New Hacker's Dictionary* describes a hacker as a person "who enjoys exploring the details of programmable systems and how to stretch their capabilities; . . . one who programs enthusiastically (even obsessively)."[1] Jude Milhon described hacking as "clever circumvention of imposed limits."[2] The limits can be the technical limits of the system one is using, the limits that someone else's security techniques impose, legal limits, or the limits of one's own skills. Her definition is a good one in that it encompasses many uses of the term. Hackers in this first era were like explorers in the new world, pushing boundaries and excited about the discoveries they made.

At many conferences and venues, "hacking" still has the early meaning of clever programming that reflects the high level of skill needed to circumvent limits. Fans of Nintendo's Wii video game console reprogram its remote controller to perform tasks Nintendo never imagined. Soon after Apple released the iPhone, hackers found ways to make it operate in ways Apple had tried to prevent. Thousands of people regularly gather for daylong "hack-a-thons" to work intensely at developing innovative new software and hardware products.

Hacking Era 2: The rise of hacking's dark side

The meaning, and especially the connotations, of the word "hacker" changed as computers became more widespread and more people began abusing them. For many, it was no longer enough to push technical and intellectual limits when hacking; they pushed or broke legal and ethical limits as well. By the 1980s, hacking included spreading computer viruses, at that time mostly in software traded on floppy disks. Hacking behavior included pranks, digital vandalism, harassment, theft (of information, software, and sometimes money), and *phone phreaking* (manipulating the telephone system). These activities drove the word to take on its malicious connotation and its most common meaning today: *breaking into computers for which the hacker does not have authorized access.*

Hacking a computer at a big research center, corporation, or government agency was a challenge that brought a sense of accomplishment, a lot of files to explore, and respect from one's peers. This "trophy" hacking was often associated with young hackers. Some, inspired by the movie *"War Games,"* were especially fond of breaking into Defense Department computers, and were very successful at it. Clifford Stoll described a more serious adult case in his book *The Cuckoo's Egg.* After months digitally investigating a 75-cent accounting error, Stoll discovered that a German hacker had broken into dozens of U.S. computers, including military systems, looking for information to sell to the Soviet Union.

In 1988, a computer program known as the Internet Worm,[*] or Morris Worm, clearly established the vulnerability of the Internet as a whole to malicious hacking. A graduate student at Cornell University wrote the worm and released it onto the Internet. The worm did not destroy files or steal passwords, and there was disagreement about whether its author intended or expected it to cause the degree of disruption that it did. However, it spread quickly to computers running a version of the UNIX operating system, slowing them down by running many copies of itself and preventing normal processing. This disrupted work and inconvenienced a large number of people. The worm affected a few thousand computers (a large portion of the Internet at the time). Systems programmers spent several days working to discover, decode, and rid their systems of the worm. This incident raised concern about the potential to disrupt critical computer services and cause social disruption and so led to the establishment of the Computer Emergency Response Team Coordination Center (CERT/CC).[3]

As adult criminals began to recognize the possibilities of hacking, they recruited hackers to commit business espionage, substantial thefts, and fraud. In what is believed to be one of the first online bank robberies, a Russian, Vladimir Levin,

---

[*]A worm is a program that copies itself to other computers. The original concept was developed to make use of idle resources, but it was adopted by people using it maliciously.

with accomplices in several countries, used employee passwords to steal $400,000 from Citicorp in 1994. He transferred another $11 million to bank accounts in other countries. Extraditing the Russian man from London, where he was arrested, to the United States for trial took more than two years, illustrating some of the difficulties the international nature of computer crimes creates for law enforcement.

Hacking Era 3: Hacking as a destructive and criminal tool

As businesses, large and small, and governments, from the national level to municipalities, moved their records online, there was an explosion of information accessible over the Internet. The interconnectedness of the Internet and the increasing use of the Web for sensitive information, economic transactions, and communications made hacking more attractive to criminals and more dangerous and damaging to the victims. With basic infrastructure systems—water, power, hospitals, transportation, emergency services, communication systems—accessible on the Internet, the potential targets for hackers massively increased, and so did the risks to everyday life.

As the World Wide Web spread, the reach of a criminal hacker could span continents. Epidemics caused by computer viruses spread rapidly and globally. The Melissa virus of 1999 used code hidden in Microsoft Word documents to email copies of itself to the first 50 people in an infected computer's contact list, quickly infecting nearly 20% of computers worldwide. Just a year later, the "Love Bug," or "ILOVEYOU" virus, spread around the world in a few hours. It destroyed image, music, and operating system files and collected passwords. This virus infected major corporations such as Ford and Siemens and infected 80% of U.S. federal agencies, including the State Department and the Pentagon, along with members of the British Parliament and the U.S. Congress. Many businesses and government agencies had to shut down their email servers to clean out the virus and repair its impact. This virus, still considered one of the most destructive to date, hit tens of millions of computers worldwide and did an estimated $10 billion in damage.[4*]

A teenager crippled a computer system that handled communications between the airport tower and incoming planes at a small airport. Hackers in England impersonated air traffic controllers and gave false instructions to pilots. Hackers modified the programming at an online gambling site so that everyone won; the site lost $1.9 million. New York City accused several people of stealing $800,000 from the city's subway system by taking advantage of a software error in the machines that sell fare cards.

Hackers execute revenge attacks. After police raided a popular pirate music site in Sweden, an apparent retaliation attack by hackers shut down the main websites of the Swedish government and police. After Sony sued George Hotz for showing how to run unauthorized applications and games on Sony's PlayStation 3, a hacker

---

*Damages from such virus attacks are difficult to value precisely; estimates may be rough.

group launched a denial-of-service attack[*] on Sony. Later, in another attack, the hackers accessed names, birth dates, and credit card information of millions of users of Sony's gaming systems.[5]

As use of smartphones and social networks grew, they became targets. Hackers steal banking credentials when people use insecure banking apps or insecure phones. Hackers gained access to Facebook member profile pages by tricking members into running malware;[†] the hackers posted pornographic and violent images on those pages. It is a common tactic for hackers to create fake offers of discounts, freebies, or just something funny or interesting to get a person to click on it and initiate malware. Social networks offer a huge pool of potential victims who are used to sharing.[6]

With the establishment of CERT, computer scientists responded to increased security threats with improved security technology, but attitudes about security in businesses, organizations, and government agencies were slow to catch up with the risks. Security techniques and industry practices did not begin to improve dramatically until the early 2000s when several devastating viruses and security breaches made the news and impacted numerous organizations. The field of cybersecurity has matured and security personnel work closely with law enforcement to counter the threat posed by hackers.

Shades of hackers

In old cowboy movies, the good guys wore white hats and the bad guys wore black hats, so the terms "white hat hacker" and "black hat hacker" are often applied to the cowboys of the computer frontier. Black hat hackers are those whose activities are destructive, unethical, and, usually, illegal; we will refer to these simply as "hackers" going forward. White hat hackers use their skills to demonstrate system vulnerabilities and improve security—these include cybersecurity experts who strive to protect systems and provide early warning of potential threats. We consider the technical and ethical challenges faced by white hat hackers in Section 5.5 and refer to them as cybersecurity experts to differentiate them from hackers. As we will see when examining these two groups in more detail, many of their activities are similar, but their motivations and results are often very different. A third group, sometimes called gray hat hackers, has elements of each.

5.2.2   HACKER TOOLS

To gain access to the email accounts of Defense Department personnel, or to the electric power grid, or to medical records, a hacker uses multiple tools. Let's look at some of the more common tools and types of malware (malicious software). In Section 5.3.2, we will examine a case in which a team of hackers used multiple tools to steal millions of credit cards numbers and more.

---

[*]In a denial-of-service attack, hackers overload the target site with requests for information. We discuss them in Section 5.2.2.
[†]*Malware* is malicious software.

Virus—software that attaches or adds itself to other software. Often a virus is a small portion of a program that can replicate itself and perform other functions such as deleting files or sending emails. Viruses often spread when someone runs an infected program or opens an infected attachment.

Worm—similar to a virus, but does not need to attach itself to another program in order to function. Worms are designed to exploit specific system flaws. Once a worm has gained access to a host system, it scans nearby systems for similar flaws so that it can spread to those systems. The Conficker worm, first detected in 2008, infected millions of computers, and, like some diseases, it lived on. A variant version was shipped in police body cameras in 2015. When one of these cameras was attached to a computer, the worm attempted to spread to the computer and contact a distant server.[7] Can we trust video from such a camera or data from the computer?

Trojan horse—malware that appears to be a benign software application but carries a malicious component. The user believes the program is safe and launches it. When the application runs, in addition to its normal functionality, it performs malicious activities such as installing a virus or sending spam to all contacts in the user's address book.

Social engineering—the manipulation of people into releasing information or performing a task that violates security protocols. A hacker might impersonate someone from the technical support office in your organization and call you and ask for login credentials or other important information. Hackers have used social engineering since the early days of computers, and it has been very successful. It was used to launch the Melissa and ILOVEYOU viruses discussed earlier and to hijack the Associated Press's Twitter account. In a scam that has been operating for years, someone calls you on the phone claiming to be from the "Windows Technical Department" and says your computer has viruses or is running malware. If you continue the conversation long enough, the caller will ask you to download software to clean it, but the software actually installs malware.

Phishing—Have you received email or a text message from PayPal, Amazon, or a bank asking you to confirm information about your account? Have you received email from the IRS telling you the agency has a tax refund for you? These are likely examples of fraudulent spam called *phishing* (in the case of email) and *smishing* (in the case of text messaging)[*]: sending millions of messages fishing for information to use to impersonate someone and steal money and goods. The message tells the victim to click or tap a link to what purports to be the website of a well-known bank or online company. The phony site asks for account numbers, passwords, and other identifying information. Hackers take advantage of our knowledge that there is a lot of online fraud: Several pretexts that appear frequently in phishing scams warn that there has been a breach in the security of your bank or PayPal account and you

---

[*]SMS is the abbreviation for Short Message Service, the method used for texting on mobile phones, hence the term *smishing*.

need to respond to determine whether someone else is misusing your account. Some messages tell the recipient they just made a very big purchase and if the purchase was not really theirs, they should click a link to cancel the order. In a panic, people do—and enter their identifying information when asked for it. *Spear phishing* is targeted, personalized phishing sometimes aimed at high-level corporate or government employees. These phishing emails or texts appear to be from a coworker, about a work-related project, or from a friend, about a topic of interest to the targeted person. Both huge Democratic Party campaign email leaks in 2016 resulted from people clicking links in phishing emails.

Pharming—luring people to fake websites where thieves collect personal data. Normally when we indicate a website we want to visit, our browser looks up the IP address[*] of the site on one of many Domain Name Servers (DNS), special computers on the Internet for this purpose. Pharming involves planting false Internet addresses in the tables on a DNS that lead the browser to a counterfeit site set up by hackers.

Ransomware—malware that encrypts some or all the files on a computer or mobile device and then displays a message demanding payment for the key to decrypt the files. Often, the hacker demands payment in bitcoins, an anonymous digital currency. Victims (individuals and large businesses), especially those with no safe backups, usually pay the fee. Ransomware attacks increased to an average of 4000 a day in 2016, according to the U.S. Department of Justice,[8] with millions of dollars going to the hackers.

Spyware—malware that can monitor and record user activities on a computer or mobile device. This includes logging keystrokes on the keyboard to capture usernames, passwords, account numbers, and other information. Spyware can log websites visited and other network activity and send the data to a remote server monitored by the hacker. More devastating, spyware can control a webcam and record activity without the user knowing—spyware can disable a webcam's "active" light while recording. Miss Teen USA 2013, Cassidy Wolf, inadvertently opened an attachment to an email from a classmate that installed a spyware package on her computer. The classmate had purchased the spyware, which required very little technical knowledge to deploy, for less than $100, and used it to watch and take photos of Wolf (and other young women). Later, he tried to extort money from her by threatening to sell the photos.[9]

Botnet—a group of computers or other devices on the Internet that have a virus or piece of malware that communicates with a central host or server controlled by a hacker—or, as journalist Sean Gallagher put it, a botnet is a coordinated army of compromised devices.[10] The infected devices are referred to as bots or zombies. The hacker issues commands from the central server directing the botnet to perform tasks such as sending spam, participating in online advertising fraud, or initiating a distributed denial of service attack (defined next). The actual owners of the zombies

---

[*]An IP (Internet Protocol) address is a string of numbers that identifies a device on the Internet.

are usually unaware of what their devices are doing. Botnets are extremely difficult to eradicate: most botnets comprise millions of computers and other devices, and the virus can reinfect devices quickly. When Conficker, Zeus, Simda, and other botnets are brought down, it is often because law enforcement agents take control of the central botnet servers through hacking activities of their own.

A sophisticated international scam involved 20 billion spam messages sent within a two-week period from more than 100,000 computers in more than 100 countries. The messages directed people to e-commerce websites where the unwary ordered products with their credit cards and received nothing. Credit card charges went to a company in Russia. This scam illustrates the growing complexity of crime on the Web combining hacking, spam, phony websites, and international fraud.[11]

In the early 2000s, botnets consisted mostly of personal computers. Now, some include phones and a variety of devices on the Internet of Things.

Denial of service (DoS) or *distributed denial of service* (DDoS) attack—an attack in which a botnet overwhelms websites, mail servers, or other Internet locations with so many requests for service that normal users cannot access the sites or services. In some cases, the attack crashes the sites. DDoS attacks are a daily occurrence on the Internet and relatively easy to implement. Targets often are large companies and websites or large swaths of the Internet but can be individuals (e.g., journalists who write about security and anger hackers or professional video gamers who are targeted by competitors during games). A DDoS attack activated by malware on smartphones caused the phones to call 911, potentially slowing responses to emergencies. An attack in 2016 used hundreds of thousands (or more) digital video recorders, cameras, and other devices on a botnet called Mirai to interrupt access to more than a thousand sites including Paypal, Twitter, Netflix, Reddit, Box.com, GitHub, Airbnb, and Sony's Playstation network.[12]

Backdoor—software that allows access to a computer system or device at a future time by bypassing the normal layers of security checks. A hacker might install a backdoor, or a software developer might intentionally write one into a system so that he or she can regain access easily for maintenance or to gather usage profiles.

Backdoors for law enforcement: Section 5.5.4

This list includes only some of the more common tools at the disposal of hackers. Creating most hacking tools requires technical skills. However, hacking scripts (sequences of instructions to be executed) and computer code for thousands of computer viruses are available for free or a small price on the Internet, thus easily accessible to teenagers and thieves.

5.2.3 IS "HARMLESS" HACKING HARMLESS?

In many cases, it is the excitement and challenge of breaking in that motivates hackers—particularly for young hackers with no malicious intent. Some claim that if they copy no data and change no files then hacking is harmless. Is it?

When a system administrator for a computer system at a university, a website, a business, or the military detects an intruder, he or she cannot immediately distinguish a nonmalicious hacker from a thief, terrorist, or spy. At a minimum, an organization will expend time and effort to track down the intruder, shut off the means of access, and attempt to verify that the intruder did not change any data or steal any files. When an organization must bring down its Internet connection to stop or investigate a breach, employees and the public are inconvenienced, and the cost, in poor publicity and lost work or lost sales, may be high. Responding to nonmalicious or prank hacking uses resources that might be needed to respond to serious threats.

Uncertainty about the intruder's intent and activities has additional costs for systems that contain sensitive data since even if an intruder copied nothing, he or she may have viewed confidential or personal data. According to the head of the computer crime unit at the Department of Justice, after a hacker accessed a Boeing Corporation computer, apparently just to hop to another system, Boeing spent a large sum to verify that the intruder changed no files. Would we be comfortable flying a new Boeing airplane if the company had *not* done this? In another incident, a group of young Danes broke into U.S. National Weather Service computers and computers of numerous other government agencies, businesses, and universities in the U.S., Japan, Brazil, Israel, and Denmark. Eventually the police caught them. It appeared they had done little damage, but let's consider the risks. Their activities caused the Weather Service computers to slow down, creating the potential that serious conditions, such as tornadoes, could have gone undetected and unreported.[13] Similarly, if system administrators detect unauthorized access in a medical records system, a credit database, or payroll data, they must stop the intruders and determine whether they copied or changed any records. Uncertainty causes harm, or expense, even if hackers have no destructive intent.

Another problem, of course, is that a hacker with good intentions can make a mistake and do significant damage accidentally. Almost all hacking is a form of trespass, so it should not surprise hackers with nonmalicious intentions that others will often view them unkindly.

5.3 Some Specific Applications of Hacking

5.3.1 IDENTITY THEFT

We buy products and services from strangers and do our banking and investing online without seeing or knowing the physical location of the company we deal with. We can travel with only a passport and a credit or debit card and can qualify for a mortgage or a car loan in minutes. As part of providing this convenience and efficiency, our identity has become a series of numbers (credit and debit card numbers, Social Security number, driver's license number, phone number, account numbers) and computer files (credit history, work history, driving record). But the convenience and efficiency engender risks. Remote transactions are fertile grounds for many kinds of crime, especially identity theft and a common result, credit and debit fraud.

Identity theft describes various crimes in which a criminal or large, well-organized criminal group uses the identity of an unknowing innocent person. Criminals use stolen credit or debit card numbers to buy expensive items (or many cheap items), or they sell the numbers to others who use them. They use personal information (such as Social Security numbers) to open new accounts in the victim's name. Identity thieves take out loans, buy groceries, get expensive medical treatment, raid the victim's bank account, apply for the victim's tax refund, pass bad checks, or use the victim's identity in various other ways for financial gain.

Collecting information useful for identity theft is the goal of a significant amount of hacking, and hacking is a significant step in some of the monetary thefts that result, for example, accessing someone's bank account and stealing the money. At the beginning of this chapter, and in Section 2.1.2, we listed a small number of incidents with loss or theft of data from large databases containing personal information. In several of those incidents, identity theft and fraud were the goals. A single cybersecurity breach often affects millions of people and results in thousands of fraud cases. In the United States, losses amount to tens of billions of dollars in a year.[14] Credit card companies and other businesses bear the direct cost of most credit card fraud, but the losses lead to higher charges for consumers. In addition, individual victims might lose a good credit rating and be unable to borrow money, cash checks, get a job, or rent an apartment—and then creditors sue the victim for money the criminal borrowed.

Identity thieves love the millions of résumés that people post on job-hunting sites. Thieves collect addresses, Social Security numbers, birth dates, work histories, and all the other details that help them convincingly adopt the identity of the job seeker. Some pose as employers and post fake job announcements; others respond to job hunters and ask for more information, perhaps saying they need it for a background check. Because identity thieves misuse such sites, job seekers must adapt and be more cautious by omitting sensitive data from a posted résumé, not providing sensitive information until they have an actual interview, or finding other ways to determine that the potential employer is authentic. Job sites, aware of the threat, offer services to keep sensitive information private.

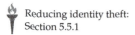
Reducing identity theft: Section 5.5.1

Although we focus on criminal groups who use hacking and other technical means to commit identity theft, family members and acquaintances of victims are responsible for a significant percentage of identity theft. Many identity theft cases result from low- or no-tech problems such as lost wallets or stolen checkbooks. We must use care in protecting our own passwords, documents, Social Security numbers, and so on, both in and out of cyberspace.

5.3.2   Case Study: The Target Breach

During a four-week period in 2013, hackers gained access to personal information including 40 million credit card numbers and approximately 70 million names, mailing addresses, and phone numbers of Target customers in the United States. How did this happen? We may never know all the details, but cybersecurity investigators have pieced together a likely scenario incorporating known facts about the breach.[15]

About two months prior to the massive data theft, hackers sent a phishing email to an employee at the company Fazio Mechanical. Fazio is a small business with about 125 employees that performs heating, air conditioning, and refrigeration maintenance for a number of companies including Target. The employee accepted the bait from the phishing email, clicked on the attachment or link, and inadvertently installed the Citadel Trojan. The Citadel malware steals usernames and passwords. Security experts do not know if the thieves chose Fazio because it is a vendor that supplies services to Target or simply because it is a small business. Small business computer systems often have weak security, and hackers use them as a gateway to bigger targets. At the time of the breach, Target had the names and contact information for many of its vendors publicly accessible, giving hackers a list of prey easier than the Target corporate network.

Over the Internet, Fazio Mechanical employees connected to at least two different internal Target applications for electronic billing and contract submission. When the Fazio employee with an infected machine logged into one of these Target systems, Citadel would have stolen the username and password and sent them to the hackers. Seeing credentials for Target would have piqued the interest of the hacking team, who may have begun additional research to discover more about how Target manages vendors.

The stolen Fazio employee credentials gave hackers access to massive amounts of internal Target information available to vendors and suppliers. At the time, Target also provided a large amount of information about itself on its public website that required no login. The hackers may have downloaded files from these sites, searching for information that gave some hint as to the internal Target network structure. For example, many Microsoft Office documents store the Windows username and domain of the person who edited the document and the server where the document is located—important pieces of data for a hacker.

To enter the Target internal network, the hackers may have logged into the contract Web application as the compromised Fazio employee. Then, instead of uploading a contract as the Web app was expecting, the hackers uploaded a program giving them control of the Target server. Now, the hacking team had access to Target's internal network, and most likely slowed down their activities. One reason was to avoid getting caught, and the second was to perform reconnaissance and probe the internal network and determine what computers were accessible.

Despite Target having a password policy, cybersecurity investigators discovered the internal network had Web and data servers with default or weak passwords that the hackers could easily crack, thus making available administrative access to systems, servers, networks, and customer data. At this point, the hackers likely gained access to the names and addresses of 70 million Target customers.

For security reasons, the point-of-sale (POS) system (the system that calculates a customer's bill at checkout and begins the payment process) was on another internal network. It is not clear exactly how hackers were able to gain access to the POS system network and its servers, but in a large organization like Target, it is not uncommon to have Web or database servers misconfigured. It takes only one crack to give the hacker an access point. Through weeks of reconnaissance and trial and error, a hacker found the crack and gained access to the internal POS system. The hackers then transferred malware called BlackPOS to Target's network and installed it on Target's POS workstations, which were Windows computers running a special POS application. To protect consumer data, after a customer swipes a credit card, the system encrypts cardholder information such as the card number before transmitting it. But, for the POS application to verify a card number and know which payment processing organization should authorize the transaction, the system must decrypt the card number and store it in computer memory for a short period. This small time window was when BlackPOS stole cardholder data. During a period of about four weeks, BlackPOS captured cardholder information for approximately 40 million Target customers.

The hacking team had one more hurdle to jump—they had to get the system to send them the card information so that they could make use of it. Using administrator privileges gained earlier, the hacking team set up its own server on the internal Target network. All the infected POS terminals sent the credit card numbers and other customer information to this server. From there, the hackers could retrieve and sell the information.

Figure 5.1 summarizes impacts of the Target breach. This breach is not unique. Eighteen months later, hackers stole more than 50 million customer credit card

---

- Hackers sold Target customer credit card data for an average price of about $27 per card.
- Between 3% and 7% of the card numbers were used for fraud before banks realized the situation and canceled the remaining cards.
- Estimated take by hackers from this crime was about $53.7 million.
- Target saw a 46% drop in profits for the quarter compared to the previous year.
- Banks and credit unions spent an estimate $200 million to reissue credit cards for about half of the compromised accounts.

FIGURE 5.1 Impact of the Target breach.

numbers and email addresses from the Home Depot chain; they used credentials stolen from a Home Depot vendor to install a variant of the BlackPOS malware on the chain's POS terminals.

5.3.3 HACKTIVISM, OR POLITICAL HACKING

Hacktivism is the use of hacking to promote a political cause. Is there ethical justification for such hacking? Should penalties for hacktivists differ from penalties for other hackers?

Just as hacking in general ranges from mild to highly destructive activities, so can political hacking. Here are some examples:

- Hackers modified the U.S. Department of Justice Web page to read "Department of Injustice" to protest the Communications Decency Act. They changed the CIA's site to read "Central Stupidity Agency."

- Three teenagers hacked into the network of an atomic research center in India and downloaded files to protest India's tests of nuclear weapons.

- Hacktivists targeted the governments of Indonesia and China for their antidemocratic policies.

- A hacker group hacked into the Bay Area Rapid Transit system (BART) and released emails, passwords, and personal information of a few thousand BART customers. They did this to protest BART's controversial shutdown of wireless communication in several BART stations to thwart a planned protest demonstration.

A fundamental problem with evaluating political hacking is that it can be hard to identify. People who agree with the political or social position of the hackers tend to see an act as "activism," while those who disagree see it as ordinary crime (or worse). Several incidents of defacement of U.S. government websites made implicit political statements. Is posting a pro-drug message on a police website a political statement against the futility, dishonesty, expense, and international intrusions of U.S. drug policy, or is it the act of a kid showing off? To some activists, any act that shuts down or steals from a large corporation is a political act and defensible. To the customers and owners, it is vandalism and theft.

Suppose we know that a political cause motivates the hackers. How do we begin to evaluate the ethics of their hacktivism? Suppose a religious group, to protest homosexuality, disables a website for gay people, and suppose an environmentalist group, to protest a new housing development, disables a website of a real estate developer. Many people who argue that one of these acts is justifiable hacktivism would argue that the other is not, because one takes a conservative position and the other takes a liberal position. Yet, it would be very difficult to develop a sound ethical basis for distinguishing them.

Some academic writers and political groups argue that hacktivism is ethical and a modern form of civil disobedience.[16] Others argue that the political motive is irrelevant and that political hacking is no more justified than other criminal hacking. Civil disobedience has a respected, nonviolent tradition. Henry David Thoreau, Mahatma Gandhi, and Martin Luther King Jr. refused to cooperate with rules they saw as unjust. Peaceful protestors have marched, rallied, and boycotted to promote their goals. Burning down ski resorts (because one would prefer to see the land undeveloped) or abortion clinics (because one opposes abortion) is quite another category of activity. To evaluate an incident of hacktivism, it is helpful to fit it into a scale from peaceful resistance to destruction of other people's property and actions that risk serious harm to innocent people.

Are hacktivists merely exercising their freedom of speech? Freedom of speech does not include the right to hang a political sign in a neighbor's window or paint one's slogans on someone else's fence. We have the freedom to speak, but not the right to compel others to listen. Crashing a website or defacing a Web page is comparable to shouting down a speaker with whom one disagrees. Those who believe that the specific content or cause is more important than the principle of freedom of speech defend such actions. People deeply involved in political causes may see their side as unquestionably morally right, and anyone on the other side as morally evil, not simply someone with a different point of view. This thought process leads to the position that the freedom of speech, freedom of choice, and property rights of people with different views deserve no respect. Peace, freedom, and civil society require that we respect such basic rights and not impose our views on those we disagree with.

Another factor to consider when evaluating hacktivism is the political system under which the hacktivists live. From both an ethical and social perspective, in free countries where almost anyone can tweet or share his or her words and video online for free, it is hard to justify hacking someone else's site to promote a political cause. Activists use the Internet and social media to organize opposition to oil exploration in Alaska that they fear will harm a caribou herd and to organize mass demonstrations against international meetings of government leaders. Human rights organizations effectively use the Web and social media, and groups supporting all kinds of nonmainstream causes promote their views in cyberspace. None of this activism requires hacktivism.

The nations in which hacktivism is likely to have the most ethical justification are those least likely to respect acts of civil disobedience. Oppressive governments control the means of communication and prohibit open political discussion, ban some religions, and jail or kill people who express opposition views. In such countries, where openly communicating one's views is impossible or dangerous, there might be good arguments to justify political hacking to get one's message out to the public and, in some cases, to sabotage government websites.

5.3.4   HACKING BY GOVERNMENTS

[K]eystrokes originating in one country can impact the other side of the globe in the blink of an eye. In the 21st century, bits and bytes can be as threatening as bullets and bombs.

—William J. Lynn III, Deputy Defense Secretary[17]

A sampling of incidents

Hacking by governments—for economic and military espionage and to disable enemies (or future enemies)—has increased dramatically. It can be difficult to prove that a government is behind a cyberattack. Sometimes, the source of an attack is traced to a specific country, but it may not be possible to determine whether the attackers work for a government or are civilian criminals. However, the nature and sophistication of attacks, as well as the type of targets can lead security researchers to believe the attacks are the work of government agencies.

An attack on the Gmail accounts of White House staffers, China policy experts, military officials, human rights activists, and others originated in a Chinese city where a major Chinese national security division is located. This attack used a very effective phishing scam with emails carefully written in government jargon about State Department reports to fool the recipients into thinking the email was authentic. High-level government officials (and other people targeted) disclosed their passwords, allowing the hackers to read their email for months.[18] In a computer attack that appeared to originate in China, hackers stole several terabytes of information about the design of one of the Pentagon's new and extremely expensive fighter jets. Other international hackers from China apparently had high-level and widespread access to the computer system of a large U.S. telecommunications company for almost 10 years. They stole technical documents, research reports, business plans, and email.

Government sponsored attacks target more than just information systems. A coordinated attack against three regional power authorities in Ukraine left hundreds of thousands of people without power. A month later, Israel's power authority was hit by an attack that required shutting down several portions of its power grid to recover. Security experts report that Russian and Chinese hackers broke into computer networks that control the U.S. electric power grid. They left behind code that could disrupt the system if activated. Hackers intruded on U.S. satellites to the point where they could control, damage, or destroy them (but did not do so), and others systematically hacked oil and gas companies worldwide.[19] The U.S. Justice Department charged Iranian hackers, who have connections to the Iranian government, with breaking into the control systems of a small dam north of New York City and launching a denial-of-service attack that affected dozens of U.S. financial institutions.

The U.S. and Israel carried out a successful cyberattack, with a virus called Stuxnet, to damage centrifuges used by Iran to enrich uranium. The computer and control systems of the enrichment facilities were not connected to the Internet, so a USB drive most likely introduced the virus. An acquaintance may have given one of the plant workers an infected drive, or the worker may have been the victim of a phishing attack at home that installed the virus on his computer and then the drive. Once on the facility's network, Stuxnet infected control hardware for the uranium centrifuges. As with many industrial devices, embedded computer chips controlled the centrifuges and workers at remote workstations in the facility monitored the output. Depending on the type of centrifuge, Stuxnet stressed the device by either spinning the centrifuge far beyond its safety limits or greatly increasing the internal centrifuge pressure. While the virus was stressing the device, it faked output to the monitoring workstations so workers did not notice anything wrong. To further hide its activity, Stuxnet did not destroy the centrifuges immediately. Through repeated random high-speed spinning or pressure increases, Stuxnet caused the centrifuges to fail periodically, but unpredictably. This made it appear to the facility staff that the centrifuges were of low quality because they were failing at a higher rate than advertised.[20]

The government of Iran attempted to hack into the computers and phones of United Nations nuclear inspectors who were attempting to learn whether Iran's nuclear facilities are for military purposes. Whether Iran's intelligence agency was able to extract sensitive information (what the inspectors found, who assisted the inspectors, and so on) was uncertain.

Leaked National Security Agency documents showed the NSA had U.S.-made communications gear, such as routers, modified prior to shipping overseas so that surveillance software or malware could be installed and used for spying.[21] The fear of China doing the same to gear sent to the U.S. is a reason there are restrictions on importing Chinese telecommunications equipment.

Cyber warfare

The Pentagon announced that the United States will treat some cyberattacks as acts of war and respond with military force. Countries targeted with cyberattacks must determine whether a foreign government, a terrorist organization, or a teenager organized the attack. There are many challenging questions about the use of cyberattacks against another country and about how to respond to one:

- When is a cyberattack justified? (Was the Stuxnet cyber sabotage against Iran justified? Would it have been better to directly attack the facilities with drones or planes to delay Iran's nuclear program?)

- When is a cyberattack an act of war? Is an attack that does significant economic damage an act of war?

- What level of certainty about the source of an attack should there be before a counterattack?

- What responses are appropriate for various kinds of attacks?

- How can we make critical systems safer from attacks?
- Wars regularly include deaths of civilians and incidents where military units accidentally kill fighters on their own side. How common and how serious will analogous side effects of cyberattacks be?

5.4 Why Is the Digital World So Vulnerable?

Why do hackers seem to easily get access to our friends' contact lists and send us spam? Why are so many hacking attacks on sensitive data and devices successful? Why are medical devices not protected from hackers? As we see repeatedly, our new tools are remarkably powerful and remarkably vulnerable.

Nearly every digital device or system, from your mobile phone and tablet to fitness monitors, Web-controlled home lights and televisions, personal computers, Web servers, and the Internet, have vulnerabilities—weaknesses or flaws that someone can discover and exploit.

A variety of factors contribute to security vulnerabilities and weaknesses:

- the inherent complexity of computer systems,
- the development history of the Internet and the Web,
- the software and communications systems that run phones, the Web, industrial systems, and the many interconnected devices we use,
- the speed at which new applications develop,
- economic, business, and political factors, and
- human nature.

Let's take a look at how our digital life became so vulnerable.

5.4.1 Vulnerability of Operating Systems and the Internet

Operating systems

One of the most important parts of any computer is the operating system. This software controls access to the hardware and makes applications and files available to the computer's users. Operating systems, such as Microsoft Windows, Apple's macOS, and Linux, all try to balance:

- giving the user as many features as possible,
- giving the user the ability to control as many features as possible,
- convenience and ease of use,
- providing a stable, crash-free system, and
- providing a secure system.

Each operating system and each version of an operating system may balance these criteria differently. Writing software to manage a computer, keyboard, mouse, touchscreen, hard disk, and memory while connecting to a network and providing a balance of the above criteria is a tremendously complex task that can require coordinating teams comprised of thousands of software designers, developers, and testers. On a mobile device or phone, the front and rear video cameras, multi-touch pressure-sensitive screens, fingerprint readers, battery usage, and wireless connectivity add to the challenges operating system designers face.

It is not unusual for there to be mistakes in an operating system or an application. Companies that write software regularly update their products with patches* to fix errors. Some companies began sending automatic updates without the user's knowledge or consent. It was the companies' view that the security of their software was critically important and they did not want to rely on nontechnical users for important security updates. Some people viewed this as "losing control" over a device they had purchased and objected to automatic updates of software. Information technology (IT) departments in businesses protested automatic updates because they frequently did not interact properly with internal applications. IT departments wanted time to control and test updates before providing them to employees. Most software companies have since made automatic software updates optional for users, resulting in an inconsistent patchwork of applied security updates for operating systems and application software.

Large organizations, businesses, and government agencies have enormous information systems that span several networks, occasionally in different parts of the world. The hardware and software on these networks are continuously upgraded and replaced. Keeping track of all that occurs in this dynamic environment and maintaining the knowledge and training of the cybersecurity staff is a daunting task. A system that was secure at one point in time may become vulnerable later.

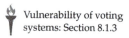
Vulnerability of voting systems: Section 8.1.3

Vulnerability of the Internet

The Internet began as ARPANET, linking together a number of universities, tech companies, and government installations. In its early years, the Internet was primarily a communications medium for researchers, so the focus was on open access, ease of use, and ease of sharing information. Many early systems did not have passwords and few connected to telephone networks; protection against intruders was not a concern. The early Internet pioneers did not expect users to intentionally try to destroy the system. Security depended primarily on trust. Designed for openness, the Internet now has three billion global users and billions of devices connecting to it.

---

*A patch is a piece of software designed to fix an error, usually for software that is already on the market and in use.

When businesses and government agencies began to set up websites in the 1990s, Internet security expert Dan Farmer ran a program to probe the sites of banks, newspapers, government agencies, and even pornography sellers for software loopholes that made it easy for hackers to invade and disable or damage the sites. Of the 1700 sites he examined, he found that about two-thirds had security weaknesses—and only four sites apparently noticed that someone was probing their security. Farmer's warnings had little effect.

One area of vulnerability on the World Wide Web is the protocol for finding the best way to route messages, for example, from your device to the website you want. The Web actually consists of thousands of smaller interconnected networks. At points where these networks connect, each sends the others a list of the sites for which it provides the shortest path. In this vast mesh of connections, there is a huge number of ways a message can travel. Having information on the shortest route greatly speeds up communications. Frequent updating of the lists of shortest paths occurs as new networks and nodes come online, but no facility verifies the updates. Each network trusts that it is getting accurate information. Several times, these lists have been falsified, intentionally and unintentionally. As a result, the Internet incorrectly routed large portions of U.S. military traffic through China in what some believe was a deliberate attempt to spy on the U.S. military. In another incident, traffic between two computers a short distance apart in Denver traveled through malicious servers in Iceland.

Many small businesses do not have an IT department and few have the resources for even a single dedicated staff person to support the business's computers, software, and networks. Employees have no formal security training, and security software at these businesses is often limited to free versions of anti-malware software. While free anti-malware software provides some protection, it is limited in scope, may not automatically scan for viruses, and seldom delivers regular updates to the list of known malware.

Many small business websites are created by small, local Web design companies or possibly a friend or family member of the business owner. Security is usually not a concern since the website simply provides information about the company and its services—*"There is nothing valuable here, why worry about security?"* These sites are easy and valuable prizes for hackers. Hackers can set up a new hidden website on a business's site and then use the hidden site to mimic bank websites for phishing scams, for pharming, as a command and control server for a botnet, or for other malicious purposes. Often hackers who steal millions of data records from banks or other large businesses start by targeting a small company and find a way to leap to the large company. We saw an example in the Target breach case in Section 5.3.2.

The Heartbleed bug

As we saw in Section 4.5, many systems use open source software or free software. One such product, OpenSSL, provides a library of computer code that programmers use to send and receive encrypted messages. Web servers using Apache software, also open source, relied on OpenSSL to provide users with secure web browsing to banks, governments, and other sites with sensitive information. The Android smartphone operating system, many email servers, and most network routers (hardware devices that forward Internet traffic from one network to another) also use this library. It was estimated that almost two-thirds of the Internet relied on this software for security when, in 2014, a catastrophic bug was found that made it possible for a hacker to access unencrypted usernames, passwords, digital certificates, and encryption keys. The bug was present in versions of OpenSSL since 2012, so hackers may have exploited this defect for almost two years before anyone found it. The defect was called "Heartbleed" because it was in the "heartbeat" section of the OpenSSL code.[22]

Many people were appalled that critical software could have such a severe defect, and conspiracy theories developed about the error being maliciously inserted. The real cause was much more benign. The nonprofit organization created to support OpenSSL had one employee and received about $2,000 annually in donations. The bug was a simple programming error made during an update by a part-time contributor and was missed when the code was reviewed before distribution. Since the code was open source, any developer who wanted to review the code was able to do so, but no one caught the mistake until years later. Since the Heartbleed defect caused critical issues for a large number of Web-based companies, several organizations, such as the Linux Foundation, have agreed to greatly increase funding to support the OpenSSL project.[23]

5.4.2 HUMAN NATURE, MARKETS, AND VULNERABILITY OF THE INTERNET OF THINGS

A significant factor leading to weak security is the speed of innovation and people's desire for new things fast. Competitive pressure spurs companies to develop products with insufficient thought or budget devoted to analyzing potential security risks and protecting against them. The culture of sharing and the phenomenon of users developing applications and games for social networks and smartphones come with vulnerabilities as well as all the wonderful benefits. Consumers buy the new products and services and download the apps with far more interest in convenience and dazzling new features than in risks and security. Hackers and security professionals regularly find gaping holes each time a new product, application, or cyberspace phenomenon appears.

Many incidents of stolen sensitive data involve stolen portable devices such as laptops and phones. This is one of many examples where individuals, organizations, government agencies, and businesses embraced an advance in technology (portable devices with huge data storage) with little thought to the risks and when few security measures were available. Companies eventually learned to use more physical protections, such as cables to secure laptops to heavy furniture in offices or hotels, and to train employees to be more careful with portable devices.

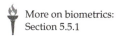
More on biometrics: Section 5.5.1

Security for mobile devices has become a fast growing business. Tracking of stolen or lost devices is now possible and the owner can remotely erase files or the entire device. Face recognition, voice prints, and fingerprint readers are becoming common biometric controls for accessing a device.

We introduced the Internet of Things (IoT) in Section 1.2.2. It includes billions of devices from mobile phones, cars, and light bulbs to sensors in roads and bridges. A study by Hewlett-Packard[24] showed that devices on the IoT have dozens of vulnerabilities on average. Many of these devices have mobile applications that store personal information that a hacker can access through their vulnerabilities. A security consultant showed that, using a device about the size of a laptop to mimic a cell tower, a person can hack into some smartphones from a distance of 30 feet and copy stored information, install software, and control the phone's camera and microphone. Researchers demonstrated it was possible to remotely gain control of early versions of Phillips Hue light bulbs and turn off lights in the victim's home. Smart televisions and DVD players that connect to the Internet have vulnerabilities that allow hackers to monitor the shows and movies people view in their homes. We saw in Section 5.2.2 that hackers can commandeer similar devices to use in denial-of-service attacks.

In some cases, the manufacturer can fix vulnerabilities automatically over the Internet, but often this is not possible. Several models of home cable modems and routers, which serve as the central hub for all Internet activity in the home, have vulnerabilities that allow hackers to take control of the device. To fix these vulnerabilities, the user must first know of them. The manufacturer cannot notify all users of the product because it knows only of those who registered it, and most people do not take the time to register products or they purchase used products. Once someone finds out that a device needs to be fixed, he or she must manually download and install the patches. This is a daunting task for the typical home user and if not performed correctly can disable the device. Sometimes, the easiest solution is to purchase a new device, but even that is not always effective: A bug in millions of new routers had been found and fixed 10 years earlier; the maker of one of the router components continued to use the old software in its chips, and router makers were unaware that the component used outdated and vulnerable software.

As cars went online, new dangers to drivers and passengers arose. Security researchers learned how to manipulate the security system in a car by sending messages over a cellular communication network, unlocking the car and starting its engine. Other researchers used simple off-the-shelf hardware to send fake traffic and weather information to navigation systems in cars. In another case, computer scientists, using a laptop computer over the Internet, broke into the controls of a car and took over operations, from the entertainment system to the transmission

Best Green Screen/Fotolia

FIGURE 5.2 How secure are drones from hackers?

and brakes, while the driver (a reporter, aware of the experiment) sat helpless in the moving vehicle. The vehicle manufacturer issued a patch that required owners to download it, place it on a USB device, and then insert the device into their cars, or ask for the patch at a dealership. It was only after the vulnerability became public that the manufacturer issued a recall for more than 1.4 million cars.[25]

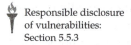
Responsible disclosure of vulnerabilities: Section 5.5.3

Millions of drones perform tasks in the sky (see Figure 5.2). Hackers can spoof* the GPS signals that drones use to determine their location. That means someone might be able to steal your package on its way from an online seller, confuse a surveillance drone tracking criminals, or capture a military drone.

While it may still seem like science fiction, the number and type of medical devices that doctors can implant in a person to monitor and control health is growing. These devices help manage a broad range of illnesses such as cardiac arrhythmia, diabetes, and Parkinson's disease. Medical devices are becoming more accessible through the Web so that doctors, patients, and family members can monitor someone's health and get an immediate alert if they need to take action. Often, you can control, not simply monitor, this equipment over the Web—from x-ray machines and lab equipment to devices used in treatment of heart patients. The Federal Drug Administration regularly issues safety alerts for medical devices after vulnerabilities are discovered. One alert was for an infusion pump, a device that controls delivery of fluids to a patient intravenously. A hacker could take control of the pump remotely and change the dosage. The potential for accidental or intentional harm to users of such devices has become a serious concern.

Perhaps this is a good place to pause for some perspective. A person who hacks, say, a pacemaker could kill someone, but the risk of that happening is probably far

---

*Spoofing means faking, tricking, or deceiving, often by making a communication appear to come from a trusted source rather than a malicious intruder.

lower than the risk of a heart attack in someone who needs a pacemaker but does not have one. At the same time, developers must continually look for vulnerabilities and reduce them.

5.5 Security

The fact that I could get into the system amazed me.

—Frank Darden, a member of the Legion of Doom,
which hacked the BellSouth telephone system[26]

We have discussed the evolution of technology and other factors that cause our digital life to be so vulnerable, and we have explored how criminals, foreign governments, and others take advantage of those vulnerabilities. With almost daily headlines announcing security breaches and cyberattacks, it may appear that no one is making any effort to protect our data, devices, and systems. This is far from true. Security is strong and sophisticated: We could not do all the shopping, banking, investing, and working online that we do if it were not. Security is also sometimes dangerously and irresponsibly weak. In this section, we consider the people and tools that protect us and also where some of the weaknesses and irresponsibilities lie. We also look into conflicts that arise when secure systems thwart law enforcement efforts.

5.5.1 TOOLS TO HELP PROTECT THE DIGITAL WORLD

As we describe a variety of security measures, we will also describe some of their weaknesses or ways hackers have found to thwart them, and then some of the responses. There is a continual leapfrogging, or cat and mouse game, that occurs with many of these tools as each side responds to the advances of the other. We can see this clearly in the discussion of credit cards and other payment technologies.

Evolution of credit card fraud and protection

Credit fraud began with simple low-tech crimes such as an individual on a shopping spree with a stolen credit card. Both well-organized theft rings and individual purse snatchers stole credit cards and continue to do so. In an early case, a group of airline employees stole new cards from mail transported on the airline's airplanes; charges on the stolen cards ran to an estimated $7.5 million before they were caught.[27] Credit card issuers instituted procedural changes to protect against theft of new cards from the mail. To verify that the legitimate owner received the card, issuers required the customer to call in and provide identifying information to activate a card, though this procedure is only as good as the security of the identifying information. At first, credit card companies commonly used the person's

Social Security number and mother's maiden name. In another early case, federal prosecutors said several Social Security Administration employees provided the Social Security numbers and mothers' maiden names of thousands of people to a credit card fraud ring so that they could activate stolen cards.[28] Now, credit card companies use caller ID to verify that the authorization call comes from the customer's telephone.

E-commerce has made it easier to steal and use card numbers and to make purchases without the physical cards. When retail sales began on the Web, thieves used software to intercept credit card numbers in transmission from a personal computer to a website. Encryption and secure servers partially solved this problem, giving e-commerce the opportunity to thrive.

Thieves install recording devices, called *skimmers*, inside card readers at stores, gas stations, and restaurants to collect credit and debit card numbers and PINs. They make counterfeit cards and raid people's bank accounts through ATM machines. Some thieves set up fake ATM machines to record card numbers and PINs; the machines have a small amount of cash to dispense so that they appear legitimate. One such machine, planted at a security conference in Las Vegas, captured card data of attendees for several days before someone discovered that it was fake.

Credit card companies now run sophisticated artificial intelligence software to detect unusual spending activity. When the system finds something suspicious, a merchant can ask a customer for additional identification or the credit card company can call a cardholder to verify purchases. For example, if you live in the United States and someone uses your card in Rome, the software might check whether you recently charged airline tickets. The vast amount of data that businesses store about our purchases and other activities—the same data that can threaten privacy—enables the credit card company to make fairly accurate conclusions about whether a charge on our card is likely to be fraudulent.

Credit card issuers and merchants make trade-offs between security and customer convenience. For purchases in stores, most customers do not want to take the time to provide identification when they use a credit card, and requesting an ID may offend customers, so many merchants did not check identity. With the introduction of self-service checkout counters, we scan our purchases and pay without any clerk looking at our card at all. Merchants and credit card companies are willing to absorb some fraud losses as part of doing business. Such trade-offs are not new. Retail stores have always accepted some amount of losses from shoplifting rather than offend and inconvenience customers by keeping everything locked up. When a company perceives the losses as being too high, it improves security.

When are merchants and credit card companies irresponsibly ignoring simple and important security measures, and when are they making reasonable trade-offs for convenience, efficiency, and avoiding offense to customers? In recent years, the balance has tipped toward security. Responding to increasingly high fraud rates, credit card companies developed a "smart" card technology called EVM (for EuroPay, Visa, and MasterCard—the companies that initiated the standard). The smart-card chip provides better authentication of the card, and thieves cannot clone the chip information to fake cards as they can with magnetic strip data. Many credit card companies issue only cards with chips now.

Services such as PayPal provide a trusted third party to increase confidence (and convenience) in online commerce and reduce credit fraud. A customer can buy from strangers online without giving them a credit card number. PayPal handles the payment for a small fee. Services such as Apple Pay, Android Pay, and Samsung Pay work with mobile devices and some desktop computers. The mobile versions use a technology called near-field communication (NFC) that allows the customer to simply pass a phone near the payment terminal; the system creates an encrypted transaction record that is unique for that purchase and does not expose any credit card information to store employees. Credit cards with chips and mobile-based NFC payment applications make fraud more difficult, so thieves have shifted more of their efforts online, resulting in an increase in so-called "card-not-present" fraud.

The many tactics used for identity theft and credit and debit card fraud, and the many solutions developed in response, illustrate the increasing sophistication of security strategies and increasing sophistication of criminal strategies. They also suggest the value of the mix of technology, business policies, consumer awareness, and law to reduce theft and fraud. Technology evolves and clever people on both sides of the law develop new ideas. For the general public and for anyone working with payment technologies, it is necessary to remain aware and flexible.

Encryption

Encryption is a particularly valuable security tool. Several early Internet designers strongly advocated using encryption. However, the core Internet communications protocol, TCP/IP, does not encrypt data because encryption requires large amounts of computing power, which was very expensive when the protocol was developed, and because the problem of safely distributing keys to decrypt messages was very challenging at that time.

More on encryption: Section 2.5.2

Now, very powerful encryption is available, but it still can be inconvenient and expensive, in both development costs and computing resources. Thus, governments and businesses often do not use encryption sufficiently or appropriately, even in applications where it is very important. For example, because the military did not encrypt the video feeds on U.S. predator drones (unmanned aircraft used in Iraq), Iraqi insurgents used $26 software, available on the Internet, to intercept the feeds. Access to the video feeds gave the insurgents valuable information about surveillance and attacks and provided the potential to modify the feeds. U.S. military officials knew the feeds were unprotected since the 1990s (when they used drones in Bosnia). They reconsidered encryption in 2004 but assumed adversaries would not know how to exploit this security hole. Adding encryption to a system after deployment is expensive, but even if omitting it as late as the 1990s was a reasonable trade-off, military officials clearly should have updated the decision.[29] Underestimating the skills of opponents and unwillingness to pay for stronger security are frequent underlying causes of vulnerabilities in both government and business systems.

Retailer TJX used a vulnerable, out-of-date encryption system to protect data transmitted between cash registers and store computers on its wireless network. Investigators believe hackers used high-power antennas to intercept data, decoded employee passwords, and then hacked into the company's central database. Over a period of about 18 months, the hackers stole millions of credit and debit card numbers and critical identification information for hundreds of thousands of people. (Stolen numbers were then used fraudulently in at least eight countries.) The investigation revealed other security problems such as the transmission of debit card transaction information to banks without encryption and failure to install appropriate software patches and firewalls.[30]

The two incidents we just described involved inadequate encryption for data in transmission. Another important use of encryption is for stored data and documents. In several major thefts of consumers' personal data from retailers, the databases included unencrypted passwords, credit card numbers, and other security numbers read from the magnetic strips on the cards. Hacking attacks on major security firms show that even such firms often leave sensitive data (including credit card numbers) on their systems unencrypted.

Another technique hackers use to gain information about a user is simply to sit in a coffee shop or other place with unencrypted Wi-Fi. The hacker scans the Wi-Fi transmissions of everyone connected to the store's network looking for personal information and login credentials. If you connect to free Wi-Fi without a password, the connection and your data are vulnerable.

Anti-malware software and trusted applications

Some tools and software assist nontechnical users to protect their own devices and files and to avoid being the weak link in the security chain. You are probably already familiar with antivirus or anti-malware software and your ISP (Internet Service Provider) or school has likely suggested you install a specific package on your computer. Antivirus software searches for malware on your computer using two techniques.

First, when you attach a new device, such as a camera or USB drive, to your computer, the anti-malware software looks at, or scans, all the files on the device. Similarly, you can set software to periodically scan files on your computer. The software searches through the computer code in the files looking for virus "signatures," that is, sequences of characters that match those from known viruses stored in its database. If it finds a match, it notifies you that one of the files has a virus and "quarantines" it, often by placing it in a special folder until you decide to delete the file or have it cleaned by removing the malicious code from the file.

Occasionally, a virus or other malware can make it past the scan undetected. So, the second technique of anti-malware software is to monitor a computer system for "virus-like" activities. Some virus-like activities are changing system files that normally would not be changed, modifying parts of the computer's memory outside the area a program is permitted to modify, or launching and modifying multiple programs simultaneously. When the anti-malware software detects such activities, it shuts down the program that is initiating the activities and warns the user.

Over time, hackers find ways to circumvent anti-malware software, such as changing the signature of the virus. Anti-malware software vendors upgrade their software; hackers find new ways to circumvent the upgrades; and so on.

Most operating system manufacturers have added a feature to their operating systems that gives users the option to require all software on their computer or mobile device come from a certified developer. A legitimate developer can apply to the operating system manufacturer, for example, Apple, Microsoft, or Google, for a digital certificate. Any application created by that developer has the digital certificate attached and is a "trusted application." With this operating system feature enabled, software run on the device must come from a certified developer or the operating system does not permit it to run. As with other protections we have described, this one is not perfect; for example, hackers found vulnerabilities in the process the Android operating system used to validate the certificates. These hackers were able to forge certificates until the operating system vendors patched the system to resolve the errors. A user might want to turn off the certification feature and use apps created by small companies or individuals who do not have certificates, but this action increases the risk of running malicious applications.

Apple's mobile operating system, iOS, requires all applications be from certified developers; it provides only such applications in its App Store. Many people believe this policy restricts creativity and adds to Apple's profit by reducing competition. Some users hack their iPhones and iPads to disable the certification requirement. Doing so is a form of jailbreaking, which we described in Section 4.3.2. While giving users more control over their iOS devices, jailbreaking increases the chance a device will get a virus. Indeed, several viruses specifically target jailbroken iPhones. Thus, again, we see a balancing act, here between security on the one hand, and flexibility, user control, or convenience on the other. The dangers of weakened security extend beyond the jailbreaker's phone: A malicious app can gain control of a phone's dialing capability as part of a denial-of-service attack.[31]

Authenticating websites

Sometimes fake websites, or emails that direct us to them, are easy to spot because of poor grammar and generally low quality. Software can determine the geographic location of a site reasonably well. If it claims to be a U.S. bank but is in Romania, it is wise to leave. Email programs, Web browsers, search engines, and add-on software (some free) can alert users to likely fraud. Some mail programs will alert the user if the actual Web address that a link will take you to is different from the one displayed in the text of a message.

Web browsers, search engines, and add-on software can filter for websites considered safe or show alerts for sites known to collect and misuse personal information. While helpful for cautious users, such tools generate potential problems. Recall in Chapter 3 we observed that we might want a filter for pornography to be more restrictive even if it meant preventing a child from accessing some nonporn sites, while a spam filter should be less restrictive so as not to remove legitimate messages. How strict should a Web tool be about marking a site as safe? When a major browser marks as safe only large companies that it has certified, legitimate small businesses on the Web suffer. Mistakes in marking a legitimate site as a known or suspected phishing site could ruin a small business and could result in a lawsuit for the company that provides the rating. It is important from both an ethical and a business perspective to be cautious when designing and implementing such rating systems.

Banks and financial businesses developed techniques to assure customers that they are at an authentic site before the customer enters a password or other sensitive identifying information. For example, when a customer first sets up an account, some banks ask the customer to supply a digital image (say, of a pet dog) or choose one from many at the bank site. Later, whenever the person begins the login process by entering his or her name (or other identifier that is not critical for security), the system displays the image. Thus, the site authenticates itself to the customer before the customer authenticates himself or herself by entering a password.

Authenticating users

Authenticating users is an essential part of security. At the beginning of this section, we described evolving security methods for protecting credit cards numbers and reducing credit card fraud; they include authenticating the user of the card. Here, we focus on users on the Web and in other applications.

A Russian man bought stock and then broke into many people's online brokerage accounts and bought the same stock through those accounts. The large number of purchases pushed the price up, and the man sold his at a profit.[32] (Note that criminal access to an investment account can be costly to the rightful owner even if the hacker cannot remove funds or stock from the account.) This and numerous incidents of theft from online bank and investment accounts led to development of better procedures to authenticate customers and users. How can such businesses distinguish the real account owner from an identity thief armed with a stolen account number and other commonly used identifying information?

Authenticating customers and users remotely is inherently difficult: Many people, businesses, and websites must receive information that is necessary and sufficient to identify someone or authorize a transaction. If authentication depends on only a few numbers (such as Social Security number and birth date), eventually, someone will lose, leak, or steal that information. We briefly describe some of the variety of better methods that developed, and then look more deeply at biometrics, a growing area.

Some sites ask the customer to provide extra information (the name of a favorite teacher, for example) when he or she first opens an account, and then they ask for some of that information at login. Some store information that identifies the device from which the customer normally logs in and ask for the additional information only when someone logs in from a different device. Some ask the customer to select from a group of several images when opening the account, and then require the customer to identify the image at login. (Note the latter is similar to the website authentication method described earlier, but used in this way it helps to authenticate the user.)

More sophisticated authentication software uses artificial intelligence techniques. The software calculates a risk score based on variation from the time of day a customer usually logs in, the type of browser regularly used, the customer's typical behavior and transactions, and so on. How would privacy advocates and the public react to the disclosure that an online bank or brokerage firm stores such information about each customer's visits to the site?

Geographic location tools, like those that tell users the physical location of a website, can, sometimes, tell an online system where a customer is. If the customer is logging in from a country other than where he or she lives, or if the customer is in a country with a high fraud rate, a retailer or financial institution can require extra identification.

Biometrics

Biometrics are biological characteristics that are unique to an individual. They include fingerprints, voice prints, face structure, hand geometry, eye (iris or retina) patterns, and DNA. Uses of DNA in the law enforcement and justice systems are well known.

Biometric technology for identification is a multibillion-dollar industry with many beneficial applications. It provides both convenience and security. You can open your smartphone, tablet, and the door of your house by touching a scanner with your finger. No passcodes to forget or keys to lose or drop while carrying packages, and the fingerprint requirement reduces access by hackers and thieves. Some smartphone applications use face or voice recognition to authenticate the owner and protect against theft of information or funds in electronic wallets. Some states use a face scanner and image matching to make sure a person does not apply for extra driver's licenses or welfare benefits under different names. To reduce the risks of terrorism, several airports use fingerprint identification systems to ensure that only employees enter restricted areas. In factories, workers no longer punch timecards; instead they use a hand scan.

Just as people have always found ways around other security mechanisms, from picking locks to phishing, hackers find ways to thwart biometric identification. In the early days of biometrics, researchers in the U.S. and Japan fooled fingerprint readers with cadaver fingers and fingers they made from gelatin and Play-Doh. A photo of a smartphone owner could unlock a phone protected by a (weak) face-recognition lock, and criminals could wear contact lenses that fooled eye scanners.[33] Today's biometric readers are much better. For example, a finger scanner can measure the capacitance of the finger and take a super high-resolution image of the subdermal fingerprint—it does not read the dead skin on top of your finger, but the living skin below. These features greatly reduce the probability the scanner can be fooled by dead fingers and fake fingerprints.

Some smartphones perform iris scans to identify the phone owners. Iris scans analyze patterns in the colored ring surrounding a person's eye pupil. A more accurate scanning method, the retina scan is not available on phones—yet. A retina scan takes a picture of and analyzes an individual's unique pattern of blood vessels in the eye's retina. Using current technology, it is nearly impossible to fake a retina scan, and the pattern in the retina fades quickly after death, so the person must be alive to be authenticated.

When a thief steals a credit card number, we can get a new account with a new number, but if a hacker gets a copy of the file with our digitized thumbprint or retina scan, we cannot get a new thumb or retina. How are such data protected and what are the risks? To prevent theft of digitized fingerprints, some phones encrypt

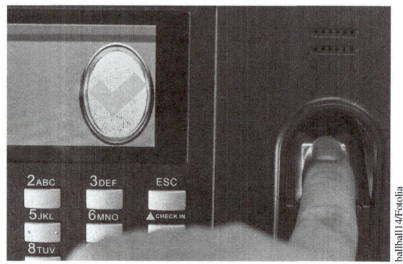

FIGURE 5.3 Scanning a fingerprint.

and store the data in a specially designed secure area of the phone. Since the digitized fingerprint does not leave the phone, a hacker cannot intercept it. Similar security techniques are designed into other biometric devices to protect the digitized identifying information. If a hacker does steal the digitization of a person's fingerprint or retina scan, is the person's identity permanently compromised? No, not currently. The digital files of biometrics are normally encrypted, so they are usable only in limited situations. Additionally, the hacker must physically bypass or fool the scanning device to transmit a copy of the file rather than performing an actual scan of the finger or eye.

As the use of biometrics continues to increase dramatically, it has the potential to increase surveillance and tracking of our activities. The fact that criminals may find ways to thwart biometrics or that biometrics can pose privacy risks does not condemn these technologies. As always, we must have an accurate view of their strengths, weaknesses, and risks, and compare them with alternatives to determine, carefully, for what applications we should use them. By anticipating both privacy risks and methods criminals may use to get around new security measures, we can design better systems. For example, anticipating that a photo of an eye can trick iris scanners, some scanners flash a light at the eye and check that the pupil contracts, as a real one would. Similarly, researchers developed methods to distinguish a photo of a face from a real one. Just as responsible businesses must use up-to-date encryption, those that provide biometric protections must update them regularly.

Multifactor authentication

We have seen there may be uncertainty in verifying a user only by a password or some biometric scan. To protect against stolen credentials, many websites and organizations use "multifactor" or "two-factor" authentication. There are three categories of authentication technologies:

1. something you know—a password, PIN, or secret key phrase
2. something you are—a voiceprint, fingerprint, or retinal scan
3. something you have—a debit or credit card, smartphone, or fob[*]

Multifactor authentication uses at least two items—from different categories. Some examples are:

- Swiping a debit card (3) and entering a PIN (1)
- Entering a password (1) and then typing a special code the website sent to your mobile phone (3)
- Speaking (2) a unique pass-phrase (1)
- Using a fingerprint (2) and a special code from a fob (3)

---

[*]In this context, a fob is a small hardware device that generates a code for access to a network.

Entering a password and a PIN would not be multifactor authentication since both items are in the same category.

5.5.2 PEOPLE WHO CAN HELP PROTECT THE DIGITAL WORLD

Cybersecurity professionals

There are millions of cyberattacks each day now—by individuals, crime organizations, governments, and automated software. Most of these efforts fail because of improved security technologies and because cybersecurity professionals work around the clock. Cybersecurity specialists can be part of an organization's information technology department, an independent security company, academia, or the government. Their activities lie in three broad areas:

- protecting systems and networks,
- testing the security of existing systems and networks, and
- investigating security breaches.

Wherever they work, they strive to achieve three goals, all of which include preventing unauthorized access to systems and devices:

- *Confidentiality*—ensuring data that should be private remain private
- *Integrity*—ensuring data are not changed without authorization and are consistent over time and in sync with the real world
- *Availability*—ensuring the system, services, and data are accessible when needed

These goals can occasionally be in conflict. For example, to safeguard the confidentiality and privacy of your email, you need a username and password to access your account. If you forget your password, your email is no longer available. System designers and cybersecurity specialists often must perform many balancing acts: A system that no one can access is very secure, but if no one can access it, it is not a very useful system.

At large private and government organizations, the cybersecurity teams create an inventory of the hardware, software, and networks that comprise their system and they research known vulnerabilities. They also determine what risks and cyber threats exist for the services and information on the systems they protect. This work leads to a cybersecurity plan that identifies a secure configuration of devices, services, and software and includes processes to maintain and update software. For cybersecurity specialists to better understand the weaknesses and vulnerabilities of their systems, they regularly test the security of their own systems and use the results to improve security; we look at some of their methods in Section 5.5.3.

Cybersecurity professionals stay well informed about technical aspects of hacking and the hacker culture. They read hacker newsletters, participate in online discussions of hacking (often undercover), and attend hacker conferences. They maintain logs of chat channels hackers use and they set up *honey pots*—websites and servers that look attractive to hackers—to record and study activities of hackers at the site. Investigators trace viruses and hacking attacks by using ISP records and many other sources of data on the Internet. Some of the same tools and phenomena that threaten privacy aid in tracing viruses and catching criminals—for example, the hidden identifying information in files and all the stored data about our online activities. Frequently, investigators can identify hackers because they brag about their exploits.

Decision makers in businesses, organizations, and government

As the Target breach illustrated, users, system developers, and managers share responsibility for securing and protecting digital systems. The hackers' success depended on a sequence of security failures, some that are difficult to prevent but some that the company should have prevented (e.g., web and data servers with default or weak passwords). In the TJX hack (Section 5.5.1), the company used out-of-date encryption and failed to install appropriate security software, according to security investigators. High-level managers in business and government have a responsibility for setting policy that places a priority on security. An organization that does not sufficiently protect its systems and sensitive data bears part of the ethical responsibility when a hacker does damage.

It is unsettling that it seems so easy to hack into military systems, other government agencies, infrastructure systems, and defense contractors. A deputy defense secretary reported that intruders have stolen plans (from the government and defense industry firms) for aircraft avionics, satellite communications systems, network security protocols, missile tracking systems, satellite navigation devices, surveillance drones, and jet fighters. Intruders broke into the email accounts of several high-ranking government officials, including a senior advisor to the president and the head of the CIA. They gained access to and published on the Internet names, phone numbers, and emails of thousands of FBI agents and Department of Homeland Security officers. During the months it took to trace the hackers, officials speculated that the attack might be the work of a foreign government; eventually the culprits were found: teenagers in the United Kingdom, aged 16 and 15. Hackers reach into even the National Security Agency; a hacker group offered for sale what appeared to be some of the NSA's own hacking tools.[34]

What shall we make of this? We cannot expect perfection. No matter how well designed security software and procedures are, the complexity of computer systems means there will be unexpected breaches. Highly skilled attackers from intelligence agencies of powerful foreign governments are likely to have some successes. Without having much more technical detail of the attacks and a high degree of security expertise, it is difficult to judge which breaches would have been truly difficult to prevent and which result from poor work or irresponsibility on the part of the people who design, manage, and operate the systems.

What about small organizations, businesses, and individuals who have websites or create apps made to work over the Internet? They often have little or no security training. As the Target breach illustrated, they can serve as an entrance for hackers to other systems. Should we require that website developers, large and small, have security training before creating a website? Or would such a requirement drastically reduce the number of websites and thus the amount of information available on the Web? Would restrictions on creating websites conflict with freedom of speech? How can managers of an organization with no technical staff keep its systems secure?

Software designers, programmers, and system administrators

Principles and techniques for developing secure devices and software exist, and responsible software designers must learn and use them. The Computer Emergency Response Team (CERT) developed coding standards for secure software development that schools should teach software developers from their first introduction to programming. Yet, many schools are not aware these coding standards exist.

System administrators have a professional, ethical, and often legal obligation to take reasonable security precautions to protect their systems. They must anticipate risks, prepare for them, and stay up to date about new risks and new security measures. This is not an easy task, but it is an essential goal and a professional responsibility. Chapter 9 focuses on responsibilities and ethics of software professionals.

Users

While it is tempting to place the blame for large data breaches on software developers, system administrators, and IT staff, users bear responsibility for some breaches. Three password practices can help us protect our own data and the systems we interact with at work and on the Web:

- Choose strong passwords.
- Change passwords periodically.
- Do not use the same password for multiple purposes.

People commonly choose poor, i.e., easy-to-guess passwords such as those in Figure 5.4. (Do *you* use any on this list?) One of the responsibilities of good system developers and administrators is to protect against poor user choices. Some systems require that a password have a minimum length, is not a word that appears in a dictionary, and includes a mix of character types (e.g., both upper and lower case). Some systems require that users change their passwords every six months. But one

123456	1234	1qaz2wsx	qwertyuiop
password	1234567	dragon	solo
12345678	baseball	master	passw0rd
qwerty	welcome	monkey	starwars
12345	1234567890	letmein	
123456789	abc123	login	
football	111111	princess	

FIGURE 5.4 Twenty-five common user passwords.[36]

system cannot stop someone from using the same password elsewhere. Why is that an issue? Here is a high-profile example: Mark Zuckerberg, CEO of Facebook, apparently used the same password on LinkedIn, Twitter, and Pinterest. After a hacker stole millions of LinkedIn credentials, someone took over Zuckerberg's Twitter and Pinterest accounts.[35] Will you use the same password for LinkedIn and online banking? Remembering a complex password, changing it frequently, and doing so for a large number of different accounts is a big inconvenience—another trade-off between convenience and security.

Some businesses have hundreds of thousands of employees, any of whom might unintentionally compromise a company system. Education and training in safe online practices and procedures is critical to security. A good cybersecurity program educates employees about cyber risks and the role each plays in the organization's security. It trains employees on the correct procedures and processes to follow in performing their tasks. Ongoing awareness initiatives, such as weekly or monthly reminders and refresher training, keep security in the front of everyone's mind.

Do we expect too much of ordinary, nontechnical users? People make mistakes. We know that we should not click on links or open attachments that arrive in suspicious email, but the email does not always appear suspicious, and we do not always remember. A company did a test mailing to two other companies of 150,000 emails with an attachment; 11% of the recipients clicked on the attachment, which, if it were not a test, could have initiated malware. To what extent is this a failure of the people who were fooled, and to what extent is it a problem in the systems themselves? We will see in Chapter 8 that programmers have a responsibility to write their programs so that a typo by a user in entering input is unlikely to crash the system (or kill someone). Perhaps selfies and face recognition will replace passwords. What else can system designers do to protect systems from common human errors that threaten security?

> *We hacked his Bitly and there was his password on gmail, and we hacked his gmail and we checked the saved passwords of his browser and we got his twitter password.*
>
> —A hacker group that sent messages from social media accounts of tech CEOs[37]

Physical security

Sometimes, breaches of physical security expose our data, block our access, or put infrastructure at risk. Thus, responsibility for security includes awareness of and protection against such risks. Here are a few examples:

- Over the course of a year, someone cut 12 major fiber optic cables in the San Francisco Bay Area knocking out service to a large number of households and businesses.

- Hard drives containing customer information were stolen from the Vudu.com office. Passwords were encrypted, but other customer information, such as name, phone number, and address, was not.

- Thieves installed credit card skimmers at night on the unsecured credit card readers at gas stations in Austin, Texas, to read data when people swiped cards to buy gas.

- Employee "tailgating" is a problem in some secure facilities—an authorized employee scans a finger or eye to open a door to a secure area and then holds the door open allowing the next person, possibly unauthorized, to enter.

5.5.3 HACKING TO IMPROVE SECURITY

Penetration testing

Even well-designed programs that have apparently been operating safely for a long time often have bugs and security flaws. Cybersecurity professionals and hackers of various sorts, within and outside of the organizations that develop or run complex systems, continuously probe for weaknesses and vulnerabilities. Security professionals perform a process called *penetration testing*, or *pen testing*, attempting to gain access to an information system or app and violate the confidentiality, integrity, or availability of the system or its services. The person or team performing penetration testing assumes the role of a hacker and uses many of the same techniques hackers use.

The cybersecurity staff of an organization can perform pen testing on the organization's systems, or they can hire an outside firm that specializes in security. In the latter case, the firm doing the testing is typically bound by a nondisclosure agreement (NDA) not to disseminate the results of the pen test to anyone except the security staff of the organization. It is a grave breach of professional ethics to violate a pen testing NDA and disclose the results to the public.

Pen testing is also a valuable part of the training for a cybersecurity professional whose job is to detect malicious hack attacks and track the hacker—to defeat a hacker, you need to think like one.

Responsible disclosure

Since the early days of computers and the Internet, there has been a subculture of hackers who, without permission, probe computer systems as an intellectual exercise to find security flaws. Some of these hackers treat this activity as a public service and refer to themselves as "security researchers" or "gray hats" to avoid the negative connotation of the term hacker. Along with academic cybersecurity researchers, they face a key ethical challenge when they discover vulnerabilities in software and digital devices: How can they responsibly inform potential victims of security vulnerabilities without informing malicious hackers who would exploit them?

Responsible disclosure of a cybersecurity flaw is more complicated than a typical whistleblowing scenario. In many whistleblowing situations, unsafe or illegal activities are already ongoing and known (or even condoned) within an organization. By publicizing these activities, the whistleblower is shedding light with the hope of improving safety or stopping a crime. On the other hand, when an outsider discovers a cybersecurity flaw, the organization that created the software may not be aware of it. Exposing the flaw publicly alerts hackers who may be able to exploit the flaw prior to the availability of a fix. It is a responsible practice to disclose a flaw privately so that an organization has time to prepare patches or close security holes.

Here are examples: A security researcher, Dan Kaminsky, discovered a major flaw in the Internet's domain name server system (the system that translates Web addresses, say, www.yourbank.com to IP addresses) that could have allowed hackers to redirect and steal any information transmitted on the Net. He kept the problem secret while working with several companies to develop a patch, and then announced the patch and said he would make details of the problem—and how to exploit it—public in 30 days. The 30-day limit, he said, encouraged companies to install the patch and encouraged others who knew of the flaw not to disclose it sooner.

A Google cybersecurity team searches for security flaws in common software and gives the developer 90 days to resolve the vulnerability before making the defect public, though if they discover hackers are already exploiting the bug, they will pressure the organization to fix it faster. Is 30 days or 90 days the right amount of time to wait? Many websites and software applications are complex and rushing out a fix before there is time to thoroughly test it can introduce additional bugs and vulnerabilities. Thus, one decision with ethical implications is how long to wait before publicizing a vulnerability.

Some companies such as Google, Facebook, and Microsoft offer rewards or "bounties" to people for privately disclosing vulnerabilities in their software. Recognizing that cars connected to the Internet have potentially dangerous security vulnerabilities, several car manufacturers also do this. On the other hand, some companies consider any hacking of their devices illegal, even if the hacker owns the device, and some sue to prevent publication of security flaws. After academic researchers discovered a flaw in the keyless ignition system of Volkswagen cars, the company successfully sued (in the United Kingdom) to prevent publication. It was almost two years before Volkswagen allowed publication of the paper and then only with modifications.[38]

Many hackers are scornful of big software companies both because of the large number of security flaws in their products and because they are slow to plug leaks even when they know of them. Some businesses and government agencies have so much confidence in their systems that they refuse to believe anyone can break in. Hackers argue that these organizations do not behave responsibly toward the public and that publicizing security problems spurs them to take corrective action. Hackers and security consultants repeatedly warn companies of flaws that allow unauthorized access, but some companies do not respond until malicious hackers exploit the flaws and cause significant problems.

As we will see in the next section, almost all unauthorized access to computer systems is illegal now, so no matter how noble the motives, hackers must consider the ethics of breaking the law. As we suggested in Chapter 1, it is not always unethical to break a law, but there must be a strong argument for doing so. Exposing security flaws is generally not a legitimate justification for illegal hacking, but, as a side effect, it does sometimes speed up security improvements.

As you read the following examples, think about how responsibly the various parties behaved.

- A man who copied patient files from a medical center said he did it to publicize the system's vulnerability, not to use the information. He disclosed portions of the files to a journalist after the medical center said that no one had copied patient files.[39] Should we view him as a whistleblower or a criminal?

- Hackers collected the email addresses of more than 100,000 iPad owners from a public AT&T website. The site displayed the email address of an iPad owner to anyone who entered the iPad ID number; it did not require a password. The hackers notified media organizations about the security flaw and discussed it on a chat channel before AT&T knew about it. Did they act responsibly or irresponsibly and criminally? One of the hackers was found guilty of identity fraud and accessing a computer without authorization, but an appeals court overturned the conviction.[40]

- A hacker broke into the website of the children's toy manufacturer VTECH and extracted personal data and photos of millions of adults and kids. He did not publish the data or contact VTECH, but instead, contacted a media outlet who then ran a story about the existence of the vulnerability and the risk to children. VTECH responded quickly, fixing the defect within a week. U.K. police arrested the hacker for violating that country's Computer Misuse Act. Did the hacker act responsibly? Was the police response reasonable?

5.5.4 BACKDOORS FOR LAW ENFORCEMENT

The introduction of secure smartphones and messaging systems—whose content even their manufacturers cannot access—revived an earlier debate from the late 20th century about "backdoors" into communications systems for law

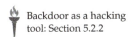
Backdoor as a hacking
tool: Section 5.2.2

enforcement. We start with a review of the context and arguments in that earlier debate because the arguments have not
changed very much.

Interception and encryption issues in the late 20th century

In the last few decades of the 20th century, new technologies, market competition, and varied customer needs generated a great diversity of telecommunications services, equipment, protocols, algorithms, and companies. Law enforcement
agencies found that new technologies made it more difficult for them to intercept
communications; the old wiretapping methods did not work anymore.

The FBI and other agencies pushed for "backdoors" in communications equipment so that they could access communications, and Congress passed the Communications Assistance for Law Enforcement Act (CALEA) in 1994. This law
requires that the design of telecommunications equipment ensure that the government can intercept telephone calls (with a court order or other authorization). In
the past, engineers designed communications equipment for its communications
purpose, and the FBI developed its tools for interception; communications providers had to assist. The significance of CALEA is that, previously, the government
could not require the design and modification of communications equipment to
meet the interception needs of law enforcement. The essential argument in favor
of CALEA (and other government programs to intercept communications) is to
maintain the ability of law enforcement agencies to protect us from drug dealers,
organized crime, other criminals, and terrorists in a changing technological environment. "The prospect of trying to enforce laws without a nationwide standard
for surveillance would turn enforcement into a nightmare," according to the FBI.[41]
The problems with CALEA, according to critics, include the side effects of backdoor access that threaten the security of communications systems. Any backdoor
increases vulnerability—to hackers, criminals, terrorists, foreign governments, and
misuse or abuse by our own government. The idea of designing communications
technology for "a nationwide standard for surveillance" is a nightmare to those
who place high value on privacy and civil liberties.

In the 1970s and 80s, the development of a new kind of encryption, called
public-key cryptography, produced encryption that is extremely difficult to crack.
Technically oriented people, and eventually ordinary people, began using encryption for email and other purposes. To ensure its access to the unencrypted content
of encrypted messages, the FBI supported a bill in Congress to require a backdoor
in all encryption products made, sold, or used in the United States. The backdoor was to permit immediate decryption of the encrypted data upon the receipt
of a court order.[42] The arguments for and against the proposed law were similar to
the arguments for and against CALEA. In addition, opponents argued that strong
encryption is essential to online commerce, providing protection against hackers
and thieves. Opponents also pointed out that sophisticated criminals and terrorists

could use illegal strong encryption without backdoors to encrypt their messages and data. Congress did not pass the proposed law.

The backdoor controversy revived

In the mid-2010s, several companies began offering products and services with very strong encryption-based privacy and security protections that prevent the company itself from accessing user data. For example, only the sender and intended recipient can read messages sent via WhatsApp, and Apple cannot unlock a user's iPhone. Law enforcement agencies are critical of this trend because it makes access to encrypted data of criminals and terrorists extremely difficult.

A terrorism case in 2015 illustrates the continuing frustration that encryption and other privacy and security technologies cause for law enforcement agencies. This case also illustrates a variety of arguments about the undelying issues. A San Bernardino, California, county health department employee and his wife killed 14 people and injured more. Police killed the attackers and recovered the employee's iPhone. The phone was locked and had a feature that would erase data after 10 failed attempts to unlock it. The FBI wanted to view the phone's data to determine if the terrorists had accomplices or ties to large terrorist organizations and if they had planned additional attacks. The FBI asked Apple to create a special version of the iPhone operating system that would not erase the data if incorrect passwords were entered. This would have allowed the FBI to repeatedly try passwords until it unlocked the phone. Apple refused, saying that providing such a program would put millions of iPhones at risk. The issue is not simply user privacy; it is security. Now that our phones can contain digital wallets, unlock doors, and control a large variety of devices in our homes and elsewhere, the security of phones is important for physical and financial security and security of everything else our phones reach.

The FBI took Apple to court to force the company to create the program, arguing that it had no other way to get the data from the phone. Are there other ways agents might get data from a phone in similar circumstances? In this case, there were. First, the phone belonged to the county, and the county was testing software that would let supervisors override the password protection on employee phones. Many companies use such software, but the county had not installed it. Second, the phone backed up data to the iCloud storage service. Apple gave the FBI older backed up data and told the FBI how to get the phone to do a current backup. This method failed because the FBI had asked county officials to change the iCloud password, and that prevented the backup. The FBI kept the third and successful method secret, dropping the case against Apple after an unspecified third party helped the FBI access the data on the phone. These methods will not work in all cases; as security techniques improve (including those that terrorists themselves develop), law enforcement agents need new techniques to thwart them.[43]

If Apple agreed to provide the software the FBI wanted, or if Apple lost in court, what else could the FBI demand? What principles are involved? An editorial in the *Wall Street Journal*, a newspaper that strongly supports antiterrorism programs, argued, "If the government can compel a manufacturer to invent intellectual property . . . in order to invade its own lawful products, there is no limiting legal principle. Could the FBI require a tech maker, for example, to send a malware worm to a user's device in the form of a routine update?"[44] And for what kinds of crimes besides terrorism?

Many basic and very challenging questions (both legal and ethical) remain: How do we balance the need to protect the security and privacy of communications systems with the government's responsibility to protect the physical security of its citizens and investigate crimes? Is it desirable to have consumer communications products and services that make access by law enforcement agents extremely difficult? Whose responsibility is it to develop techniques to access such protected data: that of law enforcement and intelligence agencies or of the companies that make the products?

5.6 The Law

5.6.1 THE COMPUTER FRAUD AND ABUSE ACT

When people started hacking for the challenge of getting into off-limits computers, there was disagreement not only about whether the activity was a crime under existing law but also about whether it should be. Gradually, state governments passed laws that specifically addressed computer crimes. Congress passed the main federal computer-crime law, the Computer Fraud and Abuse Act (CFAA), in the 1980s. As a federal law, the CFAA covers areas over which the federal government has jurisdiction: government computers, financial systems, and computers used in interstate or international commerce or communication—the last category, of course, includes computers connected to the Internet, mobile phones, and so on. Under the CFAA, it is illegal to access such a device without authorization, or to exceed one's authorization, and read or copy information.

Sections of the law address altering, damaging, or destroying information and interfering with authorized use of a computer. These sections cover denial-of-service attacks and the launching of computer viruses and other malicious programs. The CFAA is the main antihacking law, but prosecutors also use other federal laws to prosecute people for crimes related to computer and telecommunications systems. Illegal actions include access to commit fraud; disclosing passwords or other access codes to unauthorized people; and interrupting or impairing government operation, public communication, transportation, or other public utilities. State and federal antihacking laws provide for strong penalties, including prison sentences and fines.

The USA PATRIOT Act amended the CFAA, increasing penalties for a first offense and for hacking computers used by the criminal justice system or the military.

It also permits the government to monitor online activity of suspected hackers without a court order in some cases. We have observed that hacking covers a wide range of activity—some deserving serious punishment, some comparable to minor offenses kids of all generations commit, and some intended to demonstrate security weaknesses and encourage fixing them. Definitions of the actions to which the PATRIOT Act's antiterrorism provisions apply are broad and include activities some do not believe qualify as terrorism.

Unintended applications

The CFAA predates the Web, social networks, and smartphones. It was intended for malicious and prank hacking. Later applications of the law illustrate how the impact of a law can change and grow with new technology—and potentially criminalize common activities of millions of people. The problem is the lack of clear and appropriate definitions for "without authorization" and "exceeding authorization." For example, suppose a friend lets you use her password for a streaming video service. Are you committing a federal crime when you log in and watch a movie on her account? *Should* this be a crime under a federal antihacking law with stiff criminal penalties?

Is violating the terms of use of a website a crime under the CFAA's provision about exceeding one's authorized access? *Should* violating the terms of use be a crime? Consider the case of a woman, Lori Drew, who pretended to be a 16-year-old boy on MySpace. She began an online flirting relationship with a 13-year-old girl in her neighborhood (a former friend of her daughter). She later broke off the relationship and sent cruel messages to the young girl, who became depressed and committed suicide. The girl's parents and many other people wanted to see Drew punished for her malicious and irresponsible contribution to the girl's death, but it was not clear that she had broken any law. Prosecutors charged her with illegal activities under the CFAA saying she exceeded authorized access because she violated MySpace's terms of use requiring that profile information be truthful. A jury convicted the woman, but a judge later reversed the conviction stating a violation of the terms of service was too broad an application of the law. Normally, a breach of contract is not a criminal offence, and the CFAA does not state or suggest that it has become one. An ordinary, reasonable person does not expect that violating the terms of use of a website is a criminal offense.[45]

The decision of one judge, though, does not settle the legal situation. Prosecutions and lawsuits continue to treat some instances of password sharing, violation of terms of use, and other behavior as crimes under the CFAA—where application of the CFAA is questionable. We describe two cases.

Aaron Swartz was a bright, creative programmer and activist who helped develop several widely used online tools. Over a period of months while a research fellow at Harvard University, he downloaded hundreds of thousands of academic research articles from a huge digital library managed by JSTOR, a nonprofit organization. The bulk downloading violated JSTOR policies and caused temporary shutdown of the system. Since Swartz was a strong proponent of open access to information, his intent might have been to make the research, much of it paid for with government grants, publicly available. Thus, his actions may be viewed as hacktivism (discussed in Section 5.3.3). Swartz accessed the system through a guest account at MIT, a university known for encouraging openness, experimentation, pranks, and "creative disobedience." He was indicted on a variety of charges including unauthorized access under the CFAA. Facing the possibility of many years in jail, tragically, he committed suicide.[46]

Suppose you give your passwords for Facebook, LinkedIn, and other sites to a company that offers a service to collect and organize your data (e.g., contacts) in one place. A company, Power Ventures, offered such a service. However, Facebook objected to Power Ventures' access of member accounts, and a federal appeals court ruled that the company violated the CFAA because Facebook did not authorize its access.[47]

Many legal observers argue that prosecutors and judges apply the term "unauthorized access" in the CFAA too broadly. Although prosecutors are unlikely to prosecute someone for watching a movie on a friend's account, the Power Ventures decision suggests that they could. Prosecutors sometimes use threats of prosecution to pressure people, or they prosecute on easy-to-prove charges to jail people they suspect of other crimes but cannot convict. Many legal experts, computer scientists, tech companies, and civil rights organizations advocate clarifying and limiting the scope of the CFAA.

5.6.2 CRIMINALIZE VIRUS WRITING AND HACKER TOOLS?

Some law enforcement personnel and security professionals have proposed laws that make it a crime to write or post computer viruses and other hacking software. A law against writing or publishing viruses and hacking software might keep these tools from casual hackers. Criminal penalties might dissuade potential teenage hackers, but probably not serious criminals. Such a law would make security work and research more difficult. Security personnel and researchers must be able to possess security and hacker software to effectively do their job. Several companies package large numbers of viruses and other malware and hacking tools for sale to cybersecurity professionals to aid in penetration testing (described in Section 5.5.3). Courses on cybersecurity in many universities also use such packages. Should using these tools for teaching be illegal?

A law against distributing virus and hacking code would raise issues similar to some we discussed in Chapter 4 about restricting technologies to circumvent copyright protections. We saw in Section 3.2.2 that writing about how to make illegal or destructive devices, such as bombs, is not (in most cases) illegal. On the other hand, as a security professional commented, "With a computer virus, the words are the bomb."[48] A federal court ruled that software is a form of speech (see Section 3.2.1), so a law against hacking software or virus software might conflict with the First Amendment. The First Amendment does not protect some kinds of speech, such as inciting a riot. However, it does generally protect our right to encourage people to commit destructive or illegal actions in situations where the listener has time to reflect and make a decision about whether to act. A person who reads virus code has the opportunity to decide whether to activate the virus.

How do you think the law should treat virus code and hacking scripts? Is there a way to protect reasonable uses of such software while criminalizing intentional or reckless distribution in a context that encourages destructive use?

5.6.3 PENALTIES FOR YOUNG HACKERS

In his book *The Hacker Crackdown*, Bruce Sterling describes the phone phreakers of 1878. The date is not a typo. The then-new American Bell Telephone company initially hired teenage boys as operators, some of whom disconnected calls and crossed lines on the switchboard, connecting people to strangers. The boys were also, like many teenage hackers, rude.[49] The phone company learned its lesson and replaced teenage boys with woman operators. For generations, teenagers have committed pranks and minor crimes; so, pushing boundaries by hacking into school, corporate, and government computer systems was a natural step.

It benefits society to give young hackers an opportunity to mature, learn the risks of their actions, use their skills in better ways, and go on to successful, productive careers. We do not want to turn them into hardened criminals or wreck their chances of getting a good job by placing them in jail. This does not imply that we should not punish young hackers if they trespass or cause damage. Kids do not mature and become responsible without good direction or if we reward their irresponsibility. But we should remember that some of these young people may become the great innovators of the next generation—similar to Steve Wozniak who created the Apple computer and cofounded Apple Inc. Before he was building Apples, Wozniak was building "blue boxes"—devices that enabled people to make long-distance phone calls without paying for them. Nobel Prize winner Richard Feynman used hacker techniques when he was a young physicist working on the highly secret atomic bomb project at Los Alamos National Laboratory in the 1940s. He hacked safes, not computers, containing classified work on the bomb. He found or guessed the combinations and delighted in opening the safes at night and leaving messages for the authorized users informing them that security was not as good as they thought.[50]

Often the exploits of young hackers are pranks, trespasses, and small-scale vandalism with no thought of financial gain (though, as we observed in Section 4.1.5 in the context of copyright infringement, lack of financial gain is often not significant in determining whether actions are wrong). Difficult penalty issues arise for hackers who are young, who do not intend to do damage, or who, through accident, ignorance, or youthful irresponsibility, do vastly more damage than they can pay for. How can we distinguish between young hackers who are malicious and likely to commit more crimes and those who are likely to become honest and productive professionals? What penalties are appropriate? Should offenses related to unauthorized access vary in degree, and penalties likewise vary, as they do for trespass, vandalism, invasion of privacy, fraud, theft, and sabotage?

Some groups advocate heavy penalties for minor hacking offenses to "send a signal" to others who might be thinking of trying something similar. An argument for this approach is the high cost to the victims and the potential risks to the public. On the other hand, a core principle of justice is that punishment should fit the specific crime, not a potential crime that someone else might commit.

In many hacking cases, especially those involving young people, the evidence is clear, and the hacker and prosecutor work out a plea bargain. Originally, many hackers younger than 18 received relatively light sentences including a few years of probation, community service, and sometimes a fine or order to pay restitution. The first juvenile incarcerated for hacking was a 16-year-old sentenced to six months in a juvenile detention facility in 2000. He broke into NASA and Defense Department computers and was a member of a hacker group that vandalized government websites. As more young people caused more disruption, the severity of penalties increased.

Sometimes, the company whose computers a hacker invaded offers the hacker a job after he or she is caught. Give a hacker a job instead of a jail sentence? Some computer professionals and law enforcement officials are very critical of this practice of "rewarding" hackers with security jobs. Can we reduce hacking by encouraging young people to think breaking into a computer system is an acceptable alternative to sending a résumé? In some cases, the new job, the responsibility and respect that go with it, and the threat of punishment for future offenses are enough to turn the hacker's energy and skills toward productive uses. With any criminal law, there is a trade-off between having fixed penalties (for fairness, to avoid favoritism) and flexibility (to consider the particular circumstances). Penalties for minors can focus on using the hacker's computer skills in a productive way and on paying victims for damage done (if possible). Deciding on what is appropriate for a particular person is delicate, one of the difficulties prosecutors and judges face with many kinds of juvenile crime.

How can we dissuade young teens from breaking into computer systems, launching viruses, and shutting down websites? We need a combination of appropriate penalties, education about ethics and risks, and parental responsibility. Parents of many young hackers have no idea what their children are doing. How can we educate parents to prevent adolescent hacking? Just as parents have responsibility for teaching their children to avoid unsafe behavior in cyberspace, they also have some responsibility for preventing their children from engaging in malicious, destructive hacking. Certainly, finding better ways to dissuade young people from destructive hacking benefits them as well as our whole society.

5.7 Whose Laws Rule the Web?

5.7.1 A CRIME IN ONE COUNTRY BUT NOT ANOTHER

The ILOVEYOU virus infected tens of millions of computers worldwide, destroying files, collecting passwords, and snarling computers at major corporations and government agencies. Yet, prosecutors dropped charges against the Philippine man believed to be responsible. The Philippines had no law against releasing a virus at that time. (It passed one soon after.) Should police arrest the man if he visits Canada, the United States, Germany, France, or any of the other countries where the virus did damage? It is tempting to say yes, he should face arrest in any country where the virus caused damage and releasing viruses was illegal at that time. It might also be reasonable that prosecutions for other crimes take place in countries where the damage is done, not solely in the country where the perpetrator acted. But we need to look carefully at the impact of applying the same policy to all laws.

Figure 5.5 lists some of the subject areas in which national laws differ. In addition to outlawing actions that are legal elsewhere, some countries have significantly different procedural laws. For example, in the United States, the government may not appeal acquittals, but in some countries (including other Western democracies), the government may do so.

Here are a few examples of incidents where a person was prosecuted or feared prosecution for actions that were legal in the country where the person performed the actions.

- The government of Thailand arrested an American citizen while he was traveling in Thailand and sentenced him to more than two years in jail. The man had translated parts of a critical biography of the king (published by Yale University Press) and posted them on the Internet from the United States five years earlier. The Thai government had banned the book under its strict laws against insulting the royal family.[51]

- Content control/censorship (Topics include politics, religion, pornography, criminal investigations and trials, and many others.)
- Intellectual property
- Gambling
- Hacking/viruses
- Libel
- Privacy
- Commerce (advertising, store hours, sales)
- Spam

FIGURE 5.5   Some areas where national laws differ.

- A Dutch man released a controversial film critical of Islam on the Internet. The film was legal in the Netherlands; however, Jordan prosecuted the man on charges of blasphemy and other crimes. Making it difficult or dangerous for him to travel internationally was apparently one of the goals of the organization that filed the complaints in Jordan.

- Canadian courts ban reporting court proceedings in some cases—for example, political scandals and gruesome murders. When a Canadian court banned reporting in a case of alleged corruption in the Labour Party, a U.S. blogger who lived near the border reported details of the court proceedings. After his blog had 400,000 hits, mostly from Canada, he feared going to Canada even for vacation.

- The U.S. government arrests employees and executives of foreign companies whose services violate U.S. laws but not their own. (We describe some cases in more detail later.)

Consider an American or French citizen of Chinese ancestry who is a journalist and publishes a blog about the democracy movement in China. The blog is legal where written, but much of its content is illegal in China, because, in the view of the Chinese government, discussion of democracy damages the social order. Would we consider it right if China arrests the journalist on a trip there to visit relatives?

Multinational corporations and tourists have always had to learn about and comply with the laws of countries they operated in or visited. At home, in the past, they had only to deal with their home country's laws, but the Web changed that. Which country's laws should apply when Web content crosses borders? In several cases so far, governments are acting on the assumption of a principle we call the responsibility-to-prevent-access principle.

> *Responsibility to prevent access*: It is the responsibility of providers of services and information to make sure their material is not accessible in countries where it is illegal. Governments in countries where the material is illegal may prosecute, and people in those countries may sue, the providers of services and information who do not prevent access.

In the next few sections, we describe more incidents, raise questions, and discuss arguments for and against this point of view.

French censorship

The first significant case of a country applying its censorship laws to a company based elsewhere occurred in 1999 in France. Display and sale of Nazi memorabilia are illegal in France, with only a few exceptions for historical purposes. Yahoo's French sites, based in France, complied with the French law, but French people could view Nazi memorabilia offered for sale on Yahoo's U.S.-based auction sites.

A French court ordered Yahoo to block access by French people to its sites outside of France that contained material illegal in France.[52]

In Section 2.7, we described the European Union's right to be forgotten. Recall that Google had to block certain links in search results. At first, Google blocked links only from European versions of its search engine, not from google.com. The French government ordered Google to block searches not only on google.fr but also on google.com and not only for searches originating in France but also for searches originating anywhere in the world. Such blocking would enforce an EU citizen's right to be forgotten worldwide, in countries that do not recognize such a right. France has fined Google, and Google continues to appeal.

Should French law apply to google.com and Yahoo auction sites on computers outside of France? Should a speaker have an obligation not to make available speech that others do not want to hear (or that governments do not want the people of a country to hear), or should listeners have the task of covering their ears? Should France have the task of blocking access to material from outside its borders that it considers illegal?

What is the impact on freedom of speech worldwide if countries with more restrictive laws can enforce them in freer countries? Section 3.6 reminds us how restrictive and extensive censorship laws are in many countries.

Applying U.S. law to foreign companies

ElcomSoft, a Russian company, sold a computer program that circumvents controls embedded in Adobe Systems Inc.'s electronic books to prevent copyright infringement. A buyer of the program could use it for legal purposes, such as making backup copies or reading an ebook on different devices, but could also use the program to illegally make copyright-infringing copies. The program itself was legal in Russia and in most of the world, but not in the United States. Distribution of software to thwart built-in copyright protection violates the Digital Millennium Copyright Act (Section 4.3.2). When the program's author, Dmitry Sklyarov, came to the United States to present a talk on the weaknesses in control software in ebooks, he was arrested. He faced a possible 25-year prison term. After protests in the United States and several other countries, the U.S. government let Sklyarov return home but pressed a criminal case against ElcomSoft. A federal jury acquitted the company of criminal charges. ElcomSoft claimed it did not know the program was illegal in the United States and it stopped distributing the program when Adobe complained. Thus, the case did not resolve the basic issue of whether a prosecution would be successful against a company for continuing to distribute a product that is legal in its own country.

The United States arrested David Carruthers, a British citizen and then CEO of BetOnSports PLC, as he changed planes in Dallas on a flight from England to Costa Rica. The U.S. government also arrested several other executives of

BetOnSports and the chairman of Sportingbook, another large British online gambling company. Online betting is legal in England. Internet gambling companies are listed and traded on the London stock exchange. The arrests caused gambling company stocks to drop significantly. The U.S. government argues that most of the companies' customers were in the United States, where most online gambling is illegal. The companies, according to the U.S. government, should have blocked access by U.S. citizens. These arrests, under a 1961 law, are particularly aggressive because legal experts, gambling experts, and legislators disagree about whether the law applies to the Internet. Carruthers spent three years confined to a hotel room awaiting trial and a court later sentenced him to almost three years in federal prison.[53]

Foreign online gambling companies thrive with U.S. customers if their employees stay out of the United States, so Congress passed the Unlawful Internet Gambling Enforcement Act. It prohibits credit card and online-payment companies from processing transactions between bettors and gambling sites. U.S. credit card companies and online-payment companies such as PayPal had already stopped processing gambling transactions (after pressure from the government), but payment-service companies exist in other countries where online gambling, and processing payments for it, are legal. Within months of passing the new law, the U.S. government arrested the founders of a British Internet payment company that processed payments for gambling sites.

> *You just don't travel to the U.S. any more if you're in that business.*
>
> —A London business analyst, after the arrests of two British online
> gambling company executives in the United States[54]

5.7.2 LIBEL AND FREEDOM OF SPEECH

Differences among free countries

Under defamation law, we can sue a person, business, or organization for saying something false and damaging to our reputations in print or in other media such as television or the Web. Libel is written defamation; slander is verbal. In the United States, if the content is true, there is no libel. The U.S. has strong protection for freedom of speech and for expression of opinion. Public figures, such as politicians and entertainers, have less libel protection than other people. The reasoning is that vigorous, open debate—and ultimately freedom—would suffer if people feared lawsuits or prosecution when expressing strong opinions about prominent people. English and Australian law and tradition, on the other hand, place more emphasis on protecting reputations. Michael Jackson won a libel suit against a British newspaper for a statement that his plastic surgeries "hideously disfigured" him. He probably would not have won such a suit in the United States. In England, people often sue newspapers, and it can be risky to publish details about business and

political scandals. Scientists and medical researchers worry about whistleblowing and publishing criticism of research.* The burden of proof differs in different
countries. In the United States, the person who is suing has the burden of proving
the case. Public figures must prove the published information is false *and* that the
publisher knew it was false or acted recklessly. Libel law in some other countries
requires that the publisher of the statement in question prove it is true or that the
publisher reasonably believed it was true.

The result is that news publishers must block access to their articles in countries where publication of the articles violates laws. The *New York Times* did so
for the first time in 2006. It reprogrammed its geolocation tools, normally used for
targeting advertisements, to block people in England from reading a news article.
The article described the investigation of suspects arrested in an alleged plot to
carry liquid explosives onto airplanes and blow them up. Publishing information
damaging to defendants before a trial is illegal in England. It is not illegal in the
United States. Any solution to the problem of differing national laws among free
countries involves some compromise. The *New York Times*, in explaining its decision to block the terror-plot article, said that although England does not have a First
Amendment protecting freedom of the press to the extent the United States does,
England does have a free press, and it is reasonable to respect its laws.[55]

The *New York Times* action shows that major news publishers have the legal
staffs and the technical tools to handle some differences in national laws. Suppose
someone in the United States sends the blocked *New York Times* article by email
to someone in England. Suppose a U.S. blogger with readers in England repeats
some of the information in the article. What might happen to these individuals,
who do not have a legal staff and geolocation tools, who might not know the article
contains information that is illegal in another country?

Libel law as a threat to free speech

A U.S. publisher published a book in the United States by a U.S. scholar about the
funding of terrorism. Some people in England bought copies over the Web. A Saudi
banker who, according to the book, helped fund terrorist leader Osama bin Laden,
brought a libel suit in England against the author and won. Out of fear of the same
kind of lawsuit, another U.S. publisher canceled a book on a similar topic (also written by an American) that had been selling well. The relative ease of winning libel
cases in England led to a phenomenon called *libel tourism*. It has the following characteristics: The person suing for libel in England does not live or work in England.
The person or business sued is, in many cases, not located in England. The content
in question, in some cases, is not in English. The content is on servers outside of
England. But the content is accessible in England. Such lawsuits squelch freedom of

---

*In 2006, in a "landmark" ruling, the British Law Lords (similar to the U.S. Supreme Court) gave news
organizations protection from libel suits for responsible journalism of value to the public.

speech and access to information for people in countries other than England where the libel suits would probably fail. In 2014, England put restrictions on libel lawsuits to protect journalists, scientists, academics, and others and to reduce libel tourism.

U.S. courts generally enforce foreign court judgments against U.S. residents. Abuse of libel law led to passage of the SPEECH Act of 2010, which makes foreign libel judgments unenforceable in the United States if they would violate the First Amendment. But even if U.S. courts do not enforce such foreign court decisions, foreign governments can seize assets of U.S. companies that are in their country or arrest visiting individuals or executives of companies that do not comply with their censorship orders.

In U.S. libel cases where the parties are in different states, courts may rule that the libel took place where the damage occurred, and thus that is where the trial should take place. This makes sense for international cases too, for reasonably free countries, but even when the laws of two countries are similar, the location of a trial is very important. A trial in a foreign country means high travel and legal expenses, time away from work and family, a foreign attorney and jury, unfamiliar forms and procedures, and a cultural disadvantage. What happens if we generalize to oppressive governments that use strict libel laws for political purposes?

Saudi Arabia bans "anything damaging to the dignity of heads of state."[56] In Russia, it is a crime to slander government officials. Government officials in Singapore have long used libel laws to bankrupt political opponents who criticize them. The Prime Minister of Singapore and his father, the former Premier, demanded that the Hong Kong-based *Far Eastern Economic Review* remove from its website an interview with a political opponent who criticized them. They sued the publisher and editor for libel. A lawsuit or criminal charges in these countries against a foreign newspaper or a visiting journalist or blogger threatens not only the defendant but also honest, critical news coverage.

5.7.3   CULTURE, LAW, AND ETHICS

If publishers must comply with the laws of almost 200 countries, would they protect themselves by avoiding anything controversial? Will the extraordinary benefits of international news blogging shrink under the burden of learning every other country's laws, the need to block potentially illegal articles, and the chilling effect of uncertainty? Some people fear allowing governments to impose their restrictive laws outside their borders will destroy the openness and global information flow of the Web; that the Web would come to reflect some combination of Muslim restrictions on discussion of religion, U.S. opposition to online gambling, and Chinese censorship of political discussion. Others argue that companies would adapt and acquire software to handle the appropriate screening.

Jack Goldsmith and Tim Wu, in their book *Who Controls the Internet?*, argue that the "global network is becoming a collection of nation-state networks"[57] and that this is a good thing. The Net, Goldsmith and Wu believe, will be more peaceful and productive if each country controls content within its borders according to its own history, culture, and values. Goldsmith and Wu point out that many people and governments (in both totalitarian countries and democracies) consider the freedom of speech enjoyed in the United States to be excessive. U.S. publishers and bloggers should respect differing national standards and laws and prevent their publications from reaching people in countries that prohibit them.

One criticism of this point of view is that respecting culture is not the same as respecting laws. Culture evolves over time and is rarely absolute or uniform throughout a country. Governments often claim to be protecting national culture and values when they impose controls on their citizens to maintain their own power or to benefit special interests within their country. Laws, as we saw in our discussion of differences between law and ethics in Chapter 1, have many ignoble sources. Who in China wants censorship of political discussion in cyberspace—the people or the Communist Party, which is trying to maintain political control while it loosens economic control? The U.S. government defends its ban on offshore gambling websites with the argument that it has the right to ban morally objectionable activities. Certainly, there are many valid criticisms of gambling on social and ethical grounds, but this argument from the government is not convincing. The federal and state governments allow and tax many forms of legal gambling and profit from monopolies on their state lotteries. It seems likely that anticompetitiveness—not morality—motivates the governments, casinos, and racetracks that oppose offshore online poker playing.

Consider Canada's and France's restrictions on showing U.S. television programs. Some defenders of these laws in those countries emphasize preventing U.S. culture from overrunning their culture. Others (e.g., in Canada) are frank about the purpose being to provide jobs for Canadians and to protect the financial health of the small domestic broadcasting industry. Within each country that has similar protectionist laws (including the United States), there are strongly opposing opinions about whether such laws are unjust intrusions on freedom, whether they help some domestic industries while hurting others, or whether they are reasonable ways to help a local economy. Should governments enforce their protectionist laws on people outside their borders?

Where a large majority of people in a country support prohibitions on certain content, say, discussions of certain religions, is it ethically proper to abandon the basic human rights of free expression and freedom of religion for minorities? Is there a positive ethical value in thwarting a country's censorship laws and providing exactly the material that some governments ban?

5.7.4 POTENTIAL SOLUTIONS

International treaties can set common standards or means of resolving international cases among the countries that sign them. Countries in the World Trade

Organization (WTO) agree not to prevent their citizens from buying certain services from other countries if those services are legal in their own. This is a good step, a generalization of the principle in the United States that the individual states cannot discriminate against sellers (of legal products) from other states. (Recall the wine shipment and real estate sales cases in Section 3.2.5.) But this WTO agreement does not help when a product, a service, or information is legal in one country and illegal in another.

Here is an alternative to the responsibility-to-prevent-access principle that we stated in Section 5.7.1. Let's call it the authority-to-prevent-entry principle:

> *Authority to prevent entry*: The government of Country A can act within Country A to block the entrance of material that is illegal there, but may not apply its laws to the people who create and publish the material, or provide a service, in Country B if it is legal there.

This principle might be reasonable for services such as gambling, which is a prominent part of the culture in some countries, illegal in others, and regulated and taxed in still others. It has been the de facto practice for political speech for a long time. For example, the Soviet Union jammed radio broadcasts from Western countries during the "Cold War." It did not have an internationally respected right to order the broadcasters to stop broadcasting. Similarly, Iran jammed BBC programs on satellite TV. Within their borders, national governments have many tools to block information and activities they do not want. As we saw in Section 3.6.1, they require ISPs and search engine companies (within their country) to block access to banned sites. The government of Singapore made it a criminal offense for Singaporeans to subscribe to, import, or reproduce the *Far Eastern Economic Review* after it published an interview the government considered libelous. Of course, people who believe in freedom of speech do not approve of such actions. The authority-to-prevent-entry principle is a compromise. It recognizes that governments are sovereign within their territories. It attempts to reduce the impact of their restrictive laws outside their borders. If influential countries like the United States and France, for example, adopted this principle and refrained from arresting visiting foreigners, their example could apply pressure to less free countries to do the same. They do not appear inclined to do so.

Of course, this principle has weaknesses too. Countries that lack up-to-date cybercrime laws attract people who commit international online crimes, including major frauds. We want some sensible way for the victims in other countries to take action against them. One reason for the difficulty in developing good solutions to the problem of differing laws in different countries is that there are such widely different kinds of laws. As we saw in Chapter 1, some outlaw truly bad activities that victimize other people. Some impose particular views about acceptable personal beliefs, speech, and nonviolent activities. If all laws were of the first type, there might be much agreement about enforcing them. The problems would be about differences in detail (such as differences between U.S. and British libel law). The responsibility-to-prevent-access principle, the principle many governments currently follow, is dangerous primarily because there are so many laws of the second type. But many people and governments strongly support such laws. It would be quite difficult to find agreement about which laws are the "right" laws, laws a country could rightly enforce outside its borders. Compromises about which laws to enforce, unfortunately, reduce freedom for the people in the country that is freest in any particular area. Thus, we still need creative development of good solutions for the problem of determining what country's laws apply in cross-border Internet cases.

 ## Exercises

Review Exercises

5.1   What did the word "hacker" mean in the early days of computing?

5.2   Is it legal to release a computer virus that puts a funny message on people's screens but does not damage files?

5.3   What is phishing?

5.4   Give an example of hacking by a government.

5.5   Describe one method financial websites use to convince a consumer the site is authentic.

5.6   What is one technique fingerprint readers use to ensure they are not reading a fake finger?

5.7   For what Web-based service did the U.S. government arrest several business executives from England?

General Exercises

5.8   Your roommate Chris uses your computer at night while you sleep. Your roommate Robin takes your car at night while you sleep and drives it around for a while. Neither has your permission; neither does damage. List several characteristics of the two events that are similar (characteristics related to the effects of the events, ethics, legality, risks, etc.). List several characteristics of the two events that are different. Which would offend you more? Why?

5.9   Consider the analogy between occasional downtime on the Web as a result of viruses, worms, or denial-of-service attacks and vehicle traffic slowdowns on roads during rush hour or bad weather. Describe similarities; then evaluate. Are both side effects of modern civilization that we have to get used to? How can individuals and businesses reduce the negative impacts on themselves?

5.10   Describe two tools hackers used, or vulnerabilities they exploited, to steal consumer data from Target.

5.11   Some people argue that a hacker who defaces a Web page of a government entity such as the White House, Congress, or Parliament should receive harsher punishment than a hacker who defaces a Web page of a private company or organization. Give some arguments for and against this view.

5.12   Hacktivists might argue that presenting their views on their own websites and social media platforms is not enough because most people who would look there already share those views. They want to reach people who visit sites with opposing views. Analyze this argument for hacktivism.

5.13   In Section 5.3.3, we described the incident in which a hacker group hacked into the Bay Area Rapid Transit system (BART) to protest BART's shut down of wireless communication in some BART stations. Was this a form of hacktivism? Was it ethical? Give reasons.

5.14   A hacker group stole client credit card numbers from a security firm and used them to make donations to charities. Part of the purpose of the hack was to demonstrate the weakness of security at the firm. Analyze the ethics of this incident.

5.15   After terrorist attacks in Paris, the hacking group Anonymous said it disrupted Twitter accounts belonging to members of Islamic State and posted personal information about them online. List at least two questions we should ask when considering whether the group's actions were ethically acceptable.

5.16   Describe a (hypothetical) hacking attack by a foreign government that you would consider an act of war. Indicate what characteristics of the attack lead to that conclusion.

5.17   In what way is the history of the Internet responsible for its vulnerability?

5.18   To reduce scams that steal from people banking online, some people suggest creating a new Internet domain "bank," available only to chartered banks. Consider the identity theft and fraud techniques we discussed. Which ones would this new domain help prevent? For which would it be ineffective? Overall, do you think it is a good idea? Why or why not?

5.19   Some young hackers argued that, if the owners of a computer system want to keep outsiders out, it is their responsibility to provide better security. Ken Thompson, one of the inventors of UNIX, said, "The act of breaking into a computer system has to have the same social stigma as breaking into a neighbor's house. It should not matter that the neighbor's door is unlocked."[58] Which position do you agree with more? Give your reasons.

5.20   In Section 5.5.1, we gave an analogy between merchants accepting some amount of shoplifting, on the one hand, and merchants and credit card companies accepting some amount of credit card fraud, on the other hand. Identify a strength and a weakness of this analogy.

5.21   We saw that hackers and identity thieves use many techniques and continually develop new ones. Think up a new scheme for obtaining passwords or some type of personal information that might be useful in identity theft. Then describe a possible response to protect against your scheme.

5.22   In Section 5.5.1, we described a customer authentication method that calculates a risk score based on many details of a customer's typical activities on a company's website. To use this method, the site must store many details of each customer's visits to the site. Does this violate the privacy principles in Figure 2.1 of collecting only the data needed and not storing data longer than needed? Explain your answer.

5.23   Does requiring both a fingerprint and a password to log in to a system meet the criteria of multifactor authentication, described in Section 5.5.1? Explain.

5.24   In one multifactor authentication scheme, after the person types a username and password, the website sends a code to the person's mobile phone. The person must enter the code to continue. Give one argument for and one argument against using this method for access to Medicare accounts.

5.25 What penalty, from Harvard, MIT, or the law, do you think would have been appropriate for Aaron Swartz's massive downloading of research papers from JSTOR? (See Section 5.6.1.)

5.26 Suppose a 16-year-old releases automatic-dialing software that will flood the emergency 911 telephone system with calls, knocking out service. He claims he was experimenting with the software and released it by accident. What penalty do you think is appropriate?

5.27 The terms of use of the website for a major concert ticket seller prohibit automated purchases. Should a person who used a software program to purchase a large number of tickets be prosecuted for exceeding authorized access to the site? Why or why not?

5.28 Evaluate arguments in favor of and against passage of a law making the writing and publication of a computer virus a crime. (See Section 5.6.2.) Would you support such a law? Why?

5.29 Identify several issues raised by this scenario:

Someone in California posts on amazon.com a very critical review of a new book written by a British author. The review says the writer is an incompetent fool without a single good idea; he can't even express the bad ideas clearly and probably did not graduate from grade school; and he should be washing dishes instead of wasting the reader's time. The author files a lawsuit for libel in England against the reviewer and Amazon.

5.30 Using some of the ethical principles in Chapter 1, analyze the ethics of the action of the U.S. blogger who posted details about the Canadian trial (Section 5.7.1). Do you think he should have done it?

5.31 During World War II, "Radio Free Europe" broadcast news and other information into German-controlled countries. It was illegal to listen to those broadcasts in those countries. During the "Cold War," the Soviet Union jammed Western radio broadcasts into that country. In the discussion of the Yahoo/France case (Section 5.7.1), we asked: "Should a speaker have an obligation not to make available speech that others do not want to hear (or that governments do not want the people of a country to hear), or should listeners have the task of covering their ears?" Does your answer for the Yahoo case differ from your answer in the German and Soviet examples? If so, how and why? If not, why not?

5.32 Assume you are a professional working in your chosen field. Describe specific things you can do to reduce the impact of any two problems we discussed in this chapter. (If you cannot think of anything related to your professional field, choose another field that might interest you.)

5.33 Think ahead to the next few years and describe a new problem, related to issues in this chapter, likely to develop from digital technology or devices.

Assignments

These exercises require some research or activity.

5.34 The section on hacking by governments (Section 5.3.4) describes, mostly, incidents of hacking for military or strategic purposes. Find information about hacking for industrial or economic espionage. Summarize your findings. What responses are appropriate?

5.35 Find out if *Facebook* v. *Power Ventures* has been retried (after the 2016 9th Circuit Appeals Court decision described in Section 5.6.1). Tell the current status of the case. Find out if there have been recent prosecutions for violating the Computer Fraud and Abuse Act for unauthorized access in other cases that do not involve hacking. If so, describe the issues in one such case.

Class Discussion Exercises

These exercises are for class discussion, perhaps with short presentations prepared in advance by small groups of students.

5.36 Near the end of Section 5.5.3, we described three examples of disclosing vulnerabilities in computer systems. Discuss and evaluate them. Were they handled responsibly?

5.37 Some people argue that without the constant threats and challenges provided by (unauthorized) hackers, we might not learn of vulnerabilities, and security would be weak. Are hackers heroes? Do they perform a public service by finding and publicizing computer security weaknesses?

5.38 Do we have an ethical responsibility to maintain up-to-date antivirus protection and other security software on our personal computers and devices to prevent their being infected with remotely controlled software that harms others? Should a law require that everyone install such software? Consider analogies from several other technologies or areas.

5.39 Suppose a denial-of-service attack shuts down several thousand websites, including retailers, stock brokerages, and large corporate entertainment and information sites, for several hours. The attack is traced to one of the following perpetrators. Do you think different penalties are appropriate depending on which it is? Explain why. If you would impose different penalties, how would they differ?

   (a) A foreign terrorist who launched the attack to cause billions of dollars in damage to the U.S. economy.

   (b) An organization publicizing its opposition to commercialization of the Web and corporate manipulation of consumers.

   (c) A teenager using hacking tools he or she found on a website.

   (d) A hacker group showing off to another hacker group about how many sites it could shut down in one day.

5.40 Suppose a local community center has invited you, a group of college students, to make a 10-minute presentation about protecting smartphones from malicious software. Plan and give the presentation.

5.41 Consider the Target breach described in Section 5.3.2. What mistakes, if any, did each of the following people make and what was their level of responsibility?

   (a) The Fazio Mechanical employee who received the phishing email

   (b) The system administrator at Fazio Mechanical

   (c) The Fazio Mechanical website developer

   (d) The developer of Target's electronic billing system

   (e) The developer of Target's contract submission system

   (f) Target system and network administrators

   (g) Target cashiers

   (h) Target executives

   (i) Shoppers using credit cards at Target in 2013

5.42 How should the U.S. government respond to a hacking attack by China in which the hackers shut down critical military communications for several hours?[*]

5.43 Should violation of the terms of agreement of a website be a crime? Why or why not? If you think it should depend on the type of site and the type of violation, explain the criteria to make the distinction.

5.44 As we discussed in Section 5.5.4, several tech companies have added strong encryption for some user communications and stored data that can prevent (or make extremely difficult) access by phone thieves, hackers, and the government. The companies themselves cannot access the data when requested by law enforcement agencies.

  (a) Assume there is no law prohibiting or restricting use of technologies that prevent government access. You are a committee of high-level executives of a major tech company debating whether to implement such technology in your operating system for smartphones and other products. Mention several relevant issues and discuss them.

  (b) Argue that people should be free to use (and companies free to provide) the best available tools to protect privacy and security. Address the problems of investigating serious crimes and terrorism.

  (c) Argue that a law should require that the technology allow law enforcement access to communications and stored data. Address concerns of opponents of such laws described in Section 5.5.4.

5.45 A judge in the state of Kentucky seized the Web addresses of more than 100 gambling sites that allow people to gamble at online slot machines and roulette tables. Such gambling is illegal in Kentucky. The online gambling companies whose sites were seized do not have a physical presence in Kentucky. Give arguments for and against the judge's action.

Notes

1. Eric S. Raymond, ed., *New Hacker's Dictionary*, MIT Press, 1993.
2. Quoted in J. D. Bierdorfer, "Among Code Warriors, Women, Too, Can Fight," *New York Times*, June 7, 2001, pp. 1, 9.
3. Jon A. Rochlis and Mark W. Eichin, "With Microscope and Tweezers: The Worm from MIT's Perspective," *Communications of the ACM*, 32:6, June 1989, pp. 689–698.
4. Lev Grossman, "Attack of the Love Bug," *Time*, May 15, 2000, pp. 48–56.
5. The Swedish site was The Pirate Bay; Ivar Ekman, "File-Sharing Crackdown and Backlash in Sweden," *International Herald Tribune*, June 5, 2006, p. 1. Jason Scheier, "Sony Hack Probe Uncovers 'Anonymous' Calling Card," *Wired*, May 4, 2011, www.wired.com/gamelife/2011/05/sony-playstation-network-anonymous.
6. Robin Sidel, "Mobile Bank Heist: Hackers Target Your Phone," *Wall Street Journal*, Aug. 26, 2016, www.wsj.com/articles/mobile-bank-heist-hackers-target-your-phone-1472119200. Hayley Tsukayama, "Facebook Security Breach Raises Concerns," *Washington Post*, Nov. 15, 2011, www.washingtonpost.com/business/economy/facebookhack-raises-security-concerns/2011/11/15/gIQAqCyYPN_story.html.

---

[*]This is hypothetical; such an attack has not occurred.

7. Eduard Kovacs, "Conficker Worm Shipped with Police Body Cameras," *Security Week*, Nov. 16, 2015, www.securityweek.com/conficker-worm-shipped-police-body-cameras.

8. "How to Protect Your Network from Ransomware," U.S. Department of Justice, www.justice.gov/criminal-ccips/file/872771/download.

9. Aaron Katerksky, "Dozens of Arrests in 'Blackshades' Hacking Around the World," *ABC News*, May 19, 2014, abcnews.go.com/Blotter/dozens-arrests-blackshades-hacking-world/story?id=23778246.

10. Sean Gallagher, "How One Rent-a-botnet Army of Cameras, DVRs Caused Internet Chaos," *Ars Technica*, Oct. 25, 2016, arstechnica.com/information-technology/2016/10/inside-the-machine-uprising-how-cameras-dvrs-took-down-parts-of-the-internet.

11. Victoria Murphy Barret, "Spam Hunter," *Forbes*, July 23, 2007, members.forbes.com/forbes/2007/0723/054.html.

12. Dan Goodin, "iPhone Hack that Threatened Emergency 911 System Lands Teen in Jail," *Ars Technica*, Oct. 28, 2016, arstechnica.com/security/2016/10/teen-arrested-for-iphone-hack-that-threatened-emergency-911-system/. Gallagher, "How One Rent-a-botnet Army of Cameras, DVRs Caused Internet Chaos." Nicole Perlroth, "Hackers Used New Weapons to Disrupt Major Websites Across U.S." *New York Times*, Oct. 21, 2016, www.nytimes.com/2016/10/22/business/internet-problems-attack.html?_r=0. Brian Krebs, "IoT Device Maker Vows Product Recall, Legal Action Against Western Accusers," *Krebs on Security*, Oct. 24, 2016, krebsonsecurity.com/2016/10/iot-device-maker-vows-product-recall-legal-action-against-western-accusers/.

13. John J. Fialka, "The Latest Flurries at Weather Bureau: Scattered Hacking," *Wall Street Journal*, Oct. 10, 1994, pp. A1, A6.

14. Erin Fuchs, "Identity Theft Now Costs More than All Other Property Crimes Combined," *Business Insider*, Dec. 12, 2013, www.businessinsider.com/bureau-of-justice-statistics-identity-theft-report-2013-12.

15. Sources for this section include: Brian Krebs, "New Clues in the Target Breach," *Krebs on Security*, Jan. 29, 2014, krebsonsecurity.com/2014/01/new-clues-in-the-target-breach/; Brian Krebs, "The Target Breach, By the Numbers," *Krebs on Security*, May 6, 2014, krebsonsecurity.com/2014/05/the-target-breach-by-the-numbers/; Brian Krebs, "Inside Target Corp., Days After 2013 Breach," *Krebs on Security*, Sept. 21, 2015, krebsonsecurity.com/2015/09/inside-target-corp-days-after-2013-breach/; Sara Peters, "The 7 Best Social Engineering Attacks Ever," *Dark Reading, Information Week*, Mar. 17, 2015, www.darkreading.com/the-7-best-social-engineering-attacks-ever/d/d-id/1319411?image_number=8; and Thor Olavsrud, "11 Steps Attackers Took to Crack Target," *CIO*, Sept. 2, 2014, www.cio.com/article/2600345/security0/11-steps-attackers-took-to-crack-target.html.

16. Mark Manion and Abby Goodrum, "Terrorism or Civil Disobedience: Toward a Hacktivist Ethic," in Richard A. Spinello and Herman T. Tavani, eds., *Readings in CyberEthics*, Jones and Bartlett, 2001, pp. 463–473.

17. In Cheryl Pellerin, "DOD Releases First Strategy for Operating in Cyberspace," U.S. Department of Defense, *American Forces Press Service*, July 14, 2011, archive.defense.gov/news/newsarticle.aspx?id=64686.

18. Many news stories covered this incident. See, for example, L. Gordon Crovitz, "China Goes Phishing," *Wall Street Journal*, June 6, 2011, www.wsj.com/articles/SB10001424052702303657404576363374283504838.

19. Many news stories covered these and other incidents. See, for example: US-China Economic and Security Review Commission, "2010 Report to Congress," p. 243, origin.www.uscc.gov/sites/default/files/annual_reports/2010-Report-to-Congress.pdf; Alex Spillius, "China and Russia Hack into US Power Grid," *The Telegraph*, Apr. 8, 2009, www.telegraph.co.uk/news/worldnews/asia/china/5126584/China-and-Russia-hack-into-US-power-grid.html; Richard Clarke, "China's Cyberassault on America," *Wall Street Journal*, June 15, 2011, www.wsj.com/articles/SB10001424052702304259304576373391101828876; and Jim Wolf, "China Key Suspect in US Satellite Hacks: Commission," *Reuters*, Oct. 28, 2011, www.reuters.com/article/2011/10/28/china-usasatellite-idUSN1E79R1LK20111028.

20. Jonathan Fildes, "Stuxnet Worm 'Targeted High-Value Iranian Assets,'" *BBC News*, Sept. 23, 2010, www.bbc.co.uk/news/technology-11388018. David Sanger, "Obama Order Sped Up Wave of Cyberattacks against Iran," *New York Times*, June 1, 2012, www.nytimes.com/2012/06/01/world/middleeast/obama-ordered-wave-of-cyberattacks_against-iran.html.

21. Glenn Greenwald, "How the NSA Tampers with U.S.-made Internet Routers," *The Guardian*, May 12, 2014, www.theguardian.com/books/2014/may/12/glenn-greenwald-nsa-tampers-us-internet-routers-snowden.

22. Dan Goodin, "Critical Crypto Bug in OpenSSL Opens Two-thirds of the Web to Eavesdropping," *Ars Technica*, Apr. 7, 2014, arstechnica.com/security/2014/04/critical-crypto-bug-in-openssl-opens-two-thirds-of-the-web-to-eavesdropping/.

23. Steve Marquess, "Of Money, Responsibility, and Pride," Speeds and Feeds Blog, Apr. 12, 2014, veridicalsystems.com/blog/of-money-responsibility-and-pride/. Marquess is president of the OpenSSL Software Foundation. Jon Brodkin, "Tech Giants, Chastened by Heartbleed, Finally Agree to Fund OpenSSL," *Ars Technica*, Apr. 24, 2014, arstechnica.com/information-technology/2014/04/tech-giants-chastened-by-heartbleed-finally-agree-to-fund-openssl/.

24. "Internet of Things Research Study, 2015 Report," *Hewlett Packard*, Nov. 2015, www8.hp.com/h20195/V2/GetPDF.aspx/4AA5-4759ENW.pdf.

25. Elinor Mills, "Expert Hacks Car System, Says Problems Reach to SCADA Systems," *CNet News*, July 26, 2011, news.cnet.com/8301-27080_3-20083906-245/expert-hacks-car-system-says-problems-reach-to-scada-systems. Joris Evers, "Don't Let Your Navigation System Fool You," *CNet News*, Apr. 20, 2007, news.com.com. Andy Greenberg, "Hackers Remotely Kill a Jeep on the Highway—With Me in It," *Wired*, July 21, 2015, www.wired.com/2015/07/hackers-remotely-kill-jeep-highway/.

26. John R. Wilke, "In the Arcane Culture of Computer Hackers, Few Doors Stay Closed," *Wall Street Journal*, Aug. 22, 1990, pp. A1, A4.

27. Barbara Carton, "An Unsolved Slaying of an Airline Worker Stirs Family to Action," *Wall Street Journal*, June 20, 1995, p. A1, A8.

28. Saul Hansell, "U.S. Workers Stole Data on 11,000, Agency Says," *New York Times*, Apr. 6, 1996, p. 6.

29. William J. Lynn III, "Defending a New Domain," *Foreign Affairs*, Sept./Oct. 2010, www.foreignaffairs.com/articles/united-states/2010-09-01/defending-new-domain.

30. Joseph Pereira, "How Credit-Card Data Went Out Wireless Door," *Wall Street Journal*, May 4, 2007, pp. A1, A12. In 2011, hackers collected unencrypted sensitive client data from a firm that analyzes international security for government agencies, banks, oil companies, and other large companies. Source: www.telegraph.co.uk/technology/news/8980453/Anonymous-Robin-Hood-hacking-attack-hits-major-firms.html.

31. Kim Zetter, "How America's 911 Emergency Response System Can Be Hacked," *Washington Post*, Sept. 9, 2016, www.washingtonpost.com/news/the-switch/wp/2016/09/09/how-americas-911-emergency-response-system-can-be-hacked/.

32. Robert Lemos, "Stock Scammer Gets Coal for the Holidays," *The Register*, Dec. 28, 2006, www.theregister.co.uk/2006/12/28/sec_freezes_stock_scammer_accounts.

33. William M. Bulkeley, "How Biometric Security Is Far from Foolproof," *Wall Street Journal*, Dec. 12, 2006, p. B3.

34. Thom Shanker and Elisabeth Bulmiller, "Hackers Gained Access to Sensitive Military Files," *New York Times*, July 14, 2011, www.nytimes.com/2011/07/15/world/15cyber.html?pagewanted=all. Pellerin, "DOD Releases First Strategy for Operating in Cyberspace." Robert McMillan, "Security Experts Say NSA-Linked Hacking Effort Was Itself Compromised," *Wall Street Journal*, Aug. 17, 2016, www.wsj.com/articles/security-experts-say-nsa-linked-hacking-effort-was-itself-compromised-1471458035.

35. Robert McMillan, "Mark Zuckerberg's Twitter and Pinterest Accounts Hacked," *Wall Street Journal*, June 7, 2016, www.wsj.com/articles/mark-zuckerbergs-twitter-and-pinterest-accounts-hacked-1465251954.

36. Morgan Slain, "Announcing Our Worst Passwords of 2015," TeamsID, SplashData, Jan. 19, 2015, www.teamsid.com/worst-passwords-2015/.

37. Quoted in Alex Hern, "Google CEO Sundar Pichai Joins Long List of Celebrities Hacked by OurMine Group," *The Guardian*, June 28, 2016, www.theguardian.com/technology/2016/jun/28/sundar-pichai-hacked-ourmine-group-bitly.

38. Darlene Storm, "Hack to Steal Cars with Keyless Ignition: Volkswagen Spent 2 Years Hiding Flaw," *Computerworld*, Aug. 17, 2015, www.computerworld.com/article/2971826/cybercrime-hacking/hack-to-steal-cars-with-keyless-ignition-volkswagen-spent-2-years-hiding-flaw.html.

39. Marc L. Songini, "Hospital Confirms Copying of Patient Files by Hacker," *Computerworld*, Dec. 15, 2000, www.computerworld.com/article/2589907/data-privacy/hospital-confirms-copying-of-patient-files-by-hacker.html.

40. Kim Zetter, "Appeals Court Overturns Conviction of AT&T Hacker 'Weev'," *Wired*, Apr. 11, 2014, www.wired.com/2014/04/att-hacker-conviction-vacated/.

41. John Schwartz, "Industry Fights Wiretap Proposal," *Washington Post*, Mar. 12, 1994, pp. C1, C7.

42. The Security and Freedom through Encryption Act (SAFE), as amended by the House Intelligence Committee, Sept. 11, 1997.

43. Robert McMillan, "San Bernardino County Had Software that Could Have Given FBI Access to Shooter's iPhone," *Wall Street Journal*, Feb. 22, 2016, www.wsj.com/articles/san-bernardino-county-had-software-that-could-have-given-fbi-access-to-shooters-iphone-1456184504. Martyn Williams, "FBI Director Admits Mistake Was Made with San Bernardino iCloud Reset," *Computerworld*, Mar. 1, 2016, www.computerworld.com/article/3039838/security/fbi-director-admits-mistake-was-made-with-san-bernadino-icloud-reset.html. Katie Benner and Eric Lichtblau, "U.S. Says It Has Unlocked iPhone Without Apple," *New York Times*, Mar. 28, 2016, www.nytimes.com/2016/03/29/technology/apple-iphone-fbi-justice-department-case.html?_r=0.

44. Editorial, "Apple Is Right on Encryption," *Wall Street Journal*, Mar. 1, 2016, www.wsj.com/articles/apple-is-right-on-encryption-1456877827.

45. *United States* v. *Drew*, 259 F.R.D. 449 (C.D.Cal.), 2009.

46. Harold Abelson *et al.*, Report to the President: MIT and the Prosecution of Aaron Swartz," July 26, 2013, swartz-report.mit.edu/docs/report-to-the-president.pdf; Marcella Bombardieri, "The Inside Story of MIT and Aaron Swartz," *Boston Globe*, Mar. 30, 2014, www.bostonglobe.com/metro/2014/03/29/the-inside-story-mit-and-aaron-swartz/YvJZ5P6VHaPJusReuaN7SI/story.html.

47. Orin Kerr, "9th Circuit: It's a Federal Crime to Visit a Website After Being Told Not to Visit It," *Washington Post*, July 12, 2016, www.washingtonpost.com/news/volokh-conspiracy/wp/2016/07/12/9th-circuit-its-a-federal-crime-to-visit-a-website-after-being-told-not-to-visit-it/. The case is *Facebook* v. *Power Ventures* and the appeals court decision is at cdn.ca9.uscourts.gov/datastore/opinions/2016/07/12/13-17102.pdf.

48. Peter Tippett, quoted in Kim Zetter, "Freeze! Drop That Download!" *PC World*, Nov. 16, 2000, www.pcworld.com/article/34406/article.html. The article includes pros and cons of criminalizing virus writing and a discussion of other means of reducing viruses.

49. Bruce Sterling, *The Hacker Crackdown: Law and Disorder on the Electronic Frontier*, Bantam Books, 1992, pp. 13–14.

50. Craig Bromberg, "In Defense of Hackers," *New York Times Magazine*, Apr. 21, 1991, pp. 45–49. Gary Wolf, "The World According to Woz," *Wired*, Sept. 1998, pp. 118–121, 178–185. Richard P. Feynman, *Surely You're Joking, Mr. Feynman: Adventures of a Curious Character*, W. W. Norton, 1984, pp. 137–155.

51. Gareth Finighan, "U.S. Citizen Jailed for More than Two Years in Thailand," *Daily Mail*, www.dailymail.co.uk/news/article-2071468/Joe-Gordon-US-citizen-jailed-Thailand-posting-online-excerpts-book-banned-king.html, Dec. 8, 2011.

52. Lisa Guernsey, "Welcome to the Web. Passport, Please?" *New York Times*, Mar. 15, 2001, pp. D1, D8.

53. Pete Harrison, "Online Gambling Stocks Dive Again," *Reuters UK*, Sept. 7, 2006, www.gamesandcasino.com/gambling-news/online-gambling-stocks-dive-again-as-us-doj-holds-gaming-executive-again/147.htm. Pete Harrison, "Sportingbet Arrest Sparks Fears of Wider Crackdown," *Reuters*, Sept. 8, 2006, go.reuters.com. Bloomberg News, "Gambling Executive Sentenced to Prison," *New York Times*, Jan. 8, 2010, www.nytimes.com/2010/01/09/business/09gamble.html. Kristen Hinman, "David Carruthers: From House Arrest to Prison," *Riverfront Times*, Jan. 8, 2010, www.riverfronttimes.com/newsblog/2010/01/08/david-carruthers-from-house-arrest-to-prison.

54. Quoted in Harrison, "Sportingbet Arrest Sparks Fears."

55. Tom Zeller, Jr., "Times Withholds Web Article in Britain," *New York Times*, Aug. 29, 2006, www.nytimes.com/2006/08/29/business/media/29times.html.

56. Robert Corn-Revere, "Caught in the Seamless Web: Does the Internet's Global Reach Justify Less Freedom of Speech?" *Cato Institute*, July 24, 2002, p. 7.

57. Jack Goldsmith and Tim Wu, *Who Controls the Internet? Illusions of a Borderless World*, Oxford University Press, 2006, p. 149.

58. In Donn Seeley, "Password Cracking: A Game of Wits," *Communications of the ACM*, June 1989, 32:6, pp. 700–703, reprinted in Peter J. Denning, ed., *Computers under Attack: Intruders, Worms, and Viruses*, Addison-Wesley, 1990, pp. 244–252.

Work

6.1 Fears and Questions

Computers free us from the repetitious, boring aspects of jobs so that we can spend more time being creative and doing tasks that require human intelligence. Computer systems and the Internet provide quick, reliable access to information so that we work smarter and more efficiently, yet people still do the work. Nurses care for the elderly, and construction workers build buildings. Architects use computer-aided design systems, but it is still humans who design the buildings. Accountants use financial applications and thus have more time for thinking, planning, and analysis. But will computers design buildings? Can audits be automated?

Initially, many social critics, social scientists, politicians, unions, and activists saw virtually all potential effects of computers on work as highly threatening. Some predicted mass unemployment due to increased efficiency while others argued that money spent on computers was wasted because computers *decreased* efficiency. They argued that requiring workers to acquire computer skills was too heavy a burden, and that the need for increased technical training and skills would widen the earning gap between those who obtain the new skills and those who do not. They saw telecommuting as bad for workers and society. They expected a huge number of jobs to be eliminated by offshoring—hiring people or companies in other countries to perform services that workers in one's home country used to do.

Although the dire forecasts were wrong, the many widespread rapid changes raise significant social questions. How do we deal with the dislocations and retraining needs that result when technology and the Internet eliminate jobs? What are the advantages and disadvantages of working from home or a coffee shop on a mobile device rather than at the traditional company office? How does mobile work affect the physical distribution of population and businesses? What is the impact on society and on workers of smartphone apps that facilitate new forms of work, matching potential workers with potential customers, as needed, for short jobs? What risks need to be considered when employees use their own smartphones, tablets, and other devices for work?

At the same time that information technology gives some workers more autonomy, it gives employers increased power to monitor the work, communications, movements, driving habits, health, and online activity of employees and to observe what their employees do when away from work (e.g., in social media). These changes affect productivity, privacy, and morale. Why do employers monitor employees? What monitoring is reasonable and what is not?

And always, there is the returning question: will technology—now perhaps artificial intelligence and robotics—put a huge number of people out of work?

In this chapter, we explore these questions and others raised by the evolving technology we use for work.

6.2   Impacts on Employment

But nowhere is there any mention of the truth about the information highway,
which is mass unemployment.

—David Noble, "The Truth About the Information Highway"[1]

6.2.1   JOB DESTRUCTION AND CREATION

The fear that computing technology and the Internet would cause mass unemployment may seem unreasonable now. Yet, since the beginning of the Industrial Revolution, technology has generated fears of mass unemployment. In the early 1800s,
the Luddites (of whom we say more in Chapter 7) burned weaving looms because
they feared the looms would eliminate their jobs. A few decades later, a mob of
seamstresses and tailors destroyed sewing machines because of the same fears.[2]

More recently, in the 1950s and 1960s, factory automation came under (verbal)
fire from presidential candidate John F. Kennedy and industry and labor groups
for threatening to bring the menace of increased unemployment and poverty. The
quotation at the beginning of this section is about the information highway (a term
commonly used for the Internet in the 1990s), but social scientists argued that it
applied as well to all computer technology. Technology critics such as Jeremy
Rifkin consider the reduction in the human labor and time required to produce
goods and services to be one of the horrific consequences of computers and automation. In 2011, President Obama suggested that the high unemployment rate
at the time was related to people using ATMs instead of bank tellers and airport
check-in kiosks instead of live agents.[3]

There is no doubt that technology in general and computing technology in
particular eliminate jobs. Here are some examples[4]:

- Since the 17th century, engineers used slide rules, but electronic calculators
  made them obsolete; the jobs of manufacturing and selling slide rules
  evaporated.

- Jobs of building, selling, and repairing typewriters have disappeared.

- The number of telephone switchboard operators dropped from 421,000 in
  1970 to 164,000 in 1996.

- As the use of ATMs grew, the number of bank tellers dropped by about 37%
  between 1983 and 1993.

- Railroads computerized their dispatch operations and eliminated hundreds
  of jobs.

- Travel agencies closed as consumers made travel reservations online.

- Jobs of electric meter readers disappeared as utility companies installed devices
  that send meter readings to company computers. Similar technology monitors

vending machines and oil wells, reducing the number of people needed to check on them in person.

- Shopping online and self-service checkout systems in stores reduced the need for sales clerks.

- Hundreds of music stores closed and jobs in the printing industry declined as music, magazines, newspapers, and books went digital.

- As use of cellphones increased, the number of employees in the wired telecommunications industry dropped by more than 120,000.

- Thousands of journalism jobs disappeared as people began to read news online.

- Digital cameras put film processors out of work. Kodak, founded in 1880, laid off thousands of employees and filed for bankruptcy protection in 2012.

- Self-driving vehicles are likely to reduce the number of jobs for truck, taxi, and ride-sharing drivers. By reducing the need to own a car, or a second car, they may reduce the number of jobs in the auto manufacturing industry.

The goals of developing and implementing technology include a reduction in the resources needed to accomplish a result and an increase in productivity and standard of living. Human labor is a resource and technology reduces the number of workers required to carry out tasks. If we look back at our examples of lost jobs, we see that many of them accompanied an increase in individual productivity. While the number of telephone operators was dropping by more than 60% between 1970 and 1996, the annual number of long-distance calls increased from 9.8 billion to 94.9 billion. Manufacturing productivity in the United States more than doubled between 1980 and 2002.[5] Productivity growth fluctuates, but the trend is upward.

Diane Labombarbe/E+/Getty Images

FIGURE 6.1 Would we have today's phone services if human operators still connected calls?

With a sewing machine, a person could make more than two shirts a day. Rather than loss of jobs, the sewing machine meant a reduction in the price of clothes, more demand, and ultimately hundreds of thousands of new jobs.[6*] A successful technology can eliminate some jobs and create others. Today, it is clear that computers created millions of jobs through new products, services, and entirely new industries. From the electronic calculators that replaced slide rules to the networks and cellphones that replaced telephone operators (see Figure 6.1) to the social networking services that created a new phenomenon, the new devices and services all represent new jobs.

By 1998, the Semiconductor Industry Association reported that chip makers employed 242,000 workers, directly, in the United States and 1.3 million workers indirectly. The chip industry, which did not exist before the microprocessor was invented in the 1970s, ranked fourth among U.S. industries by annual revenue. Although e-commerce and automatic checkout in stores reduce demand for sales clerks, there are not fewer people in these jobs. The U. S. Bureau of Labor Statistics (BLS) forecasts an increase of 7% in the number of retail workers between 2014 and 2024. Contrary to predictions in the early 1990s, there are still approximately 500,000 bank tellers.[7]

Countless new products and services based on computer technology create jobs: medical devices, 3D printers, personal fitness devices, navigation systems,

---

Are there more or fewer musicians?

A harpist described—and lamented—how a series of technologies eliminated the jobs of musicians[8]: Piano rolls, automated player pianos, and recordings replaced the live piano player at silent movies. Juke boxes replaced live bands in bars. Records and then digital music replaced live orchestras and bands at Broadway shows, dance performances, and weddings.

Here is another perspective to consider. A few hundred years ago, listening to professional-quality music was a rare luxury for most people. Only the wealthy could hire professional musicians to perform for them. Technology, including electricity, radio, CDs, DVDs, iPods, smartphones, data-compression algorithms, and the Web brought the cost of an individual "performance" in a private home (or out on a hiking trail) down so low that high-quality music is available to almost anyone.

The effect on employment? The BLS reports more than 170,000 musicians and singers earn a median income of about $24 per hour.[9] Some make a fortune in jazz, country, classical, zydeco, new age, rock, or rap music. Independent musicians get exposure to millions more listeners through services such as Spotify, iTunes Music, Pandora, and more. As technology brings the cost of a product or service down and the market expands, more people work in the field.

---

[*]Sewing machines were first marketed to factory owners, just as computers were first used by large companies. Isaac Singer had the insight to sell them directly to women, in a parallel to the eventual shift from corporation-owned mainframes to personal computers for consumers.

virtual-reality systems, smartphones and apps for them, and so on. The app industry alone accounted for almost 1.7 million jobs in the United States by 2016. New products and services create jobs in design, marketing, manufacture, sales, customer service, repair, and maintenance for those products. New technical jobs also create jobs for support staff such as receptionists, janitors, and stock clerks. The enormous growth of retail sales on the Web contributed to an increase in jobs in the package shipping industry. Computer and Internet technology generated all the jobs at Alphabet (Google's parent company), Apple, eBay, Hulu, Amazon, Microsoft, Facebook, Twitter, Zappos—and thousands more companies. An industry research firm reported that worldwide spending on information technology was above $3.5 trillion in 2015 and forecast that it would stay above that level for the next several years. That money pays for a very large number of jobs.[10]

Some of the same technologies that eliminate jobs help people find new ones. In the past, job seekers did research on jobs and companies in newspapers and libraries and by telephone. The Web and social media make more information and services available to a job seeker with much more convenience and for a lower price. Many online training programs can help us learn new trade or professional skills. We post résumés on job websites. We research a company's reputation among its employees on a variety of forums and can investigate schools, entertainment, neighborhoods, and religious facilities in distant towns before spending time and money to travel for an interview. And then, we may not even need to travel for the interview as companies can meet us face-to-face using video-conferencing applications to reduce travel time and costs.

Airplanes, automobiles, radio, television, computers, much medical technology, and many other items we use daily did not exist before the 20th century. Throughout the 20th century, there was an enormous increase in technology and a decrease in jobs in areas such as agriculture and saddle making. If technology's overall impact was to destroy jobs, there should have been fewer people working in 2000 than in 1900. But, with a population that approximately quadrupled between 1900 and 2000, the U.S. unemployment rate was 4% in 2000, lower than throughout most of the century. (One segment of the population is working less: children. In 1870, the average age for starting work was 13; by 1990, it was 19. In the early 20th century, children worked long days on farms and in factories and mines. Technology—and laws—eliminated many of the jobs performed by children.)

Many new jobs created by computer technology are ones not imagined or possible before. They range from jobs of great social value, such as building prosthetic devices integrated into the nervous system, to entertainment and sports—computer game designers and professional computer game players. At the turn of the last century, who would have thought that people would buy (and hence others would produce, market, and sell) ringtones for their phones? Who would have imagined that there would be hundreds of thousands of job openings for smartphone software experts? In the coming decades, the new field of bioelectronics (application of electronic technology in biology and medicine) will create jobs unknown now.

What is the overall effect of computerization on employment rates? Does it create more jobs than it destroys? Measuring the effects of digital technology alone is difficult, because other factors influence employment trends, but we can look at some overall numbers. In the United States, in the 10 years between 1993 and 2002 (a decade of increasing computer and Web use), 309.9 million jobs ended—a huge number to anyone who has not seen these figures before. But 327.7 million jobs were added in the same period, for a net increase of 17.8 million jobs. This "job churn," roughly 30 million jobs opening and closing each year,[*] is typical of a flexible economy. In stagnant economies, people do not change jobs often.[11]

Consider the times of significant unemployment in the United States over the past century. Technology did not cause the Great Depression in the 1930s. Economists and historians attribute the depression to a variety of factors including "business cycles," the then-new Federal Reserve Bank's inept manipulation of interest rates, and that old standby, "greed." Unemployment was high in the early 1980s and in the early 1990s but was not consistently high, while growth in use of computers has been dramatic and continuous, especially since the mid-1970s, when personal computers began to appear. Mortgage policies (of financial institutions and the government) were a major cause of the recession that began in 2007; technology was not the cause.

The Organisation for Economic Co-operation and Development (OECD), an international organization whose members include most of Western Europe, North America, Japan, Australia, and New Zealand, studied employment trends in 25 countries. The OECD concluded that unemployment stems from "policies. . . [that] have made economies rigid, and stalled the ability . . . to adapt."[12] The study suggested that "unemployment should be addressed not by seeking to slow the pace of change, but rather by restoring economies' and societies' capacity to adapt to it." Unemployment in many European countries is often higher than in the United States, but Europe is not more technologically advanced or computerized than the United States. The differences have more to do with the flexibility of the economies and other political, social, and economic factors. The OECD report states that "history has shown that when technological progress accelerates, so do growth, living standards, and employment."[13]

New technology reduces employment in specific areas and in the short term, but it is obvious that computer technology did not and does not cause mass unemployment. Those who continually predict mass unemployment see only the old, preexisting jobs that are lost, missing the lessons of history and economics to see that people create new jobs. As major advances occur in artificial intelligence and robotics, we hear more scary projections of massive job losses to come in the next few years. Are the worriers correct this time? Will intelligent systems augment our work efforts—or replace us?

---

[*]Roughly half are seasonal jobs that appear and disappear each year.

Even if, overall, technology generates more new jobs than it eliminates, people do lose jobs due to technological advances, and the long-term social gains are not of much interest to a person who is laid off. The loss of a job is immediate and personal and can be devastating to the individual and his or her family. When large numbers of people lose their jobs in one small community or within a short time, difficult social problems occur. Thus, there is a need for people (individual workers, employers, and communities) and institutions (e.g., schools) to be flexible and to plan activities to mitigate the risks of change, such as training employees in several tasks. There are roles for education professionals who do long-range planning, for entrepreneurs and nonprofit organizations that provide training programs, for large companies that can retrain their employees, for financial institutions that fund start-up companies, and so on.

> *Why not use spoons?*
> —The apocryphal comment from a man who saw workers digging at a construction
> site with shovels. When he asked why they were not using modern excavation
> equipment, he was told that using shovels created more jobs.

6.2.2 CHANGING SKILLS AND SKILL LEVELS

Although it seems new technologies, and computing technology in particular, have not caused mass unemployment, some people believe that the impact of computing technology is different and more negative than that of earlier technologies. We describe some of the concerns and questions, then look at some positive developments.

The worries

Computers eliminate a much wider variety of jobs than any single previous technological advance. In the past, the impact of new machines or technologies tended to be concentrated in one industry or activity. The sewing machine had a direct influence on the garment industry, but computers, robots, and artificial intelligence impact a broad range of skills and activities. Earlier automation eliminated primarily manufacturing jobs, but software automates services as well. Software makes decisions that used to require trained, thinking human beings and can take over many white-collar, professional jobs. Here are just a few examples and trends:

- Computer programs analyze loan applications and decide which to approve; some such programs are better than people at predicting which applicants are likely to default on their loans.
- Software does a better job than some radiologists in detecting certain cancers.
- Design jobs have become automated. Software to design the electrical layout for new housing developments can do in several minutes a job that would have taken a high-paid employee 100 hours.

- Automated computer programming is reducing the need for trained programmers.
- Although it still requires highly trained engineers, there is a large degree of automation in the layout of computer chips.
- Advances in artificial intelligence, including the techniques of the computer program that beat a Go expert, increasingly help software do a better job than intelligent, highly trained humans.

Will such software mean fewer jobs for high-skilled workers? Will the importance of and need for human intelligence and judgment in the workplace decline?

Another concern is that the pace of improvement in capability and cost for computing and communication technology is much faster than for any previous technology. This rapid pacing causes more job disruption as people continually face job elimination and the need to retrain.

As computer systems are eliminating both high-skill jobs and low-skill jobs, will jobs diverge into two distinct groups: high-paying jobs for the most highly skilled and highly trained elite, and fewer low-paying jobs for people without computer skills and advanced education?

Positive developments

Although it often seems that our times and problems are new and different from what came before, similar concerns arose for other technologies. The steam engine and electricity brought enormous change in jobs, making many obsolete. Normally, as demand increases for new skills, people acquire them. For example, in 1900, only 0.5 people out of every 1000 in the United States worked as an engineer. After the huge growth in technology during the 20th century, 7.6 out of every 1000 people were engineers.[14] When economists Claudia Goldin and Lawrence Katz researched earlier periods of rapid technological development, they found that the education system quickly adapted to train children in the necessary skills. They pointed out that a bookkeeper in 1890 had to be highly skilled, whereas a bookkeeper in 1920 was a high school graduate using an early form of an adding machine.

Both of their observations have current parallels. Online courses, some using games, teach young children principles of programming, and programming camps are available for children of all ages. Complex interactive augmented reality[*] systems guide workers through steps of jobs that required extensive training before. Performance-support software and training software empower low-skilled workers and make the training process for complex jobs cheaper, faster, and easier. Such systems, for example, guide auditors through an audit of a securities firm, help

---

[*]Augmented reality uses a smartphone, tablet, or eyeglasses to overlay computer generated images or text on a real image captured by the device's camera.

employees at financial institutions carry out transactions, and train salespeople. The National Association of Securities Dealers reported that its auditors were fully competent after one year using such a system, compared to two and a half years without it. Programming tools enable nonspecialists to do certain kinds of programming, design Web pages, and so on. Companies are more willing to hire people without specific skills when they can train new people quickly and use automated support systems.

The benefits of performance-support systems occur throughout a wide range of job levels and benefit special populations. Several large companies, including Walgreens, hire previously unemployable people with mental and physical disabilities; they perform their jobs with the help of such systems.[15] As people live longer, they benefit from systems that help them work longer. In Japan, for example, older construction workers, farmers, and baggage handlers use high-tech exoskeletons and "smart suits" that sense their movements and help them bend and lift heavy objects.

In spite of the trend to automate high-skill jobs, the U.S. Bureau of Labor Statistics (BLS) projects that between 2014 and 2024, the number of jobs in accounting, auditing, financial analysis, computer and information technology, and other professional areas will increase more than average, with a 17% increase in the number of jobs for software developers. At the same time, the BLS expects many jobs to be available that require little, if any, computer skill. The areas in which the BLS expects a majority of new job creation through 2024 include nursing, personal care aide, retail clerks, and food preparation and service (even while automation, as in Figure 6.2, eliminates some jobs in those areas). The BLS projected job declines in two major areas: in manufacturing and in farming, fishing, and forestry.[16]

Deposit Photos/Glow Images

Figure 6.2 Some restaurants, including this one at an airport, reduce labor costs by installing self-service ordering terminals.

The printing press put scribes out of work when writing was a skill possessed by only a small, "highly trained" elite. Recall from Chapter 1 that machines that did simple arithmetic in the 17th and 18th centuries shocked and disturbed people. People thought arithmetic required uniquely human intelligence. In the past, human imagination and desires continued to find new fields of work, both physical and mental, to replace those no longer needed. This trend appears to continue today.

6.2.3 Are We Earning Less and Working More?

Various analyses suggest that wages have increased very little since the 1970s (adjusted for inflation). This is sometimes cited as an indication that the value of human work is declining as computers take over tasks people used to do, though there are many other interpretations and there are disagreements about the level of real income. Nonwage benefits have risen, now adding more than 40% of the wage amount to total employee compensation. The Economic Policy Institute, using data from the BLS, calculated that total real compensation was up 6.5% between 2000 and 2012—an increase but significantly less than the increase in worker productivity.[17]

Two researchers, Michael Cox and Richard Alm, decided to avoid the problems of using income and inflation data and, instead, they looked at a long list of direct measures of consumption and leisure. For example, they reported that between 1970 and the mid or late 1990s, attendance at operas and symphonies doubled (per person), the average size of new homes increased by more than a third (while the number of people per household decreased), the percentage of people who participate in sports and attend professional sporting events increased significantly, and spending on toys quadrupled (per child). From 1970 to 2010, the average number of televisions and automobiles per household increased, and the percentage of new homes with air conditioning rose from 49% to 88%.

Cox and Alm also calculated how much time an average worker had to work to earn enough money to buy various products and services. They reasoned that this was a better tool for measuring trends in income in a meaningful way, as opposed to looking at dollar amounts. They found that the cost, in the average worker's work time, of air travel dropped by 40%, while the cost of a coast-to-coast phone call dropped to one-tenth the work time required in 1970. In the 1970s, it would have cost more than the average worker's lifetime earnings to buy the level of computing power we carry on smartphones; in 1984, a cellphone (not particularly smart) cost 456 hours; and now, a full-price smartphone costs less than a week of an average worker's income. In 2008, a refrigerator cost about half what it did in the 1970s when measured in work hours. The cost, in worker's time, of many basic foods also dropped significantly. In addition, products have improved in quality, safety, convenience, and comfort. For example, cars are safer, and supermarkets now have shelves full of prewashed and precut salads and vegetables; this was not typical a few decades ago.[18]

Since the beginning of the Industrial Revolution, working hours have declined and most people no longer routinely work 10–12 hours a day, six days a week. Economists disagree about whether working hours have declined significantly since the 1950s. (Researchers can count working hours, like income data, in various ways, supporting different conclusions.) Some people continue to work more hours while income rises because they have higher expectations; they consider the lifestyle now possible to be essential. Another factor is that certain aspects of the tax and compensation structure encourage employers to have employees work overtime rather than hire additional workers. A third factor is that taxes take a larger percentage of income than they did in the past; people have to work more hours for the same take-home pay.

It does not appear that computerization has resulted in lower or stagnating income, or in a need to work longer hours, when measured by what products and services an average worker's time will buy. Indeed, technology is likely responsible for a large share of the improvements. For people who are earning less or working more, the causes likely include social, political, and economic factors, as well as impacts of technology.

6.3 Changing Work Patterns: From Telecommuting to Gigs

Computer and communication technologies dramatically and continually change the way we work and where we work. They facilitate nontraditional forms of work and new ways to earn income. In this section, we describe some of these phenomena and discuss benefits, problems, and opposition from businesses and workers who see threats from new competitors.

6.3.1 TELECOMMUTING

For thousands of years, most people worked at, or close to, home. The Industrial Revolution led to a major shift as many jobs moved to offices and factories, yet working at home continued to be common for certain kinds of jobs. Doctors, especially in small towns, had their medical offices in their homes and shopkeepers often had an apartment behind or above the store. Writers traditionally work at home and though farmers work in the fields, the farm office was in the house. However, in much of the 20th century, professional and office workers worked mostly in offices at an employer's location.

Computers, the Internet, and wireless communications brought about another shift in work location. People who are employees of large companies can work away from their desk and away from their company office. Many work at home, at least part of the time. Individuals and small businesses operate globally, from home, via the Web. Many people work on a laptop or other mobile devices in coffee shops, outdoors in parks, on airplanes, and in their cars. A variety of terms are used for these phenomena. *Telecommuting* refers to working at home using computing equipment instead of commuting to an employer's office. *Mobile work*, *remote work*, and *telework* also refer to this and other variations of such work paradigms.

Benefits

By replacing or shrinking large downtown offices, where real estate and office rentals are expensive, telecommuting reduces overhead for employers and can generate significant savings. Many employees report that telecommuting has made them more productive, more satisfied with their jobs, and more loyal to their employers. Telecommuting, and telecommunications in general, make it easier to work with clients, customers, and employees in other countries: At home, one can more easily work a few hours at night that are compatible with foreign time zones.

Telecommuting reduces:

- expenses for commuting and for work clothes or uniforms,
- rush-hour traffic congestion and the associated pollution and energy use,
- stress, by saving travel time that workers can use for exercise, sleep, or more interaction with friends and family,
- child-care expenses for parents,
- lost work time during and after blizzards, hurricanes, or other disasters that close roads or discourage travel, and
- the number of disabled or elderly people who cannot work because commuting is physically difficult.

In some professional fields, people no longer must live in the same city or state as their employer. Employees and employers benefit when a person can accept a job with a company in a distant state without having to move. Two-career couples can work for companies hundreds or thousands of miles apart.

The Internet made it possible for companies to locate in small towns and work with dispersed consultants instead of having hundreds or thousands of employees in larger population centers. Workers can live in rural areas instead of big cities and suburbs if they prefer (in "electronic cottages," to use futurist Alvin Toffler's words). Urban policy researcher Joel Kotkin observes that telecommuting may encourage a return to involvement in one's local community.[19] Is he correct? Will being in the neighborhood all day, doing errands locally, eating in local restaurants, and so on, generate an interest in the safety, beauty, and vitality of the community that is less likely to develop when one returns home after dark, tired from a day at the office? On the other hand, now that we can communicate with people all over the world on the Internet, will home workers stay inside, communicating with unseen business and social acquaintances, and be just as unlikely to know their neighbors as many commuters are? Or will it be a combination of the two?

Problems and opposition

Many early telecommuters were volunteers, people who wanted to work at home and were likely to be independent workers. (Many were computer programmers.) As more businesses began to require or allow employees to move their offices to their homes, problems arose for both employees and employers.

Some of the issues created by telecommuting are:

- Corporate loyalty of telecommuters can be weakened.
- Lacking immediate supervision, some people are less productive, while others may work too hard and too long. Employees need better direction about the type and amount of work expected when working from home.
- By working away from the company office, employees miss mentoring relationships and possibly opportunities for advancement.
- Employees complain that the costs of office space and overhead that were reduced for the employer simply shifted to the employee who must give up space at home for the office.
- Being at home with children is a distraction for some telecommuters.
- Reducing the boundary between home and work may cause stress for workers and their families.
- The ease of working with people around the world can lead to odd working hours that match the time zones of clients, creating more stress at home.

For many, the social interactions and camaraderie at work are a significant part of pleasant working conditions. Employers address the social-isolation problem by holding regular meetings and encouraging other activities such as employee sports leagues, where employees interact in person. Telecommuters reduce isolation by participating in activities of professional associations and other social networks.

Working at home using computer equipment is so common now that it might be surprising that local governments and labor unions attempted to stop it in its early days.* The view of various unions at the time seemed to be that most computer at-home work would be data-entry work done by low-paid women in sweatshop conditions. The AFL-CIO advocated a government ban on all computer at-home work.[20] The efforts to stop computer work at home quickly turned futile. The mistaken views about who would work at home and what the working conditions would be are reminders to be cautious about banning or restricting a new phenomenon before its applications and benefits, as well as problems, develop.

---

*For example, the city of Chicago ordered a couple to stop using a computer at home to write textbooks and educational software because Chicago zoning laws restricted home work that used mechanical or electrical equipment.

6.3.2 The Sharing Economy, On-Demand Services, and Gig Work

Evolving forms of transactions

The Web, and later smartphones, enabled a flourishing *sharing economy* by matching people offering goods or services with others who want them. Typically, without the technologies to match providers with customers, the goods or services would have been unused and not part of the economy. People sell items they no longer need via Craigslist or eBay.* Airbnb matches travelers with people who want to rent out their apartments, spare rooms, sofa beds, or, as the name suggests, air mattresses, in countries all over the world. It is especially useful when a major sporting event or a convention attracts thousands of people to a city without enough hotel rooms; some people prefer to use it whenever they travel. Organizations like Waste No Food and Community Food Rescue reduce food waste by matching farmers, restaurants, and supermarkets with charitable groups that can distribute extra food that did not sell or fruits and vegetables too small to sell legally.

Although the term is "sharing" economy, items or services may be traded, given away, or sold, and indeed, many of the well-known examples, such as Airbnb and ride-sharing services, facilitate sales of services or goods, providing extra income to people who might—or might not—have another job. Such services amount to billions of dollars of transactions each year. The key elements that enable the sharing economy are the easy *access* to potential providers and consumers and the systems that handle the details of the transactions.†

On-demand services include very quick delivery of products and services. Depending on the context, "quick" might mean a few minutes or one day. For example, some online retailers provide same-day delivery. They bypass the traditional shipping companies and use their own fleets of drivers or independent drivers who pick up assignments dynamically via mobile apps. On-demand delivery reduces one of the negative features of buying things online: waiting days for them to arrive.

The term *gig*, in the context of work, developed about 100 years ago to mean a job for a musician, usually for one evening or for a short period of time. Now, people use the term for a variety of types of work where mobile apps connect an available worker with a specific assignment. Typically, gig workers work the hours they choose and they are paid by the job, rather than hourly. The best known example is ride sharing, which is enormously popular in hundreds of cities (Uber and Lyft in the United States and elsewhere; Juno in the United States; Didi in China; Gett in Israel; Ola in India; Grab in Singapore; and others). Ride-sharing services have hundreds of thousands of drivers who provide millions of rides daily. Start-ups and well-established online sellers use gig workers for delivery of groceries, restaurant

---

*eBay seems more like a virtual shopping mall now, with full-time, high-volume sellers, but it began as a site where individuals sold things they no longer needed, and it continues to include such listings.

†The term *access economy* may be more accurate, but *sharing economy* has achieved widespread use.

meals, and packages. App-based services provide a doctor or nurse who comes to the customer, at home or elsewhere. Other gig work includes house cleaning, doing errands, walking dogs, and waiting on lines. Gig work expands a trend of self-employed people providing skills or services to many other people or companies, rather than working full time for one employer.

Clearly, there is a lot of overlap between the sharing economy, on-demand services, and gig work. An app that matches people who have snow-removal equipment with people who need it illustrates on-demand sharing. So do car-sharing companies such as Zipcar and Car2Go that provide on-demand, short-term car rental services, with cars scattered at convenient locations; they are popular in urban areas and near college campuses. Ride sharing has all three features: Apps match customers with both a vehicle and a driver, on demand (in a few minutes) at the customer's location. Because of the popularity of ride sharing, the legal and social issues it has raised, and the sometimes intense opposition to it, we use ride sharing as the main example throughout this section.

Advantages, disadvantages, and problems to be solved

The sharing economy turns unused goods, space, and labor into economic assets, thus reducing waste, providing a source of income for people who might need it, and providing goods and services to consumers at lower prices than otherwise available. Apps that connect gig workers with potential customers benefit society as a whole by reducing the overhead, and hence the cost, of forming such connections, thus making more jobs and services economically practical and available.

Advantages to consumers include quick service, convenience, and lower prices. Customers of ride-sharing services have found the drivers more pleasant than taxi drivers and their cars cleaner. Availability of quick, inexpensive rides reduces drunk-driving arrests and fatal crashes, according to several studies.[21] A few studies (in New York and Los Angeles) found that Uber provides more, faster, and cheaper service in low-income neighborhoods than taxis.[22] Risks to consumers of using gig workers include potentially dishonest or incompetent workers, though of course they can be found in traditional businesses as well. Before hiring or contracting with a potential worker, some gig services check workers carefully and set standards; some do not. Some gig services ask for customer feedback, which helps establish reputations for good (and bad) workers.

Advantages to workers include flexibility and autonomy. The new types of gig work add valuable options for earning income in addition to another job and between traditional gig jobs, such as acting. They add options for people who choose to work a small number of hours (for example, students, a parent who works while a child is in school, or retired people). Ride-sharing apps handle payment, so drivers do not carry a lot of cash, thus reducing the risk of attacks by robbers.

Gig workers have to cover expenses that employers often pay for employees. For example, many ride-sharing drivers provide their own vehicle and pay for fuel and insurance. (Some taxi drivers pay these expenses also.) To reduce this problem, several ride-sharing companies arranged agreements with car makers or rental companies to rent cars to drivers at low rates and/or waive the rental fee for drivers who work a lot of hours. Gig workers do not have employer-provided health care, sick leave, vacation days, or unemployment insurance. For some, particularly those who do not have another job, this is a problem. Some get benefits from a family member's job or another employer. (Among Uber drivers, for example, roughly half have medical coverage from another source.[23])

Home sharing illustrates other issues. As Airbnb grew in popularity, some users and their neighbors encountered problems. People in residential neighborhoods complain of noisy vacation renters. Can existing noise regulations handle this problem? Some short-term renters trashed the places they rented, and some customers complained of being spied on by hidden cameras when renting rooms. What kind of screening of potential users can be done without unreasonable intrusions on privacy? What policies should services such as Airbnb have for terminating memberships of people who generate a lot of complaints? To what extent are the problems integral to technology-enabled services, and to what extent are they problems that occur to a similar degree with traditional business structures?

Safe drivers?

In the least expensive ride-sharing services, drivers with ordinary driver licenses use their own cars. Various cities and countries ban these services because they require that anyone taking passengers for pay must have a professional driver license. License requirements vary but include training and background checks. The purpose is to protect the safety of passengers. Thus, it is reasonable to ask whether requiring a professional driving license for ride-sharing drivers significantly improves safety.

Ride-sharing services do background checks on drivers, yet some drivers were found to have serious criminal convictions. How does the number of ride-sharing drivers with criminal convictions compare to the number of taxi drivers with such convictions?[24] Publicity and lawsuits about Uber drivers with convictions led to discussion of the varying methods used to screen ride-sharing and taxi drivers. How strong should the screening process be? The publicity brought attention to difficult social policy issues such as whether convictions for certain nonviolent crimes or convictions more than a certain number of years in the past should disqualify potential drivers.

Gig apps and vehicle technology provide mechanisms for safety that were not available before. The apps allow easy feedback from passengers. (Since the app can determine if a particular passenger rode with a particular driver, fake reviews—a problem on review sites for restaurants, hotels, and other businesses—are less likely.) Sensors in phones and vehicles provide data that help ride-sharing and delivery services monitor the driving habits of drivers, e.g., speed, smoothness of braking, and whether the driver is using a phone while driving. Feedback from the data can help drivers improve and can help the services determine which drivers should have their contracts terminated. These mechanisms can provide continuing, almost constant, information about the quality of drivers.[*]

We mentioned studies showing that after Uber began operating in some cities, drunk-driving arrests and fatal crashes decreased. We do not have to determine whether a driver with a professional license is better than an Uber driver to know that the latter is better than a drunk driver. Just having a convenient, inexpensive alternative to driving when impaired can increase safety.

How does the level of safety that professional licensing provides compare to the level of safety that screening and monitoring technologies provide? Do the benefits of professional licensing outweigh the benefits of inexpensive ride sharing?

Contractor or employee

U.S. labor law, from the 1930s, makes a sharp distinction between employees and independent contractors. Law and regulations specify criteria that determine how a job is classified and require that employers provide certain benefits for employees. Small business owners, self-employed professionals (including freelance programmers), and other independent contractors do not receive employer-provided benefits. In many kinds of work, independent contractors get higher pay to cover the cost of some of these benefits.

A lot of gig work facilitated by apps does not fit into either of the two legal categories of employee or independent contractor. Many sharing-economy companies exert more control over workers than is common for independent contractors and less than is common for employees. Gig workers have sued several companies to be classified as employees and thus to receive employee benefits. A major U.S. case against Uber is still in court. In a lawsuit by two Uber drivers in the United Kingdom, a court ruled that the drivers are employees and are covered by laws about minimum wage, sick pay, vacation pay, and so on; Uber is appealing the ruling. At least one app-based start-up shut down after some of its gig workers sued to be classified as employees. Instacart, a grocery shopping service, began allowing some categories of its gig workers a choice between employee status and contract worker status.[25]

The final decisions in lawsuits about the status of gig workers will have a significant impact on app-based, sharing-economy services. The obvious advantage to workers who become employees is additional income in the form of benefits. The obvious disadvantage is the loss of flexibility and autonomy: Because of the overhead of managing employees and the employer's liability, companies are likely to set minimum hours and additional requirements about where, when, and how

---

[*]As with other monitoring tools, the information must be used sensibly. One driver reported receiving a warning after she braked suddenly to avoid a dog that ran into the road.

a person works. Some impacts are less obvious. An increase in the total cost of a worker results in a decrease in company profit and/or an increase in prices to the consumer. If consumers are unwilling to pay the higher prices or investors conclude that the return on their investment will be too low, a company stops providing the product or service. Thus, if laws or court decisions significantly restrict the model of a service company using software to match independent workers with customers, prices will go up and/or there will be fewer innovative services and jobs of this kind.

Alternatives to classifying gig workers as employees include creation of a new category, perhaps called dependent contractor, that specifies a middle ground between employee and independent contractor and is appropriate for the sharing economy. Another alternative is to amend labor law to allow more flexibility, with workers and companies deciding the status of their relationship by contract.

Opposition from governments and competitors

Established businesses that recognize the value of new business structures and the services made possible by new technologies adopt (or buy) them. For example, Zipcar was a start-up and the Avis Budget Group bought it, General Motors started a similar hourly car rental service, and some taxi companies began using mobile apps to dispatch cabs more efficiently. However, a frequent response to innovation is opposition. Various city and national governments have put severe restrictions on sharing-economy and on-demand services, particularly ride sharing and short-term home rentals. We give some examples, then discuss reasons.

Some cities ban ride-sharing services completely. Some set minimum fees for rides, thus eliminating the advantage of lower prices. Some cities prohibit ride-sharing drivers from picking up passengers at airports; airports hire people to pose as travelers and lure drivers to the airport, and then issue citations to them. The mayor of New York proposed limiting the number of Uber cars allowed in the city. In many cities, taxi companies are big campaign contributors to city officials.

In cities around the world, taxi drivers hold strikes and block roads to demand more restrictions on ride-sharing services (see Figure 6.3). In some instances, they have violently attacked ride-sharing drivers. Opposition has been especially strong in France. A French law requires ride sharing drivers (but not taxis) to return to a garage before picking up the next customer; a French court ordered Uber to pay €1.2 million to a taxi union for not clearly telling Uber drivers about this requirement. A French court convicted Uber and two French Uber executives on criminal charges and fined them €964,000. The charges included connecting prospective passengers with drivers who do not have professional licenses—that is, drivers for Uber's low-cost UberPop service, which had roughly 500,000 riders in France. Uber shut down UberPop in France and several other countries under pressure from courts and regulators. In Abu Dhabi, Uber and Careem (a ride-sharing service in the Middle East) shut down after drivers were arrested. Uber suspended operations in

YASUYOSHI CHIBA/Staff/AFP/Getty Images

Figure 6.3 Taxi drivers in Brazil protesting against Uber.

Hungary after the Hungarian Parliament passed a law allowing the government to block access to the apps and websites of ride-sharing services that do not follow its regulations and imposed heavy penalties for drivers.[26]

Taxi drivers in many cities argue that they want a "level playing field"; they want ride-sharing drivers to be subject to the same rules they must follow. A sensible approach, then, would be to examine those rules and determine which are reasonable and which unreasonably make taxi rides so much more expensive that ride sharing is such a competitive threat. If an airport charges a fee for taxis that pick up passengers, it might be reasonable for ride-sharing drivers to pay a similar fee. In many cities, taxi companies or drivers must buy a special taxi license for each taxicab, and they complain that ride-sharing drivers do not buy these licenses. The licenses were initially inexpensive, but local governments continue to severely restrict the number issued, thus driving the prices up to hundreds of thousands of dollars in some cities. The price of the license reflects the monopoly profit resulting from restricting the supply of taxi service. Should the "playing field" be leveled by eliminating anticompetitive restrictions such as limits on the number of taxis?

Like Uber, Airbnb faces strong opposition. Many communities have banned short-term rentals. For example, New York prohibits people from renting out their apartment for less than 30 days; the fine for listing such a rental on a home-sharing site is $7,500. Some cities limit the total number of days per year that someone can share their home. Are such bans, restrictions, and fines reasonable? Supporters of the bans argue that people buy multiple properties and rent them out, essentially converting residences to hotels, changing the character of neighborhoods and reducing the housing supply. Such multiple listings occur, but the vast majority of users list only one property. How does the impact on housing supply compare to the impact of other factors, such as restrictions on construction of new housing? Core opposition to Airbnb appears to come from hotels that might lose customers, local governments that might get less revenue from hotel taxes, and hotel workers who might lose jobs. To what extent should these concerns prevent or restrict competition from popular new services?

Opposition to companies such as Uber in countries outside the United States has additional sources. One is hostility to a large foreign (i.e., U.S.) company, partly because it is a large foreign company, but also because, some government officials complain, foreign companies do not pay high enough taxes within their country. Another criticism is lack of sensitivity to laws and culture in the country; for example, Uber was convicted of violations of France's privacy laws, which are much stricter than those in the United States.

In Section 3.2.5, we saw that new ways of doing business and sharing information enabled by the Internet were illegal under old laws that restricted freedom of speech. In several cases, lawsuits led to removal of the old restrictions. That seems a better solution than artificially raising the price of new services or banning them. Do you believe the popularity and benefits of sharing-economy services will, or should, lead to a reduction in opposition and restrictions?

6.4   A Global Workforce

Offshoring

Over many decades in the 20th century, as transportation and communications improved, manufacturing jobs moved from wealthier countries to less wealthy countries, especially in Asia. The difference in pay rates was large enough to make up for the extra transportation costs. The Internet reduced "transportation" costs for many kinds of information work to almost zero. The ease of working with people and companies in other countries made "offshoring" of service jobs* a phenomenon and a political issue.

Data processing and computer programming were among the first service jobs to go offshore, many to India. The lure for companies is a large pool of low-skilled workers, in the first case, and well-trained, English-speaking computer programmers, in the second. The example most well-known to American consumers is the move of customer-service call centers and software "help desks" to India, the Philippines, and other countries. Offshoring takes many other forms as well, such

---

*The term "outsourcing" refers to the phenomenon where a company pays other companies to build parts for its products or provide services (such as marketing, research, or customer service) instead of performing those tasks itself. This is very common. Generally, but not always, the companies that do the work are in the same country as the company that hires them. The term "offshoring" refers to hiring companies or employees in other countries.

as sending "back-office" jobs like payroll processing, to other countries. Actuaries in India process insurance claims for a British insurance company. Doctors in the United States and the United Kingdom dictate notes on patient visits and send digitized voice files offshore, where medical scribes transcribe them and return text files. Rather than contracting with companies in another country, some large companies set up divisions (for example, for research and development) offshore.

As offshoring of skilled work, sometimes called "knowledge work," increased dramatically, more worries arose about threats of job loss, now for high-paying jobs held by the middle class. Companies send off work in legal services, aircraft engineering, biotech and pharmaceutical research, and stock analysis and other financial services. Individuals and small businesses hire people in other countries for services such as tutoring and designing logos and websites.

In some cases, offshoring occurs because there are not enough trained professionals in the United States. For example, Steve Jobs told President Obama in 2011 that Apple had 700,000 factory workers in China because 30,000 engineers are needed on site in the factories and Apple could not find enough qualified engineers in the United States. In some cases, legal roadblocks are the problem: Jobs said it is easy to build a factory in China but very difficult in the United States;[27] Amazon and Google established drone testing facilities in other countries because the Federal Aviation Administration would not permit them to test in the United States.

The impact of offshoring

The Bureau of Labor Statistics reports that a very small percentage of mass layoffs (defined as 50 or more people for more than a month) comes from offshoring jobs. However, the impact of offshoring may increase. Economist Alan Blinder, a former vice chair of the Federal Reserve, studied the types of knowledge and service jobs that could be performed at distant places—candidates for offshoring.[28] He estimated that 28–42 million people work in such jobs in the United States. Thus, he sees offshoring as potentially very disruptive. However, Blinder emphasizes that offshoring means massive transition, not massive unemployment.

Many social scientists, politicians, and organizations view the globalization of the workforce as a terribly negative phenomenon, one of the negative results of information and communications technology and corporate greed for increased profit. From the prospective of workers in developed countries, they argue, it means millions fewer jobs, accompanied by lower pay and a reduced standard of living.

Job loss in the original country from offshoring seems obvious. Our discussion in Section 6.2.1 about jobs eliminated and created by computer and communications technology suggests we consider how offshoring creates new jobs. Lower labor costs and increased efficiency reduce prices for consumers; lower prices encourage more use and make new products and services feasible. Manufacturing of computer hardware went offshore early; this move was partially responsible for the drop in hardware costs that resulted in lower prices and contributed to the enormous growth of the industry. The same technologies that facilitate offshoring make it easier and cheaper for U.S. service companies (banking, engineering, and accounting, for example) to sell more of their services to other countries. Offshoring creates jobs for both low- and high-skilled workers in less wealthy countries. The combination of increased income and reduced prices for goods and services helps grow the economies of those countries, potentially yielding more jobs on both sides.

Blinder believes that we should plan for a major shift in the United States toward jobs that require presence. His examples include both low-skill and high-skill jobs. He opposes attempts to stop offshoring, but he also warns that we must prepare by shifting emphasis in education. He expects that the flexibility of the

---

Inshoring: Two perspectives

Americans working for foreign companies

Americans used to import cars from Japan, but now, Japanese car makers build cars in the United States. Otto Bock Health Care, a German company that makes sophisticated microprocessor-controlled artificial limbs, "offshores" research, development, and manufacturing to several countries, including the United States (and China). The German software company SAP employs thousands of people in the United States. Offshoring for a German company means "inshoring" for the United States. People in the United States work for Sony, Ikea, Bayer, Novartis, Unilever, and Toyota. Overall, about 5% of U.S. workers work for foreign companies. Indeed, as India's information technology industry grew, large Indian companies began offshoring thousands of jobs to the United States and Europe. In a global, interconnected economy, offshoring is one more way of providing products and services to consumers more effectively.

Indian perspectives[30]

For many years, Indian computer scientists and engineers flocked to the United States for jobs, wealth, and entrepreneurial opportunities, while Indian IT companies performed services and provided call centers for foreign companies. Critics, from the Indian perspective, worried that India was not growing its own high-tech industry and feared a talent drain. Indian companies that developed their own software products stopped doing so, to avoid competing with U.S. companies for which they provide services.

Over time, more positive results developed as India's information technology companies began to provide sophisticated services well beyond call centers. "Inshored" jobs provide professional training and experience, including experience working in a global business environment. These provide confidence and high salaries that permit the savings so helpful for taking risks and starting one's own company. An Indian entrepreneur observes that Indian culture generally had a negative view of entrepreneurs, but that is changing. Highly trained Indian computer scientists and engineers who went to the United States for jobs are returning to work or start businesses at home. Providing information technology services for foreign companies, from low-level services to highly sophisticated work, is now a multibillion-dollar industry in India.

U.S. economy will help it adapt more quickly and successfully to offshoring than developed countries with more rigid economies.[29] As we observed in Section 6.2.1 about technology-induced job loss, long-term gains from new jobs are little comfort to people who lose theirs. Helpful responses to the personal and social disruptions that may occur include those we mentioned in Section 6.2.1, among them: flexibility, planning, and changes in educational programs.

Problems and side effects of offshoring

As customers, companies, and workers have found, offshoring has problems. Consumers complain about customer-service call centers in foreign countries: Foreign accents are difficult to understand; service personnel are not familiar with the product or service the consumer is asking about—they just read from a manual. Though these complaints are not unique to offshored call centers, they occur more frequently at such locations. Workers in offshored call centers experience problems too. Because of time differences, customer-service workers in India work at night. Some find the relatively high pay worth the disruption to their lives and others quit. Software engineers, managers, and businesspeople need to manage people and projects remotely and schedule meetings during the work hours of workers in another country.

Some technology companies found that increased demand for highly skilled workers in India forced salaries up. One U.S. entrepreneur said salaries of engineers he hired in India went from 25% of U.S. salaries to 75% within two years, thereby reducing the cost saving and making it impractical to hire them for his company. A variety of problems of customer satisfaction, training, and less-than-expected savings led some companies to conclude that offshoring did not work well for them, and they discontinued it.

The problems of offshoring should not surprise us, as the phenomenon of new things having unexpected problems is a theme running through this book. We discover the issues, find solutions, and adapt to changes, or decide not to use certain options. Basic economics tells us that salaries rise in offshoring destinations and when the gap between salaries in the home and destination countries is no longer big enough to cover the other expenses of offshoring, the trend declines. Or, as countries develop expertise and highly skilled workers in particular areas, we might choose to use their services just as we who live in one state in the United States use services of companies based in another state.

Ethics of hiring foreign workers

Controversy surrounds both the economics and ethics of offshoring. In this section, we apply some of the ethical theories from Chapter 1 to analyze the practice from an ethical perspective. This is a good example for trying to distinguish economic advantage from ethical arguments. Several countries have passed legislation to restrict the hiring of foreign workers for some industries. The discussion here might provide insight into the ethics of such legislation. Here is the scenario we examine:

> You are a manager at a software company about to begin a large software project. You will need to hire dozens of programmers. Using the Internet for communication and software delivery, you can hire programmers in another country at a lower salary than programmers in your country. Should you do this?[31]

For the discussion, we assume the software company is in the United States and the manager is choosing between U.S. and Indian programmers.

The people most obviously affected by the decision in this case are the Indian programmers and the U.S. programmers you might hire. To generate some ideas, questions, and observations about these two groups, we will use utilitarianism and Kant's principle about treating people as ends in themselves. How can we compare the impact on utility from the two choices? The number of people hired will be about the same in either case. There does not appear to be any reason, from an ethical point of view, for placing a higher weight on the utility of one group of programmers merely because of their nationality. Shall we weigh the utilities of the programmers according to the number of dollars they will receive? That favors hiring the U.S. programmers. Or should we weigh utility by comparing the pay to the average salary in each country or by comparing the number of other job opportunities available? Those measures might favor hiring the Indians. We see that a calculation of net utility for the programmers depends on how one evaluates the utility of the job for each group of programmers.

What happens when we apply Kant's principle? When we hire people for a job, we are interacting with them in a limited role. We are making a trade—money for work. The programmers are a means to an end: producing a marketable product at a reasonable price. Kant does not say that we must not treat people as a means to an end, but rather that we should not treat them *merely* as such. And, indeed, the hiring decision does not obviously treat the potential programmers of the two countries differently in a way that has to do with ends and means.

Are you taking advantage of the Indian programmers, exploiting them by paying them less than you would have to pay the U.S. programmers? Some people believe it is unfair to both the U.S. and Indian programmers if the Indians get the jobs by charging less money. It is equally logical, however, to argue that paying the higher rate for U.S. programmers is wasteful, or charity, or simply overpayment. What makes either pay level more "right" than the other? Buyers would like to pay less for what they buy, and sellers would like to get a higher price for their goods and services. There is nothing inherently unethical about choosing the cheaper of two products, services, or employees.

We can argue that treating the Indian programmers as ends in themselves includes respecting the choices and trade-offs they make to better their lives according to their own judgment, in particular in offering to work for lower wages than U.S. programmers. But there are special cases in which we might decide otherwise. First, suppose your company is doing something to limit the other options of the Indian programmers. If your company is lobbying for U.S. import restrictions on software that Indian firms produce, for example, thus decreasing the availability of other programming jobs in India, then you are manipulating the programmers into a situation where they have few or no other choices. In that case, you are not respecting their freedom and allowing them to compete fairly. You are, then, not treating them as ends in themselves. We will assume for the rest of the discussion that your company is not doing anything like this.

Another reason we might decide that the Indian programmers are not being treated as ends in themselves, or with respect for their human dignity, is that their working conditions would be worse than the working conditions that U.S. workers expect (or that law in the United States requires). The programmers might not get medical insurance. They might work in rundown, crowded offices lacking air-conditioning. Is hiring them to work in such conditions unethical, or does it give them an opportunity to improve conditions in their country?

Whether or not it is ethically required, there are several reasons why you might pay more (or provide better working conditions) than the law or market conditions in India require: a sense of shared humanity that motivates you to want to provide conditions you consider desirable, a sense of generosity (i.e., willingness to contribute to the improvement of the standard of living of people in a country less rich than your own), and benefits for your company. Paying more than expected might get you higher morale, better productivity, and increased company loyalty.[32] Often, in various countries, a large group of potential workers (e.g., foreigners, recent immigrants, ethnic minorities, low-skilled workers, and teenagers) will work for lower than the standard pay. Some countries have laws that require the same salary be paid to all workers performing similar tasks to prevent employers from exploiting the less advantaged workers. Historically, a result of these laws is that the traditionally higher-paid group gets most of the jobs. (Often that has been the hidden intent of the law.) In this case, the almost certain result of requiring equal pay would be hiring the U.S. programmers. The law, or an ethical requirement that the pay of the Indian programmers and the U.S. programmers be the same, would protect the high incomes of programmers in the United States and the profits of companies that pay higher salaries.

Your decision affects other people besides the programmers: your customers, the owners or stockholders of your company, and, indirectly, many people in other businesses. Hiring the Indian programmers increases the utility of your company and customers and infuses money to the community where the programmers work. The customers benefit from the lower price of the product, and the owners of the company benefit from the profits. If the product is successful, your company might pay for advertising, distribution, and so on, providing jobs for others in the United States.

On the other hand, if you hire U.S. programmers, they will spend more of their earnings in the United States than the Indian programmers would, generating jobs and income for others in the United States. If the product is not profitable because of higher programming costs, the company could go out of business, with a negative impact on all its employees, owners, and suppliers. To which of all these people do you have responsibilities or obligations? As a manager of the company, you have an obligation to help make the product and the company successful, to manage the project to make a profit (not in a manner independent of ethical considerations, as we noted in Chapter 1, but consistent with them). Unless the owners of the company have a policy to improve the standard of living of people in other countries or to "Buy American," your obligation to them includes hiring competent workers at the best price. You have some responsibility for the fate of other company employees who might lose their jobs if you do a poor job of managing the project.

Although hiring lower-paid workers in other countries is often described as ethically suspect, we have not found a strong argument, using ideas from Kant and utilitarianism, to support that view. Do you agree, or can you think of a strong argument missed? We leave it as an exercise to apply some of the other ethical theories introduced in Chapter 1.

6.5 Employee Communication and Monitoring by Employers

Employers have always monitored the work of their employees. The degree of detail and frequency of the monitoring has varied depending on the kind of work, economic factors, and available technology. Most precomputer monitoring was not constant, because the supervisor had many workers to oversee and other work to do, and workers usually knew when the supervisor was present to observe them. The electronic monitoring that employers can do now can be constant, more detailed, and unseen by the worker. The vast growth of storage capabilities means that employers can store enormous amounts of information about employee activities for a long time.

Email, smartphones, social networking, and so on, make a lot of work more efficient and more pleasant, benefiting both employers and employees, but they can also be a distraction, a security leak, and a source of lawsuits. Personal social media content, outside of work, can get a person fired. We focus in this section on workplace rules for use of these tools and on monitoring employee communications, location, and behavior.

6.5.1 SOCIAL MEDIA CONTENT

Screening job applicants

Employers have long done various forms of screening, including criminal background checks, on prospective employees. The Web and social media provide a vast new collection of information on job applicants. There are companies that specialize in performing extensive background checks for employers using publicly available social media. The *New York Times* lists a variety of behaviors that one company includes in the dossiers it provides to employers about prospective employees: racist remarks, references to drugs, sexually explicit material, displays of weapons or bombs, and violent activity. (It includes positive information too—for example, charitable work.) The company does not include race, religion, and other information that laws prohibit companies from asking about, but, of course, now it is not difficult for an employer to see such information in social media even if not intentionally looking for it.[33]

Employers can use a variety of methods to protect applicants' privacy and reduce the consequences of errors when they choose to include social media information. We already mentioned one: engaging a "third-party" company to perform the screening. The screening company does not give the employer information about an applicant that is deemed to be inappropriate (by law or by the policies of the hiring company or by the policies of the screening company). This can protect the applicant's privacy and protect the employer from complaints that it used inappropriate information in the hiring decision. An employer can (and should) make its policy about searches clear to applicants. Employers or screening companies can have a policy that they perform social media searches only if the applicant consents. They can inform an applicant of negative findings, so the applicant has an opportunity to correct errors or explain the context of the information.

Many privacy advocates object to the whole idea of social media searches on job applicants, arguing that employers should restrict the information they collect about applicants to what is directly related to job qualifications. Marc Rotenberg, president of the Electronic Privacy Information Center, expressed the view that "employers should not be judging what people in their private lives do away from the workplace."[34] This view is a good policy for many employers, since it is valuable to maintain and protect a barrier between work and personal activities.[35] Most people interact daily with others whose religion, hobbies, politics, and tastes in humor differ from theirs—fellow workers, neighbors, car mechanics, shop owners, etc. Our interactions are civil and productive; we do not need to know all aspects of the other person's life nor to have similar views. There is enough human commonality and enough value in the interactions or transactions that we all benefit from them.

On the other hand, there does not appear to be a convincing ethical argument that an employer *must* consider only information related to the specific job an employee will do, ignoring all other aspects of how the employee will behave at work. There are characteristics an employer might learn about an applicant that could affect safety and security at the workplace, the image the company wishes to maintain, and the likelihood of future lawsuits related to an employee's behavior. Employers use a variety of screening methods to efficiently reduce a large pool of applicants to a small number for further consideration. Some routinely reject people who do not have a college degree, even though some people without a degree could do the job well. A particular criterion might be ill-advised, or it might work well enough to be useful, but such a criterion is not necessarily unethical.

Making a responsible and reasonable employment decision based on social media information can be difficult. A person who posts a dozen photos of himself or herself surrounded by a variety of guns might be an avid hunter or sport shooter who would be an excellent employee—or he or she might be one of those rare people who come to work one day and shoot fellow employees. Information in social media may be inaccurate since a person other than the applicant may post questionable material. Employers may be overcautious and decline to hire an applicant if something negative turns up, without exploring the context or determining the accuracy of the information. Is this an unethical activity, a poor policy, or an acceptable (if sometimes unwise) choice to emphasize caution and efficiency? An employer that frequently hires suboptimal employees (either by applying poor screening criteria or by not using—or by misusing—relevant social media information) may see its operations suffer. Employers have the most stake in choosing applicants who are likely to be an asset to the company or organization.

Some people, about to seek a job, try to clean up their online persona. They remove raunchy material, change their "favorite book" to one that appears intellectual, and so on. Some craft online profiles as carefully as job seekers craft résumés. Of course, this means that some profiles are not reliable descriptions of a person, but that is no longer a surprise. On the other hand, some people naively think their blogs are invisible to prospective employers. They criticize the companies they are interviewing with and wonder why they did not get the job. In either case, it is extremely difficult to remove all the negative information and photos a person (or his or her friends) released to cyberspace.

It is common for people to search online for information on someone they have begun to date—or almost anyone they meet, so we should not be surprised that employers learn about potential employees via social media. We might hope that as a civility, a courtesy, or a social convention we—and employers—do not look at what was not intended for us (or them). Is this foolish? Is it achievable? Is it consistent with the culture of the Web and social media?

What gets employees in trouble

Employment policies prohibit various kinds of speech in the workplace and in public, including in social media. Here is an excerpt from one company policy:

> "DO NOT make comments or otherwise communicate about customers, coworkers, supervisors, the Company, or . . . vendors or suppliers in a manner that is vulgar, obscene, threatening, intimidating, harassing, libelous, or discriminatory on the basis of age, race, religion, sex . . . or any other legally recognized protected basis."[36]

Employees are prohibited from discussing certain topics at all with anyone other than specific other employees. These include information about clients (a common restriction in health and financial fields) and information about new products or business plans. Sports teams commonly prohibit trash talking about competitors.

Almost a third of multinational companies said in a survey that they took disciplinary action against employees for misuse of social media.[37] In many instances, employers learn about questionable content after hearing complaints or after another employee shows it to a supervisor. Basing disciplinary action on personal, nonwork social media is controversial. Are there good reasons for employers to be concerned about what their employees post in such places? Is it reasonable for employers to fire employees for content of their blogs, tweets, or posts? Consider some of the wide variety of reasons for these firings:

- A school district fired a teacher because of a photo of her drinking in a bar.
- A school district declined to rehire a teacher who communicated with students on a social network and included pictures of naked men with his profile.
- An actor was fired for tweeting jokes about the horrific tsunami in Japan in 2011.
- A restaurant fired a server for complaining in social media about an inconsiderate, low-tipping customer. The server included the name of the restaurant.
- An executive was fired after he posted a video of himself berating an employee in a restaurant where he ate.
- A sheriff fired a deputy sheriff for "liking" a Facebook campaign page of a person running for election against the sheriff.
- A police department demoted two officers for a cartoon video on YouTube that poked fun at the operation of a local jail.
- A nonprofit social services organization fired five employees for a discussion on Facebook criticizing their working conditions and the job performance of another employee.[38]

These examples suggest a variety of concerns for the employer, from protection of students to protection of the employer's image and reputation (reasonably in some examples, unreasonably where criticism is deserved). A frequent question is whether employer policies restricting nonwork social media violate an employee's freedom of speech. Many such policies do not; the restrictions are conditions of the job. Certain restrictions are illegal. For example, laws protect whistleblowers and allow employees to discuss working conditions with other employees. The social service agency that fired five employees said they had violated its policy against bullying and harassment, but a judge said they were discussing working conditions and the firing was not permissible.

When the employer is a government agency, the First Amendment applies, making the legality of a firing less clear. In the case of the deputy sheriff, a federal appeals court ruled that clicking "Like" on a candidate's web page gets First Amendment protection. Was the police officer who poked fun at the local jail acting in a way "unbecoming an officer," or was he exercising his freedom of speech? Were the firings by school boards appropriate?

Although most employers have a legal right to fire employees who violate their policies about social media (so long as the policy does not violate a law), we might find some firings unethical or, simply, a bad idea. A decision about the ethics or reasonableness of a firing in many cases depends on the actual content of the material in question, how widely it was distributed, the type of employer, and other criteria. The employer, and we as outside observers, need to define a reasonable boundary between, on the one hand, the employer's property rights, protection of company assets and reputation, protection of clients or the public, and the need to monitor for possible legal and liability problems, and, on the other hand, actions that invade privacy and restrict employees' reasonable freedom of expression. The most reasonable policy is not always obvious, not always the same in the view of both parties, not the same for all types of businesses, and not always clear when new situations arise.

6.5.2 SEPARATING—OR MERGING—WORK AND PERSONAL SYSTEMS

In many work environments, employers prohibit employees from using their work email, computers, and other devices for personal use. And in many work environments, employers prohibit employees from using personal phones, tablets, and other devices for work. From the employer's perspective, content in personal messages coming from the employer address could embarrass the employer or subject it to legal problems. Also, some companies want to avoid the embarrassment of having their employees reported to be visiting pornographic sites, perhaps racist sites, or even job-hunting sites. Security is a significant issue for both types of policies. Personal use may be more likely to introduce malicious software to an employer's system that could disrupt operations or expose sensitive data about a company or customers and clients. An employee might carry a personal device to more places with more opportunity to lose it or for someone to steal it. Use of a personal device creates problems for industries required by law to closely monitor employee communications.

In government agencies, email is part of the official record and is subject to public disclosure (with some exceptions). Some government officials use their personal email specifically to keep communications "off the record." This practice subverts rules about openness in government and can have serious security risks. In Chapter 5, we mentioned that a hacking attack on the Gmail accounts of high-level government officials originated in a Chinese city where a major Chinese national security division is located. The U.S. government assured the public that personal email, not government email, was compromised. It is possible, however, that the hackers expected to find, and did find, sensitive government content.

As more people brought electronic gadgets—laptops, smartphones, tablets, and smart watches—into their daily lives, workers (especially professional workers) found the tools their employers provided to be less convenient or less versatile. Many workers viewed carrying one phone for work and one for personal use as a major inconvenience. Employers accepted the "bring your own device" trend toward using personal devices for work and developed policies and rules to reduce risks, such as requiring that employees always use a password to access their device and that specific security software be installed. Later, organizations began a move to a "choose your own device" model. Employees have a choice of device types and operating systems that the company approves, configures securely, and loads with the necessary software. Employers often install software to remotely erase a device if it is lost or stolen; employer ownership eliminates some potential legal and ethical issues of erasing an employee's personal device.

Some employers have a policy that employees may not install any software on their (work) devices other than what the employer provides. Some employers, for example, prohibit games. To someone who travels for work, this might seem silly or overly restrictive. Why not install a game to play while commuting or on a plane? Why not download music to listen to while working? Again, one of the main reasons is security: to protect against viruses or other malware that could disable the system or leak confidential company information or personal data. (In one case, investigators believe that after an Arizona police officer installed peer-to-peer software, hackers used it to collect personal information, photos, and email addresses of several police officers.) Another purpose is to keep copyright-infringing software off the employer's devices to avoid legal trouble. What degree of restrictions makes sense? How should the answer vary with the particular industry and the kind of work done?

6.5.3 MONITORING EMPLOYER SYSTEMS AND TRACKING EMPLOYEES

Monitoring employee use of computer systems

Various surveys find high percentages of employees at businesses and government agencies use the Web at work for nonwork purposes. Visits to "adult" and pornography sites, when the Web was new, gave way to sports, shopping, gambling, and stock-investment sites, then to watching videos, downloading music, and networking with friends. Many major companies use software tools that provide reports on employee Web use, ranking sites by frequency of visits or creating reports on an individual employee's activity.

Retail businesses report losing more from employee theft than from shoplifters, and they use software to monitor transactions at the cash registers looking for suspicious patterns (for example, a large number of refunds, voids, or sales of cheap items) that might indicate employee theft.[39]

Employers say they have a right and a need to monitor the use of their facilities and what employees are doing at work, but monitoring employee activity raises privacy issues. Controversies stem from disagreements about the reasons for monitoring and the appropriate boundary between the employers' rights and the employees' privacy.

Figure 6.4 lists a variety of purposes of monitoring employee activity and communications. Many large companies rank leaking of proprietary information as a serious problem. In the health industry, very strict federal rules apply to patient information to protect privacy; health businesses and organizations must ensure that employees do not violate the rules. Companies report incidents of employees sending jokes to thousands of people, running a business using the company's address, and running betting pools on sports games. Many companies that read employee communications do it infrequently, waiting until there is a complaint or some other reason to suspect a problem. Some employers routinely intercept messages entering and leaving the company, filtering all outgoing messages for content that violates laws or company policy, could damage relations with customers, or could expose the company to lawsuits. Some supervisors read employee email to find out what employees are saying about them or the company.

Is "cyberloafing"—nonwork Web use at work—a serious problem for employers, or is it the modern equivalent of reading a newspaper, listening to the radio, or making a quick personal phone call at one's desk? One large U.S. company found that on a typical day, employees viewed 50,000 YouTube videos and listened to 4000 hours of music. Another found that its employees watched about five million videos in one month. Before many employees had smartphones, they used the employer's computers, causing significant slowdowns in Internet service.[40] Even when workers use their own devices, an obvious concern about nonwork activity is that employees are not working the hours they are paid to work. On the other hand,

---

- Protect security of proprietary information and data.
- Prevent or investigate possible criminal activities by employees (work related, such as embezzlement, or not work related, such as selling illegal drugs).
- Check for violations of company policy against sending offensive or pornographic messages.
- Investigate complaints of harassment.
- Comply with legal requirements in heavily regulated industries.
- Prevent personal use of employer facilities (if prohibited by company policy).
- Training and measuring or increasing productivity.
- Locate employees.
- Find needed business information when the employee is not available.

Figure 6.4 Reasons for monitoring employee communications.

a company found that one of its top-performing employees spent more than an hour a day managing his own stocks on the Web. The company did not care because his performance was good. Some psychologists argue that allowing some personal online activity reduces stress and improves employee morale and efficiency.

Law and cases for employer systems

Monitoring for purposes listed in Figure 6.4 is generally legal in the United States and other countries.[41] The Electronic Communications Privacy Act (ECPA) prohibits interception of email and reading of stored email without a court order, but the ECPA makes an exception for business systems. It does not prohibit employers from reading employee communications on company systems. Some privacy advocates and computer ethicists advocate a revision of the ECPA to prohibit or restrict employers from reading employee email.

ECPA: Section 2.3.2

In one case, a company fired two employees after a supervisor read their email messages criticizing him. A judge ruled that the company could read the email because it owned and operated the system. In another case, a court accepted monitoring of a discussion about a boss because the discussion could affect the business environment. Courts have made similar decisions in other cases. In addition, courts generally allow employers to look at messages an employee sends or receives on personal email accounts if the employee uses the employer's computer system or mobile device to do so. Courts have ruled against employers for reading email sent at work but on a personal account between an employee and the employee's attorney. The longstanding principle of attorney–client privilege protects such correspondence. However, in a case in which the employee used the company's email system for correspondence with her attorney in violation of a clear policy that prohibits personal use of the company system, the court ruled in favor of the employer who read the messages.[42] A court ruling summed up a typical conclusion: "[T]he company's interest in preventing inappropriate and unprofessional comments, or even illegal activity, over its e-mail system would outweigh [the employee's] claimed privacy interest in those communications."[43]

Employees do not give up all privacy when they enter an employer's premises. The bathrooms belong to the employer too, but camera surveillance in bathrooms is generally not acceptable. Courts have sometimes ruled against employers if there was a convincing case that monitoring was done to snoop on personal and union activities or to track down whistleblowers. As we mentioned in Section 6.5.1, workers have a legal right to communicate with each other about working conditions, and the National Labor Relations Board, which decides cases about worker–employee relations, ruled in some cases that they may do so on company systems. Thus, employers may not prohibit all nonbusiness communications.[44]

Court decisions sometimes depend on a conclusion about whether an employee had a reasonable "expectation of privacy." Several decisions emphasize the importance of a company having a clear policy statement. An employer should inform employees clearly about whether it permits personal use of employer-provided systems and whether, and under what circumstances, the employer will access employee messages and files. A clear policy removes some of the guesswork about expectations of privacy.* Clear policy statements are important from an ethical perspective as well. Respect for an employee's privacy includes warning the employee about when someone is observing his or her apparently private actions or communications (except in special circumstances such as a criminal investigation). Giving or accepting a job in which an employee will use an employer's equipment carries an ethical obligation on both parties to abide by the policy established for that use. From a practical perspective, a clear policy can reduce disputes and abuses (by employees or employers).

Expectation of privacy: Section 2.3.2

Monitoring location, wearables, and equipment

When a government agency gave cellphones to building inspectors in Massachusetts so that supervisors could locate employees at all times while at work, the inspectors refused the phones, calling them an invasion of privacy. When trucking companies first installed tracking systems in trucks that report the location and speed of the vehicle, some truckers wrapped foil over the transmitter or parked for naps under highway bridges. Heavy equipment companies install devices that record details of the equipment operation. Nurses in some hospitals wear badges that track their location; a supervisor can see where each nurse is and locate one quickly in an emergency. Ride-sharing services track driving details such as speed, acceleration, and braking. Many companies distribute activity monitors to employees to encourage healthy activity; they record how much sleep the employee gets and many other kinds of health-related information.

These forms of monitoring have many benefits. The truck systems enable more precise planning of pick-ups and deliveries, increases in efficiency, reductions in energy use, and reductions in expenses. Location devices have helped owners recover hundreds of stolen trucks. Companies can use data on speed and rest periods to ensure that drivers follow safety rules. We observed in Section 6.3.2 that ride-sharing services can use data about driving habits of drivers to increase safety. Also, such data can settle disputes with customers or in case of an accident. A heavy equipment company learned that workers let engines run to keep the air conditioning on while they ate lunch in the vehicle's cab; the company stopped the practice, which had used up thousands of dollars in extra fuel.[45] (Was this fair to the workers?)

The risks or problems with such monitoring include intrusion on worker privacy and autonomy. For example, if medical staff in a hospital wear tracking devices, a supervisor knows who eats lunch together and how often they go to

---

*Some court decisions indicate that an employer does not have to specify each specific technology that the policy covers. The employee should assume that a policy for the employer's laptops and phones, for example, applies to a tablet or a newly invented device.

the bathroom. With the availability of a large quantity of data, some employers might try to micromanage employees in ways that are annoying and counterproductive. If data from a wearable monitor indicates that an employee did not get a good night's sleep, would an employer refrain from assigning that person to a critical task?* (Would that be a good idea? Would it be detrimental to the employee?)

Over time, reasonable distinctions develop. Is it reasonable for a city employee working out in the field or for a nurse to expect his or her location, while working, to be private? Probably not, but it might be reasonable in some jobs to turn off locating devices when employees are on a break. On the other hand, health information is more sensitive, and employers who encourage use of health and fitness trackers can hire third-party companies to collect and manage the data, providing the employer with only limited data, as agreed to by employees.

As is the case with other work-related issues we have considered, it is important for employers to develop a clear and reasonable policy about how they will use tracking and monitoring devices—and to communicate the policy clearly to employees.

 ## Exercises

Review Exercises

6.1 List two job categories where the number of jobs declined drastically as a result of computerization.

6.2 What is an advantage of telecommuting? What is a disadvantage?

6.3 What is an advantage of gig work? What is a disadvantage?

6.4 Give one reason for opposition to Uber in France.

6.5 Give two examples of material on social networking sites that got someone fired.

6.6 What is one reason employers object to employees using personal smartphones for work?

General Exercises

6.7 List four examples from Section 1.2 that reduce or eliminate jobs. Tell specifically what jobs they reduce or eliminate.

6.8 List 10 jobs that did not exist 20 years ago.

6.9 Jeremy Rifkin argued that the ability of auto makers to produce a car in less than eight hours illustrates the threat of massive unemployment from computer technology and automation.[46] Give some data or arguments that support or refute Rifkin's point of view. Give at least one argument on either side. Which do you think is stronger? Why?

6.10 Why is it difficult to determine the number of jobs eliminated and created by computers?

---

*Data from wearables can be incorrect. For example, employers who held fitness competitions for employees found that some cheated by attaching their step counters to pets or machines.

6.11   An article described a category of "physical tasks that cannot be well described in rules because they require optical recognition and fine muscle control that have proven difficult to program. Examples include safely driving a truck, cleaning a building, and setting gems in engagement rings. . . . [C]omputerization should have little effect on the percentage of the workforce engaged in these tasks."[47] To what extent is this statement true now? To what extent will it be true in five or ten years?

6.12   Suppose you run a small company and plan to replace a few dozen employees, who have worked for you for more than two years, with robotic equipment that will do the same job at lower cost. What are your ethical responsibilities to your employees?

6.13   Suppose you take a ride in a taxi and want to provide feedback (good or bad) about the driver to the taxi company. How would you carry out the steps to do so (for example, identify the company and the driver, find appropriate contact information, and make the actual contact to convey your comments)?

6.14   Give arguments for and against a legal ruling that drivers who get their customers via a ride-sharing app should be treated as employees, not independent contractors, by the app company.

6.15   Apply one of John Rawls's ideas (in Section 1.4.2) to the analysis of the scenario in Section 6.4 about whether to hire U.S. programmers or Indian programmers.

6.16   One ethical argument against offshoring jobs is that employee health and safety requirements are not as strong in some countries as they are in the United States. Evaluate this argument.

6.17   Consider an automated system that large companies can use to process job applications. For jobs such as truck drivers, cleaning staff, and cafeteria workers, the system selects people to hire without interviews or other involvement of human staffers. Describe advantages and disadvantages of such a system.

6.18   Professional baseball players are not allowed to "trash talk" their opponents in public—for example, at press conferences and in interviews. A team reprimanded a player for tweeting disparaging remarks about an opponent. Is it reasonable for the team to include Twitter in the prohibition on trash talk? Is prohibiting remarks on Twitter a violation of the player's freedom of speech? Give your reasons.[48]

6.19   Consider the case of the restaurant server fired for her social media post about a customer (Section 6.5.1). What factors would you consider in deciding if the firing was reasonable? In what ways did her action differ from that of the social service employees whose firing was reversed by a court? Do you think firing her was fair and reasonable?

6.20   Some organizations proposed federal legislation to prohibit monitoring of customer-service or data-entry employees with more than five years of experience. Give reasons for and against monitoring experienced employees.

6.21   Consider the reasons given in Figure 6.4 for employers to monitor employee communications. For which do you think it is appropriate to have regular, ongoing monitoring for all employees, and for which do you think an employer should access employee communications only when a problem occurs and only for the particular employees involved? Give reasons.

6.22   Suppose you work at a dental office filing insurance claim forms for patients. You are behind schedule and want to copy a dozen patient records and forms to your tablet to work on at home in the evening. Describe several advantages and risks of doing so.

6.23   Suppose your employer says you can use your smartphone for work purposes, but only if the employer can install software to erase the phone if it is lost or stolen or if you leave the company. Describe the pros and cons you will consider in deciding whether to accept this agreement. What is your decision?

6.24   Suppose the owner of a small business is running for the local school board and an employee is actively supporting another candidate in social media. List some criteria to consider in deciding each of these questions: Is it legal to fire the employee? Is it reasonable? Is it ethical?

6.25   The city of Philadelphia requires GPS systems in all taxicabs. Is a government requirement for a tracking system for private taxicabs a reasonable public safety measure or an unreasonable intrusion on the privacy of drivers and passengers? Identify several differences between such a government requirement and a taxicab company choosing to install GPS systems in its cabs. Is either more objectionable than the other? Why?

6.26   Assume you are a professional working in your chosen field. Describe specific things you can do to reduce the impact of any two problems we discussed in this chapter. (If you cannot think of anything related to your professional field, choose another field that might interest you.)

6.27   Think ahead to the next few years and describe a new problem, related to issues in this chapter, likely to develop from digital technology or devices.

Assignments

These exercises require some research or activity.

6.28   The Electronic Communications Privacy Act does not prohibit universities from reading student email on its computers, just as it does not prohibit businesses from reading employee email on company computers. Find your university's policy about access to student computer accounts and email (on university computers) by professors and university administrators. Describe the policy. Tell what parts you think are good and what should change.

6.29   Find a decision made in a lawsuit by an employee who was fired because of photos or other material the employer found on the employee's social network pages. Summarize the case and the result. Do you think the result was reasonable? Why?

Class Discussion Exercises

These exercises are for class discussion, perhaps with short presentations prepared in advance by small groups of students.

6.30   If someone discovers a cure for the common cold, should he or she hide it to protect the jobs of all the people who work in the huge cold-medicine industry?

If there is little controversy about the answer to the question above (as we suspect will be the case), try to identify reasons why so many people react negatively to advances in technology that eliminate jobs.

6.31   Suppose a shoe manufacturer based in the United States or Europe has decided to close a factory in Asia, where labor costs have risen, and replace it with a factory in the home country that will use mostly robotic equipment and far fewer employees.[49] Analyze the ethics of the decision using ideas from Kant, utilitarianism, Rawls, natural rights, and so on (from Section 1.4.2). You may find some useful ideas in the discussions of the ethics of offshoring jobs, in Section 6.4, and ad blocking, in Section 2.5.3.

Would the ethical arguments, or conclusions, be different for the following variations:

(i) The factory is currently in the home country, and the company will replace the workers with robotic equipment. (ii) You are starting a new business and have a choice of hiring 100 workers or using robotic equipment.

Suppose, in a factory that does not use robots, one worker accomplishes twice as much as the others in the same amount of time. Is it ethically required that he or she slow down so that another person might be hired?

6.32 Choose any three of the following employers and discuss arguments for and against a policy to do a social media search on job applicants.

(a) A private elementary school

(b) A large software company

(c) The federal government, specifically for applicants for security clearances

(d) A family-run plumbing company

(e) A major automobile manufacturer

(f) A lobbying organization

6.33 **(a)** Is it an invasion of privacy for an employer to search the Web for information by and about a job applicant? Explain.

   (b) Does refraining from hiring a person who frequently posts or tweets extreme political views violate that person's freedom of speech? Does it matter whether the employer is private or a government agency? Explain.

6.34 Age discrimination in hiring is illegal. Suppose an older person files a complaint with the federal government's Equal Employment Opportunity Commission claiming that a company that uses social media as its main tool to recruit new employees is illegally discriminating against older people, who are less likely to use social media. Give arguments in support of this claim and arguments against it.

6.35 In recent years, only about 20% of students earning college degrees in computer science in the United States were women. This is down from a peak of 37% in 1985.[50] Why do you think relatively few women major in computer science? What characteristics or images of the field might discourage women?

6.36 Walking through a public park on their way back to work after lunch, four employees of a large Internet services company begin clowning around and singing silly and raunchy songs. One of them captures the scene on his phone and later posts it on a major video site. In the video, the company logo is clearly visible on the T-shirts the employees are wearing. The company fires the employee who posted the video and has not yet decided on action against the others. Discuss arguments for and against the firing. What disciplinary action, if any, is appropriate for the other employees?

6.37 A major business newspaper ran a full-page article telling people how to get around restrictions on computer use at work. For example, the article told how to get to websites that the employer's filters blocked, how to install software the employer did not approve, how to check one's personal email from work if the employer's system blocked it, and so on. Discuss the ethics of using these techniques.

Notes

1. CPU: Working in the Computer Industry, Computer Professionals for Social Responsibility, Feb. 15, 1995, www.cpsr.org/prevsite/program/workplace/cpu.013.html.

2. J. M. Fenster, "Seam Stresses," *Great Inventions That Changed the World*, American Heritage, 1994.

3. Interview with Ann Curry, *Today*, NBC, June 14, 2011, described in Rebecca Kaplan, "Obama Defends Economic Policies, Need for Tax Increases In 'Today' Interview," *National Journal*, June 14, 2011, townhall.com/news/politics-elections/2011/06/14/obama_defends_economic_policies,_need_for_tax_increases_in_today_interview. The video of the interview is at today.msnbc.msn.com/id/26184891/vp/43391550#43391550.

4. Associated Press, "Electronic Dealings Will Slash Bank Jobs, Study Finds," *Wall Street Journal*, Aug. 14, 1995, p. A5D. W. Michael Cox and Richard Alm, *Myths of Rich and Poor: Why We're Better Off than We Think*, Basic Books, 1999, p. 129. G. Pascal Zachary, "Service Productivity Is Rising Fast—and So Is the Fear of Lost Jobs," *Wall Street Journal*, June 8, 1995, p. A1. Lauren Etter, "Is the Phone Company Violating Your Privacy?" *Wall Street Journal*, May 13–14, 2006, p. A7.

5. Cox and Alm, *Myths of Rich and Poor*, p. 129. Alejandro Bodipo-Memba, "Jobless Rate Skidded to 4.4% in November," *Wall Street Journal*, Dec. 7, 1998, pp. A2, A8.

6. Fenster, "Seam Stresses"

7. "High-Tech Added 200,000 Jobs Last Year," *Wall Street Journal*, May 19, 1998. "Chip-Industry Study Cites Sector's Impact on U.S. Economy," *Wall Street Journal*, Mar. 17, 1998, p. A20. Fatemeh Hajiha, "Employment Changes from 2001 to 2005 for Occupations Concentrated in the Finance Industries," U.S. Bureau of Labor Statistics, www.bls.gov/oes/2005/may/changes.pdf. "Retail Sales Workers," *Occupational Outlook Handbook,* U.S. Department of Labor, Bureau of Labor Statistics, www.bls.gov/ooh/sales/retail-sales-workers.htm.

8. Kimberly Rowe, in a letter to the editor, *Wall Street Journal*, Aug. 31, 2006, p. A9.

9. "Musicians and Singers," *Occupational Outlook Handbook*, U.S. Department of Labor, Bureau of Labor Statistics, www.bls.gov/ooh/entertainment-and-sports/musicians-and-singers.htm.

10. Michael Mandel, "Where the Jobs Are: the App Economy," TechNet, Feb. 27, 2012, www.technet.org/wp-content/uploads/2012/02/TechNet-App-Economy-Jobs-Study.pdf.

11. Daniel E. Hecker, "Occupational Employment Projections to 2012," *Monthly Labor Review*, Feb. 2004, pp. 80–105 (see p. 80), www.bls.gov/opub/mlr/2004/02/art5full.pdf.

12. The quotes are from "The OECD Jobs Study: Facts, Analysis, Strategies (1994)," www.oecd.org/dataoecd/42/51/1941679.pdf.

13. "The OECD Jobs Study," p. 21.

14. Phillip J. Longman, "The Janitor Stole My Job," *U.S. News & World Report*, Dec. 1, 1997, pp. 50–52. Theodore Caplow, Louis Hicks, and Ben J. Wattenberg, *The First Measured Century: An Illustrated Guide to Trends in America*, AEI Press, 2001, p. 31.

15. Longman, "The Janitor Stole My Job." Amy Merrick, "Erasing 'Un' from 'Unemployable,'" *Wall Street Journal*, Aug. 2, 2007, pp. B1, B6.

16. *Occupational Outlook Handbook*, U.S. Department of Labor, Bureau of Labor Statistics, including www.bls.gov/ooh/business-and-financial/accountants-and-auditors.htm, www.bls.gov/ooh/computer-and-information-technology/home.htm, www.bls.gov/ooh/most-new-jobs.htm, and www.bls.gov/ooh/computer-and-information-technology/software-developers.htm.

17. Caplow *et al.*, *The First Measured Century*, p. 160. Cox and Alm, *Myths of Rich and Poor*, pp. 18–19. Bureau of Labor Statistics, "Employer Costs for Employee Compensation – September 2015," Dec. 9, 2015, www.bls.gov/news.release/ecec.nr0.htm. Heidi Shierholz and Lawrence Mishel, "A Decade of Flat Wages The Key Barrier to Shared Prosperity and a Rising Middle Class," Aug. 21, 2013, www.epi.org/publication/a-decade-of-flat-wages-the-key-barrier-to-shared-prosperity-and-a-rising-middle-class/.

18. W. Michael Cox and Richard Alm, "You Are What You Spend," *The New York Times*, Feb. 10, 2008, www.nytimes.com/2008/02/10/opinion/10cox.html?_r=2. Cox and Alm, *Myths of Rich and Poor*, pp. 7, 10, 43, 59, 60. U.S. Census Bureau: www.census.gov/const/C25Ann/sftotalmedavgsqft.pdf and www.census.gov/const/C25Ann/sftotalac.pdf. For the cost of a smartphone in work hours, we used a Bureau of Labor Statistics report that in December 2014, the average worker received $850 per week. The cost, in work time, of some products and services increased. Increases for tax-preparation fees, Amtrak tickets, and the price of a first class stamp perhaps result from more complex tax laws and monopolies. Increases in the average cost of a new car are partly due to the increase in features of new cars.

19. Joel Kotkin, "Commuting via Information Superhighway," *Wall Street Journal*, Jan. 27, 1994, p. A14.

20. They might have had another motivation. An AFL-CIO official, Dennis Chamot, also commented, "It's very difficult to organize workers dispersed over a wide geographical area." (Quoted in David Rubins, "Telecommuting: Will the Plug Be Pulled?" *Reason*, Oct. 1984, pp. 24–32.)

21. Angela K. Dills and Sean E. Mulholland, "Ride-sharing, Fatal Crashes, and Crime," Social Science Research Network, May 31, 2016, papers.ssrn.com/sol3/papers.cfm?abstract_id=2783797. Gregory Ferenstein, "Ride-Hailing Apps Sharply Reduce Drunken Driving Deaths," *Newsweek*, Aug. 21, 2015, www.newsweek.com/ridesharing-apps-sharply-reduce-drunk-driving-deaths-364877. Brad N. Greenwood and Sunil Wattal, "Show Me the Way to Go Home: An Empirical Investigation of Ride Sharing and Alcohol Related Motor Vehicle Homicide," Social Science Research Network, Jan. 29, 2015.

22. Jesse Singal, "Should You Trust Uber's Big New Uber vs. Cab Study?" *New York Magazine*, July 21, 2015, nymag.com/scienceofus/2015/07/should-you-trust-ubers-big-new-study.html; Ali Meyer, "Report: Uber Serves Low-Income, Minority Neighborhoods 3X More than Taxis," *The Washington Free Beacon*, Sept. 14, 2015, freebeacon.com/issues/report-uber-serves-low-income-minority-neighborhoods-3x-more-than-taxis/.

23. Study by Alan Krueger of Princeton University and Uber, reported in Brian Solomon, "The Numbers Behind Uber's Exploding Driver Force," *Forbes*, May 1, 2015, www.forbes.com/sites/briansolomon/2015/05/01/the-numbers-behind-ubers-exploding-driver-force. The study found that almost one third of Uber drivers had a full-time job other than driving for Uber, and almost another third worked elsewhere part time.

24. In one large city, hundreds of taxi drivers were found to have criminal convictions, including for domestic violence and driving while intoxicated: Ted Oberg, "Why Does the City of Houston Allow Ex-convicts as Cabbies?" ABC13 Eyewitness News, Apr. 25, 2014, abc13.com/archive/9515494/.

25. The U.S case is *Douglas O'Connor v. Uber Technologies, Inc.*; the judge rejected a settlement in 2016. The British case and impacts on other companies are in Dara Kerr, "UK Court Rules Uber Drivers Are Employees, Not Contractors," *CNet*, Oct. 28, 2016, www.cnet.com/news/uber-uk-court-ruling-drivers-employees-not-contractors/; and Tom Mendelsohn, "Uber Drivers Are Company Employees Not Self-employed Contractors," *Ars Technica*, Oct. 31, 2016, arstechnica.com/tech-policy/2016/10/uber-drivers-employees-uk-court-ruling/. More than a million people worldwide drive for Uber, which had fewer than 7000 employees in 2016. If all the drivers became employees, Uber would be one of the five largest corporate employers in the world. Luz Lazo, "Uber Turns 5, Reaches 1 Million Drivers and 300 Cities Worldwide. Now What?" *Washington Post*, June 4, 2015, www.washingtonpost.com/news/dr-gridlock/wp/2015/06/04/uber-turns-5-reaches-1-million-drivers-and-300-cities-worldwide-now-what/. Paul Sawers, "Instacart Opens Part-time Employee Roles to Contractors in All 16 U.S. Markets, *VentureBeat*, Aug. 17, 2015, venturebeat.com/2015/08/17/instacart-opens-part-time-employee-roles-to-contractors-in-all-16-u-s-markets/.

26. Agence France-Presse, "Uber Ordered to Pay €1.2m to French Taxi Union by Paris Court," *The Guardian*, Jan. 27, 2016, www.theguardian.com/technology/2016/jan/27/uber-ordered-pay-france-national-union-taxis-paris-court. Sam Schechner, Douglas Macmillan, and Nick Kostov, "French Court Convicts Uber of Violating Transport, Privacy Laws," *Wall Street Journal*, June 9, 2016.

27. Walter Isaacson, *Steve Jobs*, Simon & Schuster, 2011, Chapter 41.

28. Linda Levine, "Unemployment Through Layoffs and Offshore Outsourcing," Congressional Research Service, Dec. 22, 2010, digitalcommons.ilr.cornell.edu/cgi/viewcontent.cgi?article=1821&context=key_workplace. Alan S. Blinder, "Offshoring: The Next Industrial Revolution?," *Foreign Affairs*, Mar./Apr. 2006, www.foreignaffairs.com/articles/2006-03-01/offshoring-next-industrial-revolution.

29. Blinder, "Offshoring: The Next Industrial Revolution?"

30. The ideas in this discussion come from Corie Lok, "Two Sides of Outsourcing," *Technology Review*, Feb. 2005, p. 33.

31. My (SB) thanks to my student Anthony Biag, whose questions in class on this issue prompted me to include it in this book.

32. However, paying too much can have a negative social consequence for the country by attracting people from more important professions. In the Philippines, call center workers can earn more than doctors, according to Don Lee, "The Philippines Has Become the Call-center Capital of the World," *LA Times*, Feb. 1, 2015, www.latimes.com/business/la-fi-philippines-economy-20150202-story.html. Foreign-owned firms usually pay more than domestic employers. For example, a study of Indonesia, "Do foreign-owned firms pay more?" by Ann E. Harrison and Jason Scorse of the University of California, Berkeley (International Labour Office, Geneva, Working Paper #98, www.ilo.org/wcmsp5/groups/public/---ed_emp/---emp_ent/---multi/documents/publication/wcms_101046.pdf), found that foreign-owned manufacturers paid unskilled workers 5–10% more and skilled workers 20–35% more than comparable domestic employers.

33. Jennifer Preston, "Social Media History Becomes a New Job Hurdle," *New York Times*, July 20, 2011, www.nytimes.com/2011/07/21/technology/social-media-history-becomes-a-new-job-hurdle.html.

34. In Preston, "Social Media."

35. Searching social media is generally legal in the United States and many other countries. Italy is an exception. Italy prohibits monitoring social network activity of employees or seeking information from social networks about job candidates, according to "Employee Misuse of Social Networking Found at 43 Percent Of Businesses, According to Proskauer International Labor & Employment Group Survey," The Metropolitan Corporate Counsel, Aug. 1, 2011, www.metrocorpcounsel.com/articles/15021/employee-misuse-social-networking-found-43-percent-businesses-according-proskauer-int.

36. Eli M. Cantor, "NLRB provides clarification of an acceptable social media policy," *Los Angeles Daily Journal*, www.dailyjournal.com, Dec. 11, 2012.

37. "Employee Misuse of Social Networking Found at 43 Percent of Businesses."

38. Kabrina Krebel Chang, "Facebook Got Me Fired," Boston University School of Management, May 18, 2011, www.bu.edu/today/2011/facebook-got-me-fired/. Chang's article mentions several cases and includes valuable discussion of the principles involved. *Spanierman*, v. *Hughes, Druzolowski, and Hylwa*, www.ctemploymentlawblog.com/uploads/file/hughes.pdf. Jacob Sullum, "Renton Police Drop Cyberstalking Investigation of Cartoon Creator, Pursue Harassment Claim Instead," *Reason Hit & Run*, Sept. 7. 2011, reason.com/blog/2011/09/07/renton-police-drop-cyberstalki. (The department tried to obtain the identity of an officer who anonymously released a series of satiric "Mr. Fuddlesticks" cartoons about the demotion of the officers and about serious police misconduct in the department. The department claimed the cartoons constituted cyberstalking and harassment and that they created a hostile work environment. The department was severely criticized and ridiculed for its behavior in this incident.) The social service organization is Hispanics United of Buffalo. The case and result are summarized in "Administrative Law Judge Finds New York Nonprofit Unlawfully Discharged Employees Following Facebook Posts," National Labor Relations Board, Sept. 7, 2011, www.nlrb.gov/news-outreach/news-story/administrative-law-judge-finds-new-york-nonprofit-unlawfully-discharged.

39. In one scam, an employee scans and charges for cheap items but bags expensive ones for the customer who is an accomplice. Richard C. Hollinger and Lynn Langton, "2005 National Retail Security Survey," University of Florida, 2006, pp. 6–8. Security Research Project, University of Florida. Richard C. Hollinger, National Retail Security Survey 2002, reported in "Retail Theft and Inventory Shrinkage," www.jrrobertssecurity.com/security-news/security-crime-news0024.htm. Calmetta Coleman, "As Thievery by Insiders Overtakes Shoplifting, Retailers Crack Down," *Wall Street Journal*, Sept. 8, 2000, p. A1.

40. Emily Glazer, "P&G Curbs Employees' Internet Use," *Wall Street Journal*, Apr. 4, 2012, www.wsj.com/articles/SB10001424052702304072004577324142847006340. Dana Mattioli, "For Penney's Heralded Boss, the Shine is Off the Apple," Wall Street Journal, Feb. 24, 2013, www.wsj.com/articles/SB1000142412788732433860457832443150023 6680.

41. Italy is an exception, as noted above.

42. *Stengart* v. *Loving Care Agency, Inc.*, New Jersey Supreme Court, Mar. 30, 2010. *Curto* v. *Medical World Communications, Inc. Holmes* v. *Petrovich Development*

Company, LLC. See also "Fact Sheet 7: Workplace Privacy and Employee Monitoring," Privacy Rights Clearinghouse, www.privacyrights.org/fs/fs7-work.htm.

43. *McLaren* v. *Microsoft*, Texas Court of Appeal No. 0597-00824CV, May 28, 1999, cyber.harvard.edu/interactive/events/conferences/2008/09/msvdoj/panel4.

44. *Leinweber* v. *Timekeeper Systems*, 323 NLRB 30 (1997). National Labor Relations Board, "The NLRB and Social Media," www.nlrb.gov/news-outreach/fact-sheets/nlrb-and-social-media.

45. James R. Hagerty, "'Big Brother' Keeps an Eye on Fleet of Heavy Equipment," *Wall Street Journal*, June 1, 2011, p. B1.

46. Jeremy Rifkin, "New Technology and the End of Jobs," in Jerry Mander and Edward Goldsmith, eds., *The Case against the Global Economy and for a Turn toward the Local*, Sierra Club Books, 1996, pp. 108–121.

47. Frank Levy and Richard J. Murnane, *Dancing with Robots: Human Skills for Computerized Work*, Third Way, content.thirdway.org/publications/714/Dancing-With-Robots.pdf.

48. Thanks to Julie L. Johnson for suggesting the idea for this exercise.

49. Paul Wiseman, "Why Robots, Not Trade, Are Behind So Many Factory Job Losses," Associated Press, Nov. 2, 2016, apnews.com/265cd8fb02fb44a69cf0eaa2063e11d9/Mexico-taking-US-factory-jobs?-Blame-robots-instead.

50. National Science Foundation, "Science and Engineering Indicators 2008, Chapter 2: Higher Education in Science and Engineering," wayback.archive-it.org/5902/20150818072824/ http://www.nsf.gov/statistics/seind08/c2/c2s4.htm.

Evaluating and Controlling Technology

In this chapter, we consider such questions as these: Does the openness and "democracy" of the Web increase distribution of useful information or of inaccurate, foolish, and biased information? How should we handle the latter? How can we evaluate complex computer models of physical and social phenomena? Is computing technology evil? Why do some people think it is? How does access to digital technology differ among different populations? How should we control technology to ensure positive uses and consequences? How soon will robots and digital devices be more intelligent than people? What will happen after that?

Whole books focus on these topics. The presentations here are necessarily brief. They introduce issues, arguments, and many questions.

7.1 Evaluating Information

A little learning is a dang'rous thing;
Drink deep, or taste not the Pierian spring;
There shallow draughts intoxicate the brain,
And drinking largely sobers us again.

—Alexander Pope, 1709[1]

7.1.1 THE NEED FOR RESPONSIBLE JUDGMENT

What is real? What is fake? Why does it matter?

We can get the wrong answer to a question quicker than our fathers and mothers could find a pencil.

—Robert McHenry[2]

There is a daunting amount of information on the Web—and much of it is wrong. Quack medical cures abound. Distorted history, errors, outdated information, bad financial advice—it is all there. Marketers and public relations firms spread unlabeled advertisements through blogs, social media, and video sites. Search engines have largely replaced librarians for finding information, but search engines rank information sources at least partially by popularity and give prominent display to content providers who pay; librarians do not. Wikipedia, the biggest online encyclopedia, is immensely popular, but can we rely on its accuracy and objectivity when anyone can edit any article at any time? On social journalism sites, readers submit and vote on news stories. Is this a good way to get news? The nature of the Internet encourages people to post their immediate thoughts and reactions without taking time for contemplation or for checking facts. How do we know what is worth reading in contexts where there are no editors selecting well-written and well-researched articles?

Faking photos is not new; photographers have long staged scenes and altered photos in dark rooms. When we see a video of a currently popular performer singing with Elvis Presley (who died in 1977), we know we are watching creative entertainment—digital magic at work. But the same technologies can deceive, and circulation of a fake photo on the Internet can start a riot or bring death threats to an innocent person. Here is an example of the latter: A young man in Canada posted a selfie he took in his bathroom mirror while holding his iPad. After a series of terrorist attacks in Paris that killed 130 people, someone modified the photo to make the iPad look like a copy of the Quran and made the man appear to be wearing a suicide vest of explosives. The person who modified the image (or someone else) then posted the fake picture with the claim that the man was one of the Paris terrorists. Two news companies republished the false photo and claim without checking them.[3]

Video-manipulation tools (and increased bandwidth) provide the opportunity for more sophisticated "forging" of people. A company developed an animation system that modifies video images of a real person to produce a new video in which the person is speaking whatever words the user of the system provides. Another system analyzes recordings of a person's voice and synthesizes speech with the voice, inflections, and tones of that person. Combined, these systems have many uses, including entertainment and advertising, but clearly people can use them to mislead in highly unethical ways.[4]

We have probably all heard of hoaxes that circulate on the Internet. In Chapter 5, we saw that governments hack into email accounts and infrastructure systems. They may also generate disruptive hoaxes. After false reports of an explosion and toxic leak from a chemical factory in Louisiana spread on social media, supported by fake videos and fake screenshots of respected news sources, a journalist traced this very sophisticated hoax and several others to a group in Russia that already had a reputation for spreading pro-Russian-government propaganda in social media in Russia.[5]

How do we know when someone is manipulating us? How carefully must we (and news organizations!) check authenticity before circulating provocative images, videos, and stories?

Example: Wikipedia

To explore some issues of information quality, we consider Wikipedia. Wikipedia is a collaborative project among large numbers of strangers worldwide. It is huge, free, participatory, noncommercial, ad-free, and written by volunteers. The English edition has more than five million articles, well more than the hundreds of thousands in the long-respected Encyclopædia Britannica, first published in 1768 and online since 1994.[6†] Wikipedia is one of the Internet's most-used reference sites. But are its entries true, honest, and reliable?

We expect encyclopedias to be accurate and objective. Traditionally, expert scholars selected by editorial boards write encyclopedia entries. Volunteers, not carefully selected scholars, write and continually edit and update Wikipedia articles.

---

†Both Britannica and World Book Encyclopedia provide free articles, but full access requires a paid subscription.

Anyone who chooses to participate can do so. People worry that the lack of editorial control means no accountability, no standards of quality, and no way for the ordinary person to judge the value of the information. They argue that because hundreds of millions of people—anyone at all—can write or edit articles, accuracy and quality are impossible. Truth does not come from populist free-for-alls. Members of the staffs of political candidates have distorted the Wikipedia biographies of their candidates to make their bosses look better. Opponents and enemies regularly vandalize profiles of prominent people. The staff of a federal agency removed criticisms of the agency from its Wikipedia article. Discredited theories about historic events such as the terrorist attacks on September 11, 2001, and the assassination of John F. Kennedy reappear regularly. A lawyer reported that one party in a legal case edited Wikipedia entries to make information appear more favorable to that party. (Jurors are not supposed to consult online sources about a trial, but some do.)

Removing false information, hoaxes, and the like requires constant effort by volunteer administrators and the Wikipedia staff. The Encyclopædia Britannica has errors and oddities, but the nature of Wikipedia makes it prone to more. Anonymity of writers can encourage dishonesty. Open, volunteer, instant-publishing systems cannot prevent errors and vandalism as easily as publishers of printed books or closed, proprietary online information sources. Several potential Wikipedia competitors, Veropedia, Citizendium, and Google's Knol project, tried to address weaknesses of Wikipedia, but none survived.

Despite the errors, sloppiness, bad writing, and intentional distortions, most of Wikipedia is, perhaps surprisingly, of high quality and extraordinary value. Why? What protects quality in large, open, volunteer projects? First, although anyone *can* write and edit Wikipedia articles, most people do not. Many who do are educated and have expertise in the subjects they write about, and they correct articles promptly. After well-publicized incidents of manipulation of articles, Wikipedia's managers developed procedures and policies to reduce the likelihood of such incidents. For example, they lock articles on some controversial topics or people; the public cannot directly edit them. We, as users, can (and must) learn to deal appropriately with side effects or weaknesses of new paradigms. Even though much of Wikipedia is excellent and useful, many articles are not up to date, and someone may have wrecked the accuracy and objectivity of any individual article at any hour. Articles on technology, basic science, history, and literature are more likely to be reliable than those on politics, controversial topics and people, and current events. We learn to use Wikipedia for background, but to check facts and seek alternative points of view. Should we judge Wikipedia (and, by extension, the mass of information on the Web) by the excellent material it provides or by the poor-quality material it includes?

Written by fools for the reading of imbeciles.

—An evaluation of newspapers, not websites, by a character in
Joseph Conrad's novel *The Secret Agent* (1907)

The "wisdom of the crowd"

People ask all sorts of questions of their digital assistants, apps, and websites such as answers.com. These queries can be about diverse personal topics such as dating, travel, food, and college ("Are online college classes as good as classroom classes?"), or wide-ranging technical, social, economic, and political issues ("If we can produce enough food to feed everyone in the world, why don't we?"). Of course, a lot of answers are ill informed. On some sites, the questioner designates the posted answer he or she deems the best. What qualifies the questioner, presumably a person who does not know the answer, to judge the worthiness of the replies? To what extent does the ease of posting a question reduce the likelihood that a person seeks out well-researched or expert information on the subject? There are obviously questions for which this kind of forum might not provide the best results. (An example might be: Is it safe to drink alcohol while using an acne medicine?) However, other questions, such as the first two sample questions quoted above, are likely to generate many varied ideas and perspectives. Sometimes, that is exactly what the questioner wants. If someone asked questions like those of only a few friends, the answers might be less varied and less useful.

Some health sites on the Web encourage the public to rate doctors, hospitals, and medical treatments. Are such ratings valuable or dangerous? Do these sites motivate doctors and hospitals to change their practices to achieve higher ratings at the expense of good medical care? Websites have sprung up to buy and sell votes to get prominent display for articles on social media sites. What are the implications of such practices for sites where the public rates medical care? Can responsible operators of sites that display material based on rankings or votes anticipate manipulation and protect against it?

Let's pause briefly to put the problems of incorrect, distorted, and manipulated information in perspective. Quack medical cures and manipulative marketing are hardly new. Product promotions not labeled as advertising date back hundreds of years. Eighteenth-century opera stars paid people to attend performances and cheer for them or boo their rivals. "Hatchet jobs" in the form of news articles, books, ads, and campaign flyers have dishonestly attacked politicians long before digital technology existed. There are plenty of poorly written and inaccurate books. Historical movies merge truth and fiction, some for dramatic purposes, some for ideological purposes, leaving us with a distorted idea of what really happened. Two hundred years ago, cities had more newspapers than they do today; most of them were opinionated and partisan. At supermarket counters, we can buy newspapers with stories as outlandish as any online. The *New York Times* is a prime example of a respected newspaper, staffed by trained journalists, with an editorial board in charge. Yet, one of its reporters fabricated many stories. Numerous other incidents of plagiarism, fabrication, and insufficient fact-checking have embarrassed newspapers and television networks.

So, the problems of unreliable information are not new, but they are problems, and the Web magnifies them. We consider two questions: How good is the wisdom of the crowd? And how can we distinguish good sources of information on the Web?

Researchers find that crowds do, in fact, generate good answers to certain kinds of questions. When a large number of people respond, they produce a lot of answers, but the average, or median, or most common answer is often a good one. This works well when the people are isolated from each other and express independent opinions. Some researchers think a large (independent) group is likely to be more accurate than a committee of experts for a variety of questions such as estimating economic growth or how well a new product or movie will do. A Canadian mining company, perhaps hoping for such a phenomenon, posted a large set of geological data on the Web and held a contest to choose areas to look for gold. The U.S. Patent Office is experimenting with online crowdsourcing to help determine if the inventions described in patent applications are truly new; people with expertise in particular technologies can alert the Patent Office to existing products that are similar.

However, the wisdom of crowds requires some independence and diversity. When people see responses provided by others, some undesirable things happen. People modify their responses so that the set of responses becomes less diverse, and the best answer may no longer stand out. People become more confident from reinforcement even though accuracy does not improve. In social networks (as well as in-person teams working on projects in businesses, organizations, and government agencies), peer pressure and dominant personalities can reduce the wisdom of the group.[7] Group settings are still useful for soliciting ideas and feedback; governments and businesses have long used open forums, town hall meetings, and focus groups for such purposes.

How can we distinguish good sources of information on the Web? Search engines and other services at first ranked sites by the number of people who visited them. Some developed more sophisticated algorithms to consider the quality of information on sites where users provide content. A variety of people and services review and rate sites and blogs. Critics of the quality of information on the Web and the lack of editorial control disdain such ratings as merely popularity contests, contending, for example, that the Internet gratifies the "mediocrity of the masses."[8] For blogs, as for Wikipedia or health care sites, they argue that popularity, voting, and consensus do not determine truth. That is correct, but there is no magic formula that tells us what is true and reliable either on the Web or off the Web. The fact that a large number of people visit a website does not guarantee quality, but it provides some information. (Why have newspapers long published "best seller" lists for books?) We can choose to read only blogs written by Nobel Prize winners and college professors, if we wish, or only those recommended by friends and others we trust. We can choose to read only product reviews written by professionals, or we can read reviews posted by the public and get an overview of different points of view.

Over time, the distinction between the online equivalents of responsible journalism and supermarket tabloids becomes clear. Good reputations develop, just as they have for centuries offline. Many university libraries provide guides for evaluating websites and the information on them.[9] One good step is to determine who sponsors the site. If you cannot determine the sponsor of a site, you can choose to consider its information as reliable as the information on a flyer you might find under your car's windshield wiper when you park in a busy parking lot. Ultimately, we must find sites, reviewers, ratings, editors, experts, and other sources we trust. Good judgment and skepticism are always valuable.

> *The only way to preserve the wisdom of the crowd is to protect the independence of the individual.*
>
> —Jonah Lehrer[10]

Vulnerable viewers

Since you are reading this book, you probably are a student, a reasonably well-educated person who is learning how to analyze arguments and make good judgments. You can develop skills to evaluate material you read on the Web. But what about people who have less education or ability? For example, what risks does bad information pose to children who find it on the Web? Some critics of the Web worry most about the impact of inaccurate information on such vulnerable people. These fears sometimes edge toward a belief that we (or experts, or the government) should somehow prevent such information from appearing. The many strong arguments for freedom of speech in general are arguments against any centralized or legally mandated way of accomplishing this. What can we do to improve the quality of information? Basic social and legal forces help (to a degree): freedom of speech (to provide responses, corrections, alternative viewpoints, and so on), teachers and parents, competition, fraud and libel laws—and people who care, who volunteer to write, review, and correct online information. What else can we do to reduce access to dangerously wrong information by vulnerable people?

Narrowing the information stream

All the problems of junk and nonsense on the Web notwithstanding, the Web now gives us access to more high-quality, up-to-date information than libraries did in the past—and much more conveniently. Consider current events, politics, and controversial issues. With the Web, we can:

- read and listen to thousands of news sources from our own and other countries, getting different cultural and political perspectives on events
- read the full text of government documents—bills, budgets, investigative reports, and congressional testimony and debate—instead of relying on a few sentences quoted from an official news release or a sound bite from a biased spokesperson

- search archives of millions of news articles from the past 200 years
- follow websites, blogs, tweets, and social media news of conservatives, liberals, libertarians, tea party activists, environmentalists, evangelical Christians, animal rights activists, and so on, far more easily and cheaply than when we had to seek out and subscribe to their print newsletters and magazines

But what do people actually do? Some get all their news and interpretation of events from a small number of apps or sites that reflect a specific political point of view. Online tools make it easy: You just set up your bookmarks and feeds and never look anywhere else, except perhaps at other sources recommended by the ones you frequent. Some critics see the Web as significantly encouraging political narrowness and political extremes by making it easy for people to avoid seeing alternative opinions.

How else do our digital tools narrow information streams? In Chapter 2, we saw that search engines personalize results for users based on their location, past searches, profile information, and other criteria. Given the huge amount of information on the Web, this fine tuning helps us find what we want quickly and can be valuable. However, it means that when we are searching for something outside our usual context, including perhaps information on controversial subjects, we might have to make an effort to look a little harder.

Sometimes, it is not that we are looking for an easy way to get information; rather, we are unaware that the information we get is filtered or biased. Facebook recognized that if we receive too much information that does not interest us, we stop reading it. To counter this problem, it set its news feed algorithms to filter updates from friends based on how recently a member communicated with them.

Idiots and dunderheads

A fool and his money are soon parted.
—Old English proverb

New technologies can have the unintended side effect of diminishing older skills. For example, computing technology reduced the use of cursive writing, and many elementary schools no longer teach it. Microsoft decided the thesaurus in Microsoft Word 2000 (and some later versions) should list the verb "trick" as the only meaning for "fool." It omitted noun synonyms "clown," "blockhead," "idiot," "ninny," "dunderhead," "ignoramus," and others that were all present in earlier versions. Standard references such as dictionaries and Roget's Thesaurus contain some of these and more choices.

Microsoft said it eliminated words "that may have offensive uses."[11*] Was this a dunderheaded decision that dulls the language and reduces literacy? Do producers of widely used reference works have an ethical responsibility to report the substance of their field accurately, or a social responsibility to remove potentially offensive words from the language?

---

*Microsoft restored some synonyms meaning a foolish person but continues to omit the more colorful and more offensive terms.

How is this relevant to political news or social issues? Here is one example: Eli Pariser, president of the liberal organization MoveOn.org, includes conservatives among his Facebook friends because he wants to be aware of views different from his own. He does not communicate with those people regularly, and, over time, he realized he was no longer receiving updates from them. Although Facebook members can turn off the filtering of news feeds, most people are not aware of it. Pariser considered the problem of filtered information so disturbing that he wrote a book about it.[12] What lessons can we learn from Facebook's filtering? Facebook's choice of a default setting (filtering turned on) might not be best, but, then again, most people might prefer it.

A study by Pew Research found that more than 60% of U.S. adults get news from social media. The question of political bias and influence arose in several instances. An article suggested a liberal bias among Facebook staff who select trending topics (assisted by algorithms). YouTube restricted access to more than a dozen short videos, sponsored by a conservative organization, on current social and political topics. (Ironically, one of the restricted videos was about methods some people use to prevent others from exercising their freedom of speech.) After the 2016 U.S. presidential election, some argued that false stories and right-wing discussions on Facebook may have affected the outcome of the election.[13]

If we want to reduce political bias, what works best: human editors, algorithms, or member feedback? Editors have biases even if unintentional. When Facebook replaced the humans with automation to select trending topics, gossip and false stories increased; the algorithms were not good enough alone, without some human judgment. YouTube explained that its algorithm considers community input in deciding which videos to restrict. Yet, putting too much weight on member or community feedback allows people with one point of view to block another. After the 2016 election, Facebook said it would use evaluations from fact-checking organizations to help determine what should be flagged as untrue. But such organizations also have biases and make mistakes. One of them changed its designation of a 2008 political campaign statement from "accurate" to "the lie of the year" after events proved its falseness. The problem of determining which statements or claims are true and fair is fundamentally difficult. Constant care and oversight are necessary to reduce bias. What features could help? One journalist suggested an "alternative viewpoints" button.

Overall, does the Internet narrow our information stream and significantly diminish access to different points of view on controversial social and political topics? Does it encourage ideological isolation? People tend to select and read articles that match their own point of view (as they have done since long before the Internet). Thus, we must consider human nature as well as biased advocates and the mechanisms of the Web when seeking ways to make it more likely that we and others see accurate information and a variety of points of view.

Narrowing academic research

The phenomenon of using the information that is easy to get occurs in other fields besides politics, of course. A researcher analyzed millions of academic articles published over 50 years and found that as journals moved online, authors tended to cite fewer articles, more recent ones, and articles from a narrower set. The speculation is that researchers using search engines to find articles related to their work select from among the ones that appear high in search results—the ones that are already cited frequently. Those articles might indeed be the most important, but this approach reinforces previous choices and can lead researchers to miss less popular but very relevant work. Researchers have far more (and easier) access to articles and journals online than they had in the stacks of libraries. However, as the author of the study says, searching online "puts researchers in touch with prevailing opinions, but this may accelerate consensus and narrow the range of findings and ideas built upon."[14] The effect of accelerating consensus and narrowing results is similar to what researchers saw with the wisdom of the crowd when crowd members were not independent, though the mechanism is different. Clearly, it is good for researchers to be aware of this phenomenon and to broaden their searches when appropriate.

The number of scholarly papers published has grown enormously to over two million a year. Is it the tendency to use search tools in a somewhat lazy way—or the sheer number of papers—that causes some valuable work to be missed? Will more sophisticated, AI-based, search tools read all the articles for us and do a better job, or will biases in their programming (intentional or not) restrict the results?

We must be extremely cautious about becoming arbiters of truth ourselves.
—Mark Zuckerberg, CEO of Facebook[15]

Abdicating responsibility

The convenience of using a computer system and abdication of responsibility to exercise judgment can encourage a mental laziness with serious consequences. A trucker in Britain got his truck stuck on a small farm road by unquestioningly following the directions of a navigation system and ignoring a sign saying the road was not suitable for large vehicles. A newspaper editor in Pakistan received a letter to the editor by email and inserted it into the newspaper without reading beyond the title. The letter contained an attack on the prophet Muhammad, and angry Muslims set fires in the newspaper office. Several editors were arrested and charged with blasphemy, in some cases punishable by death.[16] Back when newspaper content was still typeset and copyedited, such an accident would have been unlikely.

Businesses make decisions about loan and insurance applications with the help of software that analyzes risks. School districts make decisions about the progress of students and the careers of administrators based on computer-graded tests.

Doctors, judges, and pilots use software to guide decisions. When decision makers are unaware of system limitations or errors, they may make poor or incorrect choices.

Sometimes reliance on a computer system rather than human judgment becomes "institutionalized" in the sense that an organization's management and the legal system can exert strong pressure on individual professionals or employees to do what the computer says. In bureaucracies, a decision maker might feel that there is less personal risk (and less bother) in just accepting what the software produces rather than doing additional checking or making a decision the software does not support. Computer programs advise doctors on treatments for patients. It is critical to remember that, in complex fields, the computer systems might provide valuable information and ideas but might not be good enough to substitute for an experienced professional's judgment. In some institutions, when something goes wrong, "I did what the program recommended" is a stronger defense (to superiors or against a lawsuit) than "I did what my professional judgment and experience recommended." Such institutions are encouraging abdication of personal responsibility, with potentially harmful results.

A few examples above and some in Chapters 8 and 9 show dangers of depending on the results of software that is not good enough to make decisions without human oversight. On the other hand, there are many examples where the software does a better job than people do. As artificial intelligence systems improve, managing this dichotomy becomes more complex. Users have a responsibility to understand the capabilities and limitations of the systems they use.

7.1.2 COMPUTER MODELS

Likeness to truth is not the same thing as truth.

—Peter L. Bernstein[17]

Evaluating models

Computer-generated predictions based on mathematical models of subjects with important social impact frequently appear in the news. Figure 7.1 shows a few examples of such topics. A mathematical model is a collection of data and equations describing, or simulating, characteristics and behavior of the thing studied. The models and simulations of interest to us here require so much data and/or computation that they must be run on computers. Researchers and engineers do extensive modeling to simulate both physical systems, such as the design for a new car or the flow of water in a river, and intangible systems, such as parts of the economy. Models allow us to simulate and investigate the possible effects of different designs, scenarios, and policies. Simulations and models provide many social and economic benefits, from helping to train operators of power plants, submarines,

- Population growth
- The cost of a proposed government program
- The number of lives that a new drug will save
- When we will run out of a critical natural resource
- The effects of a tax cut on the economy
- The threat of global warming
- When a big earthquake is likely to occur

Figure 7.1 Some problems studied with computer models.

and airplanes to projecting trends and enabling us to consider alternatives, thus making better decisions that reduce waste, cost, and risk.

Models are simplifications. Although the models we consider are abstract (i.e., mathematical), the meaning of the word "model" here is similar to its meaning in "model airplane." Model airplanes generally do not have an engine or wiring and the wing flaps might not move. In a chemistry class, we could use sticks and balls to build models of molecules to help us understand their properties. These molecule models might not show the components of the individual atoms. Similarly, mathematical models often do not include equations for every factor that could influence the outcome, but are instead comprised of simplified equations because the correct ones are unknown or too complicated.

Physical models are usually not the same size as the real thing. Model planes are smaller; the molecule model is larger. In mathematical models, time, rather than physical size, often differs from reality. Computations done on a computer to model a complex physical process in detail often take more time than the actual process takes. For models of long-range phenomena, such as population growth and climate change, the computation must take a lot less time than the real phenomenon for the results to be useful.

Predictions from expensive computers and complex computer programs impress people, but models vary enormously in quality. Some are worthless while others are very reliable. Politicians and special interest groups use model predictions to justify multibillion-dollar programs and laws with significant impact on the economy and the standard of living and choices of millions of people. It is important for both computer professionals and the general public to have some idea of what is in such computer programs, where the uncertainties and weaknesses might lie, and how to evaluate the claims. It is the professional and ethical responsibility of those who design and develop models for public issues to describe honestly and accurately the results, assumptions, and limitations of their models.

The following questions help us determine the accuracy and usefulness of a model.

1. How well do the modelers understand the underlying science or theory of the system they are studying (be it physics, chemistry, economics, or whatever)?

How well understood are the relevant properties of the materials involved? How accurate and complete are the data?

2. Models necessarily involve assumptions and simplifications of reality. What are the assumptions and simplifications in the model?

3. How closely do the results or predictions of the model correspond with results from physical experiments or real experience?

Three different models developed to predict the change in health care costs that would result if the United States adopted a national health system gave predictions that varied by hundreds of billions of dollars.[18] Why was there such a difference? There are both political and technical reasons why models might not be accurate. Political goals can influence the weighting of many critical factors in the model. In addition to technical reasons suggested earlier (incomplete knowledge, incomplete or inaccurate data, and faulty assumptions or oversimplification), other reasons are that computing power could be inadequate for the number of computations needed to model the full complexity of the system, and the difficulty, if not impossibility, of numerically quantifying variables that represent human values and choices.

Are reusable (washable cloth) diapers better for the environment than disposable diapers? When environmentalists proposed bans and taxes on disposable diapers, this controversy consumed almost as much energy as diaper manufacturing. Several groups developed computer models to study the question. A model that attempts to consider the resource use and environmental effects of all aspects of a product, including manufacture, use, and disposal, is called a life cycle analysis model. To illustrate the difficulty of doing an accurate study of such a topic, Figure 7.2 lists a few of the questions about which the diaper modelers made assumptions. Depending on the assumptions, the conclusions differed.[19] It is worth noting also that the models focused on one quality—environmental impact. To make a personal decision, we might consider the results of such a model (if we think it reliable), and we might also consider other factors such as cost, aesthetics, convenience, comfort, and health risks.

- How many times do parents reuse a cloth diaper before discarding it? (Values ranged from 90 to 167.)

- Should the model give credit for energy recovered from incineration of waste? Or does pollution from incineration counterbalance the benefit?

- How many cloth diapers do parents use each time they change a baby? (Many parents use two at once for increased protection.) Numbers in the models ranged from 1.72 to 1.9.

- How should the model count pesticides used in growing cotton?

FIGURE 7.2 Factors in diaper life cycle modeling.

The importance of testing

Many judges use software that provides a risk assessment telling how likely it is that a person convicted of a crime will commit another crime in the future. If the model on which the software is based does a good job, this is a valuable tool to help make humane and socially valuable decisions about sentencing convicted criminals. One widely used model bases its assessment on more than 100 factors, including, for example, whether or not the person has a parent who spent time in jail. It might be known that this and the other factors in the model correlate with repeat crimes. The model does not include race or national origin. And yet, a study of the results found that the model has a bias against black people.[20] That is, the black people it rated as high risk for repeat offenses were actually significantly less likely to commit another crime than the white people with the high risk rating. The company that developed the model disputed the methodology and results of the study. We take no position on who is correct but use the example to illustrate the issue of causality and the importance of testing.

Why might the model be wrong? One possibility is that some criteria the model uses correlate with repeated crimes but also correlate with other factors such as income or race. As you may have often heard, correlation does not mean causation. For many phenomena, the causes are unknown and people work with the best information available. But with something as important as determining prison sentences, how should judges use such software? A critical task for any model is testing, in this case, comparing the later behavior of the actual criminals to the assessments. This can take many years and requires careful statistical methodology. In the meantime, such a program is a tool that might be useful, but judges need to know how it works (or, at least, how well it works) and must remain skeptical and use good judgment in incorporating its output into their decisions.

Example: Modeling car crashes[21]

Car crash analysis programs use a technique called the finite-element method. They superimpose a grid on the frame of a car, as in Figure 7.3, dividing the car into a finite number of small pieces, or elements. The model also uses data describing the specifications of the materials making up each element (e.g., density, strength, and elasticity). Suppose we are studying the effects on the structure of the car from a head-on collision. Engineers initialize data to represent a crash into a wall at a specified speed. The program computes the force, acceleration, and displacement at each grid point and the stress and strain within each element. It repeats these calculations to show what happens as time passes in very tiny increments. These programs require intensive computation to simulate the first 40–100 milliseconds of real time after the impact.

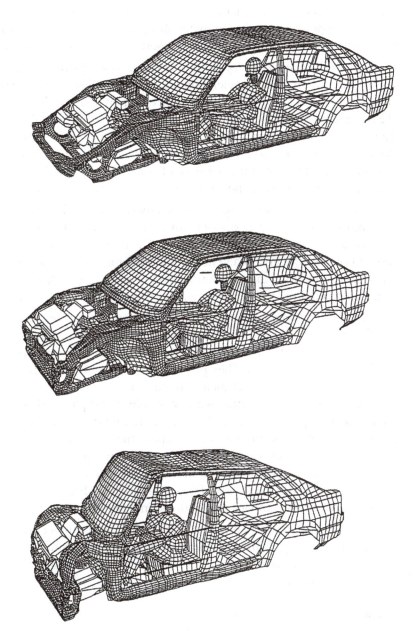

FIGURE 7.3 Simulating a frontal car crash. (The grids are simplified.) Used with permission of Livermore Software Technology Corporation.

A real crash test can include building and testing a unique prototype for a new car design and cost several hundred thousand dollars. The crash analysis programs allow engineers to consider alternatives—for example, to vary the thickness of steel for selected components, or change materials altogether—and discover the effect without building another prototype for each alternative. But how good are the models?

How well is the physics of car crashes understood? How accurate and complete are the data? Force and acceleration are basic principles. The physics involved in these programs is straightforward. Engineers know the relevant properties of steel, plastics, aluminum, glass, and other materials in a car fairly well, and there are good data on the density, elasticity, and other characteristics of materials used. However, although they understand the behavior of the materials when force is applied gradually, they know less about the behavior of some materials under abrupt acceleration, as in a high-speed impact, and their behavior near or at breaking point.

What simplifications do the programs make? The grid pattern is the most obvious simplification. A car is smooth, not made up of little blocks. Also, time is continuous; it does not pass in discrete steps. The accuracy of a simulation depends in part on how fine the grid is and how small the time intervals are. Current computer speeds allow updating the calculations on fine grids (e.g., a few millimeters per element) with small time intervals (e.g., less than one millionth of a second).

How do the computed results compare to actual crash tests on real cars? High-speed cameras record real crash tests. Engineers attach sensors to the car and mark reference points on the frame and compare the values the sensors record with values the program computes. They physically measure the distortion or displacement of the reference points, and then compare these measurements to the computed positions of the points. Starting with the results of the physical crash, the engineers use elementary physics to calculate backward and determine the deceleration and other forces acting on the car and compare these to the values computed in the simulation. The conclusion? Crash analysis programs do an extremely good job. In part because of the confidence that developed over time in the validity of the results, engineers use variations of the same crash analysis modeling programs in a large variety of other impact applications, including those in Figure 7.4.

Engineers still perform physical crash tests. The computer program is an implementation of theory. Although the crash analysis programs are excellent design tools that enable increases in safety with far less development cost, the physical crash test is confirmation.

Example: Modeling climate

Since the late 19th century, global temperatures and sea level have been rising. The average global air temperature has risen approximately 0.8°C.[*] The temperature

---

[*] Depending on the particular temperature data sets used and the specific starting year, the temperature rise is reported at various amounts between 0.72° and 0.82°C, with error ranges roughly ±0.2°C.

- Predict damage to a hazardous waste container if dropped.
- Predict damage to an airplane windshield or nacelle (engine covering) if hit by a bird.
- Determine whether beer cans would get dented if an assembly line were speeded up.
- Simulate a medical procedure called balloon angioplasty, where doctors insert a balloon in a blocked artery and inflate it to open the artery. The model helps researchers determine how to perform the procedure with less damage to the arterial wall.
- Predict the action of airbags and the proper location for sensors that inflate them.
- Design interior parts of cars to reduce injuries during crashes (e.g., from the impact of a steering wheel on a human chest).
- Design bicycle and motorcycle helmets to reduce head injuries.
- Design cameras to reduce damage if dropped.
- Forecast effects of earthquakes on bridges and buildings.

FIGURE 7.4 Other uses of crash analysis models.

increase has been particularly steep since the late 1970s. Sea level rose an average of about 1.7 millimeters per year between 1870 and 2000; the rate has increased to roughly 3 millimeters per year.[*22] The reasons for these changes include the ending of the Little Ice Age (roughly 1450–1850), natural climate variability, and human activity. Predictions for future warming and other climate changes are based, in part, on computer models of climate. We consider those models in this section. Since 1990, the Intergovernmental Panel on Climate Change (IPCC), sponsored by the United Nations and the World Meteorological Organization, has published comprehensive reports roughly every five years on the science of climate change and the quality and projections of climate models. Much of the information here comes from those reports.[23]

Throughout this section, we give numbers from the IPCC reports and other research sources to make the discussion concrete, but the numbers can be confusing and occasionally appear inconsistent because of variation in the time ranges of various data, the initialization for model runs, the variety of models used, what they are simulating, the variety of measurement techniques, and other factors. We encourage the reader not to get lost in the numbers but to use them as an aid in understanding the ideas.

Climate models, like the car crash analysis models, calculate relevant variables for grid points and elements (space between the points) for specified simulated time intervals. The grid circles the earth, rises through the atmosphere, and goes

---

[*]The error ranges are ±0.2 mm for the 20th century data and ±0.4 mm for the more recent higher data.

down into the oceans. The models contain information about the sun's energy output; the orbit, inclination, and rotation of the earth; geography; topography; clouds; sea and polar ice; soil and air moisture; and a large number of other factors. Equations simulate atmospheric pressure, temperature, wind speed and direction, moisture, precipitation, ocean currents, and so forth.

As solar radiation reaches the earth, the earth reflects some of it back and gases in the atmosphere trap some. The latter phenomenon, which warms the earth, is known as the greenhouse effect. Without it, the temperature on the earth would be too cold to support life. Water vapor is the main greenhouse gas, but several others, especially carbon dioxide (CO_2), play a significant role. Human activity (e.g., burning of fossil fuels) has increased the concentration of CO_2 in the atmosphere. Although an upward trend began roughly 16,000 years ago,[*] CO_2 concentration has been increasing at a faster rate since the beginning of the Industrial Revolution, and CO_2 emissions increased sharply after 1950. CO_2 concentration is now approximately 40% higher than in 1750.[24] One of the applications of climate models is to determine the effects of doubling CO_2 concentration in the atmosphere from its pre-industrial level. Models also project the likely increase in global temperature, sea level, and other climate characteristics in various scenarios with assumptions about population, industrial and economic activity, energy use, and so on. Another task for the models is to distinguish how much warming human activity causes and how much is from other factors.

Global warming came to public attention in the late 1980s. The models used in the 1980s and 1990s were quite limited. Here is a brief sampling of simplifications, assumptions, and factors modelers did not fully understand:

- The models did not distinguish day and night.[25]
- They used a coarse grid (with points roughly 500 kilometers apart).[†]
- They did not include the El Niño phenomenon.
- They did not include aerosols (small particles in the air) that have a cooling effect.
- The representation of the oceans was extremely simplified; computing power was insufficient to do the many calculations needed to simulate ocean behavior.
- Clouds are extremely important to climate, but many processes involved with the formation, effects, and dissipation of clouds were not particularly well understood. The IPCC summarized in 2001: "As has been the case since the first IPCC Assessment Report in 1990, probably the greatest uncertainty in future projections of climate arises from clouds and their interactions with radiation.... Clouds represent a significant source of potential error in climate simulations."[26]

---

[*]The older data come from measurements of gases trapped in ice cores drilled in Antarctica and Greenland.
[†]To understand the significance of grid size, think of a rain storm; a model might not represent the storm at all if it falls between grid points, or a model might treat it as large as an entire grid element.

When run on past data, some of the early climate models predicted temperature increases three to five times as high as what actually occurred. Thus, it should not be surprising that there has been much skepticism about the climate models and their projections.

Current models are far more detailed and complex. Increased computer power allows the use of much finer grids, fuller representation of oceans, and more experiments with the models. Increased data collection and basic science research have improved the understanding of the behavior and interactions of climate system components.

How well is the science understood? How accurate are the data? Climatologists know an enormous amount about climate. The models incorporate a huge amount of good science and data. But a lot is unknown or not well understood; we mention a few examples.

When the earth warms, water evaporates, and the additional water vapor in the atmosphere absorbs more thermal energy, warming the atmosphere farther. On the other hand, water vapor forms clouds, which reflect incoming solar radiation and thus have a cooling effect. So, clouds have positive (destabilizing) and negative (stabilizing) feedback effects. The basic science of the mechanisms is fairly well understood, but not the complexity and magnitude of all the feedbacks. The IPCC says that varying treatment of clouds is the largest factor responsible for the wide range of predictions from more than two dozen models for the long-term impact of doubling CO_2 concentration in the atmosphere from the pre-industrial level.[*] Indeed, despite all the increased model sophistication over more than 25 years, the most recent IPCC report says the impact would likely be in the range 1.5–4.5°C, the same range as in the first report.[27†]

The records of temperatures since 1850 have a variety of weaknesses, for example, few monitoring stations over the oceans and in remote land areas and variability in the quality of measuring instruments. Various research organizations have developed different temperature data sets by applying statistical methods and other techniques to make corrections and fill in gaps in the actual data.

There is insufficient data on many phenomena for the period before satellites collected data. For example, the IPCC says the shortness of the record of data on Antarctic sea ice contributes to large differences among the models in their simulation of the ice and to lack of understanding of why the ice has increased since 1979.[28]

What are the assumptions and simplifications in the models? Ideally, equations derived from the underlying science (generally, physics and chemistry) would model all the processes that affect climate. This is not possible, because it would

---

[*]The technical term for this long-range impact is *equilibrium climate sensitivity*. It includes effects of CO_2 doubling that will occur long after the doubling, after the end of this century.
[†]The IPCC considers other factors as well as model results in making this projection.

Science and fiction

Science fiction movies about global warming show the buildings of cities underwater. The entertainment industry exaggerates and dramatizes, of course. But why does an exhibit in a science museum show water up to the middle of the Statue of Liberty (about 200 feet above sea level)? A climate scientist once said: "[T]o capture the public's imagination," "we have to offer up scary scenarios, make simplified dramatic statements, and make little mention of any doubts we may have. . . . Each of us has to decide what the right balance is between being effective and being honest."[30] Although he said he hoped climate scientists could be both effective and honest, there is clearly an ethical problem when we trade honesty for something else. Is it a good idea? A 20-inch rise in sea level would be a very serious problem, but one we can tackle. Tens or hundreds of feet of sea level rise would be an enormous disaster. Exaggeration might lead people to take constructive action. Or exaggeration might lead to overreaction and counterproductive, expensive actions, draining resources from effective approaches. If we hope to solve real potential problems such as flooding in low areas, we must present them accurately.

require too much computation time and because all the underlying science is not known. Simplified equations, called parametrizations, represent many processes; they seem to give realistic results but may not be scientifically accurate. The specific parametrizations vary among the models. The IPCC points out that "every bit of added complexity . . . also introduces new sources of possible error (e.g., via uncertain parameters)."[29]

Model projections based on scenarios, rather than a specific increase in greenhouse gas concentration, include numerous assumptions about technological development, economic development, political control of emissions, population, energy use, and so on, throughout a century.

How well do predictions of the models correspond with actual experience? The IPCC says there is very high confidence that the models reproduce the general features of global average temperature changes, including the warming of the second half of the 20th century.[31] Long term trends are consistent with observed temperatures, and the models predict seasonal variations and other broad-scale phenomena. The general patterns of predictions by different models are similar. For example, they all predict warming, and they all predict that more of the warming would take place near the poles and in winter.

We can now look back and compare temperature projections for the past few decades with actual data. How well have the models done? The 1990 IPCC report indicated that temperature would increase 0.3°C per decade.* Actual temperatures increased little more than half that much per decade from 1990 to 2010.[32] The 2007 report said the models projected warming of 0.2°C per decade

---

*With a range of 0.2–0.5°C.

for the next few decades. However, since the late 1990s, and for at least 15 years, global temperature rose very little (about 0.05–0.07°C per decade, compared to 0.12°C per decade for the period 1951–2012[*]). The IPCC refers to the period of small temperature rise as a "hiatus."[†] Most of the models did not predict that this would happen. How significant is this discrepancy? The IPCC said that some 15-year periods have been below the trend of the models and some above, and that other aspects of the climate over the hiatus period are consistent with continued warming. It suggested several possible causes of the small temperature increase, including natural climate variability and various possible errors in the models. Other scientists have suggested numerous possible explanations, and some revised the analysis of temperature data and concluded that the hiatus did not happen. It will take more years to fully understand the hiatus and its implications.[33]

What about the near future? The IPCC says the models project that, with more than 50% likelihood, the average temperature during the period 2016–2035 will be 1°C higher than the average for the period 1850–1900 and very unlikely that it will be more than 1.5°C above the 1850–1900 period. We will be able to evaluate the accuracy of these projections within the next two decades.

7.2   Neo-Luddite Views of Computers, Technology, and Quality of Life

The microchip is. . . made of silicon, or sand—a natural resource that is in great abundance and has virtually no monetary value. Yet the combination of a few grains of this sand and the infinite inventiveness of the human mind has led to the creation of a machine that will both create trillions of dollars of added wealth for the inhabitants of the earth in the next century and will do so with incomprehensibly vast savings in physical labor and natural resources.

—Stephen Moore[34]

Quite apart from the environmental and medical evils associated with them being produced and used, there are two moral judgments against computers. One is that computerization enables the large forces of our civilization to operate more swiftly and efficiently in their pernicious goals of making money and producing things. . . . And secondly, in the course of using these, these forces are destroying nature with more speed and efficiency than ever before.

—Kirkpatrick Sale[35]

---

[*]With error ranges given in the reports, as usual with all these figures. Some figures vary depending on the exact start and end dates reported.

[†]Many of the years since 2000 were the hottest on record. This is not inconsistent with the hiatus: The temperature rise from the 1970s through the 1990s brought temperatures to the highest levels since the 19th century; thus any rise could set a record.

7.2.1 CRITICISMS OF COMPUTING TECHNOLOGIES

The quotations above, both from 1995, illustrate the extreme divergence of views about the anticipated value of computer technology. Evaluations cover the spectrum from "miracle" to "catastrophe." Although most of this book discusses problems that arise with the use of computers, the Internet, and other digital technologies, the implicit (and sometimes explicit) view is that these technologies are a positive development bringing us many benefits. The potential for loss of freedom and privacy via government surveillance and the building of consumer dossiers is a serious danger. Computer crime is expensive, and changes in employment are disruptive. Our discussion of system failures in the next chapter warns us that some potential applications can have horrifying risks. We might urgently try to prevent implementation of some applications and urgently advocate for increased protection from risks, yet not consider the threats and risks as reasons for condemning the technology as a whole. For the most part, we have looked at new risks and negative side effects as problems that occur in the natural process of change, either problems we need to solve or the price we pay for the benefits, part of a trade-off. Many people with quite different political views share this attitude, although they disagree about the significance of specific computer-related problems and about exactly how to solve them.

On the other hand, there are people who utterly reject the view that computing technology is a positive development with many important benefits. They see the benefits as few and overwhelmingly outweighed by the damage done. Neil Postman says that voting, shopping, banking, and getting information online while at home is a "catastrophe." There are fewer opportunities for people to be "co-present," resulting in isolation from neighbors. Richard Sclove and Jeffrey Scheuer argue that electronic communication will erode family and community life to the point that people will mourn the loss of depth and meaning in their lives.[36] A reviewer of this book objected to the "gift of fire" analogy that suggests computers can be very useful and also very dangerous; he thought "Pandora's box" was more appropriate. Pandora's box held "all the ills of mankind." Kirkpatrick Sale, author of *Rebels Against the Future*, used to demonstrate his opinion of computers by smashing one with a sledgehammer at public appearances.

In England in 1811–1812, people burned factories and mills in efforts to stop the technologies and social changes that were eliminating their jobs. Many were weavers who had worked at home on small machines. They were called Luddites.[*] For 200 years, the memory of the violent Luddite uprising has endured as the most dramatic symbol of opposition to the Industrial Revolution. The term "Luddite" has long been a derisive description for people who oppose technological progress. More recently, critics of technology have adopted it as an honorable term. Kirkpatrick Sale and many others who share his viewpoint call themselves neo-Luddites, or simply Luddites.

---

[*]The name Luddite comes from General Ned Ludd, the fictitious, symbolic leader of the movement.

What do neo-Luddites find so reprehensible about computers and digital technology? Some of their criticisms are problems that also trouble people whose view of computing technology is generally positive, problems we discussed in earlier chapters. One of the differentiating characteristics of the neo-Luddites is that they focus on these problems, seeing no solutions or trade-offs, and conclude that computers are a terribly bad development for humankind. Among their specific criticisms are the following:

- Computers cause massive unemployment and de-skilling of jobs. "Sweatshop labor is involved in their manufacture."[37]

- Computers "manufacture needs"; that is, we use them just because they are there, not because they satisfy real needs.

- Computers cause social inequity.

- Computers cause social disintegration; they are dehumanizing. They weaken communities and lead to isolation of people from each other.

- Computers separate humans from nature and destroy the environment.

- Computers benefit big business and big government most.

- Use of computers in schools thwarts development of social skills, human values, and intellectual skills in children. They create an "ominous uniformity of knowledge" consistent with corporate values.[38]

- Computers do little or nothing to solve real human problems. For example, Neil Postman, in response to claims of the benefits of access to information, argues that "if families break up, children are mistreated, crime terrorizes a city, education is impotent, it does not happen because of inadequate information."[39]

Some of these criticisms might seem unfair. The conditions in computer factories hardly compare to conditions in the sweatshop factories of the early Industrial Revolution. In Chapter 6, we saw that computers eliminate some jobs, and that the pace of computerization causes disruptions, but the case that computers, and technology in general, cause massive unemployment is not convincing. Blaming computers for social inequity in the world ignores thousands of years of history. Postman is right that inadequate information is not the source of most social problems. A computer in the classroom does not replace good parents in the home. But should this be a criticism of computers and information systems? Access to information and communication can assist in solving problems and is not likely to hurt. The main problem for ordinary people, Postman says, is how to find meaning in life. We need answers to questions like "Why are we here?" and "How are we supposed to behave?"[40] Is it a valid criticism of computing technology that it does not solve fundamental social and philosophical problems that have engaged us for thousands of years?

To neo-Luddites, the view that computers are fundamentally malevolent is part of a wider view that almost all of technology is malevolent. To the modern-day

Luddites, computer technology is just the latest, but in many ways the worst, stage in the decline of what was good in human society. Computers are worse than earlier technologies because of their enormous speed and flexibility. Computers increase the negative trends that technology causes. Thus, if one points out that a particular problem blamed on computers already existed because of an earlier technology, Luddites consider the distinction to be a minor one.

The depth of the antipathy to technology in the Luddite view is perhaps made clearer by attitudes toward common devices most of us use daily. For example, Sale has said, "I find talking on the phone a physical pain, as well as a mental anguish." Sven Birkerts, another critic of computers, says that if he lived in 1900, he would probably have opposed the telephone.* Speaking of the invention of the printing press, Sale laments that "literacy . . . destroys orality." He regards not only computers but civilization as a catastrophe. Some of us see modern medicine as a life-saving and life-enhancing boon to humanity; some Luddites point out that it gave us the population explosion and extended senility.[41]

Having read and listened to the arguments of technology enthusiasts and technology critics, we find it striking that different people look at the same history, the same society, the same products and services, the same jobs—and come to diametrically opposed conclusions about what they see. There is a fundamental difference between the world views of supporters and opponents of technology. It is more than the difference between seeing a glass as half full or half empty. It seems to be one of drastically differing views about what should be in the glass and whether it is filling or draining. Supporters of technology see an upward trend in quality of life, beginning with people living at the mercy of nature with an empty glass that technology has been gradually filling. Neo-Luddites view the glass as originally full when people lived in small communities with little impact on nature; they see technology as draining the glass.

The neo-Luddite perspective is associated with a particular view of an appropriate way of life for human beings. For example, Sale's first point, in the quotation at the beginning of this section, makes the moral judgment that making money and producing things is pernicious. His introductory remark and his second point barely hint at the unusually high valuation he places on not disturbing nature (unusually high even in the contemporary context, where there is much awareness of the importance of protecting the environment). We explore these views further.

7.2.2 VIEWS OF ECONOMICS, NATURE, AND HUMAN NEEDS

Luddites generally have a negative view of business, markets, consumer products, factories, and modern forms of work. They see the profit-seeking goals of

---

*Critics of telephones complained that they replaced true human interaction with disembodied, remote voices. Telephones actually expanded and deepened social relationships for isolated people—for example, women (farm wives, in particular) and the elderly.[42]

businesses as in fundamental conflict with the well-being of workers and the natural environment. They see work in factories, large offices, and business in general as dehumanizing, dreary, and bad for the health of the workers. Hence, for example, the Luddite criticisms of the clock. Neil Postman describes the invention of the clock as "the technology of greatest use to men who wished to devote themselves to the accumulation of money."[43]

Choice of words, making subtle differences in a statement, sometimes illustrates the difference in perspective between Luddites and non-Luddites. What is the purpose of technology? To the Luddites, it is to eliminate jobs to reduce the costs of production. To proponents of technology, it is to reduce the resources needed to produce goods and services. The two statements say nearly the same thing, but the first suggests massive unemployment, profits for capitalists, and a poorer life for most workers. The second suggests improvements in wealth and the standard of living.

The Luddite view combines a negative attitude toward business with a high estimation of the power of corporations to manipulate and control workers and consumers. For example, Richard Sclove describes telecommuting as being "imposed by business." (Interestingly, one of the common criticisms of the Industrial Revolution was that working in factories instead of at home weakened families and local community.)

Luddites make particularly strong criticisms of automobiles, of cities, and of most technologies involved in communications and transportation. Thus, it is worth noting that most of us get both personal and social benefits from them. Cities are centers of culture, wealth production, education, and job opportunities.[44] Modern transportation and communication reduce the price of products and increase their variety and availability. For example, we can look up menus and movie schedules on our smartphone to find what we want and we can shop worldwide on the Web. We can eat fresh fruits and vegetables all year and commute a long distance to take a better job without having to sell our house and move, or we can work from home. If we move to a new city for college or a job, modern conveniences such as airplanes, telephones, and the Internet make the separations less unpleasant. We can visit more often in person and share greetings and activities with friends and family members via social media. Luddites and other critics of technology do not value these advantages highly. In their point of view, the advantages are merely ameliorating other problems technology causes. For example, Postman quotes Sigmund Freud's comment, "If there had been no railway to conquer distances, my child would never have left his native town and I should need no telephone to hear his voice."[45]

Does the technology create the need for itself?

Luddites argue that technology causes production of things we do not need. Sale argued that small, portable computers do not "meet any known or expressed need," but companies produce them simply because miniaturization of computing components made it possible. People have bought many billions of laptops, tablet computers, and mobile phones. While the number of possible uses is phenomenal, does a mobile device meet a *need*? It depends on what we mean by "need." Do we need to do homework in the backyard or listen to music on a smartphone? Does an architect or contractor need a laptop at a construction site? Those who emphasize the value of individual action and choices argue that needs are relative to goals, and goals are held by individuals. Thus, should we ask whether "we," as a society, need a particular device? Or should this be an individual decision with different responses? The Luddites, who believe that advertising, work pressure, or other external forces manipulate buyers, reject an individual-oriented view.

Environmental and anti-technology groups use computers and the Web. The editor of *Wild Earth*, who considers himself a neo-Luddite, said he "inclines toward the view that technology is inherently evil," but he "disseminates this view via E-mail, computer, and laser printer."[46] An interviewer reported that, after a long career attacking computers, Kirkpatrick Sale was using a laptop. The question is: Are Sale and the editor of *Wild Earth* using the technology because of an artificial need or because it is useful and helpful to them? Sale sees the use of computers as an uncomfortable compromise. The use of computers, he says, insidiously embeds into the user the values and thought processes of the society that makes the technology.[47]

As the Internet of Things expands to umbrellas and tampons, we might want to reconsider Sale's point of view and ask: Do we really need everything connected to the Internet? Technology columnist Joanna Stern poked fun at this highly connected life by calling the IoT the "Internet of Every Single Thing."[48] Do we need a refrigerator that notifies us that we are low on eggs, or takes a photo of the inside of the fridge whenever we close the door, so we can check our current inventory while at the grocery store? Why not just make a grocery list as we did in the past? Do we need trash cans and water bottles connected to the Internet? The answer to some of these questions is no; some products will disappear because consumers will not buy them. But when we consider all the unanticipated uses of past innovations, can we be sure we or anyone can determine in advance which new gadgets will be useful and which will not? Some items on the IoT will save lives. For many, the main benefit will be convenience. Some that we might at first laugh at will be very helpful to special populations. Can you think of examples?

The argument that businesses or technologies manipulate people to buy things they do not really want, like the argument that use of computers has an insidiously corrupting effect on computer users, displays a low view of the judgment and autonomy of ordinary people. It is one thing to differ with another person's values and choices. It is another to conclude that, because of the difference, the other person is weak and incapable of making his or her own decisions. The Luddite view of the appropriate way of life puts little value on modern comforts and conveniences or on the availability of a large variety of goods and services. Perhaps most people value these things more highly than the Luddites do. To get a clearer understanding of the Luddite view of a proper lifestyle, we consider some of their comments on the relationship of humans and nature.

Walmart and e-commerce versus downtown and community

Does electronic commerce force changes on communities that no one wants? Richard Sclove and Jeffrey Scheuer think so.[49] They use the analogy of a Walmart store draining business from downtown shops, resulting in the decline of the downtown community, a "result that no consumers wanted or intended." They generalize from the Walmart scenario to cyberspace. As we conduct more economic transactions electronically, we lose more local stores, local professional and social services, and convivial public spaces like the downtowns of small towns. Consumers are "compelled" to use electronic services, "like it or not." Other strong critics of technology share the underlying point of view of Sclove and Scheuer, so it is worth examining their argument.

The Walmart analogy is a good one; it is useful for illustrating and clarifying some issues about the impact of e-commerce on communities. Suppose, say Sclove and Scheuer, that a new Walmart store has opened just outside of town and about half the town residents begin to do about a third of their shopping there, while the others continue to do all their shopping downtown. Everyone shops downtown, and everyone wants the downtown stores to remain. But downtown stores have lost about 16.5% of their sales, and many will not survive. Sclove and Scheuer describe this as an "involuntary transformation" that no consumer wanted or intended. It occurs, they say, because of a "perverse market dynamic." The changes, however, are not involuntary or perverse. The core of the problem with Sclove's and Scheuer's interpretation is their failure to make two important distinctions: the distinction between wanting something and the willingness to pay for

it, and the distinction between something being coerced or involuntary, on the one hand, and being unwanted, unintended, or unexpected on the other.

Consider a simpler situation for a moment. Suppose, we poll the adult residents of a small town with a population of, say, 3000 and ask if they would like to have a fine French restaurant in town. Almost everyone says yes. Will a French restaurant open in the town? Probably not. Almost everyone wants it, yet there is not enough potential business for it to survive. There is a market dynamic at work, but it is not perverse. The fact that consumers want a particular service, store, or product is irrelevant if not enough people are willing to pay the prices that make the business viable. In Sclove's and Scheuer's Walmart scenario, the downtown stores could stay in business if the people were willing to pay higher prices to make up for the 16.5% of revenue lost to Walmart. But we know that if the stores raise prices, they will almost certainly lose even more customers. The town residents are not willing to pay what it costs to keep the downtown stores in business. You might object: The townspeople did not have to pay the higher prices before. Why now? Because now the people who shop at Walmart—or online—*have another choice.* Whatever price advantage or convenience lured them, they were not getting that benefit before. Again, a market dynamic is at work, but not a perverse one: competition.

The second issue about the Walmart/ e-commerce scenario is whether the change is an "involuntary" transformation. Sclove and Scheuer say that, as local businesses decline, people will be compelled to use electronic services, like it or not. Is this accurate? No more so than Walmart

(continued)

shoppers or cyberspace enthusiasts were compelled to shop downtown (or from other offline stores), like it or not, before they had the new option. The new status quo is no more involuntary than the previous one. Although no one wants to see the downtown decline, the actions that could lead to that result are all voluntary. When a new store opens (online or offline), no one is forced to shop there. The impact on the downtown stores might not have been obvious to all the townspeople at the beginning (although now it is common enough that they might anticipate it), but an unexpected or unintended result is not the same as a coerced result. In a free society, individuals make millions of decisions based on their

knowledge and preferences. This decentralized, individualized decision making produces a constantly changing pattern of stores, services, and investments (not to mention social and cultural patterns). No one can predict exactly what the result will be, but (apart from government subsidies, prohibitions, and regulations) the actions of the consumers and merchants are voluntary. No one person can expect to have exactly the mix of shopping options (or other community characteristics) that he or she wants. If the result flows from the myriad decisions that consumers and producers make, it is not coerced. It is the process, not the result, that tells us whether an outside force is coercing people.

Nature and human lifestyles

Luddites argue that technology has made no improvement in life, or at best improvements of little importance. Sale's list of benefits includes speed, ease, and mass access—all of which he disdains. Sale says that although individuals might feel their lives are better because of computers, the perceived benefits are "industrial virtues that may not be virtues in another morality." He defines moral judgment as "the capacity to decide that a thing is right when it enhances the integrity, stability, and beauty of nature and is wrong when it does otherwise."[50] Jerry Mander, founder of the Center for Deep Ecology and author of books critical of technology and globalization, points out that thousands of generations of humans got along without computers, suggesting that we could do just fine without them too. While some people evaluate trade-offs between negative side effects of pesticides and the benefits of reducing diseases or protecting food crops, Mander's objections to technology lead him to the conclusion that there can be no "good" pesticide. While many people work on technological, legal, and educational approaches to reducing the gasoline usage of automobiles, Mander says there can be no "good" automobile.[51]

What are the underlying premises behind these comments by Sale and Mander? We consider Sale's comment on moral judgment first. Many debates about the environment set up a humans-versus-nature dichotomy.[52] This is not the true conflict. Nature, biodiversity, forests, a hospitable climate, clean air and water, open space away from cities—these are all important and valuable to humans. But so are life-saving medical techniques and shelter from the rain, cold, and heat. Conflicts about the environment are not conflicts between humans and nature. They are conflicts between people with different views about how to meet human needs.

In contrast to Sale's statement, moral judgment, to many people, and for many centuries, has meant the capacity to choose that which enhances human life, reduces misery, and increases freedom and happiness. Sale's comment chooses nature, not humanity, as the primary standard of moral value.

Whether an automobile or electronic device is "good," by a human-centered standard, depends on whether it meets our needs, how well it does so, at what cost (to the environment and society, as well as to our bank account), and how well it compares to alternatives. Critics of modern technologies point out their weaknesses but often ignore the weaknesses of alternatives—for example, the millions of acres once needed to grow feed for horses and the hundreds of tons of horse manure dropped on the streets of cities each day, a century ago.[53] Candles, gas lamps, and kerosene lamps filled homes with fumes and soot. Do we need electricity? Do we need hot water on tap, movies, and symphony orchestras? Or do we need nothing more than food and shelter? Do we need an average life expectancy of more than 25 years? Do we want to merely exist—do we *need* even that? Or do we want long, happy, comfortable lives filled with time for love, interesting activities, and an opportunity to use our marvelously inventive brains?

Accomplishments of technology

It is easy to miss the extreme changes in quality of life that have taken place over the past few centuries. We mention here a scattering of examples.

Technology and the Industrial Revolution have had a dramatic impact on life expectancy. A study in 1662 estimated that only 25% of people in London lived to age 26. Records from 18th-century French villages showed that the median age of death was lower than the median age of marriage. Until recent generations, parents had to endure the deaths of several of their children. Starvation was common. In the United States, life expectancy at birth increased from 47.3 years in 1900 to 79 in 2016. Worldwide average life expectancy increased from approximately 30 in 1900 to approximately 71.1 in 2015. Science and technology (along with other factors such as education and increased wealth) reduced or almost eliminated typhoid, smallpox, dysentery, plagues, and malaria in most of the world. Deaths at work, during travel, and by accidents, declined dramatically.[54]

In the early 2000s, Americans spent less than 10% of family income on food, compared to approximately 47% in 1901. Agronomist Norman Borlaug, who won a Nobel Peace Prize for his work in improving agricultural productivity, reported that when new forms of wheat and crop management were introduced in India, yields rose from 12.3 million tons in 1965 to 73.5 million tons in 1999. In about the same timeframe, U.S. production of its 17 most important crops increased from 252 million tons to 596 million tons, but used 25 million fewer acres. Nicholas Eberstadt, an expert on population, reported that food supplies and gross domestic product have been growing faster than population for decades in most areas of the world, in both developing and developed countries.[55]

Environmental impacts of computing technology

We considered including a section in this book on environmental impacts of computers, mobile devices, and the Internet. While reviewing data, we concluded that attempts to quantify environmental benefits and costs would be subject to the same weaknesses and criticisms of models that we discussed in Section 7.1.2. It is extremely difficult to measure impacts and to determine how to compare to impacts of technologies and activities that computing technology replaces. However, we can make some observations.

Production of computers is energy intensive and uses hazardous materials. Because of these materials, disposal of electronic devices is an issue, as it is for fluorescent light bulbs. Running and cooling the millions of servers on the Internet in the United States accounts for about 2% of electric power usage, more than the usage of the U.S. auto industry and less than the usage of the chemical industry.[56] There are estimates that production of computers uses roughly twice as much energy as operating them though this disparity is decreasing as major manufacturers of computers, smartphones, and other digital devices move to make their manufacturing more energy efficient.

On the other hand, digitally controlled machinery uses less power than older electromechanical controls. Digital sensors and controls for regulating lighting, heating, air conditioning, and farm irrigation (among many other examples) save resources by determining just what is needed and thus reduce waste. Microprocessors control hybrid cars, reducing gasoline use. Telecommuting, e-commerce, and online information sources significantly reduce the need for driving and flying and thus, the need for fuel. One fiber-optic cable, with about 150 pounds of silica, carries more messages than a ton of copper wire.[57]

Digital storage of documents, data, photos, and so on reduces the need for paper and the amount of trash produced. Specific examples suggest the reductions: A large insurance company reduced its use of paper by 100 million pages in a nine-month period by storing its manuals digitally instead of printing them. A computerized system for recording insurance claims replaced more than 30 million index cards. We text and send email instead of sending letters and cards on paper. Electronic payments eliminate paper bills and checks. We read books, newspapers, magazines, and so on, on tablets, e-readers, and smartphones, reducing paper use. The decline in business for the U.S. Postal Service and printed newspapers, while population and economic activity grow, are indications of these reductions. But do we actually use less paper than we did before? We could not find clear data for total paper use. However, between 2001 and 2011, annual consumption of newsprint for daily newspapers in the United States dropped by an estimated 61%, and the number of pieces of first class mail dropped by about 24%.[58]

For a long time, companies that sell furniture and appliances built rooms (e.g., kitchens) to photograph for their catalogs, and then tore them down and discarded much of the material. IKEA now uses 3D graphics programs to create some of its room images for catalogs, with obvious savings of natural resources (as well as time and money).

We take, post, and share far more photos (billions per month) than we did when we made prints and slides. This is an example of a phenomenon that occurs in many fields: As a product or service becomes more efficient and cheaper, we use more of it. We see the same effect with medical technology, education, and other services that bring us benefits.

The benefits of telecommunications and information technology are enormous in developing countries. A report of a United Nations Conference on Trade and Development, for example, observes that developing economies can make productivity gains worth billions of dollars by encouraging the growth of electronic commerce. The report said that "it is because the internet revolution is relevant not just to the high-tech, information-intensive sectors but also to the whole organisation of economic life that . . . developing countries stand a better chance of sharing in its benefits earlier than in previous technological revolutions."[59]

Technology is certainly not the only factor in improving quality of life. Progress against disease, discomfort, and early death depends on the stability, freedom, and flexibility of political and economic systems as well. Measuring quality of life is subjective, and some find other measures more important than the few we cited above. But, for many people, these data suggest that technology has contributed much to human well-being.

7.3 Digital Divides

Despite the views of Neo-Luddites, most people continue to expand their use of computing technology and the Internet. The term *digital divide* refers to the fact that some groups of people regularly use the various forms of modern information technology, while others do not and cannot. In the 1990s, the discussion about the digital divide focused on gaps in access to computers and the Internet for various groups within the United States and other developed countries. As Internet access and mobile phones spread, focus shifted to the rest of the world. The global digital divide shrank faster than many long-standing global divides in, for example, access to fresh water and toilets, but many very difficult problems still thwart access to computer and Internet technology in poor and developing countries. In this section, we review trends in access in the United States, and then look at problems of access in other parts of the world.

In most of this book, we examine problems that digital technologies cause. Thus, it is interesting to observe that this section looks at problems related to the lack of the technology; the implicit assumption is that digital technology is highly desirable for people all over the world. The question is how to get it to them.

7.3.1 TRENDS IN ACCESS IN THE UNITED STATES

When personal computers and later the Internet were first available to the public in the United States, a small minority enjoyed them. In 1990, personal computers cost nearly 10% of the average U.S. household income. We connected to the Internet using slow, noisy dial-up modems. Frequent Internet use required a second phone line since we could not make or receive phone calls while connected to the Internet. There were few applications useful to most people, and users needed technical skills. Many people could not afford computers and Internet access, and many did not see much point in having them.

As the value of computers and Internet access became clearer, people became concerned about the gaps in ownership and access. In 1990, only 22% of households in the United States owned a computer. Access in rural and remote regions lagged access in cities. Black and Hispanic households were about half as likely as the general population to own a computer. Poor children had little access to computers both in schools and at home. Only 10% of Internet users in the early 1990s were women, and people over 65 rarely used computers.[60]

Software innovations, such as point-and-click graphical user interfaces, Web browsers, and search engines, made computer use simpler for ordinary people. With lower prices, more useful applications, and easier use, ownership and access spread. By 1997, the gender gap had vanished. By 2000, most public libraries provided free Internet access for the public and 98% of U.S. high schools had Internet access—though the quality of that access still varies greatly. In 2001, 84% of homes with children in middle and high school had a computer and Internet access. By the early 2000s, the gaps among Hispanic, black, and white people almost completely disappeared among those with the same education levels. Businesses, community organizations, foundations, and government programs all played roles. Federal and local governments spent billions of dollars on technology for communities and schools. Companies such as Apple, Microsoft, and IBM contributed hundreds of millions of dollars in equipment and training programs.[61]

The price of computing power continued to drop, and the trend in ease of use continued with the development of touch interfaces for tablets and mobile phones. By 2015, 92% of adults in the United States owned a mobile phone and 67% had a smartphone.[62]

As computers, phones, and Internet access spread, the focus changed to disparity in quality of access, for example, access to a broadband, or high speed, Internet connection. In 2003, fewer than 20% of all U.S. households had what the government then defined as broadband: four megabits per second (Mbps) download speed. But as broadband spread and improved, the U.S. Federal Communications Commission (FCC) changed the definition from four Mbps to 25 Mbps.[*] As of 2016, 80% of U.S. households met the new higher standard, while 6.3% still did not have four Mbps service.[63] Slow or no access makes it more difficult to find employment opportunities, access news and information, attend online courses, and make use of online health information.

Several million households with school-age children still do not have Internet access at home. The lack of Internet connections makes it difficult for children to complete some school assignments and use online resources. As an example of one program to address this problem and of the care required in such programs, Sprint offered free data connections to low-income students, and then discovered that the

---

[*]The definition of broadband includes a minimum upload speed also; the FCC raised it from one Mbps to three Mbps.

program was not fully successful because the students lacked devices on which to use the data. Sprint then began a program to provide one million devices (phones, laptops, and tablets) *and* free data to low-income high school students.

While broadband spread dramatically in 13 years, from fewer than 20% of households having four Mbps to 80% of households having more than 25 Mbps, we need to remain aware of those in low-income households who lack the devices and connections that could help improve their lives.

7.3.2   Reaching the Next Billion Users[*]

Almost three and a half billion people worldwide can access the Internet from their homes, more than 10 times as many as in the late 1990s[64]—but about the same number of people cannot. Only a decade ago, most people in the world had never made a telephone call. There are now roughly as many mobile phone subscriptions as people in the world (see Figure 7.5). That does not mean everyone has one: In developed countries, many individuals and businesses have multiple subscriptions, while large numbers of people, especially in poor countries, do not have phones. In many parts of the world, if you give someone a free smartphone, it would be useless—there is no place to charge it.

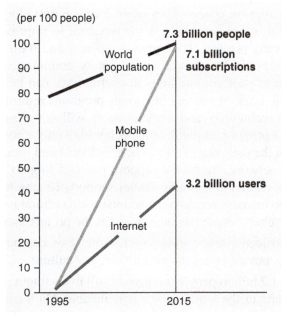

Figure 7.5 Progress in Internet and mobile phone access.[65]

---

[*]When the World Wide Web first reached a billion people around the world, roughly a decade ago, some nonprofit organizations and companies began using the phrase "the next billion users" for the people in developing countries whom they hoped would be online in the near future.

From one perspective, the spread of mobile phones and Internet access is an extraordinary accomplishment in a very short time. From another perspective, it means a large part of the world's population is missing out on technologies that could provide them with access to information, education, and healthcare—important services that can help lift individuals and communities out of extreme poverty. Here, we consider problems that thwart the spread of computer and Internet technology in poor and developing countries, some projects that attempt to help, and some reasons why such projects sometimes fail.

First, we give a little more data to provide some context. In the developing world, very approximately,[*] 50% of the population uses the Internet, compared with 87% in the most economically advanced countries. In dozens of the poorest countries, the rate is less than 10%. Broadband Internet is becoming more widely available and affordable, but is still out of reach in many developing countries. As in the early Internet days in the United States, some communities have Internet cafes where people can use computers and access the Internet, but often the equipment is old and shares a single low-speed connection. While many people around the world have a mobile phone, in poor countries few have smartphones.[66]

Lack of access to the Internet in much of the world has many of the same causes as lack of health care and education: poverty, isolation, poor economies, and politics. Many companies and organizations in the developed world have embarked on projects to improve access. They often focus on providing computers and Internet access to schools where there is the potential to improve education—a key factor in reducing poverty. They give computers and train teachers to use technology in classrooms. But providing computers, communication, and Internet access to remote and poor communities in useful ways can be very difficult, and many projects fail. Lack of success in various programs reinforces an important lesson: Giving out technology and walking away will not close the digital divide. The success of a program implementing technology into school curricula, for example, depends on the presence of supporting technical and social infrastructures such as electricity, networks, technical support, parental support, teacher attitudes toward technology, and administrative school support. To gain local community support, programs to increase access must address local cultural issues and work with community members whose business or status the project may impact negatively.

We consider a few hurdles to the spread of computer and communications technology: power, connectivity, climate, and culture.

About 1.2 billion people worldwide still live without access to electricity,[67] and in many parts of the world power is unreliable. On a game day, the Dallas Cowboys stadium draws more than three times the amount of power that the country of Liberia can supply to its power grid.[68] Mobile phone users in many regions must travel to areas that have power and then pay to charge their phones. Voltage spikes,

---

[*]The numbers change quickly, and various studies count differently; use of the Internet typically means access to the Net from home, but some figures include owning a smartphone and some do not.

brownouts, and outages damage computer equipment. Local power generation, such as from a gasoline generator or solar cells, can be expensive to install or expensive to maintain and operate. A few projects have tried innovative approaches such as human-powered bicycle generators that operate equipment or charge batteries.

Cellphone and Internet connection in many areas is available sometimes but is unreliable or slow. In response, Google developed a version of its YouTube app to work on slow networks. Clearly, more apps designed for low data transmission would be helpful. To improve access to the Web, several companies are experimenting with projects such as huge drones or satellites to provide network nodes over regions with no or poor Internet connectivity. The United Nations reports that more than 65 million people are displaced from their homes because of war or famine.[69] Communication can be invaluable to these people, but it is difficult to provide reliable power and Internet connection in refugee camps.

The nonprofit organization One Laptop per Child (OLPC) recognized a problem often overlooked: extreme climates. OLPC developed a laptop computer specially designed for elementary school children in developing countries. It works in extreme heat or cold, extremes of humidity, and dusty or rainy environments, and the power requirements are very low, but the price (approximately $200) is too high for many poor countries.[70]

Culture and social attitudes can slow the spread of technology. Women generally report that a mobile phone gives them independence, access to jobs, and access to the political system, but large gender gaps in ownership of mobile phones exist in Africa, the Middle East, and south Asia. In India, for example, 28% of women own mobile phones (see Figure 7.6) while 43% of men do. In India, Bangladesh, and Pakistan, roughly three times as many men as women use Facebook.

Jake Lyell/Alamy Stock Photo

Figure 7.6 Indian women share a mobile phone.

In some communities, men do not allow their wives and daughters to own phones. Large companies and foundations, including the Gates Foundation, are working to reduce the gender gap. Google and Tata Trusts send thousands of trained women, riding on bicycles, to rural villages in India to teach women how to use the Web.[71]

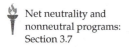

Net neutrality and nonneutral programs: Section 3.7

Political and social views affect acceptance; for example, some countries welcome programs that provide free partial or limited access to the Internet for people who cannot afford access, while others that place high value on net neutrality reject these programs.

How important are computers and Internet access in poor countries? Some governments and local officials criticize programs that promote acquisition of computer equipment because, they argue, basic health care for children and clean water are higher priorities. On the other hand, communication and access to information can contribute to solutions for these problems. In many developing countries, farmers and fishers use the Internet or their mobile phones to find nearby villages where they get a better price for their crops or catch (see Figure 7.7). As the technology spreads,

Jake Lyell/Alamy Stock Photo

FIGURE 7.7 A farmer compares prices for her crop in various markets in Burkina Faso.

food production and distribution, and thus health and economic well-being improve. In wealthier countries, although we enjoy many life-saving and life-enhancing benefits of digital technologies, most people use our tech tools far more for entertainment and convenience than for basic needs. As Internet access continues to spread to the billions of people without it, the impact can be far greater because of the potential to improve the lives of people who are devastatingly poor.

7.4 Control of Our Devices and Data

In Chapters 4 and 5, we saw that Apple tries to control which apps people can install on their iPhones and that some users found ways to deactivate the controls, but doing so can increase the risk of a hacking attack. Here, we look at situations in which the companies that provide devices, software, or data can reach into our devices and delete or modify our stuff. Their intervention may be helpful and may protect us, or it may serve needs of the company, or both. In any case, it is an example of our loss of control of our devices and data. For the situations we consider, think about the balance between benefits and disadvantages.

7.4.1 REMOTE DELETION OF SOFTWARE AND DATA

Soon after Amazon began selling electronic books for its Kindle ebook readers, the company discovered a publisher was selling books in Amazon's online store that the publisher did not have legal rights to sell in the United States. Amazon deleted the books from its store and from the Kindles of people who had bought them; it refunded customer payments. A reasonable and appropriate response? Many customers and media observers did not think so. Customers were outraged that Amazon remotely deleted books from their Kindles. People were startled to learn that Amazon *could* do so.* The response was so strong that Amazon announced that it would not remove books from customer Kindles again. Few realized at that time that Apple's iPhones already had a way for Apple to remotely delete apps from phones. When a software developer discovered malicious code in an app for Android phones, Google quickly removed the app from its store and from more than 250,000 phones. Although this was a good example of the purpose of remote deletion and a beneficial use, the fact that Google could do so disturbed people.

Perhaps this extended reach should not have been a surprise, since in many businesses the IT department has access to all desktop computers and can install— or delete—software. Software on personal devices communicates with businesses and organizations regularly, without our direct command, to check for updates of software, news, and our friends' activities. When we enable updates of software, a company remotely deletes old versions.

---

*Ironically, one of the books Amazon removed was George Orwell's *1984*—a novel about a totalitarian government that regularly sent documents down a "memory hole" to destroy them.

A main purpose of remote deletion by companies such as Google and Apple is security—to remove illegal or malicious software that the company discovers in an app after users have downloaded it. Indeed, companies that provide popular app stores see it as a serious responsibility to protect users from malicious apps. Millions of phones running a malicious app could have a devastating impact on our entire communications network. Some companies tell us about their removal capability in their terms of use agreements, but as we have noted before, such agreements can run to thousands of words and have vague, general statements and few people read them.

What are some potential uses and risks of remote deletion? Malicious hackers might find a way to use the delete mechanism for pranks or ransom. For more than 2000 years, governments and religious and social organizations have burned books that displeased them. What pressures might governments put on companies to delete material they disapprove of? Will the impact of electronic deletion be more devastating than destruction of scrolls, ancient books, and printed material?

7.4.2 Automatic Software Upgrades

We use Microsoft's upgrade from Windows 7 to Windows 10 to illustrate general problems and questions about automatic software upgrades. In 2016, users of Microsoft Windows 7 found their computers automatically and unexpectedly upgrading to Windows 10. The long upgrade time inconvenienced many who were in the middle of an important project while others had more serious problems. Some users had selected to receive operating system updates but did not expect that the entire operating system would be upgraded to a newer version. Microsoft said Windows 10 installed only if the user gave explicit permission. Some users may have allowed the upgrade without realizing they did, but some system administrators said they saw the upgrade performed on test systems where they had not given explicit permission.

Why would an operating system vendor push strongly to upgrade older systems? In this case, as in others, the newer operating system provides many improved security features and better compatibility across various hardware platforms the company supports (for example, PCs, Xbox, and Surface). It is easier for a company to provide user support when all users are on the same version of an operating system. Why would some users not want the upgrade? Some people use software that may be incompatible with the new system, some simply prefer the older user interface, and some do not want an interruption—with potential for unknown problems—in the middle of a large project. As we mentioned in Chapter 5, automatic software updates can create headaches for IT staff who have not had the opportunity to test the update for compatibility and security.

Software updates for cars, medical devices, and so forth can have serious impacts on safety. You would not want your self-driving car to pause on a highway while an update installs. One maker of semi-autonomous cars automatically downloads software updates to the vehicles, informs the owner, and lets the owner schedule installation, say, at night. If the owner does not install the update, he or she could be putting others at unnecessary risk. How should the company handle that?

Where should control of updates lie? Do software vendors do a good enough job of telling users the category of update (security patch, new features, etc.—or a whole new operating system)? How should update policies vary with the type of device—phone, tablet, television, automobile, radiation treatment machine?

7.5 Making Decisions About Technology

No one voted for this technology or any of the various machines and processes that make it up.

—Kirkpatrick Sale[72]

7.5.1 QUESTIONS

We saw in Section 7.2 that the determination of what are true needs depends on our choice of values. Throughout this book, we saw controversies about specific products, services, and applications of computer technology (for example, personalized advertising, anonymous Web surfing, and face recognition systems). How should we make decisions about the basic question of whether to use a whole technology, or major segments of it, at all? Who would make such decisions?

Most people in science, engineering, and business accept, almost without question, the view that people can choose to use a technology for good or ill. Some critics of technology disagree. They argue that technologies are not "neutral." Neil Postman says, "Once a technology is admitted [to our culture], it plays out its hand; it does what it is designed to do."[73] This view sees the technologies themselves as being in control.

In the view of some critics of computing technology, big corporations and governments make decisions about uses of the technology without sufficient input or control from ordinary people. Kirkpatrick Sale's lament at the beginning of this section expresses this view: There was never a vote on whether we should have computers, the Internet, mobile phones, or toothbrushes that tell us how long to brush. Some people argue that we should not use a new technology at all until we have studied it, figured out its consequences, and made a determination that the consequences are acceptable. The idea is that if the technology does not meet certain criteria, we would not permit its development and use.

This view leads to a few basic questions. Can a society choose to have certain specific desirable modern inventions while prohibiting others or prohibiting whole technologies? How well can we predict the consequences of a new technology or application? Who would make the decisions? We consider the first question here and the others in the next few sections.

How finely can we make decisions about acceptable and unacceptable technologies? In response to a criticism that the tribal life he extolled would have no pianos, no violins, no telescope, no Mozart, Sale replied, "[I]f your clan thought that the violin was a useful and nonharmful tool, you could choose to invent that."[74] Perhaps critics of computing technology who recognize its value to disabled people would permit development of applications for them. The question is whether it is possible for a clan or society to choose to invent a violin or a camera-equipped cane that warns a blind person of obstacles without the technological and economic base on which development of these products depends. That base includes the freedom to innovate, a large enough economy to get materials from distant sources, and a large number of potential applications that make the research, development, and production of the basic ingredients of these products economically feasible. It is unlikely that anyone would even think of developing the cane for the blind if some of the components did not already exist in prior products (for example, perhaps, small cameras in mobile phones). Nor would drones exist to quickly deliver life-saving medical supplies in Rwanda, bypassing poor roads, if companies did not sell drones for many other purposes.

7.5.2   THE DIFFICULTY OF PREDICTION

A brief look at the development of communications and computer technology suggests the difficulty of evaluating the consequences and future applications of a new technology. Early computers were developed to calculate ballistics trajectories for the military. The personal computer was originally a tool for doing computation and writing documents. Only a few visionaries imagined most of their current uses. Each new technology finds new and unexpected uses. When physicists began developing the World Wide Web, who would have predicted online auctions, social

---

Telemedicine: A bad application of technology?

In Chapter 1, we described long-distance medicine, or telemedicine, as a benefit of computer technology. Computer and communications networks make possible remote consultations and examination of patients, and they make possible remotely controlled medical procedures. You may be able to think of potential privacy and safety problems with such systems. Should we ban telemedicine?

Several states passed laws prohibiting the practice of telemedicine by doctors who are not licensed in that state. The main argument they give for the laws is safety, or concern about out-of-state "quacks." The laws will "keep out the charlatans and snake-oil salesmen," according to one supporter.[75] Also, telemedicine could increase the influence of large, well-financed medical centers—to the detriment of local physicians in private practice. Large hospitals might become the "Walmarts of medicine," says one writer. Telemedicine might make medical care even more impersonal than it is already.

Is concern for patients the real reason for the laws? The arguments about charlatans and quacks seem weak, considering that the laws target doctors who are licensed, but in another state. Many doctors who support the bans see telemedicine as a significant competitive threat. As the director of one state medical board put it, "They're worried about protecting their turf."[76] The laws restrict competition and protect established special interests—a risk of any mechanism designed to prohibit a new technology or product.

networking, or sharing home video? Would anyone have predicted even a small fraction of the ways we use smartphones? Postman's statement that a technology does "what it is designed to do" ignores human responsibility and choice, innovation, discoveries of new uses, unexpected consequences, and social action to encourage or discourage specific applications. Computer scientist Peter Denning takes a different view: "Although a technology does not drive human beings to adopt new practices, it shapes the space of possibilities in which they can act: people are drawn to technologies that expand the space of their actions and relationships."[77] Denning says people adopt technologies that give them more choices. Note that he does not say more choices of consumer products, but more actions and relationships. Don Norman also suggests that society influences the role of a technology when he says, "The failure to predict the computer revolution was the failure to understand how society would modify the original notion of a computational device into a useful tool for everyday activities."[78]

How well can a government committee, a think tank, or a computer industry executive predict the consequences of a new technology? The history of technology is full of wildly wrong predictions—some overly optimistic, some overly pessimistic. Some scientists were skeptical of air travel, space travel, and even railroads. (They believed that passengers would not be able to breathe on high-speed trains.) Consider the quotations in Figure 7.8.[*] Some of them reflect a lack of imagination about the myriad uses people would find for each new technology, about what the public would like, and about what they would pay for. The quotes demonstrate humorously that many experts can be utterly wrong. John von Neumann, a brilliant mathematician and early computer scientist, recognized this when he said, in 1949, "It would appear that we have reached the limits of what it is possible to achieve with computer technology, although one should be careful with such statements, as they tend to sound pretty silly in 5 years."[79]

We examine the prediction problem more seriously and in more depth by considering arguments made by computer scientist Joseph Weizenbaum against the development of a particular computer technology: speech recognition systems.[80] We now have more than 40 years of hindsight since Weizenbaum wrote in 1975. However, many inexpensive applications of speech recognition had already appeared by the early 1990s. Here are Weizenbaum's objections, accompanied by comments from our perspective today.

"The problem is so enormous that only the largest possible computers will ever be able to manage it." Speech recognition software runs on mobile phones.

". . . a speech-recognition machine is bound to be enormously expensive, . . . only governments and possibly a very few very large corporations will therefore be able to afford it." Millions of people use applications that include speech recognition.

---

[*]Many false or out-of-context quotes of this type circulate on the Internet. We have tried to eliminate false ones and provide context for others; the endnote on Figure 7.8 contains sources.

- *My personal desire would be to prohibit entirely the use of alternating currents. They are unnecessary as they are dangerous.*
  —Thomas Edison, 1899

- *Television won't be able to hold on to any market it captures after the first six months. People will soon get tired of staring at a plywood box every night.*
  —Darryl Zanuck, 20th Century Fox, 1946

- *Computers in the future may . . . only weigh 1.5 tons.*
  —Popular Mechanics, 1949

- *The U.S. will have 220,000 computers by the year 2000.*
  —Official forecast by RCA Corporation, 1966. The actual number was close to 100 million.

- *Cellular phones will absolutely not replace local wire systems.*
  —Marty Cooper, 1981 (Cooper, director of research at Motorola, invented an early cellphone but thought they would always be too expensive.)

- *I predict the Internet . . . will soon go spectacularly Supernova and in 1996 catastrophically collapse.*
  —Bob Metcalfe, 1995 (Metcalfe, an inventor of the Ethernet, thought the Internet infrastructure was insufficient to handle increasing traffic.)

- *Everyone's always asking me when Apple will come out with a cell phone. My answer is, 'Probably never.'*
  —David Pogue, technology writer for *The New York Times*, 2006

- *There's no chance that the iPhone is going to get any significant market share. No chance.*
  —Steve Ballmer, CEO of Microsoft, in an interview in 2007 shortly before the iPhone went on sale

FIGURE 7.8 Predictions.[81]

"What can it possibly be used for?" Speech recognition technology is a multibillion-dollar industry. Here are just few of its current uses, and we are still in its infancy:

- We can search for information, send text messages, make appointments, control home appliances, and so on with our voices. We can check airline flight schedules, get stock quotes and weather information, conduct banking transactions, and buy movie tickets on the phone by speaking naturally instead of pushing buttons.

- We can call a business, speak the name of the person we want to reach, and automatically connect to that person's extension.

- Software creates transcripts from audio tracks of video and television for deaf people to read and for search engines to index.

- Training systems (e.g., for air traffic controllers) and various tools that help disabled people use computers and control appliances in their homes use speech recognition.

- People who suffer from repetitive strain injury use speech recognition input instead of a keyboard. IBM advertised speech-input software for poets, so they can concentrate on poetry instead of typing. People with dyslexia use speech recognition software so that they can write by dictation.

- Speech translation systems recognize speech and translate it into other languages. They are very helpful to tourists, businesspeople, social service workers, hotel reservations clerks, and many others.

- Speech-activated, hands-free operation of mobile phones, music systems, and other appliances in automobiles eliminates some of the safety hazards of using these devices while driving.

- Going beyond simply recognizing words, software can analyze emotions in voice tones. One suggested application is marriage counseling. What other uses can you think of?

The military planned to control weapons by voice command, "a long step toward a fully automated battlefield." Speech recognition in a battlefield situation is still a challenging problem, but we have already automated some aspects of warfare, for example, by using drones. Some argue that we should have the best possible weapons to defend ourselves. Others argue that, if wars are easier to fight, governments fight more of them. If countries fight wars with remotely controlled automated weapons and no humans on the battlefield, is that an improvement over wars in which people are slaughtered? What if only one side has the high-tech weapons? Would that cause more wars of aggression? Is there any technology that the military cannot or does not use? Should we decline to develop strong fabrics because the military can use them for uniforms? Clearly, military use of high-tech tools raises serious ethical and policy questions. Are these questions sufficient reason to abandon or condemn a technology?

Governments can use speech recognition to increase the efficiency and effectiveness of wiretapping. And they do: Governments use speech recognition to filter thousands of hours of recorded conversations. Weizenbaum's concern was the potential for increased abuse of wiretapping; he does not explicitly mention legal wiretapping of criminal suspects. One can argue that governments can use the same tool beneficially in legal wiretapping of suspected criminals and terrorists, but it is true that speech recognition, like many other technological tools, can be a danger in the hands of governments. Protection against abuses depends in part on the recognition of the importance of strictly controlling government power and in part on the appropriate laws and enforcement mechanisms to do so.

Discussion of Weizenbaum's objections is important for several reasons: (1) Although Weizenbaum was an expert in artificial intelligence, of which speech recognition is a subfield, he was mistaken in his expectations about the costs and benefits. (2) His objections about military and government use highlight the dilemma: Should we decline to develop technologies that people can misuse, or should we develop the tools because of their beneficial uses, and use other means, including our votes and our voices, to influence government and military policy? (3) Weizenbaum's argument against development of a technology because of its expected cost is similar to arguments expressed by others about current and future computer applications and other technologies. For example, a common objection to some new medical technologies is that they are so expensive that only the rich will be able to afford them. This shortsighted view can result in the denial of benefits to the whole population. For many new inventions, prices are high at first but quickly come down.

Weizenbaum was not trying to evaluate computer technology as a whole but was focusing on one specific application area. If we are to permit the government, or experts, or the people via a majority vote to prohibit development of certain technologies, it is essential at least that we be able to estimate the consequences—both risks and benefits—of the technology fairly accurately. We cannot do this; nor can the experts do it.

But what if a technology might threaten the survival of the human race? We consider such an example in the next section.

7.5.3   Intelligent Machines and Superintelligent Humans—Or the End of the Human Race?

Prominent technologists such as Hans Moravec, Ray Kurzweil, and Vernor Vinge describe a not-very-distant future in which intelligence-enhancing devices, artificial intelligence, and intelligent robots change our society and our selves in profound ways.[82] The more optimistic scenarios include human use of intelligent machines and services of many kinds. People might acquire advanced mental powers through brain implants and computer–brain interfaces. When someone has a stroke, doctors might remove the damaged part of a brain and replace it with a chip that performs the lost functions, perhaps with a large amount of extra memory, or a chip to access the Web directly. Why wait for a stroke? Once the technology is available, healthy people will likely buy and install such implants. MIT robotics researcher Rodney Brooks, for example, suggested in 2003 that by 2020 we might have wireless Internet interfaces that doctors can implant in our heads. He says people might be just as comfortable with them as they are with getting laser eye surgery at a mall.[83] You could be reading this in 2020. Are such implants available? Do such implants make someone less human than a heart transplant or pacemaker does? What social problems could intelligence enhancement cause in the next few decades? What philosophical and ethical problems arise when we combine human and machine intelligence in such intimate ways?

Going farther into the future, will we "download" our brains to long-lasting robot bodies? If we do, will we still be human?

The technological singularity

The term *technological singularity* refers to the point at which artificial intelligence or some combined human–machine intelligence advances so far that we cannot comprehend what lies on the other side. It is plausible, says computer scientist Vernor Vinge, that "we can, in the fairly near future, create or become creatures who surpass humans in every intellectual and creative dimension. Events beyond such a singular event are as unimaginable to us as opera is to a flatworm."[84]

Some technologists welcome the idea of humanity transforming into an unrecognizable race of superintelligent, genetically engineered creatures within this century. Others find it horrifying—and others unlikely. Some see potential threats to the survival of the human race. They see the possibility of the machines themselves achieving human-level intelligence, and then rapidly improving themselves to a superhuman level. Once robots can improve their design and build better robots, will they "outcompete" humans? Will they replace humans just as various species of animals displace others? And will it happen soon, say within the next 20 years or so?

Two estimates support these scenarios. One is an estimate of the computing power of the human brain. The other is based on Moore's Law, the observation Gordon Moore, a co-founder of Intel, made in 1965 that the computing power of new microprocessors doubles roughly every 18 to 24 months. Moore's Law held true for nearly 50 years. But now, the electronics on chips are so small (less than 14 or even 10 nanometers) that chip manufacturers began running into problems in quality manufacturing and problems related to laws of physics that slowed the process. Doubling computing power now takes between 2.5 and 3 years. If the progress of hardware power continues at this rate, then by roughly 2040 computer hardware will be about as powerful as a human brain, sufficiently powerful to support the computation requirements of intelligent robots.

Both those who think an extreme advance in machine intelligence is likely in the near future and those who criticize these ideas provide several reasons why it might not happen. First, hardware progress might continue to slow down. Second, we might not be able to develop the necessary software in the next few decades, or at all. Developments in AI, particularly in the area of general intelligence, have been slower than researchers expected when the field began. (On the other hand, some experts did not expect recent achievements, such as a computer beating a Go master, for another decade.) Third, the estimates of the "hardware" computing power of the human brain (the sophistication of the computing power of neurons) might be drastically too low. Finally, some philosophers argue that robots programmed with AI software cannot duplicate the full capability of the human mind.

Responding to the threats of intelligent machines

Whether the singularity occurs within a few decades, or later, or not at all, many in the relevant fields foresee general-purpose intelligent machines within your lifetime. By its definition, we cannot prepare for the aftermath of the singularity, but we can prepare for more gradual developments. Many of the issues we explored in previous chapters are relevant to enhanced intelligence. Will software bugs or other malfunctions kill thousands of people? Will hackers hack brains? Will a large division open between the superintelligent and the merely humanly intelligent?

We saw that protections for safety and privacy in computer systems are often weak because they were not designed in from the start. It is valuable to think about potential problems of superintelligent systems and intelligence enhancement for humans well before they confront us so that we can design the best protections.

Bill Joy cofounded Sun Microsystems (now owned by Oracle) and was a key developer of Berkeley Unix and the Java programming language. In his article "Why the Future Doesn't Need Us,"[85] Joy describes his worries about robotics, genetic engineering, and nanotechnology. He observes that these technologies will be more dangerous than technologies of the 20th century (such as nuclear weapons) because they will be self-replicating and will not require rare and expensive raw materials and huge factories or laboratories. Joy foresees profound threats, including possibly the extinction of the human race.

What protections do people who fear for the future of humanity recommend? Joy describes and criticizes some before suggesting his own. Space enthusiasts suggest creating colonies in space and several private organizations are working toward that goal, but Joy believes it may not happen soon enough. If it does, it might save the human race, though not the vast majority of humans on earth. And if colonists take the current technologies with them, the threat goes too. A second solution is to develop protections that can stop the dangerous technologies from getting out of control. Futurist Virginia Postrel suggests "a portfolio of resilient responses."[86] Joy argues that we could not develop "shields" in time, and if we could, they would necessarily be at least as dangerous as the technologies they are supposed to protect us against.

Joy recommends "relinquishment," by which he means we must "limit development of the technologies that are too dangerous, by limiting our pursuit of certain kinds of knowledge." He cites, as earlier examples, treaties to limit development of certain kinds of weapons and the United States's unilateral decision to abandon development of biological weapons. However, relinquishment has the same kinds of weaknesses Joy attributes to the approaches he rejects: They are "either undesirable or unachievable or both." Enforcing relinquishment would be extraordinarily difficult, if not impossible.

As Joy recognizes, intelligent robots and the other technologies that concern him have huge numbers of potentially beneficial applications, many of which will save lives and improve quality of life. At what point should governments stop pursuit of knowledge and development? Ethical professionals will refuse to participate in development of some AI applications, but they too face the difficult problem of where to draw the line. Suppose we develop the technology to a point where we get useful applications with legal and technological safety controls. How will we prevent visionary or insane scientists, hackers, teenagers, aggressive governments, or terrorists from circumventing the controls and going beyond the prohibited level? Joy sees a relinquishment verification program on an unprecedented scale, in cyberspace and in physical facilities, with privacy, civil liberties, business autonomy, and free markets seriously curtailed. Thus, relinquishment means not only that we might lose development of innovative, beneficial products and services, but also that we would lose many basic liberties.

Although we can find flaws with all proposals to protect against the dangers of powerful technologies, that does not mean we should ignore the risks. We need to choose appropriate elements from the various proposals and develop the best protections we can.

Prediction is difficult, especially about the future.[87]

7.5.4 A FEW OBSERVATIONS

We have presented arguments against the view that we should evaluate and perhaps ban new technologies at the start. Does this mean that no one should make decisions about whether it is good to develop a particular application of a new technology? No. The arguments and examples suggest two things: (1) that we limit the scope of decisions about development of new technology, perhaps to particular products, and (2) that we decentralize the decision-making process and make it noncoercive, to reduce the impact of mistakes, avoid manipulation by entrenched companies who fear competition, and prevent violations of liberty. We cannot often predict the decisions and the results of decisions made by individual engineers, researchers, programmers, entrepreneurs, venture capitalists, customers, and teenagers who tinker in their garages, but they have a valuable robustness. The fundamental problem is not *what* decision to make about a specific technology. Rather, it is to select a decision-making *process* that is most likely to produce what people want, to work well despite the difficulty of predicting consequences, to respect the diversity of personal opinions about what constitutes a desirable lifestyle, and to be relatively free of political manipulation.

When we consider the most extreme potential developments, such as super-intelligent robots, what level of certainty of dire consequences should we require before restricting the freedom to develop technologies and products that might have marvelous benefits?

 Exercises

Review Exercises

7.1 What is one significant criticism of Wikipedia?

7.2 What questions do we use to evaluate computer models?

7.3 Give one of the neo-Luddite criticisms of electronic commerce.

7.4 What is one common use of mobile phones in rural areas or developing countries?

7.5 What is one reason Google or Apple might remove an app from people's smartphones?

7.6 Give an example of a mistaken prediction made about computers.

General Exercises

7.7   Consider a social media website on which display of news stories depends on the votes of readers. Is it an ethical obligation of the site operators to ensure that votes are not bought and sold, or is it merely a good business policy? Or is it both?

7.8   Describe a scenario in which biased or incorrect information a child finds on the Web might harm him or her. Suggest and evaluate one mechanism for preventing such harm.

7.9   **(a)**   Give an example (actual or hypothetical) of digital manipulation of an image or video for which there is no ethical problem; it is clearly ethical.

　　　　(b)   Give an example (actual or hypothetical) of digital manipulation of an image or video for which no complex argument is needed; it is clearly unethical.

　　　　(c)   Give an example (actual or hypothetical) of digital manipulation of an image or video for which deciding whether it is ethical is not simple, where there are reasonable arguments on both sides, or the context might be important. Elaborate; give an argument for each side.

7.10   We mentioned a journalist's idea of an "alternative viewpoints" button for controversial topics on the Web. What are some weaknesses of this idea?

7.11   Give an example of a bad decision or poor work that you attribute to mental laziness encouraged by computers or the Internet. (Try for one not described in the text.)

7.12   Suppose a computer program uses the following data to determine in how many years an important natural resource (say, copper) will run out.

- The number of tons in the known reserves of the resource.
- The average amount of the resource used per person (worldwide) per year.
- The total population of the world.
- An estimate of the rate of population increase for the next few decades.

　　　　(a)   List all the reasons you can think of why this program is not a good predictor of when we will run out of the resource.

　　　　(b)   In 1972, a group called the Club of Rome published a study, "The Limits to Growth," using computer models that implied that the world would run out of several important natural resources (e.g., tin, silver, and mercury) in the 1980s and several more by the end of the 20th century. Even with the enormously increased demand from China and other developing countries, we have not run out. Why do you think many people accepted the predictions in the study?

7.13   How do the opportunities for "co-present," or in-person, social interactions today compare with those of 150 years ago?

7.14   Discuss some advantages and disadvantages (to students and to society in general) of students getting college degrees online instead of at traditional colleges where they are co-present with faculty and other students.

7.15   The number of small neighborhood bookstores declined because of competition from both large chain megabookstores and online stores like Amazon.com. Should a law have prohibited Amazon.com from opening? If not, should we prohibit it from selling used books, to help preserve small neighborhood used-book stores? Give reasons. Suppose you like to shop in your neighborhood bookstore and fear it might go out of business. What can you do?

7.16   Many games that children used to play on boards with dice, cards, and plastic pieces are now computer games. Is this an example of unnecessary use of technology just because it is there? Describe some advantages and disadvantages of replacing a board game with a computer version.

7.17   Analyze the following argument that we are forced to have a mobile phone. Is it convincing?

Some people do not want to own or use a mobile phone. Technology advocates say if you don't want one, you don't have to buy one. But this is not true. We must have one. Before mobile phones became popular, there were coin-operated telephones all over, on street corners, in and near stores, in restaurants, at gas stations, and so on. If we needed to make a call while away from home or work, we could use a pay phone. Now most pay phones are gone, so we must have a mobile phone whether we want to or not.

7.18   Which of the Luddite criticisms of computers listed in Section 7.2.1 do you consider the most valid and significant? Why?

7.19   Recall the discussion in the box "Walmart and e-commerce versus downtown and community" (Section 7.2.2), and consider these questions: Do people have a right to shop in small neighborhood stores rather than online? Do people in a small town have a right to eat in a French restaurant? Distinguish between negative and positive rights (Section 1.4.2).

7.20   Identify one item on the Internet of Things that seems very silly and/or unnecessary. Then think up and describe a special situation where it might be useful.

7.21   After development of software to help parents and Internet service providers block access to material inappropriate for children, some governments adapted the software to block access to political and religious discussions. In what way does this example illustrate the views that technology will inevitably have negative uses and that, as Neil Postman said, "once a technology is admitted, . . . it does what it is designed to do"?

7.22   In the mid-1990s, approximately 70% of the computers connected to the Internet were in the United States. Did this suggest a growing gap between "have" and "have-not" nations? Give your reasons. (Try to find out what percentage of computers or websites are in the United States now.)

7.23   Approximately 6000 languages are spoken in the world. This number is declining rapidly as a result of increased communication and transportation, globalization of business and trade, and so on—all side effects of increased technology in general and of the Internet in particular. What are the advantages and disadvantages of losing languages? Overall, is it a significant problem?

7.24   Suppose you are a neo-Luddite. Argue that the spread of mobile phones to poor countries is a bad thing.

7.25   In Section 3.7, we described the Free Basics program that provides free partial access to the Internet in countries where many people cannot afford access. Compare the value of such programs for helping decrease the digital divide to the value of net neutrality.

7.26   Some writers express concern about a digital divide between content consumers and content producers on the Internet.[88] Internet users create blogs, Web pages, videos, and product reviews. Being a content creator empowers a user to communicate his or her message to a large number of people. The Internet can be a strong agent for change for those who have the skills, education, and tools to create content. Content creators tend to be more educated, and the content-production divide shows a gap among users based on socioeconomic status. How should we view the Internet content-production divide? Consider comparisons with content production before the Internet.

7.27 U.S. government traffic safety agencies want to require that all new heavy vehicles such as trucks and buses have electronic controls that limit their maximum speed. (Regulators are considering a limit of somewhere between 60 and 68 miles per hour.) Give arguments for and against such a requirement.

7.28 A philosopher writing more than a decade ago argued against the use of speech synthesis. He found it unsettling and dangerous that a person might have a telephone conversation with a machine and think it was a real person. Describe a few uses of speech synthesis. What are the benefits? What are reasons for concern?

7.29 Speaker recognition software analyzes speech to determine who the speaker is (not what words the speaker is saying, as in speech recognition). Describe some potentially useful and some potentially threatening or risky applications.

7.30 Assume you are a professional working in your chosen field. Describe specific things you can do to reduce the impact of any two problems we discussed in this chapter. (If you cannot think of anything related to your professional field, choose another field that might interest you.)

7.31 Think ahead to the next few years and describe a new problem, related to issues in this chapter, likely to develop from digital technology or devices.

Assignments

These exercises require some research or activity.

7.32 Find an article in Wikipedia on a subject that you already know a lot about. Read and review the article. Is it accurate, well done, complete?

7.33 Find websites that provide recommendations about how much Vitamin C a person should consume each day. Try to find at least one site that is extreme in some way and at least one that you consider reasonably reliable. Describe the sites and explain the basis for your characterization of them.

7.34 This exercise explores whether the wisdom of the crowd can successfully run a soccer team. In 2008, thousands of soccer fans chipped in via a website, MyFootBallClub.co.uk, to buy a British soccer team. The plan was to make management decisions by voting on the Web. Find out how well it worked and how well the team did.

7.35 Find a website that regularly reports on the validity of myths, rumors, and "urban legends" that circulate on the Internet and in social media. Give the site reference and describe any one story that you find there.

7.36 Recent predictions for population growth in the 21st century are quite different from predictions made several decades ago. Find reports of older population models (say, from the 1960s, 1970s, or 1980s), and find reports of recent population models. How do they differ? How have the assumptions in the models changed?

7.37 Three-dimensional "printers" create 3D structures, layer by layer, using glues, resins, and other materials under direction of software. Find some applications of these devices. Suppose someone described 3D printers 15 years ago as a potential invention and asked: Will they fill any real needs? How do you think most people would have answered? What is your answer now?

Class Discussion Exercises

These exercises are for class discussion, perhaps with short presentations prepared in advance by small groups of students.

7.38 Some people who consider themselves capable of distinguishing reliable information from unreliable information on the Web are concerned that most ordinary people are not educated, experienced, or sophisticated enough to do so. They are likely to believe lies, they might follow dangerous medical or financial advice, and so on. How serious a problem do you believe this is? How do you suggest addressing it?

7.39 Some critics of tools that enable us to select sources of news and information we receive on the Web or in social media argue that the tools encourage fragmentation of society along political lines. Some argue that when most people got their news from three TV networks, there was a more cohesive, shared background of information. How serious is the problem of people seeing only one political point of view on the Web?

7.40 Some people advocate a law requiring Google to make public the algorithms it uses to rank websites for display in response to search queries. Considering issues in this chapter, and any other relevant issues, discuss arguments in favor of such a requirement and arguments against it.

7.41 In a murder case, a mix of DNA from at least three people was found on a piece of evidence, making it difficult to determine if any belonged to the suspect. A computer program that analyzes DNA samples concluded that the suspect's DNA was indeed there. The defense attorneys asked to have the software examined by an expert to see how it worked and to look for errors. The company that produces the software said disclosure of the code would expose trade secrets and would harm the company. Discuss arguments on both sides. Suggest and evaluate alternative methods for judging the validity of the software without seeing the code.

7.42 Which of the following models do you think would produce very accurate results? Which do you think would be poor, and which in the middle? Give your reasons.

(a) A model developed by a team of mathematicians in 1895, using projections of population growth, economic growth, and traffic increase, to project the tonnage of horse droppings on city streets in 1995

(b) A model to determine the impact of various immigration policies on gross domestic product

(c) A model to predict the position of the moon in relation to the earth 30 years from now

(d) A model to predict how much optical fiber a major city will need 30 years from now

(e) A model to predict how much carbon dioxide the burning of fossil fuel for energy will emit worldwide 30 years from now

(f) A model to predict the speed of a new racing-boat hull design under specified wind conditions

7.43 Some neo-Luddites acknowledge that computing technology is beneficial to many people, but they see the main beneficiaries as government and big business. They say the key question is: Who benefits most? Consider the following questions and discuss the issue of who benefits most.

When a drug company develops a new cancer drug and its executives make millions of dollars as the stock goes up, while people who had that cancer live 20 extra years, who benefits most? Who benefits most from social media: governments, businesses, or ordinary users? Who benefits most from access to the Internet: you or someone your age in a rural village with no landline telephones and poor roads?

7.44 What form will the "digital divide" likely take 10 years from now? How do digital divides differ from social divisions that occurred with the introduction of earlier, nondigital information and communication technologies?

7.45 In the Prometheus myth, Zeus, the king of the gods, was furious at Prometheus for teaching science and technological skills to mankind because they made people more powerful. Zeus was jealous of his power and determined to withhold fire from mankind so that people would have to eat their food raw. Zeus and the Luddites represent different viewpoints on who benefits most from technology.

(a) Give arguments in support of Zeus' view that technology helps the less powerful, reducing the advantage of the more powerful.

(b) Give arguments in support of the Luddite view that technology helps the more powerful (e.g., governments and large corporations) most.

7.46 Read Bill Joy's article, "Why the Future Doesn't Need Us," and the reply by Virginia Postrel (see endnotes 85 and 86 for the references). Whose arguments are more convincing? Why?

Notes

1. From Pope's poem "An Essay on Criticism." In Greek mythology, the Pierian spring in Macedonia inspired the Muses and others who drank from it. Pope's poem turned it into a metaphor for knowledge.

2. Quoted in Stacy Schiff, "Know It All: Can Wikipedia Conquer Expertise?" *New Yorker*, July 31, 2006, www.newyorker.com/archive/2006/07/31/060731fa_fact. McHenry was an editor at the Encyclopedia Britannica.

3. Soraya Nadia McDonald, "How Internet Hoaxers Tricked the World into Believing this Random Sikh Guy Was a Paris Terrorist," *Washington Post*, Nov. 16, 2015, www.washingtonpost.com/news/the-intersect/wp/2015/11/16/how-internet-hoaxers-tricked-the-world-into-believing-this-random-sikh-guy-was-a-paris-terrorist/.

4. Robert Fox, "News Track: Everybody Must Get Cloned," *Communications of the ACM*, Aug. 2000, 43:8, p. 9. Lisa Guernsey, "Software Is Called Capable of Copying Any Human Voice," *New York Times*, July 31, 2001, pp. A1, C2.

5. Adrian Chen, "The Agency," *The New York Times Magazine*, June 2, 2015, www.nytimes.com/2015/06/07/magazine/the-agency.html?_r=0.

6. "Wikipedia: Size Comparisons," Wikipedia, en.wikipedia.org/wiki/Wikipedia:Size_comparisons; www.britannica.com.

7. Jan Lorenz, Heiko Rauhut, Frank Schweitzer, and Dirk Helbing, "How Social Influence Can Undermine the Wisdom of Crowd Effect," *Proceedings of the National Academy of Sciences*, May 10, 2011, www.pnas.org/content/early/2011/05/10/1008636108. full.pdf. James Surowieki, *The Wisdom of Crowds*, Anchor, 2005. A course on decision making taught by Michael Roberto and an article by Jonah Lehrer led me (SB) to these ideas and references.

8. Joseph Rago, "The Blog Mob," *Wall Street Journal*, Dec. 20, 2006, p. A18.

9. Examples include: American Library Association, "Using Primary Sources on the Web," www.ala.org/rusa/sections/history/resources/primarysources; Johns Hopkins University library, "Evaluating Information Found on the Internet," guides.library. jhu.edu/evaluatinginformation; and University of California, Berkeley, library, "Evaluating Web Pages: Techniques to Apply & Questions to Ask," guides.lib.berke-ley.edu/evaluating-resources.

10. Jonah Lehrer, "When We're Cowed by the Crowd," *Wall Street Journal*, May 28, 2011, online.wsj.com/article/SB10001424052702304066504576341280447107102.html.

11. From Microsoft's explanation of its policy, quoted in Mark Goldblatt, "Bowdlerized by Microsoft," *New York Times*, Oct. 23, 2001, p. A23, www.nytimes.com/2001/10/23/opinion/bowdlerized-by-microsoft.html.

12. Eli Pariser, *The Filter Bubble: What the Internet Is Hiding from You*, Penguin Press, 2011.

13. Jeffrey Gottfried and Elisa Shearer, "News Use Across Social Media Platforms 2016," Pew Research Center, www.journalism.org/2016/05/26/news-use-across-social-media-platforms-2016/. Georgia Wells, "Facebook's 'Trending' Feature Exhibits Flaws Under New Algorithm," *Wall Street Journal*, Sept. 6, 2016, www.wsj.com/articles/facebooks-trending-feature-exhibits-flaws-under-new-algorithm-1473176652. "YouTube and PragerU," *Wall Street Journal* (editorial), Oct. 30, 2016, www.wsj.com/articles/youtube-and-prageru-1477866319. Max Read, "Donald Trump Won Because of Facebook," *New York Magazine*, Nov. 9, 2016, nymag.com/selectall/2016/11/donald-trump-won-because-of-facebook.html. Mike Isaac, "Facebook, in Crosshairs After Election, Is Said to Question Its Influence," *New York Times*, Nov. 12, 2016, www.nytimes.com/2016/11/14/technology/facebook-is-said-to-question-its-influence-in-election.html.

14. James A. Evans, "Electronic Publication and the Narrowing of Science and Scholarship," *Science*, July 18, 2008 (Vol. 321, no. 5887, pp. 395–399), www.sciencemag.org/content/321/5887/395.abstract. I (SB) learned of this article from an article by Jonah Lehrer.

15. Isaac, "Facebook, in Crosshairs after Election."

16. Barry Bearak, "Pakistani Tale of a Drug Addict's Blasphemy," *New York Times*, Feb. 19, 2001, pp. A1, A4.

17. Peter L. Bernstein, *Against the Gods: The Remarkable Story of Risk*, John Wiley & Sons, 1996, p. 16.

18. Amanda Bennett, "Strange 'Science': Predicting Health-Care Costs," *Wall Street Journal*, Feb. 7, 1994, p. B1.

19. Cynthia Crossen, "How 'Tactical Research' Muddied Diaper Debate," *Wall Street Journal*, May 17, 1994, pp. B1, B9.

20. Julia Angwin, Jeff Larson, Surya Mattu, and Lauren Kirchner, "Machine Bias," *ProPublica*, May 23, 2016, www.propublica.org/article/machine-bias-risk-assessments-in-criminal-sentencing.

21. A much earlier version of this section appeared in Sara Baase, "Social and Legal Issues," a chapter in *An Invitation to Computer Science* by G. Michael Schneider and Judith L. Gersting, West Publishing Co., 1995. (Used with permission.)

22. T. F. Stocker *et al.*, "2013: Technical Summary," in *Climate Change 2013: The Physical Science Basis*, Intergovernmental Panel on Climate Change, Cambridge University Press, p. 37, www.climatechange2013.org/images/report/WG1AR5_TS_FINAL.

pdf. Christopher S. Watson *et al.,* "Unabated Global Mean Sea-Level Rise Over the Satellite Altimeter Era," *Nature Climate Change,* 5, 565–568, May 11, 2015, www. nature.com/nclimate/journal/v5/n6/full/nclimate2635.html. NASA, Global Climate Change: Sea Level, climate.nasa.gov/vital-signs/sea-level/.

23. The IPCC reports (published by Cambridge University Press): T. F. Stocker *et al., Climate Change 2013: The Physical Science Basis*; S. Solomon *et al.,* eds., *Climate Change 2007: The Physical Scientific Basis,* 2007 (Technical Summary at ipcc-wg1.ucar.edu/wg1/wg1-report.html); J. T. Houghton *et al.,* eds., *Climate Change 2001: The Scientific Basis,* 2001; J. T. Houghton *et al.,* eds., *Climate Change 1995: The Science of Climate Change,* 1996; J. T. Houghton, B. A. Callander, and S. K. Varney, eds., *Climate Change 1992: The Supplementary Report to the IPCC Scientific Assessment,* 1992; J. T. Houghton, G. J. Jenkins, and J. J. Ephraums, eds., *Climate Change: The IPCC Scientific Assessment,* 1990. Various IPCC reports are available at www.ipcc.ch/publications_and_data/publications_and_data_reports. shtml. I (SB) also used a large variety of other books and articles for background.

24. T. F. Stocker *et al.,* "2013: Technical Summary," p. 50 and p. 51.

25. One reason why this distinction is important is that temperature records for large areas of the northern hemisphere showed a larger rise in the nighttime winter lows than in the daytime summer highs, a potentially benign or beneficial form of warming.

26. D. L. Albritton *et al.,* "Technical Summary," in Houghton, *Climate Change 2001,* pp. 21–83; see p. 49.

27. Gregory Flato *et al.,* Chapter 9: Evaluation of Climate Models, in Stocker, *Climate Change 2013,* p. 817. The issue of clouds is mentioned in several places in the reports. Solomon, "Technical Summary," *Climate Change 2007,* p. 70. "Greenhouse Gases Frequently Asked Questions," National Oceanic and Atmospheric Administration National Climatic Data Center, www.ncdc.noaa.gov/oa/climate/gases.html. Long-term projection: Stocker *et al.,* "2013: Technical Summary," p. 81.

28. Stocker *et al.,* "2013: Technical Summary," p. 69.

29. Flato, Chapter 9: Evaluation of Climate Models, p. 824.

30. Stephen Schneider, quoted in Jonathan Schell, "Our Fragile Earth," *Discover,* Oct. 1989, pp. 44–50.

31. Stocker, "2013: Technical Summary," p. 75.

32. David J. Frame and Daithi A. Stone, "Assessment of the First Consensus Prediction on Climate Change," *Nature Climate Change,* 3, 357–359 (2013), Figure 1: Changes in global mean temperature over the 1990–2010 period, www.nature.com/nclimate/ journal/v3/n4/fig_tab/nclimate1763_F1.html. National Oceanic and Atmospheric Administration, National Climatic Data Center, "State of the Climate Global Analysis Annual 2011," Dec. 2011, www.ncdc.noaa.gov/sotc/global/2011/13.

33. 2007 projections: Solomon, "Technical Summary," *Climate Change 2007,* Table TS.6, p. 70. The 0.05°C figure (for 1998–2012): IPCC, "Climate Change 2014 Synthesis Report Summary for Policy Makers," pp. 3–4, www.ipcc.ch/pdf/assessment-report/ ar5/syr/AR5_SYR_FINAL_SPM.pdf. The 0.07°C figure (for 1999–2008): J. Knight *et al.,* "Do Global Temperature Trends Over the Last Decade Falsify Climate Predictions?" pp. 22–23, within T. C. Peterson and M. O. Baringer, eds., "State of the Climate in 2008," *Bulletin of the Meteorological Society,* 90, Aug. 2009, 1–196, journals.ametsoc.org/doi/pdf/10.1175/BAMS-90-8-StateoftheClimate. The hiatus: Stocker, "2013: Technical Summary," p. 37, p. 67.

34. Stephen Moore, "The Coming Age of Abundance," in Ronald Bailey, ed., *The True State of the Planet*, Free Press, 1995, p. 113.

35. "Interview with the Luddite" (Kevin Kelly, interviewer), *Wired*, June 1995, pp. 166–168, 211–216 (see pp. 213–214).

36. Alexandra Eyle, "No Time Like the Co-Present" (interview with Neil Postman), *NetGuide*, July 1995, pp. 121–122. Richard Sclove and Jeffrey Scheuer, "On the Road Again? If Information Highways Are Anything Like Interstate Highways— Watch Out!" in Rob Kling, ed., *Computerization and Controversy: Value Conflict and Social Choices*, 2nd ed., Academic Press, 1996, pp. 606–612.

37. Kirkpatrick Sale, *Rebels Against the Future: The Luddites and Their War Against the Industrial Revolution: Lessons for the Computer Age*, Addison-Wesley, 1995, p. 257.

38. Jerry Mander, *In the Absence of the Sacred: The Failure of Technology and the Survival of the Indian Nations*, Sierra Club Books, 1991, p. 61.

39. Neil Postman, *Technopoly: The Surrender of Culture to Technology*, Alfred A. Knopf, 1992, p. 119.

40. Eyle, "No Time Like the Co-Present."

41. Harvey Blume, "Digital Refusnik" (interview with Sven Birkerts), *Wired*, May 1995, pp. 178–179. Kelly, "Interview with the Luddite."

42. From a study by sociologist Claude Fisher, reported in Charles Paul Freund, "The Geography of Somewhere," *Reason*, May 2001, p. 12.

43. Postman, *Technopoly*, p. 15.

44. See Jane Jacob's classic *The Economy of Cities*, Random House, 1969.

45. Postman, *Technopoly*, p. 6. The Freud quote is from *Civilization and Its Discontent* (e.g., the edition edited and translated by James Strachey, W. W. Norton, 1961, p. 35).

46. John Davis, quoted in Sale, *Rebels Against the Future*, p. 256.

47. Peter Applebome, "A Vision of a Nation No Longer in the U.S.," *New York Times*, Oct. 18, 2007, www.nytimes.com/2007/10/18/nyregion/18towns.html. Sale, *Rebels Against the Future*, p. 257.

48. Joanna Stern, "Smart Tampon? The Internet of Every Single Thing Must Be Stopped," *Wall Street Journal*, May 25, 2016, www.wsj.com/articles/smart-tampon-the-internet-of-every-single-thing-must-be-stopped-1464198157.

49. Sclove and Scheuer, "On the Road Again?"

50. The quotes are from Kelly, "Interview with the Luddite," p. 214 and p. 213. Sale expresses this point of view also in *Rebels Against the Future*, p. 213.

51. Sale, *Rebels Against the Future*, p. 256.

52. This dichotomy has always struck me (SB) as strange, because it almost suggests that humans are alien creatures who arrived on earth from somewhere else. We evolved here. We are part of nature. A human's house is as natural as a bird's nest, though, unlike birds, we have the capacity to build both ugly and beautiful things.

53. Martin V. Melosi, *Garbage in the Cities: Refuse, Reform, and the Environment: 1880–1980*, Texas A&M University Press, 1981, p. 24–25.

54. Ian Hacking, *The Emergence of Probability*, Cambridge University Press, 1975, p. 108. C. P. Snow, "The Two Cultures and the Scientific Revolution," in *The Two Cultures: And a Second Look*, Cambridge University Press, 1964, pp. 82–83. The population data are from National Center for Health Statistics, Centers for Disease Control and Prevention, www.cdc.gov/nchs/fastats/life-expectancy.htm; Global Health Observatory, World Health Organization, www.who.int/gho/mortality_

burden_disease/life_tables/situation_trends/en/; *Health, United States, 2010,* Table 22, p. 134, National Center for Health Statistics, Center for Disease Control, www.cdc.gov/nchs/data/hus/hus10.pdf; and from the United Nations, reported in Nicholas Eberstadt, "Population, Food, and Income: Global Trends in the Twentieth Century," pp. 21, 23 (in Bailey, *The True State of the Planet*) and in Theodore Caplow, Louis Hicks, and Ben J. Wattenberg, *The First Measured Century: An Illustrated Guide to Trends in America,* AEI Press, 2001, pp. 4–5. Nonvehicular accidental deaths declined from 72 per 100,000 people in 1900 to 19 per 100,000 people in 1997 (Caplow *et al., The First Measured Century,* p. 149).

55. Moore, "The Coming Age of Abundance," p. 119. Eberstadt, "Population, Food, and Income," p. 34. Family income spent on food: Stephen Moore and Julian L. Simon, *It's Getting Better All the Time: The 100 Greatest Trends of the 20th Century,* Cato Institute, 2000, p. 53, and U.S. Department of Agriculture Economic Research Service, "Food CPI, Prices and Expenditures: Food Expenditure Tables," Table 7, accessible at www.ers.usda.gov/data-products/food-expenditures.aspx. Ronald Bailey, "Billions Served" (interview with Norman Borlaug), *Reason,* Apr. 2000, pp. 30–37. Julian L. Simon, "The State of Humanity: Steadily Improving," *Cato Policy Report,* Sept./Oct. 1995, 17:5, pp. 1, 10–11, 14–15.

56. Arman Shehabi *et al.,* "United States Data Center Energy Usage Report," Lawrence Berkeley Laboratory, 2016, eta.lbl.gov/publications/united-states-data-center-energy-usag. Steve Hargreaves, "The Internet: One Big Power Suck," *CNN Money,* May 9, 2011, money.cnn.com/2011/05/03/technology/internet_electricity/index.htm.

57. Optical fiber: Ronald Bailey, ed., *Earth Report 2000: Revisiting the True State of the Planet,* McGraw Hill, 2000, p. 51.

58. William M. Bulkeley, "Information Age," *Wall Street Journal,* Aug. 5, 1993, p. B1. "Newstrack" ("Claims to Fame"), *Communications of the ACM,* Feb. 1993, p. 14. Vertical Research Partners (verticalresearchpartners.com), reported in Jennifer Levitz, "Tissue Rolls to Mill's Rescue," *Wall Street Journal,* Feb. 16, 2012, p. A3. U.S. Postal Service.

59. United Nations, "E-Commerce and Development Report 2001," quoted in Frances Williams, "International Economy & the Americas: UNCTAD Spells Out Benefit of Internet Commerce," *Financial Times,* Nov. 21, 2001.

60. Most of the data in this paragraph and the next one come from polls and studies by Pew Research Center, Forrester Research, Luntz Research Companies, Ipsos-Reid Corporation, Nielsen//NetRatings, the U.S. Commerce Department, and others, reported in various news media. Susannah Fox and Gretchen Livingston, "Latinos Online," Pew Research Center, Mar. 14, 2007, pewresearch.org/pubs/429/latinos-online. Jon Katz, "The Digital Citizen," *Wired,* Dec. 1997, pp. 68–82, 274–275.

61. See the note above.

62. Lee Rainie and Katheryn Zickuhr, *"Always on Connectivity,"* Aug. 26, 2015 www.pewinternet.org/2015/08/26/chapter-1-always-on-connectivity/.

63. Micah Singleton, "The FCC Has Changed the Definition of Broadband," *The Verge,* Jan. 29, 2015, www.theverge.com/2015/1/29/7932653/fcc-changed-definition-broadband-25mbps.

64. "Internet Users," www.internetlivestats.com/internet-users/. "Human Development Report 2015," Chapter 3, United Nations Development Programme, report. hdr.undp.org. "Increased Competition Has Helped Bring ICT Access to Billions,"

United Nations International Telecommunication Union, Jan. 2011, www.itu.int/net/pressoffice/stats/2011/01/#.V_uHIneZPOY.

65. "Human Development Report 2015," Chapter 3, United Nations Development Programme, report.hdr.undp.org.

66. Jacob Poushter, "Smartphone Ownership and Internet Usage Continues to Climb in Emerging Economies," Pew Research Center, Feb. 22, 2016, www.pewglobal.org/2016/02/22/smartphone-ownership-and-internet-usage-continues-to-climb-in-emerging-economies/. "Billions of People in Developing World Still Without Internet Access, New U.N. Report Finds," United Nations, Sept. 21, 2015, www.un.org/apps/news/story.asp?NewsID=51924#.WAfmD_RjKO0. Jacob Poushter, "Smartphone Ownership Rates Skyrocket in Many Emerging Economies, but Digital Divide Remains," Pew Research Center, Feb. 22, 2016, www.pewglobal.org/2016/02/22/smartphone-ownership-rates-skyrocket-in-many-emerging-economies-but-digital-divide-remains/.

67. Marianne Lavelle, *"Five Surprising Facts About Energy Poverty," National Geographic*, May 30, 2013, news.nationalgeographic.com/news/energy/2013/05/130529-surprising-facts-about-energy-poverty/.

68. Ben Lefebvre, "What Uses More Electricity: Liberia, or Cowboys Stadium on Game Day?" *Wall Street Journal*, Sept. 13, 2013, blogs.wsj.com/corporate-intelligence/2013/09/13/what-uses-more-electricity-liberia-or-cowboys-stadium-on-game-day.

69. Euan McKirdy, "UNHCR Report: More Displaced Now than after WWII," *CNN*, June 20, 2016, www.cnn.com/2016/06/20/world/unhcr-displaced-peoples-report/.

70. One Laptop per Child: one.laptop.org. Ruy Cervantes *et al.,* "Infrastructures for Low Cost Laptop Use in Mexican Schools," *Proceedings of the 2011 Annual Conference on Human Factors in Computing Systems*, dl.acm.org/citation.cfm?id=1979082.

71. Eric Bellman and Aditi Malhotra, "Why the Vast Majority of Women in India Will Never Own a Smartphone," *Wall Street Journal*, Oct. 13, 2016, www.wsj.com/articles/why-the-vast-majority-of-women-in-india-will-never-own-a-smartphone-1476351001. Facebook data: Simon Kemp, "Digital in APAC 2016," We Are Social, Sept. 6, 2016, wearesocial.com/uk/special-reports/digital-in-apac-2016. Cherie Blair, "Women & Mobile: A Global Opportunity," p. 16, www.gsma.com/mobilefordevelopment/wp-content/uploads/2013/01/GSMA_Women_and_Mobile-A_Global_Opportunity.pdf. Newley Purnell, "How Google's Bicycle-Riding Tutors Are Getting Rural Indian Women Online," *Wall Street Journal*, Oct. 3, 2016, blogs.wsj.com/indiarealtime/2016/10/03/how-googles-bicycle-riding-internet-tutors-are-getting-rural-indian-women-online/.

72. Sale, *Rebels Against the Future*, p. 210.

73. Postman, *Technopoly*, p. 7.

74. Kelly, "Interview with the Luddite."

75. Bill Richards, "Doctors Can Diagnose Illnesses Long Distance, to the Dismay of Some," *Wall Street Journal*, Jan. 17, 1996, pp. A1, A10.

76. Richards, "Doctors Can Diagnose Illnesses Long Distance."

77. Peter J. Denning, "The Internet After 30 Years," in Dorothy E. Denning and Peter J. Denning, eds., *The Internet Besieged*, Addison Wesley, 1998, p. 20.

78. Donald A. Norman, *Things That Make Us Smart: Defending Human Attributes in the Age of the Machine*, Addison-Wesley, 1993, p. 190.

79. Matt Novak, "7 Famous Quotes About the Future That Are Actually Fake," *Gizmodo*, Sept. 8, 2014, paleofuture.gizmodo.com/7-famous-quotes-about-the-future-

that-are-actually-fake-1631236877. Novak reports that von Neumann's statement is often quoted without the second half.

80. Joseph Weizenbaum, *Computer Power and Human Reason: From Judgment to Calculation*, W. H. Freeman and Company, 1976, pp. 270–272.

81. Edison: Thomas Edison, "The Dangers of Electrical Lighting," *The Electrical Engineer*, Volume 8, 1899, page 518 (quote is on page 520). Zanuck: George F. Custen, *Twentieth Century's Fox: Darryl F. Zanuck and The Culture of Hollywood*, Basic Books, 1997. *Popular Mechanics*, Mar. 1949, p. 258. RCA: Thomas Petzinger Jr., "Meanwhile, from the Journal's Archives," *Wall Street Journal*, Jan. 1, 2000, p. R5. Cooper: Peter Grier, "Really Portable Telephones: Costly, But Coming?", *Christian Science Monitor*, Apr. 15, 1981, www.csmonitor.com/1981/0415/041506. html. Metcalfe: Bob Metcalfe, "Predicting the Internet's Catastrophic Collapse and Ghost Sites Galore in 1996," *InfoWorld*, Dec. 4, 1995, p. 61 (found in books.google. com via search). David Pogue, "Pogue's Posts: iPhone Rumors," *New York Times*, Sept. 27, 2006, pogue.blogs.nytimes.com/2006/09/27/27pogues-posts-3/?_r=0. Ballmer: David Lieberman, "CEO Forum: Microsoft's Ballmer Having a 'Great Time'," *USA Today*, Apr. 30, 2007. More information about some of these predictions appears in Kathy Pretz, "Five Famously Wrong Predictions About Technology," *The Institute*, IEEE, Dec. 19, 2014, theinstitute.ieee.org/ieee-roundup/members/achievements/five-famously-wrong-predictions-about-technology.

82. Ray Kurzweil, *The Singularity Is Near: When Humans Transcend Biology*, Viking, 2005. Hans Moravec, *Robot: Mere Machine to Transcendent Mind*, Oxford University Press, 2000. Vernor Vinge, "The Coming Technological Singularity: How to Survive in the Post-Human Era," presented at the VISION-21 Symposium (sponsored by NASA Lewis Research Center and the Ohio Aerospace Institute), Mar. 30–31, 1993, www-rohan.sdsu.edu/faculty/vinge/misc/singularity.html.

83. Rodney Brooks, "Toward a Brain–Internet Link," *Technology Review*, Nov. 2003, www.technologyreview.com/Infotech/13349/.

84. "Superhuman Imagination," interview with Vernor Vinge by Mike Godwin, *Reason*, May 2007, pp. 32–37.

85. Bill Joy, "Why the Future Doesn't Need Us," *Wired*, Apr. 2000, www.wired.com/2000/04/joy-2/.

86. Virginia Postrel, "Joy, to the World," *Reason*, June 2000, reason.com/archives/2000/06/01/joy-to-the-world.

87. This statement has been attributed to both Neils Bohr and Albert Einstein; we could not find a reliable source for either.

88. Jen Schradie, "The Digital Production Gap: The Digital Divide and Web 2.0 Collide," *Poetics*, Vol. 39, No. 2, Apr. 2011, pp. 145–168.

CHAPTER 8

Errors, Failures, and Risks

8.1 Failures and Errors in Computer Systems

8.1.1 AN OVERVIEW

"Navigation System Directs Car Into River"

"Thousands of Prisoners Get Out Early Because of a Software Glitch"

"Flaws Found in Software That Tracks Nuclear Materials"

"Software Glitch Makes Scooter Wheels Suddenly Reverse Direction"

"Robot Kills Worker"

"California Junks $100 Million Child Support System"

"Man Arrested Five Times Due to Faulty FBI Computer Data"

"Software and Design Defects Cripple Health-Care Website"

These headlines describe real incidents. Are computer systems too unreliable and too unsafe to use? Or, like many news stories, do the headlines and horror stories emphasize the bad news—the dramatic but unusual events? We hear reports of car crashes, but we do not hear that drivers completed hundreds of thousands of car trips safely in our city today. Although most car trips (and computer systems) are safe, there is a good purpose for reporting crashes: It teaches us what the risks are (e.g., driving in heavy fog) and it reminds us to be responsible and careful drivers. Just as car crashes have many causes (faulty design, sloppy manufacturing or servicing, bad road conditions, confusing road signs, a careless or poorly trained driver, and so on), computer glitches and system failures also have myriad causes, including faulty design, sloppy implementation, careless or insufficiently trained users, poor user interfaces, and many others. Often, there is more than one factor.

Most computer applications, from consumer software to systems that control communications networks, are so complex that it is virtually impossible to produce programs with no errors. In the next few sections, we describe a variety of mistakes, problems, and failures—and some factors responsible for them. Some errors are minor, such as a word processor incorrectly hyphenating a word that does not fit at the end of a line. Some incidents are funny while others cost billions of dollars, and a few are sadly tragic. Because of the complexity of computer systems, sometimes even when good procedures and professional practices are followed and no one does anything wrong, an accident occurs anyway. Other times, the irresponsibility of software developers and managers is comparable to driving while very drunk. Studying these failures, their causes, and the risks they create can help prevent future failures.

If the inherent complexity of computer systems means they will not be perfect, how can we distinguish between errors we should accept as trade-offs for the benefits of the system and errors that are due to inexcusable carelessness, incompetence, or dishonesty? How good is good enough? When should we, or the government, or a business decide that a computer system or application is too risky to use? Why do multimillion-dollar systems fail so miserably that the firms and agencies that pay for them abandon them before completion? We cannot answer these questions completely, but this chapter provides some background and discussion that can help us in forming conclusions. It should help us understand the problems from the perspective of several of the roles we play:

- *A computer user.* Whether we use our own tablet computer or a sophisticated, specialized system at work, we should understand the limitations of computer systems and the need for proper training and responsible use.

- *An educated member of society.* There are many personal decisions and social, legal, and political decisions that depend on our understanding of the risks of computer system failures. We could be on a jury or we could be an active member of an organization lobbying for legislation. We could be deciding whether or not to have surgery performed by a robot. Also, we can apply some of the problem-solving approaches and principles in this chapter to professional areas other than computer systems.

- *A computer professional.* If you are planning a career as a computer professional (system designer, programmer, security specialist, or quality assurance manager, for example), studying computer system failures should help you become a better professional. Understanding the source and consequences of failures is valuable if you will be responsible for buying, developing, or managing a complex system for a hospital, airport, or business. The discussions of the examples in this chapter include many implicit and explicit lessons about how you can avoid similar problems.

We can categorize computer errors and failures in several ways—for example, by the cause, by the seriousness of the effects, or by the application area. In any scheme to organize the discussion, there will be overlap in some categories and mixing of diverse examples in others. We use three categories: problems for individuals, usually in their roles as consumers; system failures that affect large numbers of people and/or cost large amounts of money; and problems in safety-critical applications that may injure or kill people. We will look at one safety-critical case in depth (in Section 8.2): the Therac-25. This computer-controlled radiation treatment machine had a large number of flaws that resulted in the deaths of several patients. In Sections 8.3 and 8.4, we try to make some sense of the jumble of examples. Section 8.3 looks at underlying causes in more depth and describes professional practices and other approaches to preventing failures and handling them properly when they occur. Section 8.4 puts the risks in perspective in various ways.

The incidents described here are a sampling of the many that occur. Robert Charette, an expert in software risk management, emphasizes that computer system errors and failures occur in all countries, in systems developed for businesses, governments, and nonprofit organizations (large and small) "without regard to status or reputation."[1] In most cases, by mentioning specific companies or products, we do not mean to single those out as unusual offenders. One can find many similar stories in news reports, software engineering journals, and in The Risks-Forum Digest organized by Peter Neumann.[2] Neumann collects thousands of reports describing a wide range of computer-related problems.

8.1.2   PROBLEMS FOR INDIVIDUALS

Billing errors

The first few errors we look at are relatively simple ones.

- A woman received a $6.3 million bill for electricity. The correct amount was $63. The cause was an input error made by someone using a new computer system.

- The IRS is a constant source of major bloopers. When it modified its programs to avoid billing victims of a Midwest flood, the computer generated erroneous bills for almost 5000 people. One Illinois couple received a bill for a few thousand dollars in taxes—and $68 billion in penalties. In one year, the IRS sent 3000 people bills for slightly more than $300 million. One woman received a tax bill for $40,000,001,541.13.

- The auto insurance rate of a 101-year-old man suddenly tripled. Rates depend on age, but the program handled ages only up to 100. It mistakenly classified the man as a teenager.

- Hundreds of Chicago cat owners received bills from the city for failure to register dachshunds, which they did not own. The city used two databases to try to find unlicensed pets. One database used DHC as the code for domestic house cat, and the other used the same code for dachshund.

These errors are perhaps more humorous than serious since big mistakes are obvious and they usually get fixed quickly, though even these can take up a lot of a person's time and cause stress. Small but persistent errors might be less noticeable but have serious negative impacts on people with low income, since people often pay erroneous bills, unaware of the mistake. Some errors can damage a person's reputation or credit rating.

Programmers and users can avoid some of the errors we described above. For example, programmers can include tests to determine whether a billing amount is outside some reasonable range or has changed significantly from previous bills. In other words, because programs and user input can contain errors, good systems have provisions for checking user entries and for checking the reasonableness of output. If you have some programming experience, you know it is relatively easy to include such tests and to flag cases for further review.

Some errors in billing systems cause significant expense and disruption to customers. When the Los Angeles Department of Water and Power (LADWP) implemented a new billing system, many customers received erroneous, inflated bills.

Errors in our favor, briefly

As I (TH) was working on this chapter, a computer glitch in my school's payroll system caused me to receive two payroll deposits this week. Sadly, I'll need to return one of them. And, one morning, I (SB) found an extra $10 million in my investment account. It disappeared a few hours later.

People's perspectives on errors sometimes depend on which side they are on. If you were charged twice for the same credit card purchase, you would want one of the charges canceled. If you made a deposit to your bank or investment account and it went in someone else's account by mistake, you would want the error corrected.

The bills were based on water use estimates, not actual water meter readings (a common practice in the utility industry). When thousands of customers called about the errors, the LADWP staff typically stated the error would be resolved when the meter was next read. As months passed, the errors compounded and many accounts began accruing interest on unpaid balances. LADWP officials had known of problems in the system, but they implemented it anyway. LADWP workers who normally collected late payments were assigned to handle billing errors; as a result, hundreds of millions of dollars in uncollected payments of *correct* bills were later written off as bad debt. The settlement of a lawsuit resolved the overbilling issues and required LADWP to invest an additional $20 million to overhaul the system.

How close to perfection should we expect billing systems to be? After a water-utility company sent a customer an incorrect bill for $22,000, a spokesman for the company pointed out that one incorrect bill out of 275,000 monthly bills is pretty good. It is better than a 99.999% accuracy rate. Is that reasonable? At some point, the expense of improving a system is not worth the gain, especially for applications where the impact of the error on customers is small and errors can be detected (once they occur) and corrected at much lower cost than it would take to try to prevent them.

Inaccurate and misinterpreted data in databases

Businesses are reluctant to release error rates for many major commercial databases containing information on millions of people. The businesses themselves might not have such data, and we need to distinguish between a spelling error in someone's address and an incorrect report that someone bounced several checks. Thus, it is difficult to get accurate and meaningful data. We can consider some examples.

An input error appeared to be the cause of a problem when credit bureau records incorrectly listed thousands of New England residents as not having paid their local property taxes. People were denied loans before someone identified the scope of the problem and the credit bureau corrected it. Like $40 billion tax bills, a systematic error affecting thousands of people is likely to get noticed. More serious, perhaps, are errors in individual people's records. In one case, a county agency used the wrong middle name in a report to a credit bureau about a father who did not make his child-support payments. Another man in the same county had that exact name and could not get credit to buy a car or a house. Another man applied for jobs at several retail stores and was turned down at all of them. Eventually, he learned the stores used a special database to screen applicants, and it listed him as a shoplifter. A real shoplifter had given the police the innocent man's identification from a lost wallet.

A high school excluded a 14-year-old boy from football and some classes without explanation. He eventually learned that school officials thought he had been using drugs while in junior high school. The two schools used different disciplinary codes in their computerized records. The boy had been guilty of chewing gum and being late. While this case is very similar to the case of the dachshund/cat confusion described earlier, the consequences were more significant. Both cases illustrate the problems of relying on computer systems without taking the responsibility of learning enough about them to use them properly.

Federal law requires states to maintain databases of people convicted of sex crimes and to release information about them to the public. A family was harassed, threatened, and physically attacked after their state posted an online list of addresses where sex offenders live. The state did not know the offender had moved away before the family moved in. In another case, a man murdered two men in Washington state after getting their addresses from the state's sex offender database, and another man killed two men listed in Maine's online registry. One of the murdered men was in the database because, as a teenager, he had sex with his girlfriend who was a few weeks below the legal age of consent. While technically not an error in the database, this case illustrates the need for careful thought about what a database includes and how it is presented to the public, especially if it involves a highly charged subject.

E-Verify is a system designed to verify that a worker hired in the United States is legally authorized to work. It uses data from the Social Security Administration and the Department of Homeland Security (DHS). It is voluntary for most businesses but some states require it for all workers, and the federal government requires it for federal contractors. Some people advocate requiring all employers to get approval from E-Verify for every new person hired. The U.S. Citizenship and Immigration Services agency says that E-Verify quickly verifies almost 99% of applicants, but how accurate is it? A measure of the inaccuracy of the system must include those whom the system approves but who are not actually authorized to work and those it denies who are actually authorized to work. A report by the Government Accountability Office estimated the system erroneously approves more than half of the applicants who are truly not authorized to work. Some of these applicants use stolen identities. Approximately 0.2% of all applicants are initially rejected but approved after a process to correct the error. Reasons for erroneous rejections include inconsistencies in the spelling of names, employer errors in using the system, and errors in the DHS database. (The initial rejection rate is

Destroying careers and summer vacations[3]

CTB/McGraw-Hill develops and scores standardized tests for schools. Millions of students take its tests each year. An error in CTB's software caused it to report test results incorrectly—substantially lower than the correct scores—in several states. As a result, educators endured personal and professional disgrace. In New York City, school principals and superintendents lost their jobs because their schools appeared to be doing a poor job of teaching students to read. One man said he applied for 30 other superintendent jobs in the state but did not get one. Parents were upset as nearly 9000 students had to attend summer school because of the incorrect scores. Eventually, CTB corrected the error; New York City's reading scores had actually risen five percentage points.

Why was the problem not detected sooner, soon enough to avoid firings and summer school? School testing officials in several states were skeptical of the scores showing sudden, unexpected drops. They questioned CTB, but CTB told them nothing was wrong. They said CTB did not tell them that other states experienced similar problems and also complained. When CTB discovered the software error, the company did not inform the schools for many weeks, even though the president of CTB met with school officials about the problem during those weeks.

What lessons can we learn from this case? Software errors happen, of course. People usually notice significant mistakes, and they did here. But the company did not take seriously enough the questions about the accuracy of the results and was reluctant to admit the possibility—and later the certainty—of errors. It is this behavior that must change. The damage from an error can be small if the error is found and corrected quickly.

CTB recommended that school districts not use scores on its standardized tests as the sole factor in deciding which students should attend summer school, but New York City did so. In a case with a similar lesson, Florida state officials relied on computer-generated lists of possible felons to prevent some people from voting, even though the database company supplying the lists said the state should do additional verification.[4] Relying solely on one factor or on data from one database is temptingly easy, particularly when considering the costs of additional review or verification. However, in many situations, it is a temptation that people responsible for critical decisions should resist.

significantly higher for noncitizens than for citizens.) The government considers all whose denial is not reversed on appeal to be unauthorized to work. However, an analysis done for the government by an outside research firm estimated that more than 6% of those receiving a final rejection (roughly 0.05% of the total) are actually legally authorized to work. Are these error rates acceptably low? Approximately 60 million people in the United States change jobs or enter the workforce every year. If the system becomes mandatory, an error rate of 0.2% incorrect initial rejections would affect 120,000 people who are legal workers each year. Certainly, 0.05% sounds low, but it means roughly 30,000 people who legally should be able to work would be prevented from doing so.[5]

When errors occur in databases used by law enforcement agencies, the consequences can include arrests at gunpoint, strip searches, and time in jail with violent criminals. For example, a car rental company mistakenly listed a car as stolen and, as a result, two adults went to jail and a child to a juvenile home for 24 hours—until police determined that they really had rented the car they were driving. Police stopped and frisked an innocent driver because his license plate number incorrectly appeared as the license number of a man who had killed a state trooper.

After the terrorist attacks in 2001, the FBI gave a "watch list" to police departments and businesses such as car rental agencies, banks, casinos, and trucking and chemical firms. Recipients emailed the list to others, and eventually thousands of police departments and thousands of companies had copies. Many incorporated the list into their databases and systems that screened customers or job applicants. Although the list included people who were not suspects but whom the FBI wanted to question, some companies labeled the list "Suspected terrorists." Many entries did not include date of birth, address, or other identifying information, making mistaken identifications likely. Some companies received the list by fax and typed misspelled names from blurred copies into their databases. The FBI stopped updating the list but did not tell the recipients; thus, many entries became obsolete.[6] Even if an error is corrected in one database, problems may not be over for the affected person since copies of incorrect data remain in many other systems.

Several factors contribute to the frequency and severity of the problems people suffer because of errors in databases and misinterpretation of their contents:

- A large population (Many people have identical or similar names, and most of our interactions are with strangers.)
- Automated processing without human common sense or the power to recognize special cases
- Overconfidence in the accuracy of data stored on computers
- Errors (some due to carelessness) in data entry
- Failure to update information and correct errors
- Lack of accountability for errors

The first factor is unlikely to change as it is the context in which we live. We can reduce the negative impacts of the second factor with better system specifications and training of users. The remaining factors in the list above are all within our control as individuals, professionals, and policy makers. We discuss them throughout this chapter.

> *It is repugnant to the principles of a free society that a person should ever be taken into police custody because of a computer error precipitated by government carelessness. As automation increasingly invades modern life, the potential for Orwellian mischief grows.*
>
> —Arizona Supreme Court[7]

8.1.3   SYSTEM FAILURES

Modern communications, power, medical, financial, retail, and transportation systems depend heavily on computer systems, yet these systems do not always function as planned. We give examples of failures, with indications of the causes in some cases. For computer science students and others who might contract for or manage custom software, one aim is to see the serious impacts of the failures—and to see what you want to work hard to avoid. The lessons of adequate planning and testing, of having backup plans in case of failures, and of honesty in dealing with errors apply to large projects in other professions as well. Here is a sampling of failures:

- A software bug forced thousands of Starbucks stores to close. A daily update left the stores unable to process orders, accept payments, or proceed with normal business.

- A software error at the Swiss Bank Coop resulted in banking customers receiving not only their own end-of-year statements, but also the statements of several other bank customers. The incident violated the financial privacy of thousands of customers and put the security of their accounts at risk.

- A three-line change in a two-million-line telecommunications switching program caused a failure of telephone networks in several major cities. Although the program underwent 13 weeks of testing, it was not retested after this change—which contained a typo.

- American Express Company's credit card verification system failed during the Christmas shopping season. Merchants had to call in for verification, overwhelming the call center.

- Log-ins overloaded Skype's peer-to-peer network when a huge number of people rebooted their computers after installing routine Windows updates. A majority of Skype's Internet phone users could not log in for two days.

- An error in a software upgrade shut down trading on the Tokyo Stock Exchange. A computer malfunction froze the London Stock Exchange for almost eight hours—on the last day of the tax year, affecting many people's tax bills.[8]

- A glitch in an upgrade in the computer system at Charles Schwab Corporation crashed the system for more than two hours and caused intermittent problems for several days. Customers could not access their investment accounts or trade online. New software at Knight Capital Group, an investment company, caused millions of unintended stock trades in a short time and left the company with a loss of more than $400 million, threatening its survival.

- A failure of Amtrak's reservation and ticketing system during a Thanksgiving weekend caused delays because agents had no printed schedules or fare lists.

- Virgin America airline switched to a new reservation system a month before Thanksgiving. Its website and check-in kiosks did not work properly for weeks.[9]

- The $125 million Mars Climate Orbiter disappeared when it should have gone into orbit around Mars. One team working on the navigation software used English-measure units while another team used metric units. The investigation of the loss emphasized that while the error itself was the immediate cause, the fundamental problem was the lack of procedures that would have detected the error.[10]

- In 2002, a change was made to a computer system used by the Washington State Department of Corrections to compute the release time of prisoners. The change incorrectly applied "good time" credit earned in county jails to state prison sentences resulting in the early release of more than 3000 prisoners before the error was discovered in 2012. The error was not fixed until 2016.

Voting systems

In 2002, Congress passed the Help America Vote Act and authorized $3.8 billion to improve voting systems. In many states, that meant replacing paper ballots with electronic systems, but the rush to electronic voting machines demonstrated that they, too, could have numerous faults. Here are just a few of the problems that occurred:

- Some electronic voting systems crashed—voters were unable to vote.
- One county lost more than 4000 votes because the machine's memory was full.
- In one Texas county, a programming error generated 100,000 extra votes.
- Another programming error caused some candidates to receive votes actually cast for other candidates.

Providing a secure electronic system that is resistant to vote fraud and sabotage is a significant issue in elections. Software can be rigged to give inaccurate results, and depending on the design of the system, independent vote recounting may be difficult. Validating voting software is often impossible since many companies consider the software proprietary and keep the source code hidden as a trade secret.

Security researchers have strongly criticized electronic voting machines stating that the machines have insecure encryption techniques (or none at all), insufficient security for installation of upgrades to software, and poor physical protection of the memory cards on which the system stores votes. One research group demonstrated a system's vulnerability to a virus that took over the machine and manipulated the vote results. They found that developers of voting systems lacked sufficient security training. For example, programmers omitted basic procedures such as input validation and boundary checks. Researchers opened the access panel on a voting machine with a standard key that is easily available and used in office furniture, electronic equipment, and hotel minibars. There were certification standards for voting systems, but some flawed systems were certified; the standards were inadequate. In some counties, election officials gave voting machines to high school students and other volunteers to store at home and deliver to polling places on election day.[11]

Many of the failures resulted from causes we see over and over: lack of sufficient planning and thought about security issues, insufficient testing, and insufficient training. Often in projects like these, the desire of states to obtain federal grants encourages haste. The grants have short limits on how soon the states must spend the money, and to meet the reduced timeframe, planning, testing, and training times are decreased to a point where they are nearly ineffective. In this application, the task of training users is complex because thousands of ordinary people volunteer as poll workers and must learn how to manage and operate the machines on election day.

Voting online has some benefits, such as convenience for voters, but it presents additional issues, including voter authentication, vote verification, and more vulnerability to hacking. Under direction of a computer science professor, a team of graduate students hacked an experimental online voting system and changed votes. They also found evidence of attacks on the system from Iran and China. Many states in the United States allow online voting for special populations, for example, disabled people and people in the military who are overseas. Alaska, which allows online submission of ballots by all voters (e.g., by sending a pdf file of a scanned ballot), warns that people who use the system waive their right to a secret ballot and accept the possibility of transmission errors.[12]

Online voting in Estonia began in 2005. The Estonian system is considered the most secure Internet voting system in use. An analysis by a team from the University of Michigan found poor procedural controls and serious system weaknesses that hackers could exploit to alter vote results without being detected. Many of the vulnerabilities result from election staff not following documented procedures and from carelessness with sensitive information, such as displaying Wi-Fi credentials publicly or entering passwords in view of a camera. The researchers also said the system does not use recommended encryption techniques that allow independent verification of votes. They recommended that use of the system be discontinued. The Estonian government strongly disagreed with the report. The population of Estonia is only about 1.3 million (slightly more than the state of Rhode Island), and voter authentication relies on Estonia's mandatory national ID card. It is unclear whether its system would work well in a country the size of the United States (with approximately 320 million people) and where a mandatory national ID card is controversial.[13]

Long before we voted on computers, Chicago and parts of Texas were infamous for vote fraud. In some cities, election officials found boxes full of uncounted paper ballots after an election was over. Secret ballots and reasonable accuracy and authenticity of vote counts are essential to a healthy democracy. Electronic and online systems have advantages over earlier voting systems, but they introduce a host of other problems that must be addressed. Developing them requires a high degree of professionalism and a high degree of security. What trade-offs are we willing to make with respect to secret ballots, convenience, and cost? What forms of fraud will these systems eliminate, and what new forms of fraud will they permit? What level of security is acceptable?

> *Those who cast the votes decide nothing. Those who count the votes decide everything.*
> —Attributed to Joseph Stalin (former Premier of the Soviet Union)[14]

Abandoned systems

The flaws in some information systems are so extreme that the systems end up in the trash after wasting millions, or even billions, of dollars. Some examples are[15]:

- A large British food retailer spent more than $500 million on an automated supply management system that left merchandise sitting in depots and warehouses. They hired 3000 additional clerks to move items and stock shelves.
- The Ford Motor Company abandoned a $400 million purchasing system.
- A consortium of hotels and a rental car business spent $125 million on a comprehensive travel-industry reservation system, and then canceled the project because it did not work.
- After nine years of development, Britain's National Health Service abandoned a patient record system that cost more than £10 billion. It failed because of the scope of the project, changing specifications, poor management by the Department of Health, technical issues, and disputes with vendors.
- The state of California spent more than $100 million to develop a system for tracking parents who owe child support payments. After five years, the state abandoned the system.
- Seven years after work began on what was supposed to be a four-year project, the state of Pennsylvania abandoned a system to administer unemployment compensation payments. When canceled, the system was $60 million over its original $107 million budget and did not work properly.
- After spending $4 billion, the IRS abandoned a tax-system modernization plan; a Government Accountability Office report blamed mismanagement.

Robert Charette estimates that from 5% to 15% of information technology projects are abandoned before or soon after delivery as "hopelessly inadequate." Figure 8.1 includes some reasons Charette cites.[16] As many as one in six large software projects go so poorly that they threaten the existence of the company. Such large losses demand attention from computer professionals, information technology managers, business executives, and public officials who set budgets and schedules for large projects.

- Lack of clear, well-thought-out goals and specifications
- Poor management and poor communication among designers, programmers, customers, and other project stakeholders
- Institutional or political pressures that encourage unrealistically low bids, unrealistically low budget requests, and underestimates of time requirements
- Use of very new technology, with unknown reliability and problems, perhaps for which software developers have insufficient experience and expertise
- Refusal to recognize or admit that a project is in trouble

FIGURE 8.1 Why abandoned systems failed.

Legacy systems

After US Airways and America West merged, they combined their reservation systems. The self-service check-in kiosks failed and the resulting long lines at ticket counters delayed thousands of passengers and flights. Merging different computer systems is extremely tricky, and problems are common, but this incident illustrates another factor. According to a vice president of US Airways, when the merger occurred, most airline systems dated from the 1960s and 1970s. They were designed for the mainframe computers of that era. These old systems "are very reliable, but very inflexible," the airline executive said.[17] These are examples of "legacy systems"—out-of-date systems (hardware, software, or peripheral equipment) still in use, often with special interfaces, conversion software, and other adaptations to make them interact with more current systems.

The problems of legacy systems are numerous. When old hardware fails, replacement parts are difficult to find. Connections with modern systems are another frequent failure point. Old software may run on newer hardware, but if it was written in an older programming language that programmers no longer learn, maintaining or modifying the software is difficult. Old programs often had little or no documentation, and the programmers who wrote the software or operated the systems have left the company, retired, or died. If there were good design documents and manuals, they probably no longer exist or cannot be found. Programming styles and standards have changed over the years. For example, limited memory on early computers led to obscure and terse programming practices, so a variable a programmer might now call "flight_number" would then have been simply "f." Older systems, such as a 1980s-era system that airports use to communicate with pilots, were not designed for the cyberthreats of today and have security vulnerabilities.

Users of large computer systems in the early days included banks, airlines, government agencies, and providers of infrastructure services such as power companies. These systems grew gradually to the point where a complete redesign and development of a fully new, modern system would, of course, be expensive. The conversion to the new system, possibly requiring some downtime, could also be very disruptive and require major retraining of staff. Thus, legacy systems persist.

We will continue to invent new programming languages, paradigms, and protocols—and we will later add on to the systems we develop now. Among the lessons legacy systems provide for computer professionals is the recognition that someone might be using and maintaining their software 30 or 40 years from now. It is important for system designers and programmers to document, document, document their work and plan for flexibility, expansion, and upgrades. When encouraging software development teams to document code and use good programming style, some managers remind developers to "Think of the poor programmer who has to maintain your code. Make his or her life pleasant so you are thought of kindly."

8.1.4 EXAMPLE: STALLED AIRPORTS AT DENVER, HONG KONG, AND MALAYSIA

Ten months after the $3.2 billion Denver International Airport was supposed to have opened, I (SB) flew over the huge airport. It covers 53 square miles, roughly twice the size of Manhattan. It was an eerie sight—nothing moved. There were no airplanes or people at the airport and no cars on the miles of wide highway leading to it. The opening was rescheduled at least four times. The delay cost more than $30 million per month in bond interest and operating costs. The computer-controlled baggage-handling system, which cost $193 million, caused most of the delay.[18]

The plan for the baggage system was quite ambitious. Outbound luggage checked at ticket counters or curbside counters was to travel to any part of the airport in less than 10 minutes via an automated system of carts traveling at up to 19 miles per hour on 22 miles of underground tracks. Similarly, inbound luggage would go to terminals or transfer directly to connecting flights anywhere in the airport. Scanners throughout the system tracked the 4000 carts and sent information about their locations to computers. The computers used a database of flights, gates, and routing information to control motors and switches to route the carts to their destinations.

The system did not work as planned. During testing, carts crashed into each other at track intersections; the system misrouted, dumped, and flung luggage; and carts needed to move luggage went mistakenly to waiting pens. Both the specific problems and the general underlying causes are instructive:

- *Real-world problems.* Some scanners got dirty or knocked out of alignment and could not detect carts going by. Faulty latches on the carts caused luggage to fall onto the tracks.

- *Problems in other systems.* The airport's electrical system could not handle the power surges associated with the baggage system. The first full-scale test blew so many circuits that the test had to be halted.

- *Software errors.* A software error caused the routing of carts to waiting pens when they were actually needed.

No one expects software and hardware of this complexity to work perfectly when first tested. There are numerous interactions and conditions that designers might not anticipate. Mangling a suitcase is not embarrassing if it occurs during an early test and if the problem is fixed. It is embarrassing if it occurs after the system is in operation or if it takes a year to fix. What led to the extraordinary delay in the Denver baggage system? There seem to have been two main causes:

- *The time allowed for development and testing of the system was insufficient.* The only other baggage system of comparable size was at Frankfurt Airport in Germany. The company that built that system spent six years on development and two years testing and debugging. BAE Automated Systems, the company that built the Denver system, was asked to do the entire system in two years. Some reports indicate that because of the electrical problems at the airport, there were only six weeks for testing.

- *Denver made significant changes in specifications after the project began.* Originally, the automated system was to serve only United Airlines, but Denver officials decided to expand it to include the entire airport, making the system 14 times as large as the automated baggage system BAE had installed for United at San Francisco International Airport.

As a *PC Week* reporter said, "The bottom-line lesson is that system designers must build in plenty of test and debugging time when scaling up proven technology into a much more complicated environment."[19] Some observers criticized BAE for taking on the job when the company should have known that there was not enough time to complete it. Others blamed the city government for poor management, politically motivated decisions, and proceeding with a grandiose but unrealistic plan.

Poor planning and implementation of computer systems caused the opening of new airports in Hong Kong and Kuala Lumpur to be disasters. The ambitious systems at these airports were to manage everything: moving 20,000 pieces of luggage per hour and coordinating and scheduling crews, gate assignments for flights, and so on. Systems at both airports failed spectacularly. At Hong Kong's Chek Lap Kok airport, cleaning crews and fuel trucks, baggage, passengers, and cargo went to the wrong gates, sometimes far from where their airplanes were. Airplanes scheduled to take off were empty. At Kuala Lumpur, airport employees had to write boarding passes by hand and carry luggage. Flights, of course, were delayed; food cargo rotted in the tropical heat.

At both airports, the failures were initially blamed on people entering incorrect information into the system. In Hong Kong, it was perhaps a wrong gate or arrival time that dutifully traveled throughout the system. In Kuala Lumpur, mistakes by check-in agents unfamiliar with the system paralyzed it. "There's nothing wrong with the system," said a spokesman at the airport in Malaysia. A spokesman at Hong Kong made a similar statement. They were deeply mistaken;

one incorrect gate number should not cause the magnitude of problems experienced at Hong Kong. Any system with a large number of users and a high level of user input must be designed and tested to handle input mistakes. A "system" includes more than software and hardware. It includes the people who operate it, and therefore successful implementations must consider this. Additionally, as in the case of the Denver airport, there were questions about whether political considerations, rather than the needs of the project, determined the scheduled time for the opening of the airports.[20]

8.1.5   EXAMPLE: HEALTHCARE.GOV[21]

On October 1, 2013, the U.S. Department of Health and Human Services (HHS) launched a health insurance enrollment system to give residents of more than 30 states the opportunity to sign up for health insurance under the Patient Protection and Affordable Care Act, commonly called Obamacare. People access the system via the website HealthCare.gov. The launch was a huge failure. For the first two months of operation, the website was unusable for most visitors. The first day, out of 4.7 million unique site visitors, only six people were able to complete the registration process.[22] The site had 14.6 million unique visitors in the first 10 days, but only a few thousand completed the process. Millions of people were frustrated by the exceedingly slow response times, confusing directions, and error prone website. These problems resulted in extensions to the federal registration deadlines for insurance coverage. It has been very difficult to determine what the project cost. HHS reported that by February 2014, it had spent $834 million. The HHS Office of the Inspector General gave a figure of $1.7 billion, and some later estimates were higher. Whatever the exact number, the cost was well above early estimates.[23]

How could such an important project fail so badly?

Planning, management, and testing problems

Referring to HealthCare.gov as a "website" severely understates the complexity of the project. The system is one of the largest software projects run by the federal government and has millions of lines of code. It needed to interact in real time with databases of numerous federal agencies including the Internal Revenue Service, the Social Security Administration, and the Department of Homeland Security. It had to exchange data with more than 300 private insurance companies. More than 50 different companies had contracts to work on some portion of the website, the database, and the interfaces to other agencies, organizations, and insurance companies.[24]

When the HealthCare.gov project began, the requirements were not fixed, since legislative and policy actions were still needed. The contract for the first part of the project was awarded with only two years to implement a project with unclear specifications—a very short period of time for a project of this magnitude. Because requirements were not set, the original contract was not for a fixed price, but "cost-reimbursable." This type of contract makes it easier for vendors to get paid for the additional work as details develop, but it can lead to significant cost overruns. The *New York Times* reported that in the 10 months prior to implementation, project requirements for hardware and software were modified significantly seven times.[25] Many deadlines were missed throughout the project.

Projects of the scale of HealthCare.gov need experienced project managers who understand the complexities of integrating the work of the very large numbers of contractors and organizations. Despite having limited internal staff with such expertise, the Centers for Medicare and Medicaid Services (CMS, part of HHS) decided to manage the project themselves. Internal to CMS, infighting between departments caused delay of many decisions, and vendors often received contradictory information. In some cases, CMS workers hid important information from other groups within CMS. Early in 2013, an outside contractor was brought in to evaluate the project for risks and to develop strategies to increase the chance of success. The report contained many recommendations such as limiting system functionality in order to give the project team time to complete and thoroughly test the website; additional features could be added later. The CMS project manager did not review the contractor's final report.[26]

Software coding did not start until March 2013, with only seven months to develop and test the system. Requirements changed right up until the implementation date. Changes implemented late in the development process are dangerous as even simple ones may have far reaching effects in a highly interconnected and complex piece of software. In general, testing was not adequate for the size and complexity of the system. Integration testing, a testing methodology where the system is tested to see if all pieces work together, did not begin until a few weeks before the launch date. Testing too close to the launch date does not give developers time to fix problems and then retest the system. The *Washington Post* reported, "As late as Sept. 26 [a few *days* before launch], there had been no tests to determine whether a consumer could complete the process from beginning to end."[27]

Security weaknesses

In addition to problems that were obvious to people who tried to use the site, a variety of problems were less visible, including security issues. The HealthCare.gov system has a huge collection of personally identifiable information and is certain to be the target of malicious hackers as long as it is operational, yet the project had no person responsible for overall system security, and thorough security testing was not performed before the site launched. After implementation, a security flaw was discovered that could allow a hacker to take over a user's entire insurance account. Compounding the security issues, the site required users to enter personal information to create an account before reviewing insurance plans. The site therefore captured personal information even if someone never bought insurance through the site.

This policy is in contrast to typical online marketplaces that require personally identifying information only at checkout. Overall, a Government Accountability Office report said, the site posed unnecessary risks of unauthorized access, disclosure, or modification of personal information.[28]

Another major security issue was failure to register misspelled or similar domain names (website names). Many website owners register names similar to their own as a convenience for users who mistype or misspell the name and as a protection against malicious sites. (For example, Microsoft registers not only www.microsoft.com but others such as www.microsfot.com.) Registering and redirecting similar domain names to HealthCare.gov was extremely important. Since this was not done, a customer mistyping the website address could be directed to a malicious website set up to mirror HealthCare.gov and collect user credentials and personal information for identify theft. The *Washington Examiner* reported that shortly after HealthCare.gov launched, over 200 websites appeared to exploit the domain name.[29]

Improvements and "back end" problems

Within weeks after launch, a team of technology experts identified technical and leadership issues affecting the website and oversaw hundreds of software fixes and hardware upgrades.

Within a few months, HealthCare.gov was functioning, handling more than 80,000 simultaneous users. Fixes and improvements continued. However, while CMS concentrated on the consumer interface, the system was not performing all the necessary behind-the-scenes operations. Thousands of people who believed the system had overcharged them or improperly denied them coverage filed appeals, but CMS had not developed or implemented the appeals process guaranteed in the Affordable Care Act; it just stored the filed appeals forms. Other functions that were not working several months after launch of the website included ability to exchange enrollment information with state Medicaid programs and adjust coverage when a person's family (or other) circumstances changed. Eighteen months after launch, an electronic system to pay health insurance companies was not fully working, and companies had to send estimated bills to HHS.[30]

Questions

How does this example compare to others, say the airport systems we described in Section 8.1.4? We see problems common to both the Denver Airport system and HealthCare.gov: The time allotted for the project was severely insufficient, politics affected deadlines, and significant changes in specifications increased the difficulties.

Politicians often underestimate costs for large projects to encourage acceptance. How much of the $1–2 billion for HealthCare.gov was actually reasonable for such a complex system, and how much was waste due to poor management?

How well have the security issues been resolved?

Did we perceive the launch of HealthCare.gov as worse than other poorly done large projects because it directly affected so many people?

8.1.6   WHAT GOES WRONG?

Computer systems fail for two general reasons: the jobs they do are inherently difficult, and sometimes the jobs of building and using the system are done poorly. Several factors combine to make these jobs difficult. Computer systems interact with the real world (including both machinery and unpredictable humans), contain complex communications networks, have numerous interconnected subsystems, have features to satisfy many types of users, and are extremely large. Devices and machines from smartphones to automobiles, passenger airplanes, and jet fighters contain millions of lines of computer code.[31] Whereas a small error in an analog mechanical system might cause a small degradation in performance, a single typo in a computer program can cause a dramatic difference in behavior.

The jobs of building and using a system can be done poorly at any of many stages, from system design and implementation to system management and use. (This characteristic is not unique to computer systems, of course. We can say the same about building a bridge, a house, a car, or any complex system.) Figure 8.2 lists factors in computer errors and system failures. The examples we have described illustrate many of them and we comment on a few.

Overconfidence

Unrealistic or inadequate understanding of the risks in developing and running a complex system is a core issue in software failure. When system developers appreciate the risks, they have greater incentive to use available "best practice" techniques and build more reliable and safer systems.

Some safety-critical systems that failed had supposedly "fail-safe" software controls. The basic logic of these programs was fine; the failures resulted from not considering how the system interacts with real users or real-world problems (such as loose wires, fallen leaves on train tracks, a cup of coffee spilled in an airplane cockpit, and so on).

Unrealistic estimates of reliability or safety can come from genuine lack of understanding, from carelessness, or from intentional misrepresentation. People without a high regard for honesty, or who work in an organization that lacks a culture of honesty and focus on safety, sometimes give in to business or political pressure to exaggerate safety, to hide flaws, to avoid unfavorable publicity, or to avoid the expense of corrections. These ethical issues impact a surprisingly large number of software projects.

- Design and development:
  - Poor communication with client resulting in unclear or incorrect requirements
  - Inadequate attention to potential safety risks
  - Interaction with physical devices that do not work as expected
  - Incompatibility of software and hardware, or of application software and the operating system
  - Not planning and designing for unexpected inputs or circumstances
  - Confusing user interfaces
  - Overconfidence and insufficient testing
  - Reuse of software from another system without adequate checking
  - Insufficient market or legal incentives to do a better job
  - Carelessness
  - Hiding problems during development; inadequate response to reported problems
- Management and use:
  - Data-entry errors
  - Lack of risk management
  - Inadequate training of users
  - Errors in interpreting results or output
  - Failure to keep information in databases up to date
  - Overconfidence in software by users
  - Insufficient planning for failures; no backup systems or procedures
  - Misrepresentation; hiding problems during use; inadequate response to reported problems

FIGURE 8.2 Some factors in computer system errors and failures.

Reuse of software: The Ariane 5 rocket and "No Fly" lists

Less than 40 seconds after the first launch of France's Ariane 5 rocket (see Figure 8.3), the rocket veered off course because of a software error.[32] The rocket and the satellites it was carrying cost approximately $500 million and were destroyed as a safety precaution. The Ariane 5 used some software designed for the earlier, successful Ariane 4. The software included a module to perform calculations related to velocity during the first few minutes after a launch on the Ariane 4. The module did not have to run after takeoff on the Ariane 5, but a decision was made to avoid introducing new errors by modifying a component that operated well in the Ariane 4. Because the Ariane 5 travels faster than the Ariane 4 after takeoff, the module's calculations produced numbers bigger than the program could handle (an "overflow" in technical jargon), causing the system to halt.

FORGET Patrick/SAGAPHOTO.COM/Alamy Stock Photo

FIGURE 8.3 Ariane 5 rocket.

When a woman named Jan Adams, and many other people with first initial J and last name Adams, tried to board an airplane, they were flagged as possible terrorists. The name "Joseph Adams" was on a "No Fly" list of suspected terrorists (and other people considered safety threats) that the Transportation Security Agency had given to the airlines. To compare passenger names with those on the "No Fly" list, some airlines used old software and strategies designed to help ticket agents quickly locate a passenger's reservation record (e.g., if the passenger called with a question or to make a change). The software searched quickly and "cast a wide net." That is, it found any possible match, which a sales agent then verified. As the software was intended to be used, there is no inconvenience to anyone if the program presents the agent with a few potential matches of similar names. In the context of tagging people as possible terrorists, a person mistakenly "matched" likely undergoes questioning and extra luggage and body searches by security agents.

Do these examples tell us that we should not reuse software? One of the goals of programming paradigms such as object-oriented code is to make software elements that can be widely used, thus saving time and effort. Reuse of working software should also increase safety and reliability. After all, if a module underwent field testing in a real, operational environment, we know it works—at least, we think it works. The critical point is that it works in a different environment. When a software module is used in a new system, it is essential to reexamine the specifications, assumptions, and design of the software; to consider implications and risks for the new environment; and to retest and validate the software for the new use.

8.2 Case Study: The Therac-25

8.2.1 THERAC-25 RADIATION OVERDOSES

The benefits of computing technology to health care are numerous and very impressive. Yet, one of the classic case studies of a deadly software failure is a medical device: a radiation treatment machine.

The Therac-25 was a software-controlled radiation-therapy machine used to treat people with cancer. Between 1985 and 1987, Therac-25 machines at four medical centers gave massive overdoses of radiation to six patients. In some cases, the operator repeated an overdose because the machine's display indicated that it had given no dose. Medical personnel later estimated that some patients received more than 100 times the intended dose. These incidents caused severe and painful injuries and the deaths of three patients.

Why is it important to study a case more than thirty years old? The root causes of these injuries and deaths have a continued presence in today's systems. Years after the Therac-25 incident, medical physicists operating a different radiation-treatment machine in Panama tried to circumvent a limitation in the software in an attempt to provide more shielding for patients. Their actions caused dosage miscalculations; 28 patients received overdoses of radiation, and many died.[33] It seems that dramatic lessons need repetition with each new generation. Studies of the Therac-25 incidents showed that many factors contributed to the injuries and deaths. The factors include lapses in good safety design, insufficient testing, bugs in the software that controlled the machines, and an inadequate system of reporting and investigating the accidents. The main sources for this discussion are articles by computer scientists Nancy Leveson and Clark Turner and by Jonathan Jacky.[34]

To understand the problems, it helps to know a little about the machine. The Therac-25 was a dual-mode machine. That is, it could generate an electron beam or an x-ray photon beam. The type of beam needed depended on the tumor it would treat. The machine's linear accelerator produced a high-energy electron beam (25 million electron volts) that is dangerous. Patients must not be exposed to the raw beam, so it is essential that the proper protective device be in place when the electron beam is on. A computer monitors and controls movement of a turntable that holds these devices. Depending on the intended treatment, the machine rotates a different set of devices in front of the beam to spread it and make it safe. Another position of the turntable uses a light beam instead of the electron beam to help the operator position the beam precisely in the correct place on the patient's body.

8.2.2 SOFTWARE AND DESIGN PROBLEMS

Design flaws

The Therac-25 differed from the earlier Therac-6 and Therac-20 in that it was fully computer controlled. The older machines had hardware safety interlock mechanisms, independent of the computer, that prevented the beam from firing in unsafe conditions. The design of the Therac-25 eliminated many of these hardware safety features but reused some software from the Therac-20 and Therac-6. The developers assumed, incorrectly, that the software would function properly in this new environment. When new operators used the Therac-20, there were frequent shutdowns and blown fuses, but no overdoses. The Therac-20 software had bugs, but the hardware safety mechanisms were doing their job. Either the manufacturers did not know of the problems with the Therac-20, or they completely missed the serious implications. Like its predecessor, the Therac-25 malfunctioned frequently. One facility said there were sometimes 40 dose-rate malfunctions in a day, generally underdoses. Thus, operators became used to error messages appearing often, with no indication that there might be safety hazards.

The operator interface had a number of design weaknesses. The error messages that appeared on the display were simply error numbers or obscure messages ("Malfunction 54" or "H-tilt"). This was not unusual for early computer programs when computers had much less memory and mass storage. One had to look up each error number in a manual for more explanation. However, neither the operator's manual nor the maintenance manual for the Therac-25 included an explanation of the error messages.

The machine distinguished between errors by the amount of effort needed to continue operation. For certain error conditions, the machine paused, and the operator could proceed (turn on the electron beam) by pressing one key. For other kinds of errors, the machine suspended operation and had to be completely reset. One would presume that the machine would allow one-key resumption only after minor, non-safety-related errors. Yet, one-key resumption occurred in some of the accidents in which patients received multiple overdoses.

Atomic Energy of Canada, Ltd. (AECL), a Canadian government corporation, manufactured the Therac-25. Investigators studying the accidents found that AECL produced very little documentation concerning the software specifications or the testing plan during development of the program. Although AECL claimed that they tested the machine extensively, it appeared that the test plan was inadequate.

Bugs

Investigators were able to trace some of the overdoses to two specific software errors. Because many readers of this book are computer science students, we will describe the bugs to illustrate the importance of using good programming techniques, but we simplify the discussion for readers with little programming experience.

After the operator entered treatment parameters at a control console, a software procedure called Set-Up Test performed a variety of checks to be sure the machine was in the correct position, and so on. If anything was not ready, this procedure scheduled itself to rerun the checks. (The system might simply have to wait for the turntable to move into place.) The Set-Up Test procedure can run several hundred times while setting up for one treatment. A flag variable indicated whether a specific device on the machine was in the correct position. A zero value meant the device was ready; a nonzero value meant it must be checked. To ensure that the device was checked, each time the Set-Up Test procedure ran, it incremented the variable to make it nonzero. The problem was that the flag variable was stored in a small unit of memory. After the variable was incremented to the largest number that it could hold, the variable overflowed and showed a value of zero. If everything else happened to be ready at that point, the program did not check the device position, and the treatment could proceed. Investigators believe that in some of the accidents, this bug allowed the electron beam to be on when the turntable was positioned for use of the light beam, and there was no protective device in place to attenuate the beam.

Part of the tragedy in this case is that the error was such a simple one, with a simple correction. No good student programmer should make this kind of error. To indicate the device needed checking, the program should set the flag variable to a fixed value, say 1 or "true," rather than incrementing it.

Other bugs caused the machine to ignore changes or corrections that the operator made at the console. When the operator typed in all the necessary information for a treatment, the program began moving various devices into place. This process could take several seconds during which the software checked for editing of the input by the operator and restarted the set-up if it detected editing. However, because of bugs in this section of the program, some parts of the program learned of the edited information while others did not. This led to machine settings that were incorrect and inconsistent with safe treatment. According to the later investigation by the Food and Drug Administration (FDA), there appeared to be no consistency checks in the program.

In a system controlling physical machinery while an operator enters—and might modify—input, many complex factors can contribute to subtle, intermittent, and hard-to-detect bugs. Programmers working on such systems must use good programming practices to avoid the problems and insist on testing procedures that expose potential problems.

8.2.3   Why So Many Incidents?

There were six known Therac-25 overdoses. You may wonder why hospitals and clinics continued to use the machine after the first one.

The Therac-25 had been in service for up to two years at some clinics. Medical facilities did not immediately pull it from service after the first few accidents because they did not know immediately that it had caused the injuries. Medical staff members considered various other explanations. They questioned the manufacturer about the possibility of overdoses, but the company responded (after several of the accidents) that the machine could not have caused the patient injuries. According to the Leveson and Turner investigative report, they also told the facilities that there had been no similar cases of injuries.

After the second accident, AECL investigated and found several problems related to the turntable (not including any of the ones we described). They made some system changes and recommended operational changes. They declared that they had improved the safety of the machine by five orders of magnitude, although they told the FDA that they were not certain of the exact cause of the accident. That is, they did not know whether they had found and fixed the problem that caused the accident or just other problems. In making decisions about continued use of the machines, the hospitals and clinics had to consider the costs of removing the expensive machine from service (in lost income and loss of treatment for patients who needed it), the uncertainty about whether the machine was the cause of the injuries, and, later, when that was clear, the manufacturer's assurances that they had solved the problem.

A Canadian government agency and some hospitals using the Therac-25 made recommendations for many more changes to enhance safety; they were not implemented. After the fifth accident, the FDA declared the machine defective and ordered AECL to inform users of the problems. The FDA and AECL spent about a year (during which the sixth accident occurred) negotiating about changes in the machine. The final plan included more than two dozen changes. They eventually installed the critical hardware safety interlocks, and most of the machines remained in use after that with no new incidents of overdoses.[35]

Overconfidence

Hospitals using the machine assumed it worked safely, an understandable assumption. Some of their actions, though, suggest overconfidence, or at least practices they should have avoided. For example:

- In the first overdose incident, when the patient told the machine operator that the machine had "burned" her, the operator told her that was impossible.

- Operators ignored error messages because the machine produced so many of them.

- A camera in the treatment room and an intercom system enabled the operator to monitor the treatment and communicate with the patient. (The operator console was outside the shielded treatment room.) One facility had successfully treated more than 500 patients with the machine. Then, on a day when neither the video monitor nor the intercom was functioning at that facility, an accident occurred. The operator did not see or hear the patient try to get up after an overdose. The patient received a second overdose before he reached the door and pounded on it.

The most obvious and critical indication of overconfidence in the software was AECL's decision to eliminate the hardware safety mechanisms. A safety analysis of the machine done by AECL years before the accidents suggests that they did not expect significant problems from software errors. In one case where a clinic added its own hardware safety features to the machine, AECL told them it was not necessary. None of the accidents occurred at that facility.

8.2.4 OBSERVATIONS AND PERSPECTIVE

From design decisions all the way to the response to the overdose accidents, the manufacturer of the Therac-25 demonstrated a pattern of irresponsibility. The Therac-25 is a stark reminder of the consequences of carelessness, cutting corners, unprofessional work, and attempts to avoid responsibility. A complex system can work correctly hundreds of times with a bug that shows up only in unusual circumstances—hence the importance of always following good safety procedures in operation of potentially dangerous equipment. This case also illustrates the importance of individual initiative and responsibility: One facility installed hardware safety devices on its Therac-25 because it recognized the risks and took action to reduce them. The hospital physicist at one of the facilities where the Therac-25 overdosed patients spent many hours working with the machine to try to reproduce the conditions under which the overdoses occurred. With little support or information from the manufacturer, he was able to figure out the cause of some of the malfunctions.

To emphasize that safety requires more than bug-free code, we consider other radiation treatment accidents. Two news reporters reviewed more than 4000 cases of radiation overdoses reported to the U.S. government. Here are a few of the overdose incidents they describe (not involving the Therac-25).[36]

- A technician started a treatment, and then left the patient for 10–15 minutes to attend an office party.
- A technician failed to carefully check the prescribed treatment time.
- A technician failed to measure the radioactive drugs administered; she just used what looked like the right amount.
- In at least two cases, technicians confused microcuries and millicuries.[*]

---

[*]A curie is a measure of radioactivity. A millicurie is one thousand times as much as a microcurie.

The underlying problems were carelessness, lack of appreciation for the risk involved, poor training, and lack of sufficient penalty to encourage better practices. (In most cases, the medical facilities paid small fines or none at all.) Some of the incidents occurred in systems without computers. These examples remind us that individual and management responsibility, good training, and accountability are important no matter what technology we use.

8.3 Increasing Reliability and Safety

Success actually requires avoiding many separate possible causes of failure.

—Jared Diamond[37]

8.3.1 PROFESSIONAL TECHNIQUES

The New York Stock Exchange installed a $2 billion system with hundreds of computers, 200 miles of fiber-optic cable, 8000 telephone circuits, and 300 data routers. The exchange managers had prepared for spikes in trading by testing the system on triple and quadruple the normal trading volume. On one day, the exchange processed 76% more trades than the previous record, handling the sales without errors or delays.[38] We describe failures throughout this chapter, but many large, complex computer systems work extremely well and we rely on them daily. How can we design, build, and operate systems that are likely to function well?

To produce good systems, we must use good software engineering techniques at all stages of development, including specifications, design, implementation, documentation, and testing. There is a wide range between poor work and good work, as there is in virtually any field. Professionals, both programmers and managers, have the responsibility to study and use the professional techniques and tools that are available and to follow the procedures and guidelines established in the various relevant codes of ethics and professional practices. The Software Engineering Institute and the computer security organization CERT have developed detailed coding standards to guide software developers in creating robust, safe, and secure programs.[39] The Software Engineering Code of Ethics and Professional Practice and the ACM Code of Ethics and Professional Conduct, in Appendix A, are two important sets of general guidelines for professional ethics and practices. Another important resource is the Project Management Institute's (PMI) *Project Management Body of Knowledge (PMBOK)*. PMI developed PMBOK using the input from thousands of project managers in a variety of industries; it contains best practices, processes, and other topics that can improve a project's chance of completing successfully.

Safety-critical applications

A subfield of computer science focuses on design and development of safety-critical software. Safety specialists emphasize that developers must "design in" safety from the start. There are techniques of hazard analysis that help system designers identify risks and protect against them. Software engineers who work on safety-critical applications should have special training. Software expert Nancy Leveson emphasizes that with good technical practices and good management, you can develop large systems right: "One lesson is that most accidents are not the result of unknown scientific principles but rather of a failure to apply well-known, standard engineering practices."[40]

To illustrate two important principles in safety-critical applications, we use as examples the accidents that destroyed two space shuttles, each killing the seven people onboard. Although computer systems were not the cause, these tragedies make the points well. Burning gases leaked from a rocket shortly after launch of the *Challenger* and caused its destruction. The night before the scheduled launch, the engineers argued for a delay. They knew the cold weather posed a severe threat to the shuttle. An engineer reported that, "It was up to us to prove beyond a shadow of a doubt that it was not safe to [launch]."[41] We cannot prove absolutely that a system is safe, nor can we usually prove absolutely that it will fail and kill someone. For the ethical decision maker, the policy should be to suspend or delay use of the system in the absence of a convincing case for safety, rather than to proceed in the absence of a convincing case for disaster.

In the second accident, a large piece of insulating foam dislodged and struck the wing of the *Columbia* space shuttle as it launched. NASA knew this happened, but pieces of foam had dislodged and struck the shuttle on other flights without causing a major problem. Thus, NASA managers declined to pursue available options to observe and repair the damage. *Columbia* broke up when reentering the earth's atmosphere at the end of its mission, illustrating the danger of complacency.[42]

Risk management and communications

Management experts use the term *high reliability organization* (HRO) for an organization (business or government) that operates in difficult environments, often with complex technology, where failures can have extreme consequences (for example, air traffic control and nuclear power plants).[43] Researchers have identified key characteristics of high performing HROs. These characteristics can improve software and computer systems in both critical and less critical applications. One characteristic is "preoccupation with failure," or risk management. That means always assuming something unexpected can go wrong—not just planning, designing, and programming for all problems the team can foresee, but always being aware that they might miss something. Risk management includes being alert to cues that might indicate an error or problem. It includes fully analyzing near-failures (rather than assuming the system "worked" because it averted an actual failure) and looking for systemic reasons for an error or failure rather than focusing narrowly on the detail that was wrong. (For example, *why* did some programmers for the Mars Climate Orbiter assume measurements were in English units while others assumed metric?)

Another feature of successful software project organizations is loose structure. Designers or programmers can speak to people in other departments or higher up in the company without going through rigid channels that discourage communication. An atmosphere of open, honest communication within the organization and between a company and client is essential for learning of problems early and reducing the effort required to handle them.

There is much more to the field of organizational features and project management that encourage success. It is well worthwhile for project managers, founders of start-up companies, and anyone in management to devote time to studying this topic.

Development methodologies

Computer system development teams that do well expend extensive effort to learn the needs of the client and to understand how the client will use the system. Good software developers help clients better understand their own goals and requirements, which the clients might not be good at articulating. A long planning stage can allow for discovering and modifying unrealistic goals. One company that developed a successful financial system that processes one trillion dollars in transactions per day spent several years developing specifications for the system, then only six months programming, followed by carefully designed, extensive testing. Other large projects require a more iterative approach, as it may be impossible to determine system details until the project begins development and generates feedback.

Agile is an iterative methodology popular among developers of systems in retail, banking, online services (e.g., Spotify), and throughout the software industry. Software developers wrote the *Agile Manifesto* (Figure 8.4) in response to the high failure rate of information technology projects using a traditional, sequential

---

We are uncovering better ways of developing
software by doing it and helping others do it.
Through this work we have come to value:

Individuals and interactions over processes and tools
Working software over comprehensive documentation
Customer collaboration over contract negotiation
Responding to change over following a plan

That is, while there is value in the items
on the right, we value the items on the left more.

Kent Beck	James Grenning	Robert C. Martin
Mike Beedle	Jim Highsmith	Steve Mellor
Arie van Bennekum	Andrew Hunt	Ken Schwaber
Alistair Cockburn	Ron Jeffries	Jeff Sutherland
Ward Cunningham	Jon Kern	Dave Thomas
Martin Fowler	Brian Marick	

© 2001, the above authors.
This declaration may be freely copied in any form,
but only in its entirety through this notice.

FIGURE 8.4 The Agile Manifesto.[44]

methodology. Project teams that use Agile interact with the client frequently, often daily, and deliver working parts of the system in the shortest timeframe possible, typically two to four weeks, instead of waiting for the entire system to be completed. Requirements and design are documented only to the extent necessary to begin development of the software.

Agile projects emphasize "user stories," that is, activities or ways users will interact with the system. The goal is to have a deliverable product that users can test and work with every few weeks. Developers incorporate user feedback and continue to build the system incrementally, feature by feature. Agile software development is especially helpful when most of the system features are not known at the start of the project.

In examples of poorly developed systems in Sections 8.1.3–8.1.5, we noted that changes in requirements were a major source of problems. The Agile methodology is designed to respond quickly and well to changing needs and information. Successful projects control change with a change management committee or other change approval process to ensure all changes are in line with the project's goals. Agile methodology may not be suitable for some applications where all safety features must be in place before use. Many software developers use hybrid methodologies combining aspects from each that are most suitable for their projects.

User interfaces and human factors

If you are editing a document and you try to quit without saving your changes, what happens? The program likely will remind you that you have not saved your changes and give you a chance to do so. The designers of word processors learned that people forget or sometimes click, touch, or type the wrong command. They gave us "undo" buttons. These are simple and common examples of considering human factors in designing software.

System designers and programmers can learn design principles from psychologists and human-factors experts. Well-designed user interfaces help avoid many problems. Here are a few characteristics of good user interfaces:

- simple, consistent, and purposeful display of information
- clear instructions and error messages
- checks on user input for typos and consistency with previous inputs
- well-chosen default actions and values, to reduce user workload
- feedback to the user explaining what the program is doing

The crash of American Airlines Flight 965 near Cali, Colombia, illustrates the importance of consistent and clear user interfaces. While approaching the airport, the crew intended to lock the autopilot onto the beacon, called Rozo, that would lead the plane to the airport. The pilot or copilot typed "R" and the Flight Management

System (FMS) displayed a list of beacons beginning with "R." Normally, the closest beacon is at the top of the list, but in this case Rozo was not on the list. The FMS would include Rozo only if the crew entered its full name, not just "R." The pilot or copilot selected the first beacon without checking carefully. The beacon at the top of the list was more than 100 miles away, near Bogota. The plane turned more than 90 degrees and a few minutes later, in the dark, it crashed into a mountain, killing 159 people.[45] The investigation by the Colombian aviation agency attributed the crash to errors made by the crew. The crew did not verify the beacon; continued to descend in the dark after the plane made a large, unexpected turn; and made other errors. A number of additional factors also contributed to this tragedy. However, the unexpected behavior of the FMS—not including the nearest beacon—created a dangerous situation.

We illustrate several principles that can help build better and safer systems with examples from automated flight systems and semi-autonomous cars. These points apply to many other application areas as well.[46]

The user must have sufficient understanding of the system. This can be a responsibility of the user (and those who develop training systems) and a responsibility of the system designers. In several incidents, a pilot changed a setting (e.g., speed or target altitude) without realizing that making that change caused other settings to change. For example, a pilot on Asiana Airlines Flight 214 did not realize the specific autopilot mode he selected disengaged an auto-throttle feature. As a result, the plane's speed decreased too rapidly on approach to the San Francisco airport and the tail section hit the ground and broke-off. The crash killed three passengers and injured most of the others. The airplane had multiple autopilot modes, each controlling different sets of features for different phases of the flight. How could a good user interface clearly indicate which features each mode controlled?

Lex Rayton/Alamy Stock Photo

FIGURE 8.5 The cockpit controls of a modern commercial airliner.

In several more cases, pilots inadvertently disengaged a desired control because of another design problem. We elaborate with two more examples.

Alarms, warnings, and error messages must be clear and appropriate. As we saw in the Therac-25 incidents, users ignore or override warnings that occur often, particularly if they do not understand the cause. The Indonesia AirAsia Flight 8501 crash resulted from a combination of technical failure and the crew's frustrated response. Four times during the flight, a system that controls the plane's rudder sounded an alarm. To stop the alarm, a pilot turned off a computer that controlled the rudder and several other flight systems, and then turned it back on again. Each time the computer came back up, the system operated normally, but a few minutes later, the alarm sounded again. The fourth time, someone in the cockpit removed a circuit breaker to reset the system. This disengaged the autopilot; the aircraft ascended sharply, stalled and then crashed, killing all 155 passengers and crew. Investigations found that the alarm was caused by a cracked solder joint which no one on board the aircraft could have repaired but which did not impact rudder operation.

The system should behave as an experienced user expects. Pilots tend to reduce their rate of climb as they get close to their desired altitude. The automated system on some planes maintained a climb rate far higher than pilots typically chose. Pilots, concerned that the plane might overshoot its target altitude, made adjustments, not realizing that their intervention turned off the automated function that caused the plane to level out when it reached the desired altitude. Thus, because the automation behaved in an unexpected way, the airplane did exactly what the pilot was trying to prevent. (The incidence of this problem declined with more training.)

The user needs feedback to understand what the system is doing at any time. This is important when a pilot or driver must suddenly take over if the automation fails or encounters a situation it cannot handle.

A workload that is too low can be dangerous. Clearly, an overworked operator is more likely to make mistakes. One of the goals of automation is to reduce the human workload. However, a workload that is too low can lead to boredom, overconfidence, or inattention. This can be a danger in cars that have a lot of self-driving capability but are not yet fully self-driving. The first fatal crash of a Tesla occurred while the driver was using the car's autopilot feature and not paying enough attention to traffic. Recognizing that temptation, Tesla makes its cars beep at the driver if his or her hands are off the steering wheel too long, but when a car does most of the driving, the temptation for inattention will be strong.

Human factors issues are important for semi-autonomous vehicles. Until fully self-driving cars replace most cars on the road, we will have a range of driver-assisting technologies. As car makers rush to add software controls and more features, problems occur. Screens are confusing or do not work. Owners might not install updates, particularly if installation is not convenient. Drivers do not understand the capabilities and the limitations of their smart but not perfect cars and may put too much trust in them. Distracted, confused, frustrated, or poorly informed drivers will make mistakes.

Redundancy and self-checking

Redundancy and self-checking are two techniques important in systems on which lives and fortunes depend. Redundancy takes several forms in both hardware and software. On aircraft, several computers can control an actuator on, say, a wing flap. If one computer fails, another can do the job.

Software modules can check their own results—either against a standard or by computing the same thing in two different ways and then comparing to see if the two results match or by recalculating as circumstances change. A more complex form of redundancy aims to protect against consistently faulty assumptions or methods of a programming team. In an example of this approach, three independent teams write modules for the same purpose, in three different programming languages, and the modules run on three separate computers. A fourth unit examines the outputs of the three modules and chooses the result obtained by at least two out of three. Safety experts say that even when programmers work separately, they tend to make the same kinds of errors, especially if there is an error, ambiguity, or omission in the program specifications.[47] Thus, this type of "voting" redundancy, while valuable in many safety-critical applications, might not overcome problems in other areas of the software development process.

Testing

We cannot overemphasize the importance of adequate, well-designed software testing. There are several clearly defined standards and methodologies for structured testing of software and systems. When a system is in production or in use, even small changes or updates need regression testing—a form of testing that ensures new changes do not impact activities that were working properly before the updates. Many significant computer system failures in previously working systems occur soon after installation of an update or upgrade. Unfortunately, many cost-conscious managers, programmers, and software developers see testing as a dispensable luxury, a step you can skimp on to meet a deadline or to save money. This is a common but foolish, risky, and often irresponsible attitude.

A practice called independent verification and validation (IV&V) can be very useful in finding errors in software systems. IV&V means that an independent company (that is, not the one that developed the program and not the customer) tests and validates the software. Testing and validation by an independent organization is not practical for all projects, but many software developers have their own testing teams that are independent of the programmers who develop a system. The IV&V team acts as an "adversary" and tries to find flaws, much as penetration testers (described in Section 5.5.3) try to find security vulnerabilities in a system. IV&V is helpful because teams that have developed an application tend to view

Attack on a hospital[48]

In 2015, a U.S. Air Force AC-130 gunship (aircraft) attacked a Doctors Without Borders hospital in Afghanistan, killing 30 staff and patients and wounding more. Though investigations identified human error as the principle cause, technological failures and mistrust of a computer system played integral parts in this tragedy. The night of the attack, the aircraft launched early in a hurried response to troops requesting air support. As a result, the crew did not complete a full briefing before the mission and expected mission updates once in the air. Sometime after the plane was airborne, the onboard electronics system failed, eliminating the aircraft's ability to send and receive video, email, or electronic messages. Where critical decisions depended on reliable communications from the aircraft to the command center, there was no backup for the faulty electronics system.

Because the crew believed they had been targeted by a missile as they arrived in the area, they circled at a wide distance from the target, thereby reducing the quality of the targeting images and the precision of the fire control systems. A ground team on the scene passed target coordinates for a building to the crew. When the crew entered coordinates into the targeting computer, it aimed at an open field 300 meters away from the actual target. The crew believed there was an error in the system or the coordinates had been transcribed incorrectly and, using low-quality night imagery, retargeted the system onto a building that appeared to match a physical description of the target.

As the aircraft moved in closer to fire, the targeting system correctly self-checked and realigned to the correct target building, but it did not provide information to the crew on the reasons for its actions. The crew believed the actions were in error and moved the alignment back to the building they had chosen—the hospital—in part because no one on the ground contradicted the targeting. The crew transmitted the coordinates of the building they chose to the command center shortly before the attack. Even though the coordinates matched the hospital, no one at the command center realized this at the time because of confusion related to the earlier communications failure, and there was no other automated system to compare targets to the no-strike list. The aircraft began firing and by the time the error was identified, the attack was over.

We spoke earlier of the need for a convincing case for safety. Here, with all the confusion, system failures, and perceived system failures, the crew did not have a convincing case for the correctness of their target. To what extent did technological failures contribute to the result? Were they incidental to errors the crew made by not following standard operating procedures for rules of engagement? Or had the crew become so dependent on technology that the failures and inconsistencies of the system significantly increased the risks? Does this case support or hinder the argument to integrate more technology and artificial intelligence into the battlefield? What are the responsibilities of technology professionals who design or build systems to be used in battlefields?

the application from a different perspective than a user. People who designed or developed a system believe the system works. With the best of intentions, they tend to test for problems they have already considered. Consciously or subconsciously, the people who created the system may be reluctant to find flaws in their creation;

their testing may be half-hearted. Independent testers bring different perspectives, and for them, success in finding flaws is not emotionally or professionally tied to responsibility for those flaws.

You might have used a *beta version* of a product or heard of *beta testing*. Beta testing is a near-final stage of testing in which a select set of customers (or members of the public) use a complete, presumably well-tested system in their "real-world" environment. This testing by regular users, not software experts, can detect software limitations and bugs that the designers, programmers, and testers missed. It can uncover confusing aspects of user interfaces, the need for more rugged hardware, problems that occur when interfacing with other systems or when running a new program on older computers, and many other sorts of problems.

> *We are what we repeatedly do. Excellence, therefore, is not an act, but a habit.*
> —Will Durant, summarizing Aristotle's view in his *Nicomachean Ethics*[49]

8.3.2 Trust the Human or the Computer System?

How much control should computers have in a crisis? This question arises in many application areas. We address it in the context of aircraft and automobile systems.

Like antilock braking systems in automobiles that control braking to avoid skidding (and do a better job than human drivers), computer systems in airplanes control sudden sharp climbs to avoid stalling. Some airplanes automatically descend if they detect cabin depressurization and the pilot does not take action quickly.

The Traffic Collision Avoidance System (TCAS) detects a potential in-air collision of two airplanes and directs the pilots to avoid each other. The first version of the system had so many false alarms that it was unusable. In some incidents, the system directed pilots to fly toward each other rather than away, potentially causing a collision instead of avoiding one. TCAS was improved and, according to the head of the Airline Pilots Association's safety committee, it has proved to be a great advance in safety.[50] In an example where the computer's instructions were better than a human's, TCAS functioned correctly when a Russian airplane carrying many children and a German cargo plane got too close to each other. TCAS detected the potential collision and told the Russian pilot to climb and the German pilot to descend. Unfortunately, the Russian pilot followed an air traffic controller's instruction to descend, and the planes collided. A few months after this tragedy, the pilot of a Lufthansa 747 ignored instructions from an air traffic controller and followed instructions from the computer system instead, avoiding a midair collision. U.S. and European pilots are now trained to follow TCAS instructions even if they conflict with instructions from an air traffic controller.

Pilots sometimes overreact to collision warnings and make extreme maneuvers that can injure passengers or cause a collision with other air traffic in the area; both better training and automated systems can reduce this problem. Automated systems in some airplanes prevent certain actions even if the pilot tries them (for example, banking at a very steep angle). Some people object, arguing that the pilot should have ultimate control in case unusual action is needed in an emergency. Based on accident statistics, some airlines believe otherwise: preventing pilots from doing something "stupid" can save more lives than letting them do something bold and heroic, but outside the program limitations, in the very rare cases where it might be necessary.[51]

Makers of self-driving cars believe allowing humans to override the car's decisions can lead to unsafe conditions. Autonomous cars have driven roughly two million test miles on public highways in California and other states. They have been involved in a very small number of accidents, most of them the fault of a human driver.

8.3.3   LAW, REGULATION, AND MARKETS

Criminal and civil penalties

Legal remedies for faulty systems include lawsuits against the company that developed or sold the system and criminal charges when fraud or criminal negligence occurs. Families of Therac-25 victims sued and settled out of court. A bank won a large judgment against a software company for a faulty financial system that caused problems a user described as "catastrophic." Several people have won large judgments against credit bureaus for incorrect data in credit reports that caused havoc in their lives.

Many commercial contracts for business computer systems limit the amount the business can recover to the actual amount spent on the computer system. Because fraud and misrepresentation are not, of course, part of a contract, some companies that suffer large losses because of faulty software allege fraud and misrepresentation by the seller in an attempt to recover some of the losses.

Well-designed liability laws and criminal laws—not so extreme that they discourage innovation, but clear and strong enough to provide incentives to produce good systems—are important legal tools for increasing reliability and safety of computer systems and accuracy of data in databases, as they are for protecting privacy and for protecting customers and the public in other industries. After-the-fact penalties do not undo the injuries that occurred, but the prospect of paying for mistakes and sloppiness is incentive to be responsible and careful. Payments compensate the victim and provide some justice. An individual, business, or government that does not have to pay for its mistakes and irresponsible actions has little motivation to correct problems.

Unfortunately, there are many flaws in liability law in the United States. Abuse of the liability lawsuit system almost shut down the small-airplane manufacturing industry for years. People have won multimillion-dollar suits when there was no scientific evidence or sensible reason to hold the manufacturer or seller of a product responsible for accidents or other negative impacts. The complexity of large computer systems makes designing liability standards difficult, but it is a necessary and important task.

Regulation and safety-critical applications

Is there legislation or regulation that can prevent life-threatening computer failures? A law saying that a radiation machine should not overdose a patient would be silly. We know that it should not do that. We could ban the use of computer control for applications where an error could be fatal, but such a ban is ill advised because in many applications, the benefits of using such systems far outweigh the risks.

A widely accepted option is regulation, including specific testing requirements and requirement for approval by a government agency before a new product can be sold. The Food and Drug Administration (FDA) has regulated drugs and medical devices for decades. Companies must do extensive testing, provide huge quantities of documentation, and get government approval before they sell new drugs and some medical devices. Arguments in favor of such regulation, both for drugs and for safety-critical computer systems, include the following:

- Preventing use of a bad product is better than relying on after-the-calamity remedies.
- Most people who would be at risk (e.g., patients) do not have the expertise to judge the safety or reliability of a system.
- Ordinary people find it difficult and expensive to successfully sue large companies.

If the FDA had thoroughly examined the Therac-25 before it was put into operation, it might have found the flaws before any patients were injured. However, we should note some weaknesses and trade-offs in the regulatory approach.[52] The approval process is extremely expensive and time consuming and the multiyear delays in introducing a good product may cost many lives. Political concerns can affect the approval process as does influence of competitors. There is an incentive for bureaucrats and regulators to be overcautious since damage caused by an approved product results in bad publicity and possible firing for the regulator who approved it. Deaths or losses caused by the delay or failure to approve a good new product are rarely obvious and receive little publicity.

Leveson and Turner, in their Therac-25 article, summarize some of these dilemmas:

> The issues involved in regulation of risky technology are complex. Overly strict standards can inhibit progress, require techniques behind the state of the art, and transfer responsibility from the manufacturer to the government. The fixing of responsibility requires a delicate balance. Someone must represent the public's needs, which may be subsumed by a company's desire for profits.

On the other hand, standards can have the undesirable effect of limiting the safety efforts and investment of companies that feel their legal and moral responsibilities are fulfilled if they follow the standards. Some of the most effective standards and efforts for safety come from users. Manufacturers have more incentive to satisfy customers than to satisfy government agencies.[53]

Professional licensing

Another approach to improving software quality is mandatory licensing of software development professionals. Licenses are permits to perform particular types of work and are required for hundreds of trades and professions ranging from the practice of medicine to flower arranging and fortune telling. The desired effect is to ensure competence and to protect the public from poor quality and unethical behavior. Federal agencies grant some licenses, e.g., the Federal Aviation Administration (FAA) for airline pilots, but most licensing is handled at the state level.

States typically do not accept licenses from other states, so when people who work in licensed professions move to a new state, they cannot work in their field until they get a new license. For software developers, this raises a tricky issue. Freelance programmers can work on projects in any state. Should they need to be licensed in every state where they have a client? Large software companies commonly work on projects for clients outside the state where the company and its programmers are located. Would companies need to ensure that everyone on the project team is licensed in the appropriate state? Licensing software professionals at the federal level is not an easy solution, as the United States has no department or agency for overseeing software safety, as the FAA does for air traffic.

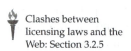
Clashes between licensing laws and the Web: Section 3.2.5

Professional licensing requirements typically include specific training, the passing of competency exams, ethical requirements, and continuing education. The field of software technology is constantly advancing and changing. Languages, tools, and development techniques are constantly in flux. What should be the standards for training and testing? How can they be kept up to date?

The history of mandatory licensing in many fields shows that the actual goals and the effects were and are not always very noble. In some trades (plumbing, for example), the licensing requirements were devised to keep black people out. Requirements for specific degrees and training programs, as opposed to learning on one's own or on the job, tend to keep poorer people from qualifying for licenses. In at least one state, licensing laws prohibit a person licensed as both a dentist and an orthodontist from providing basic dental services at discounted prices for poor people. Can you think of reasons for this? Economic analyses have shown that the effect of licensing is to reduce the number of practitioners in the field and keep prices and income for licensees higher than they would otherwise be—in many cases, without any improvement in quality.[54] Any respectable, ethical scheme for licensing software developers would need to be carefully designed and maintained to avoid such negative side effects and abuses. More fundamentally, some see a requirement for a government-approved license as a violation of the freedom to work.

There are voluntary means for judging qualifications of software personnel— for example, a diploma from a respected school and a variety of certification programs. Certifications typically are narrowly defined; they certify that an individual has reached a certain level of knowledge, skill, or expertise in a particular area, for example, a specific tool, technique, or piece of software. Certifications do not have the broad range typical of licenses. Professional associations could establish a broader, voluntary certification program to include the kinds of testing, ethical standards, and continuing education associated with licensing but without the legal ban on work by unlicensed practitioners.

Issues about licensing software professionals are hotly debated in the information technology field with the two key professional organizations each having a different view—the IEEE supports licensing software engineers and the ACM does not.

Taking responsibility

In some cases of computer errors, businesses pay customers for problems or damages without a lawsuit. For example, Intuit offered to pay interest and penalties that resulted from errors in flawed income-tax programs. When United Airlines mistakenly posted ticket prices on its website as low as about $25 for flights between the United States and Europe, it honored tickets purchased before it corrected the error. United, at first, charged the buyers the correct fare and probably had the legal right to do so, but the airline concluded that having angry customers would cost the business more than the tickets.

We noted earlier that business pressures can lead to cutting corners and releasing defective products. Business pressure can also be a cause for insistence on quality and maintaining good customer relations. Good business managers recognize the importance of customer satisfaction and the reputation of the business. Some businesses have an ethical policy of behaving responsibly and paying for mistakes, just as a person would pay for accidentally breaking a neighbor's window with a misdirected softball.

Other market mechanisms besides consumer backlash encourage a quality job and provide ways to deal with the risk of failures. Insurance companies have an incentive to evaluate the systems they insure and require that certain standards are met. Organizations whose communications are critical to public safety, such as police departments and hospitals, can take responsibility to ensure they have appropriate backup service, possibly paying extra for the higher level of service.

How can customers protect themselves from faulty software? How can a business avoid buying a seriously flawed program? For high-volume consumer and small-business software, one can consult the many websites that review new programs, or consult one's social network. Specialized systems with a small market are more difficult to evaluate before purchase. We can check the seller's reputation or consult previous customers and ask how well the seller did the job. Online user groups for specific software products are excellent sources of information for prospective and current customers. In the case of the Therac-25, the users eventually spread information among themselves. If the Web had existed at the time of the accidents, it is likely that the problems would have been identified sooner and that some of the accidents would not have happened.

8.4 Dependence, Risk, and Progress

8.4.1 ARE WE TOO DEPENDENT ON COMPUTERS?

Many people who write about the social impacts of computers lament our dependence on computing technology. Because of their usefulness and flexibility, computers, mobile phones, and similar devices are now virtually everywhere. Is this good? Or bad? Or neutral? The word "dependence" often has a negative connotation. "Dependence on computers" suggests a criticism of our use of the technology and its gadgets. Is that appropriate?

In Holland, no one discovered the body of a reclusive, elderly man who died in his apartment until six months after his death when someone noticed that he had a large accumulation of mail. This incident was described as a "particularly disturbing example of computer dependency." Many of the man's bills, including rent and utilities, were paid automatically and his pension check went automatically to his bank account. Thus, "all the relevant authorities assumed that he was still alive."[55] But who expects the local gas company or other "relevant authorities" to discover a death? The problem here, clearly, was the lack of concerned family, friends, and neighbors.

On the other hand, many people and businesses are not prepared to do without the computer systems and electronic devices they use every day. In several incidents, computer failures or other accidents knocked out communications services for extended periods of time. Drivers could not buy gasoline with their credit cards. "Customers were really angry," said a gas station manager. A supermarket manager reported, "Customers are yelling and screaming because they can't get their money, and they can't use the ATM to pay for groceries."[56] A physician commented that modern hospitals and clinics cannot function efficiently without medical information systems. Modern crime fighting depends on computers. Many drivers would be lost if their navigation system failed.

Is our "dependence" on electronic technology different from our dependence on electricity, which we use for lighting, entertainment, manufacturing, medical treatments—just about everything? Is our "dependence" on computers different from a farmer's dependence on a plow? Modern surgery's dependence on anesthesia?

Computers, smartphones, and plows are tools and we use tools because we are better off with them than without them. They reduce the need for hard, physical labor and tedious routine mental labor. They help us to be more productive, or safer, or more comfortable. When we have a good tool, we can forget (or no longer even learn) the older method of performing a task. If the tool breaks down, we are stuck and cannot perform the task until someone fixes the tool. This can mean loss of telephone service for several hours, loss of a large amount of money, or danger for some people. But the negative effects of a breakdown do not condemn the tool. To the contrary, for many applications (not all), the inconveniences or dangers of a breakdown are a reminder of the convenience, productivity, or safety the tool provides when it is working. The breakdown can remind us, for example, of the billions of communications, carrying voice, text, photos, and data, that are possible or more convenient or cheaper because of the technology.

Some misconceptions about dependence on computers come from a poor understanding of the role of risk, confusion of "dependence" with "use," and blaming computers for failures where they were only innocent bystanders. On the other hand, abdication of responsibility that comes from overconfidence or ignorance is a serious problem. There are valid criticisms of dependence when a system design allows a failure in one component to cause a major breakdown or when businesses, government agencies, and organizations do not make plans for dealing with systems failures. The wise individual is grateful for ATMs, credit cards, and smartphone wallets, but keeps a little extra cash at home in case they do not work. The driver with a navigation system might choose to keep a map in the car.

8.4.2 RISK AND PROGRESS

Electricity lets us heat our homes, cook our food, and enjoy security and entertainment. It also can kill you if you're not careful.
—"Energy Notes" (Flyer sent with San Diego Gas & Electric utility bills)

We trust older technologies when we turn on a light or ride a bicycle. Technology, overall, tends to make us safer. For example, as use of technology, automation, and computer systems increased in virtually all workplaces, the risk of dying in an on-the-job accident dropped from 39 among 100,000 workers (in 1934) to 3.3 in 100,000 in 2013.[57] But as the tools and technologies we use become more complex and more interconnected, the amount of damage that results from an individual disruption or failure increases, and we sometimes pay the costs in dramatic and tragic events. For example, if a person out for a walk bumps into another person, neither is likely to be hurt, yet if both are in cars traveling at 60 miles per hour, they could be killed. If two airliners collide, or one loses an engine, several hundred people could be killed. Despite the large loss from one accident, the death rate per mile traveled is lower for air travel than for cars.

Many new technologies are not very safe when first developed. Software engineering textbooks use the Cali crash, described in Section 8.3.1, as an example so that future software specialists will not repeat weaknesses in that airplane's flight management system. In addition, tragedies such as the Cali crash triggered improvements in ground proximity warning systems to reduce crashes into mountains. Older radar-based systems sometimes gave warning only 10 seconds before a potential impact. Newer systems (called terrain awareness and warning systems) contain a digital map of the world's topography. They can give a pilot up to a minute of warning if a plane is too close to a mountain (or other terrain) and automatically display a map of nearby mountains. These systems are likely responsible for preventing crashes in incidents in which pilots set an altimeter incorrectly, attempted to land in poor visibility, mistook building lights for airport lights, and so on. No commercial U.S. airliner has crashed into a mountain since the enhanced systems were implemented.[58]

We learn and so, overall, computer systems and other technologies have made air travel safer. If the death rate from commercial airline accidents in the United States were the same now as it was about 60 years ago, 8000 people would die in plane crashes each year.

Scientists and engineers study disasters to learn how to prevent them and how to recover from them. A disastrous fire led to the development of fire hydrants—a way to get water to the fire from the water pipes under the street. Automobile engineers used to design the front of an automobile to be extremely rigid, to protect passengers in a crash, but they discovered that people died and suffered serious injuries because the car frame transmitted the force of a crash to the occupants. In the 1950s, Mercedes-Benz engineers learned it was safer to build cars with "crumple zones" to absorb the force of impact.[59] More improvements followed, and the death rate from motor vehicle accidents in the United States declined almost 80% from 1965 to 2013 (from 5.30 per 100 million vehicle miles traveled to 1.09 per 100 million vehicle miles traveled).[60] One significant factor is increased education about responsible use (e.g., the campaign against drunk driving). Another is the introduction of a variety of devices to help drivers avoid accidents and to protect people when they occur:

- Rear-view cameras help drivers avoid hitting a child or an object when backing up.
- "Night vision" systems detect obstacles and project onto the windshield an image or diagram of objects in the car's path.
- Electronic stability systems detect a likely rollover, before the driver is aware of the problem, and slow the engine.
- Seat belts and airbags protect occupants when other devices fail and there is a crash.

The pace of change in computer technology is much faster than that in other technologies, and there are some important differences between computers and other technologies that increase risks:

- Computer systems make decisions; electricity does not.
- The power and flexibility of computers encourage us to build more complex systems—where failures have more serious consequences.
- Most software is not built from standard trusted parts as is the case in many engineering fields.
- The interconnectivity of the Internet of Things can spread failures to millions of distant devices.

These differences affect the kind and scope of the risks we face. They need our continued attention as computer professionals, workers and planners in other fields, and as members of the public.

Observations

Throughout this chapter, we have made several points:

- Many of the issues related to reliability and safety for computer systems have arisen before with other technologies.
- There is a "learning curve" for new technologies. By studying failures, we can reduce their occurrence.
- Much is known about how to design, develop, and use complex systems well and safely. Ethical professionals have a responsibility to learn and follow these methods.
- We cannot expect all large systems to be error-free. The complexity of computer systems makes oversights and mistakes likely, but we can reduce their probability.
- We must compare the risks of using computer technologies with the risks of using other methods, and we must weigh the risks against the benefits.
- Many accidents and tragedies are not the direct result of a technological failure, but instead, result from poor decisions or incorrect actions made by humans in response to flaws in the technology.

This does not mean that we should excuse or ignore computer errors and failures because failures occur in other technologies or that we should tolerate carelessness and negligence because perfection is not possible. We cannot accept poor and irresponsible work as "part of the learning process," and we cannot excuse it because, on balance, the contribution of computer technology is positive.

The potential for serious disruption of normal activities and danger to people's lives and health because of flaws in computer systems should always remind the computer professional of the importance of doing his or her job responsibly. Computer system developers and other professionals responsible for planning and choosing systems must assess risks carefully and honestly, include safety protections, and make appropriate plans for shutdown of a system when it fails, for backup systems where appropriate, and for recovery.

Knowing that one will be liable for the damages one causes is strong incentive to find improvements and increase safety. When evaluating a specific instance of a failure, we can look for those responsible and try to ensure that they bear the costs of the damage they caused. When evaluating an application area or the technology as a whole, we focus on the balance between risks and benefits.

 Exercises

Review Exercises

8.1 List two cases described in this chapter in which insufficient testing was a factor in a program error or system failure.

8.2 List two cases described in this chapter in which the provider did an inadequate job of informing customers about flaws in the system.

8.3 What was one cause of the delay in completing the Denver airport?

8.4 Give one reason why the HealthCare.gov website did not function properly in its first few weeks.

8.5 What is one case in which reuse of software caused a serious problem?

8.6 What is one characteristic of successful high reliability organizations?

8.7 Describe one principle of human-interface design that is particularly important in safety-critical applications.

General Exercises

8.8 (a) Suppose you write a computer program to add two integers. Assume that each integer and their sum will fit in the standard memory unit the computer uses for integers. How likely do you think it is that the sum will be correct? (If you run the program a million times on different pairs of integers, how many times do you think it would give the correct answer?)

(b) Suppose a utility company has a million customers and it runs a program to determine whether any customers have overdue bills. How likely do you think it is that the results of the program will be completely correct?

(c) Probably your answers to parts (a) and (b) were different. Give some reasons why the likely number of errors would be different in these two examples.

8.9 Consider the case described in Section 8.1.2 in which a school assumed a boy was a drug abuser because two schools used different disciplinary codes in their records. Describe some policies or practices that can help prevent such problems.

8.10 List several possible reasons why a car rental company might mistakenly list one of its rented cars as stolen. Which of these could better software or better policies prevent? Which are the kinds of mistakes that would be difficult or impossible to prevent?

8.11 Doctors typically enter orders for prescription drugs for their patients into a computer system. On one system, when another doctor used the same terminal after the previous doctor neglected to log out, the system assigned drugs ordered by the second doctor to the first doctor's patient. Describe two features that such systems could include to reduce this kind of error.

8.12 The FDA maintains a registry of more than 120,000 drugs. An investigation by the Department of Health and Human Services found that the information on about 34,000 drugs was incorrect or out of date. Nine thousand drugs were missing from the directory.[61] Describe several possible risks of the database being so out of date. Give as many possible reasons as you can think of why the database was out of date.

8.13 Consider the standardized-test score reporting error described in the box in Section 8.1.2. Suppose the test company had reported scores to the schools as significantly higher, rather than lower, than the correct scores. Do you think the schools would have questioned the scores? Do you think anyone would have discovered the error? If so, how? Give a few examples of situations where you think people would not report computer errors. For each example, give your reason (e.g., optimism, ignorance, gullibility, dishonesty, or others).

8.14 List some similarities between the development of the Denver Airport baggage system (Section 8.1.4) and the development of the federal health insurance enrollment system (Section 8.1.5) relevant to the problems the systems had. Describe some significant differences.

8.15 Suppose you are on a consulting team to design a voting system for your state in which people can vote online. What are some important design considerations? Discuss some pros and cons of such a system. Overall, do you think it is a good idea?

8.16 Find several provisions of the Software Engineering Code of Ethics and Professional Practice (Appendix A.1) that were violated in the Therac-25 case.

8.17 In the discussion of high reliability organizations, we said that one important practice is being alert to cues that might indicate an error. What cues were missed or ignored in the Therac-25 case by the manufacturer, and what cues were missed or ignored by some users?

8.18 Identify at least one ethical failure that occurred in both of these cases: the standardized-test score reporting error (Section 8.1.2) and the Therac-25.

8.19 Several models of a medical infusion pump in use worldwide had a defect, called "key-bounce." When a user typed the dosage on the keypad, a key pressed once could bounce and cause the digit to record twice. Thus, a dose of 2 units might become 22 units, and the pump could give a patient an overdose of drugs. More than five years after the company was warned of problems with the pumps, the FDA issued a recall notice.[62] Identify several things that various people did, or probably did, that were wrong.

8.20 Suppose you are responsible for the design and development of a computer system to control an amusement park ride. Sensors in the seats will determine which seats are occupied, so the software can consider weight and balance. The system will control the speed and duration of the ride. The amusement park wants a system where, once the ride starts, a person is not needed to operate it.

List some important things that you can or should do to ensure the safety of the system. Consider all aspects of development, technical issues, operating instructions, and so on.

8.21 After making a programming change in a major bank's computer system, an employee forgot to enter certain commands. As a result, approximately 800,000 direct deposits received by the bank were not posted to the customer accounts until the next day. What are some potential consequences of the error? If you were the bank president, what would you say in a statement to the news media or your customers?

8.22 Who are the "good guys"? Pick two people or organizations mentioned in this chapter whose work helped make systems safer or reduced the negative consequences of errors. Tell why you picked them.

8.23 We mentioned that smartphones contain millions of lines of computer code. Estimate how many pages one million lines of code would take up if printed. (State your assumptions.)

8.24 How can features such as automatic braking and lane-departure warnings make a car less safe?

8.25 Consider the following incident:

> A baby in a hospital was connected to several monitoring devices with alarms that would signal if a medical problem occurred. A nurse turned off an alarm that rang in the baby's room so that the exhausted mother could sleep. Inadvertently, her action prevented alarms from ringing at the nurse's station. A problem occurred, alarms did not ring, and the baby died.

Suppose you are investigating this incident. List several potential types of or sources of errors that might have caused the alarms not to ring.

8.26 Make a list of all the errors, failures, and mistakes you can identify in the incident in which a gunship attacked a hospital (see the box in Section 8.3.1). Try to separate them into two categories: user errors and computer system errors.

8.27 How would losing your mobile phone for one day affect you?

8.28 Choose a noncomputer activity that you are familiar with and that has some risks (e.g., skateboarding, scuba diving, or working in a restaurant). Describe some of the risks and some safety practices. Describe analogies with risks related to computer systems.

8.29 What aspects of successful high reliability organizations (Section 8.3.1) were lacking in the Therac-25 case? What factors in the space shuttle disasters (Section 8.3.1) appear also in the Therac-25 case?

8.30 Software developers are sometimes advised to "design for failure." Give some examples of what this might mean.

8.31 This exercise is for computer science students or others who write software. Describe how you could put redundancy or self-checking into a program you wrote. If you actually did so, describe the project and the methods.

8.32 Assume you are a professional working in your chosen field. Describe specific things you can do to reduce the impact of any two problems we discussed in this chapter. (If you cannot think of anything related to your professional field, choose another field that might interest you.)

8.33 Think ahead to the next few years and describe a new problem, related to issues in this chapter, likely to develop from digital technology or devices.

Assignments

These exercises require some research or activity.

8.34 Read a few items in the current issue of the Risks Digest (catless.ncl.ac.uk/risks/). Write a summary of two items.

8.35   Samsung recalled millions of its Galaxy Note 7 devices because batteries overheated and burned. As we wrote this, the cause was still unknown and speculation ranged over hardware (the batteries were faulty, or the battery compartment was too small) and software. Find out if the cause is now known and, if so, describe it.

8.36   For years, there has been controversy about whether radio waves from mobile phones increase the risk of brain cancer. Find recent studies. What were their conclusions?

8.37   Find a journalistic or scientific article published within the past year that discusses a significant failure of a computer system. Write a summary of the article and a commentary on the article's analysis of the problem. Include a full citation for the article.

Class Discussion Exercises

These exercises are for class discussion, perhaps with short presentations prepared in advance by small groups of students.

8.38   Consider the following information.

> Some drivers of a particular company's cars involved in accidents blamed the accidents on unintended acceleration caused by flaws in the electronic throttle system. A NASA study found no fault with the electronic throttle system. In some cases, the car's event recorder indicated that the driver stepped on the accelerator when intending to step on the brake. Some accidents resulted from pedals caught on floor mats. A high percentage of drivers in accidents involving unintended acceleration were 65 years old or older. A group of software experts who examined the source code for the electronic throttle made many criticisms of the code and said problems with the code could cause unintended acceleration in some circumstances.

With this varied information as background, discuss what level of cause-and-effect proof should be necessary to win a lawsuit against the car company for a crash where the driver blames the electronic throttle for unintended acceleration. What information should be considered in particular cases? What implications do your responses have for other products that include large, complex software systems?

8.39   Some critics of the HealthCare.gov website development project make comparisons with Facebook with respect to number of users, cost of development, complexity, ease of access, and so on. Discuss such comparisons and reasons for the differences.

8.40   Assume that the family of one of the victims of the Therac-25 filed three lawsuits. They are suing the hospital where their family member was treated, the company that made the machine (AECL), and the programmer who wrote the Therac-25 software. Divide students into six groups: attorneys for the family against each of the three respondents, and attorneys for each of the three respondents. Each group is to present a five-minute summation of arguments for its case. Then, let the class discuss all aspects of the case and vote on the degree of responsibility of each of the respondents.

8.41   Some states considered legislation prohibiting autonomous cars unless there is a way for a person to take control from the computer system. Discuss arguments for and against such a law. Should legislators pass it?

8.42   A factory contains an area where robots do all the work. There is a fence around the area. Human workers are not supposed to enter while the robots are working. When anyone opens the gate in the fence, it automatically cuts off power to the robots. A worker jumped over the fence to repair a robot that was malfunctioning. Another robot, bringing parts to the malfunctioning robot, accidentally pinned the worker against a machine, killing him.

Suppose your class is a consulting team hired (by a neutral party) to investigate this case and write a report. Consider several factors relevant in safety-critical systems. What was done right? What was done wrong? Is there important information not included in this summary of the case that you would ask about? If so, what? What degree of blame do you assign to the software company that designed the robot system, the company that operates the factory, and the worker? Why? What changes, if any, should the factory operators make to reduce the likelihood of more deaths?

Notes

1. Robert N. Charette, "Why Software Fails," *IEEE Spectrum*, Sept. 2005, www. spectrum.ieee.org/sep05/1685.

2. *The Risks Digest: Forum on Risks to the Public in Computers and Related Systems*, archived at catless.ncl.ac.uk/risks.

3. Jacques Steinberg and Diana B. Henriques, "When a Test Fails the Schools, Careers and Reputations Suffer," *New York Times*, May 21, 2001, pp. A1, A10–A11.

4. Andrea Robinson, "Firm: State Told Felon Voter List May Cause Errors," *Miami Herald,* Feb. 17, 2001.

5. Department of Homeland Security, U.S. Citizenship and Immigration Services, "E-Verify Performance," www.uscis.gov/e-verify/about-program/performance. Westat, "Evaluation of the Accuracy of E-Verify Findings," July 2012, www.uscis.gov/sites/default/files/USCIS/Verification/E-Verify/E-Verify_Native_Documents/Everify%20Studies/E-Verify%20Accuracy%20Report%20Summary.pdf. "Immigration: You Can't Rely on E-Verify," editorial in *Los Angeles Times*, May 27, 2011, articles.lat-imes.com/2011/may/27/opinion/la-edarizona-20110527. Government Accountability Office, "Employment Verification," Dec. 2010, www.gao.gov/new.items/d11146.pdf. Note that error percentages varied in different documents; those given here are based on the latest review but are approximate.

6. Ann Davis, "Post-Sept. 11 Watch List Acquires Life of Its Own," *Wall Street Journal,* Nov. 19, 2002, p. A1.

7. *Arizona* v. *Evans*, reported in "Supreme Court Rules on Use of Inaccurate Computer Records," *EPIC Alert*, Mar. 9, 1995, v. 2.04.

8. Reuters, "Glitch Closes Tokyo Stock Exchange," *The New Zealand Herald,* Nov. 2, 2005, www.nzherald.co.nz/tokyo-stock-exchange/news/article.cfm?o_id=272&objectid=10353098. Julia Flynn, Sara Calian, and Michael R. Sesit, "Computer Snag Halts London Market 8 Hours," *Wall Street Journal,* Apr. 6, 2000, p. A14.

9. Jack Nicas, "Jet Lagged: Web Glitches Still Plague Virgin America," *Wall Street Journal,* Nov. 23, 2011, www.wsj.com/articles/SB10001424052970203710704577053110330006178.

10. Mars Climate Orbiter, mars.jpl.nasa.gov/msp98/orbiter.

11. Davide Balzarotti, Greg Banks, Marco Cova, Viktoria Felmetsger, Richard Kemmerer, William Robertson, Fredrik Valeur, and Giovanni Vigna, "Are Your Votes Really Counted? Testing the Security of Real-World Electronic Voting Systems," *Proceedings of the International Symposium on Software Testing and Analysis*, July 2008,

www.cs.ucsb.edu/~seclab/projects/voting/issta08_voting.pdf. Ed Felton, "Hotel Minibar Keys Open Diebold Voting Machines," Sept. 18, 2006, www.freedom-to-tinker.com/?p=1064.

12. Jeremy Hsu, "Alaska's Online Voting Leaves Cybersecurity Experts Worried," *IEEE Spectrum*, Nov. 6, 2014, spectrum.ieee.org/tech-talk/telecom/security/alaska-online-voting-leaves-cybersecurity-experts-worried. "Absentee Voting by Electronic Transmission," State of Alaska Division of Elections, www.elections.alaska.gov/vi_bb_by_fax.php.

13. Drew Springall *et al.,* "Security Analysis of the Estonian Internet Voting System," *Proceedings of the 21st ACM Conference on Computer and Communications Security*, Nov. 2014, jhalderm.com/pub/papers/ivoting-ccs14.pdf.

14. Balzarotti *et al.,* "Are Your Votes Really Counted?"

15. Charette, "Why Software Fails". Virginia Ellis, "Snarled Child Support Computer Project Dies," *Los Angeles Times*, Nov. 21, 1997, p. A1, A28. Peter G. Neumann, "System Development Woes," *Communications of the ACM,* Dec. 1997, p. 160. Rajeev Syal, "Abandoned NHS IT System Has Cost £10bn So Far," *The Guardian*, Sept. 17, 2013, www.theguardian.com/society/2013/sep/18/nhs-records-system-10bn. Oliver Wright, "NHS Pulls the Plug on its £11bn IT System," Aug. 2, 2011, www.independent.co.uk/life-style/health-and-families/health-news/nhs-pulls-the-plug-on-its-11bn-it-system-2330906.html.

16. Charette, "Why Software Fails."

17. H. Travis Christ, quoted in Linda Rosencrance, "US Airways Partly Blames Legacy Systems for March Glitch," *Computerworld,* Mar. 29, 2007. Linda Rosencrance, "Glitch at U.S. Airways Causes Delays," *Computerworld,* Mar. 5, 2007, computerworld.com/article/2543659/enterprise-applications/glitch-at-u-s--airways-causes-delays.html.

18. The DIA delay was widely reported in the news media. A few of the sources I used for the discussion here are Kirk Johnson, "Denver Airport Saw the Future. It Didn't Work." *New York Times*, Aug. 27, 2005, www.nytimes.com/2005/08/27/us/denver-airport-saw-the-future-it-didnt-work.html; W. Wayt Gibbs, "Software's Chronic Crisis," *Scientific American*, Sept. 1994, 271(3), pp. 86–95; Robert L. Scheier, "Software Snafu Grounds Denver's High-Tech Airport," *PC Week*, 11(19), May 16, 1994, p. 1; Price Colman, "Software Glitch Could Be the Hitch. Misplaced Comma Might Dull Baggage System's Cutting Edge," *Rocky Mountain News*, Apr. 30, 1994, p. 9A; Steve Higgins, "Denver Airport: Another Tale of Government High-Tech Run Amok," *Investor's Business Daily*, May 23, 1994, p. A4; Julie Schmit, "Tiny Company Is Blamed for Denver Delays," *USA Today*, May 5, 1994, pp. 1B, 2B.

19. Scheier, "Software Snafu Grounds Denver's High-Tech Airport."

20. Wayne Arnold, "How Asia's High-Tech Airports Stumbled," *Wall Street Journal,* July 13, 1998, p. B2.

21. We used many sources as background for this section. In addition to specific sources cited below: Jim Hirschauer, "Technical Deep Dive on What's Impacting Healthcare.gov," App Dynamics Blog, App Dynamics, Oct. 25, 2013, blog.appdynamics.com/apm/technical-deep-dive-whats-impacting-healthcare-gov/; U.S. Government Accountability Office, "HealthCare.gov: Ineffective Planning and Oversight Practices Underscore the Need for Improved Contract Management," July 2014, GAO-14-694, www.gao.gov/assets/670/665179.pdf; "HealthCare.gov: CMS Has Taken

Steps to Address Problems, but Needs to Further Implement Systems Development Best Practices," GAO Report to Congressional Requesters, Mar. 2015, www.gao.gov/assets/670/668834.pdf; Joshua Bleiberg and Darrell M. West, "A Look Back at Technical Issues with HealthCare.gov," Brookings Institute, Apr. 9, 2015, www.brookings.edu/blog/techtank/2015/04/09/a-look-back-at-technical-issues-with-healthcare-gov/.

22. Devin Dwyer, "Memo Reveals Only 6 People Signed Up for Obamacare on First Day," *ABC News*, Oct. 31, 2013, abcnews.go.com/blogs/politics/2013/10/memo-reveals-only-6-people-signed-up-for-obamacare-on-first-day.

23. U.S. Senate Committee on Health, Education, Labor, and Pensions Hearing, Questions for Secretary of Health and Human Services, May 8, 2014, www.help.senate.gov/imo/media/050814_HELP_Burwell_QFRs-Alexander-FINAL.pdf. "An Overview of 60 Contracts That Contributed to the Development and Operation of the Federal Marketplace," Office of the Inspector General Report, Aug. 26 2014, oig.hhs.gov/oei/reports/oei-03-14-00231.asp.

24. Ariana Cha and Lena Sun, "What Went Wrong with HealthCare.gov," *Washington Post*, Oct. 24, 2013, www.washingtonpost.com/national/health-science/what-went-wrong-with-healthcaregov/2013/10/24/400e68de-3d07-11e3-b7ba-503fb5822c3e_graphic.html.

25. Sharon LaFraniere, Ian Austen, and Robert Pear, "Contractors See Weeks of Work on Health Site," *New York Times*, Oct. 20, 2013, www.nytimes.com/2013/10/21/us/insurance-site-seen-needing-weeks-to-fix.html?pagewanted=all&_r=1&.

26. David Chao (CMS project manager), Testimony given to Senate House Committee Inquiry, Nov. 19, 2013, www.youtube.com/watch?v=QKu95EnUaTs.

27. Lena H. Sun and Scott Wilson, "Health Insurance Exchange Launched Despite Signs of Serious Problems," *Washington Post*, Oct. 21, 2013, www.washingtonpost.com/national/health-science/health-insurance-exchange-launched-despite-signs-of-serious-problems/2013/10/21/161a3500-3a85-11e3-b6a9-da62c264f40e_story.html.

28. Government Accountability Office, "HealthCare.gov: Actions Needed to Address Weaknesses in Information Security and Privacy Controls," GAO-14-730, Sept. 2014, www.gao.gov/products/GAO-14-730.

29. Joel Gehrke, "Obamacare Launch Spawns 700+ Cyber Squatters Capitalizing on HealthCare.gov, State Exchanges," *Washington Examiner*, Oct. 23, 2013. Testimony of Morgan Wright Before the House Committee on Science, Space, and Technology, Nov. 19, 2013, www.projectauditors.com/Papers/Troubled_Projects/HHRG-113-SY-WState-MWright-20131119.pdf.

30. Amy Goldstein, "HealthCare.gov Can't Handle Appeals of Enrollment Errors," *Washington Post*, Feb. 2, 2014, www.washingtonpost.com/national/health-science/healthcaregov-cant-handle-appeals-of-enrollment-errors/2014/02/02/bbf5280c-89e2-11e3-916e-e01534b1e132_story.html. Rachana Pradhan and Brett Norman, "Behind the Curtain, Troubles Persist in HealthCare.gov," *Politico*, Feb. 17, 2015, www.politico.com/story/2015/02/healthcare-gov-troubles-115276.

31. Robert N. Charette, "This Car Runs on Code," *IEEE Spectrum*, Feb. 2009, spectrum.ieee.org/transportation/systems/this-car-runs-on-code.

32. The report of the Independent Inquiry Board set up to investigate the explosion is at sunnyday.mit.edu/accidents/Ariane5accidentreport.html.

33. "FDA Statement on Radiation Overexposures in Panama," www.fda.gov/radiation-emittingproducts/radiationsafety/alertsandnotices/ucm116533.htm. Deborah Gage

and John Mc-Cormick, "We Did Nothing Wrong," *Baseline,* Mar. 4, 2004, www. baselinemag.com/article2/0,1397,1543564,00.asp.

34. Nancy G. Leveson and Clark S. Turner, "An Investigation of the Therac-25 Accidents," *IEEE Computer*, July 1993, 26(7), pp. 18–41. Jonathan Jacky, "Safety-Critical Computing: Hazards, Practices, Standards, and Regulation," in Charles Dunlop and Rob Kling, eds., *Computerization and Controversy*, Academic Press, 1991, pp. 612–631. Most of the factual information about the Therac-25 incidents in this chapter is from Leveson and Turner.

35. Conversation with Nancy Leveson, Jan. 19, 1995.

36. Ted Wendling, "Lethal Doses: Radiation That Kills," *Cleveland Plain Dealer*, Dec. 16, 1992, p. 12A. (I thank my student Irene Radomyshelsky for bringing this article to my attention.)

37. Jared Diamond, *Guns, Germs, and Steel: The Fates of Human Societies*, W. W. Norton, 1997, p. 157.

38. Raju Narisetti, Thomas E. Weber, and Rebecca Quick, "How Computers Calmly Handled Stock Frenzy," *Wall Street Journal,* Oct. 30, 1997, p. B1, B7.

39. www.securecoding.cert.org/confluence/display/seccode/SEI+CERT+Coding+ Standards.

40. From an email advertisement for Nancy G. Leveson, *Safeware: System Safety and Computers*, Addison Wesley, 1995.

41. Roger Boisjoly, quoted in Diane Vaughan, *The Challenger Launch Decision: Risky Technology, Culture, and Deviance at NASA*, University of Chicago Press, 1996, p. 41.

42. For a discussion of systemic, organizational issues behind the *Columbia* failure, see Michael A. Roberto, Richard M. J. Bohmer, and Amy C. Edmondson, "Facing Ambiguous Threats," *Harvard Business Review*, Nov. 2006, hbr.org/2006/11/ facing-ambiguous-threats.

43. One of several articles that discuss characteristics of HROs is Karl E. Weick, Kathleen M. Sutcliffe, and David Obstfeld, "Organizing for High Reliability: Processes of Collective Mindfulness," Chapter 44 in *Crisis Management: Volume III,* edited by Arjen Boin, Sage Library in Business and Management, 2008, www.archwoodside. com/wp-content/uploads/2015/09/Weick-Organizing-for-High-Reliability.pdf.

44. Manifesto for Agile Software Development, agilemanifesto.org/.

45. Federal Aviation Administration, "American Airlines Flight 965, B-757, N651AA," lessonslearned.faa.gov/ll_main.cfm?TabID=3&LLID=43&LLTypeID=0. Stephen Manes, "A Fatal Outcome from Misplaced Trust in 'Data,'" *New York Times*, Sept. 17, 1996, p. B11.

46. A few of these principles are described in Barry H. Kantowitz, "Pilot Workload and Flightdeck Automation," in M. Mouloua and R. Parasuraman, eds., *Human Performance in Automated Systems: Current Research and Trends*, Lawrence Erlbaum, 1994, pp. 212–223.

47. M. Sghairi, A. de Bonneval, Y. Crouzet, J.-J. Aubert, and P. Brot, "Challenges in Building Fault-Tolerant Flight Control System for a Civil Aircraft," *IAENG International Journal of Computer Science*, Nov. 20, 2008, www.iaeng.org/IJCS/issues_ v35/issue_4/IJCS_35_4_07.pdf. (My thanks to Patricia A. Joseph for finding this reference.) "Airbus Safety Claim 'Cannot Be Proved,'" *New Scientist*, Sept. 7, 1991, 131:1785, p. 30.

48. General John Campbell, Department of Defense Press Briefing by General Campbell via teleconference from Afghanistan, Nov., 25, 2015, www.defense. gov/News/Transcripts/Transcript-View/Article/631359/department-of-defense-press-briefing-by-general-campbell-via-teleconference-fro. Matthew Rosenberg, "Pentagon Details Chain of Errors in Strike on Afghan Hospital," *New York Times*, Apr. 29, 2016, www.nytimes.com/2016/04/30/world/asia/afghanistan-doctors-without-borders-hospital-strike.html?_r=0. Sean Gallagher, "How Tech Fails Led to Air Force Strike on MSF's Kunduz Hospital," *Ars Technica*, Nov. 30, 2015, arstechnica.com/information-technology/2015/11/how-tech-fails-led-to-air-force-strike-on-msfs-kunduz-hospital/.

49. Will Durant, *The Story of Philosophy: The Lives and Opinions of the World's Greatest Philosophers*, Simon & Schuster, 1926.

50. William M. Carley, "New Cockpit Systems Broaden the Margin of Safety for Pilots," *Wall Street Journal,* Mar. 1, 2000, pp. A1, A10. Kantowitz, "Pilot Workload and Flightdeck Automation," p. 214.

51. Andy Pasztor and Robert Wall, "Airbus Scrapped 'Auto-avoid' Technology Aimed at Preventing Planes from Being Used as Weapons," *Wall Street Journal*, Mar. 30, 2015.

52. These problems and trade-offs occur often with regulation of new drugs and medical devices, regulation of pollution, and various kinds of safety regulation. They are discussed primarily in journals on the economics of regulation.

53. Leveson and Turner, "An Investigation of the Therac-25 Accidents," p. 40.

54. Walter Williams, *The State Against Blacks*, McGraw-Hill, 1982, Chapters 5–7. Council of Economic Advisors, "Occupational Licensing: A Framework for Policymakers," July 2015, p. 4, www.whitehouse.gov/sites/default/files/docs/licensing_report_final_nonembargo.pdf.

55. Tom Forester and Perry Morrison, *Computer Ethics: Cautionary Tales and Ethical Dilemmas in Computing*, 2nd ed., MIT Press, 1994, p. 4.

56. Heather Bryant, an Albertson's manager, quoted in Penni Crabtree, "Glitch Fouls Up Nation's Business," *San Diego Union-Tribune*, Apr. 14, 1998, p. C1. Miles Corwin and John L. Mitchell, "Fire Disrupts L.A. Phones, Services," *Los Angeles Times*, Mar. 16, 1994, p. A1.

57. U.S. Department of Labor, Bureau of Labor Statistics, Census of Fatal Occupational Injuries, Rate of Fatal Work Injuries 2006–2014, www.bls.gov/iif/oshwc/cfoi/cfch0013.pdf. Datum from 1934: "A Fistful of Risks," *Discover*, May 1996, p. 82.

58. Alan Levin, "Airways Are the Safest Ever," *USA Today*, June 29, 2006, p. 1A, 6A. William M. Carley, "New Cockpit Systems Broaden the Margin of Safety for Pilots," *Wall Street Journal,* Mar. 1, 2000, p. A1.

59. An excellent "Nova" series, "Escape! Because Accidents Happen," aired Feb. 16 and 17, 1999, shows examples from 2000 years of history of inventing ways to reduce the injuries and deaths from fires, and from boat, car, and airplane accidents.

60. National Highway Traffic Safety Administration, Fatality Analysis Reporting System, www-fars.nhtsa.dot.gov/Main/index.aspx.

61. "FDA Proposes Rules for Drug Registry," *Wall Street Journal,* Aug. 24, 2006, p. D6.

62. "Class 1 Recall: Cardinal Health Alaris SE Infusion Pumps," Food and Drug Administration, Aug. 10, 2006, www.fda.gov/cdrh/recalls/recall-081006.html. Jennifer Corbett Dooren, "Cardinal Health's Infusion Pump is Seized Because of Design Defect," *Wall Street Journal,* Aug. 29, 2006, p. D3.

Professional Ethics and Responsibilities

9.1 What Are "Professional Ethics"?

The terms "computer ethics" and "digital ethics" can include such social and political issues as the impact of technology on employment, the environmental impact of computers, whether or not to sell digital technology to totalitarian governments, use of computer systems by the military, and the impact of new applications on privacy. Or, they can take a more personal focus and include dilemmas about what to post on the Internet or what to download. In this chapter, we concentrate more narrowly on a category of professional ethics, similar to medical, legal, and accounting ethics, for example. We consider ethical issues a person might encounter on the job as a computer professional. Professional ethics cover relationships with and responsibilities toward customers, clients, coworkers, employees, employers, people who use one's products and services, and others whom one's products affect. We examine ethical dilemmas and guidelines related to actions and decisions of individuals who create and use computer systems. We look at situations where you must make critical decisions, situations where significant consequences for you and others could result.

Extreme examples of lapses in ethics in many professional fields regularly appear in the news. In numerous incidents, journalists at prominent news organizations plagiarized or invented stories. A famed and respected researcher published falsified stem cell research and claimed accomplishments he had not achieved. A writer invented dramatic events in what he promoted as a factual memoir of his experiences. These examples involve blatant dishonesty, which is almost always wrong.

Honesty is one of the most fundamental ethical values. We all make hundreds of decisions all day long. The consequences of many decisions are minor, yet others have huge consequences and affect people we never meet. We base decisions, partly, on the information we have (e.g., it takes 10 minutes to drive to work; this software has serious security vulnerabilities; and what you post on a social network site is available only to your designated friends.) We do not always have accurate information, but we must base our choices and actions on what we know. A lie deliberately sabotages this essential activity of being human: absorbing and processing information and making choices to pursue our goals. Lies are often attempts to manipulate people. As Kant might say, a lie treats people as merely means to ends, not ends in themselves. Lies can have many negative consequences. In some circumstances, lying casts doubt on the work or word of other people unjustly. It hurts those people, and it adds unnecessary uncertainty to decisions by others who would have acted on their word. Falsifying work is a form of theft of the payment for the work, and it wastes resources that others could have used productively. It contributes to incorrect choices and decisions by people who depend on the results of the work. The costs and indirect effects of lies can cascade and do much harm.

Many ethical problems are subtler than the choice of being honest or dishonest. In health care, for example, doctors and researchers must decide how to set priorities for organ transplant recipients. Responsible computer professionals confront issues such as *How much risk (to privacy, security, or safety) is acceptable in a system?* and *What uses of another company's intellectual property are acceptable?*

Suppose a private company asks your software company to develop a database of information obtained from government records, perhaps to generate lists of convicted shoplifters or child molesters, or perhaps marketing lists of new home buyers, affluent boat owners, or divorced parents with young children. The people who will be on the lists did not have a choice about whether the information would be widely available to the public. They did not give permission for its use. How will you decide whether to accept the contract? You could accept on the grounds that the records are already public and available to anyone. You could refuse in opposition to secondary uses of information that people did not provide voluntarily. You could try to determine whether the benefits of the lists outweigh the privacy invasions or inconveniences they might cause for some people. The critical first step, however, is recognizing that you face an ethical issue.

The decision to distribute a smartphone app for paying bills from a phone has an ethical component: Do you know enough about security? The decision to distribute software to convert files from formats with built-in copy protection to formats that people can copy easily has an ethical component. So, too, does the decision about how much money and effort to allocate for training employees in the use of a new system. We have seen that many of the related social and legal issues are controversial. Thus, some ethical issues are also controversial.

There are special aspects to making ethical decisions in a professional context, but the decisions are based on general ethical principles and theories. Section 1.4 describes these general principles. It would be good to reread or review it now. In Section 9.2, we consider ethical guidelines for computer professionals. In Section 9.3, we consider sample scenarios.

9.2 Ethical Guidelines for Computer Professionals

9.2.1 SPECIAL ASPECTS OF PROFESSIONAL ETHICS

Professional ethics have several characteristics different from general ethics since the role of a professional is special in several ways. First, the professional is an expert in a field, be it computer science or medicine, that many customers know little about. Most of the people affected by the devices, systems, and services of professionals do not understand how they work and cannot easily judge their quality and safety. This creates responsibilities for the professional as customers must trust the professional's knowledge, expertise, and honesty. A professional advertises his or her expertise and thus has an obligation to provide it. Second, the products of many professionals (e.g., highway bridges, investment advice, surgery protocols, and software that drives cars) profoundly affect large numbers of people.

A computer professional's work can affect the life, health, finances, freedom, and future of a client or members of the public. A professional can cause great harm through dishonesty, carelessness, or incompetence. Often, the victims have little ability to protect themselves; they are not the direct customers of the professional and have no direct control or decision-making role in choosing the product or making decisions about its quality and safety. Thus, computer professionals have special responsibilities, not only to their customers, but also to the general public, to the users of their products, regardless of whether they have a direct relationship with the users. These responsibilities include thinking about potential risks to privacy, system security, safety, reliability, and ease of use, and then acting to diminish risks that are too high.

In Chapter 8, we saw some of the minor and major consequences of flaws in computer systems. In some of those cases, people acted in clearly unethical or irresponsible ways; however, in many cases, there was no ill intent. Software can be enormously complex, and the process of developing it involves communications between many people with diverse roles and skills. Because of the complexity, risks, and impact of computer systems, a professional has an ethical responsibility not simply to avoid intentional evil, but to exercise a high degree of care and follow good professional practices to reduce the likelihood of errors and other problems. That includes a responsibility to maintain an expected level of competence and be up to date on current knowledge, technology, and standards of the profession. Professional responsibility includes knowing or learning enough about the application field to do a good job. Responsibility for a noncomputer professional who manages or uses a sophisticated computer system includes knowing or learning enough about the system to understand potential problems.

In Section 1.4.1, we observed that although people often associate courage with heroic acts, we have many opportunities to display courage in day-to-day life by making good decisions that might be difficult or unpopular. Courage in a professional setting could mean admitting to a customer that your program is faulty, declining a job for which you are not qualified, or speaking out when you see someone else doing something wrong. In some situations, it could mean quitting your job.

Volkswagen's "defeat device": An example of widespread ethical failure[1]

Millions of diesel cars produced by the Volkswagen group (Volkswagen, Audi, and Porsche) contained software specifically designed to falsify emissions testing in the United States and the European Union. The software sensed when these cars were undergoing emissions testing and properly engaged the emissions control system, which includes a trap for the pollutant nitrogen oxide (NO_2).[*] Operation of the trap increases the use of fuel, so to improve performance when the car was on

---

[*]Nitrogen oxide can cause emphysema, bronchitis, and other respiratory diseases.

the road, the software reduced the amount of NO_2 captured by the trap. This released into the air up to 40 times more NO_2 than is permitted by the U.S. Environmental Protection Agency (EPA). To cover the change in the trap operation, software for the on-board diagnostics system was altered to indicate the emissions system was functioning properly. The software system and corresponding control hardware were referred to as a "defeat device."

After public discovery of the existence of the defeat devices, the CEO of Volkswagen resigned over the scandal, but dozens of engineers, programmers, and other staff were involved. Audi teams developed the defeat device as a shortcut for the high cost of reengineering their cars to meet emissions standards. When Volkswagen, and later Porsche, faced similar challenges, the technology was shared and modified for other car models. Investigations show that at least six different defeat devices were implemented on numerous car models over the course of about 10 years. At a minimum, to implement a single defeat device, someone or a team must have designed it, another team programmed it, and yet another tested and integrated it into the car's systems. From testimony and numerous emails, it is clear that people working on the defeat devices and their managers knew the purpose of these systems. Even though many people inside Volkswagen knew of the device, it was not made public until a university study found emissions discrepancies and the EPA followed up.

Many questions arise from this case. An important one is: Why did no one working on the defeat devices or having knowledge of the devices become a whistle-blower and go public? The company blamed the incident on individual misconduct and a culture in some departments that tolerated breaches in rules. The government and news organizations pointed to a cut-throat corporate culture that encouraged cheating to accomplish the goal of becoming the number one automaker.

Corporate culture or peer pressure can be a powerful deterrent to ethical actions. People are tempted to blur ethical boundaries because "everyone else is doing it" or "this is the way it has always been done." Professional ethics provide a guide for us in these situations.

9.2.2 Professional Codes of Ethics

Many professional organizations have codes of professional conduct. These codes provide a general statement of ethical values and remind people in the profession that ethical behavior is an essential part of their job and that they have specific professional responsibilities. Professional codes provide valuable guidance for new or young members of the profession who want to behave ethically but do not know what is expected of them. Their limited experience has not prepared them to be alert to difficult ethical situations and to handle them appropriately.

There are several organizations for the range of professions included in the general term "computer professional." The main ones are the ACM and the IEEE Computer Society (IEEE CS).[2] They developed the Software Engineering Code of

Ethics and Professional Practice (adopted jointly by the ACM and IEEE CS) and the ACM Code of Ethics and Professional Conduct (both in Appendix A). We refer to sections of the codes in the following discussion and in Section 9.3 using the shortened names SE Code and ACM Code. The codes emphasize the basic ethical values of honesty and fairness.* They cover many aspects of professional behavior, including the responsibility to respect confidentiality,† maintain professional competence,‡ be aware of relevant laws,¶ and honor contracts and agreements.** In addition, the codes put special emphasis on areas that are particularly (but not uniquely) vulnerable from computer systems. They stress the responsibility to respect and protect privacy,†† to avoid harm to others,‡‡ and to respect property rights (with intellectual property and computer systems themselves as the most relevant examples).¶ The SE Code covers many specific points about software development, and is available in several languages. Numerous organizations have adopted it as their internal professional standard.

Managers have special responsibility because they oversee projects and set the ethical standards for employees. Principle 5 of the SE Code includes many specific guidelines for managers. Another important code of ethics for project managers is the Project Management Institute's (PMI) Code of Ethics and Professional Conduct. This code provides mandatory standards for all project managers and aspirational standards that managers should strive to uphold.

9.2.3 Guidelines and Professional Responsibilities

Here, we highlight only a few of the many principles for producing good systems. Most concern software developers, programmers, and consultants while some are for professionals in other areas who make decisions about computer systems. Many more specific guidelines appear in the SE Code and in the ACM Code, and we introduce and explain more in the scenarios in Section 9.3.

Understand what success means. After the utter foul-up on opening day at Kuala Lumpur's airport, blamed on clerks typing incorrect commands, an airport official said, "There's nothing wrong with the system." His statement is false, and the attitude behind the statement contributes to the development of systems that will fail. The official defined the role of the airport system narrowly: to do certain data manipulation correctly, assuming all input is correct. Its true role was to get passengers, crews, planes, luggage, and cargo to the correct gates on schedule—a goal at which it did not succeed. Developers and institutional users of computer systems must view the system's role and their responsibility in a wide enough context.

---

*SE Code: 1.06, 2.01, 6.07, 7.05, 7.04; ACM Code: 1.3, 1.4.
†SE Code: 2.05; ACM Code: 1.8.
‡SE Code: 8.01-8.05; ACM Code: 2.2.
¶SE Code: 8.05; ACM Code: 2.3.
**ACM Code: 2.6.
††SE Code: 1.03, 3.12; ACM Code: 1.7.
‡‡SE Code: 1.03; ACM Code: 1.2.
¶SE Code: 2.02, 2.03; ACM Code: 1.5, 1.6, 2.8.

Include users (such as medical staff, technicians, pilots, and office workers) in the design and testing stages to provide safe and useful systems. The importance of this guideline is illustrated by the discussion of computer controls for airplanes (Section 8.3.1) where confusing user interfaces and system behavior increased the risk of accidents. There are numerous "horror stories" in which technical people developed systems without sufficient knowledge of what was important to users. For example, a system for a newborn nursery at a hospital rounded each baby's weight to the nearest pound. For premature babies, the difference of a few ounces is crucial information.[3] The responsibility of developers to talk to users is not limited to systems that affect safety and health. Systems designed to manage stories for a news website, to manage inventory in a toy store, or to organize photos and video on a website could cause frustration, waste a client's money, and end up on the trash heap if designed without sufficient consideration of the needs of actual users. Numerous studies have found that user input and communication throughout the design and development of a system are critical to the system's success. The box "Reinforcing exclusion" illustrates more ways to think about your users.

Reinforcing exclusion

A speaker recognition system is a system (consisting of hardware and software) that identifies the person speaking. (This is different from speech recognition, discussed in Section 7.5.2, which identifies the words spoken.) One application of speaker recognition is teleconferencing for business meetings. The system identifies who is speaking and displays that person on everyone's screen. An early speaker recognition system recognized male voices more easily than female voices. Sometimes the system failed to recognize female speakers and focus attention on them, effectively removing them from the discussion.[4] Did the designers of the system intentionally discriminate against women? Probably not. Are women's voices inherently more difficult to recognize? Probably not. What happened? There were many more male programmers than female programmers and there typically were many more men than women in high-level business meetings. Men were the primary developers and testers of the system, so the algorithms were inadvertently optimized for the lower range of male voices.

In his book, *The Road Ahead*, Bill Gates tells us that a team of Microsoft programmers developed and tested a hand-writing recognition system. When they thought it was working fine, they brought it to him to try and it failed. All the team members were right-handed and Gates is left-handed.[5]

In some applications, it might make sense to focus on a niche audience or ignore a particular audience, but that choice should be conscious (and reasonable). These examples show how easy it is to develop systems that unintentionally exclude people—and how important it is to think beyond one's own group when designing and testing a system. Besides women and left-handed people, other groups to consider are nontechnical users, different ethnic groups, disabled people, older people (who might, for example, need a large-font option), and children.

In these examples, doing "good" or "right" in a social sense—taking care not to reinforce exclusion of specific groups of people—coincides with producing a good product and expanding its potential market.

Do a thorough, careful job when planning and scheduling a project and when writing bids or contracts. This includes, among many other things, allocating sufficient time and budget for testing the software or system and its security. Inadequate planning leads to pressure to cut corners later. (See SE Code 3.02, 3.09, and 3.10.)

Design for real users. In so many cases, systems crashed because someone typed input incorrectly. In one case, an entire paging system shut down because a technician did not press the "Enter" key (or did not hit it hard enough). Real people make typos, get confused, or are new at their jobs. It is the responsibility of the system designers and programmers to provide clear user interfaces and include appropriate checking of input. It is impossible for software to detect all incorrect input, but there are techniques for catching many kinds of errors and for reducing the damage that errors cause.

Require a convincing case for safety. One of the most difficult ethical problems that arises in safety-critical applications is deciding how much risk is acceptable. We repeat a guideline from Section 8.3.1: For the ethical decision maker, the policy should be to suspend or delay use of the system in the absence of a convincing case for safety, rather than to proceed in the absence of a convincing case for disaster.

Require a convincing case for security. As we saw in Chapter 5, the early Internet, early versions of applications, and many of the devices that comprise the Internet of Things were developed without security in mind. Systems that have security patched or cobbled on later are seldom as secure as those where developers design security in from the start. Many insecure devices, once deployed, cannot be recalled or upgraded, and thus remain vulnerable. Designers of every device or application that connects to the Internet should expect that someone with malicious intent will discover it and attempt to expose its data or take over its operations. As with safety, the policy should be to suspend or delay use of the system in the absence of a convincing case for security.

Do not assume existing software is safe or correct. If you use software from another application, verify its suitability for the current project. If the software was designed for an application where the degree of harm from a failure was small, the quality and testing standards might not have been as high as necessary in the new application. The software might have confusing user interfaces that were tolerable (though not admirable) in the original application but that could have serious negative consequences in the new application. We saw in Chapter 8 that a complete safety evaluation is important even for software from an earlier version of the same application if a failure would have serious consequences. (Recall the Therac-25 and Ariane 5.)

Be open and honest about capabilities, safety, and limitations of software. In several cases described in Chapter 8, there is a strong argument that the treatment of customers was dishonest. The line between emphasizing your best qualities and being dishonest is not always clear, but it should be clear that hiding known, serious flaws and lying to customers are on the wrong side of the line. Honesty includes taking responsibility for damaging or injuring others. If you break a neighbor's window playing ball or smash into someone's car, you have an obligation to pay for the damage. If a business finds that its product caused injury, it should not hide that fact or attempt to put the blame on others.

Honesty about system limitations is especially important for *expert systems* (also called decision systems)—that is, systems that use models and heuristics incorporating expert knowledge to guide decision making (for example, medical diagnoses or investment planning). Developers must explain the limitations and uncertainties to users (doctors, financial advisors, and so forth, and to the public when appropriate). Users must not shirk responsibility for understanding them and using the systems properly.

Pay attention to defaults. Everything, it seems, is customizable: the level of encryption on a wireless network, whether consumers who buy something online are placed on an email list for ads, the difficulty level of a computer game, the type of news stories your favorite news site displays for you, what a spam filter will filter out, and what you share and with whom in your social network. Therefore, default settings might not seem important, but they are critical. Many users do not know the options they can control or how best to configure the options. Very importantly, most users do not understand issues of security and do not take the time to change settings. As a result, system designers must give serious thought to default settings. Sometimes, protection (of privacy or from hackers, for example) is the ethical priority. Other times, ease of use and compatibility with user expectations is a priority. Balancing these priorities can lead to difficult conflicts.

Develop communications skills. A computer security consultant told me (SB) that often when he talks to a client about security risks and the products available to protect against them, he sees the client's eyes glaze over. It is a tricky ethical and professional dilemma for him to decide just how much to say so that the client will actually hear and absorb it.

There are many situations in which a computer professional must explain technical issues to customers and coworkers. Learning how to organize information, distinguishing what is important to communicate and what is not, engaging the listener actively in the conversation to maintain interest, and so on, will help make one's presentations more effective and help to ensure that the client or coworker is truly informed.

9.3 Scenarios

9.3.1 INTRODUCTION AND METHODOLOGY

The cases we present here, most based on real incidents, are just a few samples of ethical situations that occur. They vary in seriousness and difficulty, and include situations that illustrate professional responsibilities to customers, clients, employers, coworkers, potential users of computer systems in the general public, and others. Additional scenarios appear in exercises at the end of the chapter.

In most of this book, we have tried to give arguments on both sides of controversial issues without taking a position. Ethical issues are often even more difficult than some of the others we have covered, and there could well be disagreement among technology ethics specialists on some points in the cases considered here. In any real case, there are many other relevant facts and details that affect the conclusion. Despite the difficulty of drawing ethical conclusions, especially for brief scenarios, we give conclusions for some of these cases. You might face cases like these where you must make a decision and we do not want to leave the impression that, because a decision is difficult or because some people benefit or lose either way, there is no ethical basis for making the decision. (It seems ethically irresponsible to do so.)

On the other hand, in Section 1.4 we emphasized that there is not always one right answer to an ethical question—often many responses or actions are ethically acceptable. We also emphasized that there is no algorithm to crank out the correct answers. And so, we must use our knowledge of how people behave, what problems have occurred in the past, and so on, to decide what choices are reasonable. Throughout this book, we have approached many issues as problem-solving situations. For example, identity thieves get information in a certain way. How can we make it harder for them while maintaining varied and convenient services for consumers? Drivers of semi-autonomous cars may become inattentive. How can we encourage them to pay attention? We will see the same approach in some of these ethical scenarios. Rather than simply concluding that a service, product, or action is right or wrong, we, as responsible, ethical professionals, look for ways to reduce negative consequences.

How shall we analyze specific scenarios? We now have several tools. We can try to apply our favorite ethical theory, or some combination of the theories. We can ask questions that reflect basic ethical values: Is it honest? Is it responsible? Does it violate an agreement we made? We can consult a code of professional ethics. But ethical theories and guidelines might conflict, or we might find no clause in the codes specifically applicable. The preamble of the SE Code recognizes this problem and emphasizes the need for good judgment and concern for the safety, health, and welfare of the public.

Although we will not follow the outline below step by step for all the scenarios, our discussions will usually include many of these elements:

1. *Brainstorming phase*

   - List all the people and organizations affected. (They are the *stakeholders*.)
   - List risks, issues, problems, and consequences.

- List benefits and identify who gets each benefit.
- In cases where there is not a simple yes or no decision, but rather one has to choose some action, list possible actions.

2. *Analysis phase*

- Identify responsibilities of the decision maker. (Consider responsibilities of both general ethics and professional ethics.)
- Identify rights of stakeholders. (It might be helpful to clarify whether they are negative or positive rights, in the sense of Section 1.4.2.)
- Consider the impact of each potential action on the stakeholders. Analyze consequences, risks, benefits, harms, and costs for each action considered.
- Find sections of the SE Code or the ACM Code that apply. Consider the guidelines in Section 9.2.3. Consider Kant's, Mill's, and Rawls' approaches. Then, categorize each potential action or response as ethically obligatory, ethically prohibited, or ethically acceptable.
- If there are several ethically acceptable options, select an option by considering the ethical merits of each, courtesy to others, practicality, self-interest, personal preferences, and so on. (In some cases, plan a sequence of actions, depending on the response to each.)

The brainstorming phase can generate a long discussion with humorous and obviously wrong options. In the analysis phase, we might reject some options or decide that the claims of some stakeholders are irrelevant or minor. This does not imply the brainstorming effort that generated those options or claims was wasted. Brainstorming can bring out ethical and practical considerations and other useful ideas that one would not immediately think of. And it can be as helpful to think about why some factors do not carry heavy ethical weight as it is to know which ones do.

9.3.2 PROTECTING PERSONAL DATA

Your customer is a community clinic that works with families that have problems of family violence. It has three sites in the same city, including a shelter for battered women and children. The director wants a computerized record and appointment system, networked for the three sites. She wants a few tablets on which staffers can carry records when they visit clients at home and stay in touch with clients by email. She asked about an app for these tablets and the staffers' smartphones by which they could access records at social service agencies. At the shelter, staffers use only first names for clients, but the records contain last names and forwarding addresses of women who have recently left. Currently, the clinic's records are on paper and in word processing and spreadsheet applications on one of two shared desktop computers in the main clinic office. The clinic's budget is small.

The clinic director is likely aware of the sensitivity of the information in the records and knows that inappropriate release of information can result in embarrassment for families using the clinic and physical harm to women who use the shelter. But she might not be aware of the risks of the technologies in the system she wants. You, as the computer professional, have specialized knowledge in this area. It is as much your obligation to warn the director of the risks as it is that of a physician to warn a patient of side effects of a drug he or she prescribes. (See, for example, ACM Code 1.7 and SE Code 2.07 and 3.12.)

The most vulnerable stakeholders here are the clients of the clinic and their family members, and they do not take part in your negotiations with the director. You, the director, the clinic employees, and the donors or agencies that fund the clinic are also stakeholders.

Suppose you warn the director about unauthorized access to sensitive information by hackers and the potential for interception of records during transmission. You can make several recommendations to protect client privacy:

- identification codes for clients (not Social Security numbers) that the clinic will use when real names are not necessary
- security software to reduce the threat of hackers who might steal data
- encryption for transmission of records
- encryption for records on tablets
- tablets that have extra security features (such as fingerprint readers, so that only authorized employees can access the data, or remote tracking or erasing features)

You warn that staffers might be bribed to sell or release information from the system. (Suppose a client is a candidate for the city council or a party in a child-custody case.) You suggest procedures to reduce such leaks:

- a user ID and password for each staff member, coded to allow access only to information that the particular worker needs
- a log function that keeps track of who accessed and modified records
- monitoring and controls on employee email and Web activity

You cite examples of incidents of loss and theft of sensitive data to support your recommendations. Note that your ability to provide these suggestions and examples is dependent on your professional competence, currency in the field, and general awareness of relevant current events.

The features you recommend will make the system more expensive. If you convince the director of the importance of your recommendations, and she agrees to pay the cost, your professional/ethical behavior has helped improve the security of the system and protect clients.

Suppose the director says the clinic cannot afford all the security features. She wants you to develop the system without most of them. You have several options:

- develop a cheap, but vulnerable, system
- refuse and perhaps lose the job (although your refusal might convince the director of the importance of the security measures and change her mind)
- add security features and not charge for them
- work out a compromise that includes the protections you consider essential

All but the first option are clearly ethically acceptable. What about the first? Should you agree to provide the system without the security you believe it should have? Is it now up to the director alone to make an informed choice, weighing the risks and costs? In a case where only the customer would take the risk, some would say yes, it is your job to inform, no more. Others would say that the customer lacks the professional expertise to evaluate the risks. In this scenario, however, the director is not the only person at risk, nor is the risk to her the most significant risk of an insecure system. You have an ethical responsibility to consider the potential harm to clients from exposure of sensitive information and not to build a system without adequate privacy protection.

The most difficult decision may be deciding what is adequate. Encryption of personal records on portable devices may be essential while monitoring employee Web access is probably not. There is not always a sharp, clear line between sufficient and insufficient protection. You must rely on your professional knowledge, on being up to date about current risks and security measures, on good judgment, and perhaps on consulting others who develop systems for similar applications (SE Code 7.08).

Note that although we have focused on the need for privacy protection here, you can overdo such protection. You also have a professional ethical responsibility not to scare a customer into paying for security measures that are expensive but protect against very unlikely risks.

9.3.3 DESIGNING AN APPLICATION WITH TARGETED ADS

Your company is developing a free mobile app that searches Internet databases and news stories for data on food, recipes, and restaurants the user is interested in. It lets the user share this information and send text messages to friends who have the app. The app will include targeted advertising based on the content of messages, user searches, and searches done by friends (the app assumes someone's interests are similar to those of his or her friends). You are part of the team designing the system. What are your ethical responsibilities?

Obviously, you must protect the privacy of the searches and messages. The company plans a sophisticated text analysis system to scan searches and messages and select appropriate ads. No humans will read the messages. Marketing for the free app will make clear that users will see targeted ads. The privacy policy will explain that the content of user activity will determine which ads appear. So, the marketing director contends, you have satisfied the first principle of privacy protection—informed consent. What else must you consider to meet your ethical responsibility in offering this service to the public?

The fact that software, not a person, scans the searches and messages and assigns the ads reduces privacy threats. But what will this system store? Will it store data about which ads it displayed to specific users? Will it store data about which key words or phrases in messages determine the selection of ads? Will it store data about who viewed specific ads? Because the system selects ads based on content, the set of ads displayed to a user could provide a lot of information about that person. Some of it will be incorrect or misleading information because of quirks in the ad-targeting methods.

Should we insist that no such data be stored? Not necessarily, as some of it might have important uses. Some records are necessary for billing advertisers, others for analysis to improve ad-targeting strategies, and perhaps some for responding to complaints from app users or advertisers. The system design team needs to determine what records are necessary, which need to be associated with individual users, how long the company will store them, how it will protect them (from hackers, accidental leaks, and so on), and under what conditions it will disclose them.

Now, back up and reconsider informed consent. Telling customers that they will see ads based on the content of their searches and messages is not sufficient if the system stores data that can link a list of ads with a specific user. You must explain this to potential users in a privacy policy or user agreement. But we know that most people do not read privacy policies and user agreements, especially long ones. A person might give legal consent, but ethical responsibility goes further. Independent of what is in the agreement, the designers must think about potential risks of the system and build in protections.

There are ways to reduce potential damage from unintended disclosure of the ads selected for a person. For example, consider some sensitive topics: health (which might come up in searches or messages about eating disorders, diets for diabetics, vegetarianism, etc.), religion (kosher or halal food), or financial problems (which might come up in messages about the cost of expensive restaurants). If the system does not target based on these topics, then the records the system stores will have little or no information about them. Thus, for added protection, the designers should consider restrictions on the set of topics the system uses for targeting.

Should the app let users turn off ads completely? The app is free and the advertising pays for it. Anyone who objects to ads can find information in other ways. There is no strong argument that an opt-out option is ethically obligatory. Offering it is admirable, however, and it could be a good business decision, creating goodwill and attracting people who might then use other company services. You could consider developing a paid version of the app without advertising, as many companies do.

9.3.4 WEBCAMS IN SCHOOL LAPTOPS[6]

As part of your responsibilities at a tech company, you oversee the installation of software packages for large orders. A recent order of laptops for a local school district requires webcam software to be loaded. You know that this software allows for remote activation of the webcam.

Remotely operated cameras and microphones can be in televisions, game systems, tablets, mobile phones, and other appliances. Thus, issues similar to this scenario can arise in many other situations.

Is it your duty to know how your customers will use a product that you supply? Should you inform them, caution them, or even require them to take measures to protect the people who will use the product?

Perhaps one of the most challenging questions for anyone doing business is *to whom am I responsible?* The most obvious answer is the paying customer—in this case, the school district. But as we pointed out in Section 9.2.1 and as the ACM Code points out (ACM Code 2.5 and 3.4), our responsibilities go beyond customers—to employers, users, and the public. In this situation, the stakeholders include not only the school district administration but also the students, parents, teachers, and our own company. Each party has an interest in the security and proper usage of the webcam software, whether they know it or not.

First, find out more about the order. Most likely, the laptops are going to students. If so, then they and their parents need to know about the remote activation capability. If employees of the school district are the recipients, they may have agreed to some sort of privacy policy or have given informed consent.

Consider that the school district might not be familiar with the workings of the software package they ordered and is unaware the cameras can be activated remotely. Suppose a school employee activates several webcams and eavesdrops on students in their homes (as happened in at least one school[7]). When the violation is uncovered, accusations fly. Parents want to know why the school would install such software and why it did not provide proper security measures. School administrators, caught completely off guard, want to know why you did not inform them about the risks and offer them additional security. Valuable trust between families and their schools and between you and your customer evaporates—trust that is hard to restore.

Your company is ethically responsible for informing your customers of the risks of a product it sells, whether the company or a third party designed and built it. Approach this responsibility not as a burden—an obligation that might jeopardize the sale—but as a service to your customer. When you inform a customer about a security or privacy risk, suggest solutions or alternatives such as the ability to disable certain functions or an alternative product that might lower or eliminate the risk. Let your customers know that you are there to help them navigate the risks and that your goal is to deliver a product that will meet the requirements of the stakeholders.

As with many scenarios, there might not be a happy ending. It is possible that the school district will turn down your proposal for better security or cannot afford a more secure product. In these cases, you and your company must further weigh the risks to the other parties. Sometimes, your only ethical course of action is not to accept the contract. Awareness and preparation in advance can help avoid such negative situations. Become familiar with all products your company offers. If the sale of some of these products can present ethical dilemmas (security, safety, privacy, etc.), then formulate contractual requirements beforehand and present them to any potential customer up front. In the case of the webcam software, you might have a policy in place that allows for installation only on systems meeting some minimum security requirements. Moving these concerns to the front of the negotiating process helps to avoid ethical dilemmas later. In addition, it positions your company as one that is familiar with the risks and benefits of the systems it sells and as a company that subscribes to a high ethical standard.

9.3.5 PUBLISHING SECURITY VULNERABILITIES

Three MIT students planned to present a paper at a security conference describing security vulnerabilities in Boston's transit fare system. At the request of the transit authority, a judge ordered the students to cancel the presentation and not distribute their research. The students are debating whether they should circulate their paper on the Web.[*] Imagine that you are one of the students.

What are some reasons why you might want to circulate the paper? You might think the judge's order violates your freedom of speech; posting the paper would be a protest. You might want to circulate the paper for the same reasons you planned to present it at a conference: to make other security experts aware of the problems, perhaps to generate work on a security patch, or perhaps to spur the transit authority to fix the problems.

Publishing the vulnerabilities has several risks. You and your coauthors could face legal action for violating the order. The university could face negative consequences because the work was part of a school project. Publishing the vulnerabilities anonymously could reduce these risks, but many people at the university and in the security field already know who did the work. If you *could* publish anonymously, would you?

The transit system could lose a substantial amount of money if people exploit the information. If at some location in the network, the fare system is connected to

---

[*]The first part of the scenario is from an actual incident. We do not know if the students considered violating the judge's order; that part of the scenario is made up.

the system that interacts with the subway cars,[*] a hacker may gain access to that system, thereby endangering lives.

In the actual case, the transit authority requested a five-month ban to provide time for them to fix the problems, but the judge dissolved the order after a week. We have an established legal system where both parties to a disagreement have an opportunity to present their arguments. The system has plenty of flaws, but it is better than most. Maintaining a peaceful, civil society requires that we sometimes accept a decision of an impartial adjudicator. Ignoring a legal decision might be ethical in some circumstances, but not merely because one does not like the decision.

Note that we have considered, mainly, the decision of whether or not to violate the judge's order. The students still must decide whether and when to present their findings. In Section 5.5.3, we considered issues about responsibly disclosing security vulnerabilities.

9.3.6 Specifications

> You are a relatively junior programmer working on software modules that collect data from loan application forms and convert them to formats required by parts of the program that evaluate the applications. You find that some demographic data are missing from some forms, particularly race and age. What should your program do? What should you do?

Begin by consulting the specifications for the program. Any project should have specification documents approved by the client or managers of the company developing the project (or both). Your company has an ethical and business obligation to ensure that the specifications are complete and to produce a program that meets them. Ethical reasons for this include, but go beyond, doing what the company has agreed to do and has been paid to do. When data collection activities (filling in a paper or online form) are separated from data entry activities as in this scenario, system designers should always expect missing or incorrect values for required data. Many systems have an option for indicating "unspecified" values.

Suppose you do not find anything in the specs that covers your problem. The next step is to bring the problem to the attention of your manager. Suppose the manager tells you, "Just make the program assume 'white' for race if it's missing. Banks shouldn't discriminate based on race anyway." Do you accept your manager's decision? You should not. The manager's quick and simplistic response suggests that he or she is not acting with informed responsibility.

What consequences could the manager's decision have? Suppose the company later uses some of your modules in another project, say, one that evaluates patients for inclusion in research studies on new drugs. Some diseases and drugs

---

[*]Recall that hackers took over the brakes and other controls of a car after entering via the entertainment system. Systems that one might think should not be connected often are.

affect people in different ethnic groups differently. Inaccurate data could threaten the health or life of people in the studies and distort the conclusions in ways that harm other people who later use the drugs. But, you say, we emphasized in Chapter 8 and Section 9.2.3 that people who reuse existing software, especially in a safety-critical project, should review the software and its specifications to ensure that it meets the standards of the new project. That is their responsibility, you say. But if your way of handling missing data is not in the specifications, how will they know about it? Perhaps someone will notice that the specs are incomplete. Perhaps they will test the modules thoroughly before reusing them and discover what the code does. However, we have seen enough examples of human error to derive a lesson for a responsible professional: Do not count on everyone else to do their jobs perfectly. Do your best to make sure your part is not one of the factors that contribute to a failure.

In what other ways might your manager's decision be wrong? The manager might not know enough about the uses of the program to make a good decision. In this example, it is possible that the modules of the program that evaluate the loan application do not use the data on race at all. It is possible that the lender or the government wants data on race to ensure compliance with nondiscrimination policies and laws. This is an excellent time for you and the manager to discuss the situation with the customer since the application must meet that organization's needs. In addition, your company must document whatever decision it makes, especially when the specifications need a revision so that they will be complete (SE Code 3.11).

9.3.7 SCHEDULE PRESSURES

A safety-critical application

> Your team is working on a computer-controlled device for treating cancerous tumors. The computer controls direction, intensity, and timing of a beam that destroys the tumor. Various delays have put the project behind schedule, the deadline is approaching, and there will not be time to complete all the planned testing. The system has been functioning properly in the routine treatment scenarios tested so far. The only testing that remains is for rare and unexpected situations. You are the project manager, and you are considering whether to deliver the system on time, while continuing testing and making patches if the team finds bugs. Since the device has already received government approval, senior management in your company has left the decision to you, but they prefer to release it on time.

As we observed in Chapter 8, there are often pressures to reduce software testing. Testing is one of the last steps in development, so when deadlines approach, testing schedules often shrink.

The central issue here is safety. Your company is building a machine designed to save lives, but if it malfunctions, it can kill or injure patients. Perhaps the situation seems obvious: delivering the system on time benefits the company but could endanger the patients—a case of profits versus safety. But we will defer a conclusion until after we analyze the case further.

Who does your decision affect? First, the patients who will receive treatment with the machine. A malfunction could cause injury or death. On the other hand, if you delay release of the machine, some patients it might have cured could undergo surgery instead. We will assume treatment with the new machine is preferable because it is less invasive, requires less hospitalization and recovery time, has a higher success rate, and overall is less expensive. For some patients, surgery might be impossible, and they could die from their cancer without the new device. A second set of stakeholders is the hospitals and clinics who will purchase the machine. Delay could cause financial losses if they have planned on having the machine at the scheduled time. However, it is reasonable for them to expect that the design and testing are professional and complete. You are deceiving customers if you do not tell them that you have not completed testing. Third, your decision affects you and your company (including its employees and stockholders). The negative consequences of delaying delivery could include damage to your reputation for managing a project (with possible impact on salary and advancement), loss of reputation, a possible fall in stock price for the company, and loss of other contracts, resulting in reduction of jobs for the company's programmers and other employees. As a project manager, you have an obligation to help the company do well. On the other hand, if the system injures a patient, the same negative consequences are likely to occur, in addition to the injury and the human feelings of guilt and remorse as well as significant monetary losses from lawsuits.

This brief examination shows that delivering the system without complete testing could have both negative and positive impacts on patients and on other stakeholders. The issue is not simply profits versus safety. We assume you are honestly trying to weigh the risks of delivering the system against the costs of delay. However, we must consider a few aspects of human nature that can influence the decision. One is to put more weight on short-term and/or highly likely effects. Many of the costs of delay are fairly certain and immediate, and the risk of malfunction is uncertain and in the future. Also, people tend to use the inherent uncertainties of a situation and the genuine arguments for one side to rationalize making the wrong decision. That is, they use uncertainty to justify taking the easy way out. It might take experience (with both professional and ethical issues), knowledge of cases like the Therac-25, and courage to resist the temptation to put short-term effects ahead of longer-term risks.

Now that we have seen that there are arguments on both sides, we must decide how to weigh them and how to avoid rationalization. First, the machine works well in the routine tests performed so far. The Therac-25 case illustrates that a complex system can function correctly hundreds of times but fail with fatal consequences in unusual circumstances. Your customer might not know this. You, as a computer professional, have more understanding about the complexity of computer programs and the potential for errors, especially in programs that interact with real-world events such as operator input and control of machinery. We assume that careful thought went into devising the original test plan for the machine. You should delay delivery and complete the tests. (See SE Code 1.03 and 3.10 and ACM Code 1.2.)

Some patients will benefit from on-time delivery. Should their interests bear equal weight with those of the patients whom a malfunction might harm? Not necessarily. The machine represents an improvement in medical treatment, but there is no ethical obligation that it be available to the public on a certain date. You are not responsible for the care of people who rely on existing treatments. Your obligation to the people who will use the machine is to be sure that it is as safe as good professional practice can make it, and that includes proper testing. You do not have an ethical obligation to cure people of cancer, but you do have an ethical obligation to use your professional judgment in a way that does not expose people, without their knowledge, to additional harm.[*] Also, if the machine is released without complete testing and it fails, the damage to the company's and machine's reputations may prevent the machine from ever being released again, thereby denying future patients its benefits.

What about your responsibility to your company? Even if we weigh the short-term effects of the delay more highly than the risks of losses that would result from a malfunction, the ethical arguments are on the side of fully testing the machine. Yes, you have a responsibility to help your company be successful, but that is not an absolute obligation. (Recall the discussion of goals and constraints in Section 1.4.3.) Perhaps the distinction would be more obvious if the issue were stealing (from a competitor or a customer perhaps). Your responsibility to the financial success of the company is secondary to ethical constraints. In the present case, avoiding unreasonable risk of harm to patients is the ethical constraint (SE Code 1.02).

Getting a product to market

Most products are not safety-critical ones where flaws might threaten people's lives. Consider this scenario:

> You are a programmer working for a very small start-up company. The company has a modest product line and is now developing a truly innovative new product. Everyone is working 60-hour weeks and the target release date is nine months away. The bulk of the programming and testing is done. You are about to begin the beta testing. (See Section 8.3.1 for an explanation of beta testing.) The owner of the company (who is not a programmer) has learned about an annual industry show that would be ideal for introducing the new product. The show is in two months. The owner talks with the project manager. They decide to skip the beta testing and start making plans for an early release.[8]

Should you protest? Students discussing this scenario generally recognize that the decision is a bad one and that the company should do the beta testing. They ask, however, if the programmer is even in a position to protest. Are you supposed to do

---

[*]There are many situations where patients knowingly try risky drugs or treatments. Here, we are assuming that doctors and hospitals do not present the device as risky or experimental, but as a new, presumably safe treatment device.

what the project manager, your direct supervisor, says? Should you say nothing, speak up, or quit?

Consider this possible outcome: You ask for a meeting with the owner. You explain that the product is not ready, that beta testing is a very important stage of development, and that the company should not skip it. The owner accepts what you say and drops the idea of an early release. The new product, released when originally planned, is a success. You eventually become the head of quality control for the growing company.

This is not a fairy tale. It is an actual case, and the outcome just described is what actually happened. This case makes a very important point: Sometimes people will listen to you, provided, of course, you are respectful, thoughtful, and well prepared. In another actual case, a manager within a company, but not the software division, asked a programmer to do something the programmer knew was not a good idea. Although she feared that she might lose her job for refusing a manager's request, she said no and gave a brief explanation. The manager accepted the explanation, and that was the end of the incident. People often ask for things they do not necessarily expect to get. It is important to keep in mind that others might respect your opinion. You might be the only one who recognizes the problem or understands a particular situation. Your responsibilities to your company include applying your knowledge and skill to help avoid a bad decision. In the start-up scenario, speaking up might have had a significant impact on the success of the product and the company. Many people are reasonable and will consider a good explanation or argument. Many—but not all. The CEO of a small electronics company proposed producing a new version of a product within three months. The director of engineering (an excellent, experienced software engineer) wrote up a detailed schedule of all the necessary steps and told the CEO that the project would take more than a year. Note that the software engineer did not simply tell the CEO that the three-month plan was unreasonable. He documented his claim. (SE Code 2.06 and 3.09 apply.) The CEO replaced him with someone who had a "can do" attitude. Although it might seem that the result for the engineer in this case was the opposite of the two previous cases, this is also a case where doing what is professionally responsible corresponds with doing what is good for oneself. The software engineer did not want the stress of working under an extremely unreasonable schedule nor the responsibility for the inevitable failure. Leaving the company was not a bad thing.

Suppose that after hearing your arguments, the owner of the start-up company in our scenario decides the product must be ready for the trade show. Releasing the product later, as originally planned, will result in a major competitor gaining a significant market advantage that could result in your company's product not earning back its development costs. What are your options at this point? It is still not a good idea to cut the testing, but if you focus on solutions and look for alternatives, you might find one. Is it possible to reduce the number of features in the product? This can reduce development time and leave more time for testing. It also requires less testing since there are fewer features to test. This has the potential to best serve both the company, by releasing the product at the trade show, and the customer, by releasing a fully tested, stable product.

9.3.8   SOFTWARE LICENSE VIOLATION

Your company had a trial license for 10 machines for an expensive virtual reality and simulation program it was evaluating for purchase. Toward the end of the trial, your company began price negotiations with the vendor for 85 full licenses and started to copy the software onto the 85 machines that would use the application. After several weeks, the negotiations broke down and the software licenses were not purchased. At this point, several departments in your organization are regularly using the unlicensed software and want to continue to do so.[9]

The first step here is to inform your supervisor that the copies violate the license agreement. Suppose the supervisor is not willing to take any action. What next? What if you bring the problem to the attention of higher-level people in the company and no one cares? There are several possible actions: Give up; you did your best to correct the problem. Call the software vendor and report the offense. Quit your job.

Is giving up at this point ethically acceptable? Some students believe it depends in part on whether you are the person who signed the original trial license agreement. If so, you have made an agreement about the use of the software, and you, as the representative of your company, are obligated to honor it. Because you did not make the copies, you have not broken the agreement directly, but you have responsibility for the software. As practical matters, your name on the license could expose you to legal risk or unethical managers in your company could make you a scapegoat. Thus, you might prefer to report the violation to the vendor or quit your job and have your name removed from the license to protect yourself. If you are not the person who signed the license, then you observed a wrong and brought it to the attention of appropriate people in the company. Is that enough? What if the vendor sues your company for the illegal software use? What do Sections 2.02, 6.13, and 7.01 of the SE Code and 1.5 and 2.6 of the ACM Code suggest?

9.3.9   GOING PUBLIC WITH SAFETY CONCERNS

Suppose you are a member of a team working on a crash-avoidance system for automobiles. You think the system has a design flaw that could endanger people. The project manager does not seem concerned and expects to announce completion of the project soon. Do you have an ethical obligation to do something?

Given the potential consequences, yes (see SE Code 1.04; ACM Code 1.2, 2.5). We consider a variety of options. First, at a minimum, discuss your concerns with the project manager. Voicing your concerns is admirable and obligatory and is good for your company. Internal "whistleblowing" can help protect the company, as well as the public, from all the negative consequences of releasing a dangerous product. If the manager decides to proceed as planned with no examination of the problem, your next option is to go to someone higher up in the company.

If no one with authority in the company is willing to investigate your concerns, you have a more difficult dilemma. You now have the option of going outside the company to the customer, to the news media, or to a government agency. There is personal risk of course: You might lose your job. There is also the ethical issue of the damage you might do to your company and, ultimately, to the people who would benefit from the system. You might be mistaken about the flaw, or you might be correct, but your method of whistleblowing might produce negative publicity that kills a potentially valuable and fixable project. As the ACM Code (1.2) says, "[M]isguided reporting of violations can, itself, be harmful." At this point, it is a good idea to consider whether you are confident that you have the expertise to assess the risk. It could help to discuss the problem with other professionals. If you conclude that the management decision was an acceptable one (and that you are not letting your concern for keeping your job sway your conclusion), this might be the point at which to drop the issue. If you are convinced that the flaw is real, or if you are aware of a careless, irresponsible attitude among the company managers, then you must go further (SE Code 6.13). You are not an uninvolved bystander, for whom the question of ethical obligation might be more fuzzy. The project pays your salary and you are part of the team; you are a participant. Note, also, that this is the kind of situation suggested in SE Code 2.05 where you may violate a confidentiality agreement.

There have been several dramatic cases where professionals faced this difficult situation. Computer engineers who worked on the San Francisco Bay Area Rapid Transit system (BART) worried about the safety of the software designed to control the trains. Although they tried for many months, they were not successful in their attempts to convince their managers to make changes. Eventually, a newspaper published some of their critical memos and reports. The engineers were fired. During the next few years, several crashes occurred, and there were public investigations and numerous recommendations made for improving safety of the system.[10]

One of the BART engineers made these comments about the process:

> If there is something that ought to be corrected inside an organization, the most effective way to do it is to do it within the organization and exhaust all possibilities there . . . you might have to go to the extreme of publishing these things, but you should never start that way.[11]

It is important, for practical and ethical reasons, to keep a complete and accurate record of your attempts to bring attention to the problem and the responses from the people you approach. The record protects you and others who behave responsibly and could help avoid baseless accusations later.

9.3.10   RELEASE OF PERSONAL INFORMATION

We will look at two related scenarios. Here is the first:

> You work for the IRS, the Social Security Administration, a medical clinic, a video streaming company, or a social networking service. Someone asks you to get a copy of records about a particular person and he will pay you $10,000.

Who are the stakeholders?

- *You.* You have an opportunity to make some extra money. Or be sent to jail.
- *The person seeking the records.* Presumably, he has something to gain.
- *The person whose records the briber wants.* Providing the information invades his or her privacy and may threaten the person in other ways.
- *All people about whom the company or agency has personal information.* If you sell information about one person, chances are you will sell more if asked in the future.
- *Your employer (if a private company).* If the sale becomes known, the victim might sue the company. If such sales of information become common, the company will acquire a reputation for carelessness and will potentially lose business and lawsuits.

There are many alternative actions open to you:

- Sell the records.
- Refuse and say nothing about the incident.
- Refuse and report the incident to your supervisor.
- Refuse and report to the police.
- Contact the person whose information the briber wants and tell him or her of the incident.
- Agree to sell the information, but actually work with the police to collect evidence to convict the person trying to buy it.

Are any of these alternatives ethically prohibited or obligatory? The first option, selling the records, is clearly wrong. It almost certainly violates rules and policies you have agreed to abide by in accepting your job. As an employee, you must abide by the guarantees of confidentiality the company or agency has promised its customers or the public. Depending on the use made of the information you sell, you could be helping to cause serious harm to the victim. Disclosing the information is also likely illegal. Your action might expose your employer to fines. If someone discovers the leak, the employer and the police might suspect another employee, who could face arrest and punishment. (See ACM Code: 1.2, 1.3, 1.7, 2.6; SE Code: 2.03, 2.05, 2.09, 4.04, 6.05, 6.06.) What if you are under financial pressure at home and the extra money could help ease the stress on your family? Should you consider that? What if the amount was higher, say $200,000? You would be able to help not just your family but others as well. Your plans for the money do not change the ethical character of the action; no matter how tempting, it is still ethically wrong.

What about the second alternative: refusing to provide the records, but not reporting the incident? Depending on company policies (and laws related to certain government agencies; see SE Code 6.06 and ACM Code 2.3), you might be obligated to report any attempt to gain access to the records. There are other good reasons for reporting the incident. Reporting could lead to the capture of someone making a business of surreptitiously and illegally buying sensitive personal information. Reporting could protect you and other innocent employees if someone later discovers the sale of the records and does not know who sold them. (Some ethicists, e.g., deontologists, argue that taking an action because it benefits you is not ethically meritorious. However, one can argue that taking an action that protects an innocent person is meritorious, even if the person is yourself.)

ACM Code 1.2 and 1.7 suggest an obligation to report, but it is not explicit. There might be disagreement about whether you have an ethical responsibility to do more than refuse to sell the information. It is difficult to decide how much you must do to prevent a wrong thing from happening if you are not participating in the wrong act. A recluse who ignores evils and pains around him might not be doing anything unethical, but he is not what we would consider a good neighbor. Acting to prevent a wrong is part of being a good neighbor or good employee; it is ethically admirable—even in situations where it is not ethically obligatory.

Now, consider a variation of this scenario:

You know another employee sells records with people's personal information.

Your options include doing nothing, talking to the other employee and trying to get him or her to stop selling files (by ethical arguments or threats of exposure), reporting to your supervisor, or reporting to an appropriate law enforcement agency. The question here is whether you have an obligation to do anything. This scenario differs from the previous one in two ways. First, you have no direct involvement; no one has approached you. This difference might seem to argue for no obligation. Second, in the previous scenario, if you refused to sell the file, the buyer might give up, and the victim's information would remain protected. In the current scenario, you know that a sale of confidential, sensitive information occurred. This makes the argument in favor of an obligation to take action stronger (see SE Code 6.13 and 7.01). You should report what you know.

9.3.11 Conflict of Interest

You have a small consulting business. The CyberStuff company plans to buy software to run a cloud data-storage business. CyberStuff wants to hire you to evaluate bids from vendors. Your spouse works for NetWorkx and did most of the work in writing the bid that NetWorkx plans to submit. You read the bid while your spouse was working on it, and you think it is excellent. Do you tell CyberStuff about your spouse's connection with NetWorkx?

Conflict-of-interest situations occur in many professions. Sometimes the ethical course of action is clear, though at times it can be more difficult to determine.

In discussions among professionals and among students, we have seen two immediate reactions to scenarios similar to this one. One is that if you honestly believe you can be objective and fairly consider all bids, you have no ethical obligation to say anything. The other is that it is a simple case of profits versus honesty, and ethics requires that you inform the company about your connection to the software vendor. Which is right? Is this a simple choice between saying nothing and getting the consulting job or disclosing your connection and losing the job?

The affected parties are the CyberStuff company, yourself, your spouse, your spouse's company, other companies whose bids you will be reviewing, and future customers of CyberStuff's cloud storage service. A key factor in considering consequences is that we do not know whether CyberStuff will later discover your connection to one of the bidders. If you say nothing about the conflict of interest, you benefit, because you get the consulting job. If you recommend NetWorkx (because you believe its bid is the best), it benefits from a sale. However, if Cyber-Stuff discovers the conflict of interest later, your reputation for honesty—important to a consultant—will suffer. The reputation of your spouse's company could also suffer. Note that even if you conclude that you are truly unbiased and do not have an ethical obligation to tell CyberStuff about your connection to your spouse's company, your decision might put NetWorkx's reputation for honesty at risk. The *appearance* of bias can be as damaging (to you and to NetWorkx) as actual bias. If you recommend NetWorkx and one of the other bidders discovers your connection, similar negative results will likely occur.

Suppose you take the job and you find that one of the other bids is much better than the bid from NetWorkx. Are you prepared to handle that situation ethically?

What are the consequences of disclosing the conflict of interest to the client now? You will probably lose this job, but CyberStuff might value your honesty more highly, and you might get more business in the future. Thus, there could be benefits, even to you, from disclosing the conflict of interest.

Suppose it is unlikely that anyone will discover your connection to NetWorkx. What are your responsibilities to your potential client as a professional consultant? When a company hires you as a consultant, the company expects you to offer unbiased, honest, impartial professional advice. There is an implicit assumption that you do not have a personal interest in the outcome or a personal reason to favor one of the bids you will review. There should not be even an appearance of favoritism. The conclusion in this case hangs on this point. Despite your belief in your impartiality, you could be unintentionally biased. It is not up to you to make the decision about whether you can be fair. The client should make that decision. Your ethical obligation in this case is to inform CyberStuff of the conflict of interest. (See SE Code Principle 4, 4.03, and 4.05, and ACM Code 2.5.)

9.3.12 KICKBACKS AND DISCLOSURE

You are an administrator at a major university. Your department selects a few brands of security software to recommend to students for their desktop computers, laptops, tablets, and other devices. One of the companies whose software you will evaluate takes you out to dinner, gives you free software (in addition to the security software), offers to pay your expenses to attend a professional conference on computer security, and offers to give the university a percentage of the price for every student who buys its security package.

You are sensitive to the issue of bribery, but the cost of the dinner and software the company gave you is relatively small. The university cannot pay to send you to conferences. Attending one will improve your knowledge and skills and make you better at your job, a benefit to both you and the university. The percentage from the sales benefits the university and thus all the students. This sounds like a good deal for all.

A similar situation arose in the student loan business. Universities recommend loan companies to students seeking student loans. A flurry of news reports disclosed that several universities and their financial aid administrators gave special privileges and preferred recommendations to particular lending companies in exchange for payments to the universities and consulting fees, travel expenses, and other gifts for the administrators. Some financial aid officers defended the practices. Professional organizations scurried to write new ethical guidelines. Some lenders paid heavy fines. The reputations of the universities suffered. The government heavily regulates the lending industry, so we return to the security software scenario to discuss ethical issues, not primarily legal ones.

First, does your employer have a policy about accepting gifts from vendors? Even if gifts appear small to you and you are confident that they do not influence your judgment, you are obligated to follow your employer's policy. Violating the policy violates an agreement you have made. Violating the policy could expose the employer to negative publicity (and possibly legal sanctions). (See SE Code 6.05 and 6.06. SE Code 1.06, 4.03, and 4.04 are also relevant to this case.)

Who does not benefit from the arrangement with the software company? Any company that charges less for software of comparable quality or any company that charges the same or perhaps a little more for a better product and, perhaps, all the students who rely on the recommendation. The university's obligation in making the recommendation is primarily to the students. Will the benefits the administrator and the university receive sway their choice of company to the point where they do not choose the products best for the students?

People want to know when a recommendation represents an honest opinion and when someone is paying for it. We expect universities and certain other organizations to be impartial in their recommendations. When the university selects software to recommend, the presumption is that it is, in the university's opinion, the best for the students. If there are other reasons for the selection, the university should disclose them. Disclosure is a key point. Many organizations encourage their members to get a credit card that provides a kickback to the organization. This is not unethical primarily because the kickback is made clear. It is even a selling point: Use this card and help fund our good cause. However, even if the university makes clear in its recommendation that it benefits financially from sales of the software it recommends, there are good arguments against such an arrangement, arguments similar to those against what the loan administrators did. The cozy relationship between administrators and certain companies can lead to decisions not in the best interests of the students.

9.3.13 A TEST PLAN

A team of programmers at a small company is developing a communications system for firefighters to use when fighting a fire. Firefighters will be able to communicate with each other, with supervisors near the scene, and with other emergency personnel. The programmers will test the system in a field near the company office.

What is the ethical issue? Unlike earlier scenarios, there is time for testing, but here the test plan is insufficient and this is an application where lives could be at risk. Testing should involve real firefighters inside buildings or in varied terrain, perhaps in an actual fire (perhaps a controlled burn). The programmers who work on the system know how it behaves. They are experienced users with a specific set of expectations. They are not the right people to test the system. Testing must address issues such as: Will the devices withstand heat, water, and soot? Can someone manipulate the controls wearing heavy gloves? Are the controls clear and easy to use in poor light conditions? Will a building's structure interfere with the signal?

In an actual case, the New York City Fire Commissioner halted use of a $33 million digital communications system after a fireman called for help on his radio and no one heard. Firefighters reported other problems during simulation tests. The commissioner commented, "We tested the quality, durability, and reliability of the product, but we didn't spend enough time testing them in the field or familiarizing the firefighters with their use."[12]

Note that we did not indicate your role in this scenario. If you are a member of the programming team, your obligation to voice your concern is similar to that in some of the previous scenarios. If you are in charge of testing, you need to recognize that the test described is only one small step in a good test plan. If you are responsible for purchasing the communications systems for a fire department, your role might include inquiring about the testing done by the manufacturer and working with both the manufacturer and the fire department to set up a plan for field testing by firefighters.

9.3.14   Artificial Intelligence and Sentencing Criminals

> You are part of a team developing a sophisticated program using artificial intelligence techniques to make sentencing decisions for convicted criminals.

Such a program can take several different approaches. In Section 7.1.2, we described a system that examines a large number of factors about the convicted person and then produces a score to indicate the likelihood that he or she will commit future crimes. Judges consider this score when deciding on the sentence. Another approach, the one we consider here to illustrate different issues, analyzes previous similar criminal cases to "learn" how to make similar decisions.

Reviewing sentencing decisions from similar previous cases is helpful, but judges use judgment in deciding sentences (within bounds established in law). Prosecutors and defense lawyers present arguments that a judge considers, so these would need to be part of the input to the software. Years of experience provide insights that may be difficult to encode into software. A judge can consider unusual circumstances in the case, the character of the convicted person, and other factors that a program might not handle. Judges sometimes innovate creative new aspects of sentencing whereas a sentencing application would be more restricted in its options. On the other hand, some judges have a reputation for giving extremely tough sentences, while others are very lenient. Some people argue that software might be more fair than a judge influenced by personal impressions, fatigue or hunger,[13] and biases. On the other hand, again, critics of the software package we described in Section 7.1.2 argue that it produces racially biased results. Thus, for several reasons, we might not want the software to make the decisions. We modify the scenario by adding two words to the original description:

> You are part of a team developing a sophisticated program using artificial intelligence techniques to *help judges* make sentencing decisions for convicted criminals.

Let's suppose your team's system will analyze the characteristics of the crime and the criminal to find other cases that are similar. Based on its analysis of cases, should it then make a recommendation for the sentence in the current case, or should it simply display similar cases, more or less as a search engine would, so that the judge can review them? Or should it provide both a recommended sentence and the relevant cases?

This is clearly an application where it is essential to have experts and potential users involved in the design. The expertise and experience of judges and lawyers are essential for choosing criteria and strategies for selecting the similar cases on which the program bases its recommendation. The system's recommendations, if it makes them, must comply with sentencing requirements specified in laws.

The involvement of lawyers can improve subtler decisions. Consider the question of the ordering of the cases the system displays. Should it order them by relevance, case date, or by the length of the sentence? If the latter, should the shortest or longest sentences come first? Perhaps you should order the cases according to an evaluation of their similarity or relevance to the current case. That is a fuzzier criterion than date or length of sentence. Again, it is important to include a variety of experts, with different perspectives, in the design process when making such choices.

Is the ordering of the selected cases so important? When you are researching some topic, how many pages of search engine results do you look at? Many people rarely go beyond the first page. We expect a judge making a sentencing decision to be more thorough. Experience, however, reminds us that people sometimes are tired or rushed. Sometimes they have too much confidence in results from computer systems. Even when people are deliberate and careful in interpreting output, the manner in which the viewers see the data can influence their perceptions and decisions. Thus, careful planning, including much consultation with relevant experts, is an ethical requirement in a system that will have significant impact on people's lives.

A company or government agency that develops or installs this system must consider how it will maintain and update the system. Clearly, there will be new cases to add. How will the system handle changes in sentencing laws? Should it discard cases decided under the old law? Include them but flag them clearly as predating the change? How much weight should the system give to such cases in its selection criteria?

We have not yet answered the question about whether the system should recommend a sentence. A specific recommendation from the system that differs from the judge's initial plan might lead a judge to give a case more thought. Or it might influence a judge more than it should. If the system presents a recommendation, legislators or administrators might begin to think that a clerk or law student, not a judge, can operate the system and handle sentencing. This is not likely in the short term—judges and lawyers would object. It is, however, a possible consequence of apparently sophisticated AI systems making apparently wise decisions in any professional area. A potential drop in employment for judges (or other professionals) is not the main issue. The quality of the decisions is. Thus, an answer to the question will depend in part on the quality of AI technology (and the specific system) at the time of development and on the sensitivity of the application. (See Exercise 6.17 for another application area.)

Suppose judges in your state use a sentencing decision system that displays similar cases for the judge to review. You are a programmer working for your state government. Your state has just made it a criminal offense to use a smartphone while taking a college exam. Your boss, a justice department administrator, tells you to modify the program to add this new category of crime and assign the same relevancy weights to cases as the program currently does for using a smartphone while driving a car (already illegal in your state).

The first question, one for your boss, is whether the contract under which the system operates allows the state to make changes. For many consumer products, guarantees and service agreements become void if the consumer takes the product apart and makes changes. The same can be true for software. Let's assume the boss knows that the state's contract allows the state to modify the system.

Suppose you know that your boss made the decision quickly and independently. You should say no, with appropriate politeness and reasons. SE Code 3.15 states a very important, often ignored principle: "Treat all forms of software maintenance with the same professionalism as new development." That includes developing specifications—in this example, in consultation with lawyers and judges who understand the law and its subtleties. We raised a sampling of the complex and sensitive issues that go into the design of a system such as this. Modifications and upgrades should also undergo thorough planning and testing.

9.3.15 A Gracious Host

You are the computer system administrator for a mid-size company. You can monitor the company network from home, and you frequently work from home with some company files on your home computer. Your niece, a college student, is visiting for a week. Her phone battery is dead, and she asks if she can use your computer to check her email. Sure, you say.

You are being a gracious host. What is the ethical problem?

Maybe there is none. Maybe you have an excellent firewall and excellent antivirus software. Maybe you remember that you are logged in to your company system and you log out before letting your niece use the computer. Maybe your files are password protected and you create a separate account on your computer for your niece. Maybe you think of these things because you are a system administrator. But maybe not. A typical employee for a company who works from home probably would not. Most people do not think about security when a relative asks to use a personal computer or other device.

Your niece is a responsible person. She would not intentionally snoop or do harm to you or your company. But after checking email, she might check in on her Facebook friends, then look for someone selling cheap concert tickets, and then . . . who knows? Her activities could result in a virus being installed on your computer that, in turn, infects your company's network. Maybe her own computer crashed several times in the past six months because of viruses.

Your company network contains employee records, customer records, and plenty of information about company projects, finances, and plans. Depending on what the company does, the system might contain other very sensitive information. Downtime, due to a virus or similar problem, would be very costly for the company. In an actual incident, someone in the family of a mortgage company employee signed up for a peer-to-peer file sharing service and did not properly set the options indicating which files to share. Mortgage application information for a few thousand customers leaked and spread on the Web. Always be alert to potential security risks.

 Exercises

Review Exercises

9.1   What are two ways professional ethics differ from ethics in general?

9.2   What part of a car did Volkswagen's "defeat device" defeat?

9.3   Why did a program developed by Microsoft programmers to read handwriting fail?

9.4   What is one important policy decision a company should consider when designing a system to target ads based on email content?

9.5   Suppose you are a programmer, and you think there is a serious flaw in software your company is developing. Who should you talk to about it first?

General Exercises

9.6   Describe a case at work or in school where someone asked or pressured you to do something you thought unethical.

9.7   The management team of a mobile phone service company is debating options for customer retrieval of their voice mail messages. Some managers argue for providing quick retrieval, that is, access to messages without a PIN when the system recognizes that the call is coming from the customer's own phone. Some managers argue that such access without a PIN should be an option the customer can turn on or off. Others argue that the company should always require the PIN. What are some risks of not requiring a PIN? Which of the options (or others you might think of) are ethically acceptable? Which is best?

9.8   Suppose the mobile phone service company in the previous exercise chooses to provide an option for quick retrieval of messages without a PIN. What should the default setting for this option be (on or off) when someone initiates service? Why?

9.9   Your company sells a device (smartphone, tablet, or other small portable device) for which owners can download third-party apps from your app store. The company's published policy says that the company will delete an app from users' devices if and only if the company discovers that the app contains malicious software such as a virus that compromises the security of the devices or of sensitive user data on the devices. The company discovers that an app has an undocumented but easily initiated component that displays extremely offensive video showing men insulting and violently attacking Chinese people. The company immediately removes the app from its app store and alerts customers to delete the app from their devices. Should the company remotely delete the app from the devices of all who downloaded it? Give arguments on both sides. Which side do you think is stronger? Why?

9.10 Many elderly people have trouble remembering words, people's names, and recent events. Imagine a memory-aid product. What features would it have? What devices would you design it for?

9.11 Suppose you are on a panel of software professionals who investigated Volkswagen's installation of devices to defeat emissions testing. What punishments would you recommend for the engineers who designed, built, and tested the devices?

9.12 The scenarios in Sections 9.3.2 and 9.3.4 are about different situations, but they share many principles. Identify several principles that these scenarios have in common.

9.13 Consider the clinic scenario in Section 9.3.2. If you decline the job, are you responsible if the director contracts with another company to build a system the clinic can afford but is vulnerable? Present arguments on both sides and then tell what you think and why.

9.14 You work for a company that develops security products. You helped write software for a car door lock that operates by matching the driver's thumbprint. The manager for that project is no longer at the company. A local power station wants your company to develop a thumbprint-operated lock for secure areas of the power station. Your boss says to use the software from the car locks. What is your response?

9.15 Write a scenario to illustrate SE Code 2.05 and ACM Code 1.8.

9.16 You are a manager at a health maintenance organization. You find that one of your employees has been reading people's medical records without authorization. What actions could you take? What will you choose? Why?

9.17 In many cities, wills processed by courts are public records. A business that sells information from local public records is considering adding a new "product," lists of people who recently inherited a large amount of money. Using the methodology of Section 9.3.1, analyze the ethics of doing so.

9.18 You are designing a database to keep track of patients while they are in a hospital. The record for each patient will include special diet requirements. Describe some approaches to deciding how to design the list of diet options from which a user will select when entering patient data. Evaluate different approaches.

9.19 You are an expert in speaker recognition systems. (See the box in Section 9.2.3.) A company asks you to help develop a system to sift through huge quantities of sound files from intercepted phone conversations to find the conversations of specific people. The company plans to sell the system to law enforcement agencies in the United States and other countries where it expects the system to be used in compliance with the country's laws. What questions, if any, will you ask to help make your decision, and how will they affect the decision? If you would accept or reject the job without further information, give your decision and your reasons.

9.20 You are an executive at a company that provides a voice-activated home control and personal assistant system similar to Amazon's Echo and Google Home. A police department asks for everything the system recorded in the home of a murder suspect. How will you respond? What guidelines from Appendix A are relevant?

9.21   A company that is developing software for a new generation of space shuttles offers you a job. You do not have any training in the specific techniques used in the programs you will be working on. You can tell from the job interview that the interviewer thinks your college program included this material. Should you take the job? Should you tell the interviewer that you have no training or experience in this area? Analyze this scenario, using the methods in Section 9.3.1. Find relevant sections from the ethics codes in Appendix A.

9.22   A small company offers you a programming job. You are to work on new versions of its software product to disable copy protection and other access controls on electronic books. (For this exercise, assume you are in a country that does not outlaw tools to circumvent copy protection as the Digital Millennium Copyright Act does in the United States.) The company's program enables buyers of ebooks to read their ebooks on a variety of hardware devices (fair uses). Customers could also use the program to make many unauthorized copies of copyrighted books. The company's Web page implicitly encourages this practice, particularly for college students who want to avoid the cost of e-textbooks. Analyze the ethics of accepting the job. Find relevant sections from the ethics codes in Appendix A.

9.23   Find at least two examples described in this book where there was a violation of Clause 3.09 of the SE Code.

9.24   Clause 1.03 of the SE Code says, "Approve software only if . . . [it does not] diminish privacy or harm the environment." Search engines can diminish privacy. Do they violate this clause? Should the clause say something about trade-offs, or should we interpret it as an absolute rule? The concluding sentence of Clause 1.03 says, "The ultimate effect of the work should be to the public good." Does this suggest trade-offs?

9.25   Clause 8.07 in the SE Code says we should "not give unfair treatment to anyone because of any irrelevant prejudices." The guidelines for Section 1.4 of the ACM Code say, "Discrimination on the basis of . . . national origin . . . is an explicit violation of ACM policy and will not be tolerated." Analyze the ethical issues in the following scenario. Do you think the decision in the scenario is ethically acceptable? How do the relevant sections from the two codes apply? Which code has a better statement about discrimination? Why?

> Suppose you came to the United States from Iraq 15 years ago. You now have a small software company. You will need to hire six programmers this year. Because of the devastation by the war in your homeland, you have decided to seek out and hire only programmers who are refugees from Iraq.

9.26   Consider the following statements.

(1) In addition to a safe social environment, human well-being includes a safe natural environment. Therefore, computing professionals who design and develop systems must be alert to, and make others aware of, any potential damage to the local or global environment.[14]

(2) We cannot assume that a computer-based economy automatically will provide enough jobs for everyone in the future. Computer professionals should be aware of this pressure on employment when designing and implementing systems that will reduce job opportunities for those most in need of them.[15]

Compare the two statements from the perspective of how relevant and appropriate they are for an ethical code for computer professionals. Do you think both should be in such a code? Neither? Just one? (Which one?) Give your reasons.

9.27 You are the president of a small computer game company. Your company has just bought another small game company that was developing three new games. You find that one is complete and ready to sell. It is very violent and demeaning to women. It would probably sell a few million copies. You have to decide what to do with the game. Give some options, and give arguments for and against them. What will you do? Why?

9.28 Consider the first scenario in Section 9.3.7. Suppose that the company has decided to deliver the device before completing the testing and that you have decided you must inform the hospitals that are purchasing it. Discuss ethical arguments about whether to include your name and job with the information you give to the hospitals or to send it anonymously.

9.29 The first case in Section 9.3.7 concerns a safety-critical system. Suppose the software product in the second scenario is an accounting system, or a game, or a photo-sharing system. Which principles or ideas in the analysis of the first scenario apply to the second one? Which do not? Explain your answers.

9.30 You are a high-level manager at an automobile company. You must decide whether to approve a proposed project to add a screen on which the front-seat passenger will have full Internet access. The driver would not be able to see the screen easily or well from the driver's seat. What are the issues? Make a decision and explain it.

9.31 Suppose there are two large competing telecommunications firms in your city. The companies are hostile to each other. There have been unproven claims of industrial espionage by each company. Your spouse works for one of the companies. You are now interviewing for a job with the other. Do you have an ethical obligation to tell the interviewer about your spouse's job? How is this case similar to and different from the conflict-of-interest case in Section 9.3.11?

9.32 In the conflict-of-interest case in Section 9.3.11, we mentioned that future customers of CyberStuff's cloud storage service are stakeholders, but we did not discuss them further. How does your decision affect them? What are your ethical obligations to them?

9.33 In Section 9.3.12, we discussed issues about accepting gifts from vendors. Give some reasons why the policies about doing so might differ among different types of employers, for example, a small private company, a state university, a large corporation with many shareholders, and a government agency.

9.34 You are developing an app to work with browsers on mobile devices that will tag game sites as safe or unsafe based on criteria about what data the sites collect from the user's device. What ethical responsibilities do you have to the game sites you will rate and to potential users of your app?

9.35 Several professional associations of engineers oppose allowing increased immigration of skilled high-tech workers. Is this ethical? Give arguments for both sides. Then give your view and defend it.

9.36 A television manufacturer has hired your company to develop a personalization system using a camera on front of the television set and face recognition software to suggest programming and to target ads to the individual watching TV. What risks to privacy does this entail? What features should you include? How should the system or TV company inform buyers about the system? If the system recognizes that two people are watching television, which one's profile should it use to recommend programs or select ads to display?

9.37 Your company makes a system that controls household gadgets, from heating and air-conditioning to music players and garden sprinklers. The user issues commands to the system by speaking in a natural voice and the receiver for the system is a small device that sits on a table or a shelf in the home. The device listens for its "name" and begins recording and processing speech when it hears its name. The system sends the voice commands to a cloud server for processing and logging. You work on the control module that responds to speech, and you discover that similar names and certain short phrases of ordinary words will also activate it. Is this a serious problem? Why? What would you do about it?

9.38 You are an experienced programmer working on part of a project that involves processing data from wearable fitness devices. You have figured out that you can do a part of your section of the program in a way that is more efficient than the method described in the specifications. You are confident that your method is correct, and you know that the change will have no impact on other parts of the program. You understand the importance of following specifications, but you also know that any proposed revision generates a long, bureaucratic process that will take weeks and require approvals from many people in both your company and the client company. Is this a case where the trade-offs make it reasonable to use the better method without a revision of the specifications? Explain your response.

9.39 It is early December. You are the manager of the IT department of a large retail chain, and you are ready to switch all the stores in the chain to a new system for processing customer credit card payments. The new system should be quicker and more secure. Give reasons for and against installing it now rather than waiting until after the holiday season.

9.40 Analyze the following scenario using the methodology of Section 9.3.1. Is the action ethical?

> You work for a software company developing a system to process loan applications for mortgage companies. You will do maintenance on the system after delivery. You are considering building in a backdoor so that you can easily get into the system after it is installed at various customer facilities. (This is not in the specifications for maintenance; it is your secret.)

Assignments

These exercises require some research or activity.

9.41 Find estimates of how much the Volkswagen emissions scandal cost the company (in fines, lawsuits by customers, loss of stock value, or loss of business—whatever you can find).

9.42 Watch a science fiction movie set in the near future. Describe a computer or telecommunications system in the movie that does not currently exist. Suppose, in the years before the movie takes place, you are on the team that develops it. Identify issues of professional ethics the team should consider.

9.43 Research how automobile manufacturers currently perform updates of driving-assistance software in cars (including, for example, software that keeps the car within its lane and software that causes automatic braking when the car detects an obstacle). Find out if there are any government regulations controlling how manufacturers handle such updates. Suppose, a few years from now, you work for a manufacturer of fully self-driving cars and are developing policies and procedures for updates to the software in the cars. How would the update policies differ for different systems? For example, should the entertainment system have a different update policy than the steering or braking systems?

Class Discussion Exercises

These exercises are for class discussion, perhaps with short presentations prepared in advance by small groups of students.

9.44 You are the programmer in the clinic scenario (Section 9.3.2). The director has asked you to rank your suggestions for security and privacy protection measures so that she can choose the most important ones while still trying to stay within her budget. Group the suggestions into at least three categories: imperative, important, and recommended. Include explanations you might give her and assumptions you make (or questions you would ask her) to help determine the importance of some features.

9.45 Which do you think is less risky: developing fair software for sentencing criminals or developing safe software for self-driving cars? Which would you be more comfortable working on? Why?

9.46 The faculty at a large university requested that the campus store sell an electronic device, Auto-Grader, for students to use when taking machine-scorable tests. Students enter test answers into the device. When done, they send the answers to the instructor's tablet in the classroom. Once the instructor's computer receives the answers, it immediately grades the test and sends each student's score back to the student's device.

   Suppose you are a university dean who must decide whether to allow use of this system. Analyze the decision as both an ethical and practical problem. Discuss potential benefits and problems or risks of using the system. Discuss all the issues (of the kind relevant to the topics of this book) that are relevant to making the decision. Mention any warnings or policies you might include if you approve use of the system.

9.47 As we saw in Section 7.5.3, some people fear that development of intelligent robots could have devastating consequences for the human race. Is it ethical to do research aimed at improving artificial intelligence?

9.48 The Software Engineering Institute (SEI) and the computer security organization CERT have developed coding standards to guide software developers in creating robust, safe, and secure programs.[16] Do computer professionals have an ethical responsibility to follow these standards?

Notes

1. Information for this section came from the following articles: Jack Ewing and Graham Bowley, "The Engineering of Volkswagen's Aggressive Ambition," *New York Times*, Dec. 13, 2015, www.nytimes.com/2015/12/14/business/the-engineering-of-volkswagens-aggressive-ambition.html; Guilbert Gates, Jack Ewing, Karl Russell, and Derek Watkins, "Explaining Volkswagen's Emissions Scandal," *New York Times*, Sept. 12, 2016, www.nytimes.com/interactive/2015/business/international/vw-diesel-emissions-scandal-explained.html; Jack Ewing, "VW Presentation in '06 Showed How to Foil Emissions Tests," *New York Times*, Apr. 26, 2016, www.nytimes.com/2016/04/27/business/international/vw-presentation-in-06-showed-how-to-foil-emissions-tests.html; Jack Ewing and Hirroko Tabauch, "Volkswagen Scandal Reaches All the Way to the Top, Lawsuits Say,"

New York Times, July 19, 2016, www.nytimes.com/2016/07/20/business/international/ volkswagen-ny-attorney-general-emissions-scandal.html; Complaint filed by New York States Attorney General against Volkswagen, July 19, 2016, cdn. arstechnica.net/wp-content/uploads/2016/07/new_york_vw_complaint_7.19.pdf; Megan Guess, "Massachusetts, New York, Maryland Accuse Volkswagen Execs in Fresh Lawsuits," *Ars Technica*, July 19, 2016, arstechnica.com/cars/2016/07/ states-sue-volkswagen-execs-for-fraud-current-ceo-named-in-lawsuits/.

2. The somewhat outdated full names of the organizations are the Association for Computing Machinery and the Institute of Electrical and Electronics Engineers.

3. Bob Davis and David Wessel, *Prosperity: The Coming 20-Year Boom and What It Means to You*, Random House, 1998, p. 97.

4. Charles Piller, "The Gender Gap Goes High-Tech," *Los Angeles Times*, Aug. 25, 1998, p. A1.

5. Bill Gates, *The Road Ahead*, Viking, 1995, p. 78.

6. Julie Johnson contributed this scenario and much of its analysis.

7. Jacqui Cheng, "FBI, Grand Jury Now Probing High School's Webcam Spying," *Ars Technica*, Feb. 22, 2010, arstechnica.com/tech-policy/2010/02/fbi-grand-jury-now-probing-high-school-webcam-spying/.

8. I thank Cyndi Chie for giving me this scenario and telling me of the outcome in the actual case.

9. This scenario was inspired by David Kravets, "Batten Down the Hatches— Navy Accused of Pirating 585k Copies of VR Software," *Ars Technica*, July 23, 2016, arstechnica.com/tech-policy/2016/07/batten-down-the-hatches-navy-accused-of-pirating-585k-copies-of-vr-software.

10. Robert M. Anderson *et al., Divided Loyalties: Whistle-Blowing at BART*, Purdue University, 1980.

11. Holger Hjorstvang, quoted in Anderson *et al., Divided Loyalties*, p. 140.

12. Robert Fox, "News Track," *Communications of the ACM*, 44, no. 6 (June 2001), pp. 9–10. Kevin Flynn, "A Focus on Communication Failures," *New York Times*, Jan. 30, 2003, p. A13.

13. One study showed judges more likely to be lenient early in the day or after a snack: Kurt Kleiner, "Lunchtime Leniency: Judges' Rulings Are Harsher When They Are Hungrier," *Scientific American*, Sept. 1, 2011, www.scientificamerican.com/article/ lunchtime-leniency/.

14. Guidelines of the ACM Code of Ethics and Professional Conduct, Section 1.1

15. Tom Forester and Perry Morrison, *Computer Ethics: Cautionary Tales and Ethical Dilemmas in Computing*, 2nd ed., MIT Press, 1994, p. 202.

16. SEI CERT Coding Standards, www.securecoding.cert.org/confluence/display/ seccode/SEI+CERT+Coding+Standards.

Epilogue

Although most of this book focuses on problems and controversial issues, we celebrate the variety of applications and benefits that computer technology and the Internet have brought us. Very few people anticipated whole new phenomena such as portable access to the resources of the Internet, social media, and content sharing by billions of people, with their marvelous benefits and new problems.

The human mind, and hence technology, does not stand still. Change always disrupts the status quo. Technology is always shifting the balance of power—between governments and citizens, between hackers and security experts, and between people who want to protect their privacy and businesses that want to collect and use personal information. We can look to governments for solutions to some problems that technology causes, but we should remember that governments are institutions, like businesses and other organizations, with their own interests and incentives. Entrenched powers such as governments or dominant companies in an industry attempt to maintain their position.

Because technology brings change, it often brings new problems. With time, we solve or reduce many of the problems, using more or better technology, the market, innovative services and business arrangements, laws, education, and so on. We cannot eliminate all negative effects, so we accept some, adapt to new environments, and make trade-offs.

In some areas, such as privacy of personal data and activities, computer technology has brought profound changes that could fundamentally alter our interactions with the people around us and with our governments. It is essential for us to think about personal choices and their consequences. It is essential for businesses, governments, and computer professionals to think about appropriate guidelines for use of a technology. We must think ahead—to anticipate potential problems and risks and to design products and policies to reduce them. On the other hand, we must be careful not to regulate too soon in ways that would stifle innovation and prevent new benefits.

The issue of banning a tool or technology has come up in several contexts. These include encryption, devices that copy music and movies, software to circumvent copyright protection, intelligent robots, and so on. The difficulty of predicting future beneficial uses of technologies is a strong argument against such bans.

We learn from experience. System failures, even disasters, lead to better systems. However, the observation that we cannot expect all large systems to be error-free does not absolve us of responsibility for sloppy or unethical work.

There are many opportunities for computer professionals to develop wonderful new products and to use their skills and creativity to build solutions to some of the problems we have discussed. We hope that this book has sparked a lot of ideas and that the discussion of risks and failures encourages you to exercise the highest degree of professional and personal responsibility.

APPENDIX

A

The Software Engineering Code and the ACM Code

A.1 Software Engineering Code of Ethics and Professional Practice[*]

Software Engineering Code of Ethics and Professional Practice (Version 5.2) as recommended by the ACM/IEEE-CS Joint Task Force on Software Engineering Ethics and Professional Practices and jointly approved by the ACM and the IEEE-CS as the standard for teaching and practicing software engineering.

SOFTWARE ENGINEERING CODE OF ETHICS AND PROFESSIONAL PRACTICE (SHORT VERSION)

Preamble

The short version of the code summarizes aspirations at a high level of the abstraction; the clauses that are included in the full version give examples and details of how these aspirations change the way we act as software engineering professionals. Without the aspirations, the details can become legalistic and tedious; without the details, the aspirations can become high sounding but empty; together, the aspirations and the details form a cohesive code.

Software engineers shall commit themselves to making the analysis, specification, design, development, testing and maintenance of software a beneficial and respected profession. In accordance with their commitment to the health, safety and welfare of the public, software engineers shall adhere to the following Eight Principles:

1. PUBLIC – Software engineers shall act consistently with the public interest.
2. CLIENT AND EMPLOYER – Software engineers shall act in a manner that is in the best interests of their client and employer consistent with the public interest.
3. PRODUCT – Software engineers shall ensure that their products and related modifications meet the highest professional standards possible.
4. JUDGMENT – Software engineers shall maintain integrity and independence in their professional judgment.
5. MANAGEMENT – Software engineering managers and leaders shall subscribe to and promote an ethical approach to the management of software development and maintenance.
6. PROFESSION – Software engineers shall advance the integrity and reputation of the profession consistent with the public interest.
7. COLLEAGUES – Software engineers shall be fair to and supportive of their colleagues.
8. SELF – Software engineers shall participate in lifelong learning regarding the practice of their profession and shall promote an ethical approach to the practice of the profession.

SOFTWARE ENGINEERING CODE OF ETHICS AND PROFESSIONAL PRACTICE (FULL VERSION)

Preamble

Computers have a central and growing role in commerce, industry, government, medicine, education, entertainment, and society at large. Software engineers are those who contribute by direct participation or by teaching, to the analysis, specification, design, development, certification, maintenance, and testing of software systems. Because of their roles in developing software systems, software engineers have significant opportunities to do good or cause harm, to enable others to do good or cause harm, or to influence others to do good or cause harm. To ensure, as much as possible, that their efforts will be used for good, software engineers must commit themselves to making software engineering a beneficial and respected profession. In accordance with that commitment, software engineers shall adhere to the following Code of Ethics and Professional Practice.

The Code contains eight Principles related to the behavior of and decisions made by professional software engineers, including practitioners, educators, managers, supervisors, and policy makers, as well as trainees and students of the profession. The Principles identify the ethically responsible relationships in which individuals, groups, and organizations participate and the primary obligations within these relationships. The Clauses of each Principle are illustrations of some of the obligations included in these relationships. These obligations are founded in the software engineer's humanity, in special care owed to people affected by the work of software engineers, and the unique elements of the practice of software engineering. The Code prescribes these as obligations of anyone claiming to be or aspiring to be a software engineer.

It is not intended that the individual parts of the Code be used in isolation to justify errors of omission or commission. The list of Principles and Clauses is not exhaustive. The Clauses should not be read as separating the acceptable from the unacceptable in professional conduct in all practical situations. The Code is not a simple ethical algorithm that generates ethical decisions. In some situations standards may be in tension with each other or with standards from other sources. These situations require the software engineer to use ethical judgment to act in a manner which is most consistent with the spirit of the Code of Ethics and Professional Practice, given the circumstances.

Ethical tensions can best be addressed by thoughtful consideration of fundamental principles, rather than blind reliance on detailed regulations. These Principles should influence software engineers to consider broadly who is affected by their work; to examine if they and their colleagues are treating other human beings with due respect; to consider how the public, if reasonably well informed, would view their decisions; to analyze how the least empowered will be affected by their decisions; and to consider whether their acts would be judged worthy of the ideal professional working as a software engineer. In all these judgments concern for the health, safety and welfare of the public is primary; that is, the "Public Interest" is central to this Code.

The dynamic and demanding context of software engineering requires a code that is adaptable and relevant to new situations as they occur. However, even in this generality, the Code provides support for software engineers and managers of software engineers who need to take positive action in a specific case by documenting the ethical stance of the profession. The Code provides an ethical foundation to which individuals within teams and the team as a whole can appeal. The Code helps to define those actions that are ethically improper to request of a software engineer or teams of software engineers.

The Code is not simply for adjudicating the nature of questionable acts; it also has an important educational function. As this Code expresses the consensus of the profession on ethical issues, it is a means to educate both the public and aspiring professionals about the ethical obligations of all software engineers.

Principles

Principle 1: Public

Software engineers shall act consistently with the public interest. In particular, software engineers shall, as appropriate:

1.01. Accept full responsibility for their own work.

1.02. Moderate the interests of the software engineer, the employer, the client, and the users with the public good.

1.03. Approve software only if they have a well-founded belief that it is safe, meets specifications, passes appropriate tests, and does not diminish quality of life, diminish privacy, or harm the environment. The ultimate effect of the work should be to the public good.

1.04. Disclose to appropriate persons or authorities any actual or potential danger to the user, the public, or the environment, that they reasonably believe to be associated with software or related documents.

1.05. Cooperate in efforts to address matters of grave public concern caused by software, its installation, maintenance, support, or documentation.

1.06. Be fair and avoid deception in all statements, particularly public ones, concerning software or related documents, methods and tools.

1.07. Consider issues of physical disabilities, allocation of resources, economic disadvantage, and other factors that can diminish access to the benefits of software.

1.08. Be encouraged to volunteer professional skills to good causes and contribute to public education concerning the discipline.

Principle 2: Client and Employer

Software engineers shall act in a manner that is in the best interests of their client and employer, consistent with the public interest. In particular, software engineers shall, as appropriate:

2.01. Provide service in their areas of competence, being honest and forthright about any limitations of their experience and education.

2.02. Not knowingly use software that is obtained or retained either illegally or unethically.

2.03. Use the property of a client or employer only in ways properly authorized, and with the client's or employer's knowledge and consent.

2.04. Ensure that any document upon which they rely has been approved, when required, by someone authorized to approve it.

2.05. Keep private any confidential information gained in their professional work, where such confidentiality is consistent with the public interest and consistent with the law.

2.06. Identify, document, collect evidence, and report to the client or the employer promptly if, in their opinion, a project is likely to fail, to prove too expensive, to violate intellectual property law, or otherwise to be problematic.

2.07. Identify, document, and report significant issues of social concern, of which they are aware, in software or related documents, to the employer or the client.

2.08. Accept no outside work detrimental to the work they perform for their primary employer.

2.09. Promote no interest adverse to their employer or client, unless a higher ethical concern is being compromised; in that case, inform the employer or another appropriate authority of the ethical concern.

Principle 3: Product

Software engineers shall ensure that their products and related modifications meet the highest professional standards possible. In particular, software engineers shall, as appropriate:

3.01. Strive for high quality, acceptable cost, and a reasonable schedule, ensuring significant tradeoffs are clear to and accepted by the employer and the client, and are available for consideration by the user and the public.

3.02. Ensure proper and achievable goals and objectives for any project on which they work or propose.

3.03. Identify, define, and address ethical, economic, cultural, legal and environmental issues related to work projects.

3.04. Ensure that they are qualified for any project on which they work or propose to work by an appropriate combination of education, training, and experience.

3.05. Ensure an appropriate method is used for any project on which they work or propose to work.

3.06. Work to follow professional standards, when available, that are most appropriate for the task at hand, departing from these only when ethically or technically justified.

3.07. Strive to fully understand the specifications for software on which they work.

3.08. Ensure that specifications for software on which they work have been well documented, satisfy the users' requirements, and have the appropriate approvals.

3.09. Ensure realistic quantitative estimates of cost, scheduling, personnel, quality, and outcomes on any project on which they work or propose to work and provide an uncertainty assessment of these estimates.

3.10. Ensure adequate testing, debugging, and review of software and related documents on which they work.

3.11. Ensure adequate documentation, including significant problems discovered and solutions adopted, for any project on which they work.

3.12. Work to develop software and related documents that respect the privacy of those who will be affected by that software.

3.13. Be careful to use only accurate data derived by ethical and lawful means, and use it only in ways properly authorized.

3.14. Maintain the integrity of data, being sensitive to outdated or flawed occurrences.

3.15. Treat all forms of software maintenance with the same professionalism as new development.

Principle 4: Judgment

Software engineers shall maintain integrity and independence in their professional judgment. In particular, software engineers shall, as appropriate:

4.01. Temper all technical judgments by the need to support and maintain human values.

4.02. Only endorse documents either prepared under their supervision or within their areas of competence and with which they are in agreement.

4.03. Maintain professional objectivity with respect to any software or related documents they are asked to evaluate.

4.04. Not engage in deceptive financial practices such as bribery, double billing, or other improper financial practices.

4.05. Disclose to all concerned parties those conflicts of interest that cannot reasonably be avoided or escaped.

4.06. Refuse to participate, as members or advisors, in a private, governmental or professional body concerned with software related issues, in which they, their employers or their clients have undisclosed potential conflicts of interest.

Principle 5: Management

Software engineering managers and leaders shall subscribe to and promote an ethical approach to the management of software development and maintenance. In particular, those managing or leading software engineers shall, as appropriate:

5.01. Ensure good management for any project on which they work, including effective procedures for promotion of quality and reduction of risk.

5.02. Ensure that software engineers are informed of standards before being held to them.

5.03. Ensure that software engineers know the employer's policies and procedures for protecting passwords, files, and information that is confidential to the employer or confidential to others.

5.04. Assign work only after taking into account appropriate contributions of education and experience tempered with a desire to further that education and experience.

5.05. Ensure realistic quantitative estimates of cost, scheduling, personnel, quality, and outcomes on any project on which they work or propose to work, and provide an uncertainty assessment of these estimates.

5.06. Attract potential software engineers only by full and accurate description of the conditions of employment.

5.07. Offer fair and just remuneration.

5.08. Not unjustly prevent someone from taking a position for which that person is suitably qualified.

5.09. Ensure that there is a fair agreement concerning ownership of any software, processes, research, writing, or other intellectual property to which a software engineer has contributed.

5.10. Provide for due process in hearing charges of violation of an employer's policy or of this Code.

5.11. Not ask a software engineer to do anything inconsistent with this Code.

5.12. Not punish anyone for expressing ethical concerns about a project.

Principle 6: Profession

Software engineers shall advance the integrity and reputation of the profession consistent with the public interest. In particular, software engineers shall, as appropriate:

6.01. Help develop an organizational environment favorable to acting ethically.

6.02. Promote public knowledge of software engineering.

6.03. Extend software engineering knowledge by appropriate participation in professional organizations, meetings, and publications.

6.04. Support, as members of a profession, other software engineers striving to follow this Code.

6.05. Not promote their own interest at the expense of the profession, client, or employer.

6.06. Obey all laws governing their work, unless, in exceptional circumstances, such compliance is inconsistent with the public interest.

6.07. Be accurate in stating the characteristics of software on which they work, avoiding not only false claims but also claims that might reasonably be supposed to be speculative, vacuous, deceptive, misleading, or doubtful.

6.08. Take responsibility for detecting, correcting, and reporting errors in software and associated documents on which they work.

6.09. Ensure that clients, employers, and supervisors know of the software engineer's commitment to this Code of ethics, and the subsequent ramifications of such commitment.

6.10. Avoid associations with businesses and organizations which are in conflict with this code.

6.11. Recognize that violations of this Code are inconsistent with being a professional software engineer.

6.12. Express concerns to the people involved when significant violations of this Code are detected unless this is impossible, counter-productive, or dangerous.

6.13. Report significant violations of this Code to appropriate authorities when it is clear that consultation with people involved in these significant violations is impossible, counter-productive, or dangerous.

Principle 7: Colleagues

Software engineers shall be fair to and supportive of their colleagues. In particular, software engineers shall, as appropriate:

7.01. Encourage colleagues to adhere to this Code.

7.02. Assist colleagues in professional development.

7.03. Credit fully the work of others and refrain from taking undue credit.

7.04. Review the work of others in an objective, candid, and properly-documented way.

7.05. Give a fair hearing to the opinions, concerns, or complaints of a colleague.

7.06. Assist colleagues in being fully aware of current standard work practices including policies and procedures for protecting passwords, files, and other confidential information, and security measures in general.

7.07. Not unfairly intervene in the career of any colleague; however, concern for the employer, the client or public interest may compel software engineers, in good faith, to question the competence of a colleague.

7.08. In situations outside of their own areas of competence, call upon the opinions of other professionals who have competence in that area.

Principle 8: Self

Software engineers shall participate in lifelong learning regarding the practice of their profession and shall promote an ethical approach to the practice of the profession. In particular, software engineers shall continually endeavor to:

8.01. Further their knowledge of developments in the analysis, specification, design, development, maintenance, and testing of software and related documents, together with the management of the development process.

8.02. Improve their ability to create safe, reliable, and useful quality software at reasonable cost and within a reasonable time.

8.03. Improve their ability to produce accurate, informative, and well-written documentation.

8.04. Improve their understanding of the software and related documents on which they work and of the environment in which they will be used.

8.05. Improve their knowledge of relevant standards and the law governing the software and related documents on which they work.

8.06. Improve their knowledge of this Code, its interpretation, and its application to their work.

8.07. Not give unfair treatment to anyone because of any irrelevant prejudices.

8.08. Not influence others to undertake any action that involves a breach of this Code.

8.09. Recognize that personal violations of this Code are inconsistent with being a professional software engineer.

This Code was developed by the ACM/IEEE-CS joint task force on Software Engineering Ethics and Professional Practices (SEEPP):

Executive Committee: Donald Gotterbarn (Chair), Keith Miller and Simon Rogerson;

Members: Steve Barber, Peter Barnes, Ilene Burnstein, Michael Davis, Amr El-Kadi, N. Ben Fairweather, Milton Fulghum, N. Jayaram, Tom Jewett, Mark Kanko, Ernie Kallman, Duncan Langford, Joyce Currie Little, Ed Mechler, Manuel J. Norman, Douglas Phillips, Peter Ron Prinzivalli, Patrick Sullivan, John Weckert, Vivian Weil, S. Weisband and Laurie Honour Werth.

This Code may be published without permission as long as it is not changed in any way and it carries the copyright notice.

A.2   ACM Code of Ethics and Professional Conduct[*]

Adopted by ACM Council 10/16/92.

Preamble

Commitment to ethical professional conduct is expected of every member (voting members, associate members, and student members) of the Association for Computing Machinery (ACM).

This Code, consisting of 24 imperatives formulated as statements of personal responsibility, identifies the elements of such a commitment. It contains many, but not all, issues professionals are likely to face. Section 1 outlines fundamental ethical considerations, while Section 2 addresses additional, more specific considerations of professional conduct. Statements in Section 3 pertain more specifically to individuals who have a leadership role, whether in the workplace or in a volunteer capacity such as with organizations like ACM. Principles involving compliance with this Code are given in Section 4.

The Code shall be supplemented by a set of Guidelines, which provide explanation to assist members in dealing with the various issues contained in the Code. It is expected that the Guidelines will be changed more frequently than the Code.

The Code and its supplemented Guidelines are intended to serve as a basis for ethical decision making in the conduct of professional work. Secondarily, they may serve as a basis for judging the merit of a formal complaint pertaining to violation of professional ethical standards.

It should be noted that although computing is not mentioned in the imperatives of Section 1, the Code is concerned with how these fundamental imperatives apply to one's conduct as a computing professional. These imperatives are expressed in a general form to emphasize that ethical principles which apply to computer ethics are derived from more general ethical principles.

It is understood that some words and phrases in a code of ethics are subject to varying interpretations, and that any ethical principle may conflict with other ethical principles in specific situations. Questions related to ethical conflicts can best be answered by thoughtful consideration of fundamental principles, rather than reliance on detailed regulations.

Contents and Guidelines

1. General Moral Imperatives.
2. More Specific Professional Responsibilities.
3. Organizational Leadership Imperatives.
4. Compliance with the Code.

1. General Moral Imperatives.

As an ACM member I will. . .

1.1 Contribute to society and human well-being.

This principle concerning the quality of life of all people affirms an obligation to protect fundamental human rights and to respect the diversity of all cultures. An essential aim of computing professionals is to minimize negative consequences of computing systems, including threats to health and safety. When designing or implementing systems, computing professionals must attempt to ensure that the products of their efforts will be used in socially responsible ways, will meet social needs, and will avoid harmful effects to health and welfare.

In addition to a safe social environment, human well-being includes a safe natural environment. Therefore, computing professionals who design and develop systems must be alert to, and make others aware of, any potential damage to the local or global environment.

1.2 Avoid harm to others.

"Harm" means injury or negative consequences, such as undesirable loss of information, loss of property, property damage, or unwanted environmental impacts. This principle prohibits use of computing technology in ways that result in harm to any of the following: users, the general public, employees, employers. Harmful actions include intentional destruction or modification of files and programs leading to serious loss of resources or unnecessary expenditure of human resources such as the time and effort required to purge systems of "computer viruses."

Well-intended actions, including those that accomplish assigned duties, may lead to harm unexpectedly. In such an event the responsible person or persons are obligated to undo or mitigate the negative consequences as much as possible. One way to avoid unintentional harm is to carefully consider potential impacts on all those affected by decisions made during design and implementation.

To minimize the possibility of indirectly harming others, computing professionals must minimize malfunctions by following generally accepted standards for system design and testing. Furthermore, it is often necessary to assess the social consequences of systems to project the likelihood of any serious harm to others. If system features are misrepresented to users, coworkers, or supervisors, the individual computing professional is responsible for any resulting injury.

In the work environment the computing professional has the additional obligation to report any signs of system dangers that might result in serious personal or social damage. If one's superiors do not act to curtail or mitigate such dangers, it may be necessary to "blow the whistle" to help correct the problem or reduce the risk. However, capricious or misguided reporting of violations can, itself, be harmful. Before reporting violations, all relevant aspects of the incident must be thoroughly assessed. In particular, the assessment of risk and responsibility must be credible. It is suggested that advice be sought from other computing professionals. See principle 2.5 regarding thorough evaluations.

1.3 Be honest and trustworthy.

Honesty is an essential component of trust. Without trust an organization cannot function effectively. The honest computing professional will not make deliberately false or deceptive claims about a system or system design, but will instead provide full disclosure of all pertinent system limitations and problems.

A computer professional has a duty to be honest about his or her own qualifications, and about any circumstances that might lead to conflicts of interest.

Membership in volunteer organizations such as ACM may at times place individuals in situations where their statements or actions could be interpreted as carrying the "weight" of a larger group of professionals. An ACM member will exercise care to not misrepresent ACM or positions and policies of ACM or any ACM units.

1.4 Be fair and take action not to discriminate.

The values of equality, tolerance, respect for others, and the principles of equal justice govern this imperative. Discrimination on the basis of race, sex, religion, age, disability, national origin, or other such factors is an explicit violation of ACM policy and will not be tolerated.

Inequities between different groups of people may result from the use or misuse of information and technology. In a fair society, all individuals would have equal opportunity to participate in, or benefit from, the use of computer resources regardless of race, sex, religion, age, disability, national origin or other such similar factors. However, these ideals do not justify unauthorized use of computer resources nor do they provide an adequate basis for violation of any other ethical imperatives of this code.

1.5 Honor property rights including copyrights and patent.

Violation of copyrights, patents, trade secrets and the terms of license agreements is prohibited by law in most circumstances. Even when software is not so protected, such violations are contrary to professional behavior. Copies of software should be made only with proper authorization. Unauthorized duplication of materials must not be condoned.

1.6 Give proper credit for intellectual property.

Computing professionals are obligated to protect the integrity of intellectual property. Specifically, one must not take credit for other's ideas or work, even in cases where the work has not been explicitly protected by copyright, patent, etc.

1.7 Respect the privacy of others.

Computing and communication technology enables the collection and exchange of personal information on a scale unprecedented in the history of civilization. Thus there is increased potential for violating the privacy of individuals and groups. It is the responsibility of professionals to maintain the privacy and integrity of data describing individuals. This includes taking precautions to ensure the accuracy of data, as well as protecting it from unauthorized access or accidental disclosure to inappropriate individuals. Furthermore, procedures must be established to allow individuals to review their records and correct inaccuracies.

This imperative implies that only the necessary amount of personal information be collected in a system, that retention and disposal periods for that information be clearly defined and enforced, and that personal information gathered for a specific purpose not be used for other purposes without consent of the individual(s). These principles apply to electronic communications, including electronic mail, and prohibit procedures that capture or monitor electronic user data, including messages, without the permission of users or bona fide authorization related to system operation and maintenance. User data observed during the normal duties of system operation and maintenance must be treated with strictest confidentiality, except in cases where it is evidence for the violation of law, organizational regulations, or this Code. In these cases, the nature or contents of that information must be disclosed only to proper authorities.

1.8 Honor confidentiality.

The principle of honesty extends to issues of confidentiality of information whenever one has made an explicit promise to honor confidentiality or, implicitly, when private information not directly related to the performance of one's duties becomes available. The ethical concern is to respect all obligations of confidentiality to employers, clients, and users unless discharged from such obligations by requirements of the law or other principles of this Code.

2. *More Specific Professional Responsibilities.*

As an ACM computing professional I will. . .

2.1 Strive to achieve the highest quality, effectiveness and dignity in both the process and products of professional work.

Excellence is perhaps the most important obligation of a professional. The computing professional must strive to achieve quality and to be cognizant of the serious negative consequences that may result from poor quality in a system.

2.2 Acquire and maintain professional competence.

Excellence depends on individuals who take responsibility for acquiring and maintaining professional competence. A professional must participate in setting standards for appropriate levels of competence, and strive to achieve those standards. Upgrading technical knowledge and competence can be achieved in several ways: doing independent study; attending seminars, conferences, or courses; and being involved in professional organizations.

2.3 Know and respect existing laws pertaining to professional work.

ACM members must obey existing local, state, province, national, and international laws unless there is a compelling ethical basis not to do so. Policies and procedures of the organizations in which one participates must also be obeyed. But compliance must be balanced with the recognition that sometimes existing laws and rules may be immoral or inappropriate and, therefore, must be challenged. Violation of a law or regulation may be ethical when that law or rule has inadequate moral basis or when it conflicts with another law judged to be more important. If one decides to violate a law or rule because it is viewed as unethical, or for any other reason, one must fully accept responsibility for one's actions and for the consequences.

2.4 Accept and provide appropriate professional review.

Quality professional work, especially in the computing profession, depends on professional reviewing and critiquing. Whenever appropriate, individual members should seek and utilize peer review as well as provide critical review of the work of others.

2.5 Give comprehensive and thorough evaluations of computer systems and their impacts, including analysis of possible risks.

Computer professionals must strive to be perceptive, thorough, and objective when evaluating, recommending, and presenting system descriptions and alternatives. Computer professionals are in a position of special trust, and therefore have a special responsibility to provide objective, credible evaluations to employers, clients, users, and the public. When providing evaluations the professional must also identify any relevant conflicts of interest, as stated in imperative 1.3.

As noted in the discussion of principle 1.2 on avoiding harm, any signs of danger from systems must be reported to those who have opportunity and/or responsibility to resolve them. See the guidelines for imperative 1.2 for more details concerning harm, including the reporting of professional violations.

2.6 Honor contracts, agreements, and assigned responsibilities.

Honoring one's commitments is a matter of integrity and honesty. For the computer professional this includes ensuring that system elements perform as intended. Also, when one contracts for work with another party, one has an obligation to keep that party properly informed about progress toward completing that work.

A computing professional has a responsibility to request a change in any assignment that he or she feels cannot be completed as defined. Only after serious consideration and with full disclosure of risks and concerns to the employer or client, should one accept the assignment. The major underlying principle here is the obligation to accept personal accountability for professional work. On some occasions other ethical principles may take greater priority.

A judgment that a specific assignment should not be performed may not be accepted. Having clearly identified one's concerns and reasons for that judgment, but failing to procure a change in that assignment, one may yet be obligated, by contract or by law, to proceed as directed. The computing professional's ethical judgment should be the final guide in deciding whether or not to proceed. Regardless of the decision, one must accept the responsibility for the consequences.

However, performing assignments "against one's own judgment" does not relieve the professional of responsibility for any negative consequences.

2.7 Improve public understanding of computing and its consequences.

Computing professionals have a responsibility to share technical knowledge with the public by encouraging understanding of computing, including the impacts of computer systems and their limitations. This imperative implies an obligation to counter any false views related to computing.

2.8 Access computing and communication resources only when authorized to do so.

Theft or destruction of tangible and electronic property is prohibited by imperative 1.2 - "Avoid harm to others." Trespassing and unauthorized use of a computer or communication system is addressed by this imperative. Trespassing includes accessing communication networks and computer systems, or accounts and/or files associated with those systems, without explicit authorization to do so. Individuals and organizations have the right to restrict access to their systems so long as they do not violate the discrimination principle (see 1.4). No one should enter or use another's computer system, software, or data files without permission. One must always have appropriate approval before using system resources, including communication ports, file space, other system peripherals, and computer time.

3. *Organizational Leadership Imperatives.*

As an ACM member and an organizational leader, I will. . .

BACKGROUND NOTE: This section draws extensively from the draft IFIP Code of Ethics, especially its sections on organizational ethics and international concerns. The ethical obligations of organizations tend to be neglected in most codes of professional conduct, perhaps because these codes are written from the perspective of the individual member. This dilemma is addressed by stating these imperatives from the perspective of the organizational leader. In this context "leader" is viewed as any organizational member who has leadership or educational responsibilities. These imperatives generally may apply to organizations as well as their leaders. In this context "organizations" are corporations, government agencies, and other "employers," as well as volunteer professional organizations.

3.1 Articulate social responsibilities of members of an organizational unit and encourage full acceptance of those responsibilities.

Because organizations of all kinds have impacts on the public, they must accept responsibilities to society. Organizational procedures and attitudes oriented toward quality and the welfare of society will reduce harm to members of the public, thereby serving public interest and fulfilling social responsibility. Therefore, organizational leaders must encourage full participation in meeting social responsibilities as well as quality performance.

3.2 Manage personnel and resources to design and build information systems that enhance the quality of working life.

Organizational leaders are responsible for ensuring that computer systems enhance, not degrade, the quality of working life. When implementing a computer system, organizations must consider the personal and professional development, physical safety, and human dignity of all workers. Appropriate human-computer ergonomic standards should be considered in system design and in the workplace.

3.3 Acknowledge and support proper and authorized uses of an organization's computing and communication resources.

Because computer systems can become tools to harm as well as to benefit an organization, the leadership has the responsibility to clearly define appropriate and inappropriate uses of organizational computing resources. While the number and scope of such rules should be minimal, they should be fully enforced when established.

3.4 Ensure that users and those who will be affected by a system have their needs clearly articulated during the assessment and design of requirements; later the system must be validated to meet requirements.

Current system users, potential users and other persons whose lives may be affected by a system must have their needs assessed and incorporated in the statement of requirements. System validation should ensure compliance with those requirements.

3.5 Articulate and support policies that protect the dignity of users and others affected by a computing system.

Designing or implementing systems that deliberately or inadvertently demean individuals or groups is ethically unacceptable. Computer professionals who are in decision making positions should verify that systems are designed and implemented to protect personal privacy and enhance personal dignity.

3.6 Create opportunities for members of the organization to learn the principles and limitations of computer systems.

This complements the imperative on public understanding (2.7). Educational opportunities are essential to facilitate optimal participation of all organizational members. Opportunities must be available to all members to help them improve their knowledge and skills in computing, including courses that familiarize them with the consequences and limitations of particular types of systems. In particular, professionals must be made aware of the dangers of building systems around oversimplified models, the improbability of anticipating and designing for every possible operating condition, and other issues related to the complexity of this profession.

4. Compliance with the Code.

As an ACM member I will. . .

4.1 Uphold and promote the principles of this Code.

The future of the computing profession depends on both technical and ethical excellence. Not only is it important for ACM computing professionals to adhere to the principles expressed in this Code, each member should encourage and support adherence by other members.

4.2 Treat violations of this Code as inconsistent with membership in the ACM.

Adherence of professionals to a code of ethics is largely a voluntary matter. However, if a member does not follow this code by engaging in gross misconduct, membership in ACM may be terminated.

This Code and the supplemental Guidelines were developed by the Task Force for the Revision of the ACM Code of Ethics and Professional Conduct: Ronald E. Anderson, Chair, Gerald Engel, Donald Gotterbarn, Grace C. Hertlein, Alex Hoffman, Bruce Jawer, Deborah G. Johnson, Doris K. Lidtke, Joyce Currie Little, Dianne Martin, Donn B. Parker, Judith A. Perrolle, and Richard S. Rosenberg. The Task Force was organized by ACM/SIGCAS and funding was provided by the ACM SIG Discretionary Fund. This Code and the supplemental Guidelines were adopted by the ACM Council on October 16, 1992.

Index